Technology and Desire

AF478622

Technology and Desire
The Transgressive Art of Moving Images

Edited by Rania Gaafar and Martin Schulz

intellect Bristol, UK / Chicago, USA

First published in the UK in 2014 by
Intellect, The Mill, Parnall Road, Fishponds, Bristol, BS16 3JG, UK

First published in the USA in 2014 by
Intellect, The University of Chicago Press, 1427 E. 60th Street,
Chicago, IL 60637, USA

Copyright © 2014 Intellect Ltd

All rights reserved. No part of this publication may be reproduced,
stored in a retrieval system, or transmitted, in any form or by
any means, electronic, mechanical, photocopying, recording, or
otherwise, without written permission.

A catalogue record for this book is available from the
British Library.

Cover designer: Sahar Aharoni
Copy-editor: Michael Eckhardt
Production manager: Jelena Stanovnik and Claire Organ
Typesetting: Contentra Technologies

Print ISBN: 978-1-84150-461-2
ePDF ISBN: 978-1-78320-167-9
ePub ISBN: 978-1-78320-166-2

Printed and bound by Hobbs, UK

Table of Contents

Acknowledgements

The idea of organizing an international conference on the transgressive art of moving images against the background of the ever-growing body of research in visual studies, the role of imaging technologies and the impact of the digital advent in art history, media, film, and cultural studies came to us amidst our involvement in the doctoral school *Image, Body, Medium – Towards an Anthropological Perspective* that was based at Staatliche Hochschule für Gestaltung Karlsruhe (Karlsruhe University of Arts and Design). At the time, we discussed the objective to conceptually and methodologically extend the very notion of the 'life of images' (W. J. T. Mitchell) to that of reflections on the (new) technologies of images' production and their very aesthetics, as well as the sublime desire of images in motion that we felt were perpetually transgressing their very frames in the contemporary (post-)medial contexts of our time. In reference to these visually conceptual correlations, we invited a number of scholars to contribute and participate in a major international conference entitled *Technology and Desire – The Transgressive Art of Moving Images* that was held at the Zentrum für Kunst – und Medientechnologie, ZKM (Centre for Art and Media), in Karlsruhe, in close cooperation with the Art Theory and Media Philosophy department of the University of Arts and Design. Most of the papers in this volume were presented at this conference. The ZKM as an internationally renowned cutting-edge art and media research institution provided the conference's venue. This conference and publication would have not been possible without the generous financial funding of the DFG (the German Research Funding Organization) doctoral school *Image, Body, Medium – Towards an Anthropological Perspective*, to which we, in retrospect, express our sincere thanks. We owe our deep gratitude to Samantha King from Intellect Books who has acknowledged the idea and the potential of this book in the beginning. We especially thank Jelena Stanovnik, our committed editor at Intellect, who has produced and supported this project during all its different stages and navigated it to the end with Intellect's editorial team. We would like to thank Sahar Aharoni, who photographed and designed the conference's logo and poster of an abstract camera's lens and turned it into a vision of plasticity, which also serves as the cover of this volume. Our gratitude goes to Jochen Mevius, who has translated a number of chapters from German to English as indicated in this volume. Adel Iskandar has given us helpful advice in reviewing parts of the manuscript. We should particularly like to thank the staff at ZKM's library, whose help has been indispensable for the research on this collection. Elke Reinhuber and Sebastian Pelz have kindly supported the final stages of production. We are grateful to the anonymous reviewer whose precise comments have helped to amend the manuscript. Finally, our cordial thanks go to all contributors of this volume, their challenging and rigorous talks and texts, as well as their patience during the time of the preparation of this volume. Last, but never least, we sincerely thank all the artists in this collection, who have provided installation shots and images of their art works, especially Isaac Julien, Malcolm LeGrice, Rohini Devasher, Akram Zaatari, Joana Hadjithomas and Khalil Joreige, Youki Hirakawa, and Jim Campbell. Very warm thanks go to Isaac Julien for stimulating conversations, his kind support during the production of this volume and beyond, as well as the inspirational and intellectual insight into his own artistic practice that he generously shared with us in long interviews and meetings in London and Germany.

Introduction

Post-medial Technologies of Desire: Performances of Images

Rania Gaafar and Martin Schulz

In James Williamson's pioneering short film *The Big Swallow* (1901), the spectator paradigmatically encounters the physical human resistance to the capturing and signifying camera – and, by extension, to the operator's attempt to display an image of the subject in front of the camera lens. The form-and-shape-giving machinery of his very image on the screen is literally swallowed up by the actor on-screen, who is in front of the camera. The critical irony of this shot and further reflection of it will probably become more obvious today, more than a hundred years after the production of Williamson's film, and with the advent of the digital, the post-humanist and techno-scientific yet affect-induced material turn in cultural and media theory. In the very seconds following this 'big swallow' and the extreme close-up of the mouth with its almost infinitely dark antrum, what we see is basically the reappearance of the image, the continuing existence and animation of the moving image, of the film itself, despite and after the supposed disappearance of the recording camera within the moving image's *hors cadre* – and inside the subject's body. The image resists its allegedly human-operated animation and origination, as well as its time, its technologically-controlled actuality and visibility on the screen. It references an 'outside' of images in critical thought as well as in the spheres of the virtual that lie beyond the semiotic layers of signs and the external control and operation of humans. It rather transforms them to conditions of new assemblages by referencing forms of embodiment through the image's transmissive constituents and techniques. This transformational process and its embedded outcome (i.e. the continuous and uninterrupted film we see despite the killing of the camera) within the image implies to a certain extent an 'intra-action' of phenomena that performatively 'enact boundaries'[1] and seek a 'new form of realism'[2] that challenges the boundaries between subjects and objects and accomplishes matter and its vital conditions through discourse (be it cultural, technological, science-oriented or media specific).

Despite the human killing of its mechanical generator – the camera – we might reflect this very short paradigmatic and intra-relational example as a literal embodiment of the camera by the image, and hence the technological means of vision as a defiant form of agency; or we might scrutinize this so-called 'after-image' – enacted in filmic time and its duration, whilst referencing an extra-machinic movement in the plane of an ongoing transformation on the screen – as one of the many ways towards the contingent history of the virtual life of images, for it discloses that ambivalent cycle of fear and desire as part of the image's transgression of its framing and in (as well as *as*) its desire to finally and actually *become*. The disappearance of the camera is followed by the animation or, in other words, by the reanimation of the image, its resistance toward intentional disappearance and created invisibility. A man, who has swallowed up the camera that was threatening his animated organic reality, is facing an audience who has come to witness an image that has been robbed of its generically electronic source, and has undergone an allegedly anthropological resurrection. Do examples from the history of film, the likes of Williamson's *The Big Swallow,* signify and – above all – anticipate the transmedial mutation of images across the genealogies of media, this volume asks? The consumed medium finally becomes the subject of the filmic work in a performatively ontogenetic mode. It becomes the subject of the screen and, even more so, that of its plasticity which is created through affectively materialized structures.[3] A seemingly comedic film scene, performed in slapstick humour, discloses the intrinsic correlation of self and 'Other', both the technological and human. At the same time, the literal incorporation of that symbol of time-based media (i.e. the camera) by the human subject signifies agency – an affective moment of medium-based and technologically-enacted anger and resistance.

Williamson's short film offers an interesting introduction to the topic of this volume and a scenario that anticipates a new aesthetic realism of (moving) images, which represents a new turn in the medial historiography and the approach to the philosophy of contemporary images and their liveliness. It provides a perspective beyond the surface of images, a look into images and their materiality, their affective medial structure and their possibilities to account for a performatively ontogenetic mode. We might go as far as to anticipate the condition of remediation in this very sequence and consider it even further: the immediacy that is hinted at here, where time and the subjective perception of time becoming one, suggests that the after-image's interface is being interpolated and integrated in the body and its perceptual faculty. Animation in film and in the very structure of the moving image is transcended to the sphere of life. According to this aforementioned filmic example, it almost seems as if 'desires' that circle within technological projections and in medium-based formats on screens (and beyond) have the capacity to transgress any spatio-temporal boundary and be embodied as movements; movements that surpass their often apparatus-based medium and are materialized as visible phenomena; in other words, as images.

Yet there are countless examples of image's transgressive attempts to aesthetically and materially escape their frames, their media and their embeddedness in structural, often digital, networks. This form of transgression seems to have at its core the neo-phenomenological and digital shifts in film studies and beyond, which have approached the sensation, affective thickness, perception of the moving image, and the corporeality of film's – and video's – very medial structure.[4] The extension of these thoughts beyond the surface-structure of the screen and 'representation' as a form of subject-formation have been elaborated by

Laura M. Marks in her seminal study on the history and transcultural premises of an aesthetics of enfolding and unfolding images in digital topographies. Visually and philosophically Marks blends Western information technology and its interfacial aesthetics that is dynamically performed through algorithms in new media art with the geometry and materiality of non-Western art forms of abstraction and their cultural assumptions.[5]

In this volume and its theoretical output, images move across and within so-called 'relationscapes', which Erin Manning defines as articulations of thoughts in motion for 'concepts are events in the making'.[6] It is within such conceptual folds that the structure of 'assemblage', which Paul Rabinow explores as an occurrent form that discloses new methodological approaches of a contemporary anthropology, seeks to address the diametric constitution of images and their very desire. As George E. Marcus and Erkan Saka note, the term discloses an ambiguous perspective on structure as being both material and intangible (Marcus and Saka 2006). The topics of the following essays lie at these boundaries of images that evolve into vital vectoral links as a means toward agency, and they propose a revision of the desire for a material and conceptual resolution to the inquiries into the image's (and henceforth the artwork's) essential nature. The almost vague notion of scrutinizing images beyond their actual visibility and therefore beyond their medium (screens, frames, walls, mobile phone displays, radiographs, fine art's materials) reveals a perpetual desire to see beyond the visible, and to disclose the mediation of media-as-carriers and their ability to transform images as visible phenomena underneath or within their very medium.

The transgressive art of moving images has been further disclosed and enhanced by post-production aesthetics of cinematic images and by digital media technologies as such – not necessarily generated by the latter as there has always been a long history of the aesthetic transgression of media art; yet also by a recent focus in artistic research to both unite practice and theory, and hence make the conditions of the possibilities of the visual transparent and relevant for the final emergence of the visual. At the cutting edge of science, the theories of digital technology, media and film philosophy as well as art history[7], this collection contends that a new digitally enhanced 'realist turn' has emerged in the visual arts. One of the explanations for this 'new realist turn' in the visual arts is the expansion of the cinematic realm through universal machines, multi-dimensional film screens, and the conceptual approach undertaken in, for example, media art installations; their spatio-temporal aesthetic transgressions. Furthermore the emergence of new aesthetic forms in contemporary media art has challenged and reformulated theoretical concepts through art practices in a science-based framework. The theoretical departures of the form-ontological conditions of the (moving) image throughout film and media history, as well as in video and electronic cultures, have been scrutinized against the background of, among others, phenomenological, sculptural, biotechnological and agency-related approaches toward moving images. At the same time, images have not only developed an interrelation to science, they have, even more so, created a scientific imaginary condition and perspective, if not a poetic and performative strand in science studies. This can be seen as a border crossing between established academic traditions of the science of images – such as art history, new media art, film and media studies – and cultural anthropology.

Desiring Images

With the birth of Renaissance perspective,[8] seeing as the technology of knowledge in the visual arts has acquired an inherently epistemological quality, and the primacy of the visual has come to represent the authority of knowledge. At this seminal point in the rational foundation of perspectival seeing as an optical technique to relate to the world, and for the production and intentional manifestation of knowledge through images and their very iconicity, artistic, and hence reflexive, techniques of a deceptive/illusory construction of the morphology of images emerge, and introduce the artwork as a body of investigation and meta-scientific paradigm. Art and science, the various conditions of their very possibilities, have intertwined, for example, in that most paradigmatic metaphor of visual illusion, mental allusion and iconic delusion: in the anamorphosis'[9] queer condition of becoming visible, that is, the queer act of seeing that which is not visible as what it is (or is not respectively).

The anamorphosis as the possible realm within a painting might be said to embody a defining moment of virtuality at the very instant it acquires an iconographic existence through a change of perspective, allowing for an 'Other' element, even image, to come into being. It shows the riddle of what we see that is simultaneously at the boundary of epistemology and being, alluding to the visual as a spectre of presence. Yet that possibility of not only *becoming* (through a different angle of the gaze) but, even more, of *being* 'Other' ventures on the very ontological status of the image and its media as a whole, approaching or harking back to 'new ways of ontology':[10]

> Becoming is no opposite of being but is a form of being. Everything real is in flux, involved in a constant coming into, or going out, of existence. Motion and becoming form the universal mode of being of the real, no matter whether it be a question of material things, living forms, or human beings. Rest and rigidity are only found in the ideal essences of the old ontology. And if it is the first task of the new ontology to define the mode of being of the real, this means especially that we must define the mode of being that characterizes becoming.[11]

Following Deleuze the image as an art *of* and *in* time and light thus flows on a real-possible-virtual interval by creating 'acts' (or 'events') of visibilities and by extending the meaning of 'the virtual':

> For in order to be actualized, the virtual cannot proceed by elimination or limitation, but must create its own lines of actualization in positive acts. The reason for this is simple: While the real is in the image and likeness of the possible that it realizes, the actual, on the other hand does not resemble the virtuality that it embodies.[12]

The 'picture's image'[13] is a multifaceted term that has been applied to recent trends in theorizing and interpreting images in the natural sciences, and it foregrounds the division between the 'material apparition' of images and their mental as well as perceptual faculty. It discloses the endeavour of images to not only gain autonomy but, by their very appearance and essence in space and time, to become inherently autonomous creations that create new spatial dimensions for the subject viewer. W. J. T. Mitchell differentiates between image and picture, the ephemeral time-based value – *being* – of an image that cannot be reduced to its very material existence (its media), but rather resembles Ludwig Wittgenstein's notion of *Vorstellung* in conjuring up the so-called 'picture's image':

> The image is the 'intellectual property' that escapes the materiality of the picture when it is copied. The picture is the image plus the support; it is the appearance of the immaterial image in a material medium. That is why we can speak of architectural, sculptural, cinematic, textual, and even mental images while understanding that the image in or on the thing is not all there is to it.[14]

In a reciprocal and reflexive perspective on the relation between words and images, their being talked about and their actual appearance in the realm of the visible, Mitchell returns the question of the desire of pictures to the question of 'what picture we have of desire'[15] and asserts the invisibility of desire, but nevertheless its ability to be – at least in the allegorical example Mitchell employs – 'an agent (the archer) and the instrument (the bow and arrow)'[16] and therefore to have a signifying and transforming function regarding images. It is this intricate boundary between (human) desire and the abstract notion of the desire of images, their constitution of living spaces, as well as their conceptual and form-related expansion and evolution of the (realist) aestheticism of post-cinematic image-worlds that makes up the 'medial' background and argument of this volume.

Where has the meandering story and life of the moving image arrived (also historically) after the experimental phases of TV, film – and video – in the 1960s and 1970s when film-as-art was being established through the conceptualization and disruption of its factual – dematerialized – representations on-screen?[17] What 'realities' have the transformations of aesthetic orders and the medial conditions of images brought forth – especially so against the background of the 'enacted' possibilities of digital aesthetics? Following Jacques Rancière's premise of aesthetics as a methodology of identifying and seeing the ruling principles of an artwork, as well as enabling a non-hierarchical and egalitarian notion of 'a different' artistic modernity, the question of agency acquires a manifold meaning, one that is in analogy to the political element in aesthetics i.e. creating spaces of fiction in an aesthetic realm of signs. Rancière's concept of 'aesthetic sovereignty'[18] or 'reality in the age of aesthetics'[19] is one of indeterminability following the concept of an 'as if' that enables the spectator to choose and move between possible worlds. Rancière has described the spectator as an 'emancipated spectator' whose mental activity of seeing and interpreting has as much choreographing property and agency potential as the 'active' personas on stage that are being looked at.[20]

By all means, the essays in this book examine implicitly or explicitly the capacity of (moving) images to reveal and incorporate a perpetual desire to see and move beyond the visible and reshape the mediations of our perception. Where are the origins and how can the aesthetic forms of a desire that is, amongst others, perpetuated by technological means become visible? There is an all-encompassing idea of technology as a creator of (1) new forms of experiences, and (2) as the condition and possibility of the migration and circulation of form throughout medial channels. The iconicity of images, their affective materiality and their ambivalent media propose a revision of the desire of images for a material and conceptual resolution to their essential nature, their being.

In the essays that follow, the authors reflect in creative and theoretically-challenging ways all these thoughts regarding especially the advent of the digital and its influence on cinema and (moving) images in the gallery context, 'ethnographic' practices and psychoanalytic thought, as well in the history of painting and video games, the mass media, and its unconscious surplus in distributing and circulating images in electronic cultures. The idea of animism in anthropology, art and contemporary exhibition practices inaugurates to a certain extent the thoughts of this volume, for it discusses a relational – immaterial yet visible – aesthetic thickness. Anselm Franke notes in his essay:

> [...] there is the animism *within* modernity's image culture, as an aesthetic economy, and a way of imagining, which gives expression to collective desires and articulates commonsensical schemes, determining the possibilities of recognizing other subjectivities, and how life processes can be conceptualized. ('Prelude' of this volume)

It appears that images have transcended their figurations and passed beyond intrinsically semiotic networks in order to shape symbolic correlations beyond their framing, either in art history or in most recent forms and aesthetic abstractions of new media art such as experimental light-and-film installation works. The key question framing the initial discussion of this volume is whether images are predicated upon transgressing the boundaries of their framing; and whether, in the course of their history and existence in different media, their form-evolutionary altered states in the arts and in all forms of medial projection, they have developed a 'life of their own'. This volume is amongst others inspired by the theory of images and the approach set out by art and media historian W. J. T. Mitchell, which purports that images have a life and desire of their own.[21] It attempts to take Mitchell's argument further in art, film and media theory so as to critically examine the essence – even 'being' – of moving images beyond textual frameworks, notions of 'culture as text' and the linguistic paradigms of the visual. The present volume provides alternative, often indirect ways of contemplating the 'desires and drives' of still and moving images, their coming into being and their impetus to want and *be*.[22] Beyond the theoretical and historical analysis of the transgression of iconographic ways of seeing, the chapters focus on the 'substance' of images, their vectoral vibrancy and their media that are 'under suspicion'.[23]

The volume's themes emerge from a cross-disciplinary interest in experimental theoretization of the appearance of images in art, media and film and their very spatial presence, the artistic practices of moving images and the intentionality of both art and the moving image. This visual inquiry into the possibilities and functions of agency besides human subjectivity and its psychology have increasingly become embedded in critiques of the real (and 'representation') in cultures of modernity, and recently a 'practice theory' in philosophical outlook[24] is developing besides the epistemological enquiry into artistic research and its conceptualization in art theory. All these approaches toward the potentialities and the actual enactment of images' transgressive, and hence transmissive, possibilities to move beyond their frames through the aesthetic, affective and perceptual strategies they employ – or even become – lead us to an ongoing investigation of 'non-representational theory'[25] in the practice of art and the performative turn in moving image art and film. The visualization of 'traces of life' in the finished 'product' – that is, the projection – harks back to the autonomous elements of the 'becoming' of the artwork in question, as well as of its aesthetic perception: '"production", then, is used according to the meaning of its etymological root (i.e. Latin *producere*) that refers to the act of "bringing forth" an object in space.'[26]

This volume tries to rethink the role of artistic production and the assembled elements in space beyond their mere perception and rather in terms of the conditions of visual emergence. It reflects upon the spatiality of moving images in technologically-medial perspectives, and takes these reflections a step further towards the visual emergence of a material vivacity of images. Ranging from technical creation to embodiment, the chapters in this volume explore in various case studies a wide range of creative theoretical conceptualizations in anthropology and art history, media and film theory, as well as psychoanalysis and philosophy. They look at the art of the contemporary moving image and its virtualized spaces, which in the age of the digital may be seen as a passage towards the agency of moving images and as introducing an aesthetic realism. At stake here is the transformation of the zone of images beyond their very 'frames' and mere 'signs' to an access toward new knowledge and, hence, formations of cultures of knowledge of the material lives of things. Agency-network theories and the material turn in cultural studies and art theory have not been meticulously explored and dissected as artistic and theoretical 'rites of passages' for moving images as primary agents of visual cultures and different modernities across the global divide.

Film philosophy and new media art have responded to the relationship between technology, the digital and the (moving) image[27] in different ways. Yet the question of the material life of images and the approach towards such a concept intends to elucidate and further conceptualize the technological conditions and possibilities behind the moving image, and its very ability to embody that which it shows. Images have not only emerged as boundaries and paradoxical embodiment but, even more, as active agents provoking reactions from the spectator-subjects outside their apparently inanimate realm, and evoking a creative and vital referential space as soon as they are on display on screens, projection sites, in exhibition venues and in public spaces. According to Mark B. Hansen, space is a 'wearable' entity and continuum of images. It has become the focus of a transmutation in the 'co-evolution' with new technology, assigning it an affective as well as extra-affective – technologically-induced – dimension that unites both body and space in the 'medium of sensation', which is nevertheless deeply embedded if not a sign of

> [...] the defining material shift of our time – the shift to the digital – has suspended the framing function performed by the (preconstituted) technical image (photograph, cinematic frame, video scanning, etc.) and has accordingly empowered the body, in a truly unprecedented way, as the framer of information.[28]

The body acquires an initial role vis-à-vis the moving image as it becomes 'a *source* for and *activator* of a rich affective constitution of space'.[29] Within the larger intra-relational context of this volume, the body becomes a catalyst for movement and reflections on vital matters:

> Preacceleration refers to the virtual force of movement's taking form. It is the feeling of movement's in-gathering, a welling that propels the directionality of how movement moves [...]. Incipient movement preaccelerates a body toward its becoming. The body becomes through forces of recombination that compose its potential directionalities of how movements move [...]. I propose that we move toward a notion of a becoming-body that is a sensing body in the movement, a body that resists predefinition in terms of subjectivity or identity, a body that is involved in a reciprocal reaching-toward that in-gathers the world even as it worlds.[30]

In the discourse of technology and desire that this volume attempts to start, the implications for a materialization of vital practices and agency networks in an aesthetic context shifts toward a focus of what appears to be a rematerialization in post-semiotic terms of a 'life of things'. The current volume extends the Deleuzian aspect of 'the new' (O'Sullivan, 2010) that emerges from the relationship between the actual and the virtual, and rereads it in terms of an aestheticization of technology (in a wider sense) and forms of embodiment – and vice versa – on the one hand, as well as a notion of agency of an aesthetic realism on the other. The 'post-medial condition'[31] has conceptually challenged the perspective on the arts, the visual arts and their respective media to the extent that painting and sculpture, for one, have been reconsidered as old and non-technical media,[32] while their aesthetic has eventually been 'mediatized' by digital technologies, and their technically evolutionary history and relevance for tracing the genealogy of new media, respectively. The 'idea of a medium' becomes, according to Krauss, 'a set of conventions derived from (but not identical with) the material conditions of a given technical support, conventions out of which to develop a form of expressiveness that can be both projective and mnemonic.'[33]

In the approach toward the medium's 'new reality', or a novel aesthetic realism, we encounter the Bergsonian concept of the virtual as an ontological category between the 'matter' and image, which is developed by Bergson as a way toward resolving the dualism between body and mind, as well as that between reality and virtuality:

> Matter, in our view, is an aggregate of images. And by image we mean a certain existence which is more than that which the idealist calls a representation, but less than that which the realist calls a thing – an existence placed halfway between the 'thing' and 'representation.'[34]

How can we articulate the intricate and intimate, yet also 'revisioned', relationship between the technologies we employ to communicate in various ways, the aesthetic outcomes we face as an actualization in time, and the desires we express (be they intentions, longings, dreams, feelings in an art context)? These desires face models of embodiment or materialization (ephemeral as they may seem when it comes to moving images, the question of 'embodiment' acquires, among others, a sensual meaning, an affective response to seeing) as soon as they become visible or are made to become visible in public spaces and in artistic spheres in particular?

Performances of Images

'Technology' refers to a number of meanings and mechanisms, as is well known; the question this volume contemplates in a more elaborate frame is whether the interconnectivity between technology and desire can 'literally' be related to the Greek etymology of *technē*, and hence its intricate relation to a *poiesis* of technologies in their various outcomes and forms. Since the skill of 'craftsmanship' has been transformed and has extended its very meaning within new media (technology), it is continuously transforming spaces into 'living spaces' of actual experience and interconnectivity. The focus on signs and semiotics seems to have been replaced. This development is part of an emphasis on and a shift toward digital reproducibility, forms of spatio-temporal embodiment and the interest in the materiality of signs, their actuality and indexicality beyond the conventional 'real', as a reference point. What is at stake in the following is hence 'the desire for, and production of, the new.'[35] The 'and' between technology and desire presupposes a reversal and revisioning of the assumed ontological boundary between machines and affects, enacting a conceptual framework in the images and artworks in question, transgressing the boundaries of being and thing, the biological and matter,[36] and redefining the aesthetic in 'techno-scientific' terms by signifying a movement from representation to the technological embodiment of affect in/as aesthetics; from the body to the subjectivity of the immaterial, from perspectivism in the visual arts to the virtual as embodied movement, and hence from movement to time.

Dieter Mersch, for one, evokes a post-semiotic stance which argues that something that shows (itself) is not necessarily a sign, but an appearance (a visual emergence) which appropriates 'presence' and a space of perception in a threefold way: neither the structure of 'representation' nor the technology of visualization are at the core of Mersch's argument, rather the interconnectivity between the iconicity of the image and the gaze of the spectator. Thus, the transgressive art of moving images borders on the boundaries of images, their animated presence in space (still) being connected to the gaze; the thin invisible line between life and death (the image's mummification in André Bazin's terms) that signifies the transgression of the image, the plasticity of the screen, and the 'nothing behind': in short, the medium and its mediality-as-life. This invisible yet signifying boundary is embedded in a 'negative aesthetics', an *aesthetica negativa*, which Dieter Mersch elaborates on in his essay in this volume, and which signifies a play of the 'double gaze' regarding invisibility and visibility – or 'withdrawal and excess' (Mersch in this volume). The play of visions becomes an inherent quality of images and recollects the dual nature of the medium: the conditions of making things visible as images while at the same time remaining an invisible structure behind that which shows. The question of where the 'medium' hides in the encounter between the spectator and the visual remains a focus in Mersch's text, in which he shifts the argument from the iconic structures of science and different visual technologies (such as 'maps, formulas, diagrams') to iconicity as a specifically medial structure and order of 'showing'. Invisibility constitutes visibility, and the crack between both runs beyond the image itself in a different sphere. The image acquires an intricate medial status that draws attention to the unveiled (the apparent), which in turn brings about the image and the visual that we face. Iconicity, according to Mersch, is characterized by difference that becomes the condition of the possibility of iconic visuality, and technology (like pictorial immersion) as a medium is bound to negate its own mediality.

In the chapters that follow we encounter movements of images, the immanence of their very aesthetic and perceptual faculty, the affective ontologies they become beyond their very medium, and the necessity at this stage to include the immaterial signifying dimension of media technologies in the controversial documentary traditions of anthropological knowledge acquisition. Ethnographic film-making, for one, seems to continue nineteenth-century strategies of cartography and colonial rule over unknown cultures with cinematographic means. Ute Holl discloses the relationship between techniques of scientifically mapping geometrical space that were accompanied by a racially-motivated desire of authors such as Francis Galton to fetishize the physiognomy of female Otherness by measuring the female silhouettes of, for example, a young woman from the South African Khoi tribe, infamously described as 'Hottentot Venus' – the derogative and racist description European settlers chose to give Saartjie Baartman, who was brought to England in 1810. Technology is introduced to administer desire and transform it into science, laws and orders. Early ethnographic film-making could thus be regarded as the desire to stratify the Other. Upon closer examination, ethnographic film-makers like Gregory Bateson or Maya Deren have experienced filming in unknown environments as an alienation from their own cultures, and as a means to encounter a form of desire that was their own and yet also a strange and novel one: cinema's desire. Holl's contribution discloses the moments of irritation and deferral evoked in the process of seeing the Other through the camera's eye. Scientific and documentary knowledge of Otherness and the painstaking documentation of it were transferred, according to Holl, to photographic and cinematic – i.e. technically recorded – modes of projection; words were being replaced by (moving) images. Thus, cinematography considerably altered 'the epistemic frame' of scientific knowledge as 'cinema introduced the force of the imaginary into the techniques of the colonizing observer' (see Holl in this volume). Technology hence has not only altered the epistemology of alleged Otherness but, even more so, created new forms of desire for the spectator and the film-maker alike, as Maya Deren writes in her notebook from 1947. Deren's emphasis in her aesthetic practice with Margaret Mead and Gregory Bateson's Bali film material is on forms of 'psychosomatism', and hence on the tactile experiential account of the film experience – and the moving images of (racial) 'Otherness' in particular. Holl concludes that cinematic technologies – and technology as such – uncover a turning point in anthropological film-making that link the body of the film-maker to the embodiment of desire in technology.

As part of the themes and the question of the desire of images discussed in this volume, the concept of animism is revisited by Anselm Franke in his inquiry of its conceptualization and history in an exhibition context. He discovers animist practices and aesthetic ideologies in 'modern image cultures' that transgress the boundaries of difference, and thereby reformulate and relocate desire as an aesthetic practice in exhibition art and curatorial practices. Animism constitutes a relational conceptual framework that 'operates' within an 'aesthetic economy'. According to Franke, the division between subjects and objects, life and things in modernity and, hence, the very repression of forms of mediation and relationships between the living and non-living, culture and nature, has created the symptoms of anti-fetishism and iconoclasm. Against the background of these symptoms, to reinforce the boundary between representation and the real, Franke discusses the role of technological reproduction and desire in modernity and in hindsight of new strategies and reformulations of the concept of animism in an exhibition context.

Jay David Bolter characterizes today's media culture by a productive tension between two aesthetics: catharsis and flow. Popular, narrative film aims to provoke catharsis, an emotional release through identification with a main character, while video games and other contemporary cultural experiences aim through repetition to induce in their audience a state of engagement that the psychologist Mihalyi Csikszentmihalyi has named 'flow'. The two aesthetics compete and cooperate in media culture. The aesthetic of flow, however, constitutes the end of desire as it has been represented and enacted in the culture of catharsis since at least the nineteenth century (Jay Bolter). Lorenz Engell elaborates on the agency of things through analyzing moving images and film in Georges Méliès' early cinema. Alfred Gell's methodological approach is employed by Engell as a way towards an 'abduction' of agency. The key issues in this essay are the question of indexicality and cause, cinemagic as a position of agency, the primacy of disappearance and cinemagic practices. For Engell, the question of indexicality is bound to a process of projection and temporality in Méliès's films rather than iconicity or analogy. The second form of agency is 'addressing' (i.e. the camera, the spectator's gaze), which is then effaced in classical narrative film; the sign of the agency of film disappears behind the illusive mediality of it. And, finally, conceptualizations of superimposition, doubling and intermixture signify the blurring image of cinema at large as embodying an extraordinary efficacy, its agency throughout the different modes of negation, disappearance, dramaturgy and repetitions – the technological operations that lead up to the formation of the magical image as such.

The question of the materialization of emotions – and desire in particular – in film is at the core of Hinderk Emrich's essay, in which he draws a parallel between the subjectivity of the spectator and the moving image, and concludes that images do not necessarily 'show' or represent reality but, rather, they are psychologically charged with something they can only be(come) as far as they express it in turn psychologically. Following René Girard's theory of mimesis regarding desire and its potential to be realized/actualized, Emrich elaborates on the 'nature' of mediality as a mediator of sense and the intentionality of wishes, hopes, desires, all of which lose their power unless they are being fulfilled. That is why film, according to him, is only able to achieve completion or forms of implemented fulfilment by transcendentality and less by forms of sensuality; Wong Kar-wai's film *2046* (2004), among others, serves as case study for the expression of moving images *as* desires and the transcendence of the boundary to the other.

Annette Bitsch suggests a Lacanian reading of images in times of their digital- and mass-medial circulation. She focuses on the dynamization of the subjectivity of body-media relations and hence on the subject as a medium in Lacanian theory, and the conceptualization of an intangible real, which returns to the dichotomy of being and non-being, visibility and invisibility. Bitsch draws attention to Lacan's concept of a medial *a priori* of the unconscious subject, and identifies the gaze as a bearer of the desire of the 'unconscious' subject that is a moving and processing signifier disclosed in images. The world and the subject's consciousness are mediated on an imaginary level by the unconscious gaze and by the media as phantasms. According to Bitsch, Lacan disarranges the central perspective of the Cartesian consciousness and the world as seen through the ontologically charged 'eye' by transcending the stasis of immobile images toward their mobility and movement that correlate with the unconscious subject (Lacan's *je*: 'Le *je* n'est pas le *moi*'). The gaze becomes a mediatized technique of the real body to project realities at the boundary between subjectivity and objectivity in image practices. This chapter poses the question of the materialization of Lacanian theory of the unconscious desire of the gaze, which is of vital importance for this volume. Lacan has conceptualized unconscious desire as a signifying code within the body's physical reality ('the real'). Desire becomes an incorporated algorithmic concept of the body's real that applies the gaze onto the image; the visual and 'seeing' are instructed according to an unconscious medial *a priori*. Reality in the form of public images is being constructed within the subject-body's own medium, and in turn images are recharged with desire.

In his account of the ubiquitous existence of screens and the replacement of the space of cinema by galleries, biennales etc., Timothy Druckrey suggests focusing on what he terms 'media time', an inquiry into the different forms of temporality and layering in, for example, contemporary moving image art that marks a counter-strategy to the classical cinematic image in order to ascribe time a subjectivity of its own. The 'chronotropic *dispositif*' (Druckrey in this volume) provides a framework for Druckrey to conceptualize different anti-successive, frame-breaking time structures, and turn to a more elaborate concept of 'media time' that is freed from any traditional form of visual representation.

Thomas Hensel analyzes the genre of video games as an 'artistic picture medium' (see Hensel in this volume), thereby arguing for an iconological methodology in game studies, and a revision of the genre of video games in media studies and art history alike. Through theoretical assumptions around image studies, Hensel 'remediates' computer games such as *Resident Evil 4* by revealing their structural and aesthetic – iconic – resemblance to, for example, paintings and hence to art history as the famously classical discipline of iconography and decoding. Following Richard Grusin and Jay Bolter's prominent conception of remediation, he focuses on the performative and meditative potentiality of video games in relation to paintings and art history. He concludes by assigning computer images an inherently performative quality, recounting Austin's speech-act theory and extending this very notion to so-called 'image-acts'. He appeals for an iconic turn in video games and methodologically moves across the transmedial genealogies of images.

Barbara Flueckiger scrutinizes digital images and their technological production beyond the reductive view of reading digital images as mere non-representations by taking into consideration their main technological being and, above all, their different technological constructions and possibilities. The term 'digital' is technically explained for each type of image, such as '3D', 'photography', 'computer generated imagery', 'computer simulation', etc. She provides an overdue historical as well as detailed technological account of what the 'digital' is in moving images and in digital film images in particular. The post-cinematic condition in moving image art installations and the conceptualization of film in the art space as a response to cinema's replacement by ubiquitous screens, moving images and film beyond the cinematic space is elaborated by Ursula Frohne. The moving image installation meets the culture of the spectacle by representing a counteragent to mass-medial phenomena and image distributions through spatial, temporal, as well as apparatus-based, discourses and conceptualizations in the exhibition space. Film then materializes the loss of its cinematic being as an unconscious form of 'cine-culture' in the visual arts, and is recounted in post-filmic research and theory as a 'cinema on display' (Frohne in this volume).[37] Jens Schröter discovers motionless moving images, which he terms 'sequence images'. Hiroshi Sugimoto's *Radio Music Hall, NY* (1978) is depicted as a point of departure for further ontological and epistemological accounts of reflexive strategies of technological media at the boundary between movement and stillness; the difference between the temporality of the photographic image, its stillness and the moving image of film. He continues by drawing attention to several image phenomena that pay evidence to the distinction between movement and stillness in images. These are 'image types' and concepts such as holography, flip books, and lenticular images by which Schröter attempts to shift the attention from essentialist optical assumptions about the alleged implicitness and overall premise in media history, which appears to be primarily concerned with optical media and hence lens-based media systems in particular. Yet the body reappears in the sequence image and its technique interacts with the 'movement image'.

Janet Harbord's chapter poses the question of whether cinema missed its opportunity of a Coppernican revolution; that is, its opportunity to shift human-centred perception through the prosthetic devices of cinematography and cinematic scale. According to psychoanalyst Jean Laplanche, there have been three missed appointments with a revolution that would wither enlightenment myths: the Copernican decentring of 'man' as the centre of the universe; Darwin's decentring of humans as the pinnacle of evolutionary development; and Freud's overthrow of the rational, internally-constituted subject. In the beam cast by Laplanche's thought, it is possible that cinema was potentially the fourth revolution, a revolution in perspective, facilitated by its radical alteration of properties of scale and its challenge to the place from which we see. Her chapter suggests that cinema may in fact have aided the production of an internalized subjectivity, performing what Laplanche would call a critical 'going astray'. Is this, rather than the more revolutionary proposition that cinema enacts the contingent connections between individuals, how cinematic perspective came to operate? These questions of exactly what is at stake in cinematic scale and perspective are brought to bear in Charles and Ray Eames' films, whose production involved an affiliation of the famous design team with NASA and IBM (Janet Harbord).

Yvonne Spielmann's title *Out of Image* refers to a technical term that is used when images are 'out of synch', which denotes several meanings: one is the necessary synchronization in film projection, where the image projection is a projection of light values that are fixed on a material basis. Perhaps less known is the fact that video as an electronic medium does not operate with images but signals. Video is an audio-visual medium that consists of a flow of electronic signals that are produced from incoming light or generated internally using the electromagnetic energy field. From a technical perspective, electronic media produce images different from analogue recording technologies such as photography and film. Similarly, the digital sphere does not produce images in the classical sense but, rather, codes and encodes information that can optionally be displayed visually. Spielmann's chapter focuses on other forms of an 'out of synch' condition, and that is the deliberately creative disagreement and intervention of media artists into market-driven, commercial applications in private, public and global zones. These artists are interested in another kind of imagery that is highly technological but, at the same time, reflexive and imaginative. Hence, this is a shift from mere industrial mass image production toward a reflection of techniques of mobility and motion in which artists interact with computers, LED, GPS, motion- and heat sensors, etc. (Yvonne Spielmann).

Amidst the emphasis of this volume on questions of moving images and their very technological condition, Thomas Elsaesser focuses on the ethical dimension of transgressive cinematic practices regarding transculturalism and ethnicity in Fatih Akin's German-Turkish film *Auf der anderen Seite/The Edge of Heaven* (2007). Film can provide an experiential account of such (identity) border crossings and, above all, a post-ideological critique of ethical inscription, which Jacques Rancière's emphasis on the interdependence of politics and aesthetics has provided. Rereading the interrelations of self and Other, as well as questions of inclusion and exclusion in cultural and aesthetic perspectives against the background of Rancière's political aesthetics and his belief of 'radical equality' in the arts, which have replaced the political sphere of interaction, and Alain Badiou's notion of 'event', Elsaesser claims:

> [...] for Rancière, it is finally the cinema that is the most appropriate of the arts on the point of becoming 'political', because the cinema is so impure, so mechanical and so lifelike: in short, so 'thwarted' [...] that it can bring into being the singularity and visibility (and thus the value) of the ephemeral, the humble, the excluded and the abject. The cinema accomplishes the levelling of differences between art and life, as originally promised by the avant-gardes. At the same time [...] the cinema has the potential to complete this move in the direction of 'radical equality' in the political sense. (Elsaesser in this volume)

Martin Schulz's trans- and intermedial account of Bruegel's painting *The Hunters in the Snow* (1565) aims at transcending the genre of painting through film against the background of the transgressive pre-cinematic potential of paintings and their respective animation. Bruegel's immersion in Andrei Tarkovsky's film *Solaris* (1972) is a virtual and spatio-temporal account of the transgression of images across the genealogies of media and beyond their very frames. His chapter offers a transmedial account of the topography and aesthetics of painting in film and beyond. Laura U. Marks reflects upon the sources, the origins and different forms of cultural materializations of images in layers or, more specifically, 'folds' that she visualizes in different diagrams and creates within a Deleuzian context of cinematic images and the plane of immanence.[38] Marks amends a semiotic information layer (or filter) between the different planes and layers she recalls after Deleuze, and from which images arise and become visible. It is an 'enfolding-unfolding aesthetics' she attempts to constitute in an art context, in particular, and as a method to 'pull images into being' and to follow the traces of the image's coming into being, its layers of information and perception. Extending her analysis to the field of cultural anthropology, Marks rereads Islamic art and materialist cultural theories against the backdrop of Deleuze and Guattari's *A Thousand Plateaus* (1988) and involves them in her analysis of the origins and conditions of images and their digital form. Rania Gaafar reflects on the role of 'criticality' in an art context and experimental methods in the theory of science studies as an approach towards a postcolonial media theory. As a theoretical framework and inquiry into the intricate relation between media, experience and the production of new phenomena and knowledge in the visual arts, postcolonial concepts employed as a reflection to see the other in the very 'ground of the image' (Jean-Luc Nancy 2005) is still largely missing in contemporary film and media studies.[39] The formation of new knowledge, e.g. through artistic knowledge and research, in moving image art, for one, provides new experiential ways of thinking film and its sensitive mediality as epitomizing the exilic experience and its postcolonial theoretization. In the arts – and in the visual arts in particular – Gaston Bachelard's experimental technoscientific method of a 'phenomenotechnique' has hardly been scrutinized yet. In light of the current interest in artistic research and the material turn in art theory and beyond, in which more than often art and science are interrelated, Bachelard's dynamic conceptual methodology discloses new poetic configurations of knowledge. It brings experience and its technological impact in the arts back into scientific (i.e. through science theory and its relation to postcolonial studies) focus and reflects on the spaces of enunciation of knowledge – who is speaking?

Mark B. Hansen's essay explores the continually signifying divergence, yet ongoing subtle comparison, in critical film and media philosophy of the relation between 'digital cinema' and 'digital technics', thereby emphasizing the materialist conditions in the advent of the digital that radically challenge the cinema. With reference to Lev Manovich's groundbreaking work around the language of new media and the affinity between the cinema and the digital, as well as the discussion of David Rodowick's theory of cinema and the 'virtual life of film'[40] in the age of the digital, Hansen reflects the difference between digital cinema and digital technology in terms of experience, media and above all time – the 'technical mediation of worldly time' (Hansen in this volume). The relationship between technology and desire, and the moving and photographic image has always been a challenging one, and it harks back to an experimental – in the literal 'laboratory' sense and context of the word in the natural and life sciences as well[41] – history of (moving) image art, or camera-less film,[42] which has made the materialization of the celluloid strip and the making-visible of the production process of film possible, and has become an artistic method of research and a reflexive art practice well beyond structuralist film practices. Isaac Julien discusses his artistic practice against the background of the post-cinematic conceptualization of desire and the spatio-temporal dynamics and intentionality of the architecture of screens in the installation space in his moving image art. The 'contaminated sublime' (Julien in this volume) is one of the aesthetic practices and ideas he enacts in digitally-enhanced images, while montage becomes one of the key elements in 'choreographing the moving image' in an installation context in the gallery space. He discusses the relevance of a politics of aesthetics that runs counter to, and is critically detached from, the politics of representation, which has signified Otherness in film and the media, as well as research in media and film studies and in the visual arts for far too long. The unchaining of images from conventional viewing habits (in the cinema, for example) is achieved in Julien's art through what he describes as a 'cognitive dissonance (of desire)' that is disclosed at the intersection of technologically-induced affects, and the viewing habits and experiences of the spectators.

The experience of the technologies we employ fulfils desires through the various ways we, in turn, employ our own senses. This apparent 'logic' of action and reaction or, in other words, the seemingly causal relation between seeing and acting in an aesthetic context, appears to require a manual logic of 'acting' senses and applied motion. Yet movement and applied sensual action have both become habitual features of interactive ways of seeing and understanding new media art, as well as being 'affected' by contemporary moving image art and media installations in particular. The product of 'un-concealment', which Heidegger ascribed to the characteristics of technology, is situated within a context of the circulating and meandering desire of the moving image's autonomy (the residues of an aesthetics of modernity and its aspirations) from the restrictions of e.g. questions of authorship. These ideas had already been anticipated by the conceptual art movement at the end of the 1960s; as well as with the emphasis on abstraction (for example, in painting) in form beyond questions of mimesis, likeness and content. The seizure of the figurative imperative was starting to unfold, and 'medium specificity' moved to the centre of theoretical reflections before Rosalind Krauss 'located' the medium in a 'post-medium condition' and focused on the artwork's very generative structure:

> For, in order to sustain artistic practice, a medium must be a supporting structure, generative of a set of conventions, some of which, in assuming the medium is itself as their subject, will be wholly 'specific' to it, thus producing an experience of their own necessity.[43]

Post-media and Mediality

The notions of media and mediality are at a chiasm as the medium of moving images itself vanishes against the background of an aesthetic of presence and revelation. All this is happening during a time that can be characterized by an ascendancy of a philosophy of technology and with the focus on the subjectivity of the immaterial; and thereby subscribing to a negativity of the medium itself[44] by primarily focusing on the mediality of the iconicity of moving images, which has transformed and re-signified the dispositive or apparatus. Such increasingly transgressive boundaries offer a re-examination of the riddles of the image and its Janus-mentality of present absence and ephemeral animism. Images can be dealt with as phenomena of boundaries that have transgressed the rationale of a Renaissance perspective, and have also come to represent the very scientific authority of knowledge that has increasingly acquired a different, mostly performative, surplus in maintaining a proximity to different strands of a history of science.

In a much broader perspective, the topics in this volume reflect upon an aesthetic of invisibility and subscribe to an alternating gaze of the subject and therefore – in more reflexive terms – to a chiasmatic entanglement of visibility and contortion, materiality and mediality. In short, we might therefore conclude: as soon as media make something visible, they simultaneously hide their own existence, thereby calling to our attention an aesthetic of invisibility and a critical revaluation of the concept of 'virtuality' which Ann Friedberg has foregrounded in her research.[45] The inherently performative quality of images seems to pave the way for different approaches toward the agency of images as embodied artistic interventions and mediating agents. The subjectively signified materiality of the immaterial is established (specifically in the desire of images to become agents of their very medial conditions) in myriad ways.

This volume proposes a conceptual resolution to the question of the image's (and henceforth the artwork's) evidential 'ground', its desire for an immanent other and its material intermediaries. On that account this project ventures to address several seminal questions: What is an image? How do we think of its respective media when we see what is shown or what becomes visible? What *else* is an image? What remains of the image's specific medium when the boundaries between life and the inanimate are transgressed? How do images acquire an agency, and how has our perception of them changed amidst the iconic and pictorial turns in visual studies[46], and the medial and material turns in cultural and media theory? How have they in turn influenced and produced cultures of images across different media? What context does the advent of the digital provide for the disappearance of the image's medium? Media *are* alterities, according to Dieter Mersch, in so far as they always signify an absence, a third meaning, a third intermediator that is needed to make their presence, their very transgressive existence, if not visible, then ambiguously felt as suspicious. Images share that speculative suspicion.

Notes

1   Karen Barad, *Meeting the Universe Halfway: Quantum Physics and the Entanglement of Matter and Meaning*, Durham and London: Duke University Press, 2007, p. 136: 'Crucially, an agential realist elaboration of performativity allows matter its due as an active participant in the world's becoming, in its ongoing intra-activity. And furthermore it provides an understanding of *how* discursive practices matter', and p. 140: 'In my further elaboration of this agential ontology, I argue that phenomena are not the mere result of laboratory exercises engineered by human subjects; rather, *phenomena are differential patterns of mattering* ("diffraction patterns") produced through complex agential intra-actions of multiple material-discursive practices or apparatuses of bodily production, where *apparatuses are not mere observing instruments but boundary-drawing practices – specific material (re)configurings of the world – which come to matter.* These causal intra-actions need to involve humans. Indeed, it is through such practices that the differential boundaries between humans and nonhumans, culture and nature, science and the social, are constituted.'
2   ibid., p. 207. Barad terms this new realism 'agential realism'.
3   In an interview with Pascal Bonitzer and Jean Narboni, and after the publication of his seminal film philosophical work *The Time-Image* in 1986, Gilles Deleuze refers to the brain as the screen, the biology of the brain and its relevance for understanding cinema, as well as the molecular structure of thought and the inert movement of the image. The interview was originally published in *Cahiers du Cinéma*, No. 380, February 1986, pp. 25–32: 'The circuits and linkages of the brain don't preexist the stimuli, corpuscles, and particles [*grains*]

that trace them. Cinema isn't theater; rather, it makes bodies out of grain. The linkages are often paradoxical and on all sides overflow simple associations of images. Cinema, precisely because it puts the image in motion, or rather endows the image with self-motion [*auto-mouvement*], never stops tracing the circuits of the brain and the endowment of the image through cinema with movement': in Gregory Flaxman, 'The Brain is the Screen – An Interview with Gilles Deleuze' (trans. Marie Therese Guirgis), in Gregory Flaxman (ed.), *The Brain is the Screen – Deleuze and the Philosophy of Cinema*, Minneapolis: University of Minnesota Press, 2000, p. 366.

4   Cf. Vivian Sobchack, 'What my Fingers Knew: The Cinesthetic Subject or Vision in the Flesh', in Vivian Sobchack, *The Address of the Eye: A Phenomenology of Film Experience*, Princeton University Press, 1991; Laura U. Marks, *The Skin of Film – Intercultural Cinema, Embodiment, and the Senses*, Durham: Duke University Press, 1999.

5   Laura U. Marks, *Enfoldment and Infinity – An Islamic Genealogy of New Media Art*, Cambridge, MA: MIT Press, 2010.

6   Erin Manning, *Relationscapes*, Cambridge, MA & London: MIT Press, 2009, p. 5.

7   Needless to say, the migration and movement of images across different cultures, spaces, times and media have been, for one, visually enacted in Aby Warburg's mental as well as necessarily materializing arrangement of 'Atlas of Images' in the 1920s: images are always moved and moving at once, cf. most recently: Christopher D. Johnson, *Memory, Metaphor, and Aby Warburg's Atlas of Images*, Ithaka: Cornell University Press, 2012. For a discussion in art history of the myth of Pygmalion in terms of the simulacrum as 'within the very transgression of representation, within the bracketing of mimesis and the detours of desire' (p. 3) compare Victor Stoichita, *The Pygmalion Effect. From Ovid to Hitchcock*, Chicago: University of Chicago Press, 2008.

8   In his rereading, and above all rediscovery, of the history of Renaissance perspectivism, Hans Belting has uncovered the linearity and stringency of the central perspective as mistakenly based on a scientific inaccuracy by natural scientists in Greek antiquity, which has become responsible for different perceptions and materializations of the role images in East and West: light has been the medium of vision, not that of the body, which produces material objects through the lens as it was perceived by Greek antiquity in contrast to Ibn Al Haitham's abstract, form-centred cosmological theory of vision. The Renaissance hastily altered Ibn Al Haitham's theory of vision and instead constructed a theory of images with perspective as its inflexible focus, in which the spectator of images plays a determining role. Cf. Hans Belting, *Florence and Baghdad – Renaissance Art and Arab Science*, Harvard: Belknap Press of Harvard University Press, 2011.

9   One of the most famous Renaissance paintings that includes the meta-reflection of life and death in an anamorphotic skull is presumably Hans Holbeins' *Die Gesandten* (1533). Depending on the gaze and its perspective/angle, the painting either represents the erasure of life in concentrating on the anamorphosis of death, or the decision to erase death from the planarity of life. The anamorphosis as a metaphor and a reflexive image becomes a figurative embodiment of paradoxes in the discussion of a 'negative media philosophy' by Dieter Mersch. It represents a metaphor of media-reflexivity, strategies of difference in iconic structures and an embodiment of medial paradoxes that point toward Mersch's argument of

a 'negativity of media theory' which relies heavily upon the artistic/aesthetic methods and tactics of art works. These art works interfere in and with media by rendering visible the dysfunction and disorganization of what remains unknown, while recurrently showcasing it. Cf. Dieter Mersch, 'Mediale Paradoxa. Einleitung in eine negative Medientheorie', http://www.dietermersch.de/download/mersch.mediale.paradoxa.pdf, pp. 1–14; 6 f., accessed 1 April 2011.

10 Cf. Nicolai Hartmann, *New Ways of Ontology*, New Brunswick, NJ: Transaction, 2012 (originally published as Nicolai Hartmann, *Neue Wege der Ontologie*, Stuttgart: W. Kohlhammer, 1949).

11 ibid., p. 47.

12 Gilles Deleuze, *Bergsonism*, New York: Zone Books, 1988, p. 97.

13 A ZKM conference held in Karlsruhe (Germany) at the Centre for Art and Media (ZKM) in 2005 entitled, *The Picture's Image: Scientific Visualizations as Composition*.

14 W. J. T. Mitchell, *What do pictures want? The Lives and Loves of Images*, Chicago: University of Chicago Press, 2005, p. 85.

15 ibid., p. 57.

16 ibid.

17 Cf. Malcolm Le Grice's seminal work on experimental film and the digital condition: Malcolm Le Grice, *Experimental Cinema in the Digital Age*, London: BFI Publishing, 2001.

18 Jacques Rancière, *The Politics of Aesthetics: The Distribution of the Sensible*, London & New York: Continuum, 2005, p. 59.

19 Mark Nash, 'Reality in the Age of Aesthetics', *Frieze*, Issue 114, April, 2008.

20 Cf. Jacques Rancière, *The Emancipated Spectator*, London: Verso, 2011.

21 Cf. Mitchell, 2005.

22 ibid., p. 72: 'Desire versus drive: What difference does it make if we construe what pictures want as a question of desire or drive? One way to frame this issue would be to contemplate the difference between the still and moving image, the singular and the serial image, or … between the picture (as a concretely embodied object or assemblage) and the image (as a disembodied motif, a phantom that circulates from one picture to another and across media). The picture wants to hold, arrest, to mummify an image in silence and slow time. Once it has achieved its desire, however, it is driven to move, to speak, to dissolve, to repeat itself. So the picture is the intersection of two "wants": drive (repetition, proliferation, the "plague" of images) and desire (the fixation, reification, mortification of the life-form.'

23 Cf. Boris Groys, *Under Suspicion: A Phenomenology of Media*, New York: Columbia University Press, 2012.

24 Theodore R. Schatzki et al. (eds), *The Practice Turn in Contemporary Theory*, London & New York: Routledge, 2001.

25 Nigel Thrift, *Non-Representational Theory: Space, Politics, Affect*, London & New York: Routledge, 2007.

26 Hans Ulrich Gumbrecht (2004) qtd in Thrift, 2007, p. 1.

27 Cf. Jeffrey Shaw et al. (eds), *Future Cinema – The Cinematic Imaginary after Film*, Cambridge, MA: MIT Press, 2003; Mark B. Hansen, *New Philosophy for New Media*, Cambridge, MA: MIT Press, 2004; Yvonne Spielmann, *Hybrid Culture. Japanese Media Arts in Dialogue*

with the West, Cambridge, MA: MIT Press, 2013; A. L. Rees et al. (eds), *Expanded Cinema –*
Art, Performance, Film, London: Tate Publishing, 2011.

28   Cf. Mark B. Hansen, 'Wearable Space', in *Configurations,* Vol. 10, No. 2, 2002, p. 322.

29   ibid.

30   Manning, 2009, p. 6.

31   Cf. Rosalind Krauss, *A Voyage on the North Sea: Art in the Age of the Post-Medium Condition,*
London: Thames & Hudson, 1999a, p. 26 as well as ibid., 'Reinventing the Medium', in
Critical Inquiry Vol. 25, No. 2, 'Angelus Novus': Perspectives on Walter Benjamin (Winter,
1999b), pp. 289–305.

32   Cf. Peter Weibel, 'The Postmedial Condition', 2005, http://www.peter-weibel.at/index.
php?option=com_content&view=article&id=75&Itemid=35, accessed 1 February 2014.

33   Krauss, 1999b, p. 296.

34   Henri Bergson, *Matter and Memory,* New York: Zone Books, 1991, p. 9.

35   'But is such art also involved in the crisis, or critique, of representation that Owens
saw as characteristic of the allegorical impulse? Are these recastings that we see today
deconstructions? Or, is there something different in these newer practices? […] I would
claim […] that there is indeed a different attitude at stake here. Whereas the representation
of modern forms in the 1980s often operated as an ironic critique of the tenets of modernism,
what we have with some of these other practices is a repetition of the modern. A repetition
that repeats the energy, the force, of the latter. We might say then that rather than a critique
of originality and authenticity these practices repeat and celebrate the modern impulse,
which we might characterise generally as the desire for, and production of, the new (these
practices cannot be understood as parodies or pastiches in this sense). Again, for myself,
this is what is at stake in what I have been calling the aesthetic: an impulse towards the
new, towards something different to that which is already here': in Simon O'Sullivan, 'From
Aesthetics to the Abstract Machine: Deleuze, Guattari and Contemporary Art Practice', in
Stephen Zepke and Simon O'Sullivan (eds), *Deleuze and Contemporary Art,* Edinburgh:
Edinburgh University Press, 2010, pp. 193–94.

36   Cf. especially Jane Bennett, *Vibrant Matter – A Political Ecology of Things,* Durham: Duke
University Press, 2010.

37   Jean Christophe Royoux, 'Towards a Post-Cinematic Space-Time', in Sara Arrhenius
et al. (eds), *Black Box Illuminated,* Stockholm: IASPIS, Nifca, Propexus, 2003, p. 111.

38   Compare this with the figure of thought of a 'life and love of images' that transcends the divisive
line and boundary between an immanent and transcendental sphere of object and living
subject. Rather it seeks what Deleuze recounts in *Pure Immanence* that the '"indefinite", the
sphere we are trying to elaborate regarding the equivocal notion of an animation of apparently
lifeless "objects" is illustrated by the indefinite article "one" that 'is not the transcendent that
might contain immanence but the immanence contained within a transcendental field. One
is always the index of a multiplicity: an event, a singularity, a life […]': in Gilles Deleuze, *Pure*
Immanence: Essays on a Life, New York: Zone Books, 2001, p. 30.

39   This seems to be primarily the case in non-Anglophone culture, and in German culture and
media theory in particular. Cf. for a collection on the aesthetics of exile: Kobena Mercer,

Exiles, Diasporas, and Strangers, Cambridge, MA: Iniva and MIT Press, 2008. Therein in particular: Amna Malik, 'Conceptualizing "Black" British Art Through the Lens of Exile' as well as Jean Fisher, 'Diaspora, Trauma and the Poetics of Remembrance'.

40   Rodowick, 2007.

41   In reference to Bruno Latour's and Steve Woolgar's work here on the production of new knowledge by laboratory exercises: *Laboratory Life: The Construction of Scientific Facts*, Princeton: Princeton University Press, 1979.

42   Cf. an exhibition at Schirn Kunsthalle in Frankfurt am Main bearing that title: Esther Schlicht and Max Hollein (eds), *Celluloid: Cameraless Film*, Bielefeld: Kerber Verlag, 2010.

43   Krauss, 1999a, p. 26.

44   Cf. Dieter Mersch, *Einführung in die Medientheorie*, Hamburg: Junius, 2006; ibid., 'Tertium datur. Grundlinien einer negative Medientheorie', in Stefan Münker et al. (eds), *Was ist ein Medium?*, Frankfurt am Main: Suhrkamp, 2008, pp. 304–321.

45   Anne Friedberg, *The Virtual Window – From Alberti to Microsoft*, Cambridge, MA: MIT, 2006.

46   Cf. Gottfried Boehm, 'Iconic Turn: Ein Brief', in: Hans Belting (ed.), *Bilderfragen: Die Bildwissenschaften im Aufbruch*, Munich: Fink, 2007, pp. 27–36; W. J. T. Mitchell, 'The Pictorial Turn', in *Picture Theory: Essays on Verbal and Visual Representation*, Chicago: University of Chicago Press, 1994, pp. 11–35.

Prelude

Much Trouble in the Transportation of Souls, or the Sudden Disorganization of Boundaries

Anselm Franke

For most people who are still familiar with the term 'animism' and hear it in the context of an exhibition, the word may bring to mind images of fetishes, totems, representations of a spirit-populated nature, tribal art, pre-modern rituals and savagery. These images have forever left their imprint on the term. The expectations they trigger, however, are not what this project concerns. The following text doesn't exhibit or discuss artefacts of cultural practices considered animist. Instead, it uses the term and its baggage as an optical device, a mirror in which the particular way modernity conceptualizes, implements, and transgresses boundaries can come into view.

This chapter interrogates the organization of these boundaries through images, attempting to fill the space of a particular imaginary and phantasy within the dominant aesthetic economy with a concurrent historical reality. It does so because an exhibition about animism that upholds a direct signifying relation to its subject is doubly impossible: animism is a practice of relating to entities in the environment, and as such, these relations cannot be exhibited; they resist objectification. Putting artefacts in the place of the practice gives rise to a different problem: whatever way an object may have been animated in its original context, it ceases to be so in the confines of a museum and exhibition framework by means of a dialectical reversal inscribed into these institutions, which de-animates animate entities and animates 'dead' objects. Instead, the 'Animism' exhibition (see page 71 for more information on the exhibition) attempts to imagine what a quasi-anthropological museum of the modern boundary practices might look like. The exhibition sees animism as node, a knot that, when untied, will help unpack the 'riddle of modernity' in new ways, helping us to understand modernity as a mode of classifying and mapping the world by means of partitions, by a series of *Great Divides*.

The cultural particularity of modernity derives from the naturalization of these divisions and separations; that is, from their appearance as distinctions *a priori* – as if natural and outside history – which pervade all levels of symbolic production, with far-reaching effects on aesthetics and language. The positivism of the modern description of the world relies on the imagination of a negative, which is the result of the same divisions, and becomes equally naturalized. It was through the idea of animism that modernity conceived a good part of this negative, condensing that imagination in one term. Of particular importance for our project is to see this imaginary not merely as a fiction, but also a fiction made real.

Animism is a term coined by nineteenth-century social scientists, particularly the anthropologist Edward Tylor, who aimed to articulate a theory on the origins of religion, and found it in what was to him the primordial mistake of primitive people who attributed life and person-like qualities to objects in their environment.[1] Tylor's theory was built on the widespread assumption of the time that primitive people were incapable of assessing the real value and properties of material objects. Animism was explained by its incapacity to distinguish between object and subject, reality and fiction, the inside and outside, which led to the projection of human qualities onto objects. The concept was inscribed into an evolutionary scheme from the primitive to the civilized, in which a few civilizations had evolved, while the rest of the world's people, described by Tylor as 'tribes very low in the scale of humanity',[2] had remained animist, thus effectively constituting 'relics' of an archaic past. This evolutionary scheme would soon be taken up by psychology in its own terms, asserting that every human passes through an animist stage in childhood, which is characterized by the projection of its own interior world onto the outside. The colonialist connotations of the term have led some to suggest that we abandon it once and for all. This has been necessary for a related term, the 'primitive'. But in animism, there is more at stake than in the modern discourse on its primitive Other, although they overlapped at crucial points. The challenge in using the concept today is to maintain a perspective that does justice both to non-modern practices that animism presumably characterized, and to premises of modernity from which it originated. For this reason, one needs to bear the many dimensions of the term in mind and allow them enter into a constellation akin to a montage.

The first dimension is the animism of the anthropologists of the nineteenth century, like Tylor; the 'old' animism of modernity, a category in which western imagination and phantasy, politics, economy, ideology, scientific assumptions and subjectivities fuse. Between this 'old' animism and the cultural practices that it sought to describe and classify, we find a gap marked by colonial subjugation, appropriation and misrecognition. The practices at stake are ones that need to be understood independently of their description by anthropologists, although the two have, of course, become historically entangled. There is also a 'new animism', which proclaims to have come closer to the realities of the cultures in question, which seeks to take 'animist' cultural practices seriously (and often struggles to come to terms with the enduring assumptions underlying the old), considering forms of relational knowledge, and, above all, *practices* different from those predominant in modernity. This distinction between 'old' animism and 'new' animism, between the animism western anthropologists conceptualized and what they referred to, is mirrored in the relation of so-called indigenous societies to the term: while many resent the use of the term for its colonial connotations and accusations of savagery, it is also increasingly utilized in political struggles of indigenous groups within the political structures inherited from colonial modernity.[3] And on yet another register, there is the animism *within* modernity's image culture, as an aesthetic economy and a way of imagining, which gives expression to collective desires and articulates commonsensical schemes, determining the possibilities of recognizing other subjectivities, and how life processes can be conceptualized. On this plane, it is important to distinguish between an economy of images that is a symptomatic reaction to the effects of modernity, a compensatory displacement and transgression of the boundaries and fragmentation modernity inflicts, and the critical reflection of those very borders in art. As this distinction can never be absolute, it must remain in question and permanently renewed.

For the moderns, animism is a focal point where all differences are conflated. This conflation makes for the negativity of animism, which therefore breeds powerful images and anxieties: the absorption of differences is a womb-phantasy endowed with horrific as well as redemptive qualities, strong enough, however, to yield ever new separations, ever new *Great Divides*. For the so-called animists, however, animism has nothing to do with the conflation of differences, but with their negotiation in ways that, more recently, have also become of increasing importance for the former moderns. For the moderns, the animation of things destroyed the subject, and only by the destruction of animism, and of animated things, can the free subject of modernity be constituted.

What Makes Modernity Modern?

What does it mean to be modern? Social scientists generally assume it is a categorical distinction between nature and society. Only they differentiate between facts, the universal laws of nature and matter, and cultural symbolic meanings or social relations. The knowledge of the indisputable, universal truths of nature is acquired through objectification, by distinguishing what is inherent to the object from what belongs to the knowing subject and has been projected onto the object. What is not objectified remains unreal and abstract. Only what can be objectified has a right to be called 'real'; everything else enters the realm of 'culture', the subject's interior, or 'mere' image, representation, passion, fiction, fancy, phantasy. It is this dissociation of the subjective from the realm of nature and things that simultaneously constitutes the self-possessing subject, liberated from the chains of superstition, phantasy and ignorance. The very act of division, the gesture of separation, produces at once an objectified nature composed of absolute facts and a free, detached subject: the modern, Cartesian Self. Modernity is modern insofar as the destruction of superstition and its embodiments (exemplary in the figure of the fetish) resulted in the establishment of a triumphal world of indisputable facts brought to light by the power of reason applied in the sciences. As long as objects were endowed and animated by social representations and subjective projections, they annihilate the subject; only the destruction of those ignorant ties emancipates the subject and raises it to the status of the 'free' modern Self.

In his several books that engage with the modern divide between nature and culture, Bruno Latour describes the historical scenarios that can serve as a backdrop scenography to our understanding of the role of animism in the constitution of modernity. Latour asserts that the bifurcation of nature and culture, and the subsequent purification of each domain (by way of objectification), make moderns 'see double'.[4] Every modern must take sides, and perceive the world either from the side of the object (where everything is fact), or of the subject (where everything is 'made', constructed), either from nature with its determinate, indisputable and eternal laws (to which science provides access), or from the society of social agents who can construct their world freely (in politics and culture); but each perspective sees the two domains of nature and culture as absolutely separate, from mutually exclusive points of view that one cannot occupy at the same time without falling back into animism and an archaic past. The modern idea of animism must appear then as a necessary result springing from the separation between nature and culture, as a category that allowed the moderns to name those who did not make the same distinction, those who assigned social roles to non-human things, and as a category that made them imagine the collapse of the boundaries they had installed:

> For Them, Nature and Society, signs and things, are virtually co extensive. For Us they should never be. Even though we might still recognize in our own societies some fuzzy areas in madness, children, animals, popular culture and women's bodies (Donna Haraway), we believe our duty is to extirpate ourselves from those horrible mixtures.[5]

It is this extirpation, the ongoing separation and 'purification' of the two domains of subjects and objects, that characterizes the process and progress of modernization as such, which received its canonical formulation by the thinkers of the Enlightenment and the positivist, rationalist sciences: '[The] Enlightenment's program was the disenchantment of the world. It wanted to dispel myths, to overthrow phantasy with knowledge [...]. The disenchantment of the world means the extirpation of animism.'[6] The price paid by the moderns for cutting off their social ties to nature was that this nature, together with its social representations, lost its meaning; what they gained was the belief in the universality of their knowledge, and, above all, the freedom to manipulate and mobilize nature in ways unthinkable in pre-modern contexts. The moderns, Latour tells us, are literally homeless, as they live in a contradictory world composed of a 'unifying but senseless nature', while on the other, they experience a multiplicity of cultural representations 'no longer entitled to rule objective reality':

> The world had been unified, and there remained only the task of convincing a few last recalcitrant people who resisted modernization – and if this failed, well, the leftovers

could always be stored among those 'values' to be respected, such as cultural diversity, tradition, inner religious feelings, madness, etc. In other words, the leftovers would be gathered in a museum or a reserve or a hospital and then be turned into more or less collective forms of subjectivity. Their conservation did not threaten the unity of nature since they would never be able to return to make a claim for their objectivity and request a place in the only real world under the only real sun.[7]

The Great Divides

The Great Divide is what separates modern and pre-modern societies, positing civilization on one side of the abyss, and the primitive and archaic on the other: In order to understand the Great Divide between Us and Them we have to go back to that other Great Divide between humans and nonhumans [...]. In effect, the first is the exportation of the second.[8] That the internal (nature/culture) and the external (modern/pre-modern) Great Divide were mirroring each other would also mean that they were upheld by largely the same techniques: the people who found themselves on the other side of the external Great Divide would be subject to the same protocols of objectification as a nature rendered objective in the laboratory. The resulting quest for symmetry is what gave birth to modern anthropology, which had to qualify itself within the ruling milieu of the rationalist, positivistic sciences. Tylor's conception of animism therefore was firmly based in an objectivist rationalism: since the people and culture in question did not make the same categorical distinction between nature and culture – since they treated objects as if they possessed the capacity for perception, communication and agency – Tylor could conceive of animism as a 'belief', as an epistemological error, and could locate his primitive 'origin' of religion there. Nonetheless, there needed to be a supplement, since the cultures in question were still human, which meant they could not be objectified in similar ways to objects of nature. Since western ontology itself and its dualism were far from being in question at this point, however, the cultures on the other side of the Great Divide had to be inscribed into an evolutionary scheme; they had to become 'pre-modern'. Thus, Tylor located his animists among the 'lower races' and 'savages'.[9] But this evolutionary scheme was not his invention: the 'backwardness' of non-modern cultures had been a common conception as early as the sixteenth century in the context of the emergence of western modernity and mercantilist capitalism. All that Tylor did was clothe it in a scientific narrative. Animism was thus progressively inscribed in a set of imaginary oppositions that enforced and legitimized western imperial modernity, constituting a spatial-geographic 'outside', and a primitive, evolutionary 'past'.

Animism, much like the category of the 'primitive', was thus not so much a description of a social order of a past archaic or present primitive form of culture, but an expression of the need and desire to find them. The modern conception of animism says much less about those it presumably described objectively than about modernity and the distinctions that upheld its cosmography. Animism and the primitive were much sought for mirrors, by means of which modernity could affirm itself in the image of alterity. In the heyday of European colonialism, the invention of a non-existent unity of the animist primitive along an imaginary historical arrow of progress constituted a key to legitimizing the actual subjugation of the colonized as much as it was necessary to provide the moderns with an image that could confirm their identity. It mattered little whether the denigration was reversed and instead idealized as a 'paradisic state of nature'[10] (which can switch at any moment into the state of nature as the brutal struggle for survival beyond any social contracts), as compensation for the evils of modernity, or liberation from the constraints of civilization.

The Space of Death and the Theatre of Negativity

As much as that image of animist primitives and their savagery unified the 'rest' on the modern's side of the Great Divide, it inflicted terror on those locked inside of it. Imaginary appropriation licensed real subjugation; the objectivist 'tyranny of the signifier' that had enthroned enlightened reason would enact the savagery it had imputed to its others. The flipside of the disenchanted, static, enlightened realm of objective facts is equally imaginary, that darkness as of yet untouched by the light of reason. The regime of positivist signification sees its opposite in 'wildness', just as the bifurcation of nature and culture finds its negation in animism. The result, in both cases, is the creation of a space of negativity. 'Wildness challenges the unity of the symbol, the transcendent totalization binding the image to that which it represents. Wildness pries open this unity and in its place creates slippage. [...] Wildness is the death space of signification,'[11] wrote anthropologist Michael Taussig. He continues:

> This space of death has a long and rich culture. It is where the social imagination has populated its metamorphizing images of evil and the underworld: in the Western tradition Homer, Virgil, the Bible, Dante, Hieronymos Bosch, the Inquisition, Rimbaud, Conrad's heart of darkness; in northwest Amazonian tradition, zones of vision, communication between terrestrial and supernatural beings, putrification, death, rebirth, and genesis, perhaps in the rivers and land of maternal milk bathed eternally in the subtle green light of coca leaves. With European conquest and colonization, these spaces of death blend into a common pool of key signifiers binding the transforming culture of the conquerer with that of the conquered. But the signifiers are strategically out of joint with what they signify. 'If confusion is the sign of the times,' wrote Artaud, 'I see at the root of this confusion a rupture between things and words, between things and the ideas and signs that are their representation.'[12]

In his seminal study of the rubber boom in the Putuyamo region in Amazonas, Taussig describes how, through the arrival of the colonial regime and capitalist exploitation, this imaginary death space was systematically turned into a reality. It is this passage from the imaginary to reality, the process through which images turn into operational maps by means of which we understand, rule and, ultimately, create a world that this project, in seeking to explore the imaginary and the historicity of animism, must focus on.

In the death space created at the modern colonial frontier, the imagery (the social representations and the connections they uphold with the world) of the destroyed society and its cosmography fuses with the imagery of the conquering world, creating restless hybrids through which, in discontinuity, continuity and memory are preserved. The imagery brought to the colonial space of death by the Europeans has its own distinct European genealogy. The extirpation of animisms in the colonial world was preceded by the extirpation of animisms within the West: the imagination of the death space has been shaped by the struggle for Christianization, by images of martyrdom and the experiences of the witch hunt and the Inquisition, which produced a 'theatre of negativity', in which the European imaginary of evil was born. This theatre would find ceaseless continuation in the Enlightenment and secular modernity, in the progressive exorcisms of all states of mind that resisted the Christian, and later, the modern discontinuity between humans and nature.

Within Europe, the division of the modern cosmography into an imaginary black and white, night and light, was enacted as a progressive frontier. The boundary of the modern world generated an imagery at its internal margins correlative to the colonial death space, but yet articulated in more familiar morphologies of the 'night of the world' – what much later would become the 'unconscious'. This space is populated by dismembered bodies, by fragmentation, scenarios of disintegration, and the like, providing a monstrous mirror to objectification, discipline, mechanistic fragmentation and political terror. The unreal, delirious, diabolic night of darkness created by the empire of enlightened reason, however, was always also a space of transformation and transgressive phantasies, as Taussig describes in the work mentioned above; a space of heightened, even delirious animations and sensuous, mimetic ecstasies. Both aspects shaped the imaginary that would later find its conceptual expression in the concept of animism.

The Modern Boundary Replicated

The logic of the Great Divide would find another correlate in the exemplary institution of modernity, the asylum and psychiatry, and the phantasy of animism as the conflation of the modern distinctions would once again be a key accusation that sustained the power of the institutional machine. Michel Foucault wrote a history of this Great Divide, separating the normal from the pathological, reason from unreason in modernity. There are, in his exposé in the *History of Madness*, several clues to the working of the modern boundary regime. He attempts to write the history of madness starting from the point not of the later imaginary of indifference, but where madness and reason were still unseparated, where the experience of madness was not yet differentiated, not yet marked by a boundary that cut it off. He attempts to return to the gesture of partition, the caesura that creates the distance between reason and unreason in the first place, the original grip by which reason confined unreason in order to wrest its secrets, its truth, away from it:

> We could write a history of limits – of those obscure gestures, necessarily forgotten as soon as they are accomplished, through which a culture rejects something which for it will be the exterior; and throughout its history, this hollowed out void, this white space by means of which it isolates itself, identifies it as clearly as its values. For these values are received, and maintained in the continuity of history; but in the region of which we could speak, it makes its essential choices, operating the division which gives a culture the face of its positivity.[13]

What is most relevant in Foucault's description for the present context is that there arises in it an explanation how the logic of partition creates the space of silence of an exchange being brought to a halt, that is being filled by the monological discourses and institutions congruent to the division; he asserts that these discourses and institutions are indeed the result of the primary partition, spanning and administering the very abyss that made them possible. The partition lines of the Great Divides, it seems, must be replicated on different scales, without which their management and overall organization would not hold together: they must run through the interior of each subject, through the body, the family, the nation, through modern culture at large, and finally, through humankind. This replication on various scales helps us see more clearly that none of the scissions remain absolutely static; indeed, they must be negotiated and replicated permanently. Finally, their logic becomes implicit within the cognitive mapping of the world ('an obscure gesture' which constitutes the positive and negative, the social implicit and the explicit), and in order to describe them without operating within their registers, one must return to the point before the scission, before the decoupling of elements such as body and mind, subject and object, humans and non-humans, reason and unreason, in order to think their entanglement and unity. In this lies the potential significance of animism beyond its symptomatic, pathologized articulation as a transgressive phantasy where differences conflate. For there are, in the practices referred to as animist, indeed relations that constitute experiences of difference not marked by the proliferating Great Divides.

Foucault's history of the separation that gave rise to the modern institution of psychiatry also entails an aspect relevant to the question of relationality and difference. The relation established by the modern discourses to the absolute differences they postulate is monological: psychiatry speaks *about* madness, not *with* madness. Madness is objectified; what the psychiatrist speaks is the language of objective facts, which can no longer account for subjective experiences. Indeed, key symptoms of modern pathologies are a response to such objectification, which is experienced as the threat of petrification and immobilization. The boundaries of all Great Divides stir not only scientific interest, but are populated by anxieties in the form of images, figures, the threat of mimetic infections – in which the order of rationality is always put at risk – and defended by an extension of its rule. The modern subject, in its laboratory situations deprived of dialogic relatedness, becomes armoured in defence of its unity, and this defence is symptomatically displaced into the border-imagery. The anxiety about the border itself is what defines the morphology and symbolic economy of its images – and these images become templates for the inscription of Otherness. The threat of machinic dismemberment is displaced into the anxiety of the body given over to the fluid and fragmentary, and to emergent relational subjectivities against which the subject builds up an 'armor of anaesthetization'[14] that upholds its unity in a reiterated gesture of defence. These 'Others' are the symptomatic articulation of the rationalist boundaries; they encompass in the interior the so-called unconscious, the sensuous, emotional and sexual, and in the exterior, the racial Other, the subaltern:

> Whelped in the Great Divides, the principal Others to Man, including his 'posts,' are well documented in ontological breeding registries in both past and present Western cultures: gods, machines, animals, monsters, creepy crawlies, women, servants and slaves, and noncitizens in general. Outside of the security checkpoint of bright reason, outside the apparatuses of reproduction of the sacred image of the same, these 'others' have a remarkable capacity to induce panic in the centers of power and selfcertainty. Terrors are regularly expressed in hyperphilias and hyperphobias, and examples of this are no richer than in the panics roused by the Great Divide between animals (lapdogs) and machines (laptops) in the early twenty-first century C.E. Technophilias and technophobias vie with organophilias and organophobias, and taking sides is not left to chance.[15]

Life

The backdrop against which to understand the nineteenth-century conception of animism is ultimately the partition of life from non-life, and its many offsprings and differentiations. The distinction between life and non-life is perhaps the most fundamental one in modernity, explicitly as well as implicitly qualifying its notions of objectivity and the laws of nature, the divisions between subjects and objects, material and immaterial, human and non-human. It is, at the same time, the most unstable of divisions, having an instability that finds its expression in bioethical debates, technophobias, and the gothic imaginary and unique importance the experience of the 'uncanny' holds in modern aesthetics as a borderline condition in which the inanimate turns out as animate and vice versa; and which, in Freud's canonical interpretation, has consequently been explained as a 'return' of animistic convictions:

> For anyone undertaking a genealogical study of the concept of 'life' in our culture, one of the first and most instructive observations to be made is that the concept never gets

defined as such. And yet, this things that remains indeterminate gets articulated and divided time and again, through a series of caesurae and oppositions that invest it with a decisive strategic function in domains as apparently distant as philosophy, theology, politics, and – only later – medicine and biology. That is to say, everything happens as if, in our culture, life were what cannot be defined, yet, precisely for this reason, must be ceaselessly articulated and divided. [...] In our culture, man has always been thought of as the articulation and conjunction of a body and a soul, of a living thing and a logos of a natural (or animal) element and a supernatural or social or divine element. We must learn instead to think of man as what results from the incongruity of these two elements, and investigate not the metaphysical mystery of conjunction, but rather the practical and political mystery of separation. What is man, if he is always the place – and, at the same time, the result – of ceaseless divisions and caesurae? It is more urgent to work on these divisions, to ask in what way – within man – has man been separated from nonman, and the animal from the human, than it is to take positions on the great issues, on so-called human rights and values.[16]

The segmentations of life have a common background in what has dominated European Christian debates for centuries: the question over the character and composition of the soul (in Latin, *anima*, from which the word 'animism' is derived), which was seen variously as an entity distinct from the body or as its animating principle, or both at the same time. Radically simplifying the quarrels over the nature of souls, what is tantamount to the milieu of rationalist positivism in the nineteenth century was its gradual disappearance from centre stage in an evolving modernity. The soul could not be objectified since it had no apparent material reality that conformed to its latest metaphysical designs. When the anatomists during the Enlightenment opened up the body, there was no evidence of it. The soul could not be objectified, and thus it retracted into the realm of the subjective interior, and was secularized in the notion of the psyche and self. As a consequence, the very definition of 'life' was put at stake – for the 'hard' sciences, life had to be explained without making reference to an immaterial force (which the vitalists were still defending through concepts such as the *élan vital* by Henri Bergson), it had to be explained through mechanical, biochemical processes and their inherent laws alone. It is against this background of (often vulgar) materialism that one must understand the characterization of animist relations to matter and 'objects' as a 'belief' and an epistemological 'mistake' that had no objective claim to reality, disregarding the experiential dimensions of those relations and the questions they may pose:

But to describe the primitive ghostsoul as either matter or spirit is misleading; if these terms are to be applied to it, we must describe it as a material spirit. This is, of course, a contradiction in terms, which we can resolve by recognizing that the peoples who believe in the ghostsoul have not achieved the comparatively modern distinction between material and immaterial or spiritual existents.[17]

Images, Media and the Return of the Repressed

Nineteenth-century rationalist science frequently referred to the soul as an image:

> It is a thin, unsubstantial human image, in its nature a sort of vapour, film or shadow; the cause of life and thought in the individual it animates; independently possessing the personal consciousness and volition of its corporeal owner, past or present; capable of leaving the body far behind, to flash swiftly from place to place; mostly impalpable and invisible, yet also manifesting physical power, and especially appearing to men waking or asleep as a phantasm separate from the body of which it bears the likeness; continuing to exist and appear to men after the death of that body; able to enter into, possess and act in the bodies of other men, of animals, and even things.[18]

This is a description that, with minor alterations, would be applicable in almost all its features to the photographic and cinematographic image. Though substantial, the photographic image, too, moves through time and space, appears as a phantasma-bearing likeness, continues to exist after death, and has a certain physical and mediumistic power to 'possess' other bodies, as any observation of a crowd in a cinema suffices to show. Is there a relation, and if so, of what kind, between the Great Divides and modern technological media? Is there a relation between the 'disenchantment' of the world, the retraction of the soul to subjective interiority, and the objectivist stance? The canonical accounts of the industrialized, rationalized modern world frequently come to that conclusion. Is there, however, a connection, or even a similar process happening to images, regarding their status in modernity and their technologies? According to Bruno Latour, the division of nature and culture, and the subsequent purification of the two domains of subjects on the one side and things on the other, is only possible by a repression of the middle ground, the mediation that connects subjects with objects in multiple forms: 'Everything happens in the middle, everything passes between the two, everything happens by way of mediation, translation and networks, but this space does not exist, it has no place. It is unthinkable, the unconscious of the moderns.'[19] Objectification, that is, the purification of the domains of subjects and things, of life and non-life, is made possible by suppressing mediation, symbolic meanings, and images: the moderns 'had in common a hatred of intermediaries and a desire for an immediate world, emptied of its mediators.'[20] Latour accounts for these mediators and their networks in his ethnography of science, tracing the tools, technologies and chains of reference that create new associations between humans and things borne from modernity's laboratories. Latour's mediators are always graphs – modes of inscription that make things talk, and through which a reference can be mobilized.

There is another, more general aspect, however, to the realm of mediation and associations. Images – in all their aggregate conditions, as sign, work of art, inscription or picture that acts as a mediation to access something else; as social representations, symbols, schemes;

from their role in cognition, the sensuous body and mimetic exchange, to the image as an object that, as a mediator, acquires an agency of its own – are what any relation presupposes, since we have no direct access to the world. Images, whether merely mental or materialized, are, by definition, boundaries: conjunction and disjunction at the same time, creation of a difference and creation of a relation. They organize, uphold, cross, transgress, affirm or undermine boundaries. The particularity of the Great Divides, however, makes the image in modernity the subject of a particular economy, of a split, a schizophrenic regime. For the image in modernity is never allowed to embody the function of a mediator per se, organizing both processes of subjectification and objectification in ever fragile constellations. Images, too, must take sides: as neutral windows adequately representing the objective world (by way of divine or machinic inscription producing an uncontaminated mimetic accuracy that reduces the deceptive to a minimum), or as mere subjective representations with no claim to an objective world; that is, in the last instance, as an animistic mirror of sorts, a projection of interiority onto the outer world, reduced to the picture plane. The status of photography provides perfect evidence of this ever shifting status: either the photograph is seen as a merely machinic product, over which consequently no right of authorship can be claimed (as was the case in the early days of photography), or it is seen as the expression of a subject (as made constitutive at a later stage). The machine in this instance either records the world neutrally, objectively, or it is the wilful instrument of a subject's intention, although surely such division can only be maintained conceptually, never in practice. In each case, the turning point, the infrastructure of a complex chain of mediations, is blended out:

> We are digging for the origin of an absolute – not a relative – distinction between truth and falsity, between a pure world, absolutely emptied of humanmade intermediaries and a disgusting world composed of impure but fascinating humanmade mediators.[21]

The schizophrenia derived from the repression of mediation in its own right finds its ultimate articulation in iconoclasm and anti-fetishism, two distinctively modern stances to which Latour has also devoted significant work. It is in these figures that the link between the fate of the soul and the fate of the image under the rule of objectivism are linked: that is, when images are endowed with souls. On the level of pictures, the fetish is the embodiment par excellence of a forbidden hybridity, of the 'horrible mixture' outlined above. It represents what for modernity is an impossibility – at least conceptually: a fact that is also constructed. The fetish is the figure of an image-object subjectively made and falsely endowed with an objective reality – an agency, a subjectivity and life of its own. In order for it to be real, no human hand is allowed to have touched it. The desire for an unmediated, non-relational access to nature and truth calls for the destruction of false images. In the face of the fetishistic power of imagery, the moderns shift between an omnipotence and impotence that replicates their relation to nature: either 'they make everything', or 'everything is made and they can do nothing'.[22] The destruction of the accused images breeds only ever new imagery; and worse, in the last instance, it is only in the act of destruction that the image gains the power of which it is being accused: '[the] very act of critique often adds to the power of the critiqued.'[23] In modernity, there is always either too much or too little to an image. Either they are nothing or everything. Worse, in their strong belief in the power of the fetish, so much so that it demands destruction, the moderns turn into fetishists of a higher order: The fetishist knows well that fetishes are made-up, constructed, relational and mediated. The urge of the enlightened anti-fetishist to destroy the fetish reinstitutes a paradoxical belief. The facticity and rationality that inhabits the world in which fetishism has been destroyed is replaced by a new fetish, ever more powerful than the previous one: objectivity, a form of knowing that is absolute and non-relational, bracketed off from history and social context. Inscribing these facts once again into the historicity of knowing and science, Latour brings the fetishistic 'heart of darkness', which Europeans had so successfully placed in their imaginary of the other, back home again: 'But the myths which fell victim to the Enlightenment were themselves its product.'[24]

In modern technologies of mimetic reproduction, the borderline condition of all modern imagery finds its ultimate technological expression. The destruction of images and the repression of mediators not only produces the paradoxical reversal where the power of images is proliferated in the act of their destruction, but also yields unprecedented desires for the production of new images, in which the experiential dimension of modernity is expressed, confirmed and overcome. The technological media are themselves the product not merely of a technological advance, but of these desires that are the direct outcome of the logic of the divides. Modern imagery – as with any set of images – constitutes a meridian point of simultaneous association and dissociation in which objectification and subjectification blend, although this blending happens only in constellatory flashes, preparing a rescission which re-inscribes them on either side of the divides. This meridian point is a political battlefield; it holds both dystopian and utopian potential. It is a site of constant dialectical reversals, of intense unrest, nervousness and anxiety. The image becomes at once the very site of the 'horrible mixture' and its decomposition.

The key to understanding the knot at the meridian point of modern imagery is the experiential dimension of modernity. Industrialization and rationalization produced a segmentation and fragmentation of the senses, mirroring the effect of the 'disenchantment' that objectification and modern iconoclasm had on our perception of the world. The band that holds time and space together breaks, and with it symbolic unity, resulting in a generalized condition of social 'disembeddedness'. Alienation is the concept that describes the experience of the modern objectified world, and the splitting of that experience into isolated categories such as agency, object and observer, self and non-self. Social alienation is the price of modernity, as well as being the precondition and symptom of modern power relations:

Human beings purchase the increase in their power with the estrangement from that over which it is exerted. Enlightenment stands in the same relationship to things as the dictator to human beings. He knows them to the extent that he can manipulate them. [...]

Not only is domination paid for with the estrangement of human beings from the dominated objects, but the relationships of human beings, including the relationship of humans to themselves, have themselves been bewitched by the objectification of the mind. Individuals shrink to the nodal points of conventional reactions and the modes of operations objectively expected of them. Animism had endowed things with souls; industrialism makes souls into things.[25]

Unification through objectification takes the form of extinction coupled with conservation. Extinction because the conceptual denial of Otherness inscribed real Others into the continuum of objects, and if the destructive force thus unleashed did not result in direct or indirect genocides, it nevertheless destroyed the subjectivities (and cosmographies) in question (if not once and for all). The simultaneous conservation in institutions of modern knowledge, such as museums, archives and exhibitions, did not run counter to this destruction; it merely gave it an adequate expression through which the power of inscription could become manifest.

Life and Death on Display

This is where an exhibition about animism must begin. It must use the concept of animism as the mirror of modernity that it was from the outset, while at the same time disempower the relations that the powerful imaginary of the term upheld. The projection and exportation of animism onto the imagined 'heart of darkness' out there, at the other side of the Great Divides, must be reversed, and similar to the concept of fetishism, animism must be 'brought back home'. The economy of the imaginary of the Great Divides must become visible in the modern imaginary, so that the relations enforced by the foreclosing of relations can come to the fore. And insofar as the position of animism in the geography of the Great Divides links the question of life and non-life with that of the object and the subject, it must focus on the dialectics of objectification (mummification, petrification, reification, and so forth) and animation in modern imagery.

A powerful, if somewhat sentimental root-image situating the *dispositifs* of objectification within which such a dialectics unfolds is the butterfly – symbol of the psyche, of life undergoing metamorphosis. In order for the butterfly to become an object within a static taxonomy, and for it to enter the material base of such taxonomy – that is, the archive, exhibition, and so forth – it must be conserved. Its fixation requires mummification, and it is 'installed' at its place within the grid of the taxonomy (the modern cosmography) by the needle that pins it to the display. The needle is a figure for the act of objectifying signification. If this requires actual killing, there are also various forms of 'social death', which leave biological life intact, while depriving the subject/object in question of the *Umwelt* (Jakob von Uexküll translates this as 'environment') that constitutes its life, of the web that constitutes its being in relationality. This is the objectification of life we find in the ethnographic displays during the era of the grand world fairs, and such are the enclosures of the zoo. They are displays of objectification because they enclose and isolate – yet another phenotype of the disciplinary institutions and enclosures described by Michel Foucault as the engines of modern power – and because they foreclose the possibility of dialogic relationships, and deliver the object on display to consumption and spectacle clothed in educational terms.

The entire discipline of anthropology, it has been claimed, is implicated in an objectification in which extinction (cultures doomed to disappear as civilization and modern progress inevitably progress), and conservation are merely the flip sides of one and the same coin, creating what Paul Ricoeur has envisioned as an 'imaginary museum' of mankind. The intimacy of extinction and documentary inscription and conservation characterizes ethnographic film as well as photography – as famously illustrated by the case of photographer Edward Curtis and his pictures of North American native cultures, which he thought were at the brink of extinction, a 'vanishing race'.[26] The pictures themselves express the borderline, simultaneously reaching out and upholding it – the border between 'us' and 'them', and between an imagined past, a present mastered by modernity, and a future that holds no more place for 'them'. The pictures become, in an uncanny sense, the borders themselves. Curtis' pictures have frequently been invoked in debates over the myth of the camera stealing the soul.[27] This myth, ascribed to natives worldwide, once again links image with soul, and is an expression of the modern belief in the continuity, as well as the rupture, between magic and technology – an instance, once more, of the modern 'belief in belief', a blindness to the world-producing power of relational practices, which already structures the 'fetishism' discourse.[28]

On another, general register – the connection between photography and death, the 'uncanny' status of photography in that it transcends the boundaries of time and space, absence and presence, life and non-life – has been subject to intense debates that need no reiteration in detail here. Earlier, I noted that modern technological images are themselves a meridian point of sorts in regards to the separation of object and subject, a transgression or even dissolution of that very division; and that, nevertheless, this dissolution upholds, confirms and redoes the scission, having to dissolve the tension in the direction of either pole. However, the technological image cannot be wholly 'subjectified'. It is not, and cannot be, neutral with respect to the two poles of the subject and object, life and non-life, since it is itself the inscription of an objectification. Roland Barthes gives an account of this when he says:

> In terms of imagerepertoire, the Photograph (the one I intend) represents that very subtle moment when, to tell the truth, I am neither subject nor object but a subject who feels he is becoming an object: I then experience a microversion of death (of parenthesis): I am truly becoming a specter.[29]

Of spectres, we know that they are halfway between life and death, disembodied souls roaming the sphere of the living, bound to return. They are alive only in relation to the deprivation of life, having been withdrawn from the status of a subject across various registers – a 'thing', as Derrida invoked with *Hamlet*,[30] but a thing that is real only in the Lacanian sense. Spectres inhabit the space of death, the space of negativity, of the un-cohered, thus being denied entry into a circle that binds together a community of the living, and dissociates it from its outsides. Museums and photography, as two examples of modern *dispositifs* of the conservation of 'life', are haunted, afflicted by the spectres of objectification, by the return of animism, which here takes the form of the 'uncanny' return of a repressed life turned into a spectacle. This 'hauntedness' is a key to the ways in which media and institutions built the modern social imaginary – in circumscribed confines, giving way to the desires to overcome alienation, the desires for the reanimation of a deanimated, demobilized world, thus repopulating the deadened, disenchanted, objectified world with its monstrous images of hybrids, and phantasies of returns and speed-deliriums. And in so doing, ever actualizing the imaginary of animism as the 'heart of darkness', ripe with anxieties and fears of regression, which demand evermore reassuring objectifications and enclosures: no photographic image without its spectral quality, and no museum in which one is not invited to contemplate the skeleton of a dinosaur coming back to life. The node in which objectification – the fixation, conservation and mummification of life – meets the transgressive desires for reanimation, re-creation, mobilization and transformation, however, finds its ultimate technological expression in film, and what André Bazin has famously referred to as its 'mummy complex'. The 'mummy complex', it is often assumed, refers to a universal of art: the desire to provide a defence against the passing of time and, ultimately, death. The symbolic victory over death is supposedly a 'basic psychological need in man.'[31] However, we should not be too quick to agree, and instead, should return to the question of psychology and art at a later point.

It is cinema, however, that gives ultimate expression to 'the great Frankensteinian dream of the nineteenth century: the recreation of life, the symbolic triumph over death.'[32] In the cinematic synthesization of movement creating an illusion of life, the negative returns animated, redeemed in phantasmagoric and symptomatic form: images, souls, states of mediality. Having lost the right for a claim to reality, they assume the form of hybrids between life and non-life, fiction and reality. Cinema, from its outset, is populated by zombies, Frankensteins and man-machine hybrids, and mummies deserting their graves. Every coming-alive of the dead – or, in other terms, every re-subjectification of a 'dead' object – however, is a confirmation of the 'proper' boundary that keeps them firmly apart: the Frankensteinian dream does not undo the subject-object dichotomy; rather, it qualifies it. It is the symptom of a bourgeois hegemonic perspective that has internalized the logic of the divide and turns the tension, the antagonism between *rigor mortis* and phantasmagoric animation, into an aesthetic economy endlessly reiterated. The Frankensteinian dream is congruous to the structure of the commodity, and rather than overcoming its paradigms, it channels the anxieties it produces by providing a phantasmagoric displacement of relations that have previously been displaced.

Art occupies a special position within the modern geography marked by the Great Divides. It shares many of the characteristics of the status of images described above, but midway between subject and object, it is dissolved into the direction of the fictional, imaginary and subjective, where it fuels hopes for reinstituting the sovereignty of experience. The modern institution of art acquires its relative autonomy thus; for the price of being rendered politically inconsequential, its effects must remain in the realm of interiority and the imagination. Much of the history of modern art can be aligned with a contestation of that very boundary drawn around its legitimate place – the overcoming of the stigma of the fictional (leading to yet another genealogy in line with the Frankensteinian dream, the dream of total representation and a 'cosmic, fourth dimension', represented by the quest for the *Gesamtkunstwerk*, the synaesthetic total work of art), and the crossing of the boundary between art and life. This is the point of origin from which the numerous contestations of modern dichotomies in the modernist project stem, and to date, always return. There is a magic circle being drawn around the institution of art that renders it exceptional while inscribing it into the logic of separation. Objects of art always magically confirm their status as art. It can thus be explained how Sigmund Freud arrived at the conclusion that modernity preserved a place for animism in art, for in art we have retained an animistic relation to pictures and objects alike. The regression to 'earlier states' (historically and subjectively) and the conflation of differences between fiction and reality, the self and the world, all this becomes possible as long as it is institutionally framed and cannot make claims to objective reality, in which case it would likely be rendered pathological, but at least cease to be 'art' in the modern sense of the word – the form of art that, according to Adorno, was made possible by the secularization of the Enlightenment. What would elsewhere appear as outright regression can serve cultural advancement within these institutional confines, under the condition that it is bracketed off from everything else.

Insofar as aesthetic resistance to social rationalization (cultural modernity versus social modernity) takes the form of a dialectics, its attack on the latter remains bound to its own myths. This can be confirmed by a most schematic survey of the role animism plays in the modernist imaginary: a reconciliatory and transformative force in the face of alienation; a phantastic horizon for a better, utopian, animated modernity. From the Romantics to the Russian avant-garde, from primitivist modernism via the surrealists to psychedelia, animism frequently appears on a (troubled) quasi-mystical horizon in which it was inscribed by the modernist myths, variously as a displaced key or a transgressive phantasy; an engine that fuels the imaginary of a liberation, of an 'outside' to modern enclosures and identities. But the animism in question remains the phantasy of Otherness, a romantic antidote; and if one border is transgressed or even undone in a stroke, others are erected or fortified in the very same act. Insofar as aesthetic resistance in the modernist predicament was modelled on an opposition to the objectifying, partitioning stance of modernity, it remained difficult for the adversaries to act outside the modernist myths. When the surrealists staged their anti-colonial exhibition 'La Verité sur les Colonies' in 1931 in Paris, to show that Europeans had fetishes too, they succeeded less in bringing the 'heart of darkness' home, than in continuing to enhance the myth of 'childish', regressive 'relics', working towards a conflation of the Other by way of an alleged 'unconscious'. The institutions capable of exhibiting the fetish of the moderns have yet to be invented. Symmetry between modernity and its Others is never possible so long as one stays within the former's dialectical confines. As Latour asserts, the resolutely anti-modern only confirm the modern's own myths dialectically: they indeed believe that the moderns have rationalized and disenchanted the world; that it is, in fact, populated by soulless zombies.

> They take on the courageous task of saving what can be saved: souls, minds, emotions, interpersonal relations, the symbolic dimension, human warmth, local specificities, hermeneutics, that margins and the peripheries.[33]

Art and Psychology

All social representations, insofar as they bear a mythical structure, are to be explained by psychology. In canonical art history, the question of animism and the boundary between life and non-life is therefore discussed under the parameters of psychological universals. Art, it is understood, derives from the need to resist time and triumph over death. The desire to bring time to a standstill, to conserve and fix, is as much at the root of art as is the desire to animate, to recreate life, to gain access to the forces of creation. These psychological universals are inextricably linked to motion and stasis, and their negotiation and dynamics in works of art. This scenography is populated by mythical figures, captured, for instance, in the animating gaze of sculptors Pygmalion and Daedalus, on the one hand, and the chthonic monster Medusa, whose gaze petrified life, on the other. Anthropomorphic projection and visualization, objects that appear to 'return one's gaze', works of art that assume a subjectivity of sorts, or instances of 'the uncanny' in which something inanimate seems to 'come back' to life, are all perfectly familiar cases that do not present a real challenge to the discipline of art history as long as the primary boundary between reality and fiction is upheld. The question of 'life' poses itself as mere symbolic production, always in terms of the 'lifelike', and has consequences not for the 'real' world, but for the reality of the subjectivity of perception and its 'primitive roots', for which Freud gave the canonical description in relation to animism when he asserted:

> The projection outwards of internal perceptions is a primitive mechanism, to which, for instance, our sense perceptions are subject and which therefore normally plays a very large part in determining the form taken by our external world. Under conditions whose nature has not been sufficiently established, internal perceptions of emotional and intellective processes can be projected outwards in the same way as

sense projections; they are thus employed for building up the external world, through they should by rights remain part of the internal world. [...][O]wing to the projection outwards of internal perceptions, primitive men arrived at a picture of the external world which we, with our intensified conscious perception, have now to translate back into psychology.[34]

Any journey into the animist universe of the unconscious must therefore remain a confirmation of this split between the real and the unreal, as long as the unconscious remains unconscious, as long as its existence is assumed as a fact, rather than as a production resulting from a particular boundary-regime. The anti-psychological stance within modernist art history has struggled with this logic as long and insofar as it remained tied to gestures of transgression. The paradigm of psychology as laid out by Freud led to another symptomatic genealogy – that of ecstasy. Once again, it is inextricably linked to the imaginary of animism (in this book, the question of ecstasy, animism and aesthetics is discussed in an exemplary way through Sergei Eisenstein's analysis of the art of Walt Disney). In states of ecstasy and intoxication, the very boundary that separates the self from the world is undone, and interiority is exteriorized. The trip is a figure of transgression in which remobilization, reanimation, re-enchantment and metamorphosis are brought about by an unleashing of the boundaries that confine the subjectivity of perception, providing an immediate experience of the world-making power of images, transforming a mute world into dialogic excess. This 'dialogue' temporarily unleashes experiences of mediality, in which subject and object appear as mutually constitutive and keep changing sites. The ecstatic undoing of the boundaries of the subject through intoxication, extreme physical states, eroticism or spiritual ecstasies represents a major resource for modernist art. There is, however, a different trajectory, perhaps more fruitful for a re-evaluation of animism; one that is less caught up in the logic of the symptomatic and compensatory transgression and the dialectical confirmation of the modern's own myths. This different trajectory makes clear that the modernist cultural response to the objectifying stance derives from a similar set of configurations. An influential part of the modernist iconography is directly derived from the rationalization of the movements of the living body, and the objectifying 'inscription of life'. This link is discussed in the frame of situating modern animation in the present book by the exhibition's co-curator Edwin Carels. The physiological motion studies of Étienne Jules-Marey and Eadweard Muybridge gave expression to the experiential dimension of the modern fragmentation of time and space. Such expression, however, was not their primary aim; instead, their target was a rationalization of the economy of the working body to achieve increased efficiency in production – these inscriptions of life served as the blueprint for Taylorism, the theory of management that analyzes and synthesizes work-flows. Not merely the decomposition of the visual field characteristic of modernist iconography, cinema also passed through this applied science that would have the most profound impact on the body and the human sensorium.

Technology at the Meridian Point

It was Walter Benjamin who conceived of these two registers of modernity together, for Taylorism and the related emergence of a variety of physiological and psychological tests placed technology at a meridian point in which subject and object were no longer separated, but subjected to management, giving rise to new forms of subjectivities. Benjamin maintained a perspective that saw more than merely a dystopian dimension in these configurations that linked subjectivity and technology. He proclaimed the necessity of inversing the Taylor system, and changing it from a system of optimizing subordination to the machine into one of creative invention: if a subject was tested for its specific aptitudes that found no application within the given system, these applications and professions would have to be invented. His thinking of technology in relation to the subject bears the characteristics of a profane form of ecstasy; it rejects the psychological essentialism attached to the critique of modern technology from the outset. And, indeed, the physiological and psychological tests were a blueprint for thinking the animation of subjects through their actualization by means of technological inscriptions. Nor has the question of their creative use, in times where the paradigm of the test has been universalized in the form of digitized profiling, lost any of its actuality since. This is a form of technologically-aided animation through subjectification, which presents a different paradigm from the compensatory, symptomatic one of the Frankensteinian dream and aesthetic economy of animation it gave rise to.

'In the cinema, people whom nothing moves or touches any longer learn to cry again.'[35] In his work on technology and the cinema, Walter Benjamin conceived of a possible emancipatory potential of the mass media, envisioning a process inverse to the inscriptions of Marey: from image/technology to physiological motion and experience. Benjamin insisted that technology has to be transformed from a means of mastering nature into a medium for 'mastering the interplay between human beings and nature.'[36]

> The expropriation of the human senses that culminates in imperialist warfare, fascism can be countered only on the terrain of technology itself, by means of perceptual technologies that allow for a figurative, mimetic engagement with technology at large, as a productive force and social reality.[37]

Yet rather than redeeming experience at the price of 'rationality', he made the registers of human embodied experience the measure of technology and media, with a view on new forms of collectivity and transformed relations between nature and humanity. The very impulse to theorize technology is part of Benjamin's techno-utopian politics, through which he seeks to re-imagine the aesthetic in response to the technically changed sensorium. Benjamin conceived of the body as a medium in the service of imagining new forms of subjectivity. Negotiating the historical confrontation between the human sensorium and technology as an alien and alienating regime requires learning from forms of bodily innervation. 'Innervation' is understood as the conversion of affective energy into somatic, motoric form; such as the transformation of the experience of an image into physiological motion and emotion; where bodily sensation and technologically-produced images constitute not irreconcilable counterparts, but an integral 'body-' and 'image-space'.[38] Benjamin invested cinema with the power of innervation, by means of which the technological apparatus can be brought to social, public consciousness as the 'physis' of a transformed collectivity, which has its 'organs' in technology.[39] Experimenting with psychotropic substances, such as hashish, was for Benjamin one way of subjecting the experience of innervation to auto-experiments and self-regulation. Unlike several of his contemporaries and successors who experimented with drugs, Benjamin treated the effects of intoxication as symptoms and effects rather than metaphysical truths. The experience of intoxication destabilizes the boundaries of the self, and transforms the parameters of time-space perception as well as the relation between people and things, exhibiting a structural affinity with the synaesthetic effects of the cinematic experience at the intersection of the physiological and psychological. 'Innervation', in Benjamin's terms, was ultimately linked to his notion of a collective sphere of imagery, in which, by means of constellatory flashes – the dialectics of seeing, profane illumination – he conceived of a sphere of 'absolute neutrality' with respect to the notions of subject and object. What Benjamin conceived of, in other words, is a politics of the meridian point; the dissolution of modernity's notorious 'seeing double' by means of a 'stereoscopic vision' that brings the two domains of subjects and objects into the dialectical constellation in which they came to be historically productive, and by means of which they gave birth to the modern world. In this attempt, he preceded Bruno Latour, who proclaimed the need for a 'symmetric' anthropology of modernity. He refers explicitly to anthropology for it is the only discipline that is used to thinking together the most diverse boundary practices in one great whole (the cosmographies of the 'Others', for whom nature and culture and so forth are not distinct), a virtue that no other discipline, by way of their implication in the modern logic of division, is capable.

We Have Never Been Modern

An anthropology of the modern world; that is, a comprehensive, synthetic view of the organization of its boundary-practices, becomes possible only once we have come to realize that 'we have never been modern':

> Century after century, colonial empire after colonial empire, the poor premodern collectives were accused of making a horrible mishmash of things and humans, of objects and signs, while their accusers finally separated them totally – to remix them at once on a scale unknown until now.[40]

The practice of modernity, Latour asserts, is diametrically opposed to its conceptualization and self-description. While accusing other collectives of the mishmash they make between categories whose distinction for us holds sacred values, they set up a practice that intertwined culture and nature on a previous unknown scale. The 'official' version of modernity is but a mode of classification that allows one to do the opposite of what one says. Modernity also made an absolute split between theory and practice, between de facto practices and their juridical, conceptual framework. The conceptual register of modernity keeps on erecting borders, purifies fields of knowledge, insists on disciplines, and so forth; while in their practices, they work on creating assemblages, 'hybrids', or 'collectives that conceptual machines cannot simply account for. This allowed the moderns to mobilize nature without due democratic discussion on the impact of this mobilization, without mediation and representation of 'things', thus producing an unprecedented amount of new 'hybrids', of 'quasi-objects', of chains of associations in which subjects and objects are mutually constitutive, which contain both subjective and objective aspects, and span the divide between culture and nature in multiple ways. It is only with the proliferation of these 'hybrids', overwhelming us in the form of the ecological crisis, that protocols of strict division – of 'purification' – gradually lose ground and cease to be operational, thus enforcing a re-evaluation of modernity, and an inscription of all that it bracketed off – the unified nature of non-relational facts – back into history:

> The essential point of this modern Constitution is that it renders the work of mediation that assembles hybrids invisible, unthinkable, unrepresentable. Does this lack of representation limit the work of mediation in any way? No, for the modern world would immediately cease to function. Like all other collectives it lives on that blending. On the contrary (and here comes the beauty of the mechanism to light), the modern Constitution allows the expanded proliferation of the hybrids whose existence, whose very possibility, it denies.[41]

According to Latour, science, by way of its construction of 'indisputable' facts, holds democratic politics in an iron grip, limiting the collective concerns that can be negotiated to human affairs alone, while bracketing off all other agencies that participate, and indeed hold together, the 'common world'. To bring the sciences back into politics, Latour calls for a 'parliament of things',[42] in which the work of the sciences is not the presentation of objective facts that supposedly 'speak for themselves' and end all other debate by suppressing the necessary mediation that makes them 'speak' in the first place, but rather the 'socialization of nonhumans', their enrolment and subsequent mediation in a social realm extended to 'things'. Is Bruno Latour suggesting yet another 'return' to animism, a form of political order that is based on a dubious animation of things? Is the 'parliament of things' not a regressive fiction reminiscent of the animated universes of Walt Disney, where everything comes to life and things act like people, or to one of the techno-utopian phantasies of a Charles Fourier?

> Before my readers begin to get a disquieting impression that they are being pulled into a fable where animals, viruses, stars, and magic are going to start chattering away like magpies or princesses, let me emphasize that we are in no way dealing with a novelty

that would be shocking to common sense. [...] I am proposing, very reasonably, to make this mythic contradiction [between mute fact things and speaking facts] comprehensible by restoring all the difficulties that a human encounters in speaking to humans about nonhumans with their participation. [...] I do not claim that things speak 'on their own,' since no beings, not even humans, speak on their own, but always through something or someone else. I have not required human subjects to share the right of speech of which they are so justly proud with galaxies, neurons, cells, viruses, plants and glaciers.[43]

Latour calls for a parliamentary model – composed of 'spokespeople', mediators and mediums – that accounts for the enrolment of non-humans in the constitution of the common world. For the modern imagination, this is nothing short of a horror scenario. Not only does Latour ascribe things agency, but with their agency, he lets them get so close to subjects that the subject becomes virtually unimaginable other than in a communion with things, taking us right back into the realm of those 'horrible mixtures'. And nevertheless, this is not a 'return' to animism, not to the 'old'; that is, the modern version of animism, to be sure. For what we confront here has nothing to do with the conflation of differences, but with their increase, and with the demand to equally increase the tools for political representation that are capable of accounting for, and recognizing, what were previously mere mute objects, as social agents that have a significant share in the making of the common world. Taking into account things as co-authors of the social means asking the question of social constructivism, of our making of the world, of the production of relations anew, always maintaining the stereoscopic view that keeps the mutual constitution of humans and non-humans in sight. This does not require a 'return' to historically surmounted ways of relating to the world, but taking into account the submerging of relational modes of knowledge through modern boundary-practices. What Latour does not account for, in this respect, focusing as he does on the chains of references and steps of mediation undertaken through the inscriptions of scientists in their laboratory, is the realm of sensuous correspondences, the importance of non-linguistic embodied communication which were so central to Benjamin's investment with both technology and the 'language of things'.

For Benjamin, the language of things refers to the manner in which we are addressed by an object, the way in which an entire structure for the living world finds expression in the world of things. Being affected by the language of things has its roots in the 'mimetic faculty'.[44] For there is no dialogic form of relationality if there is no account of the very dependence of human language on the address we receive from things, deriving from a non-linguistic form of knowing, in which the relationship between subjects (active) and objects (passive) is reversed; who, in everyday custom, translate their texture into human language, into faculties. There is no such thing as ecstasy: we are always already outside ourselves with things because they structure our habits, experiences and, finally, our language, which, according to Benjamin, contains an archive of sensuous correspondences. For Benjamin, there is thus a continuum, not a rupture, between sensuous correspondences, the body as a medium and the medium of language.

In ascribing language only to humans, in submerging mediality across the registers of experience, in denigrating sensuous knowledge to mere 'relics', we submerge our capacity for 'relatedness', and we gain a freedom of a paradoxical nature, the freedom to modernize. For it is in this domain of the a-semiotic that the question of relationality will always also pose itself if one doesn't want to run into the danger of a new form of politically hazardous positivism that accepts as speech only what can be positivised by means of a writing device. This is, of course, also the field in which the questions discussed above become relevant to the field of aesthetics, understood as encompassing the whole spectrum of possible relationality between the registers of the sensuous, affective and cognitive. This domain, in its political implications, concerns the entire realm of habitual behaviour, of the internalization of modes of relation and emotional dispositions, the very schemes by which we make sense of the world. It is in this realm that the boundary between the implicit and explicit is being drawn by way of the entire spectrum of everyday gestures and practices. This boundary defines the margin of political negotiation in any parliamentary setting – for what is implicit, what 'goes without saying', what is taken for granted as background condition, that which organizes perceptions, skills and actions before mobilizing 'positive', declarative knowledge, defines what can be recognized, responded to and negotiated. According to Donna Haraway, the language of bodies produces its own truth, particularly in the realm of relationality between different species:

> The truth or honesty of nonlinguistic embodied communication depends on looking back and greeting significant others, again and again. This sort of truth or honesty is not some tropefree, fantastic kind of natural authenticity that only animals can have while humans are defined by the happy fault of lying denotatively and knowing it. Rather, this truth telling is about coconstitutive natural cultural dancing, holding in esteem, and regarding open those who look back reciprocally. Always tripping, this kind of truth has a multispecies future.[45]

Beyond Mirror Worlds

Once animism is released from the modern cage that defines it as either 'erroneous thinking' with the respect to the reality of objects, or as a question of projecting subjectivity, the concept opens up a very different set of problems, at the core of which lies not subjectivity of perception (leading to ever new mirror games), but perception of the subjectivity of the so-called object. These subjectivities are not to be conceived in anthropomorphic forms, but rather in relation to the available and possible forms and *dispositifs* of recognition. Trying to give an answer to the question of defining 'human', Latour answers:

> The expression 'anthropomorphic' considerably underestimates our humanity. We should be talking about morphism. Morphism is the place where technomorphisms,

zoomorphisms, phusimorphisms, ideomorphisms, theomorphisms, sociomorphisms, psychomorphisms, all come together. A weaver of morphisms – isn't that enough of a definition?[46]

Besides the concept's potential to act as a stereoscopic mirror for the understanding of modern boundary-practices, anthropology has revived the concept of animism, understood as 'relational epistemology'. There is, as anthropologist Rane Willerslev asserts, a danger in these accounts of replicating the projection of a romantic sentiment, paired with assertions of scientific universality escaping cultural relativism, that still denies the very claim of the ontologies in question; that the relations they uphold to non-human subjects are real, and not merely a transference of social metaphors onto the world, by means of which the difference between self and Other is absorbed:

> We can only have an experience of a world if we are conscious subjects of experience who can distinguish between ourselves as subjects and an external world that transcends our subjective experience of it. Otherwise, the experiencing subject and the object of experience would conflate, would become one, thereby making any experience of the world impossible.[47]

To be sure, all cultures draw boundaries, and organize and negotiate differences. All cultures objectify, and draw a line between what is real and what is imaginary in ways that constitute these realms mutually. However, they differ in the way these differences are organized, and only the moderns are known for having operated through the bifurcation of nature and culture, and the derived system of equally categorical Great Divides, monologic in their structure and form of relationality. That the societies described as animist do not ascribe to such forms of difference *a priori* does in no way mean that these differences do not exist; rather, they have to be created constantly through everyday practices. These practices are basically mimetic, if mimesis is understood as a faculty and sensuous-cognitive process:

> Mimesis is essentially relational in that the imitator has no independent existence outside or separate from the object or person imitated; and yet the imitator is constantly being thrown back on himself reflexively, without ever achieving unity. Thus mimesis offers assimilation with otherness while also drawing boundaries and distinguishing oneself. Animism demands both, and without mimesis the very basis of animistic relatedness is therefore likely to break down. This is not to say that mimesis is identical with animism. We can and do imitate things without being animists for that reason. Rather, what I am arguing is that mimesis is and must be a prerequisite for animistic symbolic world making. [...] Mimesis, therefore, is the practical side of animism, its worldmaking mechanism par excellence.[48]

Control Society

Since the 1970s, the question of relationality has taken on new forms within the realm of what previously was characterized as industrialized modernity. With the decline of industrialism, the rise of post-Fordist modes of production and immaterial labour, and the end of the 'disciplinary regime', the very site occupied by animism previously as a romantic counterpart to the objectified, disenchanted world has experienced a significant shift. From being the negative of modernity – the focal point of its imaginary opposites – animism has become a resource for the expansion of capitalist modes of production into the realm of relationality governed by affects and subjectifications. It is now most common again to talk about souls and communicative, collaborative practices; government papers speak of the embodied mind and the unity between body and soul. Mimetic and passionate engagement has become a quotidian request through which conformity is being produced. In the passage from the 'disciplinary society' to the 'society of control', the relation between inside and outside has partially been reversed – it is only that the self, the subject, remained at its place, and now finds itself in a position of negativity, in constant need of positivity itself by means of inclusion into the existing web of productive social relations.

What had been achieved by feminist theoreticians and practitioners, among those whose attacks on the notorious modern dualisms have shown significant effects, became increasingly incorporated standards in the mantras of a capitalist mode of immaterial production, now centring on the production of social relationality. This has given rise to new forms of 'clinical animisms', in which the paradigm or relatedness has become a modality of social production, which no longer has an articulate dimension of negativity, of imaginary outsides. In the society of control, it is negativity that is interiorized, as the conditioning through the disciplinary enclosures is replaced by increasingly implicit forms of self-management. Power now operates by the fear of falling outside, no longer by enclosing an inside. It operates by means of implication and innervations, providing the frames in which the productive relations are to take place, while the very frames remain out of the reach of being negotiable. Yet these frames are flexible and can adapt if a critical mass applies force. Critique, already hurt by the waning power of its iconoclastic gestures, must remain local and responsive. The relational paradigm has long entered the officially accepted doctrines of culture in which few of the old oppositions can be upheld.

The field of social production has turned increasingly into an animist mirror world of sorts, with the subject being the animating frame of its own world. Looking into the world as the mirror of the self has become the modality of interiorization. The rise of the green economy as the next capitalist frontier will do its part in creating new quasi-animist forms of governmentality. All this can be explained as a mimetic, morphological adaptation of power, spinning the wheel of dialectics between resistance and form of power further, now in the process of appropriating the transformative forces of relationality and the mimetic. The outlines of the new regime, as in the old, can once again be traced negatively, by means of its congruent pathologies. The neurotic boundary-syndrome is replaced by the mode of depression, which Jennifer Church has described in terms of being able to see a reflection of the romantic, transgressive role animism had once played: as 'false one-ness with the world.' It is false, because it is a oneness in which the subject is ultimately deprived of agency, of the possibility to act and relate, a subject being locked into an immobilized time-space by means of subjectification, rather different from the immobilization experienced by objectification that gives rise to neurosis and paranoia, yet which is strictly correlative. One battlefield of the future will be the boundaries of the self in search for the tools to resist the interiorization of the structures of power implicated in the flows of relationality. And yet one must not forget that these developments remain rather local phenomena, and that outside the 'postmodern' mobilization of 'clinical' animism induced in new forms of subjectification, what awaits us everywhere is history. Despite the postmodern amnesia of a capitalism turned green, the conflicts of modernity are far from pacified. History's battlefields need new modes of recognition, and understandings of production and transformation of relational cosmographies under the modern traditions and conditions of war. It is against this backdrop

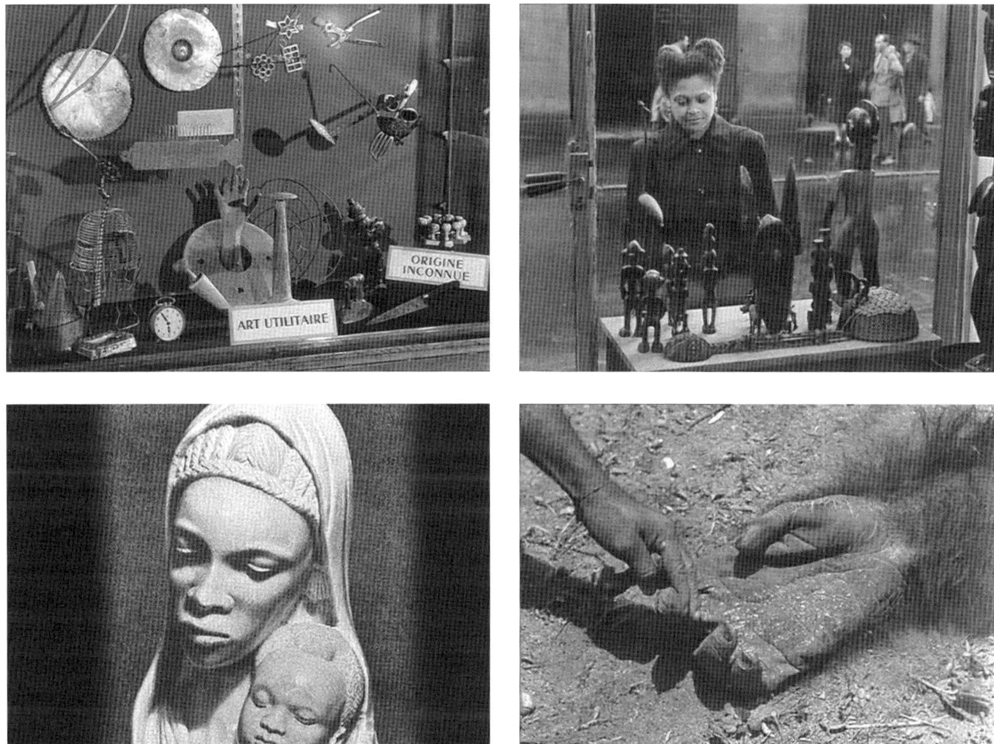

Figure 1: Chris Marker and Alain Resnais, *Les Statues Meurent Aussi*, 1953, video (original 16mm), 30 min. Courtesy of Argos Films and Présence Africaine.

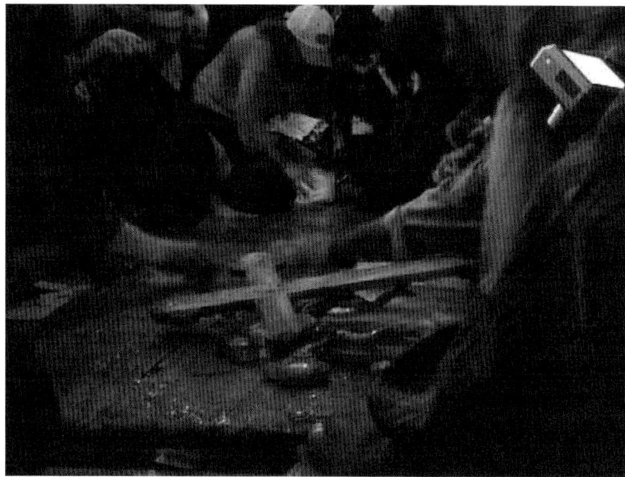

Figure 2: Harun Farocki, *Übertragung/Transmission*, 2009, video, 43 min. Courtesy of the artist.

that animism, as a grand narrative of sorts, may become a necessary epic for the society of control, a tool for the tackling of the qualitative, political aspects of relationality.

'When men die, they enter history. When statues die, they enter art. This botany of death is what we call culture.' *Les Statues Meurent Aussi/Statues Also Die* (Chris Marker and Alain Resnais, 1953), which was censored for more than a decade, was commissioned by the literary review and publishing house, Présence Africaine, which was set up in 1947 in Paris as a quarterly literary review for emerging and important African writers. Présence Africaine's publications signalled a new, postcolonial status for French and francophone thought, embracing the notion of *négritude*. *Les Statues Meurent Aussi* strives to connect the death of the statue with the rise in the commercialization of African art.

At the centre of Harun Farocki's video *Übertragung/Transmission* (2009) is the touching of stone, as he makes portraits of monuments all over the world with which people interact in performative exchanges of sorts and with different purposes, from the Vietnam Memorial in Washington to the Devil's Footprint in the Frauenkirche in Frankfurt. In *Ein Tag im Leben der Endverbraucher* (1993), Farocki constructs the twenty-four hours of a day of an average consumer through German advertising films from forty years ago.

African Judaism and Christianity were enriched by writings not included in the Hebrew bible, such as *The Book of Jubilees*. *The Book of Jubilees*, also known as *The Little Genesis*, is thought of having been composed at some point between 175 and 140 BCE, and it is preserved in the Ethiopian language Ge'ez, which is still the liturgical language of the Ethiopian Orthodox Church. From *The Book of Jubilees* we learn that before the Fall, animals were able communicate with each other in a 'common tongue'. It was only on their expulsion from the Garden of Eden that the mouths of cattle and birds and of 'everything that walks or moves, were shut'. The picture by an anonymous Ethiopian painter invokes a tradition of church-trained artists

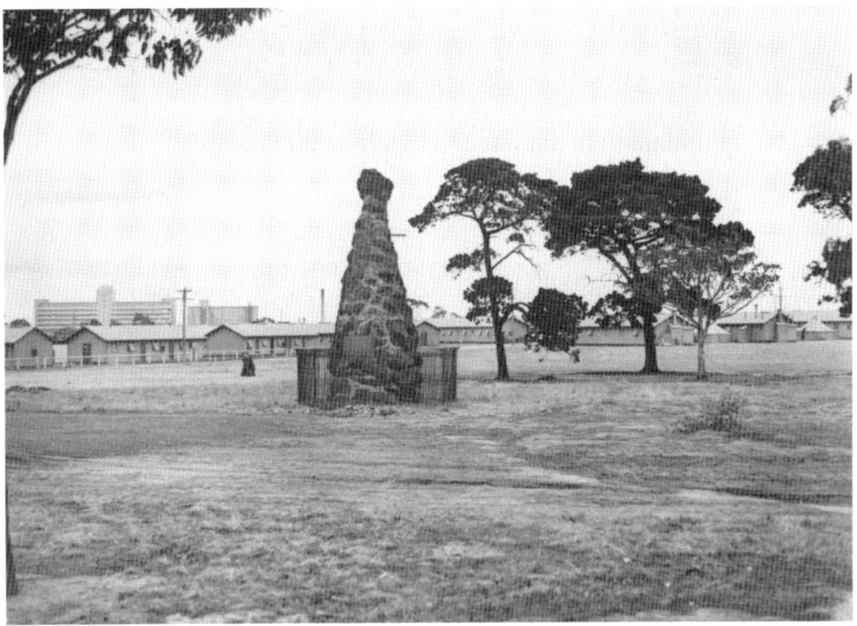

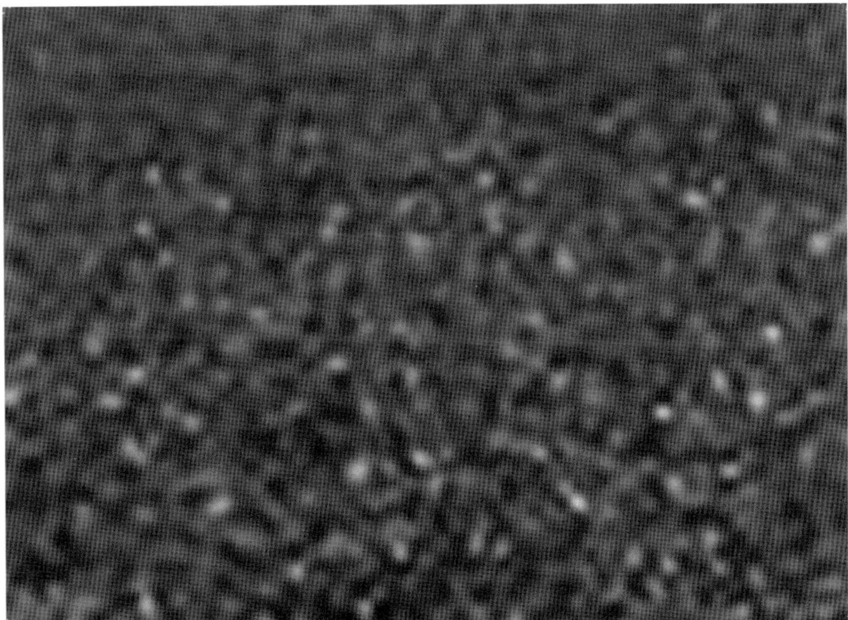

Tom Nicholson, *Monument for the Flooding of Royal Park*, 2009, inkjet prints. Courtesy of the artist and Anna Schwartz Gallery, Melbourne.

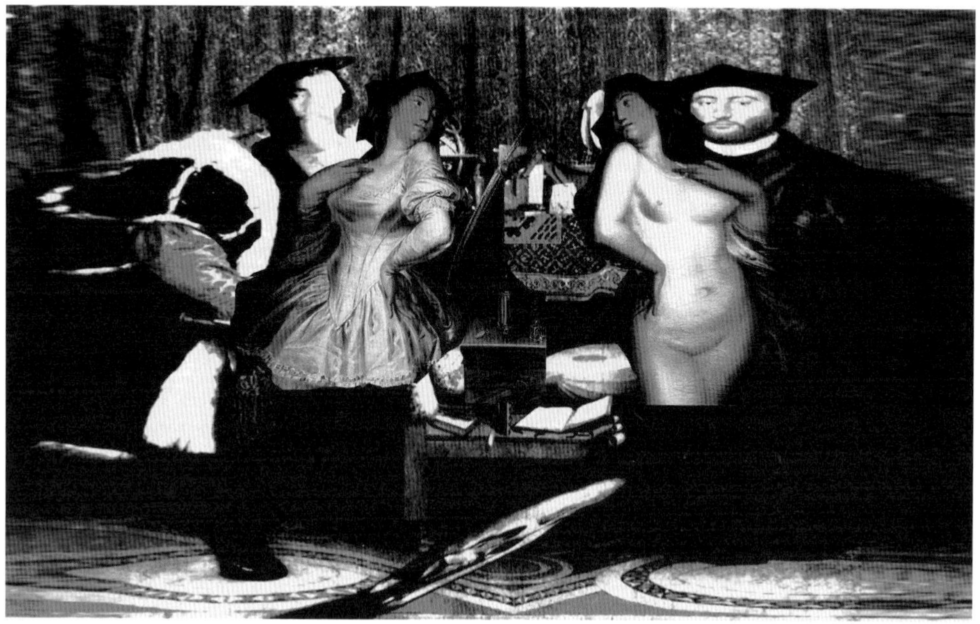

Anne-Mie Van Kerckhoven, *Stranger than Life, 2009–10*, video stills. Courtesy of the artist and Zeno X Gallery, Antwerp.

who follow and actualize century-old conventions to this date. The line that separates the communion of animals in the upper half of the picture from the lower half inevitably also calls forth speculations and associations about the mythical origins of the modern divide between culture and nature, between the communion mediated by social contracts and the 'state of nature' in which every creature, in its struggle for survival, is ultimately at war with others.

Tom Nicholson's *Monument for the Flooding of Royal Park* (2009; see p. 51) is a work about colonial Australian history, telling the story of the expedition by the infamous explorers Burke and Wills, who started in Melbourne in 1860 to cross the interior of the continent for the first time. Until today, the numerous monuments that were erected for these two men continue to physically impose themselves in public space. *Monument for the Flooding of Royal Park* is a proposal for an imaginary monument referring to a part of the history that is usually left untold – the death of the two explorers through their misuse of a particular plant – nardoo – a desert fern prepared as food by Aboriginals. Burke and Wills failed to add an essential step in the preparation of nardoo that would gradually lead to their death. The proposed monument consists of the temporary flooding, and subsequent growing of nardoo in Royal Park in the centre of Melbourne creating a red field of nardoo plants.

Anne-Mie van Kerckhoven has been working with the image-space situated right under the surface of the representations of women in mass media, structured by the relation between sex and technology (see illustration above as well as in the section colour plates, p. 2). Her imagery explores layers of deep memory that bear the force to collectivize private interiority.

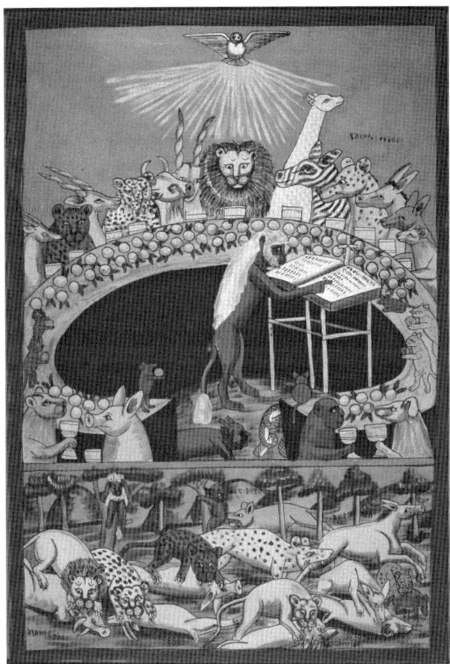

Figure 3: Anonymous, *Assembly of the Animals*, 1965–75, oil on linen. Geographical origin: Adis Abeba, Ethiopia. Courtesy of Tropenmuseum, Amsterdam.

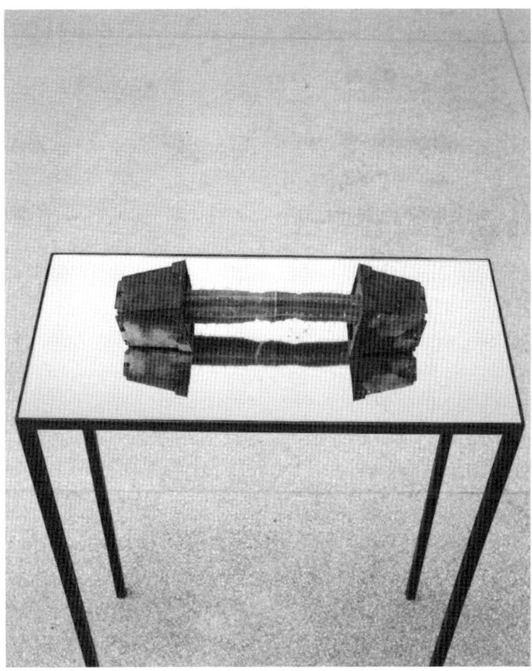

Figure 4: Klaus Weber, *Doppelkaktus/Double Cactus*, 2006, two grafted San Pedro cactuses, blued iron, mirror. Courtesy of the artist.

She investigates the dynamic forces of language, and the politics in the aesthetics of ecstasy and the obscene.

Many of Klaus Weber's works are reflections on the nodes between bodily perception (nature) and states of mind (culture), for which he frequently turns to the borders between human and vegetative and animal life. He explores biochemical aspects of social life, and subverts normative perceptions as well as understandings of art by transferring them into the registers of other-than-human forms of life, and inscribes them into systems of intoxication. *Doppelkaktus/Double Cactus* (2006) is a piece consisting of two San Pedro (*Trichocereus pachanoi*) plants, which contain mescaline, grafted together at the top end, thus reversing the very direction of their growth. Mescaline was first synthesized in 1919, and is best known through the Peyote cactus, which was used in ancient Mexico and is a vital part of the ceremonies of today's Native American Church.

These works on paper consist of pages from the Vatican daily *L'Osservatore Romano* (2001–07), featuring articles on modern life and morality overlaid with old images of the Apocalypse, the Last Judgment and the Expulsion from Eden, as well as engravings of the Inquisition. The horrors of hell interpreted by the Old Masters become here the illustration

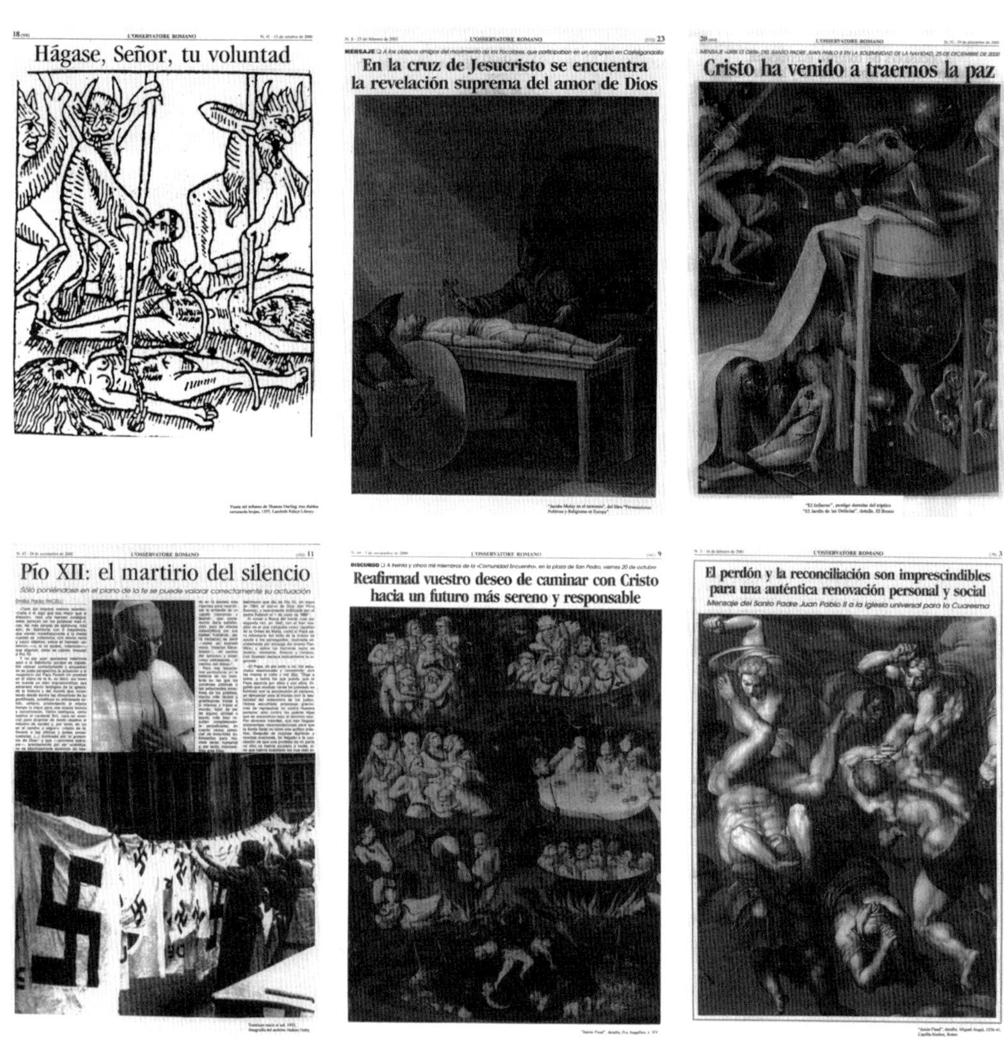

Figure 5: León Ferrari *L'Osservatore Romano*, 2001–07, collages on paper. Courtesy of the artist.

of ecclesiastical news. Ferrari's collages refer to the historical role of Christian institutions in the colonizing of the Americas, and the continuity of terror in later forms of suppression such as the military dictatorships and fascism.

Jan Švankmajer is internationally known for his animation films, among the best known are his version of Lewis Caroll's *Alice's Adventures in Wonderland* from 1988. Švankmajer's surreal, Kafkaesque, nightmarish and yet humorous journeys into the unconscious are populated by things and hybrid figures that lead uncanny lives of their own. In parallel to his film-making, Švankmajer has always produced artworks and objects, ranging from drawing

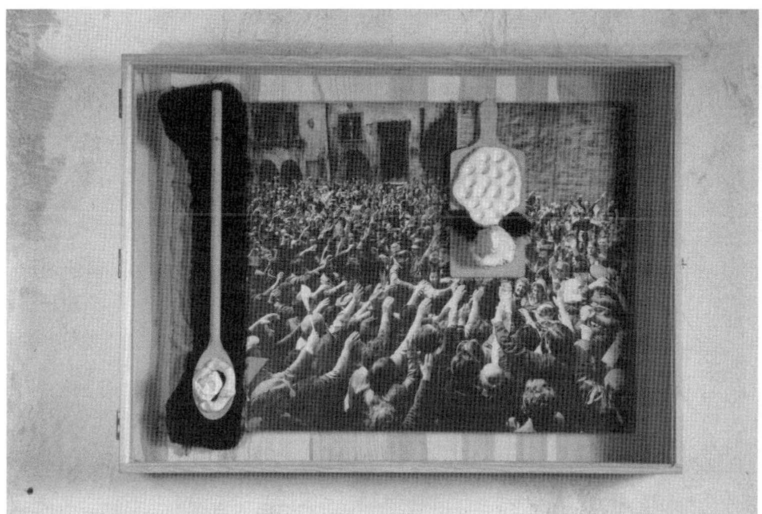

Figure 6: Jan Švankmajer, *The Power of a Request*, 1990, mixed media. Courtesy of Athanor – Film Production Company, Llc.

and collage to sculptures, ceramics and tactile objects, which equally inhabit the borderlines of familiar physiognomic worlds.

Soft Materials (2004) by Daria Martin shows an encounter between machines and humans. This video work was shot in the Artificial Intelligence Lab at the University of Zurich where scientists research 'embodied artificial intelligence'. What looks like an extraordinary choreography is a laboratory process through which the robots acquire new functions by interacting with human bodies. The woman and the men in the laboratory are highly trained in movement and body awareness. These performers shed skins of soft fabric, bearing their joints like the frank structure of a machine, and then,

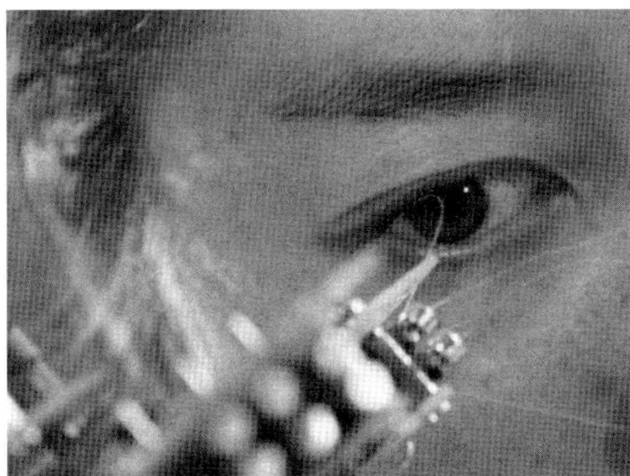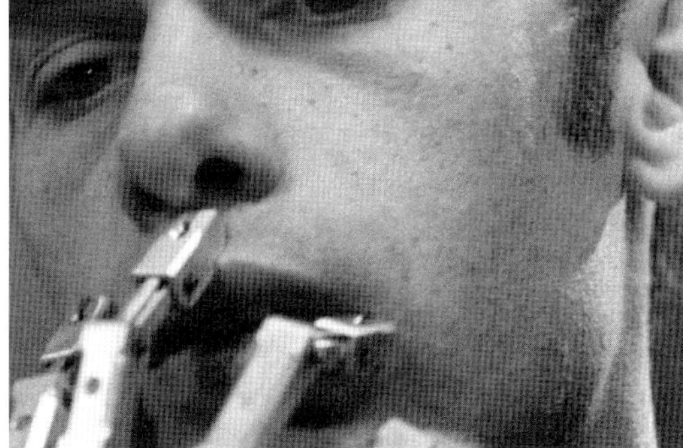

Figure 7: Daria Martin, *Soft Materials*, 2004, 16mm film, 10:30 min. Courtesy of Maureen Paley, London.

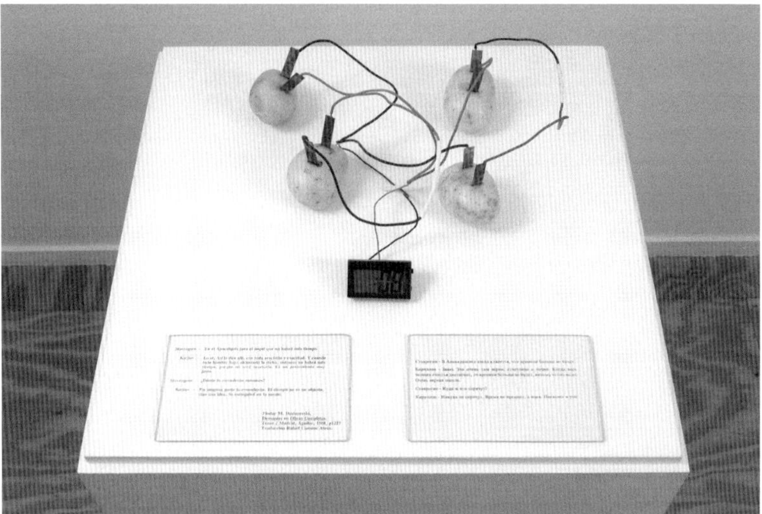

Figure 8: Victor Grippo, *Tiempo*, 1991, potatoes, zinc and copper electrodes, electric wires, digital clock, painted wooden base, glass vitrine and text. Courtesy of Alexander and Bonin, New York.

naked, they perform a series of dances with the robots. Creating intimate relationships that are in turn tender, funny and eerie, they bend flexible human phantasy around tough materials. The film provokes speculative responses around the notorious question of 'man and machine', the animate and the inanimate, blurring traditional borders between technological and human media through seductive and unexpected sensual and mimetic interactions.

Victor Grippo was a major figure in Argentinean art in the second half of the twentieth century, a period characterized by the military dictatorship and poverty. Grippo's work instilled a political resonance in domestic items such as tables, and he maintained an alchemical interest in workaday materials and natural objects. Among the materials he frequently worked with were potatoes: 'The potato-battery related to the generative energy of a native foodstuff that became the staple food of the poor the world over, in a certain sense the constitutive matter of the world.'

The work by Art & Language refers to Lewis Carroll's perhaps best-known poem, *The Hunting of the Snark* (1876), which evolves around an empty map of an ocean. In *Map of the Sahara Desert after Lewis Carroll* (1967), Art & Language transform Carroll's map of the ocean into a map of a desert – a map, that is, with the exception of cardinal points and scale, empty, thus creating a short-circuit between the internal and external sign-relations. And as much as the systematizing demonstration of the coordination among sign-relations leaves us in permanent oscillation between its various registers, the iconoclastic emptiness of *Map of the Sahara Desert after Lewis Carroll* breeds new images, inevitably inviting the imagination to populate a blank territory.

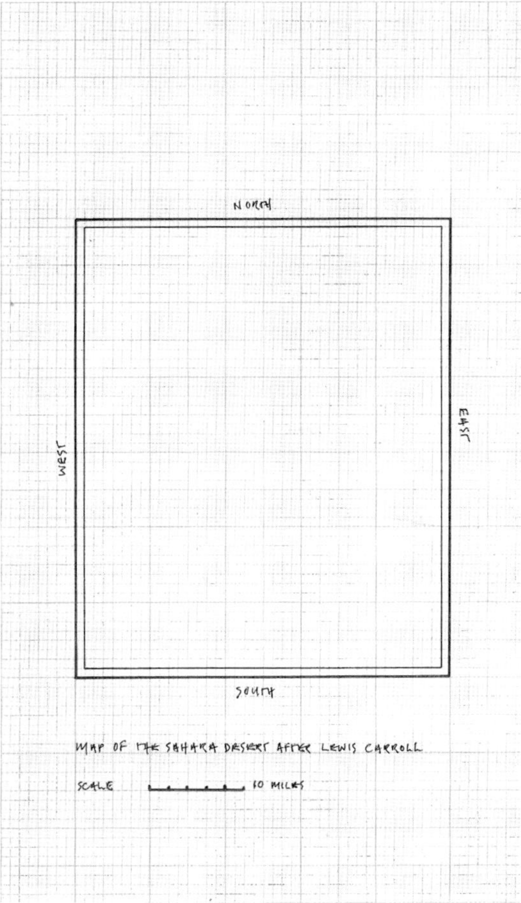

Figure 9: Art & Language, *Map of the Sahara Desert after Lewis Carroll*, 1967, ink on graph paper. Courtesy of the artist and Lisson Gallery, London Private Collection, Nantes.

What are the techniques of isolation? [...] [A] common denominator of those techniques was the visualisation of the object. [...] So any method of creating an image of someone or something [...] begins with pointing a spotlight at the object. It becomes brighter than its surroundings, more detailed, easier to observe. [...] [Y]ou can exchange the spotlight in vice/ virtue with a camera, or a microscope but the mechanism stays the same. [...] I found a photo of a prison yard. It was lying upside down. The spotlight was pointing at the sky and first I thought the image depicted a stage. Then I turned it 180 degrees and found it was a prison. [...] I used the photo as a blueprint for the drawing. For the animation I choose a centrifugal spin, as it's a common scientific method of isolating cells from each

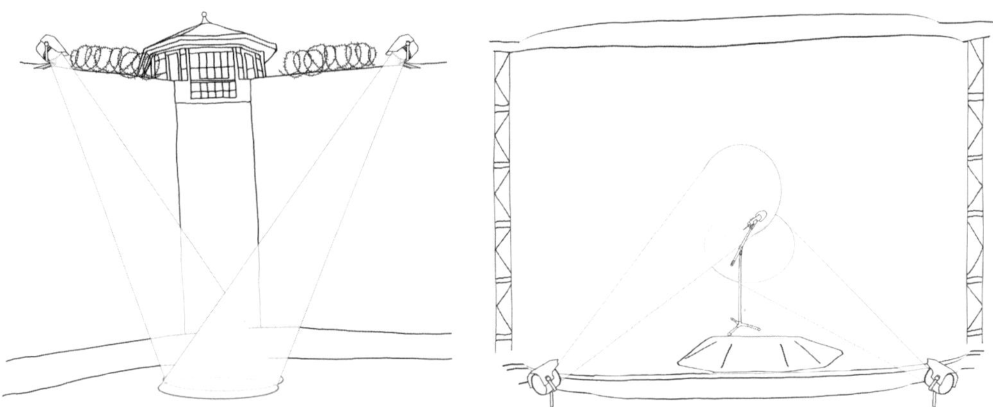

Figure 10: Natascha Sadr Haghighian, *Vice/Virtue*, 2001, digital video projection, 1:05 min. Courtesy of Johann König, Berlin.

other. [...] [T]he presentation involves a video beam with which the drawing is projected onto the paper. It utilizes the technique of the lightbeam as is used in the prison yard and on stage. The artwork is part of the very same system that it's criticizing.[49]

Wesley Meuris' series of designed cages for animals are derived from the artist's engagement with zoological classifications, taxonomies and systems of knowledge. As architectural

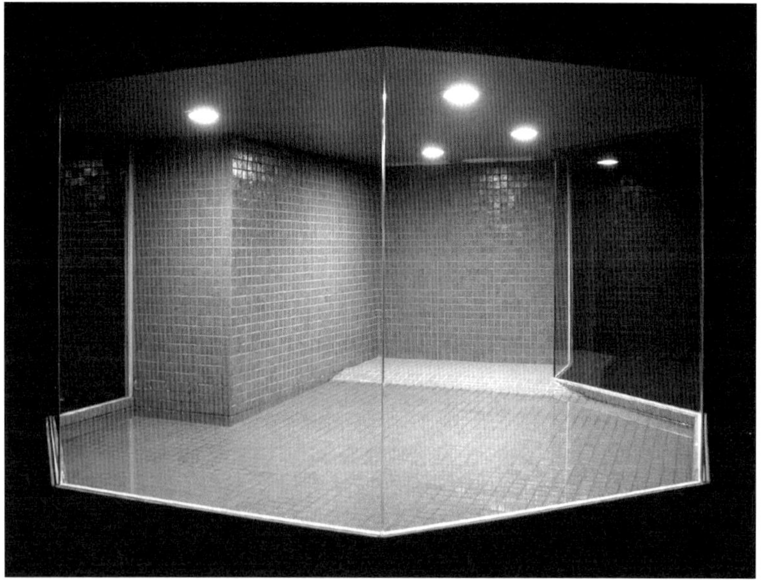

Figure 11: Wesley Meuris, *Cage for Pelodiscus Sinensis*, 2005, wood, glass-tiles, glass, water, lighting and ventilation. Public collection, Alcobendas, Madrid.

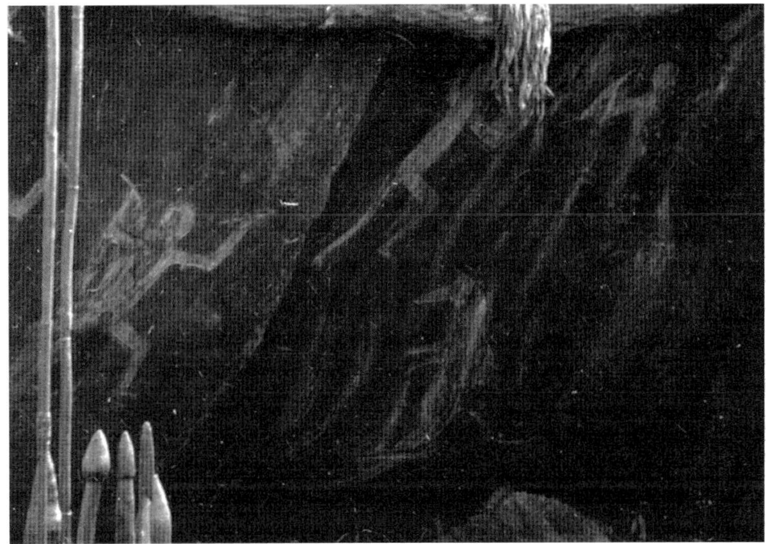

Figure 12: Tom Nicholson, *Drawings and Correspondence*, 2009, charcoal drawings and off-set printed artist's book, excerpt. Courtesy of the artist and Anna Schwartz Gallery, Melbourne.

propositions, they turn these meditations on scientific classification into a question of relationality: what is the mode of knowing we have about the object on display, and what creates the spectatorial enjoyment of seeing animals in captivity? Since the cages are empty, however, the scene of such reflection is transferred to the imagination: we have to give shape to the animal in question in our minds, using the enclosed architectural habitat as

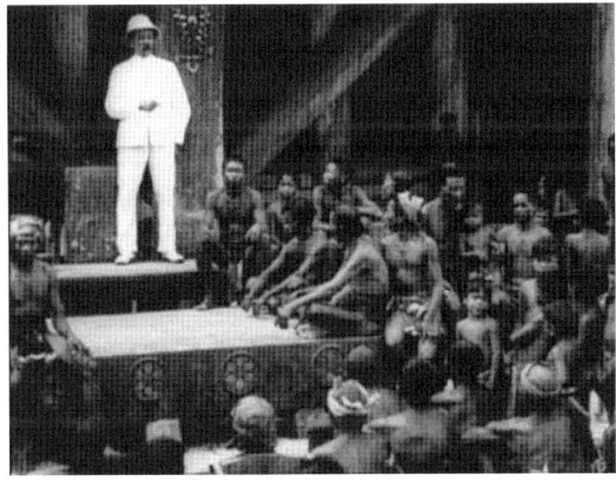

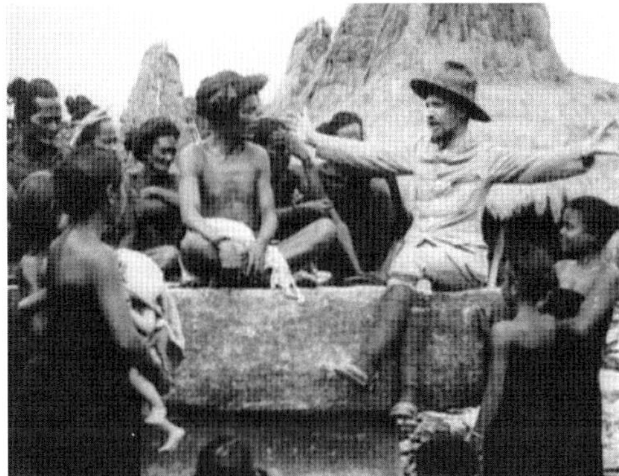

Figure 13: Vincent Monnikendam, *Mother Dao, The Turtlelike*, 1995, film transferred to video, 87:36 min. Courtesy of the artist.

an inversed script that gives shape to a life form, thus engaging in a form of spectatorial empathy that displays like these normally foreclose.

The piece *Drawings and Correspondence* (2009) by Tom Nicholson evolves around a particular drawing and its history. The drawing is found on photographs taken of an ethnographic display at the Melbourne Zoo in the 1880s, inside a *mia-mia* (temporary shelter). It is supposedly an 'authentic' native work. The research into the micro-history of the drawing and its shifting symbolic meanings open a panorama of Australian colonial history and the *dispositifs* that uphold its continuity.

In *Mother Dao, The Turtlelike* (1995), the viewer sees how the colonial machinery was implanted in the Dutch West Indies between 1912 and about 1932. More than 260,000 meters of 35mm documentary nitrate-film footage from the Dutch film archives served as Monnikendam's source material. The documentary starts with a shortened version of the legend of the inhabitants of Nias, an isle to the west of Sumatra. It was told that the Earth was created by Mother Dao, who:

> [...] collected the dirt off her body and kneaded it on her knee into a ball. This was the world. Later, she became pregnant, without a man, and gave birth to a boy and a girl. They were the first people. They lived in a fertile world.

Much of the footage used to be shown in the Netherlands as an illustration of the beneficial effect of the Dutch presence in the East Indies. Monnikendam lifts the original travelogue and colonial documentary out of its original context, showing the extent of the capitalist exploitation of the native's bodies, and reversing the relations inscribed in these images.

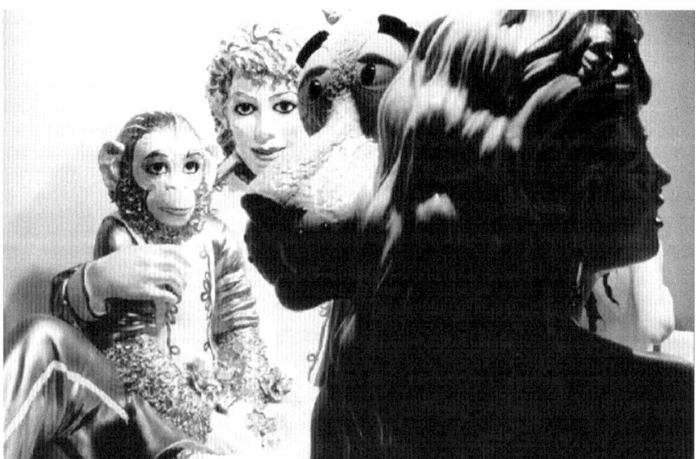

Figure 14: Louise Lawler, *All Those Eyes*, 1989, gelatin silver print. Courtesy of the artist and Metro Pictures.

Louise Lawler's *All Those Eyes* (1989) shows the brightly lit Jeff Koons sculpture of Michael Jackson with his chimp Bubbles, and the Pink Panther in the foreground. From another photograph of the same scene but taken from a different angle, we realize the setting is not a museum hall, but a private storage room. If the viewer assumes a subject, it is that of the collector, whose relation and proximity to objects contends with the 'value' invoked by the authorship of the work. Lawler leads us into a mirror cabinet not merely of gazes, but also of what Karl Marx has famously referred to as the phantasmatic 'fetish' character of the commodity, the capitalist animation of things.

In 1981 Paul Sharits sent the sheet of a film score to Josef Robakowski, suggesting he use it to shoot a film. Eventually, the film was made in 2004, in memory of the American structuralist with whom Robakowski collaborated at the end of the 1970s. Sharits based its structure upon close synchronicity between musical and visual layers. During the screening subsequent tones of Frederic Chopin's 'Mazurka op. 68 nr. 4' are accompanied on the screen by eight corresponding colours.

In his video work *Untitled (After St. Caravaggio, 2003–06, see colour plates, p. 3)*, Paul Chan refers to the genre of the still life, denying the *nature morte* of stillness and immobility by exploding the composition as the figs and their leaves, the grapes, and, finally, the basket itself levitate into air.

Poet and painter Henri Michaux experimented with drawing under the influence of various psychoactive substances, above all mescaline. He asserted that the effect of the

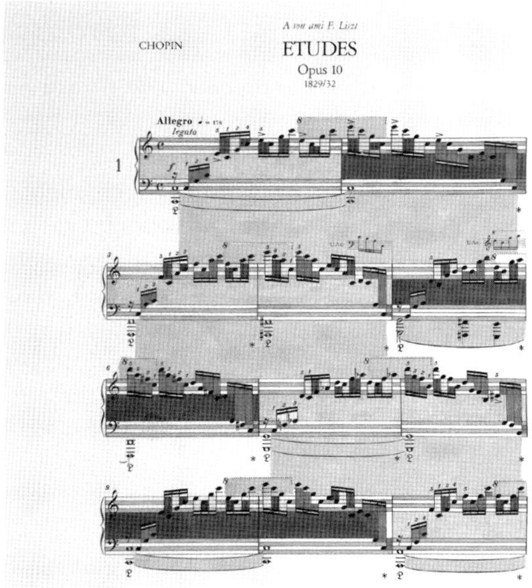

Figure 15: Paul Sharits, *Transcription*, 1990, felt pen on paper. Courtesy of private collection and M HKA, Antwerp.

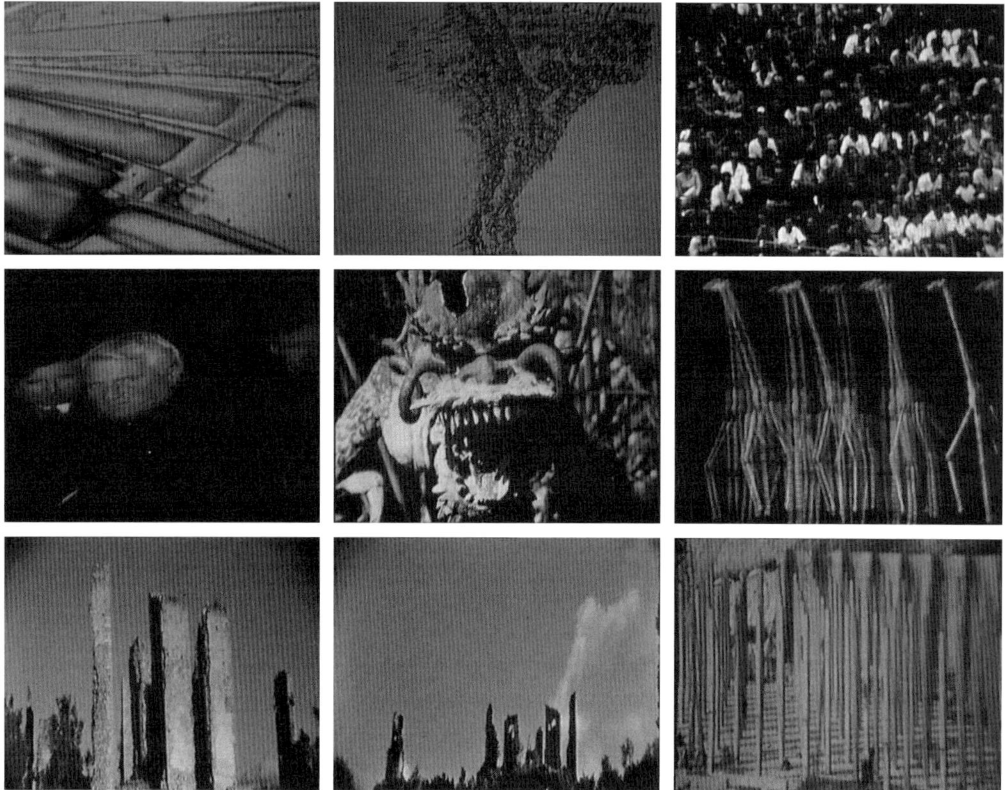

Figure 16: Henri Michaux and Eric Duvivier, *Images du Monde Visionnaire*, 1963, video, 38 min. Courtesy of the artists and Novartis AG.

drug was 'so wholly visual that they are vehicles of the purely mental, of the abstract', further explaining that 'mescaline diminishes the imagination. It castrates, desensualizes the image. It makes images that are 100 percent pure. Laboratory experiments.' Although Michaux asserted that the experience of mescaline 'eludes form', that 'it cannot be seen', he agreed to collaborate on a film commissioned in 1963 by the Swiss pharmaceutical company Sandoz (best known for synthesizing LSD in 1938) in order to demonstrate the hallucinogenic effects of mescaline. It is the only venture in film by Michaux. In charge of the filmic translation of Michaux's prescriptions was director Eric Duvivier whose other films include an adaptation of Max Ernst's collage novel *La Femme 100 Têtes*.

The photographs from *Bialowieza Forest* (2001) depict a location that has been greatly infused with myths and metaphors throughout history. The forest dates back to 8000 BCE, and is the only remaining example of the original lowland forest that once covered much of Europe. Situated in Eastern Poland, it contains a great diversity of plants, animals and

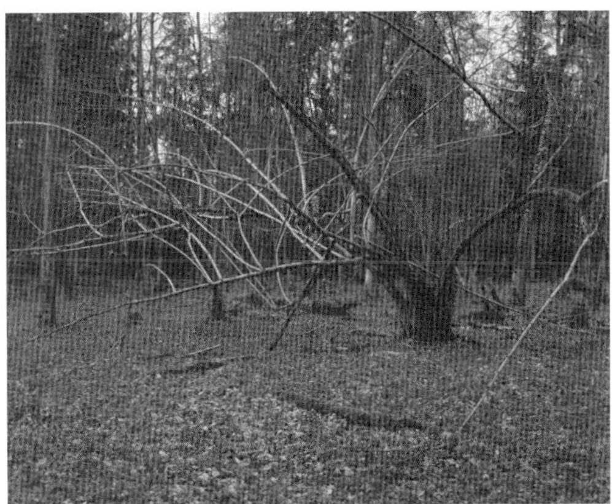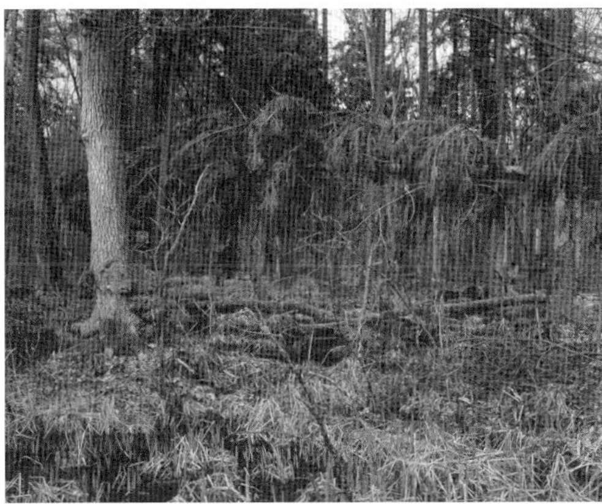

Figure 17: Joachim Koester, *Bialowieza Forest*, 2001, laminated photographs. Courtesy of the Musée des Arts Contemporains de la Communauté française de Belgique, Grand-Hornu.

insects, as well as thousands of species of fungi and vascular plants, many of these elsewhere extinct. Over the years the forest has been described in literature and travel accounts as a sylvan Arcadia, an asylum, a pristine Eden, a sacred grove, and a dark and alien impenetrable wilderness. This work can be seen as a continuation of Joachim Koester's practice in which an imaginary site is paradoxically investigated through its material reality.

The First Intermediate Period, around 2000 BC, was the occasion for a remarkable constellation of innovations in Egyptian thought and civil order. For the first time both men and women won rights of private ownership, of marriage, and of entry to the afterlife (with a proper burial). Remarkably, individuals began reflecting in writing on the world around them, and the first introspective literature appeared. Egypt 2000 invokes this mixed space of gender, identity, and death, from which it literalizes the visual seduction of the viewer.[50]

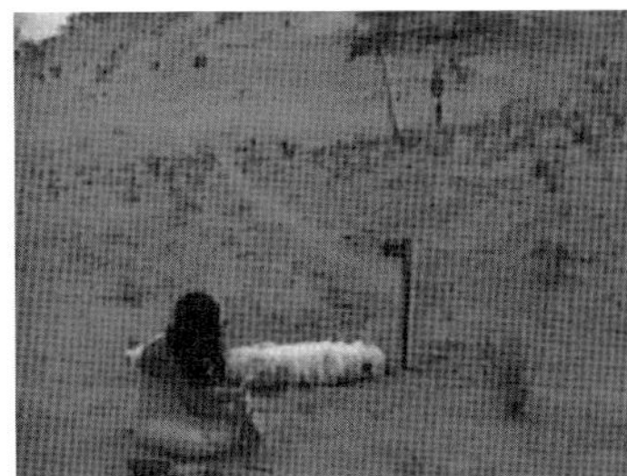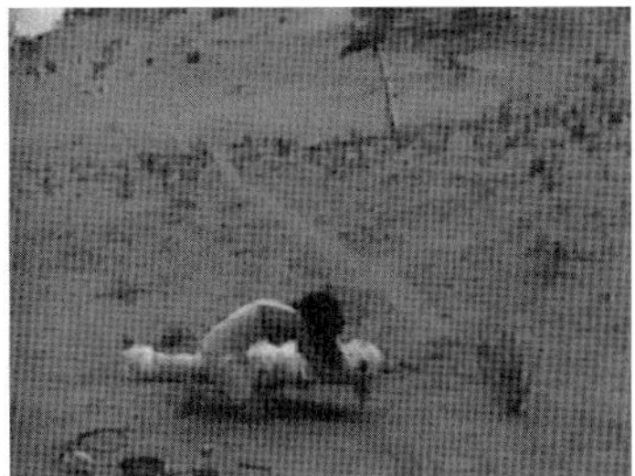

Figure 18: Tony Conrad, *Egypt 2000*, 1986, digital video projection, 13 min. Courtesy of the Galerie Daniel Buchholz, Cologne.

Félix-Louis Regnault (see colour plates, p. 4) was a physician who applied chrono-photography to study culture specific human locomotion, and produced what is widely recognized as the first 'ethnographic footage' at the Paris Exposition 'Ethnographique de l'Afrique Occidentale' in 1895. He attempted to create a scientific index of race, suggesting in 1900 that all museums collect 'moving artefacts' of human behaviour to study and exhibit:

All savage people make recourse to gesture to express themselves; their language is so poor that it does not suffice to make them understood [...]. With primitive man, gesture precedes speech [...]. The gestures the savages make are in general the same everywhere, because these movements are natural reflexes rather than conventions like language.

Poet and painter Brion Gysin, the inventor of the cut-up technique and a major source of inspiration for the Beat generation, was a life-long promoter of the Sufi trance master musicians, to whom he was introduced by Moroccan painter Mohamed Hamri. Gysin and Hamri opened the restaurant The 1001 Nights in Tangier (which closed in 1958), where the musicians would regularly perform.

Ken Jacobs is a film-maker who works as a quasi-archaeologist of the effect media and technology had on the human sensorium. He equally takes into consideration the modes of production and forms of power congruent with technological media and their history. *Capitalism: Slavery* (2006) pictures a stereograph image of a cotton plantation, whose

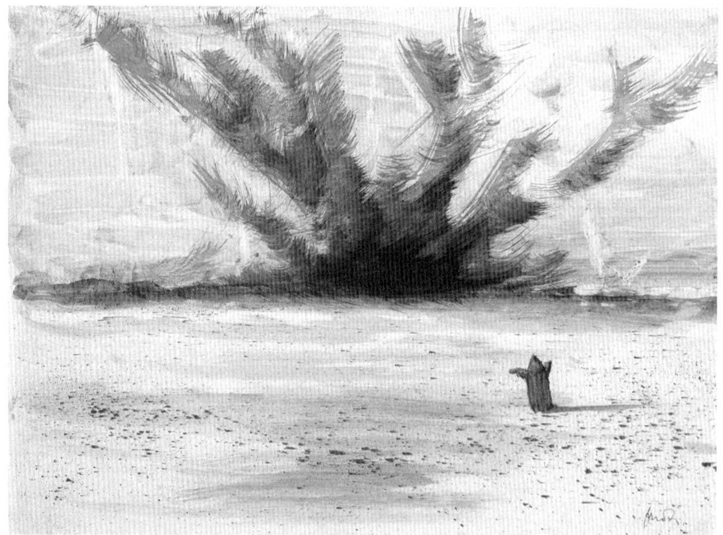

Figure 19: Brion Gysin, *Untitled (Man in the desert)*, n.d., Chinese ink, felt pen and watercolour on paper. Courtesy of the Galerie de France, Paris.

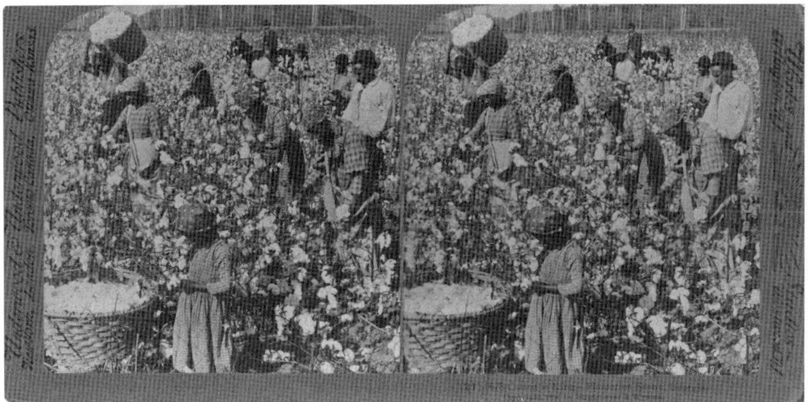

Figure 20: Ken Jacobs, *Capitalism: Slavery,* 2006, digital video projection, 3 min. Courtesy of the artist.

animation by means of digital technology endows these images with a spectral presence – brought back to life, but still mute.

'The Romanticism of the nineteenth century already contains this fantasy that we now confuse with scientific reality.' The work of French caricaturist J. J. Grandville, who satirized the ambitions and pretensions of modern man in his illustrations of the 1830s

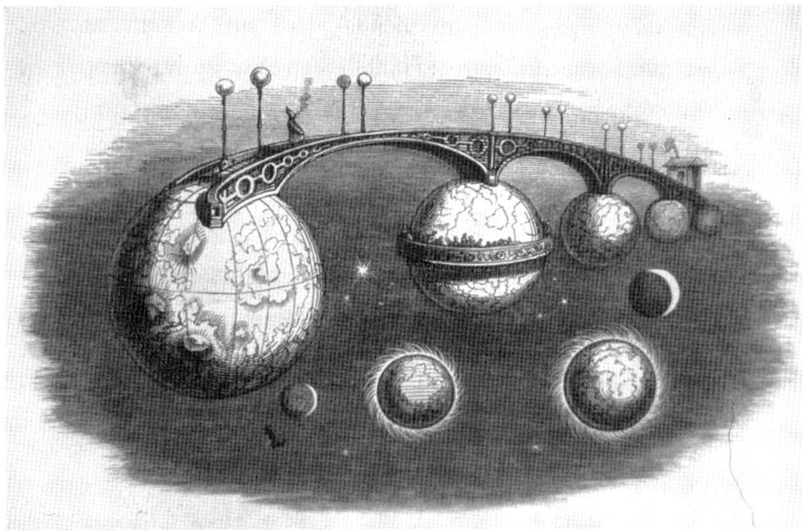

Figure 21: Marcel Broodthaers, *Grandville,* 1967, slideshow, 80 slides. Courtesy of Estate Marcel Broodthaers, Brussels.

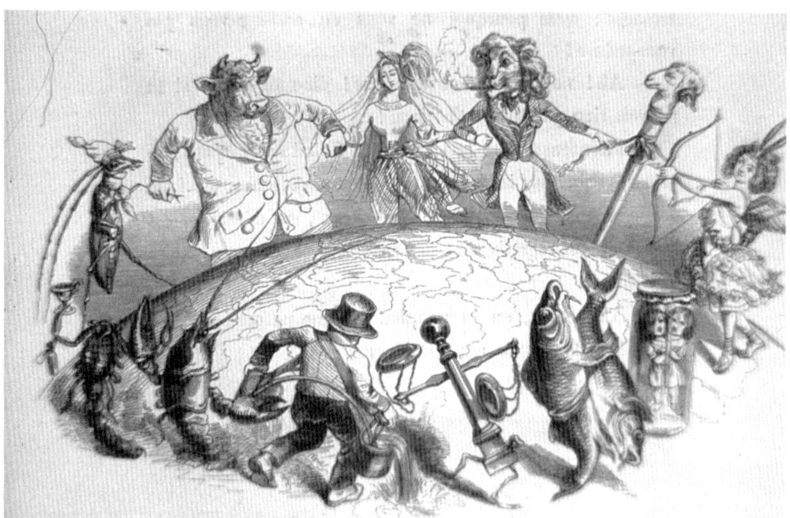

Figure 22: Marcel Broodthaers, *Grandville*, 1967, slideshow, 80 slides; Courtesy of the Estate Marcel Broodthaers, Brussels.

and '40s by way of personified animals and plants, was a favoured source for Marcel Broodthaers. He appropriated Grandville's satirical images in two slide projections of 1966 and 1968. The 1968 projection *Caricatures-Grandville* juxtaposed slides of satirical drawings by Grandville and Daumier, among others, with photographs of the 1968 student demonstrations.

Jean-Ignace-Isidore Gérard (1803–47), better known by the name of his comedian grandfather, Grandville, is synonymous today with the twin methods of the personified animal and the 'bestialized' human in modern illustration. In his satirical caricatures of the 1820s and early 1830s, but also in his later book illustrations such as those of the La Fontaine fables, J. J. Grandville addressed the question of social groups and types. In this, he was strongly influenced by physiognomist theories of the day, including the writings of Lavater and Gall. While the 'animal metaphor' already held some currency in French social satire during his lifetime (see Louis Huart's *Museum Parisien* of 1841), Grandville stands out for his thorough exploitation of the theme of organic metamorphoses from man to animal, man to plant and vice-versa. Along with the exploits of Honoré Daumier and Gustave Doré, Grandville's daring use of anthropomorphism in illustration had an influence on generations of illustrators and animators to come, from the Frenchman Ernest Griset, the Englishmen John Tenniel and Edward Lear, the Pole Ladislaw Staerwicz and finally the American Walt Disney.

'Our things in our hands must be equals, comrades.' (Alexander Rodchenko, 1924)

For Hungarian film theorist Béla Balázs, film gives visual shape to a physiognomic quality in both the animate and inanimate: '[In film,] all things make a physiognomic impression

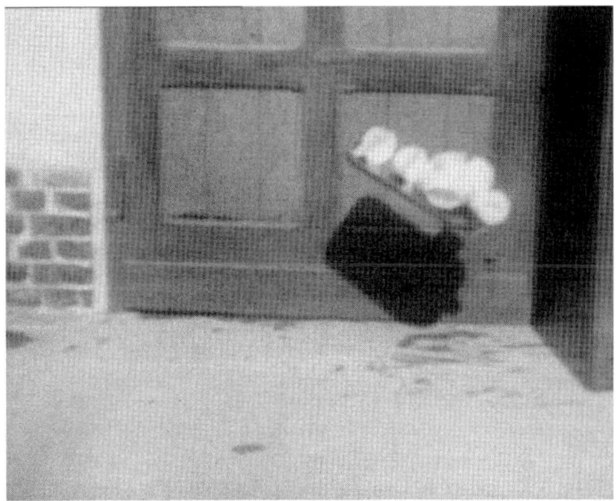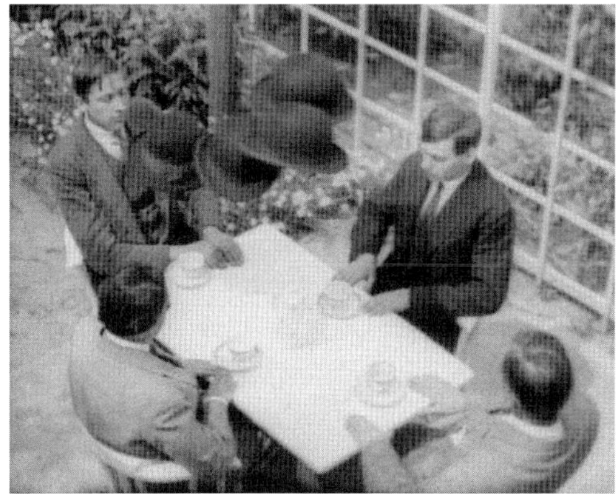

Figure 23: Hans Richter, *Vormittagsspuk/Ghosts Before Breakfast*, 1928, video (original: 35mm film), 7 min. Courtesy of the artist.

on us, whether we are conscious of it or not.' This physiognomic quality, however, was, for Balázs, an anthropomorphic projection in line with expressionist theories that saw an 'animated mirror' (Georg Simmel) in all modern art. For French film theorist and film-maker Jean Epstein, they are not merely mirrors, but also assume the status of characters in the (human) drama:

> Through the cinema, a revolver in a drawer, a broken bottle on the ground, an eye isolated by an iris, are elevated to the status of characters in the drama. [...] To things and beings in their most frigid semblance, the cinema thus grants the greatest gift: life. And it confers this life in its highest guise: personality.[51]

In *Vormittagsspuk/Ghosts Before Breakfast* (1928), Hans Richter stages a revolt of things, showing everyday objects turning against their users in a cinematic ghost hour of sorts. Teacups and saucers drop on the floor and break, beards appear and disappear, positive film changes into negative. Clothes desert their wearers, and strip them of the all-important markers of their bourgeois identity and dignity: the absence of hats releases a state of anarchy and 'unreason'. But before noon strikes, reason, order and serenity are restored: 'In the end the old hierarchy of person-master over the object-slave re-established itself. But for a short time, the public entertained a niggle of doubt about the general validity of the usual subject-object order.'

Vertov's *Soviet Toys* (1924) is generally assumed to be the first Soviet animated film. It is a propaganda film in which Vertov reacts to the introduction of limited forms of capitalist enterprises by Lenin's New Economic Policy, and is both an iconoclastic and a literalist illustration of the animated fetish-character of commodities described by Marx. The theory of animism as one of the animation of 'dead' matter was developed in the midst of the consolidation of commodity capitalism in Europe and North America. The commodity,

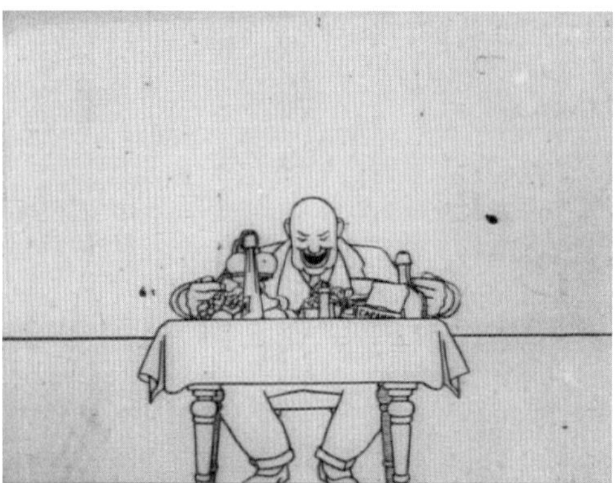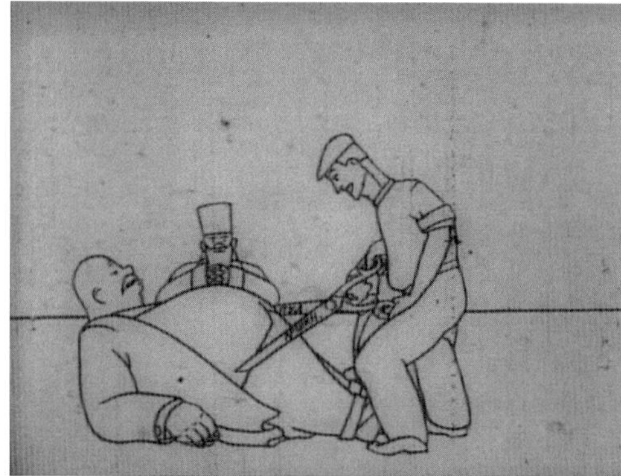

Figure 24: Dziga Vertov, *Soviet Toys*, 1924, video (original: 35mm film), 10:40 min. Courtesy of the artist.

as Karl Marx provocatively proposed, was not dead matter because it was animated by a 'fetishism of commodities'. There is a structural parallel between the commodity fetish and the cinematic image. Marx's commodity fetish derives its uncanny animation by displacing a social relation (of labour) into an inert object: 'A definite social relation assumes [...] the fantastic form of a relationship between things.' Hiding its means of production equally grants the cinematic image the animated quality it has for the viewer.

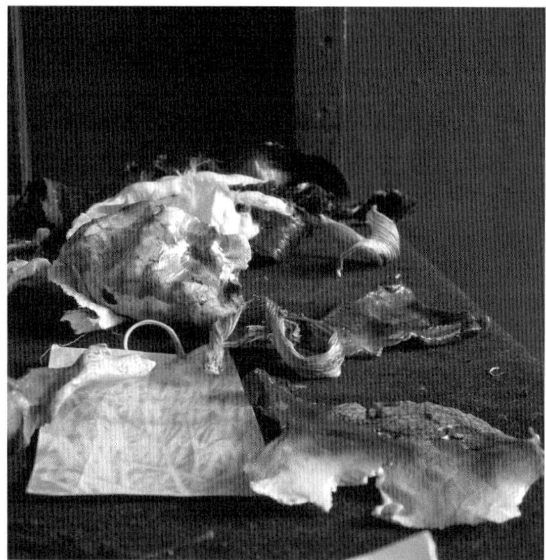

Figure 25: Reto Pulfer, *Dichtr mit Fugulit und Hydrgraph*, 2007 (detail), Raku-ceramics, b/w analogue photo fibre paper, silk, organic materials, black velvet, wooden board. Courtesy of the artist and Balice Hertling, Paris.

In Reto Pulfer's works, things press close onto consciousness, and states of consciousness dynamize things. No interior, but passages between states of mind, words, materiality, things. In these passages, there are multiple forces at work, elementary as well as symbolic, that produce a drifting and shifting of signs and sensations, uncohering and re-cohering meaning, experience and memories. Those drifts can be intensified through further short-circuits between signs and things, between sounds and textures, structured by systems of notations that become templates for a space that calls various presences forth.

Without Persons (1999–2008) consists of two computer-generated male and female voices discussing the concepts of 'being-in-the-city' and 'being-with-others'. Two monitors show a liquid – reminiscent of milk – whose shape is generated in response to the voices. The plasmatic liquid assumes ever-new forms, seemingly organic and animated by the mechanical voices, while the text contrasts the yet undifferentiated experience of the world of the early infant with the vision of a world devoid of persons. A dissonance is created between the content of the spoken word– a discussion about 'being' and relating to

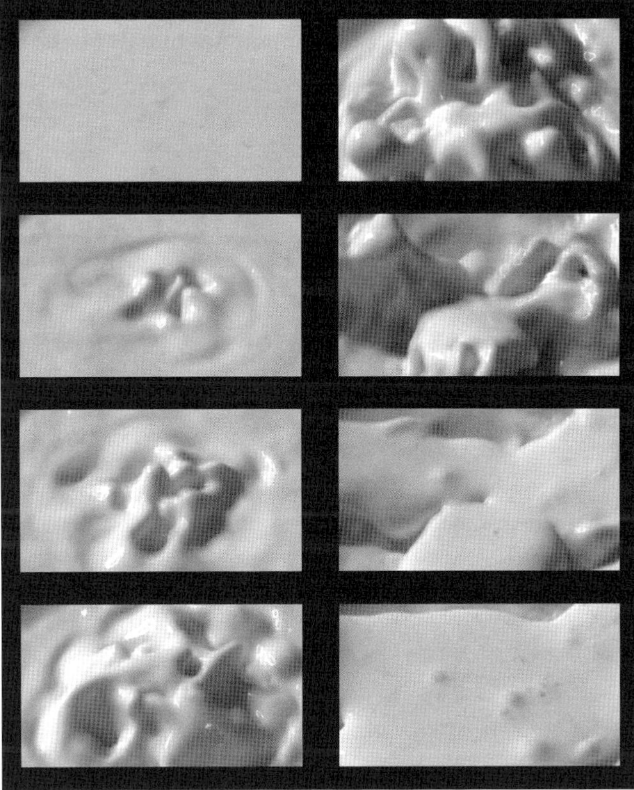

Figure 26: Luis Jacob, *Without Persons*, 1999–2008, two-channel video installation video, 22:45 min. Courtesy of the Birch Libralato, Toronto.

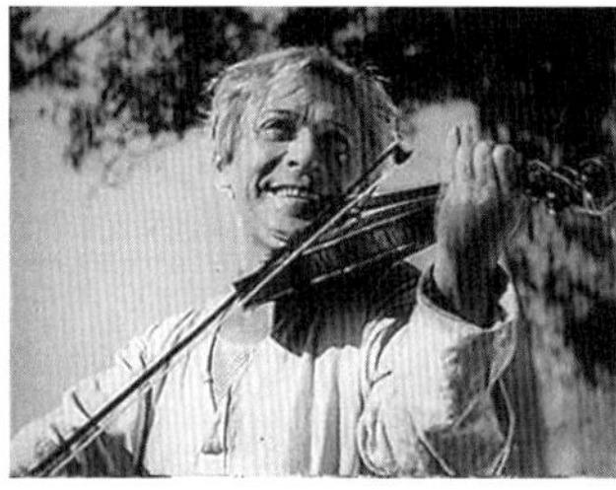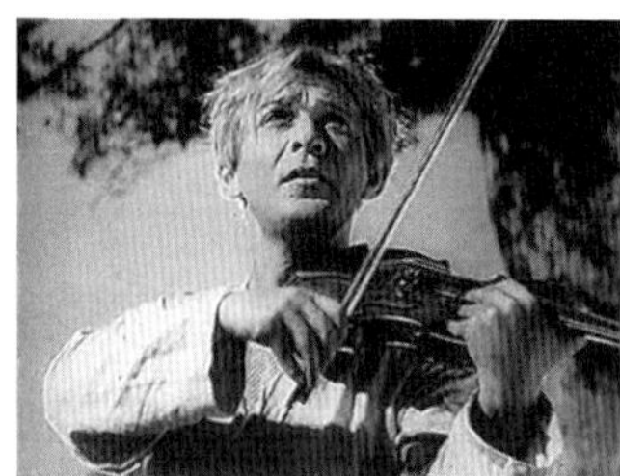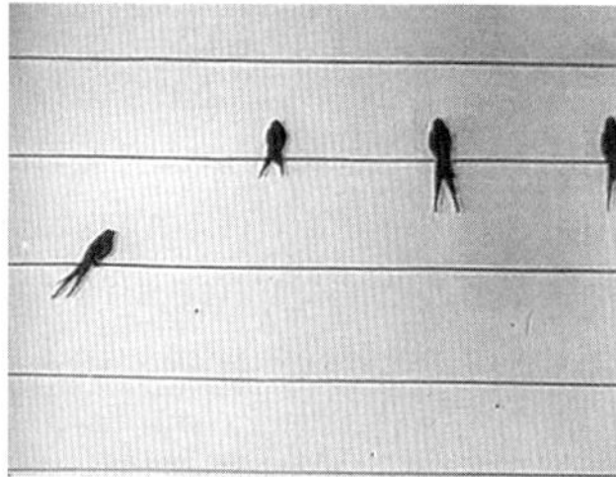

Figure 27: Grigory Alexandrov, *Jolly Fellows*, 1934, video (original: 35mm film, 96 min. Courtesy of the artist.

others – and the 'disembodied', clearly synthetic voices. This disaccord is further enhanced by the semblance of an organic link between the images and the sound, which refers to living beings, and the obvious machine support of the installation.

Certain tropes govern animated worlds. One of the laws can be described as exaggeration of cause and effect. A second rule emphasizes the animation itself: everything turns out to be more alive than you think. A third and most fundamental principle of animation is that the whole 'animated' world is joined together, bound not merely by the ropes of 'cause and effect' but by the 'carcass' upon which it is all constructed, the phonogram. The animated

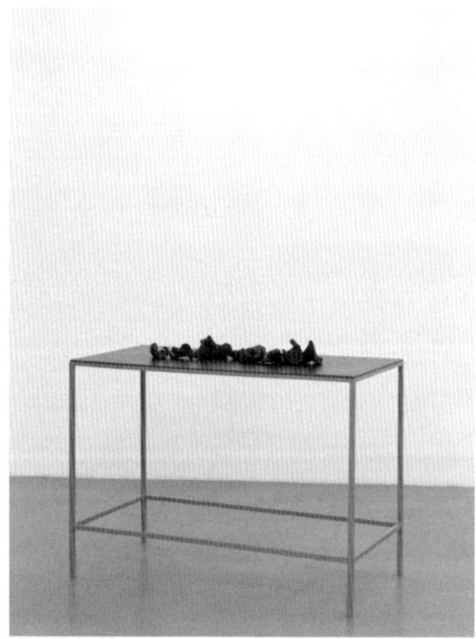

Figure 28: Lili Dujourie, *Initialen der Stille/Initials of Silence*, 2008, MDF, metal and clay. Courtesy of the artist and Galerie Nelson-Freeman, Paris.

universe sings, with its many voices, a single, very catching tune. When Grigory Alexandrov (the assistant to Sergei M. Eisenstein for more than a decade) made his first film in 1931, he translated the laws of animation derived from the study of the art of Walt Disney, among others, to the real-life universe of the Soviet utopia, creating a genre of musical comedies that has been referred to as 'Stalinist animation'.[52]

Initialen der Stille/Initials of Silence (2008) consists of a gray functional table upon which a heap of objects is laid out. They are earthen in colour and resemble scraps of clay peeled off of a rolling pin – curved little flakes of earth, the edges of which are gently ripped. From afar, the table looks like an operating table or a doctor's instrument tray, and the jumble of earth-like, curled skin or broken body parts. The haphazard placement of the curved flakes means that some appear convex, some concave. A dynamic is created; the individual elements appear to be in movement like the limbs of one body. Both in mythology and in the scriptures, clay was the material with which divinity made man. There is, in Dujourie's use of clay, the idea of a return to the very beginnings. Under the work's title, we may read the scraps of clay as testimony to the gods' and God's shaping of man and woman, to the essence of the body, which, through the ages, has been objectified and silenced.

The exhibition 'Animism' was first shown at MuHKA and Extra City Antwerpen (curated by Anselm Franke, co-curated by Edwin Carels and Bart de Baere) in 2010, then at Kunsthalle Bern (co-curated by Philippe Pirotte) in 2010, at the Generali Foundation Vienna (co-curated by Sabine Folie), in 2012 at the HKW Berlin and at e-flux in New York, and in 2013 at OCAT Shenzhen in 2013 and Ilmin Art Museum in Seoul.

This text was first published in Anselm Franke (ed.), *Animism* (I), Sternberg Press, 2010.

Notes

1   Edward Tylor, *Primitive Culture*, 2 Vols, London: John Murray, 1871.
2   Edward Tylor, *Primitive Culture*, London: John Murray, 1929, p. 426.
3   Notably the frequent indigenous uprisings in Ecuador since 1990, which evolve around struggles for the legalization of land holdings, and in which animism is posited as a social and political alternative to neo-liberal economic reforms. In 2008 Ecuador was the first country to approve a constitution that includes nature, alongside human beings, as a subject of law. The 'animist' conception of this legal text grants fundamental rights to elements such as rocks, mountains, river deltas and the seas.
4   Bruno Latour, *We Have Never Been Modern* (trans. Catherine Porter), Cambridge, MA: Harvard University Press, 1993, p. 53.
5   ibid., pp. 99–100.
6   Theodor W. Adorno and Max Horkheimer, *Dialectic of Enlightenment – Philosophical Fragments* (trans. Edmund Jephcott), Stanford: Stanford University Press, 2002, pp. 1–2.
7   Bruno Latour, *War of the Worlds: What about Peace?* (trans. Charlotte Bigg), Chicago: Prickly Paradigm Press, 2002, p. 9.

8   Latour, 1993, p. 97.

9   Tylor, 1871, pp. 20–21.

10   Cf. Tylor, 1871.

11   Michael Taussig, *Shamanism, Colonialism, and the Wild Man: A Study in Terror and Healing*, Chicago: University of Chicago Press, 1987, p. 219.

12   ibid., p. 10.

13   Michel Foucault, *History of Madness*, London: Routledge, 2006, p. xxix.

14   Cf. Susan Buck-Morss, 'Aesthetics and Anaesthetics – Walter Benjamin's Artwork Essay Reconsidered', in *October*, Vol. 62, Autumn 1992, pp. 3–41.

15   Donna Haraway, *When Species Meet*, Minneapolis: University of Minnesota Press, 2008, p. 10.

16   Giorgio Agamben, *The Open: Man and Animal*, Stanford: Stanford University Press, 2004, pp. 13–16.

17   William McDougall, *Body and Mind: A History and A Defense of Animism*, London: Methuen, 1911, p. 3.

18   Tylor, 1871, p. 429.

19   Latour, 1993, p. 37.

20   ibid., p. 143.

21   Bruno Latour and Peter Weibel (eds), *ICONOCLASH: Beyond the Image Wars in Science, Religion and Art*, Cambridge, MA: MIT Press, 2002, p. 16.

22   Cf. Latour, 1993.

23   Michael Taussig, *Defacement: Public Secrecy and the Labor of the Negative*, Stanford: Stanford University Press, 1999, p. 43.

24   Theodor Adorno and Max Horkheimer, *Dialectic of Enlightenment* (trans. Edmund Jephcott), Stanford: Stanford University Press, 2002, p. 5.

25   ibid., p. 6 & 21.

26   Cf. Edward Curtis, *The Vanishing Race. Selection from Edward S. Curtis' The North American Indian*, New York: Taplinger, 1977.

27   For further elaboration on the myth of the camera stealing the soul, see *The Museum of the Stealing of Souls*, http://stealingsouls.org/, accessed 1 November 2010.

28   Cf. Latour and Weibel, 2002.

29   Roland Barthes, *Camera Lucida: Reflections on Photography* (trans. Richard Howard), New York: Hill and Wang, 1981, pp. 13–14.

30   Jacques Derrida, *Specters of Marx, the State of the Debt, the Work of Mourning & the New International* (trans. Peggy Kamuf), London: Routledge, 1994, p. 6.

31   André Bazin, *What is Cinema?* (trans. Hugh Gray), Vol. 1, Berkeley & Los Angeles: University of California Press, 1967, p. 9.

32   Noël Burch, *Life to Those Shadows*, Berkeley & Los Angeles: University of California Press, 1990, p. 12.

33   Latour, 1993, p. 123.

34   Sigmund Freud, *Totem and Taboo* (trans. James Srachey), London: Routledge and Kegan Paul, 1950, p. 64.

35 Walter Benjamin qtd in Miriam Bratu Hansen, *Cinema and Experience: Siegfried Kracauer, Walter Benjamin, and Theodor W. Adorno*, Berkeley, CA: University of California Press, 2012, p. 196

36 Miriam Bratu Hansen, 'Benjamin and Cinema: Not a One-Way Street', in *Critical Inquiry*, Vol. 25, University of California Press, 1999, pp. 306–345.

37 Miriam Bratu Hansen, 'Of Mice and Ducks: Benjamin and Adorno on Disney', in *South Atlantic Quarterly*, Vol. 92, 1993, pp. 27–61.

38 Cf. Walter Benjamin, 'Surrealism', in Michael W. Jennings (ed.), *Selected Writings*, Vol. 2, Cambridge, MA: Belknap Press of Harvard University, 1997–2003, p. 209.

39 Walter Benjamin, *One-Way Street and Other Writings* (trans. Edmund Jephcott and Kinsley Shorter), London: New Left Books, 1979, p. 104.

40 Latour, 1993, p. 39.

41 ibid., p. 34.

42 ibid., p. 142.

43 Bruno Latour, *Politics of Nature: How to Bring the Sciences into Democracy* (trans. Catherine Porter), Cambridge, MA: Harvard University Press, 2004, p. 39.

44 Cf. Walter Benjamin, 'On the Mimetic Faculty', in Michael W. Jennings et al. (eds), *Walter Benjamin – Selected Writings*, Vol. 2, Part 2, 1931–34, pp. 720–27.

45 Haraway, 2008, p. 27.

46 Latour, 1993, p. 137.

47 Rane Willerslev, *Soul Hunters: Hunting, Animism, and Personhood among the Siberian Yukaghirs*, Berkeley and Los Angeles: University of California Press, 2007, p. 187.

48 ibid., p. 191.

49 Natascha Sadr Haghighian interviewed by Solvej Helweg Ovesen, 2001, http://www.johannkoenig.de/inc/02_art_texts_popup.php?publication_id=71 (accessed 11 April 2013).

50 Tony Conrad, 1986, unpublished text.

51 Jean Epstein in Richard Abel, *French Film Theory and Criticism, 1907–1939: Volume 1, 1907–1929*, New Jersey: Princeton University Press, 1988, p. 317.

52 Based upon extracts from Anne Nesbet, *Savage Junctures: Sergei Eisenstein and the Shape of Thinking*, London: I. B. Tauris, 2007.

PART I

Post-Medial Image Cultures and New Media Philosophies

Chapter 1

Technical Repetition and Digital Art, or Why the 'Digital' in Digital Cinema is not the 'Digital' in Digital Technics

Mark B. N. Hansen

Film-makers have long worked with technical supports other than film. Certainly since the advent of video, arguably earlier in experiments involving filmless cameras or flicker effects, and, in a different sense, for the long history preceding its actual invention, cinema has operated beyond film. While this extra-filmic operation of cinema can be retrospectively viewed as multiply and differentially anticipating the moment we are now in – the moment of digital convergence of media and of the advent of a properly post-filmic cinematic situation – what is at stake today is, in some important sense, radically discontinuous with such anticipations. The reason, to put it quite simply, is that cinema's contemporary extra-filmic support – the digital computer – comprises a materialization that radically challenges cinema's identity. It is this challenge – which is simultaneously the promise of what has, for the most part uncritically, been called digital art, that I propose to explore here.

The Cinematic Metaphor and the Temporal Object

Let me begin at what for us, in this context, is the beginning: Lev Manovich's *The Language of New Media* (1999). More specifically, let me begin by quoting Manovich's assessment of the centrality of cinematic grammar in the present and the foreseeable future of new media practices:

> The fact that computer games and virtual worlds continue to encode, step by step, the grammar of a kino-eye in software and in hardware is not an accident, but rather is consistent with the overall trajectory of the computerization of culture since the 1940s – the automation of all cultural operations. This automation gradually moves from basic to

more complex operations: from image processing and spell checking to software-generated characters, 3-D worlds, and Web sites. A side effect of this automation is that once particular cultural codes are implemented in low-level software and hardware, they are no longer seen as choices but as unquestionable defaults. […] Now we are witnessing the next stage of this process [after the encoding of linear perspective] – the translation of a cinematic grammar of points of view into software and hardware. As Hollywood cinematography is translated into algorithms and computer chips, its conventions become the default method of interacting with any data subjected to spatialization. […] Element by element, cinema is being poured into a computer: first, one-point linear perspective; next, the mobile camera and rectangular window; next cinematography and editing conventions; and, of course, digital personas based on acting conventions borrowed from cinema, to be followed by make-up, set design, and the narrative structures themselves. Rather than being merely one cultural language among others, cinema is now becoming *the* cultural interface, a toolbox for all cultural communication, overtaking the printed world. Cinema, the major cultural form of the twentieth century, has found new life as the toolbox of the computer user. Cinematic means of perception, of connecting space and time, of representing human memory, thinking, and emotion have become a way of work and a way of life for millions in the computer age. Cinema's aesthetic strategies have become basic organizational principles of computer software. The window into a fictional world of a cinematic narrative has become a window into a datascape. In short, what was cinema is now the human-computer interface.[1]

Manovich's characterization of cinema as the cultural dominant of the computer age circa 2000 quite literally set the stage for what, more than a decade hence, we can now recognize – and perhaps partition off – as a first wave of theorization of digital media. Whether the topic in question is the cinematic aesthetics of video game cutscenes or point of view in relation to purely synthetized images, the formula proposed by Manovich – cinematic surface + digital core – seemed, at the time of its appearance, not simply fruitful for characterizing new media objects of various sorts, but in some sense simply 'necessary' to our incipient efforts to make sense of the techno-cultural revolution presented by digital technics. Cinematic conventions, in sum, furnished a familiar cultural interface for us to understand, and to deploy many of the new facilities ushered in by the massive cultural dissemination of digital computing.

With well more than a decade standing between us and Manovich's prescient diagnosis, it is time again to ask after the elective affinity between cinema and new media. Does the cinematic metaphor continue to do service as a means of transitioning to a new, digitally-supported lifeworld? Or does it now rather stand in the way of such a transition, forming a kind of cultural hangover that prevents us from grasping just what is so promising – and perhaps also so disturbing – about the digital? I propose to approach this question by exploring the divergence between 'digital' cinema and 'digital' technics that, as I see it, has progressively widened over the previous decade. What is ultimately at stake in this divergence, as I shall argue below, is time, or more exactly the correlation of time, media and experience: for whereas cinematic media inscribes time as past duration in order to re-present it to present consciousness, digital technics operates on the 'time of the now'[2] and makes time available for experience beyond the reference frame of consciousness. At stake in the divergence, then, is nothing short of an opportunity to open a new collective relationship to time, one in which consciousness relinquishes its longstanding privilege over the experience of time, and comes to be replaced by enworlded body-minds acting in concert with digital artifactualizations of time.

The divergence in question here – between digital cinema and digital technics – has emerged as a result of our increased familiarity with, and deployment of, digital technologies in our everyday lives. What we have learned about digital technics over the last decade cuts against the grain of the cinematic metaphor. We have learned that the digital – or digital technics – is not a time-based medium like film and video, and perhaps is not a medium at all. And, indeed, debate continues to rage about what exactly the digital is if not a medium, with one plausible account arguing that it is a new platform where all prior media converge, a kind of 'super-medium' that (like the alphabet before it) is in fact not one (there being no medium in the singular).[3] Perhaps more radically still, the digital has been designated the infrastructure of our global culture, forming a 'technological unconscious', to invoke the felicitous term proposed by Nigel Thrift, that remains asynchronous with, and heterogeneous to, the rhythms of human experience (both conscious and unconscious) and of the media that exteriorize them.

Notwithstanding its double break with twentieth century's time-based media (double in the sense that it is neither time-based nor yet another medium), digital technics is all about time, which is to say, all about new modes of measurement and artifactualization of time in our world today. And because the human is necessarily involved in any invocation of the world as 'our' world, digital technics is furthermore all about our changed human relation to the artifactualization of time. To summarize the conclusion of my current work on twenty-first century media, digital technics impacts the experience of time in a way that is, in large part, outside the frame of media: the digital inscription of time today occurs at an infrastructural level and at temporal scales that are beneath the threshold of consciousness and perception, and also of the various media – cinema being the most significant – that extend their retentional and memorial agency.

Accordingly, digital technics poses a challenge for phenomenological and neo-phenomenological approaches to media experience, which emphasize the surrogacy media lends time-consciousness. Specifically, digital technics no longer supports a framing of the temporal flux (which is also to say of time-consciousness, self-affection and subjectivity) as a Husserlian 'temporal object', a surrogate object that 'objectifies' the flux of time through the brain. As such, digital technics challenges efforts, like that of philosopher Bernard Stiegler, to update Husserl's model of time-consciousness for our technological age. No more than the melody it is introduced to update, the cinematic temporal object can only mirror 'lived experience' and can only objectify the 'contents of consciousness' ('the lived'). As a temporal object premised on its homology with the time frame of consciousness, it remains by definition powerless to capture temporal fluxes that occur at more fine-grained level, which is to say, precisely those fluxes introduced by the digital computer and deployed in the best of today's digital media artworks. In light of this situation (to which I return in some detail below), the burden of sustaining the experience of temporal flux falls onto the spectator, or more precisely, onto the spectator's (passive) receptivity or responsiveness to heterogeneous digital artifactualizations of time. This is, as I shall emphasize below, necessarily to mark a shift in the 'economy' of time: no longer first and foremost an 'intimate' domain of human phenomenological experience, time now attains the cosmological dimension attributed to it by Paul Ricoeur (following Aristotle) and, in an altogether different register, by Alfred N. Whitehead; from this point on, the human experience of time can always only be a co-temporalization involving both embodied mind 'and' physical (technical) artifactualization, one over which the former no longer holds mastery and in which the 'bounds of experience' no longer coincide with the 'total temporal phenomenon'. Otherwise put, the human experience of time in the digital era always involves some element or dimension which escapes that experience, something ulterior or heterogeneous to experience itself.

The 'Digital' Automatism of Post-cinematic Media

To pinpoint exactly what is at stake with respect to time in digital technics, and more generally what is at stake in widening the divergence between digital cinema and digital technics, let us turn to a recent argument that seeks to open up to the digital future without throwing the cinematic baby out with the bathwater. It hardly comes as a surprise that self-proclaimed *cinefils* D. N. Rodowick frames his exploration of 'digital cinema' in relation to the 'cinematic metaphor' introduced by Manovich:

> [...] today most so-called new media are inevitably imagined from a cinematic metaphor. Undoubtedly, the art of cinema is renewing and refashioning itself through the incorporation of digital processes, while a certain idea of cinema informs and insinuates itself into the development of interactive entertainments. Here, the arts of analogy are not displaced by digital technologies; rather an idea of cinema persists or subsists within the new media as their predominant cultural and aesthetic model for engaging the vision and imagination of viewers.[4]

Rodowick goes so far as to acknowledge the blinders this 'cinemato-centrism' places on the development of new media aesthetics:

> But this also means that it is difficult to envision what kinds of aesthetic experiences computational processes will innovate once they have unleashed themselves from the cinematic metaphor and begin to explore their autonomous creative powers, if indeed they eventually do so.[5]

Notwithstanding the unequivocal force of this cautionary note, I would submit that today, and indeed already by 2007 or 2006, the singular aesthetic potentials of digital technics are (were) well on the way toward being tapped, not in the sense of being exhausted, but rather of being opened to a highly divergent and innovative set of deployments.

What we learn from Rodowick's ambivalence is precisely that the digital in digital cinema is not the same as the digital in digital technics. While this was perhaps not readily apparent in 1999, at the time of Manovich's writing, it simply cannot be overlooked today. Indeed, to my mind, this reality explains Rodowick's penchant to recognize the need for a break with cinema as the avenue for a responsible approach to digital media at the very moment that he asserts the persistence, indeed the deep cultural entrenchment, of the cinematic metaphor. This ambivalent penchant literally shapes Rodowick's book, in the sense that it informs the marked cleft dividing its first two chapters (focusing on film and duration) from its final chapter on digital media.

Nowhere, however, do the stakes of Rodowick's oscillation become more significant than with regard to the question of time. We find him arguing at different moments that digital processes are and are not images,[6] that the digital is and is not a medium,[7] and perhaps most consequentially, that the digital is and is not capable of provoking the kind of ontological insecurity that emerged in the wake of film's advent.[8] For, as we shall see, Rodowick's fixation on the diminished indexicality of the digital 'image' leads him to pursue a false question – whether the digital can inscribe duration; and this in turn causes him to forget his own call for an alternate approach to digital technics, foreclosing any possibility that digital technics might open a different relationship to time than the inscription of past duration in the process.

Rodowick's argument involves at least two stages. His first, and enabling, move is to isolate the temporal dimension of the technical processing of digital information, a move that becomes possible in the wake of his argument – correct in my opinion – that the primary 'automatism' of digital technics is transcoding or the manipulation of quantized information.[9] Focusing exclusively on the technical processes at work in transcoding, Rodowick finds a cyclical temporality wholly decoupled from any experienced (or potentially experienced) spatial-durational object:

> [D]igital capture should be understood in contrast to analogical transcription as a process of calculation in which time is measured as the *conversion* of light into code ('Quantizing' is the technical term). [...] [T]ranscoding introduces a temporal discontinuity into the recording process, experienced by most of us as shutter lag or other computational indicators of wait time: miniature clocks and spinning rainbow wheels. These signs are indexes of another sort; they designate the operation of computing cycles, applying algorithms while converting space and time into code.[10]

And, in a concise statement that perfectly sums up his claim about computational time and indexicality: 'time itself is transformed as a purely quantitative function defined by calculation. Analog media transcribe time as duration; digital capture or synthesis *consumes time as processing cycles*.'[11]

In a second move, Rodowick grafts this purely technical temporality (this temporality decoupled from reference to human experience) onto film-maker Babette Mangolte's claim that, because digital cameras register layers of pixels rather than succession of images, they have difficulty representing the passage of time.[12] What results is Rodowick's claim – to my mind, the fundamental claim of his book – that digital technics cannot inscribe duration:

> In what does the digital event consist? Digital capture, synthesis, and compositing are the three principle creative operations of digital cinema. Digital capture may be considered as analogous to video recording in a number of ways. Yet, even here the image is not 'one,' for light recorded on charge-coupled devices is already fragmented into a discrete mosaic of picture elements, which are then read off as distinct mathematic values. The process of conversion or transcoding separates the image into mathematically discrete and modular elements whose individual values are open to any number of programmable transformations. The separation of outputs from inputs, and the process of calculation converting light into code, unravel the unity of the profilmic spatial event unfolding in a unique duration. As befits the mathematical basis of information processing, the digital event corresponds less to the durations and movements of the world than to the control and variation of discrete numerical elements internal to the computer's memory and logical processes.[13]

Reading this, one cannot but wonder whether it matters that the force of Mangolte's argument concerns the aesthetic properties of digital imaging, things like the 'brightness of the LCD screen', the 'relentless glare of the digital image', the absence of shutter reprieve and of the back-and-forth, every forty-eighth of a second, between dark and image. In Mangolte's argument, it is precisely these aesthetic lacunae that occasion the movement 'deeper' into the machine, which means, ultimately, that her claim for the decoupling of digital pixelization from time is offered as an explanation for a change in the phenomenological experience of viewing, rather than an entailment of the logic of indexicality. As against Rodowick, that is, Mangolte's aim is not to think the digital, but to explore what it is like 'to work with' digital cameras, and this leads her to make what is ultimately an 'aesthetic evaluation' about digital film: that it is 'unable to establish and construct an experiential sense of time passing', or, at the very least, that it is at a 'disadvantage' where it is a question of evoking such a sense.[14]

How – the question cannot be avoided – do we move from Mangolte's narrowly focused claim about the aesthetic properties of a particular imaging technology (the digital camera) to Rodowick's blanket claim that digital technics cannot inscribe duration? The answer, of course, is via an operation of theorization involving the conversion of an aesthetic question into a logical and, in this case, purely technical constraint. At the heart of this operation is a certain inversion of aesthetics and technics: in contrast to Mangolte's procedure (seeking a technical explanation for an aesthetic failure), Rodowick starts with a technical 'automatism', which functions in an almost automatic fashion to dictate necessary aesthetic consequences, or better, limitations. How else indeed could the looped temporality of computing cycles directly determine the range of temporal inscription available to digital technics?

What falls out here is precisely the role of the aesthetic, which is to say, the very operation that, in the account otherwise so central to Rodowick's argument – that of Stanley Cavell – transforms automatisms into expressive forms, if not indeed into full-fledged, self-differing mediums. We thus need to ask anew the questions first asked by Rodowick: 'Can information processing be considered a creative medium? Can the computer [...] give rise to creative automatisms?'[15] Any attempt to answer these questions must begin from the specificity of the computer as an automatism, which is to say, following Rodowick's own analysis, from its defining capacity for quantization and manipulation (transcoding). With digital technics, in short, we are dealing with a radically different automatism than mechanical recording, the automatism characteristic of cinema, and any effort to develop the aesthetic dimension of digital technics must recognize – and indeed take off from – this difference.

It is all the more surprising then to find Rodowick himself shifting gears and focusing on recording in order to unpack the aesthetic development of digital technics. He gives as examples the images from Abu Ghraib, which:

> [...] exhibit powers possible only in the age of computers. Like all other forms of digital information, these images express a new, accelerated relationship with time – of copying and transmission – where the present gains in density and scope. Indeed, the images from Abu Ghraib are provocative examples of how the powers of digital capture and diffusion have transformed not our sense of the past, but our relationship to the history of the present and what it means to occupy *present* time.[16]

Just in case one holds any lingering doubts concerning Rodowick's appreciation for this new temporal modality of digital recording, we need only cite his correlation of it with information: 'One way to characterize digital documentation, then, is to examine how the image is treated more and more as information to be accumulated, stored, sorted, and analyzed.'[17] The underlying logic here seems to be that we no longer select images to store based on their value as images – which is to say, for Rodowick as for Barthes, as images of the reality of the past; consequently, we don't exercise the same vigilance in selection as we formerly did.

Yet, notwithstanding the clear critical thrust of Rodowick's characterization of this shift in temporal modality of recording, it has two interesting implications for our understanding of the experience of images in the digital age: on one hand, the registration of images now exceeds the scope of the individual, yielding a kind of collective retention that can no longer be a function of unified consciousness; and, on the other hand, the exponential increase in the 'archive of the immediate present' means not only that we now overwhelmingly document 'situations that are more banal than eventful', but also that recording typically occurs, as it were automatically, independently of attentive human interest. This line of thinking culminates in Rodowick's characterization of digital images as:

[...] no longer [...] capable of producing the existential or ontological perplexity of which both Barthes and Cavell were so keenly and philosophically aware. Digital photographs have become more social than personal, and more attuned to the present itself than to the present's relation to past and future. Symbolic and notational at their core, they provoke discussion of images as *information* [...] The hermeneutic circle of interpretation becomes here an ethical circle of responsiveness or unresponsiveness.[18]

Experience Beyond Phenomenology

Everything Rodowick here claims about the digital seems to me fundamentally correct, except for its evaluative aspect, which, to my mind, is a direct function of his displacement of the technical dimension of digital technics, and thus of its potential to open new relations between information and time. It is as if Rodowick simply forgets everything he had argued concerning the purely cyclical, technical time of digital technics so that he can differentiate – through (dis)analogy – contemporary digital images from earlier cinematic ones.

To get a sense for how massively Rodowick's evaluative conclusion overinvests in the traditional function of the image as a form of capture at the expense of everything Rodowick explores under the rubric of digital automatism, let us turn to a pioneering digital film-maker and theoretician, Malcolm Le Grice, who builds a double career on the impossibility of segregating technics from aesthetics (and vice versa). Well in advance of his work with digital technics, but no doubt anticipating it, Le Grice formulated a concept – 'durational equivalence' – that perfectly expresses the inseparability of digital technics and an aesthetics of presencing. As LeGrice explains, he initially developed the concept 'through comparison with the representation of time in conventional narrative film':

In the representation of extensive time scales within the relatively short duration of a film's presentation, time becomes irrevocably illusionistic. Not only is the duration of the film's represented action unrelatable to the duration of its presentation, but through subversion by illusionistic continuity between shots, the shots themselves lose their durational documentality. In other words, the material duration of the film's presentation, production and represented action becomes entirely dissociated; the spectator, with no way of integrating the relations of present, retrospective record, and fiction, can only give in to the fictional duration which subsumes all others. In this way any concept of reality in the field of durational experience is undermined by the temporal compression of narrative convention.[19]

In order to appreciate its potential contribution to the aesthetic possibilities of the digital automatism, it is important that we fully grasp what is at stake here: not only is Le Grice affirming the 'primacy for the spectator of the *reality of duration at the moment of the film's presentation*', he is linking it to the experience of time scales that are heterogeneous to the psychological-phenomenological timescales characteristic not simply of narrative cinema, but of human time-consciousness itself.[20] Within the realm of pre-digital cinema, this fundamental temporal illusion of narrative cinema can be broken through experiments that expand cinematic materiality by including not simply the physical substance of the filmstrip and projector, but the 'conditions of [...] presentation and the mechanism of [...] perception by the spectator.'[21] But it is really only in the realm of digital technics that this temporal heterogeneity can be exploited for the possibility it affords to open alternate temporal experiences that are both post-phenomenological and correlated more or less directly with the cyclical, yet always differentiated temporal processes of the computer.

By 'post-phenomenological', I mean experiences, which violate the correlation, theorized by contemporary French philosopher Bernard Stiegler (in the wake of Edmund Husserl's groundbreaking research), between the cinematic flux and the flux of consciousness. The power of cinema – by which Stiegler means, above all, narrative cinema – stems from the experiential impact of its grammatization of time's flux: according to Stiegler, when we give ourselves over to the double coincidence at the heart of cinema – the coincidence of the past and reality (Barthes's *ça a été*: 'that was') and the coincidence of real-time global media fluxes and time consciousness – we submit the affective passivity that, on the western philosophical narrative, lies at the heart of subjectivity, to a well-nigh Frankfurt School standardization. Post-phenomenological experiences can be defined, then, as temporal experiences that are not mediated by what Husserl, and Stiegler after him, call the temporal object: a surrogate object – a melody or a real-time media flux – that materializes the evanescent flux of time through the brain.

And by 'correlated with the cyclical computational processes', I mean that these experiences comprise a temporal aesthetic of digital technics that has its root in the decoupling of input and output so central to Rodowick's account.[22] To put it in Stiegler's terms, the homology between the cinematic grammatization of time and the flux of consciousness no longer holds for digital technics. The result is a loss of the double coincidence constitutive of cinema (and a total displacement of the problematic of indexicality[23]) which however, at least according to Le Grice, is more than recompensed by the quotient of aesthetic difference introduced by digital grammatization of time (real-time, which is to say, fine-scaled computing):

For art also [the computer] represents a kind of third stage following the direct media of the hand and body – painting – music – sculpture – dance, then the media of mechanical reproduction – the printing press – photography – film – the phonograph. A major characteristic of the program is that its outputs change depending on the data or procedures selected. The program is a set of instructions to manipulate data in a particular way which can include responding to new input of data or new input of the way in which it may be manipulated. As a consequence, the resulting works will follow a consistent pattern formed by the program but each particular version of the work may have differences. These differences are a component of the work and may be based on a range of factors or strategies within the program. [...] In all these cases, the resulting work goes *beyond the singularity of the hand-made object or the multiple but identical copy* of mechanical reproduction.[24]

What starts out like a reprise of Kittler's important and influential claim regarding digital convergence turns into a celebration of the temporal accident, the fine-scaled differences that differentiate each version of a work from others, and indeed, the work as such from itself. What we experience, in short, in aesthetic mediations of digital technics, and more specifically, of computational temporal cycles, is something other than a temporal object that could form a surrogate for the more or less unified experience of time-consciousness. Indeed, Rodowick himself comes to roughly the same conclusion when he announces that:

> [...] *there are no new media 'objects' or images.* A better term might be 'elements' which may vary in terms of their outputs and underlying algorithmic logics. Thus, it bears repeating that electronic art involves not the making of a thing, but variations in a process or transformations of a signal.[25]

Indeed, to appreciate this difference in the form that time, along with the aesthetic experience of time, takes in the digital, I want to recall one of the claims advanced by Rodowick with which I wholly concur: that the aesthetic of digital information foregoes interpretation for an ethics of responsiveness. I would want to add to this a specifically Levinasian twist, and say that responding to the heterogeneity of time's computational physicality is precisely what we are called upon to do in much of what I take to be the most interesting contemporary work in 'digital cinema' (and which I would, as I have said, prefer to call 'the aesthetic of digital technics'). On this score, it is of great interest that Le Grice's concept of the 'film splice' enacts, almost literally, the criticism Levinas launches against the great Husserlian motif of the retentional and protentional thickness of the now. For Levinas, you may recall, this motif guarantees the capture of time 'on this side of being', which is also to say, in the form of philosophical (time-) consciousness; in the process, it loses contact with the heterogeneity – indeed, with the cosmological, asubjective physicality – that gives time its grandeur as a philosophical topic and its power as a core dimension, perhaps the core dimension (at least for the last Levinas), of ethical experience.[26]

For Le Grice, the capture of the 'film splice' by the system of continuity editing central to narrative cinema actually 'inscribes a *fissure of discontinuity*'[27], which it is beyond the power of cinema to present, but also – crucially – beyond its power to efface:

> In any film sequence there is a period before and after 'shoot-ing', and within the conventions of montage there is a further framing through the discarding (editing out) of the moments before and after the 'intended' action. Both picture frame and particularly the time frame of each shot is suppressed in cinema by the continuity of the montage. Indeed the replacement of an absence (loss of the before and after of the shot) at the moment of the splice is exchanged for a new and illusory continuity in the narrative.[28]

Now, it is clear that digital technics, and specifically the physical instantiation of temporal flux in the fine-grained cycles of the computer, afford vastly more powerful opportunities to bring the temporal power informing this 'fissure of discontinuity' – the very heterogeneity so central for Levinas – into the range of aesthetic experience. And, importantly, it does not do this phenomenologically, which is to say, through the form of a temporal object or any other artifactualization that subordinates temporal heterogeneity to the thresholds of conscious experience. Rather, it lends aesthetic primacy to the temporal accidents constitutive of the specificity of any given digital process, and in so doing, brings into the domain of experience the 'technological unconscious' itself,[29] by which I mean the changed relation between humans and the world that is, in my opinion, at stake in digital technics and that manifests most centrally in the passage from a mediatic (or technical) phenomenology of time-consciousness to an asubjective phenomenology of time itself.

Put another way, what is at stake in digital technics is not yet another new medium, nor a new platform for media writ large, where the latter is understood as an exteriorization of human consciousness, nor even a support for a cultural metaphor (cinema). Rather, what lies at the core of the inseparably technical and aesthetic singularity of digital technics is a new 'compact' between experience and the artifactualization of time. Experience is no longer the capture of time by some unified (or, for that matter, fragmentary) subjective agent or mediatic object, but rather the singular affects that comprise our response, to stick with the Levinasian chord introduced above, to the temporal accidents of computing. We must, in other words, keep experience separate from the forms of capture and control theorized by Deleuze, and with particular application to digital networks and our desire to control information, by Rodowick.[30] And while this means following Deleuze's path for a while, a path that has been significantly extended by some important contemporary critics (Alexander R. Galloway and Eugene Thacker, as well as Brian Massumi), it also means insisting on the inviolability of experience, and insisting on it not on the basis of some new affirmation of embodiment, but on the basis of the coupling of aesthetics and technics 'beneath' or 'beyond' the scope of coherent, unified perception and embodied enaction. In other words, the technical singularities of computing cycles have aesthetic correlates which generate asubjective affects that do not contribute to narrative understanding, whether this is centred in a media object or a subject, but that yield singular asubjective experiences of the technical infrastructure of our digital worlds.

Technical Repetition, or Beyond 'Editing-in-the-Brain'

New media art holds a privileged place in the aesthetico-technical economy characteristic of our contemporary culture. Without being able to develop this claim fully, let me simply enumerate three sources for (or symptoms of) this privilege:

- New media art participates in, and perhaps even exemplifies, the current culture-wide reversal that focuses on aesthetics in its original Greek sense, as perceptibility or sensibility: if and when new media production is able to claim aesthetic status in the narrow sense (e.g. as determined by institutions of art preservation, selection and criticism), this is (or will be) because, and only because, it attains its broader aesthetic (i.e. perceptual) existence through its deployment of extra- (not intrinsically) aesthetic technical networks.

- New media art mediates between the domains of presencing and self-reference: indeed, its claim to status as art has everything to do with its capacity to bring what normally remains beneath the threshold of perception – the myriad technical temporalizations that inform the infrastructure of our world today – into the horizon of (human) experience.
- New media art, precisely in performing this feat of mediation, enframes time 'directly', which is to say, *not* in itself (for there is no time-in-itself), but by designating as its proper content the contingencies that are associated, irreducibly though always in concrete forms, with specific technical temporalizations.

This privilege of new media art hinges on the distinction between 'capture' and 'enframing' media, where the former designates media that mime or 'objectify' the passage of time, and the latter designates media that mediate – or better, participate in – time differentially and that encompass time 'as minimal change enframed'. As exemplified by Wolfgang Staehle's *Empire 24/7* (1999), a continuous webcam feed of the Empire State Building, new media art displaces – or has the power to displace – the correlation of media and time central to the program of today's culture industries; thus, as I argue elsewhere,[31] Staehle's work technically inscribes not the passage of time through consciousness, but rather a specific technical regime of temporalization which is produced by the webcam's artifactualization of time. In contrast to our experience of Warhol's massively attenuated film *Empire* (1964), to which Staehle's work clearly responds, our experience of this latter is emphatically not a self-reflexive encounter with the granularity of our own thinking, but a confrontation between the internal rhythms of our living and the external, relatively alterior, rhythms of technical mediation of worldly time.

What I now need to add to this picture is a full appreciation for the centrality of the operation of repetition – and specifically, technical repetition – in this regime of enframing media. That this shift directly implicates the digital goes a long way toward explaining why new media art opens up what amounts to a new experience of repetition: put bluntly, the act of experiencing (certain) new media artworks engages a form of repetition that is both responsive and adequate to the technical infrastructure of new digital environments. Eschewing repetition as sameness, which privileges the stability of the technical medium over the force of reception, new media art solicits an experience of repetition as difference – an experience that recompenses the instability of the (digital) medium by underscoring the partiality and the singularity of reception.[32]

Concerned with the rampant embrace of film on the part of contemporary artists, art critics, curators, and historians have begun to show an interest in the role of repetition. Consider, for example, the roundtable discussion, initiated by the editors of the journal *October*, on the topic of 'the projected image in contemporary art', and in particular, the crucial moment where Malcolm Turvey describes his own experience of the 'qualitative' differences between film as viewed in its 'proper' context and as it is repurposed for gallery viewing:

> I think one of the great things about seeing a film such as (Anthony McCall's) *Line [Projected on a Cone]* in the gallery is the way in which repetition enters the viewing experience. I loved seeing *Line* in [the Whitney Museum exhibition] *Into the Light* because you could walk in on it halfway through, review it again, and then come back again after having looked at other works around the corner, thereby creating all sorts of associations with other works. I would argue that the possibility of seeing something again, several times, really opens up film spectatorship in a way that's not possible in a theatrical venue, and that this is a really good thing about the current use of the projected image in contemporary art.[33]

What remains a purely extrinsic (though certainly fortuitous) modification of a work like McCall's *Line* (which dates from the 1970s and was 'intended' to be viewed, in a single viewing, in its entirety) has, as the *October* discussion demonstrates, become nothing less than the structural basis for a set of contemporary aesthetic strategies that encompasses everything from sculptural projects deploying short (easily consumable) image loops to monumental works permitting only 'partial engagements'.[34] Through this varied deployment, repetition as difference becomes associated with the affordances offered by new institutions and conventions of spectatorship (consumption): these new settings and contexts empower viewers to exert a certain degree of agency – a certain agency of repetition – on a technical medium ('film'), the consumption of which has for the better part of a century been stabilized or, depending on one's angle, ossified (in the form of those conventions we associate with the 'cinema').[35] Empowered in this way by repetition, viewers become the editors of their own experience (or, as it were, of their own 'films'): the choices they (cannot help but) make as they move through the gallery space 'quite literally' displace the selections that are pre-inscribed in the objects of their consumption.

Notwithstanding its significance as a response to changing consumption practices and the institutions/conventions supporting them, we cannot overlook the partiality of this art historical account of repetition as difference: without necessarily confining it to a simple strategy for handling the concrete difficulties associated with exhibiting moving images in gallery spaces, the art critical embrace of repetition focuses almost exclusively on the changing institutional status of 'cinema'. What is left out here is any consideration of how technical transformations of the medium (e.g. the transposition of film to the digital environment) impact institutions, institutions of cinema and the fundamental role repetition plays in their (re)production; across the myriad contemporary configurations that its digital transposition facilitates, film (on this account) remains a surprisingly stable object.

In stark contrast to this art critical take on repetition, medial transformation is (or at least appears to be) precisely what is at issue in Bernard Stiegler's account of repetition as the basis for the becoming-cinematographic of consciousness. For Stiegler, as I mentioned earlier, cinema furnishes the technical support for the process of selection that, following Husserl's account, constitutes time consciousness in our world today. Encompassing everything from classical Hollywood film to contemporary global television, cinema comprises the latest instantiation of the Husserlian 'temporal object' by which the temporal flux constituting consciousness can objectify itself. More precisely, cinema perfectly embodies the operation of selection whereby personal memories ('secondary memory', in Husserl's terminology) and techno-cultural artefacts or traces (what Stiegler calls 'tertiary memory') come to impact, and thus to guide, the production of new impressions (Husserl's 'primary retention'). More than its concrete specificity as one specific type of moving image among others, what is fundamental about cinema is simply its exemplification of technical inscription, which is to say, its role in the new, technically-supported economy of repetition introduced in the wake of the gramophone and cinematograph. It is, as Stiegler explains, only following the invention of these recording technologies that the constitutive selectivity of consciousness can appear as such:

> [H]ow can it be that a consciousness listens twice to the same temporal object? In fact this is impossible as long as the analog recording technique inscribing a melody on a phonogram does not exist. In other words, it is the phonogram *qua* tertiary memory that originally highlights the fact of the selection of primary retentions by consciousness. [...] Image consciousness – here the phonogram (but it could just as well be a film) – is that in which the primary and secondary are both rooted, owing to the technical possibility of repetition of the temporal object (and one cannot overemphasize the fact that before the invention of the phonograph and cinema, such repetitions were totally impossible). In the same stroke, the rooting of the second primary memory in the memory of the first primary memory, now secondary, becomes evident. Such evidence can only be due to the fact of recording. Recording is the phonographic revelation of the structure of all temporal objects.[36]

The constitutive selectivity of time-consciousness can only be discovered and (quasi-scientifically) isolated in the wake of the technical stabilization of the temporal object, which is to say, only once technical recording has secured the possibility for consciousness to experience one and the same temporal object more than one time. Despite the dizzying terminology put into play by both Husserl and Stiegler, the logic here is quite straightforward: if distinct experiences of a self-same, technically-stabilized temporal object are qualitatively different, the reason can only be because the former experience, transformed into memory, selectively impacts the latter. A second (or n^{th}) hearing or viewing of a melody or a film cannot but be impacted by a previous hearing or viewing. In short, consciousness is formed selectively, through feedback of past experience into the present.

Yet, for all the attention he pays to the technical dimension of media, Stiegler ends up sanctioning an altogether stable conception of the medium: from its proto-origin in the phonogram to today's fully digitized global televisual flux, 'cinema' designates the monolithic technical support for the operation of editing that constitutes time-consciousness. Far from being some specific set of practices associated with a concrete medium, Stiegler's concept of 'cinema' is the contemporary name for what Husserl calls a 'temporal object', an object that is not simply in time, but is constituted from time itself.[37] In the context of Stiegler's account of media history, the epoch of cinema coincides with the reign of the technical temporal object as the basis for the constitution of time-consciousness.

This coincidence imposes certain constraints on the extension of Stiegler's theory, which, as I shall argue shortly, become problematic in the context of today's digital technologies. We can already get a clear glimpse of these constraints in Stiegler's account of the media transformations of the late nineteenth and twentieth centuries; on this account, technical transformations of media are repeatedly subsumed into a dialectic of the industrialization of consciousness:

> The 20th century is the century of the industrialization, the conservation and the transmission – that is, the selection – of memory. This industrialization becomes concretized in the generalization of the production of industrial temporal objects (phonograms, films, radio and television programs, etc.), with the consequences to be drawn concerning the fact that millions, hundreds of millions of consciousnesses are every day the consciousnesses, at the same time, of the same temporal objects. To the extent that, with such objects, one can play with the collective and individual relation between primary, secondary and tertiary retentions, probably without ever being able to completely control them, but certainly being able to influence them considerably – as the influence of advertisement shows – the question of cinema and its new epoch in television is the crucial question of the future.[38]

In near complete accord with his colleagues from the art world, Stiegler readily – perhaps too readily – subordinates the technical dimension of media to the institutions and conventions that support cultural practices of consumption. What Stiegler adds to the above discussed art critical account of repetition as the basis for new forms of spectatorial agency is an appreciation for the technical infrastructure of repetition: consumer editing of the temporal object, or 'editing-in-the-brain', can only occur within a context of exact, technically-secured iteration. In this way, Stiegler's analysis asserts an important check on overly utopian visions of art as liberation from media: insofar as it depends on a technics of repetition, editing can never be autonomous from the 'culture industry', nor fully in control of itself.

What neither Stiegler nor the art-critic historians manage to grasp, however, is the possibility of there being more at stake in digitization than a simple transposition of the medium of film, and more generally, of analogue media as such. This neglect of the scope of digitization's contemporary impact is altogether evident in Stiegler's reduction of digital technology to the 'analog-digital image', which is to say, to the specific process of digitizing the analogue image;[39] here clearly, and in contrast to the keen appreciation for the global digital infrastructure of contemporary capital that he displays elsewhere, Stiegler's vision remains restricted by his commitment to the identification of consciousness and temporal object. What is thereby overlooked is the way that digital technology undermines the very stability of the media (temporal) object itself.

Digital Cinema as Digital Art

This technical fact, which informed my account of digital art in *New Philosophy for New Media* (2004), is brought home to us by a remarkable contemporary film-maker who has herself recently embraced the digital revolution in its full scope. In her film, *The Fourth Dimension* (2001), Trinh T. Minh-ha has deployed digital technology not as a simple support for film as a stable medium, but precisely as a 'bridge between film and video', a bridge that allows for the de-specification not simply of static institutionalized conventions, but of technical properties of media. What such an approach makes available is, in the first place, a markedly different approach to the image than what reigns in the marketplace created by today's culture industries: because the digital 'image' is 'always "in the making," always incomplete – partially present and partially absent' (as one of Trinh's interlocutors notes),[40] it supports aesthetic practices that overcome conventional *and* technical limits of the cinema. That is why Trinh describes her film as an image mediated by a concrete audio-visual technology, and in the end, as a particular technical access to time: the subject of *The Fourth Dimension* (2001), she notes, is:

> [...] not exactly Japan or Japanese culture, but the Image of Japan as mediated by the experience of 'dilating and sculpting time' with a digital machine vision. What characterizes the digital image is its inherent mutability – the constant movement of appearing and vanishing that underlies its formation.[41]

And what makes Trinh's example remarkable is her success in deploying digital technology to undo both the conventions associated with the film medium – what we call 'cinema' – as well as the rigidity of film as a technical medium.

One would be hard-pressed indeed to imagine a practice more antithetical to the picture of repetition discussed above: far from simply transposing film into a new environment replete with new affordances for viewer editing, what Trinh's deployment of digital technology transposes is the very temporal basis of cinema itself. Trinh places *The Fourth Dimension* squarely within the lineage of an aesthetic program dedicated to getting rid of 'the illusion of the third dimension (illusory depth of field – as in Hollywood's film realism)' so as to 'produce flat, two-dimensional images that open to the fourth and fifth dimensions of Time and Spirit.' 'Rather than promoting a greater depth of field, as in the case of film,' digital technology offered her the 'possibility of working intensely with time and with the indefinite coexisting layers of past, present, and future.' As a film that works 'with both the temporalities in the image and with the image as a time-form', *The Fourth Dimension* accordingly allows viewers to experience 'not motion, but time as a form of its own.'[42]

That Trinh's is resolutely a practice of the 'time-image' is made evident by her joint repudiation of realism, and of the 'nobility of vision' that holds sway in both commercial *and* experimental film, even as these practices are themselves entering the digital age.[43] If Trinh's work vindicates Deleuze against Stiegler's criticism,[44] it is precisely because it brings (digital) technics to bear on the practice of repetition that comprises film-making, and in so doing, exposes the limits of the equation of cinema and temporal object, along with the latter's wholesale inadequacy as a contemporary support of time-consciousness. Once absolved of its realist burden – precisely the dimension which, on Stiegler's account, motivates spectatorial belief – the digital-cinematic time-image 'documents' (nothing other than) 'its own time'[45], what Trinh calls the 'liquid time' of digital layering and composition.[46] As such, the digital-cinematic time-image no longer directly models the temporal flux of the spectator. Rather, precisely by presenting time independently of the flux of consciousness, it opens the latter to time's 'essential' heterogeneity and to the power of alterity bound up with it.[47] It elicits or solicits a confrontation of our 'onboard' spectatorial time with the heterogeneous temporality of a world that is robustly technical in its operational infrastructure.

We might say then that digital technology facilitates an access to time, if not independently of the image altogether, then at least independently of its representational dimension. In this sense, Trinh's practice exemplifies the difference between what I called the 'digital-image'[48] and the Deleuzian time-image: where the latter gives a direct image of time (rather than an indirect image of time as movement), the former involves the process of unpacking how the image is made, a delving into the time of the image, the image as 'time', as itself a temporally-extended, technically-constituted process.[49]

No one has better expressed the singularity – the true technical specificity – of digital cinematic practice than Trinh's collaborator and fellow media artist Lynn Kirby, whose work in the digital environment spans more than a decade:

It's not about the image per se, it is not about the lyricism of a certain notion of experimental work. The interesting thing for me about working in the digital realm is that moving in time is so fluid. In film we can go forward, we can optically print to go backward, but the form is still linear. In film I worked hard to create the sense of cyclical time, meetings of present moments mapped onto and through larger cycles of time, both structurally in linear films and with looping the film itself. Now we can work with these gestures in time so fluidly, we can move backward and forward and loop so easily. This time sense of the gesture, this quality where objects and materials are time, is more available because it's so easy for us to see and manipulate. It's always been there and certain filmmakers have been exploiting this area in film, where the temporality is not determined by characters or drama, but the 'in-time-ness' of things – objects, frames, etc. – experiencing time. […] through this technology, this way of working with time has become more available.[50]

What is fundamental about each of Kirby's digital projects – her various attempts to 'get inside the image' – is her willingness to embrace a mediation of time that is not only extra-human, but also, emphatically, extra-objectal: just as time cannot be constrained in the form of a static image, so too does it evade any lasting capture in the form of an object. In digital cinematic practice, that is, the 'in-time-ness' of things and objects is contained not by the work as an autonomous temporal object, but by the experience it solicits.[51] The point, as Kirby takes pains to emphasize, is not that there is no object whatsoever in digital cinematic practice, nor that the object is simply replaced by experience; rather, in the digital cinematic excavation of time exemplified by Kirby and Trinh, the work as object becomes dissociated from the experience it generates, which means that the media object it generates can no longer play the role of 'temporal object', can no longer be a mere mimetic mirror for the flux of viewer consciousness.

In the wake of this liberation of the 'in-time-ness' within or beneath the image, the technical basis of repetition – precisely that aspect isolated by Stiegler – begins to matter, which is to say, to wield some agency over the experience it makes possible. Following the exposure of its 'essential' technicity, repetition thus acquires a degree of autonomy from viewer activity that, on Malcom Turvey's above-cited account, quite literally dictated its occurrence. Far from being a rhythmic experience rigidly bound to human activity, repetition here appears as the general technical punctuation of time, the 'technical' essence of its temporalization. As such, the repetition involved in the viewer 'editing' facilitated by installation environments (Turvey) and (analogue and digital) video-editing equipment (Stiegler) is only part – indeed, a very small part – of the larger scope of repetition, understood, if not as time itself, then as the basis of its measurability – what renders time accessible to measurement. And as is the case with time, there is no repetition-in-itself, which is simply to say that repetition is transductively correlated with measurement; that it always occurs through technical mediation and it is 'essentially' technical.

If Stiegler's work begins to tap this technical core of repetition, which however dates to the invention of time-keeping technologies, his approach is constrained to the horizon of human-machine synchronization, to the horizon, that is, of the 'temporal object'. By contrast, what is accomplished in Kirby's concession of agency to the digital computer is precisely the liberation of repetition's technicity from this condition of synchronization. In works like *Six Shooter* (2002) and *In Search of the Baths of Constantine* (2002), Kirby deploys the constitutive limits of the computer to shatter such synchronization from within, through the very technicity that would, in other potential deployments, support it. These works involve Kirby's manipulation of recorded material, but always, as she explains, with the aim of liberating time from the flux of the image track:

> I have made a number of pieces in which I edited live (live output of what I was doing out to tape) by moving back and forth in the time line, scratching, much like DJs do with records, but here by moving my 'pen' (I use a Wacom tablet) through the image in the time line. This would cause the image to jump and skip, creating time holes as the hard drives couldn't keep up with how quickly I moved through the time line. Each live improvisation was with a 'gesture in time' (one take) laid down in the time line. Moving back and forth created time gaps and new time relationships, often not linear. These time/space relationships were not determined only by me, but by the hardware/software of the machine.[52]

Works like *Six Shooter* and *In Search of the Baths of Constantine* elicit contingent moments within a digital 'time gesture' when digital technology fails; not only do these moments rupture the synchronicity that binds repetition to the flux of consciousness, but they open consciousness – including the artist's own consciousness – to 'time holes' that materialize time's alterity as a concrete technical artefact.

I can imagine no better illustration of the 'essential' obsolescence of time, the structural delay endemic to time's inescapable artifactualization and, through it, to whatever experience might arise from it.[53] By artifactualizing the computer's failure to operate in 'real time', its structural incapacity to coincide with 'time itself', Kirby's work correlates time, or rather the temporalization of time, with the ineliminable, though constantly shrinking, material delay of computational processes. I can also think of no better expression for the categorical instability of the image in the digital environment: not only does Kirby's work explore the temporal infrastructure of the image in ways that move beyond its surface – the image being only a 'map to other ways of looking'[54] – it recompenses this instability by facilitating, that is, by technically-mediating, the viewer's experience of 'time holes' and other phenomenalizations of time's 'essential' alterity. What is lost at the level of the image – the stability of the moving image as temporal object – is more than made up for by the opening up of time's heterogeneity to (human) experience, to an embodied materialization (in the form of the viewer's experience) that simply cannot coincide with the temporal power, the temporal alterity, it materializes.

Far from yielding a felicitous solution to the problem of the 'projected image in contemporary art' (and to the underlying problem of digital technology), the renewed scope and function of repetition in art today calls for a stark line of demarcation to be drawn between the 'cinema' and the 'digital', or, more precisely, between 'digital' cinema and 'digital' technics. In the wake of such a demarcation, cinema would be defined neither by a specific material support (film), nor a specific semiotic or rhetorical mode (indexicality), nor even as a loose set of cultural conventions, but, rather, according to a precise temporal criterion. Thus what we call 'cinema' encompasses all time-based media that operate within the temporal thresholds of human perception, including deployments of digital technology to transpose analogue media like film into installation environments. And what we call 'digital', on the other hand, specifically designates media that operate outside of any synchronization with human time-consciousness and at a scale finer than that of image perception. While this demarcation largely coincides with the distinction between capture-media and enframing-media that I have addressed elsewhere,[55] what it adds is the crucial role of repetition. Accordingly, what differentiates the 'cinema' and the 'digital', 'digital' cinema and 'digital' technics, is not – emphatically not – a simple technical difference (analogue versus digital), but rather the way in which repetition as difference is technically-supported in the respective cases: though facilitated by recording technology, repetition in cinematic media – repetition as editing – remains the prerogative of human agents, of human time-consciousness; in properly digital mediation, by contrast, repetition coincides with technical singularity, with (for example) the contingency of a computer malfunction, and, as such, only enters human time-consciousness from the outside, as an extrinsic accident, as what I have elsewhere called a 'diachronic thing'.[56]

That this demarcation of cinematic and digital art practices coincides, in the final instance, with the media-theoretical distinction between media proper and 'real-time' computing powerfully foregrounds the limitations of the 'temporal object' for theorizing contemporary techno-culture. For what artworks like Trinh's *The Fourth Dimension* (2001) and Kirby's *Six Shooter* (2002) bear out is the undeniable impact of the digital revolution on the operation of time, not simply in our experience, but in the world (the cosmos) that facilitates such experience. Far from being wholly wilful manipulations of a neutral technology, these artworks express a fundamental transformation in the texture of time, the very materiality of the cosmos itself. That they can do so has everything to do with their own 'essential' technicity, which, to be sure, operates as an instance of the contemporary specification of time's 'essential' technicity. These artworks, in short, express the inexorable digitization of time, the simple reality that our access to time (including our capacity to temporalize) is increasingly supported technically – which is to say, facilitated – by real-time computational networks. That the constitutive time of such networks is properly 'inhuman', in the sense of evading synchronization with the rhythms of human life, attests to the contemporary imperative for a post-phenomenology of time (or sensation) to replace the phenomenology of time-consciousness. Like the artwork compelling its articulation, such a phenomenology arises directly from the ashes of the temporal object.

Notes

1   Lev Manovich, *The Language of New Media*, Cambridge, MA: MIT Press, 1999, pp. 85–86.
2   I use this expression to indicate a scale of time that is incomposable with the time of human experience as this has been theorized in philosophy from empiricism to phenomenology. The time of the now should not be understood as instantaneous, for – in its contemporary artifactualization in the processing cycles of the digital computer – it still takes time. Something similar could be said for the term 'real time' that has been applied, often without sufficient critical reflection, to characterize digital computation. Despite its name, real time,

like the time of the now, takes time, albeit a time that has no direct correlate in human experience.

3   Friedrich Kittler, *Grammophone, Typewriter, Film*, Stanford, CA: Stanford University Press, 1999.

4   David N. Rodowick, *The Virtual Life of Film*, Cambridge, MA: Harvard University Press, 2007, p. 97.

5   ibid., pp. 97–98.

6   For example, he argues that there are no digital images, properly speaking, while at the same time continuing to speak of them incessantly: '[T]he electronic image is a time-based image not only because it is capable of succession, but also because it is never fully present in space or in time; it occupies a state of continuous present becoming. Thus, even a "photograph" displayed on an electronic screen is not a still image. It may appear so, but its ontological structure is of a constantly shifting or self-refreshing display. Electronic images are in constant movement or states of dynamic change, even when they appear to be static. In this manner, the electronic image challenges not only commonsense notions of what an image is, but also what an object or aesthetic object might be as a static present in space and in time. In a sense, *there are no new media "objects" or images.* A better term might be "elements," which may vary in terms of their outputs and underlying algorithmic logics. Thus, it bears repeating that electronic art involves not the making of a thing, but variations in a process or transformations of a signal' (my emphasis): in Rodowick, 2007, p. 138.

7   'The presumed newness of digital practices refers less, then, to the creation of a new medium than to a large-scale historical process wherein existing textual and spatial media are transcoded into digital form so as to be manipulable by computational processes and communicable through information networks': in Rodowick, 2007, p. 99; 'Just as the nature and extent of the historical novelty of "new media" must be reexamined, so also must we ask: Can information processing be considered a creative medium? Can the computer as a simulation machine or information processor give rise to creative automatisms?' (ibid.). He quickly resolves (or appears to resolve) this issue: 'The computer is a medium, then. (How could it not be?)': ibid., p. 129.

8   '[D]igital images may no longer be capable of producing the existential or ontological perplexity of which both Barthes and Cavell were so keenly and philosophically aware. Digital photographs have become more social than personal, and more attuned to the present itself than to the present's relation to past and future': in Rodowick, 2007, p. 149. This claim must be juxtaposed with the crucial claim that I have been exploring in my reading of Rodowick: namely, that digital media is incapable of inscribing duration. It is this claim that lies at the heart of Rodowick's anxiety in the face of our cultural shift to the digital age.

9   'If analog media record traces of events and digital media produce tokens of numbers, the following may also be asserted: *digital acquisition quantifies the world as manipulable series of numbers.* This is the primary automatism and the source of the creative powers of digital computing', in Rodowick, 2007, p. 116.

10   ibid., pp. 117–18.

11   ibid., p. 118.

12 'In the world of the digital, time is encoded in a bit-map, and there can be no entropy. In the compression algorithm of a digital image, only what changes in the shot is renewed. That which is the same in the shot stays the same in the digital image, in contrast to the constantly changing emulsion grain from one frame to the next in the film image. The inscription of the decaying body in *Wavelength* is therefore not possible in digital, even in HD DIGI. Time is not transformation anymore, the essence of film in which there is a change twenty-four times a second. Now time is geography and is inscribed in layers on a set screen with bit-size slots. When you dig into these bit-size slots to see what is there, you find bits of time memory one on top of the other without chronology. You travel through time now by traveling through layers of pixels. And the space is totally in front of you without shadow. [...] Time is fixed as in a map in digital and is totally repeatable with no degradation due to copying loss, while silver-based film is structured by time as entropy, therefore unrepeatable. The unpredictability of time passing and time past, the slippage between one and the other, and the pathos of their essentially ineluctable difference are lost': in Babette Mangolte, 'Afterward: A Matter of Time. Analog versus Digital, the Perrennial Question of Shifting Technology and its Implications for an Experimental Filmmaker's Odyssey', in R. Allen and M. Turvey (eds), *Camera Obscura, Camera Lucida: Essays in Honor of Annette Michelson*, Amsterdam: Amsterdam University Press, 2002, p. 264.

13 Rodowick, 2007, pp. 165–66.

14 Mangolte, 2002, p. 263.

15 Rodowick, 2007, p. 99.

16 ibid., p. 146.

17 ibid., p. 147.

18 ibid., p. 149.

19 Malcom Le Grice, *Experimental Cinema in the Digital Age*, London: BFI, 2001, p. 199.

20 ibid., p. 198 (my emphasis).

21 ibid., p. 191.

22 'Digital capture may be considered as analogous to video recording in a number of ways. Yet, even here the image is not "one," for light recorded on charge-coupled devices is already fragmented into a discrete mosaic of picture elements, which are then read off as distinct mathematic values. The process of conversion or transcoding separates the image into mathematically discrete and modular elements whose individual values are open to any number of programmable transformations. The separation of outputs from inputs, and the process of calculation converting light into code, unravel the unity of the profilmic spatial event unfolding in a unique duration. As befits the mathematical basis of information processing, the digital event corresponds less to the durations and movements of the world than to the control and variation of discrete numerical elements internal to the computer's memory and logical processes': in Rodowick, 2007, pp. 165–66.

23 This comes, for Le Grice, as a fruit of the critique of the past-orientedness of cinema: 'The primary illusion of cinema is neither the photographic illusion of a space which is not present, nor the photocinematic illusion of a time which is also not present, but the illusion that we are implicated, through presence, in the actions of another time and place. [...] The illusion of a space and time not physically present is counteracted by an assertion of the presence of the substance

of the film image. However, the distinction between reality and illusion should not originate in the question of the physical presence or absence of signifier or signified. Materialist reality is to be found in the relationship between the action of the subject (subject, individual, person, ego) and implication in its consequence – the arena of irreversibility and the reality of realization': in Le Grice, 2001, p. 202. Indeed, for Le Grice – and here I wholly concur – the indexicality of the photographic image is a red herring even in the case of cinema, once its expanded materiality, and specifically the primacy it lends to the spectator, is taken into account: '[W]hile the photographic recording may be considered as a form of indexical signifier, its condition as such (in the experience) is not simply assured by the mechanism of photography. In the photographic realm this indexicality tends to be (immediately) counteracted as its resemblance encourages the trace of an object (or event) to be treated as the object itself': in Le Grice, 2001, p. 192.

24   Le Grice, 2001, p. 314 (my emphasis).

25   Rodowick, 2007, p. 138 (my emphasis).

26   Emmanuel Levinas, *Otherwise than Being: Or Beyond Essence*, Pittsburgh: Dusquesne University Press, 1998.

27   Le Grice, 2001, p. 303.

28   ibid.

29   Nigel Thrift, 'Remembering the Technological Unconscious by Foregrounding Knowledges of Position', in *Environment and Planning D: Society and Space*, Vol. 22, No. 1, 2004, pp. 175–90.

30   Cf. David N. Rodowick, *Reading the Figural, or, Philosophy after New Media*, Durham, NC: Duke University Press, 2001, particularly Chapter 7.

31   Cf. Mark. B. N. Hansen, 'Living (with) Technical Time: From Media Surrogacy to Distributed Cognition', in *Theory, Culture & Society*, Vol. 26, No. 2–3, March/May 2009, pp. 294–315.

32   Here, to be sure, we converge with Deleuze's concept of difference in repetition. Indeed, with his deployment of the distinction between differentiation and differenciation, Deleuze opens a framework that makes common cause with my own insistence on the irreducibility of temporalization in any configuration of time. A full consideration of this convergence is beyond the scope of my current exploration; let me simply say here that, because it is introduced to support a concept of 'difference-in-itself', Deleuze's tripartite model of time (following his differentiation of three syntheses in *Difference and Repetition*) is a model of 'time-in-itself'. On this point, I concur wholeheartedly with Dominique Janicaud who remarks on Deleuze's convergence with Heidegger: 'In a different manner, and yet comparable to that of Heidegger, Deleuze destitutes the third synthesis of its cognitive role in order to discover in it [*en faire*] the emergence of a pure form of time, in the Hölderlinian sense. After *Habitus* (the first synthesis), *Mnemosyne* (the second), Deleuze bends the third back on time as caesura. It is by stripping the future bare that difference is made to happen as such in the heart of temporal experience – a conception that is perfectly illuminating when it is a question of tragic time, but which no longer corresponds to the Kantian procedure: to understand the "binding function" of judgement and to elicit a rule that allows for the thinking of the articulation between the formal and the informal, transcendental time and the empirical running off of becoming': in Janicaud, *Chronos: Pour l'intelligence du partage temporal*, Paris: Grasset, 1997, pp. 213–14.

33 George Baker et al., 'Round Table: The Projected Image in Contemporary Art', in *October*, Issue 104, Spring 2003, p. 90.

34 Not insignificantly, the contribution of artist Matthew Buckingham echoes what I claimed in reference to Staehle's work above; namely, the correlation of infinity with the renunciation of the artist's agency over the experience stimulated by his work: 'I think this distinction [between sculptural image installations and monumental works] is really key. Giving up control over the duration of the audience's experience can create the opportunity to work totally differently with cause and effect. Doing so gives you, as an artist, all this material to work with – who's seen how much, the disruption of other people entering, and so on, although a lot of work doesn't consider this': in Baker, 2003, p. 90.

35 I borrow this differentiation of film and cinema from Anthony McCall: '[...] I think we tend to talk interchangeably, and not very usefully, about film and cinema, as if they were the same thing. *Cinema is a social institution, while film is a medium.* And I think while the medium may change, the institution will be just fine. I don't see how the institution of cinema – which involves the social act of looking at moving images, and talking about them – is going to be threatened by new technology. Of course, it will be affected by it in terms of how films are made, distributed, and exhibited, but it won't be destroyed by it. I can quite easily imagine film as a medium disappearing quietly in the next ten years with scarcely a blip in terms of the practices of cinema': in Baker, 2003, p. 90, my emphasis.

36 Bernard Stiegler, 'The Time of Consciousness: On the 'New World' & 'Cultural Exception' (trans. G. Collins), in *Tekhnema: Journal of Philosophy and Technology*, Issue 4, 1998, pp. 72–76.

37 Husserl defines the temporal object in paragraph 7 of his 1905 lectures on time consciousness: '[A] phenomenological analysis of time cannot explain the constitution of time without reference to the constitution of the temporal Object. By *temporal Objects*, in this *particular sense*, we mean Objects which not only are unities in time but also include temporal extension in themselves': Husserl qtd. in Stiegler, 1998. In his gloss on Husserl's concept, Stiegler emphasizes the role of the object as a surrogate for consciousness: '[T]he properly temporal object is not only in time: it is constituted temporally, it receives its warp on the woof of time – as what appears in passing, as what passes, as what manifests itself in disappearing, as flux fading away in each moment of its production.' Moreover, 'it is the right object for an account of the temporal tissue of the flux of consciousness of which it is the object. To give an account of the constitution of the flux of the temporal object will be also to account for the constitution of the flux of consciousness of which it is the object': in Stiegler, 1998, p. 68.

38 Stiegler, 1998, p. 106.

39 For example: 'I call analog-digital image making the technique permitting the digital compression of analog images, their conservation on multimedia optical supports, their transmission by networks of worldwide telecommunication, and their treatment by algorithmic analysis of images. [...] it is a matter of digital technologies of analysis. Analysis, that is, de-composition: the digital analysis of the moving analog image by the use of algorithms of shape recognition [...] is the beginning of a delinearization of the flux of images and a systematic "discretization" of movement. That means that these analog-digital

technologies of image and sound analysis open an epoch of the grammatization of the audio-visual field […].': in Stiegler, 1998, pp. 100–02; 'Analog de-composition by digital analysis is the possibility, for the first time in history, to objectively delinearize, decompose, instrumentally and systematically break up the flux, to bracket the phenomena of belief, that is, to observe (and not only watch) the flux of images while neutralizing the belief effects which, in the same stroke, is to understand them. This is the beginning of a new epoch in the intelligence of movement and of what is emotionally moving, of what sets into movement': ibid., p. 104; 'Today, owing to the digitization of the analog, the conditions of a grammatization and the grammaticalization of the audiovisible are present': ibid., p. 110.

40 Interview with Elizabeth Dungan in Trinh T. Minh-ha, *The Digital Film Event*, New York: Routledge, 2005, p. 4.

41 ibid., p. 3.

42 ibid., p. 10.

43 'Cinema is commonly thought of as being essentially visual. As it is practiced in the film industry and in the experimental arena, digital cinema tends to reinforce such a definition, even though the two milieux may differ radically in their eye-dominant treatment of film. On the one hand, you have the story-image – an image *re-produced* so as to advance the plot or to illustrate the story most efficaciously – and on the other, you have the painting-image – an image activated in its plastic form, or de-formed and made unrecognizable so as to claim its status as pure vision. […] *The Fourth Dimension* departs from such popularized expectation [of the use of digital technologies] because its approach to new technology neither indulges in the virtuosity of special retinal effects nor does it rely on distorting, fracturing, or transfiguring images in order to defamiliarize the subject it is engaged with. On the contrary, what partly constitutes the unseen dimension underlying the images offered of Japan is the mutability of relations between the ordinary, the extraordinary and the infraordinary as captured in the mutability of the digital image itself': in Minh-ha, 2005, pp. 4–6.

44 'Deleuze is undoubtedly right to object to Bergson's saying that the reproduction of illusion is also its correction in one respect.' However, Deleuze fails to draw all the consequences of this objection, precisely because he does not take into account the specificity of reproduction *qua* analogue-photographic recording technique, incorporating the Barthesian 'it has been', and *qua* fusion of instantaneous stills in the flux of a temporal object. This is the reason why, it seems to me, Deleuze fails to explain what 'having always been engaged in cinema without knowing it' means and fails to account for the impact of the moving image: cf. Stiegler, 1998, p. 66. It is, Stiegler later reiterates, solely on account of tertiary memory that 'Deleuze can ask himself if the reproduction of what Bergson calls "cinematographic illusion" is not also its correction, in a way. Deleuze's question cannot really be answered because, no more than Husserl or Bergson, he does not thematize the question of recording. He speaks of the reproduction of illusion but, despite his precise knowledge of the history of cinematographic techniques, he never elaborates the question precisely. And that is why he mires in the question of the "semiology" of cinema, which he attempts to transform into a "semiotics." He rightly objects to Metz's importation of linguistic concepts into the theory of the moving image with the substitution of 'an enunciation for an image, but does he himself do anything

different in persisting in speaking of signs, opsign, soundsign, "chronosigns," "lectosigns" and "noosigns"? Prior to semiotics or semiology, the question of regularity must be asked, the question of the rule, that is, grammar': in Stiegler, 1998, p. 92.

45 Minh-ha, 2005, p. 28

46 ibid., p. 10.

47 On this point, Trinh's analysis converges with my above account of the technical 'essence' of time, which is to say, of the non-existence of a 'time-in-itself' wholly independent or autonomous from the activity of measure. Notwithstanding the crucial role of concrete technical temporal regimes in constituting our subjectivity ('Our life situations are regulated by time – by instituted work time or television time, for example': in Minh-ha, 2005, p. 28), Trinh insists on the multiplicity of time and, specifically, on the irreducibility of its cosmological dimension: '[T]ime does not come in one unifying form; not only does it exist in a multiplicity of forms and rhythms (biological, physiological, geological, and so on) at any single moment, it is also not limited to what humans can perceive. Time leaves traces in a multitude of layers and scales in the realm of life. Everything is time – stone, tree, mountain, ocean; thoughts, doubts, clouds – we are time': in Minh-ha, 2005, p. 34. Digital technology comprises a support for the aesthetic deployment of these extra-human rhythms: '[T]oday's new technology can promote a sense of time that has always been available to us, but which we've grown blind to with the pervasive rationality and linearity of modernization: cosmic time': in Minh-ha, 2005, p. 65.

48 Cf. Mark B. Hansen, *New Philosophy for New Media*, Cambridge, MA: MIT Press, 2004.

49 I discuss the Deleuzian 'time-image' (and its relation with the digital-image) in Hansen, 2004, Chapter 7.

50 Lynn Marie Kirby, 'Time Paths' (interview with Trinh T. Minh-ha), in Minh-ha, 2005, p. 63.

51 ibid., p. 79

52 Kirby, email to author, 1 March 2007.

53 For an account of this 'essential' obsolescence, see Hansen, 2009, pp. 294–315.

54 Kirby, 2005, p. 65.

55 Hansen, 2009.

56 ibid.

Chapter 2

Arrest and Movement[1]

Timothy Druckrey

I.

> [T]here is no visual image that is not more and more tightly gripped, even in its essential, radical withdrawal, inside an audiovisual or scriptovisual (what horrid words) image that envelops it, and it is in this context that the existence of something that still resembles art is at stake today. We are well aware, as Barthes and then Eco have been pointing out for some time now, and as was so admirably reformulated by Deleuze with an extraordinary emphasis on the image, that we are not really living in 'a civilization of the image' – even though pessimistic prophets have tried to make us believe that it has become our evil spirit par excellence, no doubt because it had been mistaken for an angel for such a long time. We have gone beyond the image, to a nameless mixture, a discourse-image, if you like, or a sound-image ('Son-Image', Godard calls it), whose first side is occupied by television and second side by the computer, in our all-purpose machine society.[2]

The many histories weaving their way through contemporary arts are largely inflected by retrieving, reclaiming and reframing discourses and technologies, and that oscillate between the deconstruction of precedent, the 'triumph' of media populism, and the pursuit of aesthetic frameworks where critical reflection can assail the increasingly transient flow of fleeting experience.

It is sure that for more than a half of a century (longer some might argue), the projected image of cinema – the effects of the screen (from television to the mobile phone) – has dominated the social sphere. Indeed, the staggering, astonishing and continuing role of the screen (in all its meanings) is as ubiquitous as it is inescapable, as potential as it is numbing, as powerful as it is ominous.

Yet rather than daunting, we find an impressive horizon where the history of the effects of screens, screening and the screened are confronting nearly all of the lingering tropes that the mainstream media are crudely (and mostly unsuccessfully) attempting to circumvent. Of all the media of the past century, this is most evident in rethinking the cinematic. So entrenched in its formulas, the mainstream cinema industrial complex has become subsumed by hardly disguised repetitions, dependent on mechanical narratives and addicted to special effects. Little surprise that its audiences, even though cajoled and coaxed by social networks, streaming and the trivial attempts to make cinema social again, have been abandoning the movie house for the gaming console, the cellular sphere, the biennale.

In these spheres the evolving systems for immersing attention into 'fugitive', 'situated' and 'situational' realities has come face-to-face with radically transformed expectations that can reframe the cinematic imaginary as one differentiated from inevitable 'effects', and, instead, propose complex configurations of intention and experience. It isn't merely that we exist in 'continuous partial attention', as Linda Stone diagnosed more than a decade ago,[3] but that the conditions for sustained attention have been dismantled in the face of the bleak populism of transient meanings, and assumptions that the tidal waves of information are merely to be consumed without reflection; that the effect of newness is merely its cumulative and empty consequence – the unbearable triteness of being.

II.

From the optical theatres of the phantasmagoria to the troubled omnipresence of Google Earth to the instantaneously remixed 'cinemas' of YouTube, to the real consequences of artistic investigation of the very presumptions of cinema and its radical difference from the (moving) image, the sweeping impact of time-based media has reanimated the 'singular' image, reformulated the 'singular' viewer, reconsidered the 'singular' effect, reintroduced temporality into the 'singular' – and failing – myth(s) of modernity.

In this rethinking of singularity we bear the larger responsibility for sustaining an experimental atmosphere that has distinguished a 'media art' whose immediate collaborative formation challenged and displaced the hierarchies of lingering auteur theories in favour of stagings with broad social and artistic meanings. Accounting for this explosive potential will necessitate serious reconsiderations of the 'media' as either unique or new. In its place we have now reached a stage in which the rewriting, rethinking and re-evaluation of modernity comes as the crucial method in which to focus our approach and expand 'media studies', and to evolve a more fully articulated approach to the communicative sphere in which circulation, interaction, 'virtualization', computability, etc., are no longer mystifications, but necessary components for any coherent understanding of – or artistic intervention into – the reverberations of an omnipresent, omnivorous and increasingly omnipotent media-sphere.

Image as time, time as image, time as memory, time as effect, time liberated from linear causality, time emptied of succession, time reconstituted, time as 'real', time as 'virtual', time compressed, intensive time... there is no doubt that the conceptualization of temporality in the twentieth century was crumbling into forms only expressed by contingent means – the cut, montage, superimposition, flashback, non-linearity, special effects, dislocation, compression, multiplicity, reversibility, etc.

In this sense, spurred on by the collapse of the chronicity of time, by its radical conditionality, a revised theory of media temporality is necessary, one coincident with the development of communication, instantaneous exchange or probability; 'media time', a time delineated by formulations unimagined by the dilettantes of merely digital cinema, the grandiose dabblers of crass immersions, the supercilious engineers of 'time-based' media as an end in itself. A theory of 'media time' would refocus attention away from the nonsensical assumption that the objective of the media arts is merely to regenerate or reconstitute some variation on temporal representation enveloped in cinematic succession, scientific notions of evolving form, rendered visual processes, 'open-closure', or just plain old sensory overload.

Between the cinema and the moving image a difference is emerging that emphasizes temporal formations, that challenges assumptions about the relationship between the photographic and the cinematic – but more as a discourse that interrogates feasible temporalities, ostensible temporalities, probable temporalities, indeterminate temporalities, combinatorial temporalities. This break from the cause and effect limitations of much cinema study acknowledges the kind of temporal layering made possible not just as an after-effect of the digital, but of an investigation of the performative, ironic, situational, fugitive, contingent forms in which a link can be made between the image and its ability to express time itself not merely as an effect (as Mary Ann Doane argues in *The Emergence of Cinematic Time*, 2002), not merely as a framework, but as a full subject.

A full assessment of the temporal trajectory of the image would necessitate a rethinking of the many histories of the pre-cinema, a rethinking of the origins and presumptions of photography, and an integrated analysis of the nineteenth-century's 'frenzy' for both visibility and emerging temporal regimes enveloping and transforming modern experience.

Suffice it to suggest that the rapid-fire image technologies of the day, the pre-cinema in the eighteenth century (that demonstrated conclusively that the trajectory of representational practices were time-based), photography in the nineteenth century (which triumphed over the instantaneous ocular trace with its optical substitute), and early cinema in the twentieth century (that temporalized both recording and reception) provided an accelerating correlate to cultures inebriated by temporality, mobility, and sciences exploding every convention of fixed, linear equilibrium. Time itself became the central code in a new chronoscopic regime, the gaze and the clock, the shutter and the stopwatch, linked in an attempt to penetrate the uncanny, imperceptible or contingent durations in everything from astrophysics to zoology.

In the essay, 'Chronocracy',[4] Peter Weibel offered important comments on the political economy of time. Weibel's text occurred in conjunction with a lecture at the Dutch Electronic Art Festival (DEAF) in 2000, *Machine Times*. In departures from his prepared text, Weibel pointedly identified the kinds of temporal reshuffling that figure so broadly in the media arts.

Two examples were of particular relevance: Pierre Huyghe's installation *L'Ellipse* (1998); and Sam Taylor-Wood's *Killing Time* (1994). Huyghe's *L'Ellipse*, a three-screen projection, enacts a specific 'rupture' in cinema – the ellipse (the 'time' between cuts) – by reconstituting 'lost time'; the centre screen is flanked by 'before ' and 'after', and 'contains' the time suspended by them. More specifically, the centre projection reinserts the specific ellipse in Wim Wender's film *Der Amerikanische Freund/American Friend* (1977), in which Bruno Ganz, 20 years older, completes the ellipse by precisely restaging the duration and action eliminated from the film. Taylor-Wood's *Killing Time* (a four-screen projection) is dramatized by an operatic soundtrack (Richard Strauss' *Elektra*). The four 'ordinary' characters, distracted and restless, inhabit non-descript domestic situations – yet intervene in an otherwise tedious flow by suddenly lip-synching to passages in the opera in an odd collision between the temporal expanse of the opera and the incidental drama of the unanticipated player privately staging a performance.

Weibel thus characterizes 'elliptical time' as 'the basic structure of cinema', and outlined an economy of time that directly identified it as the 'abstract element' of the division between 'industrial' and 'personal' temporalities. The 'orchestration of time' was a reciprocal engagement with production and consumption. Weibel continues, in an essay titled 'Narrated Theory: Multiple Projections and Multiple Narrations (Past and Future)': 'The narrative universe becomes reversible and no longer reflects the psychology of cause and effect. Repetitions, the suspension of linear time, temporal and spatial asynchrony blast classical chronology apart.'[5] 'Non-remunerative' time was the 'waste of time' in an economy that is heightened and eluded (elided?) in Pierre Huyghe's *L'Ellipse*, or jettisoned in Taylor-Wood's suspension of mechanistic mimesis. Anticipation – time's rationale – is deferred, a time code denied its inexorable numerical or sequential logic.

Pierre Huyghe's work indeed posits important considerations of the cinematic in its relation to film, but especially in the early work there is a specific relation to cinematic temporality. In an evocative essay, 'Free-Time Workers and the Reconfiguration of Public Space: Several Hypotheses on the Work of Pierre Huyghe', Jean-Christophe Royoux delineates both Huyghe's position regarding cinema, and leads this towards what is clearly a rendezvous with the time effect. For Royoux, Huyghe 'enables the spectator to enter into the image [and that] Huyghe's initial problematic [is] – how to inhabit the narrative [...]'[6]; that 'modes of consumption bring new forms of appropriation'[7] and that 'cinema remains a special reference point [...] because it was the first to make credible the possibility of producing an almost exact stand-in for the real time of life [...].'[8] But, most interestingly, for Huyghe, '[f]ilm did not simply introduce the possibility of double reality; it also gave birth to a second time frame, parallel to the first, like his inverse double: free time, lining or flip side of work time.'[9] Indeed Nicholas Bourriaud, writing on Huyghe's work, cites a revealing comment by Luigi Pirandello: 'The reversibility of appearance and reality is the only means of artistic access to the real.'[10] Temporal reversibility is an anti-narrative strategy, that uses 'phase shifts' (in Weibel's words) in the service of an anti-illusionistic – or perhaps, paradoxically, redemptive – chronicity that instantiates 'difference and repetition'. Or as Deleuze writes: 'We know that modern art tends to realize these conditions: in this sense it becomes a veritable *theatre* of metamorphoses and permutations.'[11]

Yet, Royoux makes another important point:

Moreover, if reification means the transformation of reality into fiction, an enterprise transforming reality into spectacle, is this not also what we are confronted with in Huyghe's 4x3 pseudo-advertising posters, in relation to the micro-events they represent, actualizing the definition of simulacrum, whereby events are 'proceeded by the model with which their processes merely coincides' (Baudrillard)? This, indeed, is what seems to be confirmed by the blurring of relations between an event, its cinematographic image, and media commentary characterized by *The Third Memory* (1999).[12]

Many approaches to the reciprocity between the image and the cinema broach the problematic still/moving issue. These roughly divide into conceptual and technical readings of the transformation of cinema before and after the digital. Maybe most famous is Roland Barthes' essay 'The Third Meaning' (thus Pierre Huyghe's *The Third Memory*) that postulates 'the filmic', which perhaps serves as the 'punctum' – the static marker of the cinematic. For Barthes, 'the filmic, very paradoxically, cannot be grasped in the film, "in situation," "in movement," "in its natural state," but only in that major artefact, the still. [...] Finally, the still throws off the constraint of filmic time'.[13] But this textual approach complicates considerations of the distinct difference between image and movement or between image and image.

This complication is cogently approached by Deleuze in numerous passages:

[A] camera-consciousness which would no longer be defined by the movements it is able to make, but by the mental connections it is able to enter into. And it becomes questioning, responding, objecting, provoking, theorematizing, hypothesizing, experimenting, in accordance with the open list of logical conjunctions ('or', 'therefore', 'if', 'because', 'actually', 'although'[. . .]).[14]

What is in the present is what the image 'represents,' but not the image itself, which [...] is the system of the relationships between its elements, that is, a set of relationships of time from which the variable present only flows.[15]

[A]n image never stands alone [...]. Instead of a linear development, we get a circuit in which the two images are constantly chasing one another round a point where real and imaginary become indistinguishable. The actual image and its virtual image crystallize, so to speak [...]. There are many ways images can crystallize and many crystalline signs. But you always see something in the crystal. In the first place you see Time, layers of time, a direct time-image. Not that movement's ceased, but the relation between movement and time's been inverted. Time no longer derives from the combination of movement-images (from montage), it is the other way round, movement now follows time.[16]

Raymond Bellour's work, in a sense, bridges the divide with a deep awareness of the explosive possibility of (moving)-images and cinema. This is evident in long-standing work stemming from his essential text: 'The Double Helix', written for the *Passages de L'Image* (1990) exhibition catalogue at Centre Georges Pompidou. Even in this seminal text Bellour is resolute:

There is no visual image that is not more and more tightly gripped, even in its essential, radical withdrawal, inside an audiovisual or scripto-visual (what horrid words) image that envelops it, and it is in this context that the existence of something that still resembles art is at stake today.

His continued support of experimental 'cinemas' confirms a particular grasp of the shifting significance and broader implications of 'the image' as it extends from a psychological to a cognitive phenomenon. A recent essay, 'Concerning "The Photographic"', suggests a nuanced understanding of the moving (in every sense of the word) image:

The characteristic of the mental image is not so much its essential poverty [...] but a wildly fluctuating, moving discontinuity: this continuity, in its very unreality, appears to situate the mental image between photography's somewhat too-complex fixity and cinema's often too-calm illusion of movement. It is through successively grabbing, fixedly and fleetingly, inferring a discontinuous movement (movement no sooner begun than it is interrupted) that mental reality captures and memorizes a movement whether real or invented: the movement of life, or of a technology or an art appropriate to capturing within itself an illusion of truth; or the very movement of a dream, as soon as it is thought [...]. As soon as we fix on the images themselves, they yield to us in fits and starts, like a broken film.[17]

Further, he writes on Barthes' distinction between photography and cinema:

On the one side, there is movement, the present, presence; on the other immobility, the past, a certain absence. On the one side the consent of illusion; on the other, a quest for hallucination. [...] As soon as you stop the film, you find time to add to the image. You start to reflect differently on film, on cinema. You are led toward the photogram – which is itself a step further in the direction of the photograph. In the frozen film (or photogram), the presence of the photograph burst forth, while other means exploited by the mise-en-scene to work against time tend to vanish. The photo thus becomes a stop within a stop, a freeze-frame within a freeze frame: between it and the film from which it emerges, two kinds of time blend together. Always and inextricable, but without becoming confused. In this, the photograph enjoys a privilege over all other effects that make the spectator of cinema, this hurried spectator, a pensive one as well.[18]

Yet it is important to acknowledge more than adaptations of reception theory, and concede that the shift from analogue to digital technologies is playing a decisive role beyond the production, formulation and distribution of images. It demands a rethinking of spectatorship and narrative formations beyond those invoked or constrained by adaptations of traditional cinema theory.

For our purposes, the most significant shift lies within the implications of temporalities that are increasingly open-ended, contingent and perhaps unconditional – what might be called anti-chronological, or perhaps suspended chronologies; time that disappoints succession, that is anti-illusionistic or that might be identified as temporal elision propagated within the framework of a differentiated chronotropic *dispositif*. In this sense, the recurring theories of the apparatus remain static – lingering in material cause and effect models. This is evident even in Giorgio Agamben's argument in *What is an Apparatus?*, in which he continues to suggest that 'this is the reason why apparatuses must always imply a process of subjectification, that is to say, they must produce their subject.'[19] But this process of subjectification is less the issue here than looking merely at the substantive conception of the apparatus (or at the histories of the ideology of the apparatus since Foucault), than it is reconceptualizing temporalities as constitutive frameworks not of the legitimating strategies of chronometrics, but of a kind of Deleuzian 'crystallization' – however one in which the classical movement/time reciprocity is less relevant than formulations of temporal flow expressed in elided, compressed, relativized, disintegrated, 'probabilized', indeterminate, subversive, unstable, asynchronous temporalities that are a mix of succession, reversibility and contiguity. What emerges in this temporal cut or interstice is not mere stasis but rather shattered narrativizations – like the 'blasted allegories' of postmodernism – whose drive is not towards fulfilment or resolution, but towards more immediate and/or circumstantial consequences or events.

Garret Stewart, in his thoughtful book *Framed Time: Towards a Post-Filmic Cinema* (2007), evokes the transformation with the electronic media as related to the breaking of 'frame time' and the development of 'framed time':

But what was once the universal principle of such frame time in cinema no longer holds. In the fantastic turns and reversals of many recent narratives, whether openly digitized or merely contextualized in the cultural surround of electronic transmission and interactivity, frame time gives way, on several fronts at once, to that flashpoint of mediation I am calling framed time. This is the spatialized configuration of time itself as in its own right a malleable medium. [...] In regard to cinematography giving way to electronic representation as image paradigm, and even as a model of temporality itself, we are not concerned with narrative intentions but with certain ad-hoc conventions that seem to be growing up around the digital unconscious of not just a wired globe but a now only residually mechanical medium [...].[20]

Of the numerous approaches to the shift towards what George Lucas once called the 'immaculate reality' of digital cinema, most have focused on the potentials of either it's liberations from the constraints of traditional production, or on the diversification of the possibilities for exhibition or distribution. These hybridizations proliferated through the 1990s, and established important linkages emerging alongside innovations in computer graphics and the emergence of virtual reality technologies, and, ultimately, with the rapid developments in networks and on the web. The incorporation of interactions, immersive spatializations, delinearized narratives and investigation of possibilities of the database became driving forces in re-evaluations of cinema.

These involved what Paul Young in *The Cinema Dreams its Rivals* (2006) identifies as the 'decidedly uncinematic agendas of interactivity (versus voyeuristic classical spectatorship), collective engagement (versus spectator individuation), and information consumption (versus narrative consumption).'[21] Holly Willis, in *New Digital Cinema: Reinventing the Moving Image* (2005), established several categories to explain the effects of the transition from traditions of cinema and the systems of 'digital cinema': 'Reduction and critique'; 'Ambient'; 'Episodic'; 'Spatialization'; and 'Immersion'.[22] These critical assessments, among several others, found their realization in the encyclopaedic exhibition and accompanying book *Future Cinema: The Cinematic Imaginary After Film* (2002). Jeffrey Shaw and Peter Weibel's important exhibition probed the 'surmounting of cinema's traditional constraints', and aimed at the deconstruction of the 'total apparatus of the cinema [...] to allow different relations between spectator and screen, different representations/constructions of reality[...].'[23]

And yet, while the discourses of the 'post-filmic' attempt to conceptualize the splintering of narrative, the possibilities of redefining or exploding spectatorship and integrating new forms of the *dispositif*, a long history of experimental film, video and projection clearly shows that distinct artistic strategies have interfered with the singular conception of either the photographic or the cinematic – rupturing long-standing assumptions/presumptions that either system defined or established fixed differences that limited them to shaky notions of temporal fixity or chronological progression.

Two important exhibitions, 'Into the Light' (2001) and 'Slide Show' (2005), remind us that the presumed trajectory has a long and substantive history, that investigations into multiple forms of projection have deep roots, and that the narrative drive was not the only force driving the cinematic into an electronic future.

'Into the Light: The Projected Image in American Art – 1964–1977' (2001) at the Whitney Museum (curated by Chrissie Iles) included William Anastasi, Dan Graham, Gary Hill, Beryl Korot, Anthony McCall, Paul Sharits, among others, in a dazzling exhibition that highlighted important works that stretched well beyond the craze for sheer projection, and explored works that challenged the cinematic in decisive forms. It also squarely posed a significant historical assessment into a discourse that would fall under the sway of assumption that the projected images were either the privilege of cinema or of a generation of video artists competing with the scale of cinema. It also reminded us that the history of experimental film and experimental video is a complex of initiatives ranging from the experimental films of the 1920s to structuralist and post-structuralist film, the use of video in Fluxus or in the situationist movement.

Instead, Iles conceptualized the exhibition in continuity with ideas of projective space, rather than as an extension of the projected image. This linked it within an art-historical framework that situated vision or visuality conceptually, rather than as merely perceptual. Iles concludes her curatorial essay 'Between the Still and Moving Image':

> The Projective installation thus continues the mission of Duchamp's Large Glass: to make visible a model of consciousness in which as George Quasha and Charles Stein have observed, we recognize that we exist within a continuous projection of our own 'event.'[24]

(This 'event', not incidentally, comes in a remark linked with the work of Pierre Huyghe.) Elsewhere Iles has written that 'a major shift has taken place, away from the object and towards a more internal, psychological experience, in which space is no longer tangible and theatrical, but illusory and filmic.'[25]

'Slide Show: Projected Images in Contemporary Art' (2005) (curated by Darsie Alexander for the Baltimore Museum of Art) worked literally with works that utilized the 'slide as medium'. It was a striking exhibition. Alexander posed both the nostalgic and conceptual framework: 'The first audiences to walk into the space of slides discovered not only images thrown onto the wall but also the obvious presence of the mediating technology employed to disseminate them.'[26] The slide flashing introduced both appearance and disappearance, posed the idea of photography as a 'cumulative medium',[27] and simultaneously invoked both the pedagogical history of the slide in the class room, the dependence of art history on drawers of slides, and powerfully demonstrated how a range of artists (Robert Barry, Marcel Broodthaers, Jan Dibbets, Nan Goldin, Robert Smithson, Kristof Wodiczko, and others) exploded the limitations of the 'singular'. Alexander writes that 'instead of creating dramatic narrative arcs, many focused instead on the regulated succession of frames in which no single element is any more or less important than the others.'[28] If, as Weibel suggested, 'elliptical time is the basic structure of cinema' these 'flickering chrono-punctums' (to play on a phrase of Katherine Hayles) punctuate the cinematic as itself an effect of the photographic. This is well expressed by Sean Cubitt's remark that cinema 'does not represent time, but originates it'.[29]

This wide array of exhibitions – 'Into the Light', 'Slide Show', 'The Turbulent Screen', 'Future Cinema', 'The Cinema Effect' – have been complemented by a series of books: *Still/Moving: Between Cinema and Photography* (2008); *Art and the Moving Image* (2008); *Saving the Image: Art after Film* (2003); *The Cinematic Experience* (2003) – just to name a few – which strongly argues for a specific difference between the cinema, the cinematic, the filmic, the photographic and the moving image. And though these projects have largely extended the rich tradition of the link between cinema studies and the histories and margins it engendered, they do confirm a willingness to expand on the cinematic *dispositif* outside of an on-going Metzian 'hangover' that, as Paul Young expresses it, reflects 'a subject position that rewards voyeuristic absorption', or that attempts to limit itself to worn notions of narrativity, linearity or theories of the cinematic gaze as sacrosanct in the face of transformations that bust their assumptions and shatter classic cinematic ideologies; setting the conditions for other cinemas, not cinemas of attraction, not auteur cinema, not structuralist cinema, but cinemas of contingency, eccentric cinemas, ephemeral and performative cinemas, elegant micro-cinemas that are delicately subversive, demolishing the mere special effect as a spectacle of visibility, jettisoning tropes and proposing instead that the temporal schemas of imagination can be probed in configurations unimagined within cinema. Alternatively we can be confronted by an array of 'temporalities' engaged with the interrogation of systems that defy the normative flows of representability. Here, we are urged not merely to experience banal phenomenal time, but rather to engage in behaviours, assess momentary conditions, interfere with stasis, investigate the instantaneous states of information, probe transitory visibilities, survey the cumulative and relative structures of the archive, measure the effects of presence, consider indeterminate identities, examine the decay of memory, inspect the 'flow' of the event, dissect the repercussions of infinitesimal fluctuations, scrutinize the representation of codes, reflect on seemingly inert systems of surveillance, scan – and perhaps synchronize with – tidal streams of images, experience 'unstable' sonic atmospheres, and so forth. Flowing images, flowing information, flowing texts, information flows, economic flows, routes, signals, traces, porous borders, currents, boundaries – the metaphors for the current 'state' of the post-industrial, post-electronic, postmodern circuit we inhabit is enveloped in forms of contingency and mobility. Unremitting transience has substituted itself for stasis. Forms of representation undergo constant transformation to account for shifting conditions. This has become as increasingly true for economics as it has for the kind of instantaneous valuation of the crescendo of events that eclipse judgment as they disappear into the subliminal; memories that are barely formed.

In order to grasp the situation, reflection now comes in the forms of interference, rupture, or cut – a chrono-interface. This comports with emerging notions that we are embedded in mental states of 'continuous partial attention' – interstices between perception and cognition,

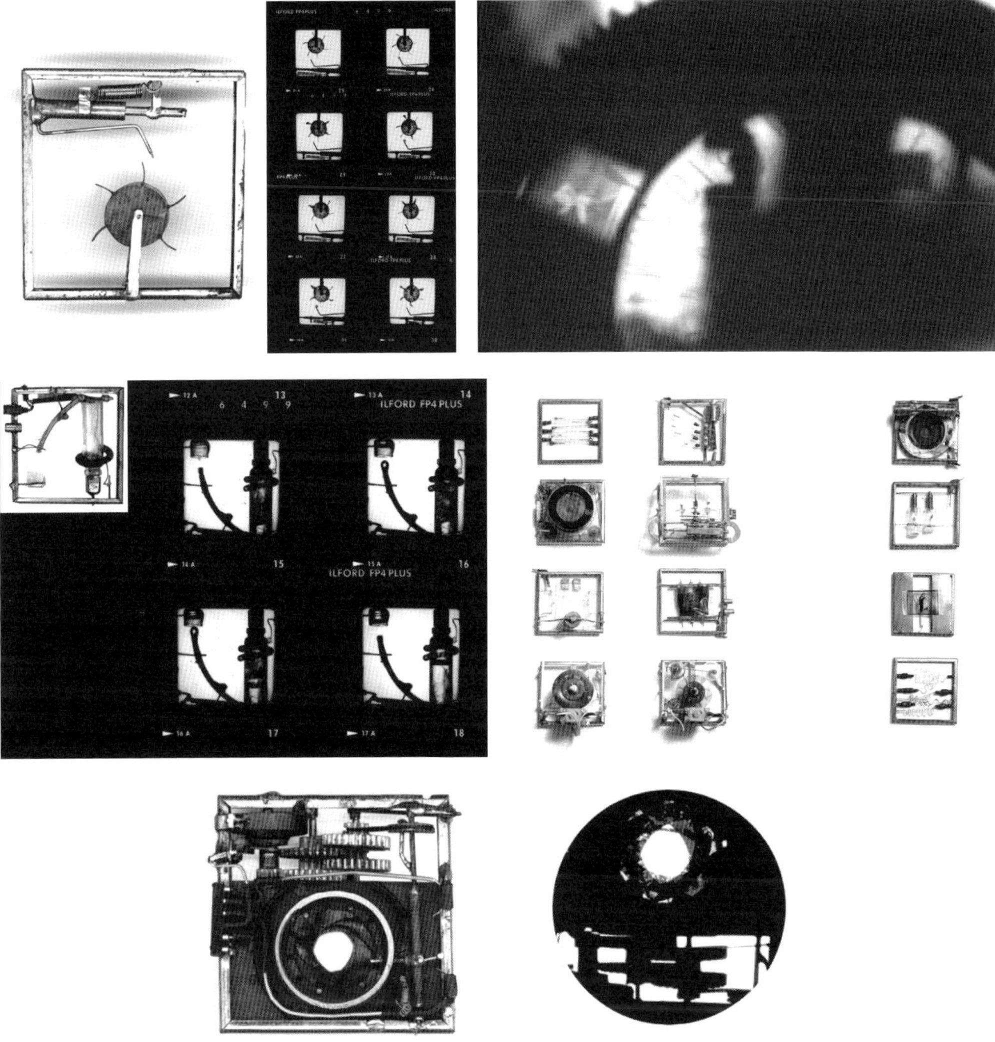

Figures 1–5: Julien Marie, *Diapositives*, 1995–98. Performance. Courtesy of the artist.

awareness and understanding, seeing and acting – Deleuze's 'chronic time', or what Virilio calls 'the dictatorship of the short-term, the tyranny of real-time',[30] a time emptied of its urgency – or perhaps representability!

'Media time' is not apodictically bound to the stable, the fixed or the certain. It is time that exceeds, extends and shatters normal perceptual limits; it is time freed of its parasitic dependence on the clock; time unburdened of its cinematic addiction.

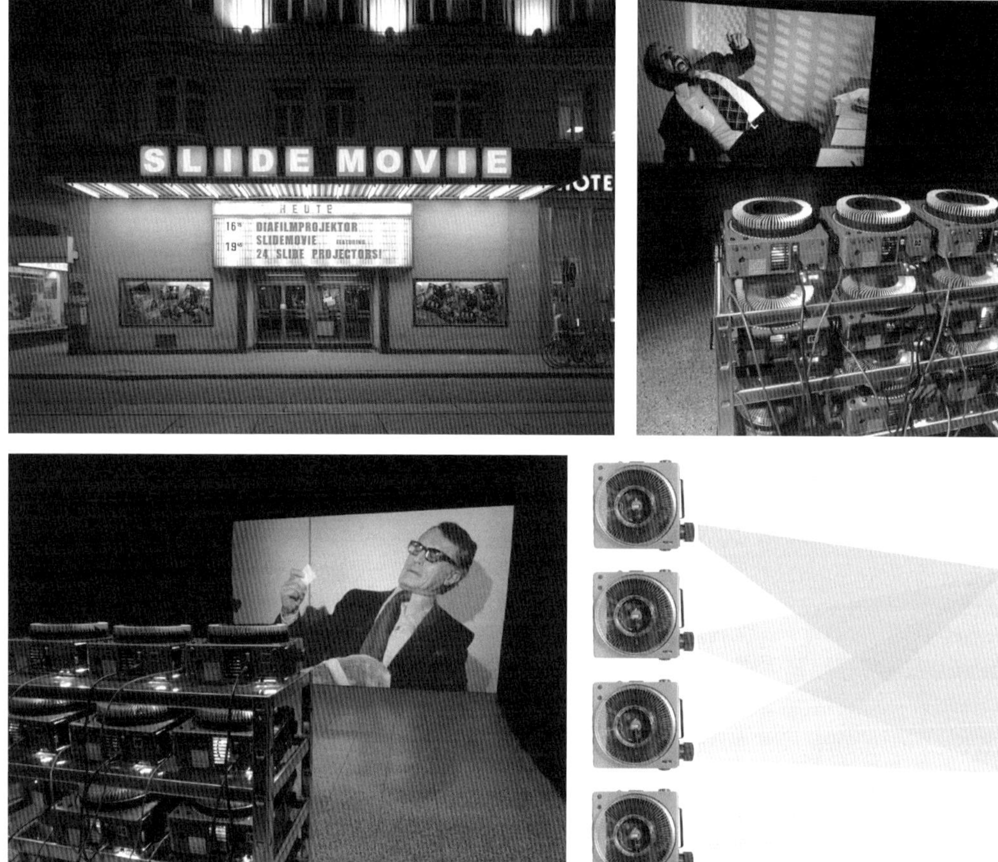

Figures 6–9: Gebhard Sengmüller, *Slide Movie*, 2005. 35mm film, installation. Courtesy of the artist.

Four Examples

Julien Maire's entire *oeuvre* is an autopsy for the apparatus, a dismantling of the 'camouflage of illusion'[31] (Adorno). His intricate and delicate post-mortem is unconcerned with retrieving the effect-ploys of optical illusion, but of re-functioning the apparatus as itself illusory, one in which the 'image' and its operation are meticulously exposed. From his earliest works, the machine itself stood as a stark signifier whose cosmetic surfaces were stripped bare so that its functions were as visible as the images they projected. The salvaged displays of *Low Resolution Cinema* (2005), the detonated machine of *Exploding Camera* (2007), the re-functioned projectors of *Memory Cone* (2009) conspire with the formation of frail 'images' from the remains of machines whose fixed purposes have been revoked, repurposed, repudiated – and yet machines whose remnants continue to produce fragile illusions. His late '90s performances of *Diapositives*, actually themselves meticulously crafted miniature machines, performed the uncanny achievement of allegorizing not just the image, but the machine itself.

Gebhard Sengmüller's works (often in collaboration) are an ongoing expropriation of strangely (un)realized techniques. Among the projects – *VSSTV*, *VinylVideo*, and more recently, *Slide Movie* and *A Parallel Image* – are spurious, and yet 'real', technologies that play with limits, toy with illusions, and enact the ploys of performativity. The techniques – slow-scan television, video encoded onto vinyl records, the deconstruction of the 24 frames per second of cinema, the wired link between image and transmission – are all too familiar, but here are torn asunder in Sengmüller's idiosyncratic historiography. Writing specifically about *Slide Movie*, Felix Stalder rightly observes:

> As fictive archeology, apparatuses are set back in time, so that the scope of action is radically expanded. If we can allow ourselves the freedom to reinvent the past, would it not then also be possible to imagine a future beyond the high-gloss techno-fetishism that the industry overwhelms us with?

He continues by invoking McLuhan: 'This is a media-theoretical statement, articulated so vehemently that its message becomes a massage that is not only intellectually comprehensible, but can actually be physically experienced.'

Philipp Lachenmann's works are delicately incisive. His early works – *Space Surrogates I and I, Corporate Space (LA), Level-8* – emerged as incisive assessments of images whose real meanings reside well outside the mere state of visibility. By extending time and demanding contemplation, his works command a kind of reflection that often requires a disquieting search of memory (private and public). Indeed his piercing works balance on the tightrope between cinema and moving images precisely as they provoke: by lulling the viewer into a cross between hypnosis and revelation. *SHU (Blue Hour Lullaby)* is exactly this kind of work. Within the desert landscape, a maximum security prison looms: its gates, its Security Housing Units (SHU), it's changing of the guard, and the accumulating passage of airlines leaving their oblivious traces above the enclosure and its impervious presence.

Shelly Silver's works (Figures 13 to 19) continually encounter the borders between the quotidian, the unremarkable, the mundane and the extraordinary; the unanticipated, the eccentric interplay of intentions. Early works such as *We, April 2nd* and *1* tackle the intricacy of seeing, and how it is guided by the urge to find the whole fragment. More recent works like *5 Lessons 9 Questions about Chinatown* are more deliberate. Indeed the description of this work announces it as '10 square blocks [...] 3 languages, 13 voices, 152 years, 17,820 frames, 9 minutes, 54 seconds, 9 questions, 5 lessons [...].' A scenario of descriptions that make contingent both the place and it's numerical representation. This too is the question concerning *What I'm Looking For* – a 'film' of stills made of photographing people and encountering people who want to determine how they want to be photographed – two forms of contingency caught between the gaze and it's subject, two forces constantly at odds…

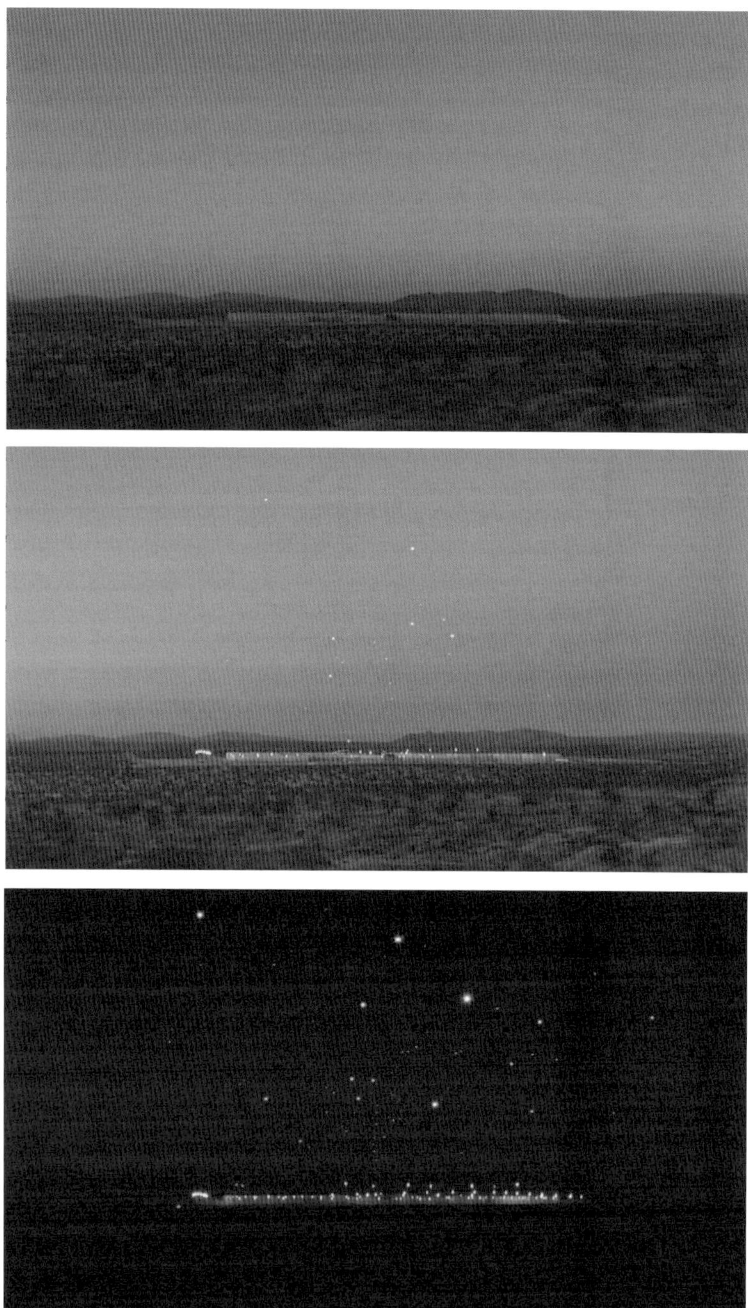

Figures 10–12: Philipp Lachenmann, *SHU (Blue Hour Lullaby)*, 2002/07. HD video, 12 min. Courtesy of the artist.

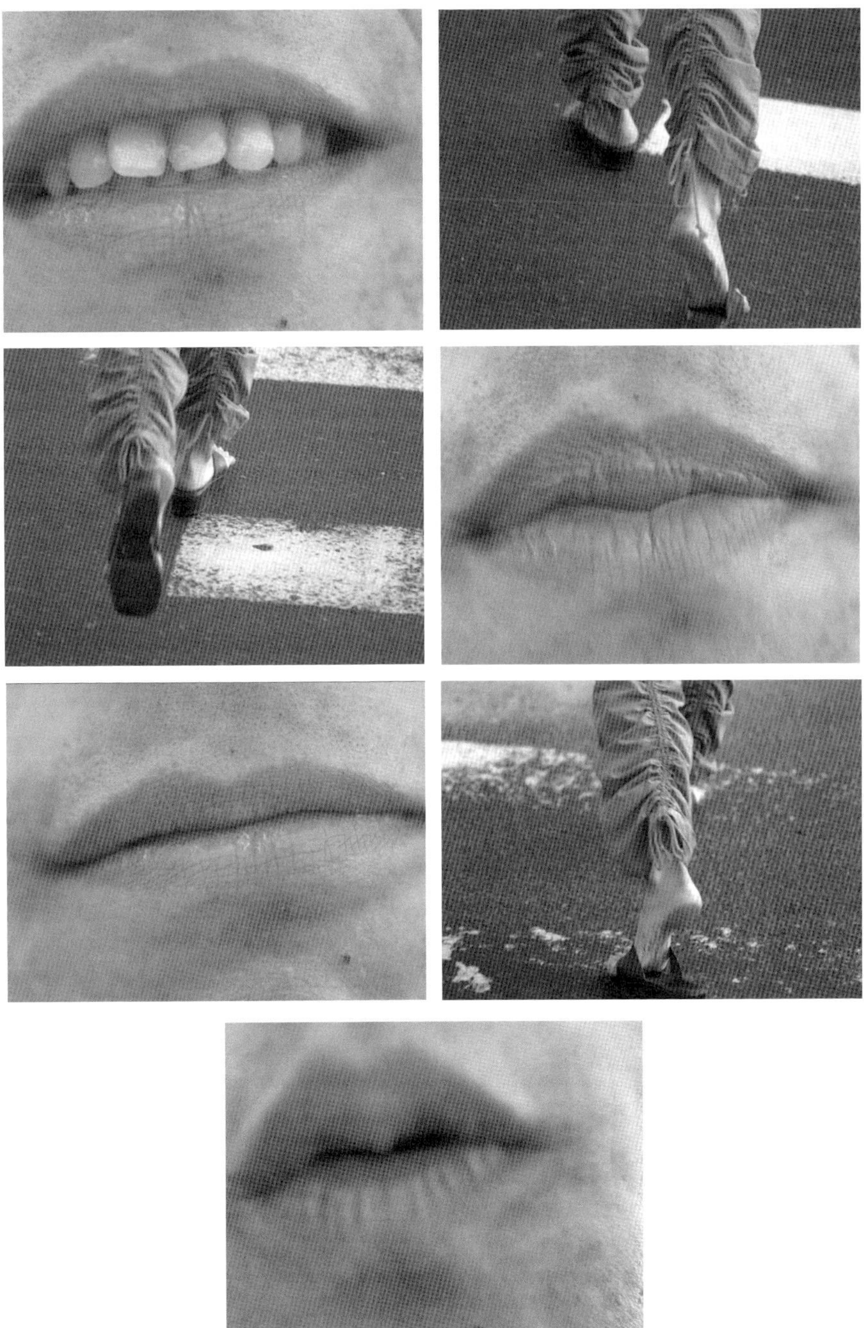

Figures 13–19: Shelly Silver, *What I'm Looking For*, 2004. HD video, 15 min. Courtesy of the artist.

Notes

1 The title 'Arrest and Movement' is indebted to T.S. Eliot's poem 'Burnt Norton' published in *The Four Quartets* (1943) which includes the lines:

At the still point of the turning world. Neither flesh nor fleshless;
Neither from nor towards; at the still point, there the dance is,
But neither arrest nor movement. And do not call it fixity,
Where past and future are gathered. Neither movement from nor towards,
Neither ascent nor decline. Except for the point, the still point,
There would be no dance, and there is only the dance.
(Also available here: http://www.artofeurope.com/eliot/eli5.htm, accessed 4 October 2012).

My title is also directly influenced by Henriette Antonia Groenewegen-Frankfort's book *Arrest and Movement: An Essay on Space and Time in the Representational Art of the Ancient Near East*, Cambridge, MA: Harvard University Press, [1951] 1987.

2 Raymond Bellour, 'The Double Helix', in Timothy Druckrey (ed.), *Electronic Culture: Technology and Visual Representation*, New York: Aperture, 1996, p. 199.

3 Cf. Linda Stone, http://lindastone.net/, accessed 25 November 2010.

4 Peter Weibel, 'Chronocracy', in Joke Brouwer et al. (eds), *Machine Times*, Rotterdam: NAI/V2, 2000, pp. 150–77.

5 Peter Weibel, 'Narrated Theory: Multiple Projections and Multiple Narrations (Past and Future)', in Martin Rieser et al. (eds), *New Screen Media. Cinema/Art/Narrative*, London: British Film Institute, 2002, pp. 42–53.

6 Jean-Christophe Royoux, 'Free-Time Workers and the Reconfiguration of Public Space: Several Hypotheses on the Work of Pierre Huyghe', in Tanya Leighton and Pavel Büchler (eds), *Saving the Image: Art After Film*, Glasgow: Centre for Contemporary Arts, 2003, p. 186.

7 ibid., p. 189.

8 ibid., p. 192.

9 ibid., p. 193.

10 Nicholas Borriaud, 'The Reversibility of the Real' (1 May 2006), http://www.tate.org.uk/tateetc/issue7/pierrehuyghe.htm, accessed 15 September 2011.

11 Gilles Deleuze, *Difference and Repetition*, New York: Columbia University Press, 1995, p. 56.

12 Royoux, 2003, p. 189.

13 Roland Barthes, *Image, Music, Text*, New York: Hill and Wang, 1977, pp. 65–67.

14 Gilles Deleuze, *The Time-Image*, London: Continuum, 2005, p. 22.

15 ibid., p. xii.

16 Gilles Deleuze, 'On the Time Image', in *Negotiations*, New York: Columbia University Press, 1997, p. 53.

17 Raymond Bellour, 'Concerning "The Photographic"', in Karen Beckman (ed.), *Still/Moving: Between Cinema and Photography*, Durham, NC: Duke University Press, 2008, p. 270.

18 Raymond Bellour, 'The Pensive Spectator', in *Wide Angle*, Vol. 9, No.1, 1987, p. 6–10.

19 Giorgio Agamben, *What is an Apparatus?*, Stanford: Stanford University Press, 2009, p. 11.

20 Garret Stewart, *Framed Time: Towards a Post-Filmic Cinema*, Chicago: University of Chicago Press, 2007, p. 2.

21 Paul Young, *The Cinema Dreams its Rivals*, Minneapolis: University of Minnesota, 2006, p. 195.

22 Cf. Holly Willis, *New Digital Cinema: Reinventing the Moving Image*, London: Wallflower Press, 2005.

23 Peter Weibel, 'Preface', in Jeffrey Shaw and Peter Weibel (eds), *Future Cinema: The Cinematic Imaginary After Film*, Cambridge, MA: MIT Press, 2003, p. 17.

24 Chrissie Iles, *Into the Light: The Projected Image in American Art*, New York: Whitney Museum, 2001, p. 65.

25 Chrissie Iles, qtd in 'The New Cinematic Aesthetic in Video', in Leighton et al., 2003, p. 132.

26 Darsie Alexander et al. (eds), *Slide Show: Projected Images in Contemporary Art*, Baltimore & London: Baltimore Museum of Art and Tate London, 2005, p. 17.

27 ibid., p. 23.

28 Darsie Alexander, 'Slide Show', in *Slide Show: Projected Images in Contemporary Art*, Philadelphia: Penn State University Press, 2005, p. 19; pp. xxi, 17, 23.

29 Sean Cubitt, *The Cinema Effect*, Cambridge, MA: MIT Press, 2005, p. 35.

30 Paul Virilio, *Lost Dimension*, New York: Semiotext(e), 1991, p. 31.

31 Cf. Theodor Adorno, 'On the Fetish Character of Music and the Regression of Listening', in Andrew Arato et al. (eds), *The Essential Frankfurt School Reader*, London and New York: Continuum, 1982, pp. 270–300.

Chapter 3

The Aesthetics of Flow and the Aesthetics of Catharsis

Jay David Bolter

Christopher Nolan's *Inception* (2010) is a blend of Hollywood genres: science fiction, action-adventure, and 'heist' film. It centres on a criminal team, whose task is to break into the dreaming mind of an Australian businessman and plant an idea. The planting or inception of an idea can only be accomplished by inducing an intense emotional release, a catharsis (the film's term), in the subject's mind. Like many recent Hollywood films, *Inception* makes reference to video games in substance and style. The team has to operate simultaneously on three dream levels, like the levels in a first-person shooter (FPS), each of which has its own architecture, set of obstacles and anonymous assassins. There are goals on each level and puzzles to solve along the way, and the film ends with an instantaneous 'levelling-up' that ostensibly brings both the characters and the audience back to the world of waking reality.

Inception is not only a genre film, but also one that reflects on the nature of film-making in an age of digital media. Hollywood has obviously been promoted for decades as a cultural 'dream machine'; in this case the film is premised on a technology that makes it possible to share dreams, and it repeatedly shifts between a world characterized as a dream and the waking world. Hollywood film and television dramas are understood as vehicles for eliciting appropriate emotions in the audience through their identification with the characters in the drama. They are cathartic in the sense that they promise an emotional climax, and catharsis is what *Inception* both represents as its goal and offers to its audience. Classic Hollywood films may deal in dreams, but they do not need to present the dream technology in the film itself: the camera remains behind (or rather in front of) the scenes. In *Inception*, the dream box is visible, and it does not look or function like a film camera. A box with leads that are connected to the wrists of all the dreamers, this technology looks suitably medical or forensic, like a lie detector. It must certainly have computer technology and may remind some viewers of, for example, the game box in David Cronenberg's *eXistenZ* (1999).

As in *eXistenZ*, the dreamers tunnel into a shared dreamworld that suggests the ultimate 3D video game. One of the members of the team, Ariadne, has in fact 'designed' all the levels of this dreamworld. Her act of design can refer to the *mise-en-scène* of traditional film, but in today's culture of game engines and first-person shooter, it also refers to 3D game design. Once the team gets into the dreamworld, it spends much of its time in firefights and chase scenes that action-adventure films now share with video games. The anonymous shooters threaten the success not only of the team's mission, but of the film itself, because they threaten to block the cathartic ending that the team and the film aim for.

Inception invites an allegorical reading – as a film that stages the anxiety of traditional film-makers at the cultural reception of new dream-machine technologies, such as the video game. The allusions to scenes from classic films – including Dziga Vertov's folding city at the end of *Man with a Movie Camera* (1929) and the enigmatic final scenes of Stanley Kubrick's *2001: A Space Odyssey* (1968) – suggest that we read *Inception* as standing for the tradition of film at this moment of its reconfiguration in digital culture. In its anxiety of the digital, *Inception* is the latest in a series of films since the 1990s, including *Strange Days* (Kathryn Bigelow, 1995), the previously mentioned *eXistenZ* and *The Matrix* (Andy Wachowski and Lana Wachowski, 1999). Those other films focused on the danger posed by the virtual reality or video games to our grasp of reality, and that theme certainly remains important in *Inception*, although it is figured in a somewhat different way. The dream technology threatens our perception of reality and the authenticity of our emotions – our ability to experience the catharsis that film promises. *Inception* may borrow stylistic and thematic elements from contemporary FPS videogames, but it is ultimately a film.

On the other hand, Nolan is not a reactionary film-maker. The film's presentation of dreams as an embodied experience, and its interest in the tactile and aural as well as the visual dimension of dreaming, suggests that Nolan understands how our media culture has changed since the classic days of Hollywood cinema in the middle of the twentieth century. Contemporary audiences encounter film differently than in the past because they are now accustomed to receiving media in what has been called a 'polyaesthetic' fashion.[1] Nevertheless, *Inception* does affirm the aesthetic function of traditional film: to evoke a cathartic response in the audience though a climactic narrative. The main character, Dom, has his own cathartic moment at the end of the film, although this moment seems particularly contrived. A spinning top at the film's end suggests that the familiar Hollywood traditions for manipulating the audience's emotion through narrative may themselves be unstable.

Inception exposes an important tension in contemporary media culture – between an aesthetic of catharsis and one of flow. If Hollywood film, television drama and most theatre (as well as some popular music and fiction) are all characterized by narrative techniques that aim at catharsis, video games and other contemporary culture forms aim instead to evoke a feeling that the psychologist Mihaly Csíkszentmihályi has named 'flow'.[2] These two aesthetics (catharsis and flow) cooperate and compete in today's culture: both remain vigorous. With its relatively long tradition in popular media forms, however, catharsis may now appear somewhat old-fashioned. Flow is the aesthetic of first-person shooter games and techno and ambient music. Flow is the state induced by selecting one short YouTube video after another or by monitoring Twitter and Facebook feeds for minutes or hours on end. Catharsis aims at the achievement of a desired emotional state, whereas the state of flow wants to continue forever, with minor variations in the intensity of involvement. Flow is the negation of desire, as it has been represented in the nineteenth- and twentieth-century narrative and drama, because it does not move toward its own repletion.

I am not suggesting that the dichotomy between catharsis and flow can completely characterize today's media culture. Our culture is best described as a plenitude, in which almost every understanding of the relationship between media and content, and between art and entertainment, is still supported by some community in the developed world. The communities may vary in size from thousands to millions, or tens of millions of viewers, users and writers, but there is no cultural centre that can succeed in marginalizing the other communities. Among writers on digital media today, modernist assumptions about creativity and the function of art have been particularly resilient. At the same time these writers are willing to modify or distort these assumptions, usually to prescribe what the future of media should or will be. A good indication of both the tenacity and flexibility of modernist assumptions can be the found in all the various uses of the term 'avant-garde' today, whose meaning now ranges from radical disruption in the sense of the historical avant-garde to successful commercialization of new digital technology.

Precisely because our culture's ideas about media today consist of a jumbled excavation of historical layers, it is useful to start with this simplifying dichotomy. I draw this distinction between catharsis and flow in order to create end points against which we can map the aesthetics of different media forms. If catharsis characterized the aesthetic goal of popular media in the twentieth century, the aesthetic of flow promises to be even more important for digital media in the twenty-first.

The Aesthetics of Catharsis and Flow

[Suggested music to accompany the reading. This characterization of catharsis could be accompanied by the soundtrack to any of hundreds of dramatic Hollywood films, especially those in the classic orchestral tradition. Among recent films, the score of *Agora* (Alejandro Amenábar, 2009) by Dario Mariniello is a fine example.]

Nolan's film addresses the status of film in an age in which the dream machine is changing. For the past century, dreams were projected on a screen in a darkened theatre; now, for many viewers, they are also generated by a small box filled with electronics. *Inception* invokes the term catharsis, whose history from Aristotle to the present is long and complicated. I will use the term to describe a set of assumptions about the function of popular narrative forms in the twentieth century. The aesthetic of cathartic narrative in my sense is captured in popular screenwriting manuals such as Dan Decker's *Anatomy of a Screenplay* (1998) or Syd Field's *Screenplay: The Foundations of Screenwriting* (2005). These manuals aim to be utterly conventional. Their authors claim that their vast experience (they have read thousands of film scripts and participated in the making of Hollywood films) allows them to codify successful practice into a set of conventions. A successful film tells a story in three acts: the first act establishes the main character and sets up the conflict; the second develops this conflict toward a climax; and the third resolves it. The resolution brings about an emotional release in the audience, which has identified with the main character and become involved in his or her dilemma. The Hollywood style is also transparent: what is happening on the screen is a sequence of possible or at least coherent events.

Twentieth-century narrative film derives these aesthetic principles from theatrical melodrama and the nineteenth-century novel, and has passed them along to so-called 'serious' television drama, e.g. *The West Wing* (1999–2006) and *Mad Men* (2007–). Film and television therefore frame the viewer's desire as a longing for narrative closure and emotional release. Formally, this is a desire for immediacy (as the erasure of mediation) – to be drawn into the action and the space of the film. The elements of the film should conspire to make the visual world of the story seamless. Hollywood film avoids unconventional editing techniques, breaks in the logic of the story and unbelievable characters: they are defamiliarizing techniques of what mark a film as 'experimental'; they constitute the difference between an 'art film' and a serious popular film. Popular film comedies, on the other hand, are allowed to use such distancing techniques because they are not expected to promote the same emotional identification in their audience. Even serious films can sacrifice some degree of visual transparency and narrative logic for 'emotional truth'. Developed over the past hundred years of film, these practices remain compelling in today's popular culture. James Cameron's *Titanic* (1997) and the 'serious' films of Steven Spielberg draw audiences whose size should astonish us even in the age of cultural plenitude.

[The reader is now invited to switch to music appropriate for flow, such as the minimalism of Philip Glass or the ambient music of Robert Rich's album *Somnium* (2001)]

Although video games have a shorter history than film, they have developed considerable diversity in the past thirty years. Genres (each with player bases in the millions or tens of millions) include: puzzle games; platform games; role-playing games; first-person shooters; and others. Many of the most popular genres continue to be single-player games. If the paradigmatic situation of film (now complicated by television, the DVD and Internet delivery) was an audience seated in a darkened hall watching a large screen, the paradigmatic situation of the video game (now complicated by the Internet and mobile phones) is still a single player seated in front of a personal screen engaged in a loop of play. As digital writers constantly remind us, video games are 'interactive', which means that through her participation the player is subsumed into the procedural circuit of the game. Interactivity promotes a different form of identification from the catharsis of popular film, for the player experiences the games as a flow of events, in which she participates. In a first-person shooter, such as the *Doom* (1993) series, the player falls into a consistent frame of mind for relatively long periods, as she moves along each level and engages and dispatches enemies. A game may offer some variety between levels – for example, with cinematic 'cutscenes' in action-adventure games, some of which are based on films – but such scenes are felt as breaks in the flow that is the principal attraction in playing. The elaborate photorealistic shooters are not the only games that pursue the aesthetic of flow. Two-dimensional platformer games (such as the venerable, absurdly-named *Super Mario Brothers* series, 1980–) or even puzzle games (*Tetris,* 1984; *Bejeweled (2),* 2004) also insert their players into a potentially endless event loop.

Games designers understand the importance of this loop and the psychological state it induces. Designer Jesse Schell notes that '[i]t pays for game designers to make a careful study of flow, because this is exactly the feeling we want the players of our games to enjoy.'[3] The key is to manage the player's sense of flow:

> Flow activities must manage to stay in the narrow margin of challenges that lies between boredom and frustration, for both of these unpleasant extremes cause our mind to change its focus to a new activity. Csikszentmihalyi calls this margin the 'flow channel'.[4]

Schell is referring to Mihaly Csíkszentmihályi, the psychologist who as early as the 1970s appropriated the term 'flow' to describe this state:

> I developed a theory of optimal experience based on the concept of flow – a state in which people are so involved in an activity that nothing else seems to matter; the experience itself is so enjoyable that people will it even at great cost, for the sheer sake of doing it.[5]

Critics of video games point to this intense, autotelic engagement as a problem, even an addiction. For Csíkszentmihályi, however, it constitutes the essence of the experience of a variety of the most enjoyable and meaningful human activities. Csíkszentmihályi does not mention video games himself, instead pointing to traditional games and sports as flow activities. Designers and writers, including Schell, have applied Csíkszentmihályi's term and description to digital versions of games.[6] As generators of flow, video games may have a winning state, but winning itself is not the point, especially in a single-player game. Many video games are designed to be repeated after a win or a loss; in others, the player simply resets the game and starts over. The point is the player's engagement in the activity itself.

What Csíkszentmihályi describes is not a new phenomenon. Flow can be evoked by activities that are common to many ages and cultures, and the flow state has something in common with states induced by forms of meditation or religious experience. But it does seem that our current cultural moment is pursuing the aesthetics of flow with special enthusiasm. Video games are such important exercises in flow because of the status that these games (in contrast to earlier games or forms of play) now enjoy. In the past two decades, the economic importance of video games has led to a rising cultural position. Video games are no longer a pastime only for adolescent boys; some genres – for example, online 'casual' games such as *Bejeweled* (2001) – are extremely popular among women over 30. Game studies is now a recognized academic discipline. Video games have also become 'serious': they are used in education and training, in the communication of health issues, and in politics for propaganda and for motivational purposes.[7]

The dichotomy of catharsis-flow, like all such analytic dichotomies, is valuable in that it serves as a starting point. Although Hollywood film definitely aims for catharsis and video games seek to achieve flow, many forms of media culture today pursue these aesthetics in some combination. The remediating relationships between video games and film, for example, involve cooperation as well as competition. Action-adventure films often include game-like action sequences, which continue for minutes at one tense emotional register. Such scenes recall, if not they do not entirely recreate, the flow of first-person shooters and seek to appeal to the much same audience as video games. At the same time, video games based on films (such as the *Lord of the Rings* games and the James Bond games) try to imitate the catharsis of film, although the attempts are generally half-hearted. As mentioned above, the cutscenes and trailers for video games do evoke the dynamic emotions of film, which is the reason why such scenes seem alien to the experience of the gameplay itself, and why hardcore game-players and game studies writers tend to be critical of cutscenes. The remediating chains of the contemporary media industry often blend the two aesthetics. If *The Matrix* films (1999–2003) are primarily cathartic, with some significant but veiled references to games, *The Matrix* 'series' also includes short animated films called *The Animatrix* (Peter Chung and Andrew R. Jones, 2003), some of which were first released on a website where the viewer was encouraged to adopt a relationship to the material that is better characterized as flow. There have been three video games: *Enter the Matrix* (2003) and *The Matrix: Path of Neo* (2005) – two single-player action games; and *The Matrix Online* (2005) – a massively multiplayer online role-playing game. Although the films enjoyed larger audiences, certainly most of the game players would have seen the films, which suggests that the same viewer/player can appreciate both aesthetics.

If television drama is, like Hollywood film, cathartic, today's television as a whole is a complex mix of styles, and many programmes (infomercials, music-video channels, the weather channel, and so on) want to flow. Csíkszentmihályi regards flow as an active state: a person is doing something that induces the feeling of flow. In this sense, channel surfing is still perhaps one of the most common flow activity in our culture. The sociologist Raymond Williams used the term 'flow' decades ago to describe the programming of (American) television, which abhors a break in the steady stream of sound and image.[8] However, for Williams, the flow of programming induced a passivity in the viewer over whom this stream washes. We could argue that experience of watching television is a blend of the two aesthetics because inside this flow of programmes and commercials the viewer may be watching cathartic dramas. At any rate, the experience of television viewing is becoming more hybridized now because viewers can choose among many different ways of consuming television programmes: watching them live (or when broadcast); recording them on DVRs for later viewing; choosing programmeees on demand from services on the Internet, and so on.

Each of these modes changes the flow of the viewing experience. Finally, nascent forms of interactive television often convert cathartic programmes into flow experiences, as they divert the viewer's concentration from the narrative and encourage her to develop her own rhythm in moving between the narrative and the additional materials (games, background information, product purchases) on the Internet.

Like television, popular and historical music illustrates the dichotomy of catharsis and flow as well as its complications. The reader who followed the musical suggestions and has listened first to film music and then to ambient music will have noticed the contrast between the emotionally dynamism of catharsis and the monochromatic quality of flow. Cathartic film music inherited the affective conventions of what we call in English 'classical music', where catharsis was dominant between 1750 and 1900 (and for some styles much later). This music establishes a tonal centre, moves away, and then returns in a gesture of cadence. Each cadence in classical music is a tiny catharsis, which contributes to larger music structures and more significant catharses. The Romantic symphonists of the nineteenth and twentieth centuries explored dissonance, and delayed the return to catharsis as long as possible, and this Romantic tradition dominated Hollywood in the mid-twentieth century through the work of such composers as Miklos Rozsa, Franz Waxman and Bernard Hermann. Orchestral film music lost favour in Hollywood in the 1960s and '70s, but was revived in the era of Spielberg, particularly by John Williams. Film music now is quite eclectic, but the romantic score is still favoured for dramatic Hollywood blockbusters, such as *Titanic* and *Lord of the Rings* (Peter Jackson, 2001). If the classical style is cathartic, baroque music could be said to flow: a baroque fugue could in principle continue forever with the endless variations of the fugal subject. To appreciate flow in music, we can also appeal to recent styles: minimalist music in the 1970s; techno and ambient music today; all of which reject catharsis in favour of a continuous affect or emotional state (they are like baroque music in this sense only). Techno and ambient music never need or want to end. The background music of most video games too is endless, even when it borrows orchestral colour from Hollywood action-adventure genre. Such music cannot have larger structures or rounded forms because it is impossible to predict the progress of the game, which the music is presuming to track. These are only general characterizations, however. Music can combine flow and catharsis: for example, Ravel's *Boléro* is characterized by minutes of repetitious flow before reaching its bombastic catharsis.

Although the history of music suggests that flow has long been available as an alternative aesthetic, video games and other digital forms have nevertheless helped to make that alternative important in popular media culture today. If films such as *Titanic* or *Avatar* (James Cameron, 2009), with their carefully calibrated dynamics of identification and emotional release, continue to engross audiences, millions are also drawn to the endless crescendo of games such as *Halo 3* (2007) and *Tomb Raider* (1999). The aesthetic of catharsis frames desire in the historically familiar terms of a lack to be filled both for a main character as the audience's proxy and for the audience itself. Flow is emotionally monochromatic, and there is no lack to be filled: all the user wants is for the current state of satisfaction to be prolonged.

Catharsis in Contemporary Media Culture

In popular culture, catharsis is usually associated with narrative or drama, as the film manuals by Decker and Fields, mentioned above, indicate. The manuals are secure in the conviction that character defines plot and that the shape of the plot involves the change (enlightenment, dissolution, etc.) of the main character. These manuals codify a widespread cultural assumption that all of our lives are constituted as 'stories that we tell one another' – an assumption apparent in the way 'ordinary' people are presented as subjects in the American morning shows, each with his or her own story of injustice or triumph. The assumption is also apparent in the unquenchable public interest in auratic film stars and other celebrities, whose lives are supposed to have the same dramatic shape as their films. Almost everywhere we look in media culture, we can find the trope 'life as cathartic narrative' – in every 'human interest' story on television news, every self-help manual of the kind that truly top the bestseller lists, and, for that matter, in the contemporary readings of at least the American versions of Christianity and Judaism.

It is more surprising that in recent decades philosophers and psychologists have sought to affirm the truth of catharsis culture by arguing that story-telling is essential to the human condition. The psychologist Jerome Bruner suggested that '[...] narrative imitates life, life imitates narrative. "Life" in this sense is the same kind of construction of the human imagination as "a narrative" is.'[9] The philosopher Daniel Dennett has claimed similarly that we are all novelists who seek to give our lives the shape of an autobiography.[10] In *After Virtue* (1981), Alasdair MacIntyre went farther and asserted that the unity of life is:

> [...] the unity of a narrative quest [...] [and] the only criteria for success or failure in a human life as a whole are the criteria for success or failure in a narrated or to-be-narrated quest. A quest for what? [...] a quest for the good [...] the good life for man is the life spent in seeking for the good life for man.[11]

In his article 'Against Narrativity', Galen Strawson cites these and others as he sets out to disprove the idea that everyone must see his or her life as a narrative.[12] But the fact that he can find so many on the other side indicates how powerful this cultural trope still is, even among academic humanists (though not necessarily among literary scholars).

An increasingly popular variation on this trope is that story-telling is not (or not only) a psychological or moral imperative, but a biological one. A number of writers with varying science credentials explain story-telling as a Pleistocene-era adaptation conferring a selective advantage: poor story-tellers died out, leaving only us novelists. For Boyd, story-telling is a kind of cognitive play that sharpens the mind in various ways.[13] More specifically for Dutton, '[s]tories encourage us to explore the points of view, beliefs, motivations, and values of other human minds, inculcating potentially adaptive interpersonal and social capacities'.[14] (In fact, only certain kinds of psychological narrative aim at this intersubjectivity; wherever else this technique may have developed, it surely comes to us though the modern novel.) The point of such Darwinian arguments is to insist on the universal nature and power of narrative. By framing their definition on the basis of recent popular narrative, the adaptionists vindicate catharsis as a universal aesthetic experience.

All of these writers are operating under the literary assumptions of what we might call the 'industrial age of print', the period (roughly 1800 to the recent past) in which the printed novel developed from a (relatively) elite literary form into a series of popular genres, codifying certain forms of climax and catharsis. Dennett's claim that we are 'novelists' cannot help to recall for us the tradition from Austen to the twentieth century. And when Marya Schechtman speaks of a 'narrative self-conception',[15] she is depending on her readers' shared understanding of organic plot and development of character inherited from the German *Bildungsroman* and the Victorian novel. These notions of coherence and transparent representation were exactly the ones that the avant-garde challenged throughout the twentieth century in their repeated rejection of narrative forms of painting, literature and film. Postmodern writers and artists also obviously challenged them in less strident ways from the 1960s onwards.

Is catharsis still possible in digital media forms? The plenitude of media culture should warn us not to be categorical in denying that possibility. For one thing, films can be remediated in digital technology, most obviously by being streamed in various forms. If I watch *Titanic* on my iPad, I may still have a cathartic experience. But some who are committed to this popular tradition go much further and insist that catharsis must be the teleology of digital media, as it has been for film. In 2004, Hollywood directors Steven Spielberg and Robert Zemeckis attended the opening of the Electronic Arts video game lab at the University of Southern California: the topic of the evening was bringing video games and film together as an entertainment form: 'Discussing the coming fusion of games and film, they said video games are getting closer to a story-telling art form – but are not quite there yet. "I think the real indicator will be when somebody confesses that they cried at level 17," Spielberg said.'[16]

In the same year, Spielberg announced that he would work with Electronic Arts to develop emotionally engaging games. Given his success as a film-maker, it is not surprising that Spielberg would assume that film is the standard to which games must rise. There is also a community of writers and computer specialists who work on 'interactive narrative', and they too take cathartic narrative as their model. In *Hamlet on the Holodeck* (1997), Janet Murray claims that the computer constitutes the next great narrative medium after drama, the novel and cinema. Because it is 'participatory' and 'procedural', the digital medium makes possible a new form of story-telling. In a novel or a film, the reader or viewer can be intimately involved in the story, but she cannot intervene to affect the outcome.[17] In Murray's vision, the player will participate in a simulation that is immersive and responsive (like the Holodeck in the *Star Trek* series), becoming a character in the 'story-world'. Murray imagines that this ultimate cyber-drama can evolve from current genres of video games.[18] For Murray, who is an essentialist like the adaptionists or the philosophers mentioned above, interactive narrative would unite the essence of the digital medium with the essence of the human story-telling. It would be radically new and yet affirm the continuity of human nature, the universality of human story-telling.

The interactive narrativists are really seeking to remediate the power of Hollywood popular film in a video game form. For them, today's games only point the way to a new expressive form that will ultimately give the player an emotional experience similar to that of film and literature. Yet, if the narrativists are waiting for the game that will make the player cry at level 17, there are reasons to think that they will have a long wait. The diversity of video games today makes it foolish to predict their future, and it is possible that a genre will develop, presumably from role-playing games that imitate the narrative form of Hollywood film. But in order for such games to become the 'cinema of the twenty-first century', they will have to reconcile the interactive freedom of the player with the constraints of a narrative arc and emotional climax. There is little evidence that game developers know how to do this or are even working in this direction. The proposals for interactive narrative by computer specialists and digital media writers are prescriptive rather than descriptive; their goal is to secure the new digital media for traditional catharsis culture.

Flow culture

The manifestations of 'flow culture' seem more novel than those of catharsis culture not because flow is a new phenomenon, but rather because digital media forms have helped to elevate the status of flow practices, and extend them to communities of almost inconceivable size and economic importance. Some of the most prominent and popular social media forms, such as YouTube, Twitter and Facebook, seem to appeal to their tens of millions of users precisely through the promise of flow.

YouTube remediates television and video for the World Wide Web and in the process refashions an interactive version of the experience of flow that Williams described for television decades earlier. A typical session with YouTube begins with one video, which the user may have found through searching or as a link sent to her through e-mail or perhaps Twitter. The page that displays that video contains links to others, established through various associations: the same subject, the same contributor, a similar theme, and so on. Channel surfing on traditional television can be addictive, but the movement from one channel to another is more or less random. The YouTube's lists of links and its invitation to search for new videos give the viewer's experience more continuity, with the opportunity for repetition or endless minimal variation. In *The Language of New Media* (2001), Lev Manovich argued that the digital era presents us with an alternative to narrative film: 'database cinema', in which video segments can be selected from a larger repository and put together in a particular order:

After the novel, and subsequently cinema, privileged narrative as the key form of cultural expression of the modern age, the computer age introduces its correlate – the database. Many new media objects do not tell stories; they do not have a beginning or end [...].

Instead, they are collections of individual items, with every item possessing the same significance as any other.[19]

YouTube is the realization of 'database' video or cinema, and is now both an alternative and a companion to the cathartic experience of the Hollywood film.

The microblogging sites, of which Twitter is the most popular, also offer a flow experience, in which a personalized stream of SMS-length messages is delivered to each user. The stream depends on whom that user has chosen to 'follow', including personal friends, celebrities, news organizations, universities, companies, and so on. If she follows enough sources, her stream of messages will change as fast as she can refresh her screen. And she can contribute to her own stream and those of her followers. The resulting stream of 'tweets' is an unexpected combination of public and private communication. SMS texts were intended to be very short private messages between two mobile phone users, but Twitter interleaves the messages from all the sources so that there is no coherence between consecutive messages and no need for the process to ever end. Those who are educated in traditional writing practices find the individual tweets and the stream almost meaningless. But for millions of Twitter regulars, the constant rhythm of short texts seems to be satisfying in its own right. When we look to other participatory social websites (such as Facebook, MySpace and Orkut), we find another, yet similar version of the flow aesthetic. A user's Facebook page consists of a series of channels that she can monitor: a wall for Twitter-like posts to and from friends, a private message service, a photo-hosting section, and repetitive games and contests in which the user is constantly challenged to participate.

Social media such as Facebook and YouTube are often said to be exercises in online identity construction. The slogan of YouTube, for example, is 'Broadcast Yourself', which suggests not only that the user has the opportunity to distribute her own broadcasts, but also that she can create a version of her own identity through these short videos that she sends into cyberspace. The original genre of YouTube video, and still one of the most common, is the talking head, in which a user faces a webcam and delivers an ad-lib or prepared presentation. There must be millions of such videos on the site (out of a total of over 100 million). Some users create their own YouTube channels and become YouTube personalities on the obvious model of television personalities on the daytime or late-night talk shows. Facebook began as a site where college students presented themselves for flirting or friendship with other students, and these roots are still apparent. Each user creates a profile, which includes such information as whether he or she is 'in a relationship' and which can be changed at any time. The Facebook channels (texts and images) are information flows that present facets of the user's personality, activities and relationships. The character that emerges from a Facebook page is a mosaic of these channels, each of which is constructed according to templates provided by the Facebook interface. The user's identity develops according to the flow of slightly varied images and posts, and the whole format works against the presentation of a climactic and singular life story. In its framing of user's identity, Facebook offers nothing like the structure of the *Bildungsroman* or biopic.

We have defined 'flow' as a cultural aesthetic, but for Csíkszentmihályi, somewhat surprisingly, flow has a more important cultural purpose. In our secular and hostile world, flow gives individuals a feeling of control in their own smaller domains (games, hobbies, work activities). Flow becomes 'the process of achieving happiness through control over one's inner life.'[20] Csíkszentmihályi's flow culture is one in which individuals aim at nothing more than personal satisfaction. The psychology of flow does not encourage them to think of ourselves as actors in a larger social or political drama. At least since the Renaissance, such a drama would be by definition cathartic: the movement toward a resolution through victory or defeat. At least from 1800 to the middle of the twentieth century, politically-aware citizens were encouraged, if not compelled, to see their own history as marked by the same dramatic curve as that of his state or nation. Flow culture takes no such view. Instead, the identity constructed on Facebook and YouTube is homeostatic: it does not see itself participating in any larger history or driven by any collective destiny. Instead, its modest goal is to keep itself within bounds, within the channels provided by a Facebook page.

Reflective Culture as a Third Way

The dichotomy between catharsis and flow can be presented as a contrast between traditional media (film) and new (video games), between older audiences and younger players, or even between an older and newer understanding of human identity and social engagement. But these are only first approximations. For one thing, flow and catharsis can blend in the same media experience, as they clearly do in many forms of popular and even traditional music. Analyzing the blending of the two aesthetics can give in fact us insights into the peculiar appeal of certain films and digital artefacts. The seemingly endless chase scenes in action-adventure films are an intrusion of flow aesthetics into film, just as the use of cutscenes introduce cathartic elements into video games. In addition, the audience for cathartic films and television series may tend to be older than the player-base for action-adventure games, but the success of *Titanic* or the Harry Potter books and films indicates that young audiences can still be won over to traditional narrative forms. Figure 1 illustrates the notion of blending by placing various media artefacts mentioned in this paper along a spectrum: from pure catharsis on the left, to pure flow on the right. Thus, the film *Titanic* is very cathartic with very little flow; the game *Bejeweled* (2001) is very nearly an experience of pure flow. The relative placements are obviously open to interpretation.

Finally, we have left out of consideration many cultural practices that do not fit on the spectrum of catharsis and flow. Catharsis and flow both describe totalizing aesthetics, in which the ideal is to command the viewer's complete attention. Csíkszentmihályi makes this focus a condition of a true flow experience, and catharsis is also understood as an encompassing experience. Murray, a champion of catharsis, claims that immersion is one of the essential properties of the digital medium. An interactive narrative will immerse the player/viewer both perceptually and emotionally, so that she is absorbed in a story-world that

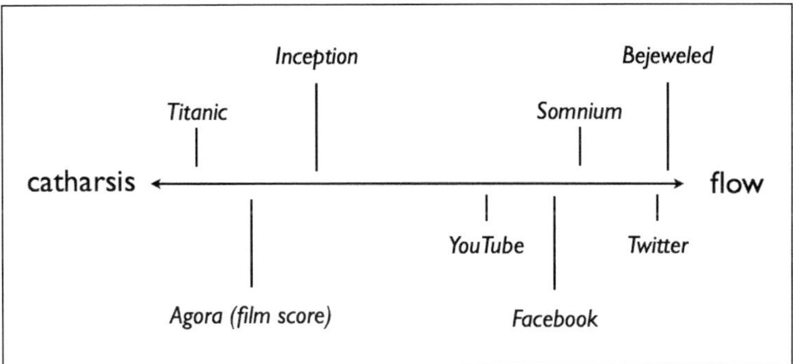

Figure 1: Media artefacts that are blends of flow and catharsis.

she experiences as real. We recognize the aesthetics of immersion in popular film, television and fiction: the movie that the audience does not want to end (but it must end); the page-turner that the reader cannot put down; and the addictive television series. Such immersion in compelling narrative forms has been a characteristic of popular twentieth-century forms, and for that very reason experimental art throughout the twentieth century has generally aimed to be reflective rather than immersive. We could offer this as one possible definition of avant-garde art in the twentieth century: that it rejects transparent representation and the immersion of the viewer in a story-world. Formal avant-garde art encourages the viewer to adopt a critical distance from the work itself, or at least to become aware of the process by which the work was created. And what Peter Bürger and many others call the 'political' or 'historical' avant-garde (such as the Futurists and Dada) want the viewer to critique the function of art in culture.[21] Brecht of course drew a contrast between cathartic, Aristotelian theatre and his own 'epic theatre'. In Aristotelian theatre, the viewer became involved in the story and identified uncritically with one or more of the characters; the techniques of epic theatre were calculated to encourage in the audience a critical distance from the characters and the action.[22] Following Brecht, Augosto Boal is perhaps even more explicit in condemning the politically reactionary ideology of Aristotelian theatre.[23] Similarly, film theorists in the 1970s and (to some extent) experimental film-makers themselves argued against Hollywood film, which is narrative and immersive (and therefore capitalist and sexist), and for structuralist film, which compels the viewer to confront the process of its own making.[24] Postmodern theory and practice, in literature as well as the visual arts, take the reflective nature of art as a given, though in different ways from high modernism and with a different relationship to popular culture.

In the era of high modernism, reflective practices were understood in opposition to the aesthetics and politics of mainstream culture. In today's media culture, however, this reflective aesthetic can also be hybridized not only with its traditional nemesis – catharsis – but also with popular expressions of flow. We can envision a triangle with flow, catharsis and reflection as the vertices, and place various popular and experimental forms along the edges or in the interior of the triangle as they combine elements of flow, catharsis and reflection. An obvious case is the music video, which appropriates filmic techniques that were once regarded as avant-garde to create a fragmented and associative visual experience that serves as a background for popular music (which is itself a combination of catharsis and flow).

In acknowledging this third aesthetic, we are also acknowledging the troubled distinction between popular and elite culture. Catharsis and flow aesthetics often belong to forms that have been considered popular in the twentieth century, while reflective art is usually positioned as elite (in spite of the fact that the avant-garde often attacked the conventions of high art). This distinction has become increasingly unstable since the middle of the twentieth century and has almost (but not quite) lost its meaning for contemporary media culture. At the same time, although the aesthetics of catharsis and flow still seem to be overwhelmingly more popular and economically important than reflective art today, neither catharsis nor flow can function as an undisputed cultural centre. Catharsis may be associated primarily with film and television; flow with games and social media. Yet digital culture hybridizes forms easily and eagerly. So it is sometimes possible to watch entire films that have been (illegally) uploaded and divided into segments on YouTube. Cathartic Hollywood personalities like Oprah Winfrey have Facebook pages and millions of followers on Twitter. There is little evidence that the aesthetic of catharsis will disappear, just as there is little evidence that video games, social media or other new digital forms are evolving toward a teleology – a single aesthetic principle, as many popular writers on digital media seem to assume.

Notes

1 Maria Engberg, 'Polyaestheticism', http://polyaesthetics.net/, accessed 15 September 2010.

2 Mihlay Csíkszentmihályi, *Flow: The Psychology of Optimal Experience*, New York: Harper Perennial, 1991.

3 Jesse Schell, *The Art of Game Design: A Book of Lenses*, Amsterdam & Boston: Elsevier/ Morgan Kaufmann, 2008, p. 118.

4 ibid., p. 119.

5 Csíkszentmihályi, 1991, p. 4.

6 Brian Schrank is studying the phenomenon of flow in video games, particularly in relation to highly creative and unusual 'avant-garde' games. I am indebted to him for making me aware of the importance of flow in games today. Cf. his dissertation, 'Avant-garde Videogames: Play Beyond Flow', Atlanta, GA: Georgia Institute of Technology, 2010.

7 Ian Bogost, *Persuasive Games: The Expressive Power of Videogames*, Cambridge, MA: MIT Press, 2007.

8 Raymond Williams, *Television: Technology and Cultural Forms*, London: Fontana, 1974.

9 Jerome Bruner, 'Life as Narrative', in *Social Research*, Vol. 71, No. 3, 2004, p. 692. Originally published in *Social Research*, Vol. 54, No. 1, 1987, pp. 11–32.

10 Daniel Dennett, 'Why Everyone is a Novelist', in *Times Literary Supplement*, 1988, pp. 16–22.

11 Alasdair MacIntyre, *After Virtue: A Study in Moral Theory*, London: Duckworth, 1981, pp. 203–04.

12 Galon Strawson, 'Against Narrativity', in *Ratio*, XVII(4), 2004, pp. 428–51.

13 Brian Boyd, *On the Origin of Stories: Evolution, Cognition, and Fiction*, Cambridge, MA: Belknap Press of Harvard University Press, 2009.

14 Cf. Denis Dutton, *The Art Instinct: Beauty, Pleasure and Human Evolution*, New York: Oxford University Press, 2009, p. 110.

15 Marya Schechtman, *The Constitution of Selves*, Ithaca, NY: Cornell University Press, 1997; cited by Strawson, 2004, p. 447.

16 Anthony Breznican, 'Spielberg, Zemeckis say video games, films could become one', *San Diego Union-Tribune*, 15 September 2004, www.signonsandiego.com/news/features/20040915-1336-ca-games-spielberg-zemeckis.html, accessed 15 September 2010.

17 Janet Murray, *Hamlet on the Holodeck: The Future of Narrative in Cyberspace*, New York: Simon & Schuster/Free Press, 1997.

18 For related views, see Marie-Laure Ryan, *Avatars of Story*, Minneapolis: University of Minnesota, 2006; Chris Crawford, *Chris Crawford on Game Design*, San Francisco: New Riders Games, 2003.

19 Lev Manovich, *The Language of New Media*, Cambridge, MA: MIT Press, 2001, p. 118.

20 Csíkszentmihályi, 1991, p. 6.

21 Peter Bürger, *Theory of the Avant-Garde* (trans. M. Shaw), Minneapolis: University of Minnesota Press, 1984.

22 Bertolt Brecht, 'Theatre for Pleasure or Theatre for Instruction' (trans. J. Willett), in *Brecht on Theatre: The Development of an Aesthetic*, New York: Hill and Wang, 1964, pp. 69–77.

23 Augusto Boal, *Theater of the Oppressed*, New York: Theatre Communications Group, 1985.

24 David N. Rodowick, *The Crisis of Political Modernism: Criticism and Ideology in Contemporary Film Theory*, Berkeley: University of California Press, 1994.

Chapter 4

Digital Images and Computer Simulations[1]

Barbara Flueckiger

In the wake of William J. Mitchell's influential text *The Reconfigured Eye* (1992), the discussion of digital images has focused mainly on the ethical implications of their truth claims. This text will focus on some different aspects, namely the process of digital image construction and its underlying representational and epistemological principles. Or to put it differently, not on the question of how digital images 'distort' what they represent, but on an understanding of how digital images 'construct' their representations.

Mitchell diagnosed a profound crisis in representation, which has its origin in the blurred truth status of digital images. However, in his statements Mitchell implicitly includes at least three different types of digital images: compositing, image processing, and computer-generated imagery (CGI):

> Although a digital image may look just like a photograph when it is published in a newspaper, it actually differs as profoundly from a traditional photograph as does a photograph from a painting.[2]
>
> The traditional origin narrative by which automatically captured shaded perspective images are made to seem causal things of nature rather than products of human artifice [...] no longer has the power to convince us.[3]

Furthermore he barely mentions semio-pragmatic aspects of image reception, i.e. the culturally coded frame in which an image is presented. But this frame deeply shapes the viewer's response. Most CGI is used in contexts that are clearly marked as fictional – motion pictures or advertisements – and which therefore call for a different culturally-determined mode of perception and interpretation. One of the best examples to illustrate this fact is *Forrest Gump* (Robert Zemeckis, 1994), which draws much of its fascination from the wit and irony of addressing a double consciousness in the viewer. While the viewer certainly knows that he is watching a fiction film and that the fictional character Forrest never encountered Kennedy, at the same time he marvels at the perfect illusion which unfolds on the screen. This kind of compositing triggers admiration similar to how we feel when watching a perfectly executed magic trick without knowing how the trick was performed. In his reflections on 'trucage', Christian Metz already referred to this play with *duplicité* (duplicity)[4], asking whether we should not regard cinema as one big special effect.[5]

Unfortunately, following the publication of Mitchell's text, a very narrow discussion has emerged, which does not take into account that Mitchell himself has also considered the continuity of the development from analogue to digital images. For instance, he uses Robert Capa's famous snapshot from the Spanish Civil War to discuss traditional photography in Roland Barthes' terms: as a floating signifier whose meaning can be changed by montage or by anchoring it with text.

Despite the sophisticated reasoning by Mitchell himself, many scholars have treated digital images as pure deception. The German media scholar Friedrich Kittler, for example, has claimed that they are pure forgery because they fool the eye with their pixel structure that does no more than evoke the appearance of an image.[6]

A Framework for the Classification of Digital Images

In my research project on CGI in film,[7] I devised a framework for the classification of different types of digital images according to their production technology. While these types vary greatly, they share some common properties, which will be the topic of my further investigation. Beyond the variations in digital image production as established in the framework, my research project has yielded a model of underlying principles that govern this exceedingly hybrid field: recording, modelling and painting. In this paper I will also investigate computer simulation as a special, but arguably the most illuminating, case of digital image production, both with regard to the epistemological questions connected with CGI, and in comparison to analogue modes of representation.

As indicated in the introduction, digital images are heterogeneous: not only in their mode of production, but also – and as a result – in their very different relationships with the depicted objects and/or scenes, and their differing aesthetic appearances and functions.

Much of the confusion in the discourse on digital images stems from the fact that there is no digital image as such, but a plurality of images, which we can attribute to the following variations:

1. Photography: digital image acquisition by a camera; produces images that are hardly distinguishable from analogue photographs.
2. Scanning: digital conversion of analogue images (photographs or paintings) into digital ones; these images are marked both in function and aesthetics by their analogue origin.

3. 2D drawing: creation of digital images with a graphics tablet and the use of tools such as 'brushes' or 'pens', etc.; with these techniques one can emulate almost any look of traditional painting, but also deviate greatly from anything possible in the analogue domain.

4. 2D image processing: corresponds to classic forms of retouching, although – of course – the range of possibilities is much greater with digital means of processing.

5. Computer-generated imagery (CGI): objects and scenes built by the use of 3D modelling and animation software in the computer and then rendered as 2D images, whether still or in motion; these images can be rendered according to the rules of photography or in non-photographic, deliberately stylized fashion; in most cases the term 'digital image' is meant to denote CGI.

6. Compositing: integration of various image parts from different sources; compositing can either provide fully illusionistic, seamless images, or heterogeneous ones that clearly stress the fact that they are forms of image montage, and anything in between these two extremes.

Often the variations 3, 4 and 6 are all labelled as 'image processing'.

In most cases, though, based on its aesthetic properties it is quite simple to determine which process an image has been produced by. Until now it is rarely the case that we confuse CGI with digital photographs. Only very few high-level renderings are so photo-realistic that we do not notice their origin in the computer. Furthermore, the fact has to be stressed that we do not judge images on the basis of their appearance alone, but include our knowledge of the world to decide whether or not an object or a scene could really have existed. When we see the grazing dinosaurs in *Jurassic Park* (Steven Spielberg, 1993), we are fully aware of the fact that these creatures were added digitally, not only because the press material and the making-of film informs us about it, but also because we know that they became extinct millions of years ago.

Common Properties of Digital Images

Despite their great variety, digital images share some common features. Most of them are raster graphics, which consist of horizontally and vertically organized pixels. These pixels are coded by a binary value consisting of 1 and 0. This value has to be defined by a filtering process that maps the continuous phenomena of the real world onto discrete steps – a process that is called 'quantization', and that relies on an arbitrarily devised relationship between the phenomena and their codification. In contrary to digital signals, analogue representations can continually adopt an infinite number of values. Mitchell has illustrated this difference as follows: 'Rolling down a ramp is a continuous motion, but walking down stairs is a sequence of discrete steps – so you can count the number of steps, but not the number of levels on a ramp.'[8] However, this distinction is currently in the process of becoming obsolete or at least questionable since digital systems provide a resolution, which far surpasses the range of analogue representation and the scope of perceptive differentiation by humans. To put it differently: are there still steps, if we perceive them as a ramp? For example, high-quality scans of analogue photographs depict every single grain, therefore the pixel structure is less visible than the grain structure of the original material.

According to Mark J. P. Wolf, the binary coding system was invented in 1670 by the Spanish Cistercian monk Juan Caramuel y Lobkowitz.[9] In general, however, its invention has been attributed to Gottfried Wilhelm Leibniz, who conceived it in 1701 as a universal principle of metaphysical dimension between being and non-being. This metaphysical dimension received additional support when Leibniz learned from a missionary that the Chinese book *I Ching* also relied on the binary system. With the invention of Boolean algebra by George Boole in 1854, complex mathematical operations became available to the binary coding system, which are the foundations of today's image processing by the computer. In Nelson Goodman's terminology, binary coding is described as an explicit notation system, a fact that will be considered later.[10]

As mentioned above, before binary values can be calculated they have to be mapped onto a scale consisting of discrete units which are integers of a fundamental one. Such filtering and mapping occur in human perception in many domains, for example in colour perception – as Eleanor Rosch (1973) has shown in her famous study – or in the social construction of time and space, as Norbert Elias (1988) has demonstrated.[11]

In digitization, this filtering and mapping calls for an explicit protocol that governs the conversion process, and defines the phenomenon-data relationship as well as the data themselves. This includes the assignment to a definite position in time and space. The values of each section of this space-time grid – i.e. for each pixel – define their tonal and colour information. In order to form an output on a display, these data have to be recombined, which means an assembly of an analogue output in accordance with the requirements of the human perception system. In other words, what is at work here is a combination of analysis and synthesis.[12] And this combination of the two complementary processes is the very foundation of computer simulation, as I will show in the corresponding paragraph.

With the binary coding system, digital data enter a universal digital ecosystem. Wolf has compared this coding system to a currency, which allows for the circulation and conversion of money.[13] In a similar fashion, digital data's common code supports transmission – i.e. feeding into a variety of media – and transformation – i.e. the conversion or processing of digital data. Random access, a further specificity of the digital domain, is based on the possibility of directly addressing the mathematically-coded elements. Unlike linear coding systems such as text or films, these data are distributed equidistantly in the time-space system. As Vilém Flusser has pointed out in his essay 'Krise der Linearität'/'Crisis of Linearity' (1988)[14], random access is the foundation of network structures, such as the Internet, and in turn leads to non-linear thought models.[15] But in contrast to other scholars, Flusser stresses the historical, culturally-determined process that started in the early Enlightenment, with its preoccupation for mathematically-substantiated descriptions of processes in terms of zero-dimensional, numerical entities. According to this view, what we witness now is not a digital revolution, but an evolution that began several centuries ago: a notion that proposes a historical model of feedback loops instead of a linear, teleological techno-determinism. In a similar fashion, Wolf (2000) suggests that digital technology was developed on the basis of an encompassing quantization of life that has emerged in many domains. In turn, this technology now supports a quantizing way of thinking, and thus exerts an influence on the perception of the world. In consequence, we should conceive this development as a complex, dynamic interaction of technology with sociocultural forces.

CGI between Recording, Painting and Modelling

In addition to the classification framework mentioned above, computer-generated images can also be classified on a deeper level according to their connection to the world they depict. In my research on the different technical strategies and their epistemological foundations, I have devised three basic modes: recording, painting and modelling. A fourth one is measurement, which usually plays a minor role, but is of prime importance in computer simulation, which will be the target subject of the study presented here. Measurement means the gathering of explicit data, for example to reconstruct objects or architecture in the computer.

By recording, I understand the translation of a physical structure according to an implicit or explicit protocol. We can assign digital photography to this category, but also motion capture as the recording of motion data in a 3D space. A further technological strand includes all the image-based approaches whose prime proponent is Paul Debevec. Image-based modelling is a technique to extract 3D data from a series of photographs,[16] while image-based lighting calculates light values for the rendering process based on a photographed light dome.[17] These approaches gain increasing importance when complex structures of the real world are to be imported into the 3D space of CGI, most prominently so in the construction of digital characters.[18]

Painting refers to image generation and processing with emulated tools such as brushes and pens. It is used in CGI, for example in the creation of texture maps, which describe the colour distribution on the surface of objects.

Model building[19] is the dominant practice in CGI. It is a rule-based, explicitly formalized system to generate 3D objects and animations. The rules apply either mathematical or physical principles, or stem from empirical observation and reconstruction. Examples of such model-building processes are procedural animations of flocks of animals like birds and crowd animation.[20] Furthermore, procedural approaches include the modelling of landscapes and plants based on algorithms from fractal geometry – for example the L-systems by the biologist Aristid Lindenmayer that apply the formal grammar of plant growth.[21] And finally, all the rendering algorithms that calculate the interaction of light with objects to provide the final image of a 3D scene are based on model building.[22] By their very nature, models are simplifications of complex phenomena. They suppress those details, which are deemed unimportant, or work with shortcuts that simply deliver the required results while neglecting some aspects.

In fact, most CGI are hybrid composites of the strategies differentiated here. For example, animation can be based on motion capture – a recording process – while the texture maps might be painted, and all the rendering processes belong to the category of model building. But model building remains at the core of CGI and especially of computer simulation. It is this principle that divides CGI most fundamentally from other, earlier forms of representation such as painting. While painting emulates phenomena and their perception based on observation, model building requires an explicit understanding of the physical principles. However, there is a small field wherein formalized knowledge is required in painting: the construction of the central perspective. As I have analyzed in a text about the depiction of cities in film, early bird's-eye views – like the famous woodcut view of Venice (1500) by Jacopo de' Barbari and Anton Kolb – necessitated a deep understanding of geometrical relationships because, like maps, they depict a view that was not available to observers at the time.[23]

Computer Simulation – A Case Study

According to Paul Humphreys, computer simulation is a subset of computational science to serve the purpose of 'modeling, prediction, design, discovery, and analysis of systems.'[24] Most scholars define simulation's underlying principle as a system that is mathematically equivalent with another one.[25] As Gottfried Boehm has suggested, it is an analogy with little or no similarity.[26] Gottfried Boehm illustrates this relationship with a beam balance, where one puts an object – for instance a fruit like an apple – on one side, and an often dissimilar, other object – a standardized weight made of metal – on the other side.[27]

Furthermore, computer simulations are most often dynamic and time-based. Therefore they depict their results in the form of computer animations, which we can understand as rule-based imitations of processes from the real world.[28] In many respects, this use of the term 'simulation' differs distinctively from Jean Baudrillard's conception of simulation's deceptive function in a decadent postmodern society, where it denotes images without a referent.[29] As we will see, the kind of simulation discussed in this paper is defined by an explicit, albeit complex relationship to the phenomena of the real world. The question of how computer-generated images refer to and produce knowledge is of great concern in a period of the iconic turn, called for by proponents such as art historian Gottfried Boehm or William J. Mitchell. Both Stephan Hartmann (2005) and Paul Humphreys (2004) have investigated the functions of computer simulation in natural and social science, where they serve as a heuristic tool to 'develop hypotheses, models and theories' or 'support experiments.'[30] The computer simulations discussed here have a similar function, but do not apply in such a profound way to general theories as formulated in natural or social science. Rather they picture certain situations, processes or events. Familiar examples would be 3D visualizations of architecture, which allow planners to explore or show buildings while they are not yet built, or computer reconstructions of crime scenes, which serve as forensic evidence in the courtroom. Mark J. P. Wolf has described such computer simulations as 'subjunctive documentaries' because they represent 'what could be, would be or might have been.'[31]

As early as 1988, Vilém Flusser wrote that CGI creates *Vorbilder*, a German term meaning both 'role models' and 'pre-images' of possible objects or events, like blueprints.

In a close analysis of a specific computer simulation, I will discuss some exemplary aspects of this form of depiction. In the broadcast *Peter Jennings Reporting: The Kennedy Assassination – Beyond Conspiracy* (2003) for ABC News, a portion of the reconstruction *Secrets of a Homicide: JFK Assassination* by journalist and 3D artist Dale K. Myers was shown. This computer simulation served to investigate and illustrate the Kennedy assassination that took place on 22 November 1963 in Dallas, at Dealey Plaza.[32] The most important source for Myers' reconstruction of the events at Dealey Plaza was the film shot on regular 8mm by Abraham Zapruder, known as the 'Zapruder film'.[33]

As is usually the case, a variety of additional sources were applied, according to Dale K. Myers:

- A survey map of Dealey Plaza, prepared by Drommer & Associates for the House Select Committee on Assassinations in 1978, was used to plot the layout of the plaza in 3D space.
- Blueprints of the Texas School Book Depository, prepared by Burson, Hendricks & Walls for the Dallas County Depository restoration project in 1978, were the basis for the 3D model of the infamous warehouse.
- The original body draft of the modified 1961 Lincoln convertible, prepared by The Hess & Eisenhardt Company, served as a guide in modelling the presidential limousine.
- More than 500 personal photographs and measurements gathered by Myers during multiple trips to Dallas, Texas were utilized in the construction and placement of all fixed structures, including the records, Criminal Court and Dal-Tex Buildings. Contemporary photographs were studied in order to ensure that the model matched Dealey Plaza circa 1963.
- The model of the Texas School Book Depository was based on blueprints and took three months to create. Dallas Police Crime Lab photographs and local TV news film were used to position over 5000 boxes on the Depository's sixth floor.
- The presidential limousine began as a digitized model of a 1961 Lincoln convertible. The resulting computer model was then modified to match the dimensions of the presidential limousine's original body draft, provided by Hess and Eisenhardt. Details were created based on a multitude of photographs taken during the 1963 Dallas motorcade. Particular attention was paid to the seating arrangement as depicted in photographs taken by the Secret Service and FBI in the White House garage the night of 22 November 1963.
- Sculptor Mark Stuckey was commissioned to create life-size clay busts of President Kennedy and Governor John B. Connally. Rubber moulds and plaster castings were created from these sculptures.
- Once the virtual model of Dealey Plaza was completed, the process of recreating the path and motion of the presidential limousine and its occupants began, based on the Zapruder film and other evidence recorded during the event.[34]

All this information and source material was analyzed and selected to reconstruct the incident using the software LightWave 3D with modelling, texturing, animation, lighting and rendering. The rendering process allows the selective use of details and the omission of parts of the 3D geometry. Finally a commentary was added with an affirmative tone supplied by expressions such as 'exactly the way they were' or 'an accurate representation of exactly what happened.'

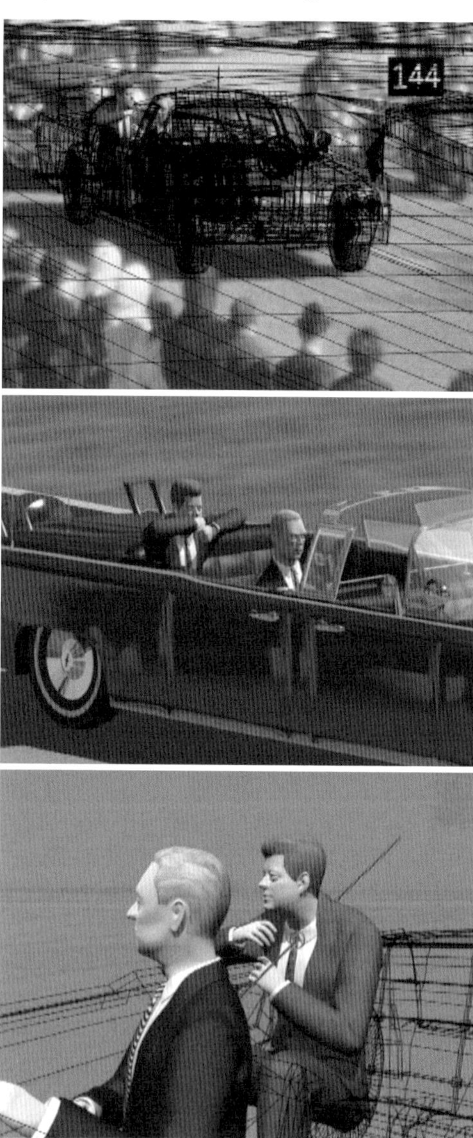

Figures 1–3: Stills from the computer simulation of the Kennedy assassination.

It is very interesting to compare this computer simulation to the Zapruder film. Abraham Zapruder's short film manifests a set of aesthetic features which are almost universal in this kind of documentation captured by a casual bystander. It consists of 486 frames[35] that unfold in one uninterrupted take of 26.56 seconds, at the original frame rate of 18.3 FPS; or, in other words, it captures the event as a *plan-séquence* or a long take which, as André Bazin argued in his essay 'The Evolution of the Language of Cinema' (1950),[36] enhances the impression of reality. Furthermore, Zapruder worked with a handheld camera, thus producing shaky images. In these shaky images both the excitement of the bystander and the close body-camera connection are present. They produce a lively, anthropomorphic view of the events, thus indicating the presence of an actual witness. Many images are blurred: an effect enhanced by the low-resolution of the regular 8mm stock. In fact, it is often difficult to discern clearly what was really happening in front of the camera. The blurriness, in conjunction with the low resolution, add to an aesthetics of the sensational which is often also found in paparazzi footage.[37] Finally, important and critical events occur behind a traffic sign or foliage or between individual frames, for example between frame 223 and 224 where – as Myers explains in the broadcast – Governor Connally's jacket pops open. In sum, although the Zapruder film has been used as a principle source of evidence not only for the computer simulation put under scrutiny here, but for the whole process of investigation, it actually hides and omits crucial information, a fact which is even more relevant given the absence of acoustic information in this film shot without sound.

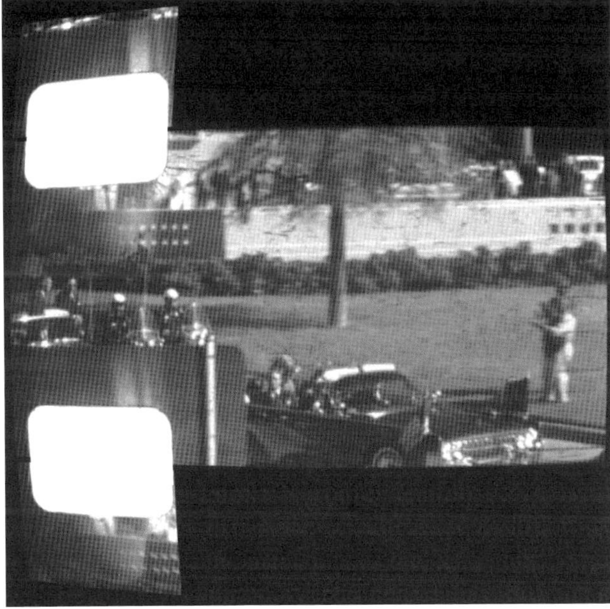

Figure 4: Frame 223 from the Zapruder film.

In contrast to the Zapruder film, one of the most remarkable properties of the computer simulation is the great flexibility with respect to the space-time coordinates of the event depicted. The virtual camera defies all the constraints of a physical camera, and offers multiple perspectives. A similar flexibility is also at work in the very selective use of details and their partial omission in the rendering process: for instance the car in the computer simulation, which is only indicated as a wire frame, and the addition of argumentative relationships like the arrow which shows the trajectory of the bullet.

Photorealism would be an option in principle, but while Myers claims his animation to be 'hauntingly realistic',[38] it operates – like most computer simulations – with a rather crude style of visualization. It also avoids integrating analogue artefacts like grain, depth of field or motion blur, which are an important part of photorealism.[39] The surface structures of the objects, the buildings and the landscape are greatly simplified. In sum, it aims to a greater or lesser degree at abstraction, and it exposes the origin of the images from the computer – a fact that has to be considered later.

At the core of the construction process of computer simulation is an interplay of analysis and synthesis. It thus mirrors on a macro-level what has been described as a characteristic of digital images on the micro-level of each pixel. As has been shown, a vast amount of information from different sources – photographs, maps, blueprints, films, etc. – has to be considered and evaluated before the reconstruction of the dispersed data can be carried out. According to Nelson Goodman (1978) these complementary strategies form part of our everyday cognitive activity in constructing our understanding of the world:

> Much but by no means all worldmaking consists of taking apart and putting together, often conjointly: on the one hand, of dividing wholes into parts and partitioning kinds into subspecies, analyzing complexes into component features, drawing distinctions; on the other hand, of composing wholes and kinds out of parts and members and subclasses, combining features into complexes, and making connections.[40]

Furthermore, a selection process that governs the combination of analysis and synthesis is necessary. We can consider this selection process as filtering and cleaning of the data with regard to the specific aims of computer simulation. While some data are suppressed or sorted out as irrelevant, others are emphasized. This selection process becomes instantly obvious in the above-mentioned image of the beam balance proposed by Boehm,[41] where only the weight of the two objects is selected as a criterion of reference. Such selection processes guide both our cognitive operations in perception, and any scientific observation and interpretation of data:

> And even within what we do perceive and remember, we dismiss as illusory or negligible what cannot be fitted into the architecture of the world we are building. The scientist is no less drastic, rejecting or purifying most of the entities and events of the world of ordinary things while generating quantities of filling for curves suggested by sparse data, and erecting elaborate structures on the basis of meager observations.[42]

Selection results in a more or less obvious level of abstraction, which appears to be cleansed of anything not necessary for the task to be accomplished. The key concept for the discussion of the range between abstraction and a fully photo-real depiction is resemblance. While 'resemblance' is a controversial concept in the theory of representation, it remains useful for the discussion of computer simulation. As Nelson Goodman, who questioned the concept vigorously, has pointed out, resemblance must always be put in relation to something, for example the weight in the beam balance metaphor.

In the case of the computer simulation of the Kennedy assassination, surely the most important frame of reference is the photographic image as depicted in the Zapruder film. In comparison with photographs, however, modelled images can cover a range from strong to weak resemblance. If these representations were purely abstract, they would need contextual support – be it a text, or a specified protocol that defines the relationship between the depiction and the objects depicted, as is the case with diagrams. For example, we could generate a computer simulation of the migration and evolution of a reindeer population, where each individual animal would be represented as a shiny dot on the screen. When such a high degree of abstraction is applied, additional – usually linguistic – information is necessary to explain the relationship between an object; for example, the reindeer and its representation, the dot. A similar case in point is the flu spreading simulation depicted in Figure 5.

In addition to the range of abstraction, photographs and computer simulations differ in regard to their connection with the objects and events depicted. While photographs – like

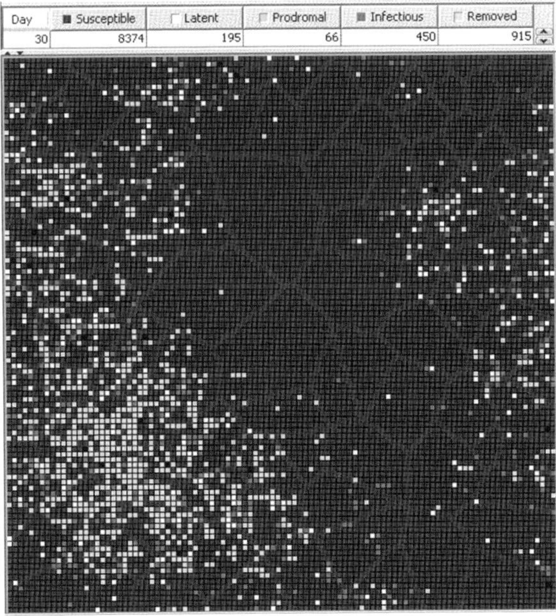

Figure 5: Flu spreading simulation.

all other forms of recording mentioned above – rely on their mechanical and physical connection to the scene in front of the camera, computer simulations often involve a myriad of distributed references – like the maps, photographs, blueprints, films and other sources in the case of the Dealey Plaza simulation. Regardless of whether the resemblance is weak or strong, then, the relationship between the objects and their representation is highly mediated. It ranges from a mediated iconicity in the case where we recognize the objects, to a symbolic relationship in the case of pure abstraction. Thus computer simulation is very autonomous vis-à-vis the depicted world. It is marked by an obvious loss of details; it is – one could say – purified of the complexity of the real world. It presents generic information rather than particulars. It expresses more an understanding of the world and its underlying principles than a pictorial representation of actual things or events: 'Any definable range of phenomena including definable characteristics of human psychology or social relationships can be given values und be mapped into a virtual, multidimensional space.'[43] But even the most abstract representation needs an anchoring in mental schemes to communicate something and not be perceived as mere patterns. As early as 1968, the computer and Internet pioneer J. C. R. Licklider described this relationship between technical principles and cognitive operations in communication:

> [...] Modelling, we believe, is basic and central to communication. Any communication between people about the same thing is a common revelatory experience about informational models of that thing. Each model is a conceptual structure of abstractions formulated initially in the mind of one of the persons who would communicate, and if the concepts in the mind of one would-be communicator are very different from those in the mind of another, there is no common model and no communication.[44]

Following Mitchell, the autonomy of CGI has been compared to paintings or written texts. But while paintings are highly subjective interpretations of actual or imagined phenomena, computer simulations rely on a formalized and rule-based description that materializes not as written texts, but as images. It has become clear that these images differ profoundly from paintings when one considers both the construction process and its results.

Like film, computer simulation offers multiple perspectives. In contrast to film, however, these multiple perspectives cover the whole range of space-time coordinates present in the constructed scene. Space and time therefore become navigable dimensions. In this respect computer simulation possesses the flexibility of cognitive operations with random access to any point in the space-time system. While in film the space-time representation consolidates as a definite trajectory, in computer simulation it remains potentially fluid – as is most evident in the real-time rendering of video games. In other words, the space-time system remains open as a field of potentialities that may or may not materialize as animation.

Surely the most important aspect of computer simulation is its potential to transcend both the scope of human perception, and of recording by a technical apparatus. It thus allows us to observe the unobservable, something that lies beyond direct access to the senses whether because of time constraints – an event can have happened in the past or might be projected into the future – or because of constraints in scale, be it that the scale is too small or too big to be grasped by human perception or by traditional systems of image recording.

Notes

1   This paper presents some findings of my research project 'Analog/Digital: Hybrid Forms of Cinematic Representation' that was funded by a grant from the Swiss National Science Foundation and published as *Visual Effects. Filmbilder aus dem Computer*, Marburg: Schüren, 2008.
2   William John Mitchell, *The Reconfigured Eye: Visual Truth in the Post-Photographic Era*, Cambridge, MA: MIT Press, 1992, p. 4.
3   ibid., p. 31.
4   Christian Metz, *Langage et Cinéma*, Paris: Larousse, 1971, p. 181.
5   ibid., p. 187.
6   Friedrich A. Kittler, *Computergraphik. Eine halbtechnische Einführung*, 1998, http://hydra. humanities.uci.edu/kittler/graphik.html, accessed 29 June 2012.
7   Cf. Flueckiger, 2008.
8   Mitchell, 1992, p. 4.
9   Mark J. P. Wolf, *Abstracting Reality: Art, Communication, and Cognition in the Digital Age*, Lanham, MD: University Press of America, 2000, p. 31.
10   Nelson Goodman, *Languages of Art*, Indianapolis: Hackett Publishing Company, 1976, p. 161.
11   Eleanor Rosch, 'Natural Categories', in Noel Sheehy and Anthony J. Chapman (eds), *Cognitive Science*, Aldershot: Edward Elgar, 1973; Norbert Elias, *Time: An Essay* (trans. by Edmund Jephcott), Oxford: Blackwell, 1992.
12   Malcolm Le Grice, 'Digital Cinema and Experimental Film', in Yvonne Spielmann and Gundolf Winter (eds), *Bild – Medium – Kunst*, München: Wilhelm Fink Verlag, 1999, p. 2010.
13   Wolf, 2000, pp. 15–16.
14   Vilém Flusser, 'Crisis of Linearity' (trans. Adelheid Mers), in *Boot Print*, Vol. 1, 2006, pp. 19–21, http://bootscontemporaryartspace.org/blog/bootprint/, accessed 1 October 2012.
15   For a more detailed investigation on Flusser's analysis and the impact of non-linearity in digital culture, see Barbara Flueckiger, 'iPhone Apps. A Digital Culture of Interactivity', in Pelle Snickars and Patrick Vonderau (eds), *Moving Data: The iPhone and the Future of Media*, New York: Columbia University Press, 2012.
16   Flueckiger, 2008, p. 70ff.
17   ibid., p. 164ff.
18   ibid., p. 417ff.
19   The German term *Modellbildung* (literal meaning: 'model building') is more accurate than modelling, because the technical process of modelling may include painting and recording, which are distinct in the system proposed here.

20   Flueckiger, 2008, p. 131ff.

21   ibid., p. 65ff.

22   ibid., p. 101ff.

23   Barbara Flueckiger, 'Städtebilder aus dem Computer', in *Cinema*, No. 54, 2009.

24   Paul Humphreys, *Extending Ourselves: Computational Science, Empiricism, and Scientific Method*, Oxford: Oxford University Press, 2004, p. 104ff.

25   Norbert Wiener (1948) cited in Bernhard J. Dotzler, 'Simulation', in Karl-Heinz Barck et al. (eds), *Ästhetische Grundbegriffe. Historisches Wörterbuch in sieben Bänden*, Stuttgart: J. B. Metzler, 2003; Humphreys, 2004; Stephan Hartmann, *The World as a Process: Simulations in the Natural and Social Sciences*, 2005, http://philsci-archive.pitt.edu/archive/00002412/, accessed 5 June 2009.

26   Gottfried Boehm, *Die Macht des Zeigens. Wie Bilder Sinn erzeugen*, Berlin: Berlin University Press, 2007, p. 135.

27   ibid., pp. 135–36.

28   Cf. Flueckiger, 2008, p. 279.

29   Cf. Jean Baudrillard, 'Simulations' (trans. Paul Foss, Paul Patton and Philip Beitschman), New York: Semiotext(e), 1983; Humphreys, 2004.

30   Hartmann, 2005, p. 6.

31   Wolf, 2000, p. 262.

32   Information from Dale K. Myers related to the construction of the computer simulation can be found on the *JFK Files* website, http://www.jfkfiles.com/, accessed 3 June 2009. The broadcast is available on YouTube: http://www.youtube.com/watch?v=DSBXW1-VGmM, accessed 29 June 2012, or on DVD.

33   The Zapruder film is available on YouTube: http://youtu.be/1q91RZko5Gw (a version that includes out-of-frame area between the sprocket holes), accessed 29 June 2012.

34   Cf. http://www.jfkfiles.com/, accessed 3 June 2009.

35   The individual frames are available as magnifications on http://www.assassinationresearch. com/v2n2/zfilm/zframe001.html, accessed 3 June 2009. This is also the source of the illustrations of this text.

36   André Bazin, 'The Evolution of the Language of Cinema', in *What is Cinema?*, Berkeley & Los Angeles: University of California Press, 2005, pp. 23–41.

37   Cf. Wolfgang Ullrich, *Die Geschichte der Unschärfe*, Berlin: Klaus Wagenbach, 2002, p. 90.

38   Dale K. Myers, http://www.jfkfiles.com/jfk/html/models.htm, accessed 11 July 2009.

39   Cf. Flueckiger, 2008, p. 334ff.

40   Goodman, 1976, p. 7.

41   Boehm, 2007, pp. 135–36.

42   Goodman, 1976, p. 15.

43   Malcolm Le Grice, *Experimental Cinema in the Digital Age*, London: BFI, 2001, p. 284.

44   J. C. R. Licklider and Robert W. Taylor, 'The Computer as a Communication Device', in *Science and Technology*, April 1968, p. 22.

Chapter 5

Enfolding-Unfolding Aesthetics, or the Unthought at the Heart of Wood

Laura U. Marks

Imagine the realm of images that populates our world as a vast, variegated surface, containing everything: holiday snapshots, action movies, medical images, pictures of the surface of Jupiter, everything. This field contains sounds and smells and other perceptible, too, from chairs to music to the scent of vanilla, but let's bracket them out for now. Imagine that this field surrounds you like a bubble, translucent, and you are looking out through it. You look through the field of images to their sources, distant in time and space: the holiday afternoon, the movie set, the ultrasound of your internal organs (also distant in a certain way), the planet Jupiter. You realize that this source is infinitely vaster than the field of images that arose from it.

But some of the images do not come to you directly from the source. They seem to get twisted or caught on the way 'in' to your perception, for they reflect not a perceptible experience, but a calculation, a procedure. For example, the camera that took the snapshot was digital, and so the visible scene at the source has been assigned pixel values in order to be expressed as a snapshot. The action movie was shot against a blue screen and keyed in to a digital background; its star was chosen on the basis of a calculation of her audience appeal. The ultrasound consists of a translation of sound waves into visual information. The picture of Jupiter is an artist's rendering based on astronomical data. These calculations constitute an intervening layer between the world and the images that convey it to us. I am going to call that layer information.[1] Beyond it lies the infinite.

What is the infinite? Well, 'infinite' is a negative term: the not-finite; and most definitions of it are negative: limitless, boundless, uncountable, inconceivable. We cannot conceive of the infinite except as the ground from which we distinguish certain figures – or, the noise from which we receive certain signals.

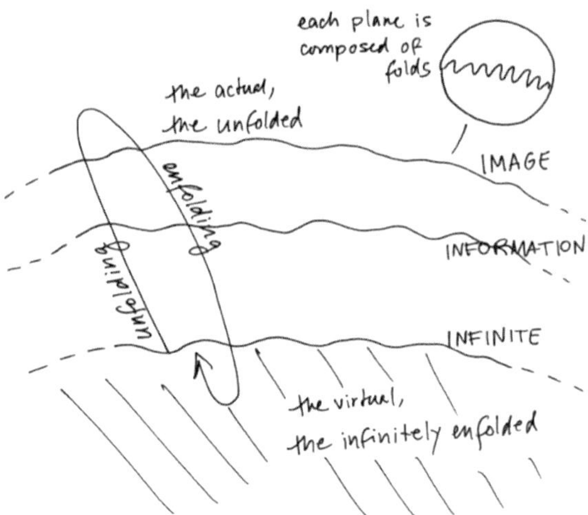

Figure 1: Enfolding-unfolding aesthetics. Diagram by Laura Marks.

But also I like to think of the infinite as constituted of innumerable folds; and when we perceive something, we unfold some small part of the infinite. Every perception is an unfolding.

Enfolding-Unfolding Aesthetics

An aesthetic, in its simplest and most old-fashioned guise, is simply an account of how we engage with the perceptible world. Baumgarten wrote in 1750 that aesthetics is the 'science of sensuous cognition'.[2] Enfolding-unfolding aesthetics deals with the coming and going of perceptibles, a kind of recycling or conservation of mass. It answers the question: where do images come from? Where do they go? By 'image' I mean not only the visible, but all that is perceptible: visual, audible, tactile, olfactory, etc. When I suggested this idea to artist/scholar Susan Schuppli, she grasped it instantly: 'I love the idea of a cosmic composite heap that is in active state of remolecularizing itself to create images yet-to-come.'

Enfolding-unfolding aesthetics starts from Deleuze's investigation, in the cinema books, into how certain images arise to us (or to the more disinterested perception of the cinema), by being selected from the infinite. Images that unfold directly from the infinite include our own perceptions, as well as things like photographs, brushstrokes and iconic images.[3] Each line in the diagram represents a plane of immanence.

My intervention in Deleuze's theory of signs is to insert another image-plane between images and the infinite, namely information: a plane through which the semiotic process passes before images can arise. This information layer is most evident in digital and other quantified media, where there is a layer of code underlying the perceptibles we see, hear and touch – like the holiday snapshot I mentioned earlier. But it is also evident in anything industrially produced, anything whose physical being is the result of research that has been quantified. Gregory Bateson famously defined information as 'the difference that makes a difference'; that is, a meaningful organization of noise into a signal.[4] In information theory, those aspects of the infinite that do not interest us – that is, almost all of it – are 'noise'.

Note that unfolding requires a certain force, a desire to bring something into actuality. Some things resist unfolding. To emphasize that resistance – and that images are the manifest, outer layer of a deeply enfolded source – I introduce two terms used in Islamic thought, principally in Shi'ism and Sufism, to describe manifest and latent states: *zâhir* and *bâtin*. 'Zâhir' implies outer forms, a surface, that which is manifest and explicit; it is used to describe the meanings of the Qur'an that are available to all. 'Bâtin' signifies enfoldedness, and the deeper, implicit meanings that may potentially be explicated. In enfolding-unfolding aesthetics, images are relatively *zâhir*, or manifest; the infinite is relatively *bâtin*, or latent; and information has both qualities. As an imam can reach into the words of the Qur'an and unfold latent meanings (some Muslims believe), so we can reach into an image and unfold, bring out onto the surface, some of its latent contents.

Information thus organizes noise into something considered meaningful. Information is a quantitative unfolding from the infinite that precedes our perception. Information is what has been selected from the infinite as valuable and unfolded. The rest (so, almost everything) remains enfolded. In turn, what we finally perceive with our senses, in many cases, is unfolded from information. In our society, much of what we deal with first-hand has already been encoded as information. When you drink Starbucks coffee, you're drinking information. When you smell Chanel or Bounce Dryer Sheets on a passer-by, you are smelling information. When you sit in a moulded plywood Eames chair (or a copy of one), you're sitting on information.

Enfolding-unfolding aesthetics is useful for critical thinking: what is deemed useful information, what is forgotten as mere matter? What continues to be taken up, to generate new signs as it circulates? Enfolding-unfolding aesthetics is useful for thinking about art, in particular, because it helps us observe how artworks select certain elements to unfold (from the infinite or information), or will certain elements to remain latent. A triadic aesthetics, it informs the way an artwork makes a viewer/participant aware of the relationships between the image/object and information, and between information and the world, or it obscures those relationships. And enfolding-unfolding aesthetics emphasizes that, even in this world so oversaturated with images, it is still a creative struggle to pull images into being.

Things are Hardened Information

Sometimes it seems our universe consists entirely of the smooth, designed, commodified surfaces of information-based media. This is especially so for people who live in urban and suburban environments in the post-industrial world. It seems we are trapped in a world not of our invention.

However, remember that the information level is not the fundamental source of images. It is a filter. It forms an interface to something else: the world in which programmers write code, artworks are dreamed up, coffee is picked and roasted, perfumes are distilled, profits are reaped or lost – and infinitely more. This world is what I call the infinite. In enfolding-unfolding aesthetics, image is an interface or filter to information, and information is an interface, or filter, to the infinite. To figure out where an image comes from, we need to find out how it arose from the infinite; and, often, we need to find out how it arose from information, too – information that itself arose from the infinite.

I like to use the most material examples here. Certainly we can consider the ways in which images are encoded, or the news is encoded, or the stock market encodes material processes. The latter is an example of information that is dense with meaning yet yields almost nothing in the way of image. But let's think about how socks are encoded. A sock is quite material. If you knit the sock yourself, the sock is the direct actualization of a virtuality that starts with you: the time spent knitting, the source of the wool, the factory where the wool was spun…an ever-expanding field of virtualities whose actual outcome is your home-made sock. Most of us buy our socks in a store, though. And here we confront the paradox that socks are made of information. In its colour, texture, pattern and packaging, a sock encodes branding and market research. Logos are images that encode information quite densely, for they embody thousands of hours and millions of dollars of research: the Calvin Klein logo, for example. On the diagram on page 152, you can see that socks are an 'image of information', which in turn draws on cotton, wool, elastic, machines, labour, factories, marketing, etc. – an infinite number of variables: from infinite, to information, to image.

So now you are looking at my Calvin Klein socks. You can kind of perceive the relationship between image – the logo, colour, and trendy stripes – and information, right? Do they look

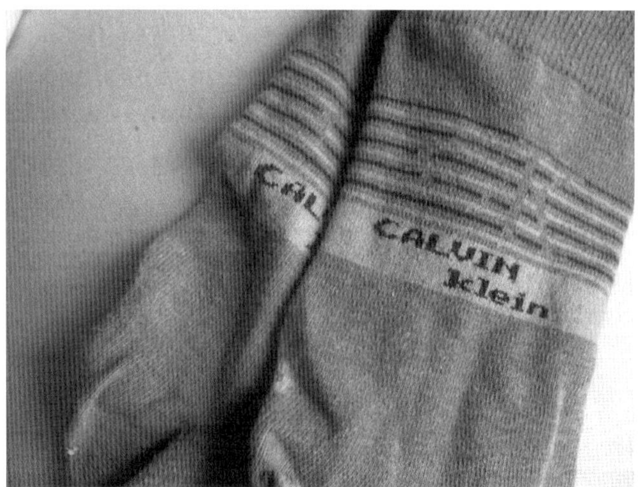

Figure 2: Calvin Klein socks. Photograph by Laura Marks.

a little off? Yes. The socks are knock-offs, made in Syria. The colours are not quite right, the knit type looks wonky, and inside there is tight, uncomfortable elastic. Also, they have holes in them. If the real Calvin Klein sock was the source image, then it is an image that has rolled back around into the infinite, and a new image or sign has been produced from it. Somebody carried it in their suitcase to Damascus. The Syrian knock-off factory (which also makes shirts with a Calvin Klein logo and a Nike swoosh) modelled a new sock on it. But their equipment is not perfect, and also the knock-off designers had ideas about beauty and rightness: these circumstances are all part of the infinite from which the new, knock-off sock arose.

I bought the socks and wore them for years and now they are slowly returning to the infinite, and eventually they will be decomposing in a landfill. Another cycle around the diagram.

The Virtual, the Unthought at the Heart of Wood

Ultimately, the enfolded model of the image does not distinguish between material and immaterial. All of these levels – image, information and infinite – are real, in Deleuze's sense that the real encompasses the virtual and the actual. The actual is what exists – a thing, an event or a concept. The virtual is that which conditions the emergence of the actual. The virtual is the truly infinite ground against which the fewest actual entities emerge. It consists of all that cannot presently be thought; it is an asymptote for thought: 'the powerlessness at the heart of thought.'

Most materiality is virtual, too. Things exist physically while remaining mostly virtual. As Elizabeth Grosz writes, philosophers who are sympathetic to matter (i.e. don't see it as something to dominate), such as Bergson, (Peirce,) Henry James and Deleuze, argue that we 'carve out' things in experience. So most of what exists in the world does not exist as things for us. Simple experiments bear this out. Other people's experience is mostly virtual to us. But there are ways we can make their experience more actual for ourselves if we want to. The Calvin Klein sock is real, but the machine on which it was knit is an inaccessible part of the machinic phylum, thus in some way virtual, as far as we're concerned; its molecular structure is similarly virtual; the tightness of the elastic is virtual to you, but not to me.

I have suggested that the infinite can also be considered the Earth.[5] Materially, the Earth is what precedes all things and to which all things return. The objects that cycle through our lives return to the Earth in a literal sense. Thinking of the Earth as the virtual is compatible with Bergson's concept of the virtual, for Bergson argued that matter is composed by duration – the way it persists, decays, and transforms: 'Matter is [...] an infinitely dilated past.'[6] And it helps us consider that the virtual lies in matter.

Materialistically, we could call the virtual 'thought's powerlessness at the heart of wood.' In fact, this is an ancient idea. Since the ancient Greeks philosophers have used wood as the ideal of something means little in itself, but is full of potentiality. The tenth-century Shi'ite theologian Abu Yaq'ub al-Sijistâni argued that the Qur'anic revelation

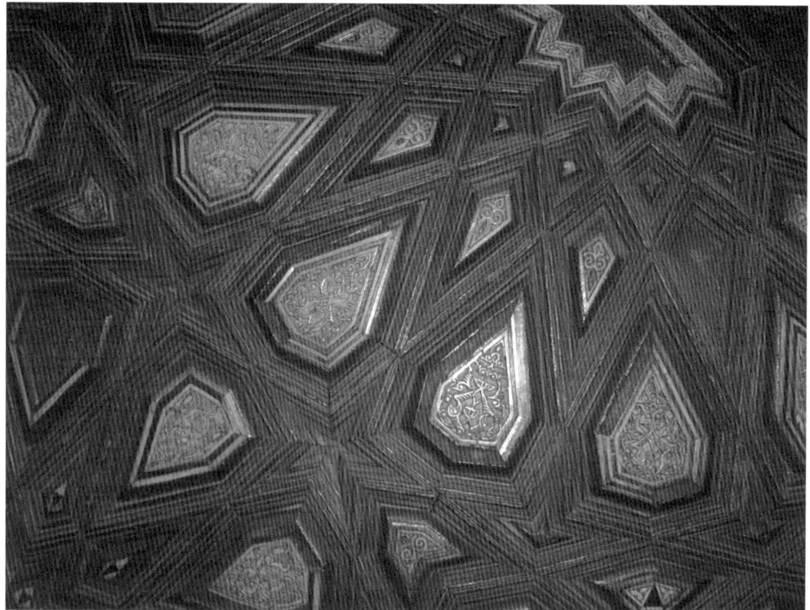

Figure 3: Detail of minibar for Sultan Qaitbay (1468–96), of cedar with ivory and wood inlay. Victoria and Albert Museum. Photograph by Laura Marks.

required interpretation, comparing it to wood that must be worked in order to be made into something useful.[7] St. Thomas Aquinas wrote that a piece of wood was a finite form containing infinite potential, in that an infinite number of forms could be potentially carved from it.

This detail of the minbar of Sultan Qaitbay mosque suggests the infinity internal to wood. It also indicates the cooperation between the carver's ideas about form and the wood's material. So, again, my notion of materiality is not exactly Marxist materialism, but closer to Deleuze and Guattari's characterization of the *machinic phylum*[8] as that material that, like the grain of wood, guides the artisan to invent and to come up with thoughts that she would not have had in the absence of this obdurate, densely enfolded material.

Bergson, in *Creative Evolution* (1998), pointed out that, far from being the rational masters who should dominate dumb creatures, we humans are more similar to animals and plants than we are different from them. He wrote: 'Our intellect [...] is intended to secure the perfect fitting of our body to its environment, to represent the relations of external things among themselves – in short, to think matter.'[9] We humans are not so different from the things we think about, and that is why we are able to think (alongside) them. That's why we can anticipate their reactions: from massaging a dog based on where you think it might ache, to sectioning the muscles of a slaughtered animal, to responding mimetically to a potato plant infested with bugs, and calling on our plant nature to find a way to cure it. (Though if we responded mimetically to the bugs we would behave differently.) This response to the world, according to Bergson, is instinct: what we have in common with animals and plants.[10] So, when we get in touch with the heart of wood, we are using our instinct to call on our internal cellulose-like nature.

Most philosophy privileges what actually exists, and who can blame it? However, Deleuze and Guattari emphasized again and again, using many different metaphors, that the relevant category is not Being – what exists, but Becoming – what changes.[11] This can be traced to the influence of Bergson, and Bergson's emphasis that all things change in duration, become something else, evolve in unforeseen ways. The moment of becoming is what fascinated Deleuze and Guattari, so they were interested in phenomena just when they are getting started: like the 'free marks'[12] with which Francis Bacon began a painting in order to ward off clichés. These are all moments where the virtual becomes actual; where something entirely new comes into the world. For these thinkers, the virtual is the engine of change, and of life itself. Hence the paradox of privileging the virtual, or what does not actually exist, over the actual.

Now the question is: what is the difference between virtual immaterialities, such as potential concepts, and a materiality that is also somehow virtual in that it is inaccessible, inconceivable to us? What is virtual and yet material? Deleuze and Guattari deal with these in various ways. In *A Thousand Plateaus* (1987) and *Cinema 1 – The Movement-Image* (1983), the monism of Bergson permits a material definition of the universe: the plane of immanence is 'flowing-matter', adding Peirce's concept that the universe is composed of signs, flowing-signs. However, these are fairly dematerialized ideas of matter: Bergson's universe is composed of light, Peirce's signs are ultimately composed in the mind.

Deleuze and Guattari's concept of the *machinic phylum* dignifies matter by recognizing that it too is infinite, and thus in a way virtual. The machinic phylum is 'the flow of matter in continuous variation [this is Bergson], conveying singularities and traits of expression.' It is 'a destratified, deterritorialized matter': matter that is not yet formed.[13] Certain aspects of this flowing-matter are taken up by humans (I will say for now, though want to keep open to other agents) as an *assemblage,* 'a constellation of singularities […] deducted from the flow – selected, organized, stratified – [....].'[14] All human culture is assemblage, invention: identifying aspects of the machinic phylum to take up, refine, discover, invent: metal, wood, clay, plants, electrons.

Here is the heart of wood of my title. Matter, Deleuze and Guattari write, is 'an entire energetic materiality in movement, carrying *singularities* or *haecceities* that […] combine with the forces of deformation: for example, the variable undulations and torsions of the fibers guiding the operation of splitting wood.'[15] Plus variable intensive effects, e.g. the wood's porosity, resistance: 'At any rate, it is a question of surrendering to the wood, then following where it leads.'[16]

So the radical materiality of the machinic phylum is the unthought at the heart of wood. When we think about where images come from, I want us to be thinking about the virtual, the infinite, and also something so physically real that it is utterly unknowable to us.

What happens when we impose laws on matter; for example, in computer-aided design? Deleuze and Guattari write:

> One may link the materiality's power of variation to laws adapting a fixed form and a constant matter to one another. But this cannot be done without a distortion that consists in uprooting variables from the state of continuous variation, in order to extract from them fixed points and constant relations.[17]

Matter is forced to act like an idea and loses its singularity and internal energy. So a question for genetic modification, AL algorithms, and additive manufacturing or 3D printing is: do they impose form on matter or go within matter and let matter inform them? When calculations are imposed on matter, how does matter resist and contribute?[18]

Connective Tissue: The Virtue of Mediation

Now I draw your attention in the diagram to the way images cycle from infinite, to (the optional step of) information, to image, and then back to infinite. We can look at the life cycle of an image in terms of how many times it cycles around, changing as it goes. This process is very much like Peirce's semiotic process, whereby signs necessarily mutate as they circulate; they still reference their source, but it becomes more and more distant. The most interesting kinds of image are those that bear the traces of their own unfolding.

This cycling is what we usually call mediation. For example, here's a still from DVD of *Christ Stopped at Eboli* (Francesco Rosi, 1979), based on the 1945 book by Carlo Levi.

The image we see is the most recent iteration of a life cycle that has taken several turns around the diagram. A 35mm film (adaptation of book); subtitled in English; transferred to DVD (with unsettling Doppler effect in sound); a scratch on one frame of the film; that

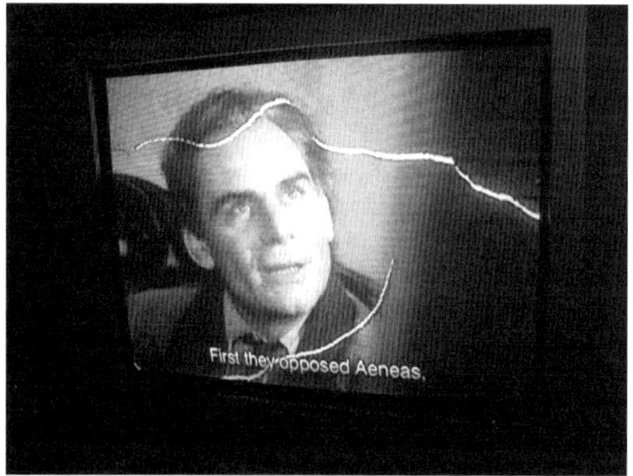

Figure 4: Still from DVD of Francesco Rosi, *Christ Stopped At Eboli*, 1979.

scratch, translated into digital scratch, becomes an entirely new shape. While all these new turns block our access to the original text, they thicken the mediating space, allowing the material history of the image to speak.

Obviously, there is only so far that we can go in celebrating decay before image gives way entirely to noise; returns to an entirely undifferentiated state; dies. I have celebrated decaying images a lot in my work, but obviously this can be a rather romantic and defeatist gesture. Nevertheless, it is also exciting and productive to consider mediation as the life cycle of the image. Thinking of mediation as thickening allows us to consider it not a block between us and the source, but as a new source.

Thus, I argue that mediation is not a block to the infinite but a fold between the infinite and our perception. Many scholars argue that digital media are independent of technology, because their foundation is a non-physical array of numbers of signals. But as you know this is not true, for every digital medium rests on an analogue base. In practice, digital media are always and entirely physical. Those numbers, or on-off impulses, are usually carried by electrons, which are as physical as can be and rife with unpredictable effects. Data compression, software conventions, software mistakes, hardware qualities, transmission properties, all of these processes are entirely physical and historical properties of digital media. And the remote servers that hold all our data, giant warehouses in the desert, account for 2 per cent of the world's energy use. That's a lot of coal powering our non-physical media. All these real phenomena leave their traces on the image. The great thing is the image itself sometimes allows us to detect them.

Mediation does not destroy 'nature' but is part of it; it is an extra set of folds, a surface complication, codifying and altering nature, and contributing its own materiality.

Images constitute a connective tissue between their perceivers and their source. Mediation connects us even further – to the image and to the human actions that modified it. I am suggesting, in the exact opposite of Baudrillard's argument about the simulacrum, that the more images circulate, the realer they get. Peirce argued that a sign becomes stronger as it 'spreads among the peoples.'[19] The more an image is seen, passed on, commented upon, even parodied, the more it exists (the more times it spins around the diagram). So-called 'viral media' exult in the endless reproduction of images. How much an image has circulated – for example, how many times a video has been viewed on YouTube – becomes part of the image, the thick folds of the information layer. Where an image has circulated constitutes its information folds.

In June 2009, following Ahmadinejad's re-election, Iranians posted hundreds of videos and photographs of demonstrations to YouTube. They may be small files, but they are dense with reality. In fact these cell-phone photographs' 'pixelly' look, as well as the blurring and shaking of the camera, attested to the fact that they have had to be pulled from the source event, with strong will and against strong resistance – pulled through information in order to reach existence as image. The Iranian demonstration videos asked us viewers, in turn, to make our eyes and ears bear witness, and feel that we are part of a chain of witnessing. Since March 2011, Syrians have been uploading videos that document government attacks on civilians. These images also witness their own struggle to be born and make strong demands on viewers. In talking about where images come from, in desiring to know their source and how they got the way they are, we strengthen their bond with their object – with, in this case, clear political effects.

The creative struggle to pull images into being creates thick folds in the connective tissue between the beholder and the beheld, between us and the infinite. I would also include the agency of non-human perception, and also non-animal, organic perception, and even the perception of non-organic entities. For, of course, there are always plenty of beings to 'hear' when a tree falls in the forest.

All this is to emphasize the thickness of communication among entities of all sorts. And the purpose of that is to underscore how important it is that we perceptually unfold the most pressing and meaningful parts of the world to respond to. Rather than what has been unfolded for us.

Notes

1   This initial explanation and some following points also appear in Laura U. Marks, 'Noise in Enfolding-Unfolding Aesthetics', in Amy Herzog, John Richardson and Carol Vernallis (eds), *The Oxford Handbook of Sound and Image in Digital Media*, Oxford: Oxford University Press, 2013.

2   Wolfgang Welsch, 'Aesthetics Beyond Aesthetics', in Francis Halsall, Julia Jansen and Tony O'Connor (eds), *Rediscovering Aesthetics: Transdisciplinary Voices from Art History, Philosophy, and Art Practice*, Stanford: Stanford University Press, 2009, p. 178.

3   Though the latter, insofar as they are conventional images, are relayed through information. I discuss this kind of image in 'Experience – Information – Image: A historiography of unfolding. Arab cinema as example', in *Cultural Studies Review*, Vol. 16, No. 1, March 2007, pp. 85–98; 'Enfolding and Unfolding: An Aesthetics for the Information Age', an interactive essay produced in collaboration with designer Raegan Kelly, in *Vectors: Journal of Culture and Technology in a Dynamic Vernacular*, Vol. 1, No. 3, 2006, http://vectors.usc.edu/projects/index.php?project=72, accessed 30 September 2012; and 'Invisible Media', in Anna Everett and John T. Caldwell (eds), *New Media: Theories and Practices of Digitextuality*, New York: Routledge, 2003 pp. 33–46.

4   Gregory Bateson, *Steps to an Ecology of Mind: Collected Essays in Anthropology, Psychiatry, Evolution, and Epistemology*, Chicago: University of Chicago Press, 1972, p. 315.

5   Cf. Laura U. Marks, 'Information, Secrets, and Enigmas: An Enfolding-Unfolding Aesthetics for Cinema', in *Screen*, Vol. 50, No. 1, Spring 2009, pp. 86–98.

6   Gilles Deleuze, 'Bergson, 1859–1941', in David Lapoujade (ed.), *Desert Islands and Other Texts*, New York: Semiotext(e), 2004, p. 31. It also helps consider that what was once conceivable becomes inconceivable.

7   Paul E. Walker, *Early Philosophical Shiism: The Ismaili Neoplatonism of Abû Ya'qûb al Sijistânî*, Cambridge: Cambridge University Press, 1993, p. 27.

8 Gilles Deleuze and Félix Guattari, *A Thousand Plateaus: Capitalism and Schizophrenia* (trans. Brian Massumi), Minneapolis: University of Minnesota Press, 1987, p. 409.

9 Henri Bergson, *Creative Evolution* (trans. Arthur Mitchell), Mineola, NY: Dover, [1911] 1998, p. ix.

10 ibid., pp. 182–87.

11 Becoming was already a subject for the ancient Greek philosophers. Plato privileged Being, and all idealisms tend toward it. But Being is too easily set against Nothingness, and establishes the fiction of identity and the reactive category of resemblance. Cf. Deleuze, 2004.

12 Gilles Deleuze, *Francis Bacon: The Logic of Sensation,* (trans. Daniel W. Smith), London & New York: Continuum, 2003, p. 66.

13 Deleuze and Guattari, 1987, p. 407.

14 ibid., p. 448.

15 ibid., pp. 408–09.

16 ibid.

17 ibid., p. 408.

18 I hazard an answer in Laura U. Marks, 'Thinking like a Carpet: Embodied Perception and Individuation in Algorithmic Media', *Deautomatization,* ed. Annette Brauerhoch Paderborn: University of Paderborn Press, 2013.

19 C. S. Peirce, 'The Nature of Symbols', in *The Collected Papers of Charles Sanders Peirce,* Volume 2 'Elements of Logic', Book 2 'Speculative Grammar', Chapter 3, 'The Icon, Index, and Symbol', Cambridge, Massachusetts: Harvard University Press, 1931–1958.

PART II

Fugitive Images and Transmediality

Chapter 6

Animated and Animating Landscapes: Space Voyages and Time Travel in the Art of Pieter Bruegel the Elder

Martin Schulz

This first large painting of a winter landscape in European art is at the same time the most influential and best known of its genre. Few other paintings are more popular and have been reproduced more often than *The Hunters in the Snow* by Pieter Bruegel the Elder, which he painted in 1565 as part of the cycle of the 'Seasons', as it is called today (Figure 1). By now this painting's motif can be found on innumerable T-shirts, handbags, postcards and calendar pages, as well as in the form of countless art prints in waiting areas and children's books. At the same time, the tremendous spatial effect of its landscape – where a fairy-tale microcosm is unfolding – is of a peerless quality. Although the painting is not in a very good condition, and its colours, through which the support can be seen in places, were applied very thinly with a nearly dry brush via a very rapid painting technique, the disappointment of the observers, who up to then knew the picture only through its glowingly colourful reproductions, is held in check.

But while this painting is familiar to the collective memory of images – and this is decidedly no longer limited to European memory – its interpretations still remain contradictory and open.[1] The circumstance that we do not know many facts about the life of Pieter Bruegel, who was born between 1526 and 1530 in Belgian Brabant, and verifiably died 1569 in Brussels, further contributes to this.[2] Without question he was counted among the most coveted artists of his time. The cliché of the 'bucolic Bruegel' has long been revised. He may have left some representations of peasants and paintings of rural motives,[3] although he lived and worked in Antwerp and Brussels, wealthy metropolises of trade and art at the time, and counted the best-known humanists of his country among his friends – first and foremost Abraham Ortelius, *the* exceptional cosmographer of the sixteenth century; but was he himself, in his function as a visual artist, a stoic humanist? A Catholic or a reformer? A detractor of the Spanish occupation?

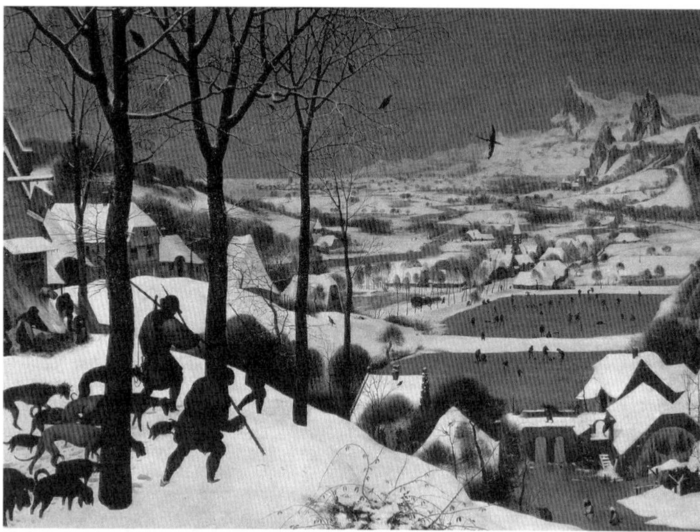

Figure 1: Pieter Bruegel the Elder, *Hunters in the Snow*, 117 x 162 cm, Vienna, Museum of Art History, 1565 © Kunsthistorisches Museum Wien.

Was he a *pictor christianus*, who painted a Bible-abiding, ironic as well as paradoxical – and thus multiply 'readable' – aesthetic of the folksy, low, grotesque, simple and ugly in opposition to the classical canon and its ideal of beauty? Or was he rather a spiritualist and a dissenter, who had to encrypt his heretical messages in a very particular way? Was he, as he came to be characterized quite early in a eulogy by Lampsonius in 1594, a 'second Hieronymus Bosch reborn', who did not care much, if at all, for the aesthetic standards of the Italian Renaissance, and invented his own world of images instead?[4] Or must he be understood as one of the first modern landscape artists, as the co-inventor of a completely new art form?

Many of these questions will be dealt with as hypotheses in this essay; and this is not only concerning an iconographical and functional sense, as the change from the religious image to the more or less profane artistic image, not least from an image that is understandable in an objective sense to an image of subjective mood, can be observed here in a critical phase. In an 'intermedial' passage that transcends the respective media, an animation and translation of images can be traced. In the case of Bruegel's winter painting, as I will have to show below, the image's passage runs from illumination via drawing to panel painting and finally, in a long leap ahead, to the immersive possibilities of film. Its particular technique and logic succeed in translating the intrinsic movements of the ultimately static painting into a medium of the moving image, as well as the desire of the observers, which is linked to the pictorial technique of immersion. The transgressive art of moving images is already present in Bruegel's landscape and thus appears, carefully put, as a pre-cinematic quality. In addition, this painting also exists within the continuum of a voyage through time, which is inspired less by motifs, but rather by the fascination of the imaginary space of the landscape and the immersion of the gaze: a travel through time and space from the depictions of the months in a book of hours up to the cinematic adaptation and transformation of the painting, as it was accomplished by Andrei Tarkovsky in his film *Solaris* (1972). This leads to a crystalline compression consolidation of space and time, in which past and present, actual and virtual space, material and mental images, painting and film and, not least, technology and desire permeate and determine each other.

I.

Bruegel's painting was created in the southern Netherlands, which were suffering under the oppressive rule of Spain; shortly before the start of the devastating Calvinist iconoclasms in the north and not long before the Dutch struggle for liberation, which would last eighty years and consist of countless military operations and their victims; during the cruel peak of the inquisition with its mass executions; and, finally, during a time of exceptionally cold winters, a period lasting from about 1560 into the eighteenth century, which is actually compared to a 'little ice age' today and, as current research shows, indeed has had considerable cultural consequences as well.[5]

It seems to be appropriate to recapitulate some well-known facts: the winter painting is part of the cycle which is called 'Seasons' today, and which was only recognized as such in the 1880s.[6] Five paintings have survived: *The Hunters in the Snow* (1565), *The Gloomy Day* (1565) and *The Return of the Herd* (1565), which are in the Kunsthistorisches Museum Wien/ Vienna; as well as *The Hay Harvest* (1565), nowadays a part of the Lobkowicz Collection at the National Gallery in Prague as an item on loan; and finally *The Harvesters* (1565) in the Metropolitan Museum of Art in New York.[7] This cycle was – most likely – commissioned by the Antwerp merchant *Nicolaes Jonghelinck* (1515–70) and was originally located in a luxurious country villa outside Antwerp's gates together with an ensemble of other series of paintings.[8] But by 1570 Jongelinck had died. His estate and its whole inventory were auctioned off, and his villa was completely destroyed by Spanish soldiers in 1584 during the Siege of Antwerp.[9]

And this is the source of the questions which stood at the centre of discussion for a long time and were characterized as the crucial 'Bruegel enigma' as late as 1986.[10] How many paintings existed at the outset? How were they arranged and which paintings are missing? Although these almost 'criminological' questions only concern one notion among many – and are therefore only mentioned in brief – they have nevertheless driven a deep, lasting wedge between two camps: between those who think that, according to the number of months and following the tradition of the books of hours, it once must have been a series of twelve paintings;[11] and others who follow the notion – initially articulated by Charles de Tolnay and shared in the context of this essay – that there were only six paintings in total.[12] Therefore the paintings do not represent a cycle of months, but of 'seasons', divided in the

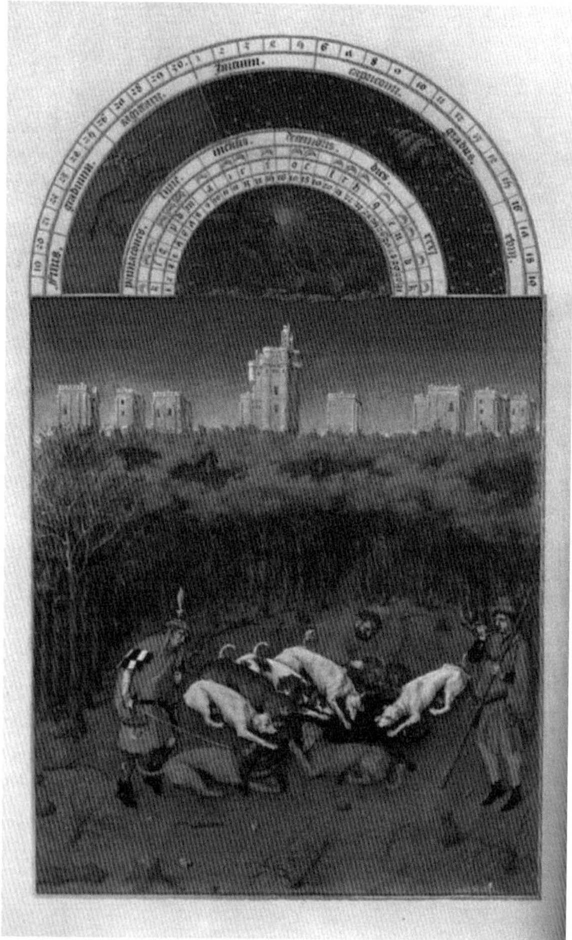

Figure 2: *Book of Hours, Duc du Berry,* '8 December', Musée Condé, Chantilly, 1410–16 © Musée Condé.

pattern of six parts which was as common for Northern Europe as the usual division into four periods: early spring, spring, early summer, midsummer, fall and winter.[13] Following this assessment, the representation of spring has to be considered as the lost painting – a circumstance which is, in turn, the basis for a suspenseful and well researched crime novel well worth reading by author Michael Frayn, where the enigmatic painting of spring seems to reappear for a short time, only to be irrevocably destroyed at last.[14]

Some facts should be established to begin with: first, that this cycle was situated in the country villa of a wealthy merchant, who was at least able to afford furnishings inspired by humanism; secondly, these paintings are, without question, standing in the tradition of the labours of the months which clearly refer to the calendar illuminations to be found in the late-medieval books of hours. Exceptional examples are present in the famous book of hours of the Duc du Berry from the beginning of the fifteenth century (Figure 2). These miniatures went through their last flowering in the middle of the sixteenth century – especially with regard to the works of Simon Bening – before they vanished entirely. But here a motivic legacy definitely became available for the art of the large-format panel painting; its schemes, however, could be freely adapted, combined and translated.[15]

Eventually, Bruegel's paintings depict typical weather phenomena of the respective season together with the requisite rural labours, which are viewed each in front of a phantastical panorama; and they possess a recognizable iconography. However, they do not tell a story for which a preceding or referring text exists. Once they are detached from possible symbolic indications, the paintings primarily depict events which are staged freely, and which the beholders can freely conceive according to their own imagination. In this manner, the paintings already transgress the framework of iconographical conventions.

II.

The Hunters in the Snow (1565) bears a modern, mostly freely invented title.[16] The painting shows one of the first representations of winter in the history of European art, which is possibly unique in its infinitely wide ambience of snow, ice and green-blue frozen light. The gaze of the beholder is effectively drawn into the image by the terrific spatial effect of this painting. This is, not least, achieved by a row of truncated large trees, which suggests a bulging of the hill and thus a flowing (and not an abrupt) transition into the middle ground of the painting. Their diagonal line towards the middle of the painting, which leads from a snow-covered elevation into the depth and width of an icy winter landscape, has the effect of a central-perspectival construction, while, at the same time, this panorama is created by many different perspectives. In the foreground, which is in turn viewed from a bird's-eye view, three hunters with shouldered pikes are pacing down the incline towards the village. They are accompanied by a pack of twelve quite emaciated dogs of different sizes and races, which tiredly slink home with their tails between their legs; they only bagged a fox. To the left is a family owning an inn; showing a stag and St. Eustace, one of the Fourteen Holy Helpers and patron saint of hunters, the sign dangling down denotes it as 'Dit is in den Hert' – meaning 'The Stag Inn'. The hunt of the returning stalkers was not particularly blessed; a fact to which ramshackle state of the sign might refer. The family is busy burning a pyre of brushwood, in the hissing flames of which one can recognize the contours of a pig's head with a bit of imagination; thus one is seeing the procedure of scorching a pig. This is a common motif for the month of December, while the hunt can be an emblem for December as well as January.[17]

Concerning the figures, which evoke their medieval precursors very clearly with their shortening, their smallness and stockiness, which seems partly to follow a template, it is remarkable that, apart from a few exceptions and in contrast to most of Bruegel's other paintings, their faces remain covered and hidden. The arrangement of the landscape, however, turns out to be far more differentiated and rich in detail.

The row of trees with their filigree branches, which offer optically powerful vistas of a row of humpbacked houses with hipped roofs, leads into the middle ground of a true microcosm of a world in winter. On the eye level of the observers, a crow flies down into the valley, and its flight emphasizes the spatial illusion of the image. A downright infinite plenty of precisely rendered details of frozen nature can be seen, and the spoken description of the single elements would just add up to a brittle list, but would not be able to represent its visual density and the totality of its effect. Iciest cold, which dominated the winters from about 1560, has covered the world and frozen lakes and rivers solid. A frozen river winds itself through the winter landscape, which reaches up to the cragged and pointed rocks of a distant mountain range. In a wide sweep, passing a sturdily built castle, the gaze is led even further into the misty distance to a town at the edge of the sea. But apparently, in spite of the harshest living conditions in a permanent frost, which at the time led to the extinction of whole villages, adults as well as children amuse themselves with skates, ice hockey, old-style curling and whipping tops. The closeness of the people and the distance of the landscape into which life is embedded – man and nature, village, castle and town, hill, plains, river, lake, mountain range, sea and sky –coalesce into a cosmic panorama.

There have been suggestions concerning a closer topographical determination, but these have been unanimously refuted at this time.[18] Simultaneously, one has to consider the high probability that Bruegel's own experiences while travelling through the Alps and, more importantly, the cosmography and the cartographical gaze of the sixteenth century, which perceives, outlines and records from a flying vantage point, had some influence; and, consequently, the dialectic confirming that imagination and truthful image, phantasy and document, allegory and chorography, measurable quantity and visual quality, practical purpose and sensuous experience and thus science and art were not in contradiction with each other.[19] Obviously, one is dealing with a composed landscape, the type called *Mischlandschaft* ('mixed landscape') in modernity, which combines freely invented places with those ones that were precisely observed and drawn beforehand;[20] or, also using a modern expression, with a *Überschaulandschaft* or 'world landscape', which is arranged by the use of colours, with a brown foreground, green middle ground and a blue background, as it has been introduced into art history especially by Joachim Patinir (1485–1524).[21]

III.

With the above descriptions we have already touched upon questions concerning possible unresolved interpretations of the painting. Initially, the winter painting seems to conflict with the numerous other works by Bruegel, which are dominated by pessimistic allegories, criticism of the world as such, humour, derision, caricature and irony. But, in fact, Bruegel originally reveals himself as a landscape artist in his earliest works that we know of today.[22] The *View of Walterspurg* in the Swiss Graubünden Alps (size: 31 x 26 cm), created in 1553 during his return from Italy and on view in Brunswick nowadays, is an impressive example (Figure 3). It shows the exceptional and, apart from that, advanced drawing artistry of Bruegel, which creates an atmospheric illusion of space with nothing but finest, non-diffused hatching using darker and lighter lines as well as points. Up to his death, Bruegel had drawn landscapes, in which the artistic genre of 'landscape' was fully distinct and divided into many subgenres: mountain ranges, rivers, forests, regional villages, *vedute* of cities, natural curiosities or untamed landscapes.[23] Drawn with the intention of selling them and making a living, they allowed Bruegel to live comfortably.[24] Together with cosmographical maps, atlases and countless travelogues from the New World, which were produced and sold by the same publishers, landscapes had a large and profitable market as print products in international Antwerp as early as the sixteenth century. Landscapes became nothing less than specialties and trademarks of Dutch art production, not least because of the competition with Italy.[25] As a freelance artist, Bruegel drew and painted for the art market of a metropolis of the time: in the heated economic climate of competition and volatile prices, for an

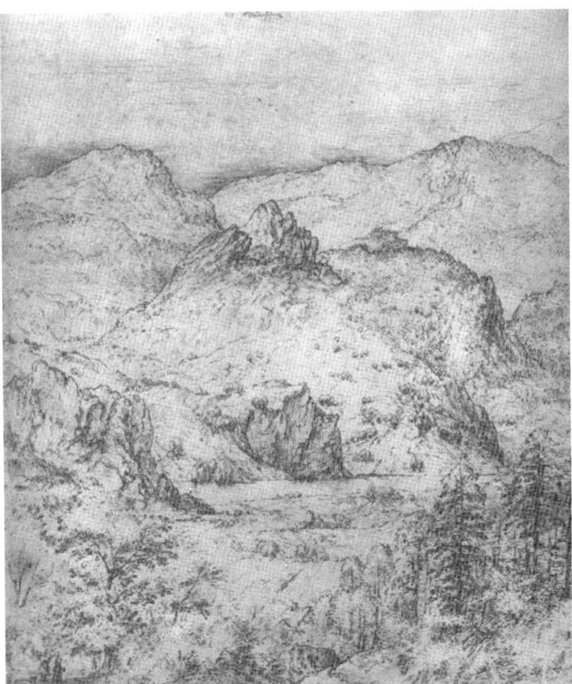

Figure 3: Pieter Bruegel the Elder, *View of Walterspurg*, Drawing 31 x 26 cm, Bowdoin College Museum of Fine Arts, Brunswick, Mains, 1553 © Bowdoin College Museum of Fine Arts.

international audience that was keen to buy, and whose interests, in turn, affected the motifs and forms of the pictures. For the self-conception of the landscape artists following in the seventeenth century, Bruegel achieved nothing less than a mythical prominence.[26]

But in this particular case of a large-format panel painting which is part of a cycle that picks up on the traditional calendar-related motifs present in the books of hours, and which was painted for a country villa, one has to ask what other ideas and desires concerning nature are presented to the educated and worldly observer. The cartography of his time offers an important clue. But does it, as is suggested nowadays, completely legitimate the aptness of the landscape as subject for a painting, which by modern visual arts is so often perceived as moody, atmospheric and romantic?[27]

There are close similarities and cross-dependent interrelations between the map and the painting of a landscape, between the artistic demands of cartography and the scientific accuracy of the painting.[28] A the same time, two different cultural techniques concerning the image are involved, which are mutually dependent, but are based on different intentions: the map, without mentioning its political, military, and economical significance, is a diagrammatic image, the representation of a data space, which has been calculated and surveyed, (Figure 4) tagged with token-like symbols, which have to be read and understood; it serves practical purposes, additionally, as it is a view from above, from a vertical height, without a horizon and equally precise in each place; whereas the landscape painting basically offers an illusionary vista, shows a horizon, and enables the gaze to experience a panoramic space with different distances.[29] In addition, landscape painting is able to look back on its own tradition, which is independent from cartography.

The question remains: what did the historical observers see apart from this? Did they focus on the imagination of a bucolic landscape and a counter-world as well which kept

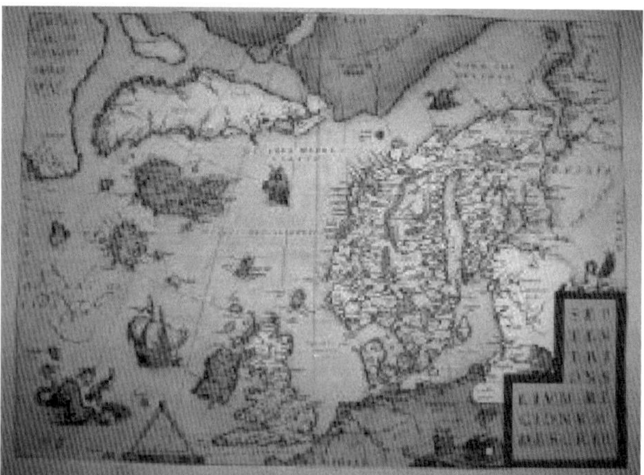

Figure 4: Abraham Ortelius, *Septentrionalium Regionum Descrip.*, Folio 45, reprint of Theatrum Orbis Terrarum (1577), Darmstadt 2007, p. 101.

its utopian allure in contrast to the licentious life of the noisy city? Are there cracks of political reality in this otherwise idyllic picture? Does it possibly formulate an implicit criticism of the Spanish occupation and violent oppression which could only be endured by acquiring a noble distance and stoic calm? Had the flashpoint, where the assumption of meek restraint must turn into a militant reaction, been already reached? Do the Dutch Geuzen hide among the armed hunters, with the foxtail as their symbol? Is the dangling sign of the inn a hint at the humiliated Dutch? Is the crow gliding into the plains a bird of death?

But one should not expect overly explicit criticism from this painting, as its owner Nicolaes Jonghelinck had close business relations to the Spanish court, and the hated cardinal and Governor Perrenot de Granvelle, leading the Spanish repression, was at the same time an important patron of Bruegel.[30] Is it therefore rather an aesthetically and technically masterful and effective as well as philosophically and poetically inspired artistic picture, which, viewed politically, has to be assigned to some extent to the category of necessarily opportunistic fair weather paintings? During the time of their creation, Bruegel's works seemed to be surrounded by an aura of the inscrutable; and, tongue-in-cheek, Max Friedländer made the speculative point: 'Concerning Bruegel, he was less brilliant than those who interpreted him, but his humor outclassed theirs.'[31]

The approach introduced by Max Dvorak in the 1920s and refined by Charles de Tolnay, which perceived Bruegel's landscape as pantheistically animated, Neoplatonically inspired and therefore philosophically observed images of nature, was accepted for a long time but has been put into perspective only today.[32] It is possible to delineate at least three recent approaches towards a more exact understanding concerning the historical meaning and references of the 'Seasons' in particular – with all their subtle differences and larger overlaps. First of all, there is an approach that proceeds iconologically in the broadest sense, and searches for a textual foundation of these paintings; for the intellectual background, which is linked to Antwerp's late humanism and its stoic character, and especially to Abraham Ortelius, the highly educated 'Geographus Regius' of Philipp II, who showed a multitude of talents, interests and activities.[33] Two frequently quoted sentences, which Ortelius added belatedly to Bruegel's epitaph in his handwritten *Album Amicorum* (1574), are borrowed nearly verbatim from Plinius' history of art in the *Naturalis Historia*.[34] They have given rise to a fair bit of speculation about hidden layers of meaning present in the paintings, while they turn out to be classical truisms at a closer look.[35]

In addition, citations from Cicero's and Seneca's works, which appear in the painted cartouches of the sheets of the *Theatrum Orbis Terrarum* (1570), are indications for cosmology which would have to be interpreted as possessing a stoic background, and would link Bruegel closely to Ortelius once more: especially the maxim of an *imitatio* and *contemplatio mundi* that is perceived as a beautiful and rationally ordered universe.[36] In addition, the artistic ensemble of Nicolaes Jonghelinck's villa, where cycles about the twelve labours of Hercules and the 'seven liberal arts' by the 'romance philologist' Frans Floris were present next to depictions of the planets and months, is a further criterion for a humanistic

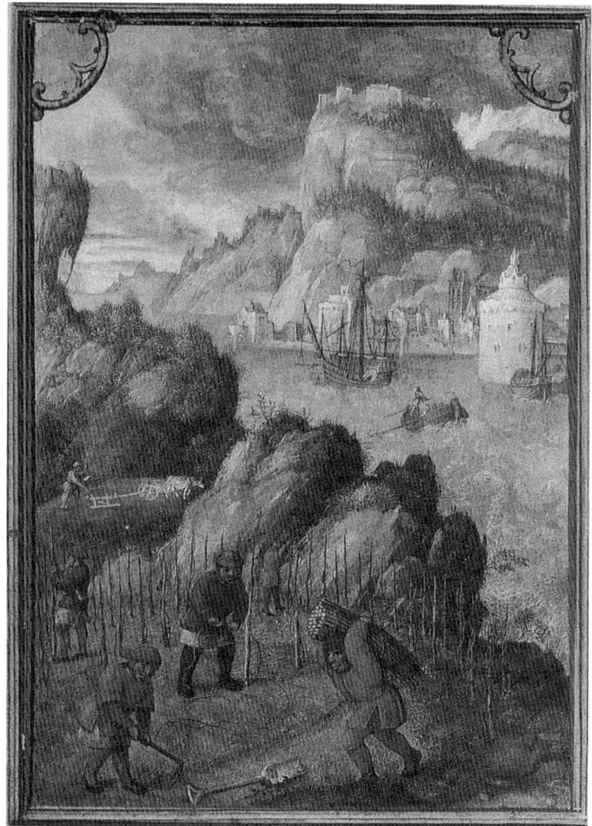

Figure 5: Simon Bening, *Flemish Calender*, 'February', 11 x 15 cm, cod. lat. 23638, Folio 8 v., Bayerische Staatsbibliothek München, ca. 1550 © Bayerische Staatsbibliothek.

aspiration.[37] Another classical source, which possibly served as the base for citations, appears even more obvious, as it was more apt to emphasize a bucolic poetry and therefore also a political utopia: Virgil's *Georgica* and *Bucolica*, for one, glorifies rural life and depicts diligent farm labour as the foundation of peace and a new golden age. Some passages almost read like descriptions of the 'Seasons'. Bruegel certainly knew this text, which was verifiably part of Jongelinck's library.[38] Can the paintings of the months therefore be understood as a kind of 'Flemish Georgica'? Does nature appear here as a classically Arcadian counter-space to the foolishness of the world and the tumultuous hustle of the city? These are indications for a humanistic background of the 'Seasons': but they remain indications, because, on the one hand, one cannot readily assume that a text is cited or illustrated via the paintings; and, on the other, one has to take into consideration that they seize on motifs present in medieval calendar paintings which are based on a specific iconography, but are not based on a text.

The chorographic or – as one would call it today – ethno- and geographical understanding of the genre of 'landscape', which was mentioned above, is connected to an iconological interpretation, and yet follows a completely different approach, which historicizes the modern aesthetic gaze regarding the landscapes. According to Nils Büttner, this view towards nature is closely linked to the fascinating reports – real as well as fictitious – about world voyages and the great demand for cartographical images; for works that were also created to allow purely imaginary, but also contemplative journeys into the distance while sitting in an armchair, without being subjected to the hardships and dangers of a real voyage.[39] The text *Utopia*, published in 1516 by Thomas More, where an imaginary, ideally-ordered island kingdom is described, as well as the *Theatrum orbis terrarium* (the first modern atlas from 1570 in its first edition of many) by court cosmographer and Bruegel's friend, Abraham Ortelius, mark the brilliant cornerstones of this era (Figure 5).[40] Therefore it is possible to speak equally of an invention as well as a discovery of landscape.

A third perspective on these paintings reflects an aesthetical comprehension. It does not proceed from textual foundations, but recognizes the development of a new artistic genre in these paintings – and with it the liberated possibilities of subjective imagination, of mood, but also the visual realization that reveals itself in the becoming-visible of nature.[41] In this they appear as the first autonomous images representing landscapes, and consequently demonstrate a 'generic awareness', as Werner Busch calls it: a new consciousness regarding images, which are either in the final process of 'liberation' from *historia* and allegory, or can already be understood as subjective images of nature in a modern sense, and do without textual references and traditional patterns of interpretation.[42]

IV.

It seems unnecessary to add anything more to this 'state of the art' with its characteristically open and multi-layered possibilities concerning the interpretations and references arising from the historical context. And yet the transfer between media or, as has been suggested recently, 'inter-iconicity', as well as intercultural time travel of the images, are both aspects that have been ignored in various analyses of Bruegel's art.[43] Hence, the particular historical conditionality of these images could be conceived within a larger cultural framework, where the movement of the images between their media and different periods plays an especially crucial role. Disregarding, as matter of principle, the many technical reproductions of the winter painting and their proliferation as easily sellable kitsch objects – an disregarding these transformations into the popular culture of images, which would necessitate a separate analysis – it is first and foremost the artistic translation which is of interest in this context.

The focus here is on the aesthetic image of nature: the imagined cosmos, the vision and the panorama of an artificial landscape; its depth effect, which, as a particularity of European image culture, is set up for the immersion of the gaze practically on an objective level as well as individually on a subjective level.[44] It is the offered and accurately calculated potentiality of the immersing gaze which has always been sought and has been as long in existence as there have been images, but which in this intensity has scarcely been an invention of the baroque staging on walls and ceilings or even of the virtual realities of modern panoramas – of films and all picture worlds which are based on digital technology; not to mention the massively popular immersive worlds of computer games, the contemporary sales of which have long left behind those of CDs and DVDs containing music and film.[45]

Once again, one has to point out the tradition concerning the labours of the month, where the painted landscape in particular obtained a new atmospheric effect.[46] In a miniature painting by Simon Bening from the *Flemish Calendar* (1550), which has an original size of barely 11 x 15 cm, and represents the month of February, a foreground appears which, compared to the picture, has been put diagonally into the painting (Figure 6).[47] Starting from an elevation surrounded by rocks, which is seen from slightly above and where some wine growers are busy with the care of their vines, the gaze is led via a roiling sea

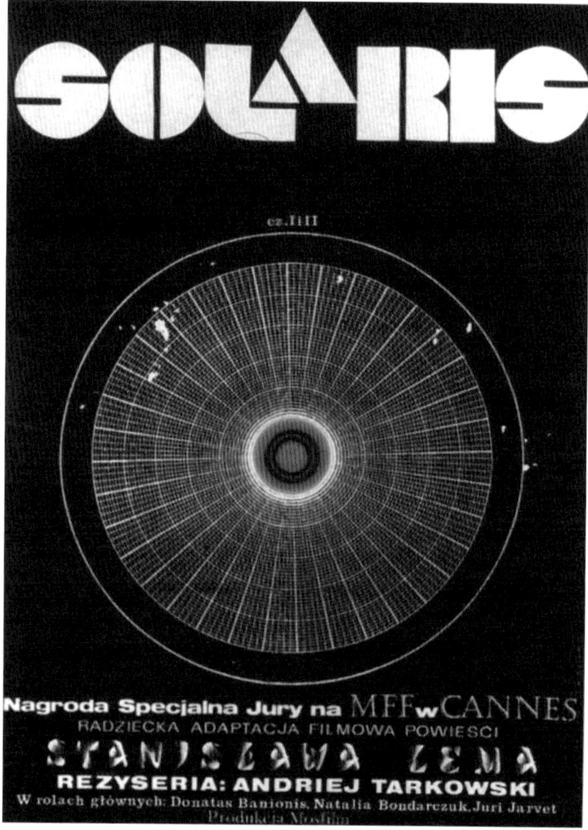

Figure 6: Polish film poster for *Solaris* © Martin Schulz.

towards a city in front of a blue, misty massif with a dark, storm-lashed sky full of clouds arching above it. Once again, there is interplay between closeness and distance, figure and landscape. The iconographical details of the farm labours, the sea navigated by ships and boats, the city situated in the distance, the aristocratic castle positioned high above and the stormy weather of early spring are also characteristic for this illustration of the labours of the month. Moreover Simon Bening, who died in 1561, was the last of Flemish masters of illumination, which has literally vanished in media history. Bruegel the Elder was probably well acquainted with his works; and they have long been perceived as a link between the medieval art of illumination and Bruegel's 'Seasons'.

The iconographic borrowings in the paintings of Bruegel, which were freely taken from the traditional labours of the month and combined with each other, have been identified and clarified to a large extent.[48] The functional change of the labours of the months is always discussed in this respect: from the book of devotions which still was more or less a religious item to the already profane artistic object of a panel painting. One also has to consider the transfers of the images concerning media history and their consequences: from a little book via the drawing to the large panel painting; from personal contemplation happening in private to an accessible room, usable by a group of people; thus, from sitting to walking; from browsing to standing; further, from paper to wood; while the representations assembled in this context are photographical or even digital reproductions anyhow, in which views and details of a different medial quality become visible that were not possible with regard to the original.

Many writers have tried time and again to transfer the preeminent winter painting into the medium of language by describing it; to use language to translate, depict and classify the graphic, atmospheric and that which is shown; and yet this is always coupled with the knowledge that the abilities of language, which proceeds successively, show a deficiency compared to the simultaneously and infinitely provided wealth as well as the spatial effect of the painting.[49] And, with exception of *Landscape with the Fall of Icarus*, no other of Bruegel's paintings has elicited so many poems. The most well-known poem is by William Carlos Williams, written in 1960 and referring to *The Hunters in the Snow*:

The over-all picture is winter
icy mountains
in the background the return

from the bunt it is toward evening
from the left
sturdy hunters lead in

their pack the inn-sign
hanging from a
broken hinge in a stag a cruxifix

between his antlers the cold
inn yard is
deserted but for a huge bonfire

that flares wind-driven tended by
women who cluster
about it to the right beyond

the hill is a pattern of skaters
Brughel the painter
concerned with it all has chosen

a winter struck brush for his
foreground to
complete the picture [...].[50]

For a rigorous historian who wants to explore the exact historical background, such a poem has only little worth as evidence, as it tries for a poetically equivalent depiction and an analogue linguistic translation of the image, and thus rather serves as an indication for a falsifying subjective and romantic view from the present. But how modern may or must the interpreting gaze be? How present and close the distant historical image? Williams, who sought inspiration from paintings a number of times, aspired – quite classically, but irrespective of the historical distance – to use words in order to achieve the effect which visual artists create with brush and paint. For American literary scholar Wendy Steiner this poem is the 'most penetrative interpretation of the painting.'[51] Beyond the boundaries and barriers between text and image which were introduced by Lessing's *Laokoon*, she recognizes close structural and 'inter-artistic' analogies which remain valid across different epochs. Whether or not one agrees to this interpretation – which will not be elaborated further in this essay – whether one is close to the hermeneutics of Heidegger or Gadamer's 'fusion of horizons' or deconstructs them completely, the 'old' image possesses, undeniably, a historical point in time at which it originated; it has a past tradition to which it relates, the history of its reception which is formative for the cultural memory, and at the same time a persistent present and an approaching future, in which other perspectives will develop, and thus insights which will reveal a new, as yet unknown history.

V.

Finally, an imaginary time travel to a distant future shall be attempted, to a ramshackle space station on a far-flung planet and to the quintessential cosmic limits of human expansion and knowledge; more precisely, to the filmic conversion of a literary fiction which itself is more than 30 years old. I am referring to the science fiction film *Solaris* by Andrei Tarkovsky, where Bruegel's winter painting occupies a virtual key role. The film is based on the eponymous novel by Stanislav Lem from 1968. At first, Lem collaborated on the script, but later he was deeply irritated by several elementary dramaturgical changes, and Tarkovsky's capricious ambitions to turn the epistemological, partly anti-anthropocentric and yet ethical novel into a – as he perceived it – rather mystical and melodramatic salvation tale.[52] The film was finished in 1972, after many humiliations, change requests and harsh criticism by the Soviet state committee for cinematography, which ultimately took little note of the special prize of the jury in Cannes on an official level: the film was just too opaquely religious for socialist realism.[53] At the same time, *Solaris* could indeed be perceived as a Russian answer to Stanley Kubrick's *2001: A Space Odyssey* (1968), which set new standards for the genre of the science fiction film in the West, especially on the technical level; but this was the one aspect that Tarkovsky did not focus on, as he wanted to film a philosophical parable – not necessarily a futuristic 'projection'.[54] Is has to remain a vague, if compelling, speculation to imagine a certain symmetry between the totalitarian political system surrounding Tarkovsky's life and work, and the Netherlands of the sixteenth century under centralistic occupation. The director arguably fell back on Bruegel's winter painting because of reasons which, in all openness, have to be sought primarily in the atmosphere and structure of the painting. In nearly all his films, particularly in the film *Andrei Rublev* (1966), Tarkovsky time and again relates to the history of painting; not so much in a sense of comparing media, or even a competition, or in the sense of a meta-discourse about the fundamentally different conditions and possibilities of filmic and painted images, as they are shown, for example, in Jean-Luc Godard's *Passion* (1982).[55] The back link, the memory and the close historical, spiritual and media-related connections between the images seem rather more important to him. Just as one refers to 'film as poetry' and 'poetry as film' – meaning that Tarkovsky was looking for analogies to the mental images of poetry and thus all but turned poetry into film[56] – it is equally possible to speak of 'film as painting' and of 'painting as film'.[57]

The plot of the film is to be outlined in short: Solaris is the name of a mysterious planet that is covered with a seemingly intelligent substance. The investigation of the planet is one of the most ambitious projects of natural science, which also meets its absolute limits in this context. 'Solaristics', once the source of high hopes, has been stagnating for a long time. Kelvin, a strict empiricist and the protagonist of the film, has the task of shutting down the local space station, which has only been sending confusing messages to Earth for some time as no one receives them. He only discovers chaos and disintegration; and the station appears more or less like a scrapheap of the scientific age (Figure 7). The only two scientists to survive appear erratic and downtrodden. Soon after, Kelvin himself shares the experiences that made these people completely lose their composure. Via an inexplicable planetary force, dreams, fears, ideas and memories, in short the un- and subconscious are materialized. Specifically, his former wife Harey, who committed suicide because of him years ago, appears to him. He tries to kill the ghostly 'stranger' several times, but she returns again and again. He feels

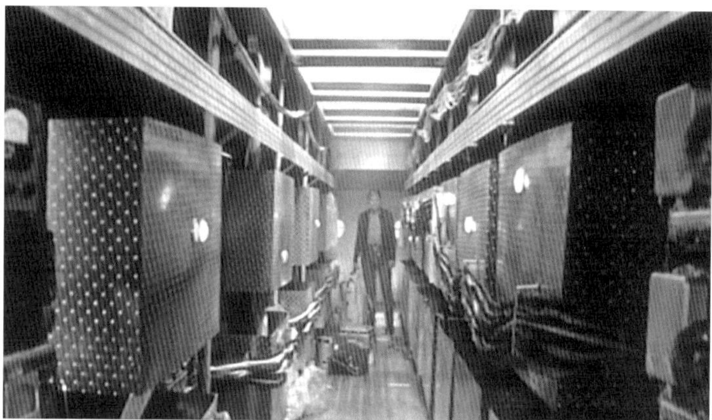

Figure 7: Andrei Tarkovsky, still from *Solaris*, 1972 © DVD icestorm.

guilty for her death, which is metaphorically and actually repeated and annulled. The voyage to an outer cosmos, into the far and unknown distance, into unfeeling space, where the different and completely incomprehensible laws of an anonymous intelligence reign, is turned into a voyage into the deep inner self of his own memory, to the ethical conflicts of responsibility and conscience.

A key scene takes place, which significantly plays in the library of the station (Figure 8). It is not by chance that it resembles a humanist study, decorated with old furniture, antique statues, books, globes and telescopes; and also with five of Pieter Bruegel's paintings. In the otherwise highly technical ambience of the space station, which is necessary for the survival in space, this room appears equally as a window in time and a heterotopia, which has archived the cultural memory and provides it as well. In fact, a peaceful birthday party

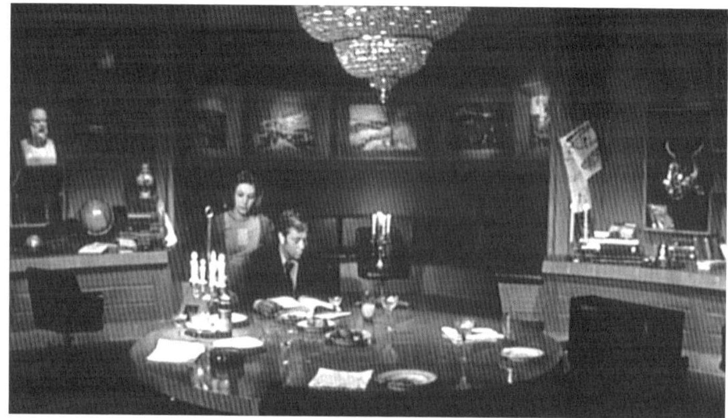

Figure 8: Andrei Tarkovsky, still from *Solaris*, 1972 © DVD icestorm.

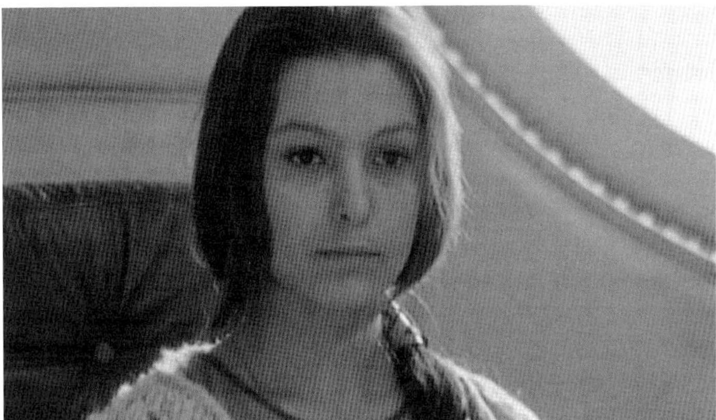

Figure 9: Andrei Tarkovsky, still from *Solaris*, 1972 © DVD icestorm.

was planned. But the presence of Kelvin's wife in particular – of whom one does not know whether she is just a shadowy eidolon, a living dead, the creation of an overstretched imagination, a cynical citation by the planet or a true incarnation of Kelvin's memory – leads to another argument about the sense and value of science and technology. These have pushed forward to the limits of the cosmos and are now confronted with a different form of existence, which no longer can be understood using human categories. The cyberneticist Snaut is able to accept this Socratically, and likewise everyone has to realize that, ultimately, one knows nothing and falls back on him or herself in the end. The party is over, the host completely drunk. Kelvin hurries back to the library and sees his wife in a truly mystical immersion and hallucination (Figure 9).

The site of the winter painting is no longer a room of Jonghelinck's luxurious villa outside the gates of Antwerp, where one would have to imagine the cycle of the paintings originally: no longer a room in the Kunsthistorisches Museum Wien/Vienna, but a space station somewhere in the cosmos. Only reproductions are left of Bruegel's paintings, which are also much smaller than their originals. Furthermore the cycle is no longer complete: only the winter paintings, *The Harvesters* (1565) and *The Gloomy Day* (1565), are on display, complemented by *Landscape with the Fall of Icarus* (ca. 1560) and *The Tower of Babel* (1563), which apparently represent the punishment of human hubris. Kelvin can do nothing but stare at his wife in bewilderment, who seems to be an uncanny materialized creation of his imagination (Figure 10). At first, he perceives her from the back, similar to many constellations in paintings by Caspar David Friedrich, as she is absorbed in the observation of a painting (Figure 11). He is unable to see what she is seeing and is, quite literally, not clued in the picture like she is. The vision she experiences while facing Bruegel's painting only plays out in front of her inner eye, partly along with remembered images of her own re-experienced history; a vision that signifies her complete development into a human as well as Kelvin's catharsis. The framed sixteenth-century landscape painting at the wall and her

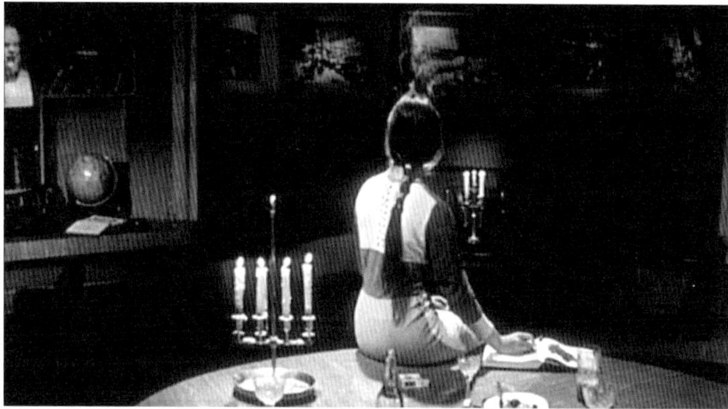

Figure 10: Andrei Tarkovsky, still from *Solaris*, 1972 © DVD icestorm.

trance-like gaze, which suggest an extraordinary vision that is completely immersed in the image, can be said to trigger a stream of inner images which seem to fuse with the painted image. A highly energetic transfer between the imaginary gaze of a painted image and her mental images takes place (Figure 12). The painting revives memories of life on earth, which appears as infinitely remote and as different as life and death in this alien cosmos. One could speak of an activated and enlivened *durée intérieure* – by all means in the sense of Henri Bergson, to which the complex terms of the 'time-image' and the 'crystal-image' by Gilles Deleuze are connected; of a compression of time, where present and past, presence and memory, the mediated and the immediate, actual and virtual image, subject and object, the 'here and now' and the 'then and there', the place of the space station and the imaginary space of the landscape painting from the sixteenth century melt into each other.[58] In a related sense, Tarkovsky writes about 'sealed time' as the fundamental principle of the film,

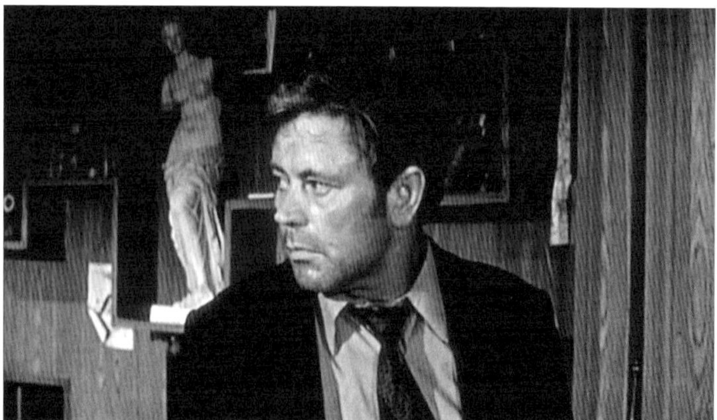

Figure 11: Andrei Tarkovsky, still from *Solaris*, 1972 © DVD icestorm.

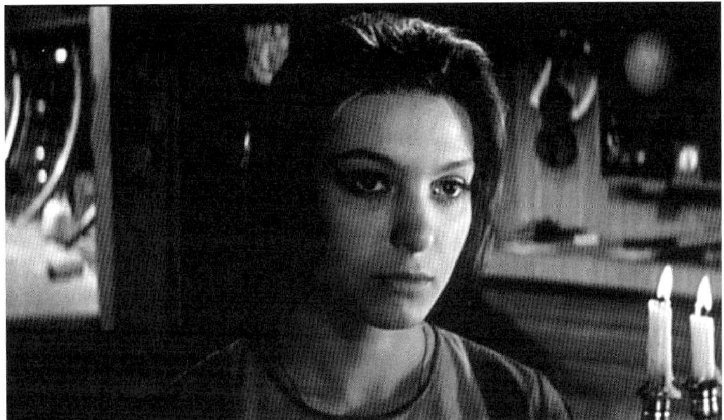

Figure 12: Andrei Tarkovsky, still from *Solaris*, 1972 © DVD icestorm.

which – although clearly different concerning the specific media – would have close and transcending connections to poetry, music, painting, basically to the conditions of human existence and to the patina of all things, which makes experience itself possible, at the same time.[59] This does neither denote metrical time, which progresses in a linear way, nor historical time; but rather a time that has permanent and consequential effects, a time that is never past, an 'achronological time' and 'time crystals' (Deleuze), which can be experienced, remembered and repeated, and which becomes alive under special circumstances that form the dramatic framework of the film. Thus, this is scarcely referring to the symbolic background of the winter painting, but it is transforming questions of time and space into an experiential journey instead, as is shown by the inner images of the female protagonist.

In turn, the viewer of the film, who in relation to the two filmic figures is in a third position, sees what the protagonist is unable to see: the interior, permanently speechless images of her immersing gaze, which obscures the limits and transitions between interior and exterior, past and present; but also, it appears, the lines of sight and their potential intersections, as they exist in the painting itself and can be conceived from it (Figure 13).

The viewers themselves slip from the (normally) large silver screen into the microcosm of the painted image. Similar to the colourful final sequences of *Andrei Rublev* (1966), which show nothing but the fresco of the Trinity, the painting fills the complete filmic image and thus no longer functions simply as a picture within a picture. The painted image, which no longer seems to have a frame and no longer appears as an illusion on a surface, and the filmic image have been joined. The static and expansive, surface-like quality characteristic for the art of painting is suspended by the sliding movements and focusing of the camera's eye, and also by the added cross fades. The art of painting – in terms of a projection onto a surface – does not represent a mere symbolical gaze in a more or less allegorical space, but rather makes its very experience possible; as a voyage into an imaginary, external as well as interior cosmos; which is not simply represented in a scenic narration, reproduction or illustration,

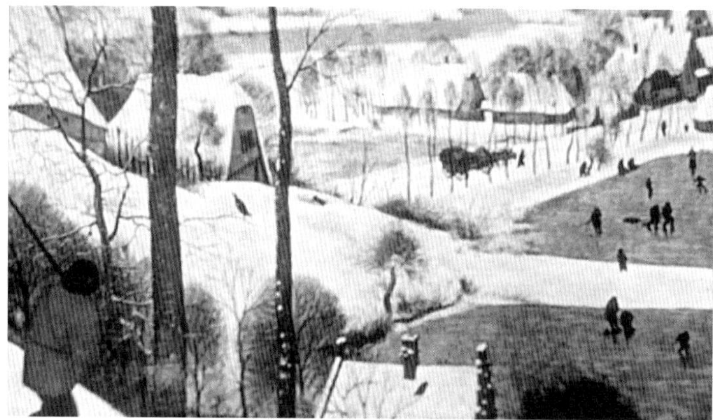

Figure 13: Andrei Tarkovsky, still from *Solaris*, 1972 © DVD icestorm.

but opened up in all directions. In this way, the art of painting is transcended and shifted to a different movement and time, just as it transforms the film in turn, and which is translated into the potentialities of painting. Synaesthetically incited and synergistic qualities like the twittering of birds and the barking of dogs, which can only be imagined when standing in front of to the painting, are added. The filmic translation of the painted image suggests, in a way, a continuum that is open in all directions, in which the couple, accompanied by an electronically modified prelude by Johann Sebastian Bach, ultimately seems to float (Figure 14). Instead of words that are spoken and exchanged with each other, only pictures are shown, only the bodies 'speak' and only the music sounds.

This filmic transformation, which is embedded in an ethical, epistemological, psychological, as well as romantic, travel through time and space and presents the highest

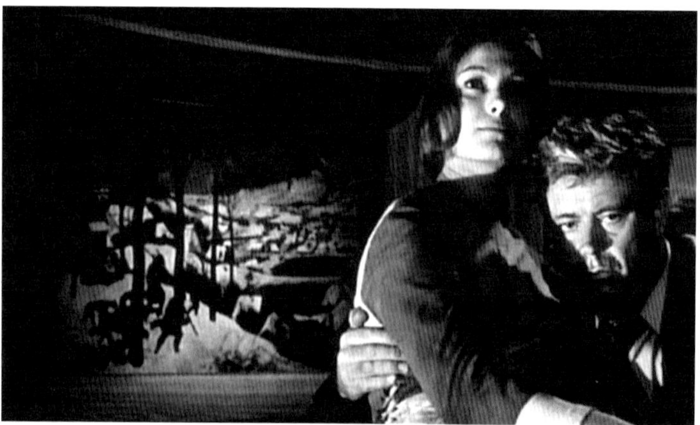

Figure 14: Andrei Tarkovsky, still from *Solaris*, 1972 © DVD icestorm.

level of filmic craftsmanship, seems to offer no clue for a genuinely historical understanding of Bruegel's winter painting at first. It proceeds too subjectively and, furthermore, with very specific intentions within a filmic fiction; in addition, it does not reason discursively within the medium of language, hardly within a meta-language of its own medium and not within historical frameworks. But, concerning the history of images, it is interesting in itself that a well-known picture of the traditional art of painting is not simply quoted at a dramatic point of a film, but is completely incorporated within the spatiality and temporality of the filmic image. Of course, this is still the particular case of a Russian, well-educated, conservative director, who attributed materialism, pragmatism, and mere intellectualism, as well as spiritual illiteracy, to modern western society; with the common polemic attacks against modern art, its avant-gardes and demands for progress, which would deem mere 'method itself as the purpose and goal of art'.[60] In contrast, he adheres – entirely in the style of a prophetic and demiurgic genius of art – to the view that art works with 'the hieroglyphs of absolute truth' to turn 'infinity into something that can be experienced'[61]; believes in 'the parallel between the impression of an artwork on a spiritually sensitive person and a religious experience'[62]; and can 'only assert that the image is striving towards the infinite and leads towards the absolute.'[63] Against the reification of the natural science he put – wholly within an idealistic tradition – a transcending subjectivity that adheres to a kind of natural poetry. It recognizes the technological possibilities and desires of a purely imaginative space voyage precisely in this image, set in an old medium – a space voyage that is therefore decidedly non-scientific and non-technological. For him, films as well as the visual art of painting are first and foremost moral authorities and spiritual media, which are deliberately structured to be open for respective subjective experiences.[64]

Tarkovsky's 'mystical art of film' – as it has been referred to – and his statements related to it, even if they were meant to be serious, metaphysical and 'absolute', need to be translated and put into a political, semantic and historical perspective, which is not the aim of this essay.[65] But the transgressive connections and contexts of Bruegel's winter painting have to be pointed out: from illumination to the art of drawing via the panel painting to the film; from the Middle Ages via early modern times to the present; from Burgundy to the Netherlands, to Austria and Russia. It is not only different techniques which exist between the media of different ages and cultures, not only the dividing barriers of culture and competition, but rather the exchange and the movement of the images themselves. Thus, Tarkovsky's idiosyncratic filmic translation of the painting is to be understood neither as a mere citation nor as a *paragone* between film and painting, but rather as an intermedial conjunction in which present and past, subject and object, the personal gaze and the gaze of the Other and – not least – painting and film interlace. Tarkovsky therefore does not simply reproduce the art of painting, but transforms it and adds the imagined gaze, as well as the simulated shifting and sliding gaze that is implemented in the painting, but cannot be experienced in front of the painting itself, other than being imagined at best. Thus, it is first of all a 'filmic' interpretation of the painting, which, like any interpretation, is a translation into a different medium. In contrast to a scientific language-based interpretation, which describes, makes use of certain theories and methods, is based itself on historical sources and weighs different plausible approaches, Tarkovsky succeeds in creating a truly congenial 'translation'. It remains completely in and close to the painting and emphasizes that which is predetermined in the painting and not simply adapted from its historical consideration: the rambling and diving of the gaze into the depth and width of space, the merging and transgression of internal and external images, of present and virtual space, of the time of one's own remembrance and the animated time of the historical image; furthermore the focusing on countless details, the dreamlike vision, the imagined noises and synaesthetic effects. And consequently, the citation of Plinius in Ortelius' *Album Amicorum*, along with its reference to an ancient topos referring to Apelles, has an up-to-date significance with regard to the transgressive art of moving images: *Multa pinxit, hic Brugelius, quae pingi non possunt* translates as 'He painted much, this Bruegel, which in fact cannot be painted at all'; and one could add: for this, film would have to be reinvented.

Translated by Jochen Mevius

Notes

1 For the range of interpretations, see most recently Inge Herold, *Pieter Bruegel der Ältere. Die Jahreszeiten*, Munich: Prestel, 2002.

2 A detailed overview concerning these sources can still be found in Fritz Grossmann, *Bruegel. Die Gemälde*, Cologne: Phaidon, 1955, p. 7–36; Bob Claessens and Jeanne Rousseau, *Pieter Bruegel*, Herrsching: Pawlak, 1969; Wolfgang Stechow, *Bruegel*, Cologne: DuMont, 1974; Max J. Friedländer, *Pieter Bruegel*, Berlin: Propyläen, 1921. The statements in Carel van Mander's *Schilderboeck* from 1604, of literary quality and enriched with rhetorical topoi, as well as legends, remain an important source.

3 This notion can still be found in, for example, Wilhelm Fraenger, *Der Bauern-Bruegel und das deutsche Sprichwort*, Erlenbach-Zurich: Rentsch, 1923. This understanding can be traced back to Karel van Mander's *Schilderboeck* from 1604, where Bruegel is characterized as 'droll Pieter', as a realist painter and entertainer in rustic company. If nothing else, this is an evaluation of the landscape painting and the comical genre, which appear as inferior genres when compared to Italian art. For a recent approach, see Jürgen Müller, *Das Paradox als Bildform. Studien zur Ikonologie Pieter Bruegels d. Ä.*, Munich: Fink, 1999. For a history of reception up to the 1950s, see Grossmann, 1955, p. 21ff.; lately, however, see Walter S. Gibson, *Pieter Bruegel and the Art of Laughter*, Berkley, Los Angeles & London: University of California Press, 2006, who, although his approach was criticized, emphasizes the rustic genre and thus the pure and non-moralistic humour in Bruegel's works. In this context, compare also Margaret A. Sullivan, *Bruegel's Peasants: Art and Audience in the Northern Renaissance*, Cambridge: Cambridge University Press, 1994; also see Svetlana Alpers' differing view: 'Bruegel's *Festive Peasants*', in *Simiolus*, No. 6, 1972/73, pp. 163–76; and finally, see Jürgen Müller, 'Pieter der Drollige oder der Mythos vom Bauern-Bruegel', in *Pieter Brueghel der Jüngere – Jan Brueghel der Ältere.*

Flämische Malerei um 1600, exhibition catalogue, Villa Hügel Essen, Lingen: Luca 1997, pp. 42–53.

4   This eulogy, which Karel van Manders refers to shortly thereafter for the first time, is reprinted in Grossmann, 1955, p. 10.

5   Cf. Wolfgang Behringer, Hartmut Lehmann and Christian Pfister (eds), *Kulturelle Konsequenzen der 'Kleinen Eiszeit'*, Göttingen: Vandenhoeck & Ruprecht, 2005.

6   Cf. Klaus Demus, *Flämische Malerei von Jan van Eyck bis Pieter Bruegel dem Älteren*. Katalog der Gemäldegalerie des Kunsthistorischen Museums Wien, 1981, p. 88; Eduard v. Engerth, 'Über die im Kunsthistorischen Museum neu zur Aufstellung gelangenden Gemälde, III. Niederländische Schulen', in *Jahrbuch der Kunsthistorischen Sammlungen des Allerhöchsten Kaiserhauses*, No. 5, 1884, pp. 145–66.

7   Images in Klaus Demus, 'Pieter Bruegel d. Ä. im Kunsthistorischen Museum Wien', in Wilfried Seipel, *Pieter Bruegel d.Ä. im Kunsthistorischen Museum Wien*, Ostfildern: Hatje & Milan: Skira, 1997.

8   For a detailed examination based on the most recent source material, see Iain Buchanan, 'The Collection of Nicolaes Jonghelinck: The "Months" by Pieter Bruegel the Elder', in *Burlington Magazine*, No. 132, 1990, p. 541–50. Such a large and elaborate series is only conceivable as a commissioned work, as is noted by Claesens and Rousseau, 1969 p. 32. The important question how the relationship between artists and patrons was structured, and what kind of influence they had on the works, has still not been answered satisfactorily.

9   For a detailed examination of all sources concerning origination, see Buchanan, 1990.

10   Cf. Hans J. van Miegrot, 'The "12 Months" Reconsidered: How a Drawing by Pieter Stevens Clarifies a Bruegel Enigma', in *Simiolus*, No. 16, 1986, pp. 29–35.

11   Among others, Grossmann, 1955; Wolfgang Stechow, *Pieter Bruegel the Elder*, New York: Abrams, 1968, pp. 96–118.

12   Cf. Karl von Tolnai, 'Studien zu den Gemälden P. Bruegels d. Ä', in *Jahrbuch der Kunsthistorischen Sammlungen in Wien*, No. 8, 1934, p. 105–36, who was the first to decidedly speak in favour of every image showing two months. Still, there is an ongoing discussion about the exact two months to be seen in the respective paintings; for suggestions, see a table with proposals in Buchanan, 1990. It seems to be clear that Bruegel refers to the tradition of the labours of the months, while also adapting, completing and varying them freely. The bagged fox is a peculiar motif that has to be understood in a political context as a sign of the Geuzen; similarly Bruegel's oil on wood painting *The Return of the Herd* (1565). Concerning the exact iconographic allocation, for the time present the last word belongs to Klaus Demus, who advises against searching for definite signs of determinate months, and understands the paintings – in a modern sense – as moody and atmospheric representations of the respective seasons instead: cf. Demus, 1997, p. 84ff.

13   Cf. Demus, 1997, p. 84.

14   Michael Frayn, *Headlong*, London: Faber & Faber, 1999.

15   See Christian Vöhringer, *Pieter Bruegel der Ältere. Landschaft mit pflügenden Bauern und Ikarussturz*, Munich: Fink, 2002, pp. 48–74. Here – and one will have to return to this topic – Vöhringer emphasizes the formal and iconographic borrowings from the illuminations in

the books of hours, especially as a counterargument to the philological and political interpretation of the painting showing the fall of Icarus, as maintained by Beat Wyss: Beat Wyss, *Pieter Bruegel. Landschaft mit Ikarussturz. Ein Vexierbild des humanistischen Pessimismus*, Frankfurt am Main: Fischer, 1990.

16   This title was introduced by René Bastelaer-Hulin de Loo, *Peter Bruegel L'Ancien, son oeuvre et son temps*, Brussels: van Oest, 1907, p. 303.

17   Cf. the compiled motifs in Wilhelm Hansen, *Kalenderminiaturen der Stundenbücher. Mittelalterliches Leben im Jahresverlauf*, Munich: Callwey, 1984.

18   Cf. Fritz Novotny, *Die Monatsbilder Pieter Bruegels d. Ä.*, Vienna: Deuticke, 1948, p. 9.

19   For a comprehensive overview, see Nils Büttner, *Die Erfindung der Landschaft. Kosmographie und Landschaftskunst im Zeitalter Bruegels*, Göttingen: Vandenhoeck & Ruprecht, 2000. The close interrelationship between artistic landscape painting and scientific cartography, especially with regard to the seventeenth century, was highlighted by Svetlana Alpersin *The Art of Describing: Dutch Art in the Seventeenth Century*, Chicago: University of Chicago Press, 1983. From the perspective of conceptual history, it appears enlightening that 'landscape' denoted both that which was mapped by the cartographers and that which was painted by the landscape artists. Cf. Christine Buci-Glucksmann, *Der Kartographische Blick der Kunst*, Berlin: Merve, 1997. For a larger cultural-historical context, also comprising a phenomenological view on Chinese and Japanese landscape painting, see Edward Casey, *Representing Place: Landscape Painting and Maps*, Minneapolis: University of Minnesota Press, 2002; cf. Robert Stockhammer, *Kartierung der Erde. Macht und Lust in Karten und Literatur*, Munich: Fink, 2007; Tanja Michalsky, *Projektion und Imagination. Die niederländische Landschaft der Frühen Neuzeit im Dialog von Geographie und Malerei*, Paderborn: Fink, 2010. Based on modernity, Joachim Ritter's well-known hypothesis concerning the relation between natural science and aesthetical experience presents a different approach. He perceives the aesthetical and 'complete' visualization of nature as a dialectical antipode, as a purpose-free and subjective complement to the modern objectifying natural sciences, although these created the leeway for this in the first place: 'Nature as landscape [is only possible] under the prerequisite of liberty under the framework of modern society': in Joachim Ritter, *Landschaft. Zur Funktion des Ästhetischen in der Modernen Gesellschaft*, Münster: Aschendorff, 1963, p. 30 (translated by Jochen Mevius). Concerning conceptual history, see Renate Fechner, *Natur als Landschaft. Zur Entstehung der Ästhetischen Landschaft*, Frankfurt am Main: Lang, 1986; for additional layers of meaning in this context, see Denis Cosgrove and Stephen Daniels (eds), *The Iconography of Landscape*, Cambridge: Cambridge University Press, 1988; Denis Cosgrove (ed.), *Mappings*, London: Reaktion Books, 1999; *Geographical Imagination and the Authority of Images*, Stuttgart: Steiner Verlag, 2006.

20   Cf. Fritz Novotny, 'Über das 'Elementare' in der Kunstgeschichte', in *Plan I*, Vol. 3, December 1945.

21   The term *Weltlandschaft* ('world landscape'), which proceeds from a rather symbolic understanding, and is still not thoroughly clarified in this regard, was initially introduced by Ludwig von Baldass, 'Die niederländische Landschaftsmalerei von Patinir bis Bruegel', in *Jahrbuch der Kunsthistorischen Sammlungen des Allerhöchsten Kaiserhauses*,

No. XXXIV, 1917, p. 111–58. Concerning this topic, see also Justus Müller Hofstede, 'Zur Interpretation von Pieter Bruegels Landschaft. Ästhetischer Landschaftsbegriff und Stoische Weltbetrachtung', in Otto von Simson and Matthias Winner (eds), *Pieter Bruegel und seine Welt*, Berlin: Mann, 1979, p. 73–142, especially p. 84ff. 'World landscape' was equalled with and aesthetically modified by *Überschaulandschaft* ('panorama landscape'): cf. Atanazy Raczynski, *Die Flämische Landschaft vor Rubens*, Frankfurt am Main: Prestel, 1937, p. 14; see also Franzsepp Württemberger, *Pieter Bruegel der Ältere und die deutsche Kunst*, Wiesbaden: Steiner, 1957; Detlef Zinke, *Patinirs 'Weltlandschaft.' Studien und Materialien zur Landschaftsmalerei im 16. Jahrhunderts*, Frankfurt am Main: Lang, 1977, p. 28ff; Walter S. Gibson, *Mirror of Earth: The World Landscape in 16th Century Flemish Painting*, Princeton: Princeton University Press, 1989; see especially the exhibition catalogue *Patinir und die Erfindung der Landschaft*, Prado, Madrid, 2007. The question lingers if Patinir's landscapes have to be understood symbolically (which is suggested, not least, by the many Christian motifs that remain) or rather more as aesthetical experiences.

22   Concerning the surviving collection of these drawings, see Ludwig Münz, *Die Zeichnungen Pieter Bruegels*, Cologne: Phaidon, 1962; Hans Mielke, *Pieter Bruegel: Die Zeichnungen*, Turnhout: Brepols, 1996; see also Büttner, 2000, p. 172ff.

23   Cf. Stefan Bartilla, *Die Wildnis: Visuelle Neugier in der Landschaftsmalerei. Eine Ikonologische Untersuchung der Niederländischen Berg - und Waldlandschaften und ihres Naturbegriffs um 1600*, Freiburg: Rombach, 2005.

24   Concerning this and the following deliberations, cf. Büttner, 2000, p. 72ff.

25   In this context it is necessary to object to an older hypothesis by Ernst H. Gombrich: while the North developed the landscape painting in practice, the aesthetical concept and theory of art as related to the landscape painting could only be provided by Italy and its classical tradition; see Ernst H. Gombrich, 'Die Kunsttheorie der Renaissance und die Entstehung der Landschaftsmalerei', in *Die Kunst der Renaissance I. Norm und Form*, Stuttgart: Klett-Cotta, 1985, pp. 140–57; on the same topic, cf. also Otto Pächt, 'Early Italian Nature Studies and the Early Calendar Landscape', *Journal of Warburg and Courtauld Institutes*, No. 13, 1950, pp. 13–47, who makes a similar connection; cf. also Alexander Perrig, 'Die theoriebedingten Landschaftsformen in der Italienischen Malerei des 14. und 15. Jahrhunderts', in Wolfram Prinz and Andreas Beyer (eds), *Die Kunst und das Studium der Natur vom 14. zum 16. Jahrhundert*, Weinheim: VCH, Acta Humaniora, 1987, pp. 41–60.

26   Cf. Bartilla, 2005, especially p. 30ff.

27   See footnote 19 (above).

28   One has to point out Dürer's *Map of the World*, which he drew in cooperation Johann Stabius in 1515. Holbein worked in cartographical workshops. In Italy, artists were tied into large-scale projects of cartographic mural paintings; for instance, the one headed by the cartographers Ignazio Danti and Stefano Buensignori 1565 in the Palazzo Vecchio in Florence. The painting of the *Galleria delle Carte geografiche* in the Vatican came into existence between 1580 and 1583. On this topic, see also Büttner, 2000, p. 72ff.

29   Cf. also Gottfried Boehm, 'Offene Horizonte. Zur Bildgeschichte der Natur', in *Wie Bilder Sinn erzeugen. Die Macht des Zeigens*, Berlin: University Press, 2007, pp. 72–95; Buci-Glucksmann, 1997.

30 Concerning the collection, see Maurice Piquard, 'Le Cardinal, les Artistes et les Évrivains', in *Revue Belge*, Vol. 17, 1947/48, pp. 133–47; see also Buchanan, 1990. Possibly, Granvelle was the motivation for Bruegel to move to Brussels. But as early as 1564, Granvelle was forced to leave Brussels due to the machinations of Philip II. Cf. also Anabella Weismann, 'Das Bild als Waffe im Elitekonflikt. Graphik und Malerei als Medien des öffentlichen und privaten Widerstands gegen die spanisch-katholische Herrschaft über die Niederlande im 16. Jahrhundert am Beispiel des Werkes von Pieter Bruegel', in *Mitteilungen aus dem Schwerpunktbereich Methodenlehre*, Vol. 36, 1994, pp. 1–46. Weismann also notes that Granvelle indeed promoted and protected unorthodox artists and scientists as well.

31 Max Friedländer, *Pieter Bruegel*, Berlin: Propyläen, 1921, p. 82 (translated by Jochen Mevius).

32 Cf. Max Dvořák, 'Pieter Bruegel der Ältere', in *Kunstgeschichte als Geistesgeschichte*, Munich: Piper, 1924, p. 219ff; Charles de Tolnay, *Die Zeichnungen Pieter Bruegels*, Munich: Piper, 1924/1952; 'Studien zu den Gemälden Pieter Bruegels d. Ä.', in *Jahrbuch der Kunsthistorischen Sammlungen in Wien*, Vol. XLIV, 1935, p. 105ff; cf. also Jan Bialostocki, 'Die Geburt der modernen Landschaftsmalerei', in *Bulletin du Musée de Varsovie*, Issue XIV, 1973, p. 9ff. Concerning a comprehensive criticism of these approaches, see Müller-Hofstede, 1997, especially p. 80ff.

33 The humanist background of Bruegel's works and their time is an accepted foundation of most of the research on Pieter Bruegel. Compare also with references in Tanja Michalsky, 'Imitation und Imagination. Die Landschaft Pieter Bruegels d. Ä. im Blick der Humanisten', in Hartmut Laufhütte (ed.), *Künste und Natur in Diskursen der Frühen Neuzeit*, Vol. 1, Wiesbaden: Harrassowitz, 2000, pp. 383–405. Concerning Ortelius, see Robert W. Karrow, *Mapmakers of the sixteenth century and their maps bio-bibliographies of the cartographers of Abraham Ortelius*, Chicago: Speculum Orbis Press, 1993; also the examination and references in Müller-Hofstede, 1997; Arthur E. Popham, 'Pieter Bruegel and Abraham Ortelius', in *Burlington Magazine*, No. 59, 1931, pp. 184–88.

34 *Album Amicorum*, Cambridge, Library of Pembroke College, P12 verso. The complete text is reprinted and reproduced in Michalsky, 2000, pp. 384–85. See also Müller-Hofstede, 1997, p. 74ff. Concerning the classical topic of the artist in the first part, where nature is praised as the true teacher of his art, but also as a jealous rival, see also Mark A. Meadow, 'Bruegel's Procession to the Calvary. Aemulatio and the Space of Vernacular Style', in Jan de Jong (ed.), *Pieter Bruegel*, Zwolle: Waanders, 1997, pp. 180–205.

35 On this topic, see also Michalsky, 2000. The first sentence reads: 'Multa pinxit, hic Brugelius, quae pingi non possunt, quod Plinius de Apelle'. But this does not point to a mysteriously veiled layer of viewing – although one could easily misunderstand it thus. It rather refers to ephemeral and acoustic natural phenomena like thunder and lightning. Plinius, in Naturalis historiae libri, XXXV, 96, accordingly depicts Appeles thusly: '[...] pinxit et, quae pingi non possunt, tonitrua, fulgetra, fulgura.' The second sentence, initially referring to Timanthes famous painting showing Iphigenia in Aulis: 'In omnibus eius operibus intelligitur plus semper quam pingitur.' If one proceeds from the original, nothing refers to an esoteric background here as well, but the reference is rather to invisible emotions which one has to follow with one's imagination. Agamemnon's daughter stood

before the altar of Artemis, to whom she was to be sacrificed, while the faces of the surroundings figures displayed grief and terror – and this in a variety and heightening that could not be surpassed in its range concerning the facial representation of emotion. But it is the face of the father, the one most deeply distraught, which is covered by his own garment, thus rendering the expression of his face imaginable to the observer alone. For a dctailed examination of this topic and the particular context concerning Plinius, see Müller-Hofstede 1997, p. 74ff. Plinius, Nat. Hist. XXXV, p. 74 reads: 'atque in unius huius operibus intelligitur plus semper quam pingitur'. It remains open if the latter citation finds a translated political meaning in the sign that the faces of the hunters (as Geuzen) – and thus their emotions – remain invisible.

36 Müller-Hofstede, 1997, p. 138. He also relativizes this specific interpretation – which still remains speculative – as he attributes both the modern consciousness of a purely aesthetic perspective on nature and a new artistic genre to Bruegel at the same time.

37 Buchanan, 1990.

38 ibid.

39 Büttner, 2000; concerning the close interrelation between landscape painting and cartography see also the references in footnote 29.

40 The possible influence of Thomas More and his *Utopia* on the *Garden of Earthly Delights* by Hieronymus Bosch is described by Hans Belting, *Hieronymus Bosch. Garten der Lüste*, Munich: Prestel, 2002.

41 Fritz Novotny goes as far as this: 'There are only a few works of the XVI. century which make a historical consideration seem as superfluous as this series of landscapes by Bruegel. [...] The turn towards the profane, which takes place in Bruegel's complete work, corresponds – in the particular sphere of landscape painting – to the creation of an image of nature which is based on visibility to an extent that was unknown before': in Novotny, 1948, pp. 25–26 (translated by Jochen Mevius); on this topic, see also Tanja Michalsky, 'L'Atelier des Songes. Die Landschaft Pieter Bruegels des Älteren als Räume Subjektiver Erfahrungen', in Klaus Krüger and Alessandro Nova (eds), *Imagination und Wirklichkeit. Zum Verhältnis von Mentalen und Realen Bildern in der Kunst der Frühen Neuzeit*, Mainz: von Zabern, 2000, pp. 123–37.

42 Cf. Werner Busch (ed.), *Landschaftsmalerei*, Berlin: Reimer, 1997, p. 13ff. With regard to some selected drawings by Bruegel, Busch also points out the (still existent) symbolic layers, cf. Michalsky, 2000; Christopher Braider, *Refiguring the Real. Picture and Modernity in Word and Image 1400–1700*, Princeton: Princeton University Press, 1993, p. 71ff. For a different perspective, see David H. Brumble, 'Pieter Bruegel the Elder: The Allegory of Landscape', in *Art Quartely,* No. 2, 1979, pp. 125–39.

43 Regarding the concept of inter-iconicity (as a counterpart to intertextuality), see Thomas Hensel, 'Der Regisseur als Autor als Maler. Zu Andrej Tarkowskijs Poetik einer Interikonizität', in Hensel et al. (eds), *Das Bewegte Bild. Film und Kunst*, Munich: Fink, 2005, pp. 217–56; Christoph Zuschlag, 'Auf dem Wege zu einer Theorie der Interikonizität', in Silke Horstkotte and Karin Leonhard (eds), *Lesen ist wie Sehen. Intermediale Zitate in Bild und Text*, Cologne, Weimar & Vienna: Böhlau, 2006, pp. 89–101; Valeska von Rosen, 'Interpikturalität', in Ulrich Pfisterer (ed.), *Metzler Lexikon Kunstwissenschaft. Idee, Methoden, Begriffe*, Stuttgart & Weimar: Metzler, 2003, pp. 161–64.

44 Cf. Hans Belting, *Florenz und Bagdad. Ein Westöstlicher Blickwechsel*, Munich: Beck, 2008.

45 Concerning the historical dimension, see Oliver Grau, *Virtuelle Kunst in Geschichte und Gegenwart. Visuelle Strategien*, Berlin: Akademie, 2001.

46 Of course, one should not ignore that a similar change and a comparable transfer has taken place in Dutch painting over a century before: from the book of hours of the Duc du Berry, and even more so from the *Turin-Milan Hours* to the Madonna of Chancellor Rolin by Jan van Eyck from 1435. Here, too, the landscape appears as a view that is open and infinitely detailed. The gaze of the observer towards the exterior becomes a part of this. But here, it also becomes linked to the interior, meditative gaze of the chancellor. In the first third of the fifteenth century, it is also quite possible to speak of an aesthetical realization of nature in a landscape painting, which is no longer subject to theological control, and only represents a conceptual arrangement; instead, an open and liberated aesthetical space is created, the pictorial evidence of a unity within a microscopic multiplicity. Concerning this topic and a possible connection to the theological crisis caused by nominalism, see Ruth Groh, 'Van Eycks Rolin-Madonna als Antwort auf die Krise des mittelalterlichen Universalismus', in Christiane Kruse and Felix Thürlemann (eds), *Porträt – Landschaft – Interieur: Jan van Eycks Rolin-Madonna im Ästhetischen Kontext*, Tübingen: Narr 1999, pp. 115–30; Karlheinz Stierle, 'Die Entdeckung der Landschaft in Literatur und Malerei der italienischen Renaissance', in Heinz-Dieter Weber (ed.), *Vom Wandel des Neuzeitlichen Naturbegriffs*, Konstanz: University Press, 1989, pp. 33–52.

47 *Flämischer Kalender*, cod. lat. 23638, Bayerische Staatsbibliothek München; Lucerne: Faksimile, 1987.

48 Vöhringer, 2002; Deborah Povey, 'Abel Grimmer's Twelve Month and Fours Seasons: towards the clarification of a Bruegel dilemma', in *Umění*, No. 51, 2003, pp. 484–94.

49 Klaus Demus speaks of a 'representation of something that is hardly sayable, and thus only showable': in Demus, 1997, p.85 (translated by Jochen Mevius); concerning the general problem of 'the versifying reproduction of works of art', see Otto Pächt, 'Das Ende der Abbildtheorie (1950)', in *Methodisches zur kunsthistorischen Praxis. Ausgewählte Schriften*, Munich: Prestel, 1977.

50 William Carlos Williams, *Selected Poems* (ed. Charles Tomlinson), London: Penguin, 1976, p. 87.

51 Wendy Steiner, 'Williams' Brueghel. Eine vergleichende Analyse', in Volker Bohn (ed.), *Bildlichkeit*, Frankfurt am Main: Suhrkamp, 1990, pp. 229–53, especially p. 232 (translated by Jochen Mevius).

52 Cf. Maja Josifowna Turowskaja and Felicitas Allardt-Nostitz, *Andrej Tarkowskij. Film als Poesie – Poesie als Film*, Bonn: Keil, 1981, p. 52.

53 Andrej Tarkowskij, *Martyrolog, Tagebücher 1970–1986*, Frankfurt am Main & Berlin: Limes, 1989, p. 85ff.

54 Turoskaja/Allardt-Nostitz, 1981, p. 58.

55 Cf. Jürgen E. Müller, *Intermedialität. Formen moderner kultureller Kommunikation*, Münster: Nodus, 1996, p. 197ff; Joachim Paech, 'Ein-BILD-ungen von Kunst im Spielfilm', in Helmut Kort and Johannes Zahlten (eds), *Kunst und Künstler im Film*, Hameln: Niemeyer, 1990, p. 46ff.

56 The most prominent example for this context certainly is his film *Zerkalo/The Mirror* (1974/75).

57 Cf. also Jaques Aumont, 'Projektor und Pinsel. Zum Verhältnis von Malerei und Film', in *montage/av. Zeitschrift für Theorie & Geschichte audiovisueller Kommunikation*, No. 2, 1993, p. 77ff. Nevertheless, Tarkovsky also emphasizes the existing media-related differences with regard to a pure cinematic art in his own book, *Sculpting in Time: Reflections on the Cinema*, Austin: Texas University Press, 1989.

58 Concerning this topic, cf. Henri Bergson, *Materie und Gedächtnis. Eine Abhandlung über die Beziehung zwischen Körper und Geist*, Hamburg: Meiner, [1896] 1991; Gilles Deleuze, *Das Zeit-Bild*, Frankfurt am Main: Suhrkamp, [1985] 1991, especially pp. 95 & 132ff.

59 Tarkovsky, 1989, p. 63ff.

60 Cf. Tarkovsky, 1989, especially p. 122ff.

61 ibid., p. 45.

62 ibid., p. 47.

63 ibid., p. 110.

64 Cf. Hans-Dieter Jünger, *Kunst in der Zeit und des Erinnerns. Andrej Tarkowskijs Konzept des Films*, Ostfildern: Edition Tertium, 1995, p. 88ff.

65 Cf. Hensel, 2005.

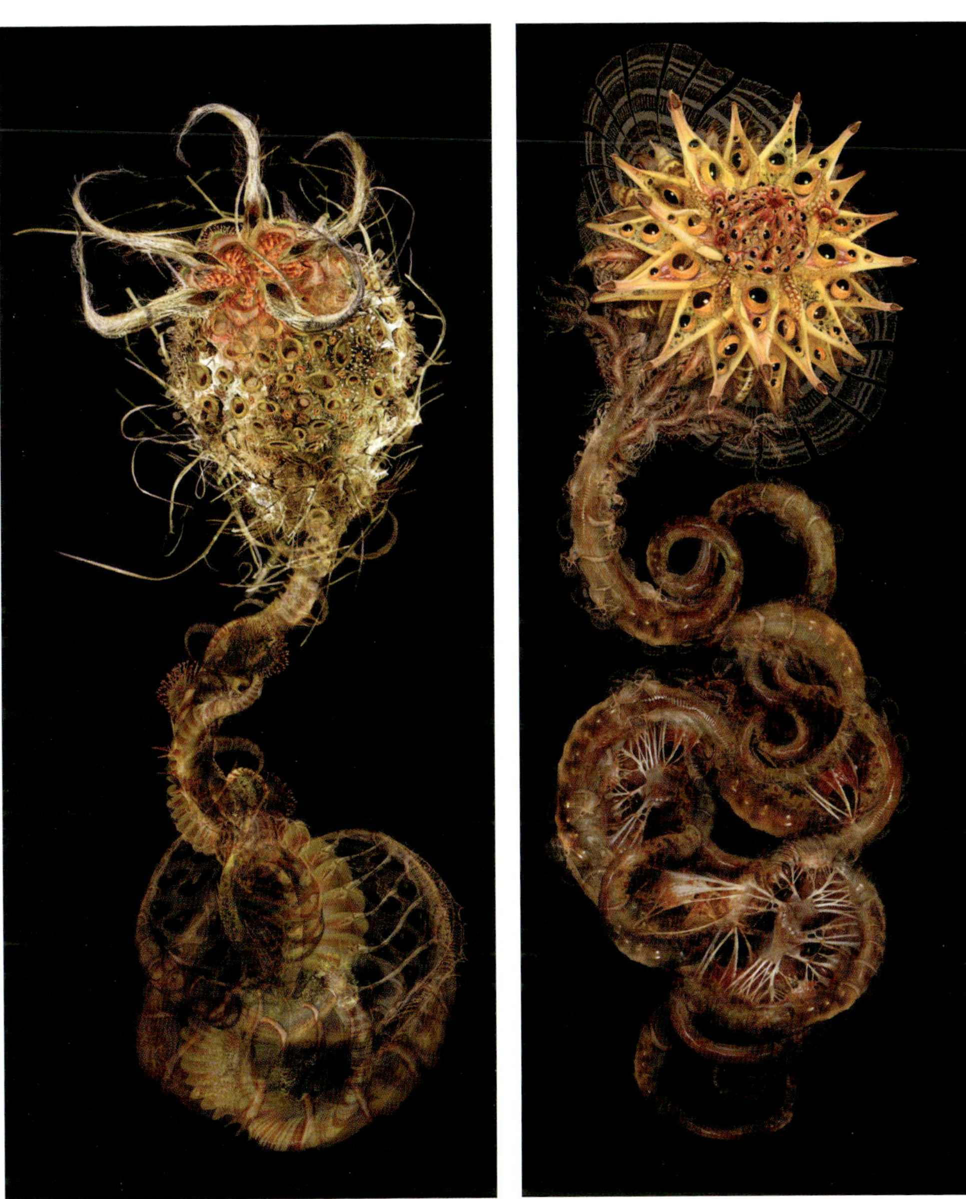

Rohini Devasher, *Archetype I and II*, colour pencil on archival pigment print, 44" × 114" inches 2007. Courtesy of the artist.

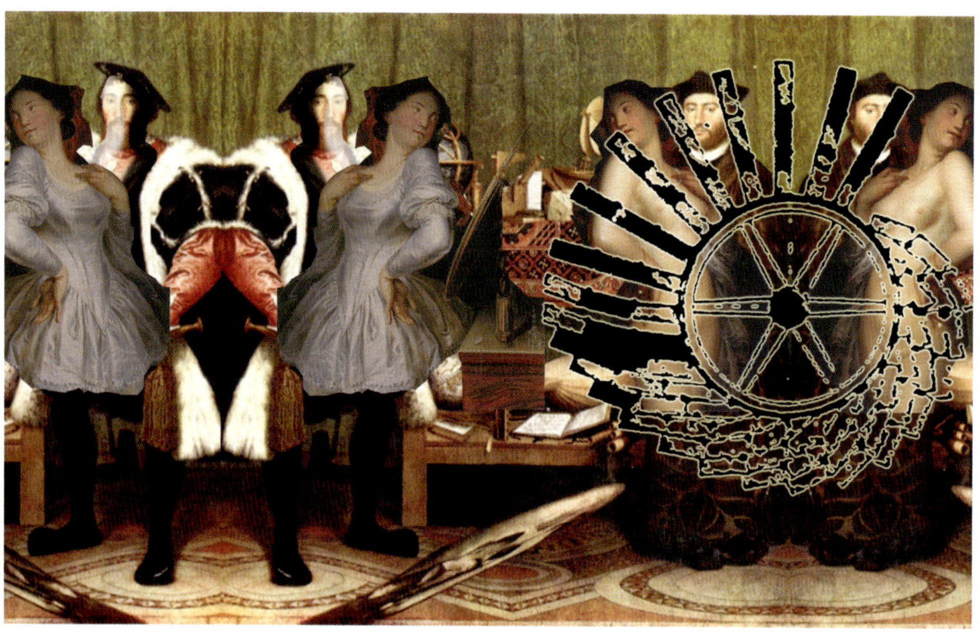

Anne-Mie Van Kerckhoven, *Stranger than Life,* 2009–10, video stills. Courtesy of the artist and Zeno X Gallery, Antwerp.

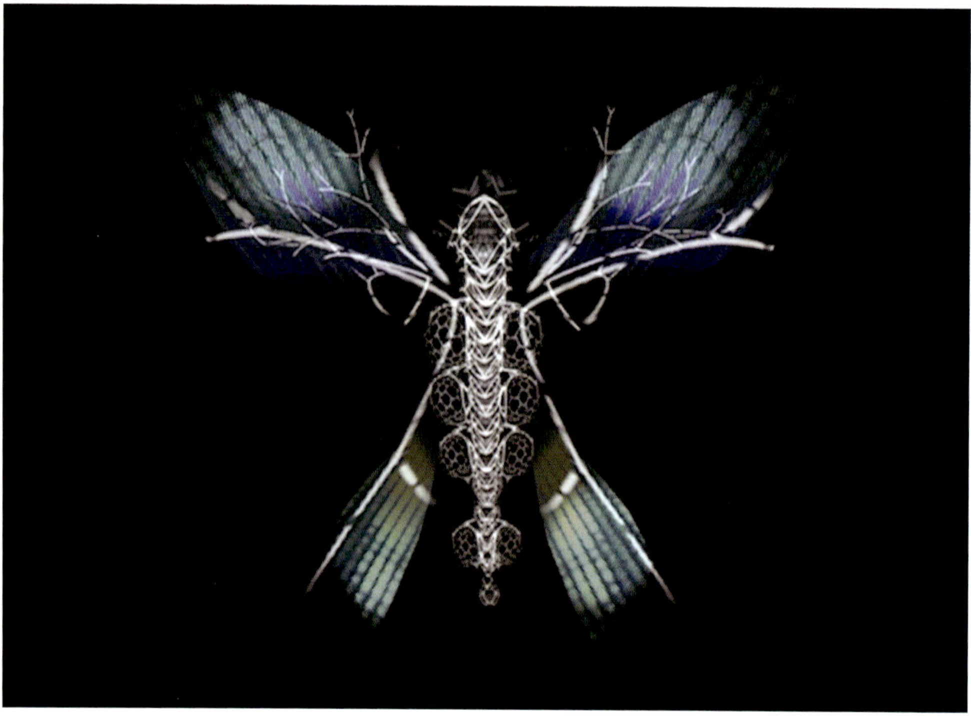

Rohini Devasher, *Doppelgänger,* double channel video, duration 7 min. each, 2011. Courtesy of the artist.

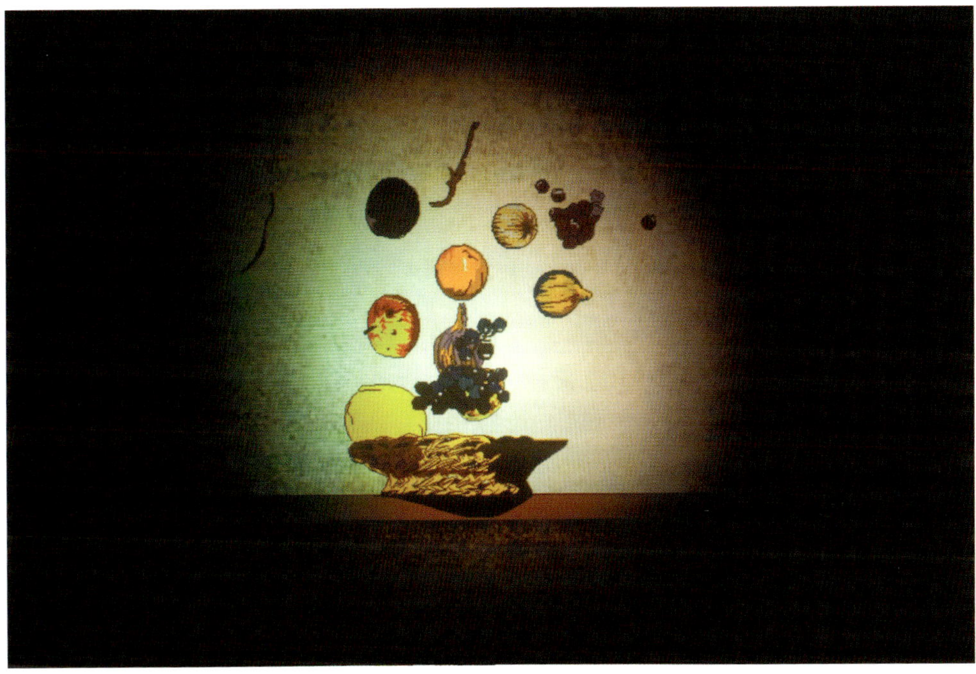

Paul Chan, *Untitled (after St. Caravaggio)*, 2003–06, digital video projection, 2:58min. Courtesy of Greene Naftali, New York.

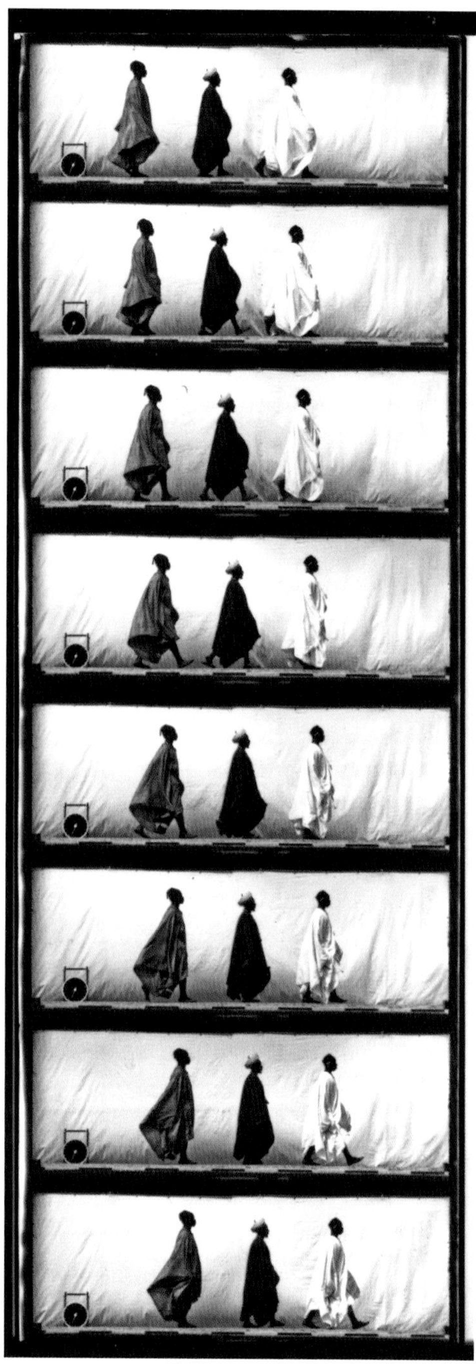

Félix-Louis Regnault, *Hommes nègres, marche*, n.d., duplicate on flexible transparent film. Courtesy of the Cinémathèque Française, Paris.

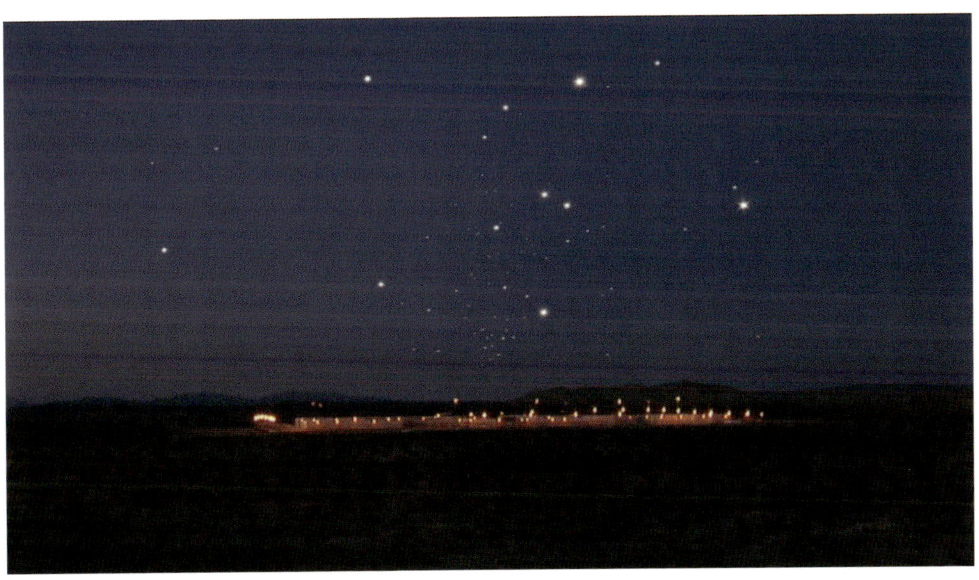

Philipp Lachenmann, *SHU (Blue Hour Lullaby)*, 2002/07. HD Video, 12 min. Courtesy of the artist.

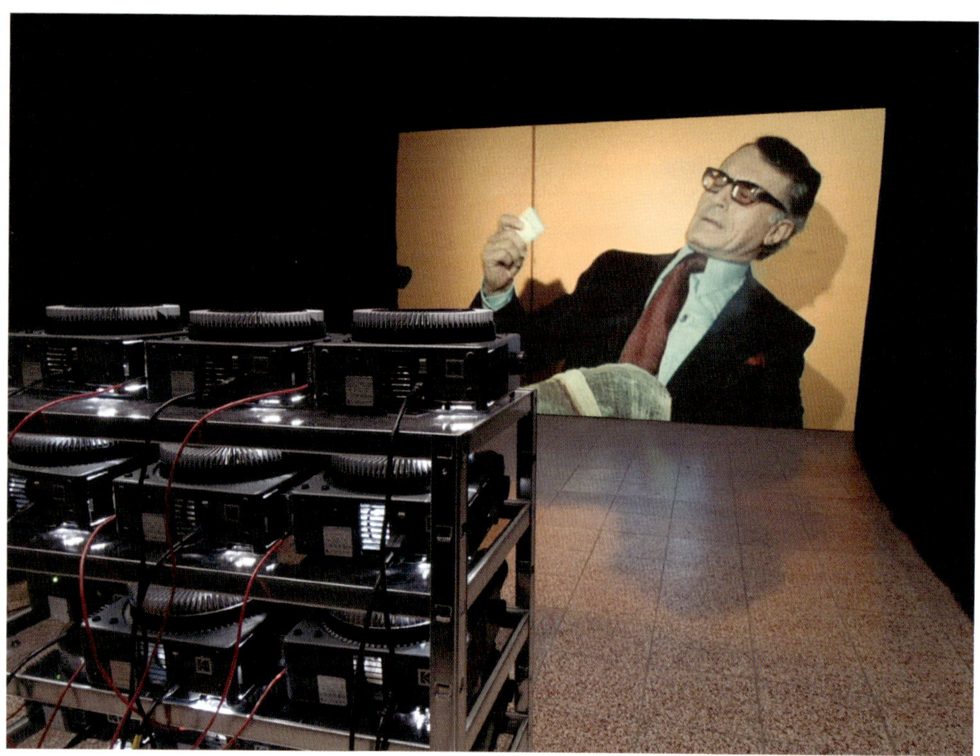

Gebhard Sengmüller, *Slide Movie*, 2005, 35mm film, installation. Courtesy of the artist.

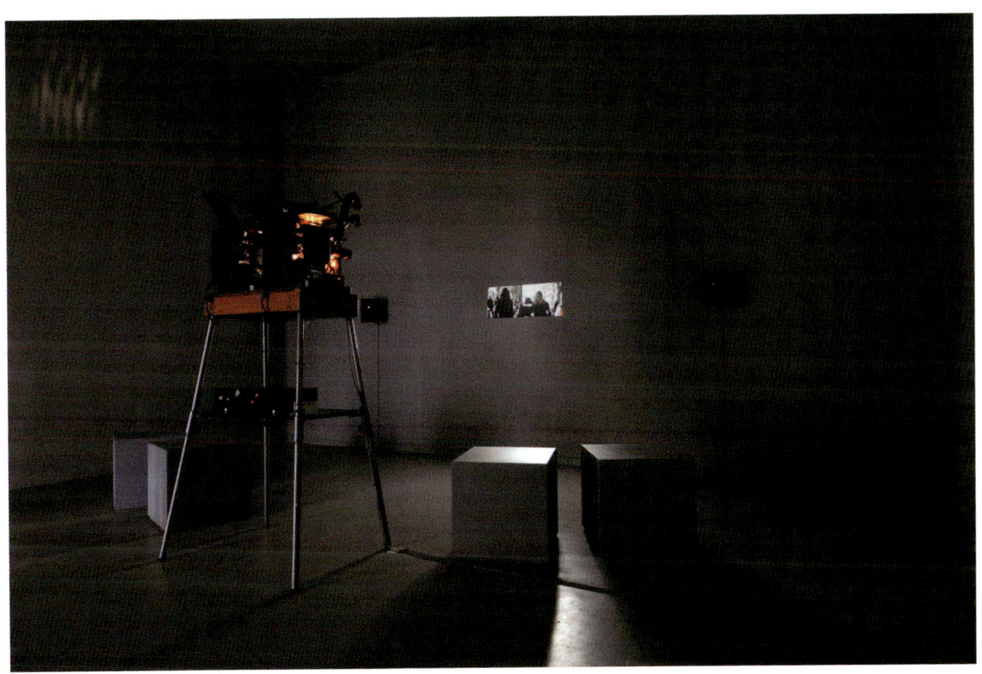

Rosalind Nashashibi, *The Prisoner*, 2008. Installation view, Manifesta 7, Trentino, 2008. Two-screen installation, 16 mm film, 5 min. Courtesy of the artist, commissioned by Manifesta 7. Photograph: Andrea Pozza.

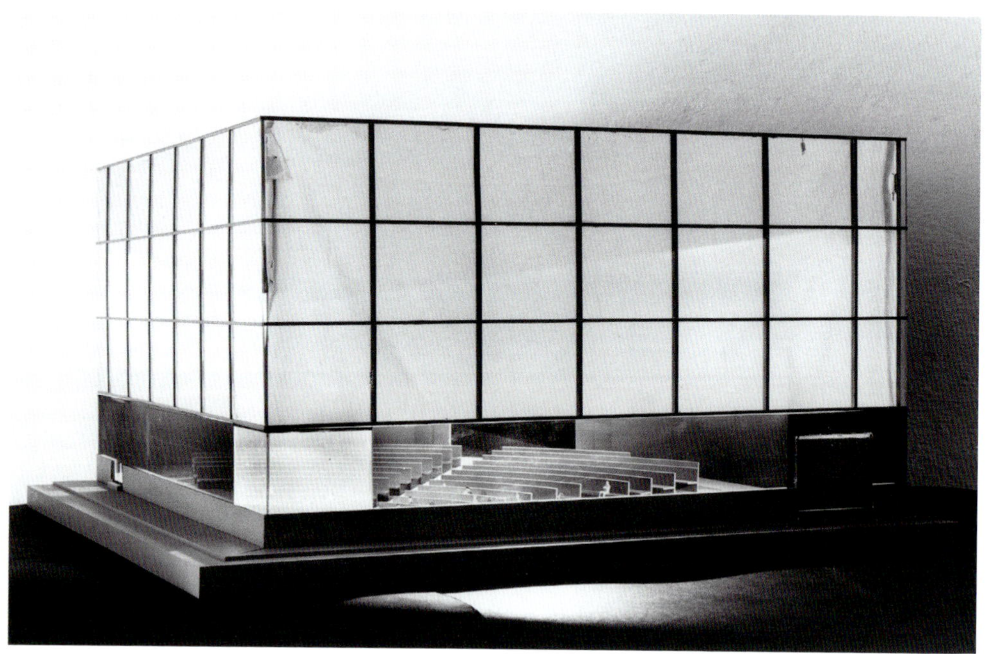

Dan Graham, *Cinema*, 1981/2000 Architectural model, 13 × 21-13/16 × 21-13/16 in. Courtesy of the artist and Marian Goodman Gallery, New York/Paris.

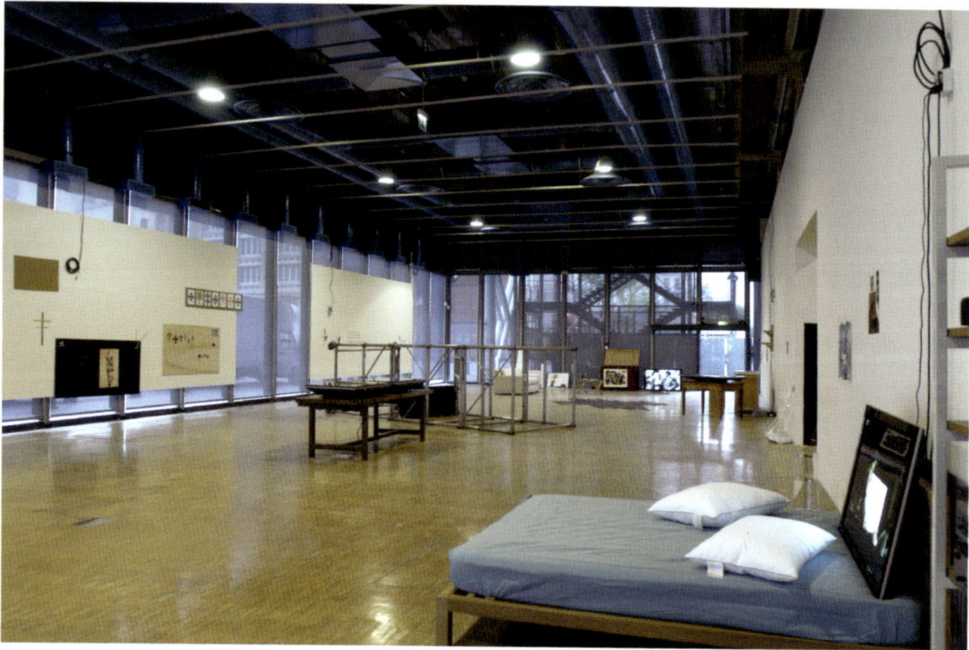

Jean-Luc Godard, View of the exhibition *Voyage(s) en utopie. Jean-Luc Godard 1946–2006, à la recherche d'un théorème perdu.*, Paris, Centre Pompidou, 2006. © Jean-Claude Planchet, Centre Pompidou, 2006.

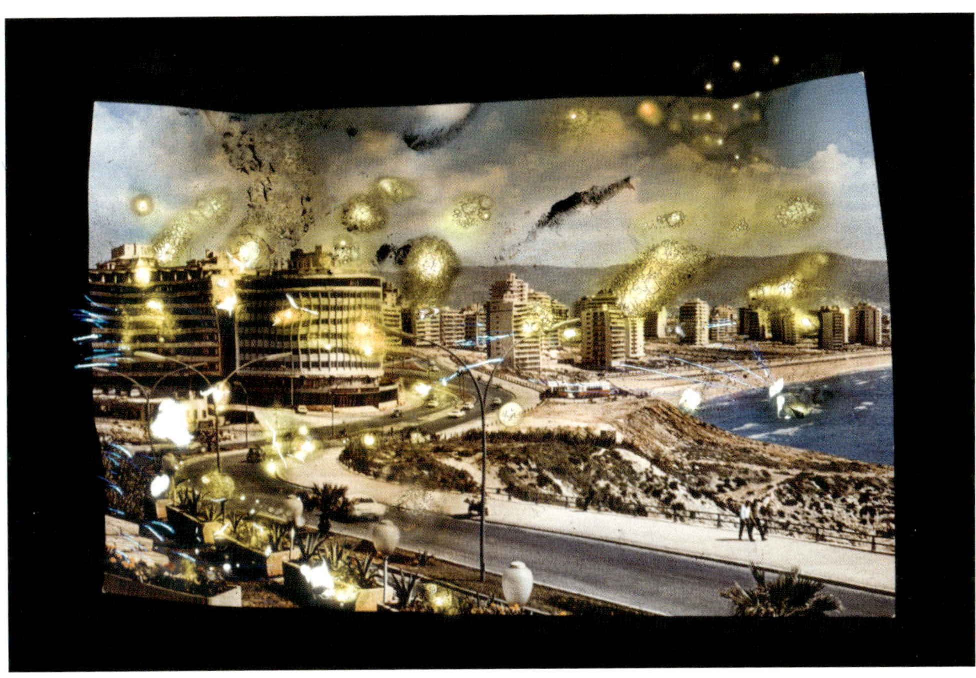

Joana Hadjithomas and Khalil Joreige, *Wonder Beirut: The Story of a Pyromaniac Photographer*, 1998–2006. Courtesy of the artists.

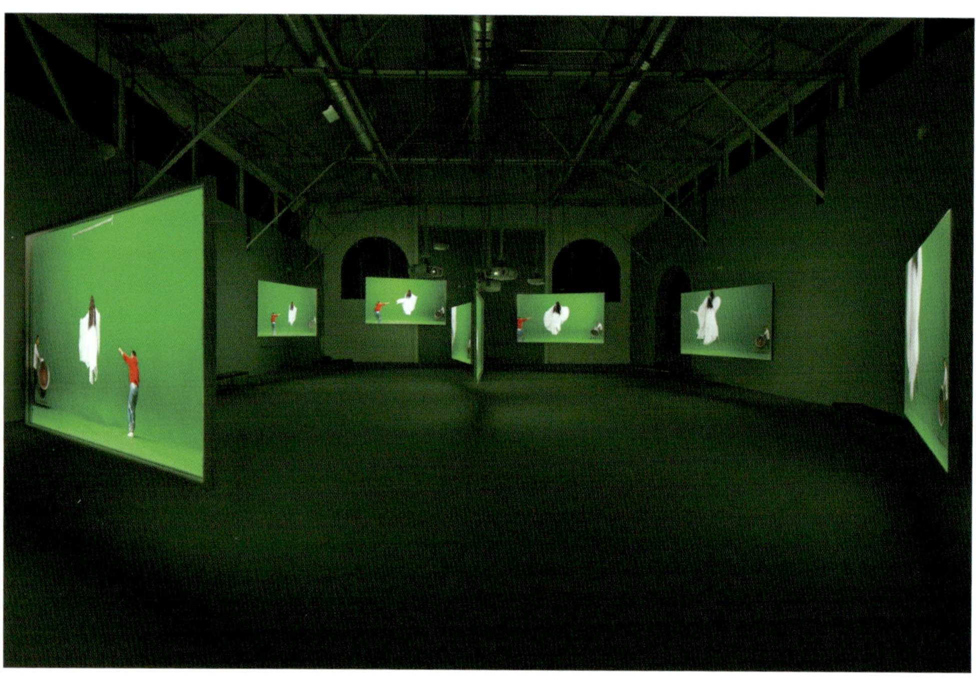

Isaac Julien, *Ten Thousand Waves I*, 2010. Installation view, Museum of Contemporary Art, San Diego. Nine-screen installation, 35mm film transferred to HD, 9.2 surround sound, 49:41 min. Courtesy of the artist and Victoria Miro Gallery, London.

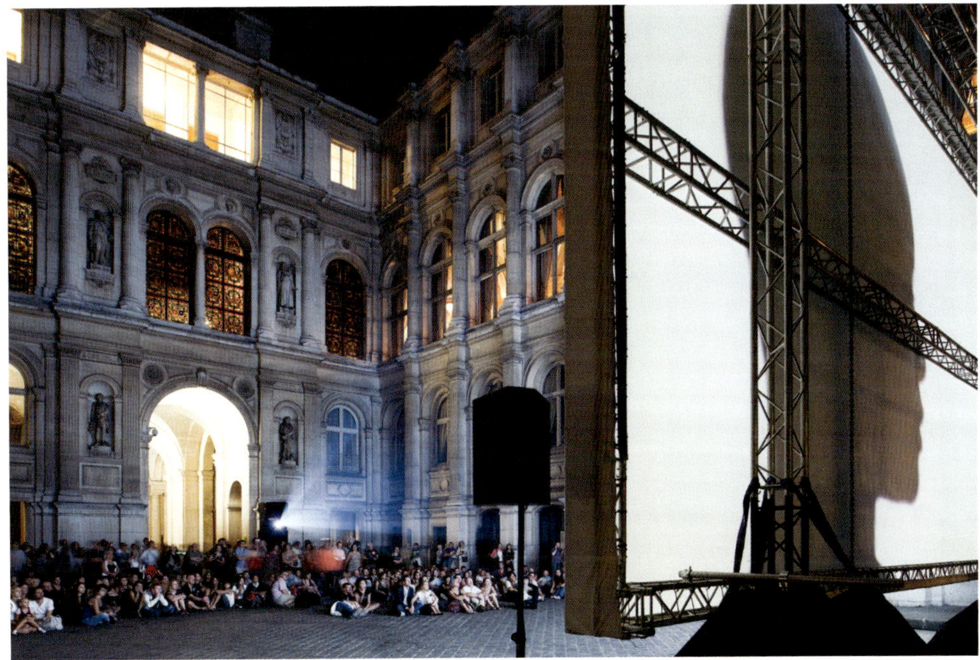

Isaac Julien, *The Leopard I*, 2007. Installation view, Nuit Blanche, Cour de L'hôtel de Ville, Paris. Single-screen installation, super 16mm colour film transferred to HD, sound, 19:51 min. Courtesy of the artist and Victoria Miro Gallery, London. Photograph: Martin Argyroglo.

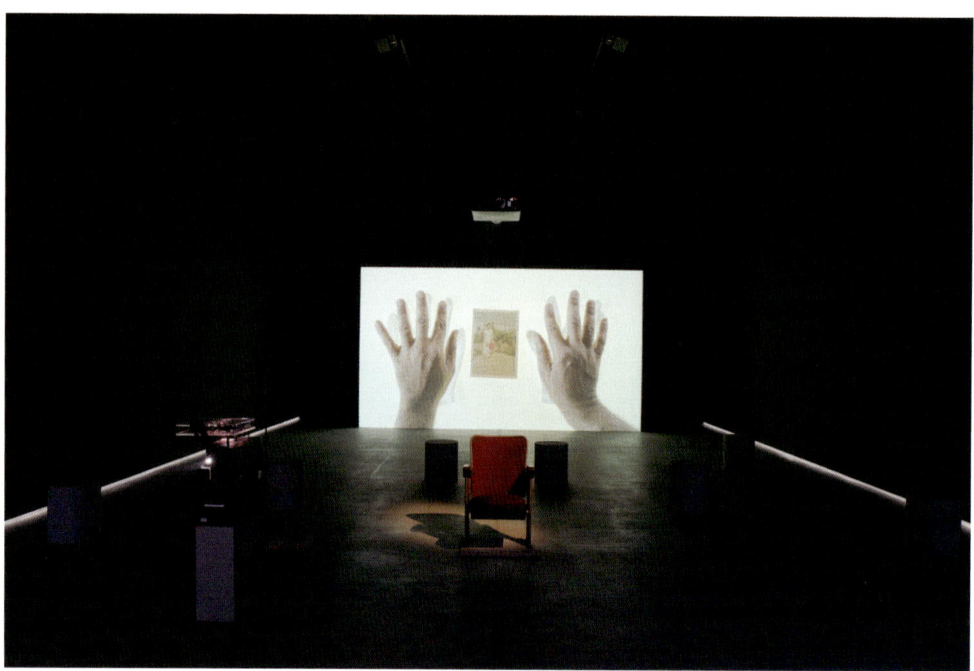

Akram Zaatari, *Letter to a Refusing Pilot*, 2013. Installation View at the Venice Biennale, 2013.
Photo credit: Marco Milan.

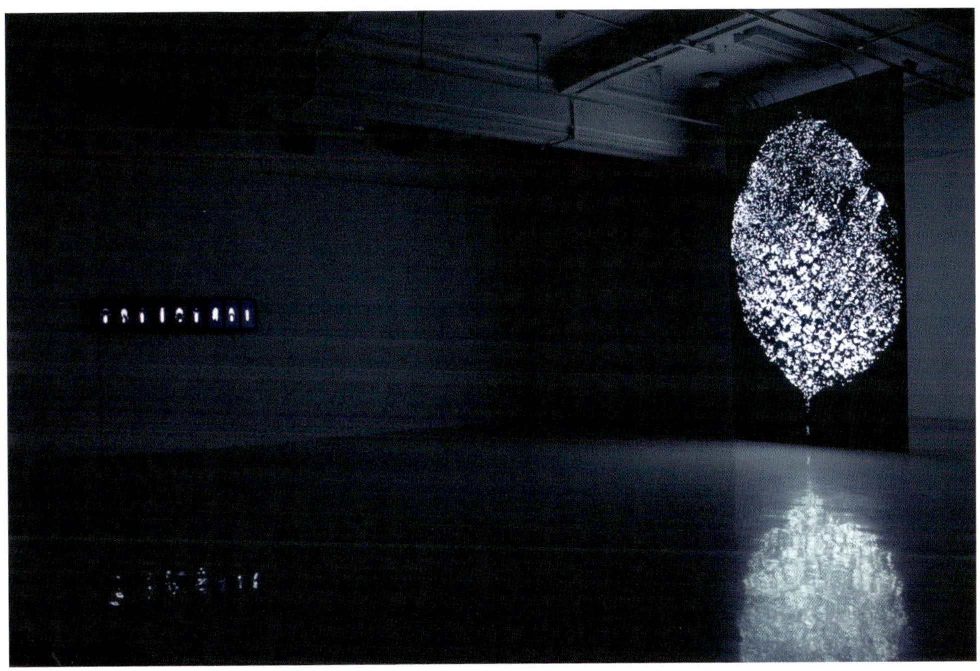

Youki Hirakawa, *Frozen Leaf*, 2012. Installation view. Single-channel, full HD video, vertical projection, 8 min., loop, silent. Courtesy of the artist.

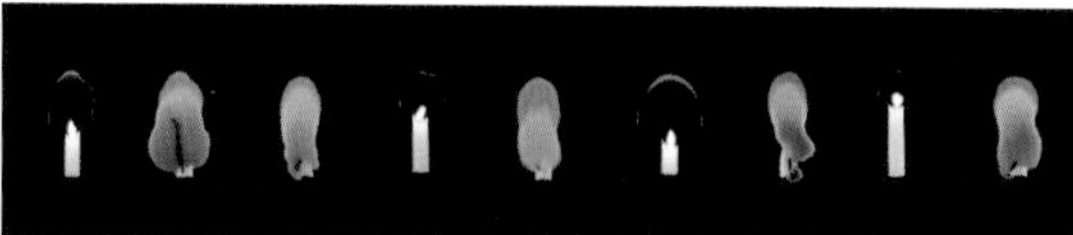

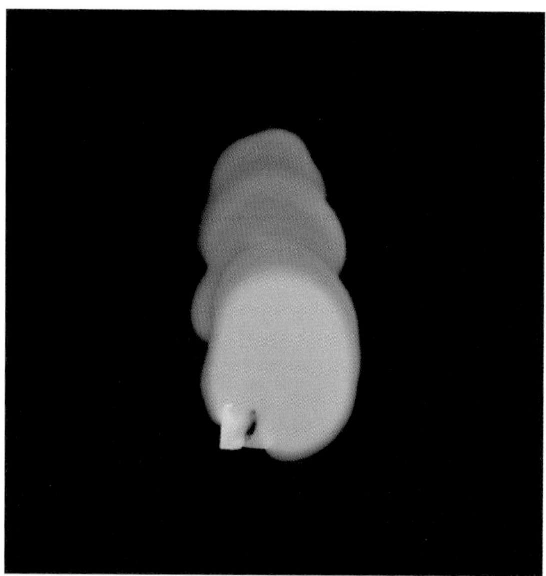

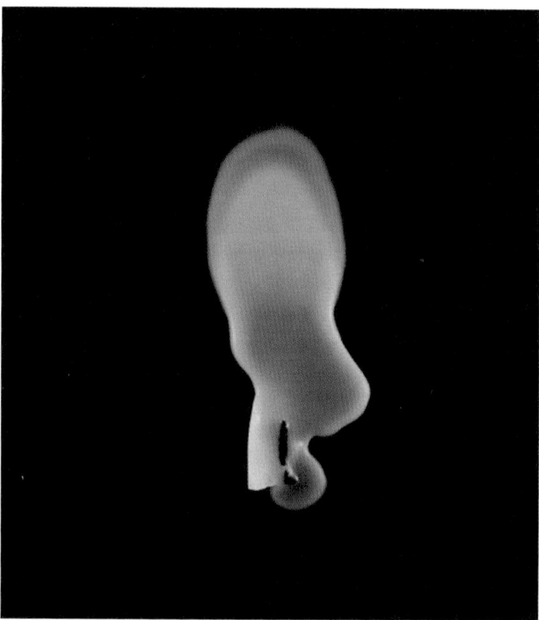

Youki Hirakawa, *Fallen Candle*, 2012, nine-channel full HD video, 15 min. each channel, silent. Courtesy of the artist.

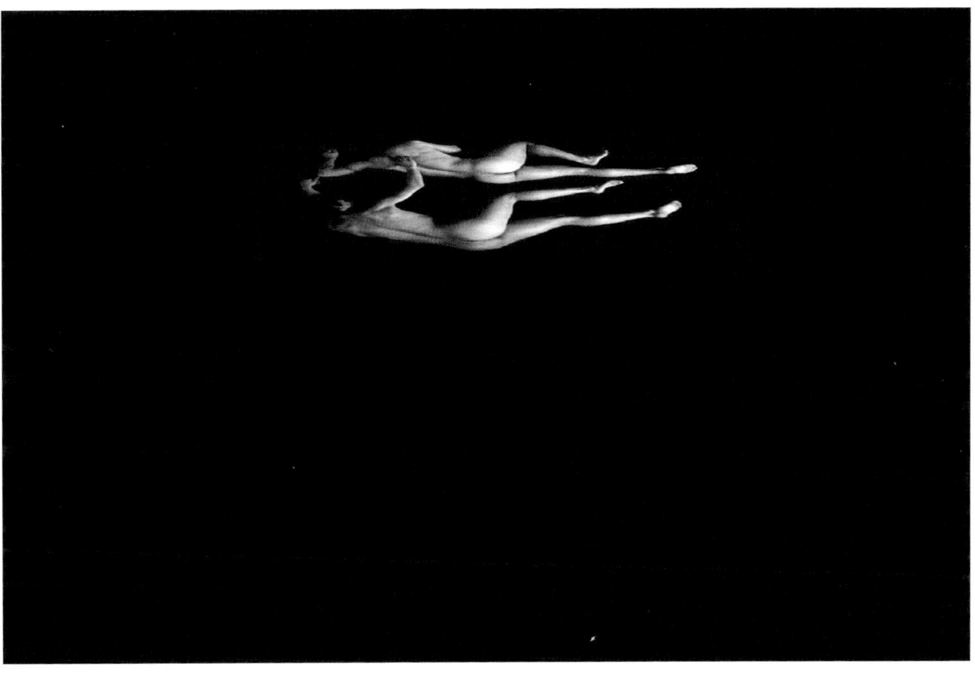

Jim Campbell, *Untitled (for Heisenberg)*, 1994–95. Room-sized installation, dimensions variable. Eight ultrasonic sensors, salt, laser disc player, computer, custom electronics. Courtesy of the artist and Hosfelt Gallery, San Francisco, California.

Chapter 7

Copernicus and I: Revolutions in Perception
and *The Powers of Ten*

Janet Harbord

I.

The psychoanalyst Jean Laplanche notes that during the time in which Copernicus wrote his treatise *On the Revolutions of the Celestial Spheres* (1543), the term 'revolution' had but one meaning, that of rotation (from Latin *revolvere*: 'to turn, to roll back, again, to revolve'). By the time of Kant, some two hundred years later, the prospect of revolution as change or radical transformation had stabilized as a second meaning. To 'turn around' and to 'overturn' become activities etymologically linked by the mid-seventeenth century, according to Laplanche. Yet the effect of Copernicus' treatise in the time of its publication was to invoke the second of the two meanings of revolution far earlier than Kant: the theory of a heliocentric universe, situating the sun as the centre around which other planets rotate, displaced the notion of Earth (and humankind) as the centre of the universe, revolutionizing the understanding of celestial-human relations. Copernicus, through the notion of what planet revolved about what, produced an overturning of ideas that, for many, inaugurated the foundation of modern science.

Laplanche, however, is less concerned with Copernicus and his revolution and more interested in Freud's and his lost revolutionary moment, an interest in potential or opportunity overlooked. According to Laplanche, Copernicus and Freud share a common potency in their work, which is the ability to dislodge the figure of man from the centre of the world – an astronomical world and a psychic one respectively. In a seminal essay, 'The Unfinished Copernican Revolution', Laplanche accuses Freud of discovering, and then burying, the insight that the human subject is both riven by and constituted through the figure of the Other, haunted by a spectral transmission of seduction that registers below the radar of consciousness. Freud's original 'discovery' is nothing less than the founding of the unconscious through the Other, as the Other inside the self, an always-alien presence that comes from elsewhere and disrupts the centred ego of the subject. Citing Freud's famous dictum that Copernicus had struck the first narcissistic blow to mankind by removing him from the centre of the universe – followed by Darwin's demotion of man as sovereign in the order of divine descent – Laplanche argues that Freud in fact missed his moment with history. Retreating from the theory of seduction, Freud went astray in covering over the radical implications of seduction, thus failing to fully reveal the fragile work of ego-formation and its constant undoing by 'the gravitational pull' of the unconscious, 'the obscure way it drags the apparent coherence of our discourse into its orbit'[1].

One might also argue that cinema presented a fourth potentially radical decentring of the human subject, not inconsequently during the period in which Freud was writing. The ghostly apparitional quality of the earliest moving images and their haunting effect is well documented, but what is left as a residual trace in this moment of shock is the means of seeing mechanically: that is, the displacement of the human eye by the camera, a machine that not only mimicked human perception, but extended its reach and provided perceptions that were beyond the ability of the human organ. The camera could literally see from the position beneath a speeding train, as one of the first celebrations of cinema as a mechanical form, Vertov's *Man with a Movie Camera* (1929), reveals.[2] But more suggestively, the camera evinced modes of seeing that the eye alone could not produce: the close-up revealed the breaking instant of a smile in its muscular detail; the moving image could frame movement as gestures isolated in their singularity, or locate the vibrations of the world through objects. Cinema not only allowed the human subject to see again, but presented a form of perception that was radically different from naturalized versions of human perception; in short, cinema as a mechanical form of seeing was potentially alien and excessive to received ideas of human perceptual normality. In its excessive nature, early cinema could be seen to imply that human perception was not necessarily a standard, or indeed a reliable, way of seeing.

There is something of a mirroring of anxieties produced both within cinema and within the discourse of psychoanalysis at more or less the same moment. Both practices, one might note, became locked into certain binary formations in response to anxieties. For cinema, the question of whether the image conformed to a version of the real that could be regarded as a veracity, a document of truth, was radically problematized by the bag of tricks exploited famously by Méliès, but which were nonetheless inherent to cinematic production: framing and selection, in-camera stoppage and techniques of superimposition and post-production more generally. The objective/subjective, indexical/creative split that has reverberated down the century of film theory had its correlation in psychoanalytic debate of the theory of seduction. Freud, according to Laplanche, vacillated between two 'equally inadequate' theories. One deemed seduction to have taken place, therefore it is accorded the status of a real event, and memory is some form of imprint; the other theory reduced the possibility of seduction to the subjectivist phantasy of the individual, a trick enacted retrospectively as it were. In the cinema auditorium and the psychoanalyst's room at the end of the nineteenth and beginning of the twentieth century, whispers of a similar nature could be heard.

In both the cinema and in psychoanalysis, it is not clear where the image is seen from, nor who or what is at the centre of this account. Laplanche directs our attention to the fact that this was also the case in the development of astronomy, and that the decentring of 'man' was only the first step. More radically, the Copernican treatise opened up the universe as an immense and infinite thing, beyond which other solar systems existed, an Otherness beyond the perceptual and calculable possibilities of the human subject. The concept of a potentially unknowable and infinite space emerged through the simple problematic: if the Earth pivots and constantly changes its point of view, how would it be the case that seemingly fixed stars do not undergo some form of change? The answer to this is that the stars are at distance so great from the Earth that this distance is 'incommensurable with the internal distances of the solar system'.[3] The Copernican treatise reveals not only that this solar system opens onto other solar systems, a universe of universes without a centre, but that the dimensions of such Otherness serves to report the limits of human calculation and knowledge.

My aim here is to excavate the traces of a centre-less universe, that exists obliquely in the margins of film culture, and, for Laplanche, in the abandoned ruins of Freudian psychoanalysis, aided by a third discourse that enters the other two by the middle of the twentieth century – that of space travel. These three strands become braided in a particularly suggestive way in the work of American architect-designers, Charles and Ray Eames, who rose to prominence in the mid-twentieth century. The Eameses provide a peculiarly domestic, quotidian version of the decentred world by insisting on the relational quality of living, their design a rehearsal for a potential choreography of being between objects, materials, atmospheres and bodies. In their many projects, man is not the measure of all things, and calculation has its limits. Most poignantly for a genealogy of perception, the Eameses experiment with a range of cinematic, astronautical and cartographic modes of production that question the status of the human figure through displacement; the human body is not necessarily (or consistently) the ideal instrument within which vision is located. Indeed, the corporal is a site constructed through, and dependent upon, various 'Other' technologies. Similarly, we find in Laplanche's reworking of seduction and alien encounters, a concept of 'being human' that undercuts the idea of autonomy, and envisages the subject as part of a web of transmissions and relations. At stake here is the imagining of a different history for film, of how film may have evolved as a technology predicated on sending rather than representing, on elaborating external dependencies rather than the expression of internal worlds, that may have broken with the Romantic notion of selfhood rather than reproducing its negative dynamic of self-Other.

II.

Charles and Ray Eames, a couple who met in 1940 and married the following year, were designers concerned with bodies and how they inhabit space. Most famous for the design of a particular chair whose streamlined feature became the hallmark of neo-modernist taste,

Charles and Ray Eames promoted the belief that design delivered and enhanced the objectives of democracy. With an approach that is proximate to ingenuous, the couple retained a simplicity in their mission and their method, despite their dealings with corporate America and government commissions. The notion of simplicity is however misleading, a disguise for the practice of crossing conceptual, disciplinary and political lines of thought to produce radically different affiliations, clusterings and perspectives. Design is in many ways the Trojan Horse of the Eameses. As a practice, it enabled experimentation and the development of prototypes, a system of modelling that presented scaled down or approximate versions of more complex and potentially destabilizing ideas. Their peculiar career of designing toys, games, houses, furniture, making films of airports, shells, the Mexican Day of the Dead, producing installations and multimedia provides an approach to cultural production that mixes the material and the virtual, calculation and experiment, and embodiment and abstraction. The Eameses' approach to a subject – to create an inventory of its many facets and then to connect elements in a path through complexity – works against the grain of dichotomous thought in the post-war period.

When Charles met Ray in 1940, Ray was a student of his and five years his junior. Charles, trained in architecture, was head of Industrial Design at Cranbrook Academy of Art. Ray was a painter, had studied art and was deeply influenced by a modernist aesthetic. When the pair married they moved to Los Angeles where Charles worked for MGM studios and Ray designed covers for *Art and Architecture* magazine. Los Angeles was the centre of the US aviation industry at this time, and in a powerful identification with the modernist sensibility crossed with aspirational impulse, Charles commented in 1941: 'In the airplane, one feels strongly the appropriateness of its streamed lines and they seem healthy and good'.[4] Charles and Ray, who appear in all of their photographs, and to borrow Beatriz Colomina's description, as 'the ecstatic couple',[5] began to work together on the design and manufacture of toys, chairs, houses, films, and to partner scientific research for which they received numerous awards, including two awards for film at the Edinburgh Film Festival in the 1950s. Charles received much of the acclaim for their collaborative efforts, and despite the iconic photograph of the pair riding a motorbike with Charles seated behind, it is unclear whether Charles ever rode pillion to Ray's front rider.

Appearing to operate at the periphery of corporate and political life, their practice resides at the powerful intersection of computer development and domestic life in the post-war period. The Eameses were in a sense vectors, manufacturing the relations between things, skilfully holding in play the traction between the material and the virtual, the embodied viewer and abstract calculation. In a period of nascent computer culture, they revealed the enigmatic nature of information and its visualization, relocating the problem of meaning within the space of relative positions rather than in the discrete spaces respectively of the body, the subject or the machine. In so doing, the Eameses allow us to ask retrospectively a series of questions about how we conceptualize perception and its relation to mechanization, knowledge and exteriority. My method here draws on that of Charles and Ray Eames, in assembling a range of seemingly disparate and oppositional modes of thought and enacting a process of cross-referencing and association[6] between texts, 'facts', faction and philosophies, including psychoanalysis and space travel.

In so doing, I aim to disrupt the interpretation of the concept of perception as a mode of attention securing a disciplined subjectivity. In drawing on a range of discursively different texts, from space travel, an educational science film turned cult object, psychoanalysis and philosophy, I aim to reinsert the instability of perception as the site of knowledge. Perception here is a dynamic correspondence with various forms of Otherness or beyond-knowing, which the field of visual culture mobilizes.

III.

Space travel provided one of the greatest adjustments to the self-perception of the human species. It is also perhaps the most dramatic performance of the interdependency of human and machine, self and Other. In 1957, this performance involved a dog as a surrogate for the human figure in the launch of the first (Russian) satellite; Laika, a mongrel from the streets of Moscow, was the companion species, whose return was not planned for – a calculated collateral loss. The purpose was to monitor the sensory affects of space travel on a living organism. Her legacy endures as a trace of the corporeal, a sound recording of her heartbeat now survives on the Internet. As a result of this experiment, in 1961, Russian cosmonaut Yuri Gagarin orbited the Earth for 108 minutes in the Vostok 3KA and became the first man in space. In moving beyond the Earth's 'atmosphere', Gagarin's journey conversely reflected back the significance of the atmosphere as a shared set of conditions necessary for the continuation of life.

On 14 March 1962, Jacques Lacan, in a seminar on identification, speculated on the voyage of Gagarin, pitting the soft flesh of the human body against the frail tin container. The cosmonaut was suggestive for the psychoanalyst, who regarded the spectre of man inside of a machine, which is itself in space, as symptom of the modern subject floating free in a universe of significations with no recourse to foundation. For Lacan, we are all 'erotic cosmonauts', navigating between the matter of bodies and the computing apparatus of the symbolic order that channels and delimits our desires. If the space capsule is a metaphor for the desiring body, it is a natural step to speculation on the effects of a lack of gravity on the body's sexual functions. 'What happens,' asks Lacan, 'in the state of weightlessness to the sexual drive, which usually manifests itself as going against gravity?';[7] or in what way is desire constituted if not through the dichotomous structure of gravity? Yet as metaphor, the scenario beholds the terrible isolation of the Lacanian desiring subject.

IV.

Prior to this cross-interference of space and psychoanalysis, in 1946, a rocket-borne 35-millimetre camera attached to a V-2 missile had provided the first image of Earth from space at a distance of 65 miles. These images of the Earth from space register in various ways in the Eameses' work, but their overall effect is consistent with a project that 'breaks with a fixed perspectival view of the world', proffering a point of view with no privileged site of perception.[8] The image of world-from-space resonated with a technologized way of seeing that was located in calculated projections, dependent on a culture of computing that was in the mid-twentieth century, about to cross from military into domestic use. The Eames office was the centre of a hub of industry, government, design and architectural interests leading to projects that encouraged, explored and demonstrated the interrelations of these domains. In 1953, the Eameses made the film *A Communication Primer* that sought to explain the use of the computer in everyday life. A successful film attracting the attention of IBM, the couple were commissioned to make *The Information Machine* in 1957. The film was one in a long series that the Eameses made for the computer company IBM, along with dozens of exhibitions and books created over the course of two decades. Corporate America funded much of the Eameses' output. In addition to IBM, the companies Polaroid, ABC, CBS, Westinghouse, Time Inc and Boeing commissioned the Eameses to make cultural models that explained the corporate intention and their products to the public. Conceiving of their office as a communications system, the Eameses' career reflects the changing terrain of the post-war period in America, moving from an industrial economy to one of information and knowledge. The most flagrant demonstration of this was their exhibit for the 1959 American National Exhibit in Moscow, *Glimpses of the USA*, a multi-screen installation on seven suspended screens, upon which more than 2200 still and moving images of quotidian America were projected. The project was key to their practice, utilizing both the computer and film; the installation operated along an axis of proximity (domestic interiors) at one end to extreme distance (aerial views of a city) at the other. Vision, it would seem, was not on the ground, nor located within a body.

V.

In 1968, the first prototype of the film *The Powers of Ten* was made, a shorter version than the more famous later film, using a female voice-over and situating the picnic on a golf course in Miami. The 1977 version relocated the scene to Lake Michigan, Chicago. It took a year to make. The only live sequence is the picnic scene, the first thirty seconds of the film. The most onerous part of the production was the remaining 40 images, drawn from aerial photography and images from space travel in collaboration with NASA. The film is patched together from photographs of photographs, photographs of composites, photographs of paintings based on scientific photographic images[9] to produce an imaginative sequence rather than a photographically indexical one. To create the animated film odyssey, the images were arranged as a storyboard on a 40-foot long animation stand. The images that take us into the epidermis, the collagen, the capillaries, cell nucleus, an atom and a quark were made through an electron microscope and painted over to simulate what the human eye cannot see. These pictures of boundary surfaces are given a diagrammatic rendition, for what they represent is form without stability, structures that are in constant motion.

In this film of calculated travelling, the conventions of narrative film create a dramatic, if somewhat skeletal, structure. The use of voice-over both narrates and comments on the action, generating a story in two parts. The first establishing shot of a couple having a picnic constructs the ground beneath our feet, the quotidian scene of leisure but for the weightily marked *mis-en-scene*: on the chequered blanket are placed a clock, and books on science and time. The man sleeps in the sun, and it is from his body that we take our leave, as though the film may be inhabiting his dreams – a trope typical of 1950s Hollywood. The scene is idyllic, Edenic, and indeed it is Adam who sleeps whilst Eve remains alert to the possibilities of the immediate environment. As we leave the environment and rise further out, the scenes are described in terms of a measurement consistent with the human body – how far a man can run in the space of a minute. But as we pull away from the scene of the picnickers, the explanation strains to find an equivalent human measure. What the viewer is given to experience is the sensory rush of being pulled backwards rather than simply up. The use of a backwards zoom animates the images to produce a smooth line of motion, yet we are being pulled in a direction whilst being denied a view of what we are approaching. It is a camera action reminiscent of Hitchcock's simultaneous backtracking forward zoom, a disorientating combination of movements that brings the object into greater focus whilst retreating from the scene. The sense of uncertainty in this movement works against the calculation of the controlling explanatory voice, which, as the film unfolds, becomes a type of incantation.

It is unclear how far we will or can go, of whether there is a limit in this sequence or the possibility of endless mathematical description. In what begins as an acceleration away from the quotidian scene of the picnic and into the scene of space travel, it becomes a sequence about loss. The transporting effect of the journey gives way to disorientation and loss, for to move away from the Earth is also to diminish it to the point of disappearance. The further we go, the greater the sense of surrounding alienation. 'As we approach the limit of our vision, we pause to start back home, this lovely scene, the galaxies like dust, is what most of space looks like,' the voice tells us, adding, 'this emptiness is normal'. It is unclear whether this emptiness belongs to the galaxies or to the viewer. This pause is also what we might call the first act turning point of this micro-drama, a pause about ocular limits. The pause is also to float momentarily before the reverse motion sets in, zooming us into familiar territory. If the film had ended here, it would have provided a clear binary opposition, of man and the universe, micro and macro. But as the camera enters the hand of the man, the second turning point occurs. The hand, in a somewhat Lynchian mode, leads us into another world of scale, one that the human eye again cannot see. In a film that purports to expand our knowledge, it evolves into a film about what we cannot know, or what we can know but not see. Subsequently, and in a rupture of the epistemological from the ontological, what we cannot see may contradict what we believe we know.

VI.

In an essay entitled 'The Unfinished Copernican Revolution' published in 1992, the psychoanalyst Jean Laplanche is concerned with journeys that meander off course, with Freud as his central protagonist. Laplanche's reading of the Freudian trajectory travels through Copernicus, or Freud's fascination with the 'Copernican moment' of a narcissistic wounding. Up until the mid-fifteenth century, the question of what turns around what planet follows a line set out by Ptolemy in the second century AD, and taking in a tradition that was to include Aristotle, Plato and Pythagorous. The Ptolemaic thesis postulated that the Earth was the centre of the universe, and from this false hypothesis, set out on a path of inventing supplementary ad hoc explanations that support the error rather than allowing the detail to call it into question. Laplanche dwells on this period of astronomy for its illustration of what he calls a radical 'going astray', a move that prefigures Freud's initial thesis on seduction, and subsequent withdrawal from this, choosing a path that Laplanche calls 'Ptolemaic': detail is added to detail in order to support the wrong supposition. If Laplanche posits an analogy between himself and Copernicus in the correction an original wrong turning, the parallel in astronomy and psychoanalysis is also the difficulty of living with a knowledge of displacement and decentring; a question of the relation between epistemology and ontology.

'What is at stake in what we neatly term the "Copernican revolution"', writes Laplanche, 'is a question of centring which at the outset seems limited to a change of astronomical centre [...] but which actually opens onto far vaster consequences.'[10] Beyond establishing heliocentrism, Copernican thought opened the door to the idea, noted above, of a centreless universe. If the centre of the world could be everywhere and 'its circumference is nowhere',[11] there are no limits, or rather, there is infinity. The paradox of this moment is that in the so-called advance of knowledge about the functioning of the universe, the limits to knowledge become apparent: infinity is the spectre of an infinite knowledge that is infinitely unknowable. And 'man' is not, spatially or astronomically, the centre of what, in whatever limited capacity, he does know. Furthermore, 'man is in no way the measure of all things', and there is the rub in Laplanche's interpretation of bodily empiricism. For the original going astray of Ptolemaic astronomers, Laplanche attributes to their method as philosophers, lacking in empirical observation. The productive line of descent traced through astronomers, mathematicians and geographers, the Copernican line, is 'closer to observation', a result of the empiricism that in another context condemns man as the creature who cannot see beyond his empirical self.

But the real critique of the essay is saved for Freud rather than man. In a moment that could (according to Laplanche) have initiated the Copernican revolution of psychoanalysis, as early as 1897, Freud had both discovered and abandoned the idea of seduction as a foundational element of psychic life. The discovery and its abandonment set in play the paradoxical displacements and swerves in Freudian thinking that lead to what Laplanche regards as the domestication of the 'Other', and the predominance of the biological drives as explanatory forces. In this essay (and in his work more broadly), Laplanche returns to this scene to insert the seduction of the other's communication, its translation and repression as a constitutive event in the formation of the unconscious. The dynamic state of the unconscious remains so precisely as a result of the enigmatic message from the 'Other' that is never assured in its meaning: '[T]he other thing (*das Andere*) that is the unconscious is only maintained in its radical alterity by the other person (*der Andere*): in brief, by seduction.'[12]

The Copernican move that Freud makes and then retreats from sets up a dialectic in his work between a conservative interpretation and a radical one. For Laplanche, this is not a matter of retrospective debate and interpretation. Rather, Freud's model of the unconscious ceases to wield an explanatory force once the domestication of the alien Other (seduction) is removed.

VII.

Between the first and second versions of *The Powers of Ten*, the Eameses made a film about Copernicus in 1973, in commemoration of the 500th anniversary of the astronomer's death. The short film is located in northern Italy, where Copernicus studied. The film traces the relation between the study of astronomy and the advent of the printing press. Copernicus is attributed with the revolutionary model of astronomy partly as a result of his engagement with a new technology, a technology of record and reproduction that circulated his text to many others, although Copernicus was purportedly reluctant to publicize his work for fear of garnering hostility. One might pause for thought at this crossroads, between the domestic or private life and the public arena, to note that the Eameses, unlike Copernicus, unlike Freud, had made a virtue in erasing the boundary.

VIII.

Despite his reluctance to be put into circulation, Copernicus appears in many philosophical texts in the following centuries, not least in Nietzsche's *Beyond Good and Evil* (1886), warning of the dangers of totalizing forms of scientific and philosophical thought. Copernicus appears in the first section as a prized opponent of ocular evidence. Copernicus is in part a springboard for Nietzsche's attack, a few pages further on, of the narcissism of the subject articulated as a unified 'I':

> As for the superstitions of the logicians, I shall never tire of underlining a concise little fact which these superstitious people are loath to admit – namely, that a thought comes when 'it' wants to, not when 'I' want; so that it is a *falsification* of the facts to say: the subject 'I' is the condition of the predicate 'think'. *It* thinks: but this 'it' is precisely that famous old 'I' is, to put it mildly, only an assumption, an assertion, above all not an 'immediate certainty'.[13]

The 'I' that Nietzsche attacks as self-present in thought is undone by thought itself, an alien thing that arrives at its leisure. The critique prefigures the trail that Freud was about to embark on several years later, tracing a radical disruption of consciousness emanating from elsewhere.

IX.

Towards the end of 'The Unfinished Copernican Revolution', Laplanche threads together the beads of space travel, alien Otherness and unconscious processes.[14] Citing the 1972 Pioneer 10 rocket, Laplanche refers to the decoration on the side of the rocket as an attempt 'to send across interstellar space a message which would signify my intention to communicate – and this beyond any sharing of codes with the possible recipient'.[15] Laplanche does not elucidate the detail of the message, which was an image of man and woman, Adam and Eve, painted in naked and vulnerable form on the side of the craft. Adam has his hand raised in the air as a sign of greeting, a curious gesture given the ambiguity of the meaning of this sign. Even when one shares the code of communication, it is unclear whether he is waving hello or goodbye. Laplanche, placing himself in the position of the alien 'receiver', finds two possible interpretations. The first is that this may read as an index of intelligent life inside the rocket. The second interpretation is that the alien understands the sign as a desire of the sign, the desire to communicate, to address, transmit or signal *something* in the absence of a shared code. For Laplanche, the image of Adam and Eve, it would seem, is an irresistible illustration of the recognition of the alien Other, toward whom a communication is sent, and 'perhaps, to conscious and even unconscious reasons for such an intention'.[16]

X.

The pause of the film as it hovers at the edge of the galaxies is also the point of pivot, the turning back towards home. And so the journey speeds us towards the Earth, through the frames of calculation that bear witness, like milestones, to our journey out. Falling back into the Earth's atmosphere as though we were in fact in the capsule of a rocket, we return home. Home is the body of the man regarded from a distance of one metre (ten to the power of zero), a framing that incorporates the whole body. Only the film does not stop here, but insists on a continuation of this simple line of motion-based calculation, permeating the skin as though it were not a boundary, to reveal microns, angstroms and fermi. The spiralling shapes and textures of each frame are narrated in detail.

Where the journey into the cosmos held out the phantasy of human seeing inside of a space craft, this sequence of the film thoroughly problematizes that idea. What we may have phantasized as the location of perception – the body of the man dreaming this voyage – is now the object of investigation, his role as perceiving subject put into question:

can one both see and see inside of oneself? Conventionally, the perception of the body through the skin purports to a kind of seeing that exposes what is hidden. The journey through the skin in *The Powers of Ten* reveals nothing other than patterns, rhythms and vibrations. The alien environment of outer space centres back to the subject, an internal alienness inside of the self.

XI.

At this point, I want to circle back to Laplanche and the essay on Copernicus once more in order to critique the description of the relation that he sets in play between alienness and the subject. In his elaboration of the ex-centric subject, Laplanche describes it thus:

> Internal alien-ness maintained, held in place by external alien-ness; external alien-ness, in turn, held in place by the enigmatic relation of the other to his own internal alien – such would be my conclusion concerning the decentering revolution I have proposed here in continuation of the Freudian discovery.[17]

In the language that Laplanche chooses to describe this rebounding set of phantasized states of the self via the Other, the image proposes a subject internally enclosed, a unification modelled on the image of the body as an autonomous organism. The body here is separate in its existence, containing inside of itself the phantasized relation with the external Other. Although Laplanche is keen to expose how the state of autonomy is radically compromised by the existence of an alien Other internalized, the spatial integrity of subject and object remain in place. Reading this description through the lens of the Eameses' film, another possibility emerges – of a state of phantasized relations that exist in the movement of away and towards, residing in the realm of between rather than inside,[18] giving rise to another set of questions concerning psychoanalytic modelling, image production and space travel. Can the unconscious be imagined as existing between subjects rather than inside of them?[19] Are images but one manifestation of enigmatic messages sent towards the Other? Is the rigorous scientific calculation of distances and relations between bodies, planets and atoms ever free of the desire to communicate enigmatically?

XII.

In the 1970s, and between the making of the two *Powers of Ten* films, the Eameses were commissioned by Polaroid to make four films about the new instant cameras. In 1972, the first of these, the film *SX-70*, was made. Diagrams of the camera's components and its chemical process were intercut with scenes of people using the cameras and offering each other the photographs. Charles worked closely with Edwin H. Land, the inventor of the camera and president of Polaroid. Land wrote of the instant camera: 'A new kind of relationship between people in groups is being brought into being by the *SX-70* when the members of a group are photographing and being photographed and sharing the photographs.'[20] By the 1970s, photography is not only a representational practice, but a vector for relations between people, making visible the connections between subjects and Others through exchanging perceptions in the form of material images. Polaroid photography was conceived by the Eameses' at least as a fundamentally social media.

XIII.

Returning to the question of Copernicus and revolutions that revolve around the question of the eye of perception, the biological eye, the subjective 'I' and the mechanical eye of the camera, each of these questions are nestled inside of one another and in orbit. It may be instructive here to recall that the Copernican revolution did not create an immediate overturning of the experience of the world. The next morning, the world turned on its axis and the sun came up, or appeared to. Obtaining the knowledge that the world was not the centre of the universe did not necessarily transform experience of it; rather it produced a doubling of systems of thought as the Ptolemaic and the Heliocentric that continue to coexist.

This doubling of systems of perception and thought might also be a pertinent description of the 'revolution' of cinema, and the subsequent splitting of the medium into documentary film and narrative film at the beginning of the twentieth century. The question of where we see from is raised by any prosthetic extension of viewing, and where the mechanical enters the scene in the form of the camera, seeing is engaged with a prosthesis. Perception is dependent on another thing, and in the early part of the century, graphic forms of representation that revealed their machinic vision[21] became a genre of their own, of science, put to work in the service of medicine and military applications. The other line of descent, arguably, translates the automated vision of the camera into the Ptolemaic, domesticated infrastructure of narrative cinema, where the positions of seeing and the field of representation mimics the perspective of the human subject. The existence of alienness in the field of perception is concealed in this splitting, and only in popular science films do the two traditions converge again, as well as, more recently, in electronic cartography programmes such as Google Earth. For this reason, *The Powers of Ten* is a significant visual experience, reminding us that perception is at once virtual and embodied.

Did the Eameses have this in mind, and is the film an example of their intuitive feel for what IBM and a nascent computer culture was ushering into the frame as popular culture? We cannot know. In the image of the Eameses that I have in mind as I write, of the couple standing on a low parapet, holding hands and their outer arms raised as they dangle ornaments, they appear to distil a certain period of American-ness. Homespun optimists, able to turn their hands to anything, Charles and Ray were born into the era of the Depression only to find themselves in an Eden of unprecedented manufacturing and innovation. They are waving something at us. But their communication, sent into the future, remains enigmatic. With arms raised, they seem to be telling us something, but we cannot be sure of what it is.

Notes

1 Jean Laplanche, 'The Unfinished Copernican Revolution', in *Essays on Otherness* (trans. Luke Thurston), London & New York: Routledge, 1999, p. 83.

2 The opening credits describe the film as an 'excerpt from the diary of a cameraman', rather than the creation of a director or writer. It continues 'For viewers' attention, the film presents an experiment, in the cinematic communication of visible events.'

3 Laplanche, 1999, p. 56.

4 Charles Eames, 'Design Today', in *California Arts & Architecture*, September 1941, cited in *The Work of Charles and Ray Eames: A Legacy of Invention*, Washington: Abrams Inc in association with the Library of Congress and the Vitra Design Museum, 1997, p. 14.

5 Beatriz Colomina, 'Reflections on the Eames House', in *The Work of Charles and Ray Eames: A Legacy of Invention*, Washington: Abrams Inc in association with the Library of Congress and the Vitra Design Museum, 1997, p. 127.

6 Laplanche, 1999. For Laplanche, Freud overlooks the enigmatic call of the unconscious that determines the method (rather than vice versa); the process of cross-referencing and association is the only way in which the unconscious allows, and thus determines an approach.

7 Aaron Schuster, 'The Cosmonaut of the Erotic Future', in *Cabinet,* Issue 32, Winter 2008/9, p. 10.

8 Beatriz Colomina, 'Multi-screen Architecture', in Chris Berry, Janet Harbord and Rachel Moore (eds), *Public Space, Media Space*, Palgrave Macmillan (2013).

9 This description borrows from the essay by Philip and Phylis Morrison, 'A Happy Octopus: Charles and Ray Learn Science and Teach it with Images', in *The Work of Charles and Ray Eames: A Legacy of Invention*, Washington: Abrams Inc in association with the Library of Congress and the Vitra Design Museum, 1997, p. 108.

10 Laplanche, 1999, p. 55.

11 Laplanche is citing Hermes Trismegistus in his description of divine infinity to insert a reverberation with the idea of infinity in religious thought, cited by Nicholas Mulerius, 1617. Cf. Laplanche, 1999, p. 56.

12 ibid., p. 71.

13 Friedrich Nietzsche, *Beyond Good and Evil* (trans. R. J. Hollingdale), London: Penguin Books, [1886] 1973, p. 47.

14 John Fletcher provides an editor's note to the 1999 Routledge edition, detailing the translation of the term *etrangerete* – 'strangerness' – translated as alienness: 'The English "strange" has a subjective dimension that is relative and reducible [...] the stranger can become over time familiar, whereas "alien" denotes an irreducible strangerness, the result of an *external* origin [...]. The hyphenated form "alien-ness" allows the reader to hear

the noun in Laplanche's neologism – *étrangèreté* – and distinguishes it from the usual abstraction "alienness" – étrangeté [...].': in Laplanche, 1999, p. 62.

15 Laplanche 1999, p. 79.

16 ibid.

17 ibid., p. 80.

18 The concept of relationality draws heavily on the writings of Michel Serres and his attention to the importance of thinking with prepositions, declensions and inflections: 'Has not philosophy restricted itself to exploring - inadequately - the "on" with respect to transcendence, the "under", with respect to substance and the subject and the "in" with respect to the immanence of the world and the self? Does this not leave room for expansion, in following out the "with" of communication and contract, the "across" of translation, the "among" and "between" of interferences, the "through" of the channels through which Hermes and the Angels pass, the "alongside" of the parasite, the "beyond" of detachment [...] all the spatio-temporal variations preposed by all the prepositions, declensions and inflections?': in Michel Serres, *Atlas I*, Paris: Editions Julliard, 1994, p. 83.

19 Lacan's work posits this exterior unconscious functioning through language. A more fluid version appears in a recent conversation between psychoanalyst Adam Phillips (AP) and artist Paul Chan (PC):

> AP: 'It's as though we're educated to believe that there must be something inside; as though there's a terrific anxiety in believing there's no inside. How could we imagine ourselves or what goes on between us if there's nothing inside us? But really, our words aren't beside us; they're between us [...]. Can you imagine living as if there's nothing inside you?'
>
> PC: 'Yes. But only because of my experience of working… [My work] doesn't come out of me per se; it's me rubbing against this thing I want to make. It's a border conflict that creates whatever it is we call "ourselves"': in *Paul Chan: The 7 Lights*, Serpentine Gallery, Köln: Walther König, 1997, p. 100.

20 Donald Albrecht, 'Design is a Method of Action', in *The Work of Charles and Ray Eames: A Legacy of Invention*, Washington: Abrams Inc in association with the Library of Congress and the Vitra Design Museum, 1997, p. 38.

21 For an elaboration of this term, see John Johnston, 'Machinic Vision', in *Critical Inquiry*, Vol. 26, No. 1, Autumn 1999, pp. 27–48.

Chapter 8

Cinema *Mise en abyme*: Contingencies of the Moving Image

Ursula Frohne

The time is out of joint.
William Shakespeare, *Hamlet*

Reflections of the cinema experience and of film in its mainstream representations have entered the exhibition space as a constituting element both of post-conceptual art and post-cinematic film. On the one hand interconnected with the aesthetic experience of the contemporary art installation that references spatial concepts from the historical avant-garde to site-specificity; on the other hand responding to the omnipresence of the moving-image screens in the public sphere, the new type of 'cinematographic installation'[1] highlights the significance of cinema's cultural puissance. As a central facet of the contemporary art exhibition, multi-screen video projections employ a repertoire of technical possibilities and contextual features whose production and presentation modes have rapidly diversified since the early 1990s.

The much-debated 'incorporation' of traditional art forms by the film medium since its emergence returns as a reflexive concept in contemporary art installations, placing on display the cinematographic *dispositif* in a variety of analytical framings, often by adaptation and manipulation of iconic film scenes or entire feature films. This increased presence of the moving image in the exhibition space apparently correlates with the ubiquity of screen projections in the post-cinematographic public sphere, pointing to a threshold situation that emerges, according to Walter Benjamin's observation, when a medium undergoes a renaissance in response to its advancing cultural decline.[2] This impression of an almost melancholic fetishization of the precursor media – film and the cinematic experience – is sustained by the inflation of references in the art context to mainstream movie icons. As Jean-Christoph Rouyaux, among others, has asserted, the charged forms of hyper-invested artistic references to the production and consumption processes of film in dramatized display modes that reanimate the cultural significance of cinema suggest a psychoanalytical reading of film's 'endgame' state within the ineluctable post-cinematic era.[3] The concomitant loss of film's emphatic avant-garde status has been addressed elsewhere in conclusive delineations of the 'work of mourning' dedicated to the film medium, as it were, which assert that the introduction of cine-material into the contemporary art space brings to the fore the filmic unconscious by translating cine-culture into the field of art as a way of conserving its fragmentary afterlife.[4] With the horizon of this discourse in mind, the following discussion investigates the conceptual distinctness of cinematographic art installations in relation to the ongoing blurring of the boundaries between film and other media. The omnipresence and multiple formats of screen-visuality conveying the 'intertextual commodity' of film suggest that cinema no longer possesses a specific place of its own, but occurs everywhere in the public and private spheres, intertwined with and integrated into other cultural forms. How does this extension of the cine-aesthetic into the field of art relate to the current ubiquity of film in the various forms, by which it is split up into countless media and modalities based on various technologies and motives? The replacement of the analogue image by the digital media, leaving behind the materiality of video and film, has led to the production and distribution of more visual material than ever before, transforming the ways we watch, listen to, and experience film as a fragmented and highly individualized event. Can both phenomena – contingent cinema and cinematic installations – be subsumed under the same development of increasingly differentiated display modes and subjective forms of experiencing the film medium? Do these parallel processes constitute merely two sides of one cultural tendency within which film transforms from a 'self-contained commodity' into a gradually less solid 'intertextual commodity'? Although the familiar opposition between the 'black box' and the 'white cube', between cinema culture and museum display, seems to be dissolving by shifts in meaning and evolutions that alter the way we look at and reflect upon art and film, the question arises whether visual arts provide a zone in which the 'radical elsewhere'[5] of the contingent spectacle survives, or whether the field of art functions like a transit zone – an intermediate stage in the rethinking of the cinema project. The implications of these both economically and socially reconfigured reception constellations of the cinematic experience are explored below in terms of the historical dispositions and paratextual interconnections among film, installation, cinema and gallery space.

Cinema on Display

The significant revival of film we are witnessing today is visible not only in the conjured features of the 'future cinema' that Peter Weibel characterized as a three-step transformation of classical cinema,[6] but also in the great number of artworks reflecting the challenges of contemporary visual culture in conceptualized cinematic settings. In various approaches to the aesthetics of film and the audio-visual arts, the ubiquity of the screen hallmarks cinema and the exhibition display likewise; historically, too, they can be viewed as 'systemic neighbors,[7] both representing paradigmatic spaces of modernity. Film appears not as an addition to the field of visual art, but as integral to its formation since the onset of the avant-garde. Its omnipresence is not primarily a question of acquired artistic mastery of its rapidly changing technologies, but symptomatic of its formative role for contemporary visual culture. Whereas film-theoretical approaches regard post-cinematic constellations in the light of film's twofold secession – first, from its historical representational *dispositif*; second, from its photographic materiality (namely the celluloid film and its potential for indexical visuality) – my discussion aims to highlight the fact that the filmic *dispositif* in multi-screen video installations has not been adequately described as a mere extension of the 'cinema without walls' yet. Rather, the *dispositif* pursues a variety of conceptual framings of the mainstream visual regimes, of their institutional and social conditions and their economic imperatives, mostly by concentrating on deconstructions or alterations of the familiar notions of projection and identification – neither within the classical cinematic experience, nor its post-cinematic successor alone. This paper focuses on analyzing the productive friction between the visual arts and cinema,[8] with *déconstruit remontages* and re-*mises-en-scène* of feature films or mainstream fiction being just some of the methods used by visual artists to (re-)interpret the cultural and collective experience of cinema, dissecting film and its cinematic apparatus for epistemological means. In spite of some superficial overlappings with ubiquitous screen technology and contingent filmic insertions in the public sphere,[9] my argument emphasizes that the cinematographic installation breaks with the culture of the spectacle, its representational, immersive and commodified modes, and even operates as an agent of opposition to the mass distribution and contingent availability of film and video. This opposition is accomplished over singular presentation in the exhibition space, moreover by the conceptual focusing on the apparatus, by the narrative or temporal structure, and by the interlinkage in site-specific settings of moving-image components and the surrounding environment.[10] Inasmuch as the conceptual interventions in the filmic material and the display modes of the cinematographic apparatus are identifiable as significant features of art installations – their constellations often consisting of multiple projection screens with sculptural props in a defined spatial surrounding, rather than affirming the fragmented modes of production and perception of film in general – they genuinely counteract the aesthetics of post-cinematic ubiquity by bestowing the aura of art on the filmic material.[11] In this discussion, Mieke Bal's translation of the literary *mise en abyme* concept into a visual context becomes relevant as further support for the elucidating potential of the installation *dispositif*, and in order to pinpoint the meaning production and epistemological surplus of its various forms of dislocation and multiplication of film within the field of art.[12]

Many examinations of the cinematographic installation have addressed the synthesis of film and art, while exhibitions have functioned as platforms for the discussion of post-cinematographic reflections in contemporary installation art. Jean-Christophe Royaux characterizes this as a development towards a 'Cinéma Exposition' and mainly a catalyst for new narrative modalities enabling the work of art to be defined as an intermediary between the author and the viewer, a structure for activating the reading and experiencing of the process of thought and memory. It has also been argued that cinematographic installations present a new take on the twentieth century through the history of cinema. Accordingly, there has been talk of cinema being 'musealized', of the practice becoming established among contemporary artists and making increasing inroads into public and private collections as well as the exhibition landscape. Critics of this development consider the institution of cinema to be moving closer to museum structures, detecting in this increasing self-definition over the museum signs that post-cinematographic film, or cinema, is internalizing the expiry of its media-historical half-life: 'The Film Library – cinema – *becomes* the museum',[13] as Ian White asserts, thus enabling film, that medium of industrial entertainment, to share in the singular aura exclusive to the work of art.[14] Paradoxical though it may seem to attribute such potential to film – the very medium on which Benjamin, in 'The Work of Art in the Age of Mechanical Reproduction', diagnosed the paradigmatic decay of aura in modernity – the cinematographic installation represents a return to the possibility of auratization at the end of cinema's classical era inasmuch as the contemporary musealization of film[15] does not perpetuate the tendency to make things available to the 'masses' by reproduction, but instead restores the auratic uniqueness of the work of art.

The blurring of boundaries within the visual arts – and the arts in general – that has become so explicit in installation art, and which Juliane Rebentisch, approaching the aesthetic of the installation from a philosophical perspective, has plausibly shown to be a misconceived dispensation from modernity's claims of autonomy[16], has meanwhile been demonstrated not only by the artistic praxis of reflecting the border-transgressing categories of entertainment media and film, especially; there are also increasing numbers of converse examples in which directors deploy installation concepts to adapt and restage their films for the aesthetic spaces of art. The recurring presentation in contemporary exhibitions of works by film-makers like Harun Farocki or Chantal Akerman point to comparable ambitions to secure for film a status aloof from the mainstream of ubiquitous contact zones, by incorporating into the performative museum presentation the context of the filmic fiction, particularly those aspects of the conditions of production and audience reception that remain off-screen. This rapprochement of cinema and exhibition, two fields long separate in terms of theoretical examination, was assertively documented by the Jean-Luc Godard retrospective at the Centre Pompidou in Paris in 2007. For this filmographic project, Godard developed a complex dramaturgy whereby his film works were associatively embedded in complex spatial settings. Using prop-heavy scenarios that reinforced the importance of installation-based art in its relationship of exchange with the off-screen, the multi-layered referential system of the staging – a system derived from various contexts – emphasized the montage of the film-internal set pieces as a paradigmatic requirement for the aesthetic experience of film (see colour plates, p. 8). Displaying startling analogies with the idiosyncratic pictorial arrangements of his *Histoire(s) du Cinéma* (1988–98), Godard's material-rich exhibition concept placed reproductions of Francisco de Goya's or Henri Matisse's paintings alongside mobile phone screens and television broadcasts from the Eurosport channel running parallel with his own films, and ranking equally within the overall installation context. It was a prophetic pointer to the ubiquitous and mutually competitive pictorial forms of contemporary culture, and their fragmented, non-binding modalities of reception. One may equally assume that Godard's staging alluded to the earlier 'Les Immatériaux' show curated at the same venue by Jean-François Lyotard in 1985, and in which set-like display was already deployed as a means to sensitize the audience to imminent radical changes in visual and social culture.[17] Already Lyotard's project applied installation-based staging as a system for analyzing philosophical models of thought, as well as a method of depicting invisible networks of relationships, with the exhibition space functioning as a heterotopic place of which the aesthetic dramaturgy brought to performance, but did not simply affirm, the dynamics of everyday culture. Both exhibition concepts marked the threshold to a new epoch: Lyotard's project anticipated the virtualization of the social, while in its excessive multiplication of perspectives and projections, Godard's epic fanning-out of his 'Voyages en Utopie'[18] illustrated the foundations of his filmic thinking. At the same time, the disparate nature of these elements advanced the realization that the domain of the immersion aesthetic is no longer the museum or the cinema, both of which have been usurped by the promiscuous visual relationships of the spectacles of everyday culture.

Cinematic (re-)*mise-en-scène*

It is not surprising that the (media-)reflexive installation phenomena discussed in this essay should become more visible in a historical situation amounting to the high point of the society of the spectacle critically envisioned by Guy Debord in 1967. Debord's prophecy of a world in which images increasingly replace visual relationships with the factual reality forecast a diminishing of the distinction between that which takes place in reality and that in the media.[19] The methods of intervening in established structures of perception and habit used by the cinematographic installation are comparable with those already brought into play by the Situationist International movement, which, via its incommensurable praxis of *dérive*, sought to enhance reflection upon the totality of the everyday. And yet, the linkage of filmic material with the aesthetic of the installation strives neither to assert a new, intermedia cinematographic ideal, nor to advance the de-differentiation of the arts by synthesizing disparate aesthetics. With their structural insistence on time and space, however, the installation concepts reconfigure the raw material of the spatio-temporal parameters of the cinematic experience.[20] Especially on a semantic level, awareness of the spatial dimensions as determinants of the cinematographic illusion clearly emerges, articulating itself as a principle: space and time prove to be plastic categories in artistic praxis. In cinematographic installations, the spatial framework aligns itself as a hybrid figure in which the formal structure of cinema combines with the spatial interventions of minimalist sculpture. This combination reveals a crucial difference between the cinema projection of a feature film and its restaging in the context of cinematographic installations. The former endeavors to neutralize media conditions within the complete referential illusion, and in this way negates its own materiality. The cinematographic installation, however, foregrounds the negated technical dimension of filmic space, which presupposes an image-fixated viewer mode by showing it to be an aesthetic experience: for instance, by underscoring the intrinsic sculptural value of the installation and/or the video, film, or slide projectors (from Bruce Nauman to De Rijke/de Rooij and Janet Cardiff); or thanks to the vivid presence of the celluloid strip that meanders through the installation space (as e.g. in the film installations of Stan Douglas, Rachel Khedoori, Rosa Barba or Rosalind Nashashibi, see colour plates, p. 7). The projections often beamed directly onto a white wall likewise point to a formal-aesthetic accentuation of an image-and-space connection that goes beyond the functional spatial references of cinema presentation, suggesting a removal of the boundaries of the picture area to create a visuality that shapes the space. Apart from the overall atmospheric impact, the projection aimed at the bare wall thematizes the institutional nature of the performance venue – the white cube – as the framework of technical presentation, and a field of discourse for forms of cinematographic expression expanded in this direction since the onset of the avant-garde. This aesthetic space that has no wish to simulate cinema but develops further the latter's 'numinous' atmosphere as a *dispositif* condition of projection,[21] on the one hand, serves to depict the material structures of the filmic apparatus. Equally, however, the aesthetic operations of the installations react by performing alienating interventions in the structures of the cinematographic aesthetic of illusion. Whereas a film aims to produce an assimilatory reading in which the purported naturalness of the film image and its spatio-temporal synthesis can be experienced as a totality, the 'cinematographic installation'[22] treats them as phenomena of difference in which the non-identical nature of the spatio-temporal categories is illuminated as a paradigm of the representation of the film narrative 'itself'[23], and therefore functions in the 'artistic' variant as an instrument of analysis and knowledge. The essay addresses these oblique off-centre visions of film and cinema in contemporary art and culture. It situates the charged forms of hyper-invested artistic references to the production and consumption processes of film in dramatized display modes that offer an opening onto what lies at the heart of the cinematographic experience. The concept of anamorphosis also offers a useful model to review the transgressions between the filmic *dispositif* and the spatial setting of the installation, since the display may provide new insights, never seen as such, and often more significant and original than the cinematic view on film is prone to yield, and may prove to be epistemologically more penetrating than to observe the screening prudently from the front. Thus, to grasp something of cinematographic aesthetics, it is revealing to enter the projection space – once defined by the cinema experience – through the side door of the installation. The off-site displays of film in contemporary art and post-cinematic settings, I want to argue, inserts the viewer into the fold (in Deleuze's sense) at the intersection of the transgressive relation between art and film. Rather than affirming the spatio-temporal effect of the film, which is geared along the lines of the plot logic, the re-*mise-en-scène* in an installation brings to representation the film-immanent *mise-en-scène* and the plurality of its references; that is to say, film's structural intermediality. It identifies the constructions of 'verisimilitude' in the film-immanent ruptures and fragmentations of the narrative space that is based precisely on the screening-out of the *hors-champ*, which it couples to the installation-based reception context of the filmic performance as a reflexive figure. The artistic focuses on and intervenes in the intermediate spatio-temporal zones and constructed joints that, thanks to the *découpage*, allow the film to appear like a narratological unit, desynchronize perception. This coincides in film with the course of the depicted plot. And so the installation mode complies with Gilles Deleuze's theory regarding the montage aesthetic of film as the becoming real of the invented, since seeing appears as movement: an interval perception, as it were, which takes account of the space and time zones that exist between the filmic images and scenes. Current adaptations and restaging of feature films in gallery as well as museum spaces result in anamorphotic views of canonized filmic works, in the sense of the Greek term 'ana-morphis' which etymologically suggests a 're-arranging/ shaping', which demands a transformation of the viewers' standpoint, if they want to recognize the features of the displaced and conceptually defamiliarized filmic shape.

La Recherche du Temps Perdu

This aesthetic principle has been illustrated in other connections with reference to Douglas Gordon's *24 Hour Psycho* (1993), Sam Taylor-Wood's *Third Party* (1999), Steve McQueen's *Deadpan* (1997), Pierre Huyghe's *The Third Memory* (1999) and Eija-Liisa Ahtila's *The House* (2004),[24] and for that reason will be mentioned here only briefly in regard to the *dispositif* characteristics of the installation concept of Pierre Huyghe's *L'Ellipse* (1998) (Figure 1).[25] In an allusion to the film term 'jump cut', Huyghe's title broaches the principle of topological and impact-aesthetic ruptures of the narrative space, and by that refers to the basic structural categories of an aesthetic of illusion generated by the medium film.[26] As is well-known, the work is based on key scenes of Wim Wenders' film *Der Amerikanische Freund/The American Friend* (1976),[27] and combines parallel projection displayed over three screens, setting footage from the feature film with newly produced scenes showing Bruno Ganz, the main protagonist of Wenders' movie, more than twenty years later at the film's original locations in Paris. Two consecutive scenes, which are in Wenders' film, connected by a jump-cut (also called in the film jargon 'ellipsis'), appear in the installation on two separate screens. This kind of narratological separation that is shunt out by montage nevertheless creates a simultaneity of two consecutive scenes, and highlights their topographically as well as temporally segregated locations. By insertion of an eight-minute sequence on a third screen in-between the scenes on the left and on the right screens, Huyghe shows the protagonist as actor in the role of Jonathan Zimmermann in an elevator on the one side, and upon entering his apartment on the other. On the centre screen, Bruno Ganz, the actor, appears obviously aged by at least two decades. Here he walks, followed by the camera, across a bridge in an extended tracking shot, which bridges, as it were, the spatial as well as temporal distance between both locations that are also topographically separated by the parallel installation of the screens. The actor, who physically recapitulates the path, moves like the time and space

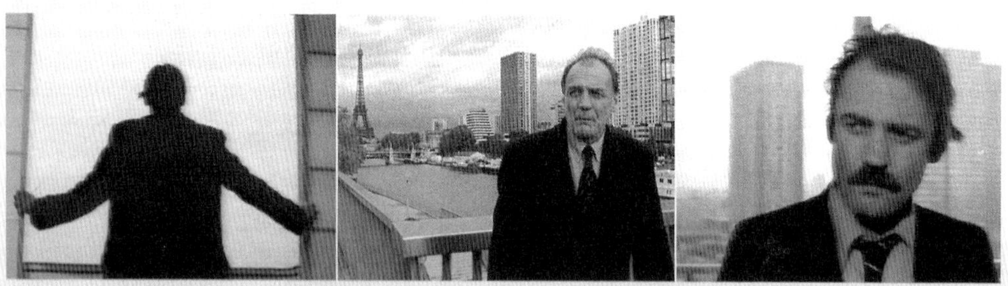

Figure 1: Pierre Huyghe, *L'Ellipse*, 1998. Three-channel video installation, sound. © VG Bild-Kunst, Bonn 2010.

relation, which the jump-cut conceals by suture of the spectators' identification. Bruno Ganz who has significantly aged since 1977 when the film was produced, moves between the temporally decoupled, however topographically and logically related, film locations. The spectators observe this unedited eight-minute sequence showing his path across the bridge toward the building, which is displayed in the feature film as the meeting place between Zimmermann and his client. The real-time tracking of the recent Bruno Ganz appearing on the centre screen is positioned within the filmic narrative exactly at the point where the jump-cut (ellipsis) connects the temporally distant sequences to a logical unit. The principle of this montage, which is actually concealed by the elision, is made explicit by insertion of the real-time sequence in the screens' parallel display. Positioned between both scenes of the jump-cut, it highlights the dissection of the audio-visual continuity as characteristic of the filmic *mise-en-cadre*: the living actor enters into the pictorial space of the artificial character and indicates his irreversible temporality as the real-lifeness, which in fiction is annihilated by the repeatability of the most famous scenes. Whereas the video sequences document an authentic excerpt from the life of Bruno Ganz, he seems to memorize the fictional plot of his previous performance. His return to the shooting locations of the film leads to a double encounter with his role on the one hand, and his own biographical history on the other. Moments of memories seem to move him as if *en recherche du temps perdu*. In a journey through time, during which he is reeled-in by his *memoire involuntaire*, making him pause and muse for brief moments, Bruno Ganz realizes the lapse of time, which is negated by the filmic jump-cut. In his memory, he experiences the passed span of life, reaching from the time of the film production to the recent moment that he physically as well as psychologically perceives at a distance. Re-encountering the *genius loci* of his previous film performance, he experiences the time lapse as a dramatic encounter, with his own past displayed by his astonished and likewise elegiac expression. In this process of re-enactment, the boundary between the man and the actor becomes blurry, and the fiction appears to be inseparably concatenated with the protagonist's personal history.

When Bruno Ganz arrives at his destination, the video sequence at the centre of Huyghe's installation ends. The projection then continues on the right screen with the scene following the jump-cut in Wenders' film, while the left and middle projection screens remain blank. The fiction returns and closes the elliptic storyline, extended between the fictional and the factual, between historical and biographical time levels. Huyghe's reoganization of the scenes transforms the meaning of the film sequences insofar as these now serve as a story which forms the framework of the new setting, and which becomes readable within the installation concept as an order of recollective images. With Deleuze's reflections on the *Time-Image*, this constellation could be seen as a closed-circuit, reaching from the present to the past, and from there again to the present.[28] On his path recapitulating the fictional scene in real time, Bruno Ganz hence attains from one epoch (1977) to another (1998), while the time passing during his walk across the bridge overlaps with his emerging feeling of his passed lifetime. The title, *L'Ellipse*, thus references the filmic arc of suspense which is constituted in transition from one scene to the next beyond temporal or topographical breaches. Instead of connecting the diverse stations of the narrative by the principle of suture, Huyghe's installation creates a convergence between fictional time and the lifetime of the protagonist. He punctuates the function of the filmic montage, and by revealing the logic of the suture, he imparts on the film its own temporal logic and grants filmic time a reality that literally reaches into lifetime. As is illustrated by the spatially fanned out order of the sequences in Wenders' film, the elliptic montage is based on the fact that the causality of the storyline, always omitting occurrences of the plot, interrupts the linear process of the events[29] to condensate the real-timely settings in an accessible/commodified filmic narrative time.

Permanency

At the end of Wenders' filmic narrative, Zimmermann dies. Bruno Ganz's revisiting of the filmic locations and his entry in-between the elements of the filmic montage make him therefore appear as a revenant who performs in just that space, where for an almost imperceptible moment the illusionary dimension of the scenically-coalesced locations and temporal levels breaks open in the conventional reception of the filmic narrative. In confrontation with the protagonist's subjective lifetime, Huyghe's *L'Ellipse* addresses the phantom character of filmic phantasy figures that animate the memory of the filmic narrative in an imaginary space and time zone. More or less unchanged, like mythological figures embalmed in filmic time and according to their own laws, their cultural existence alternates between historical aging and nostalgic juvenescence that remains present as icons of their own genuine 'timelessness'. Huyghes meta-montage of the filmic document also refers to the film characters' virtual immortality thanks to the prevention of their aging by an allegedly timeless medium, which agelessly conserves their present state. At the same time, however, the conceptual accentuation of these filmic characteristics points to their transience, as the appearance of the actor is always bound to the temporality of the film screening, and the herein grappled pictorial existence commemorates its actual mortification in the moment of its recording.[30] Huyghe's confrontation of the found footage with the newly produced pictures of the aged actor brings this awareness to the fore.

Cinema *Mise en Abyme*

More than just producing a breach of the filmic illusion, Huyghe's *L'Ellipse* aims at identifying a concept of filmic temporality that takes its own course by an endless precipice. This incompletable (in principle) *mise en abyme* frames the momentary character of the picture formation and entails the herein appearing levels of reality. Originally applied theoretically in the field of literary studies, this concept of the *mise en abyme* has first been further developed by Craig Owens to highlight the potential of photography, which by its reflections and reduplications is capable of creating meaning beyond its representational readability.[31] In contrast to an image-within-the-image-structure, the ambiguous *mise en abyme* in cinematographic installations is essentially disposed as a spatial-temporal dimension, and breaches the fiction by complex interrelations between the internal narrative and the story which forms the framework. Huyghe's insert of a sequence occupies exactly the interspace which is generated by the film editing and which exceeds the filmic temporality. Therefore it envisions, similar to a déjà vu, the diegesis of a past time, and functions like a mirror image to the unchanged present of the past conserved within the filmic medium. In such a way, the aesthetic boundary, which separates the filmic and real space in manifold manners, becomes an oscillating reflexion of the aesthetic experience. The installation loosens those stitches that, according to suture theory,[32] connect the fragmented filmic image via the viewer's perceptual activity to produce a coherent diegetic space-and-time-relation. Thus, Huyghe's work signals that the reception of film has always been based on the active interaction of the viewer's imagination. His separation of the film scenes, by means of parallel projection, alludes to the consumable spatio-temporal syntheses generated by abrupt changes of scenes. Such deliberately disillusioning interference in the filmic logic forces the viewer to analyze the ontological status of the place that 'exists' in the film, just as the historicity of the filmic fiction moves to the centre of perception thanks to the artistic exposure of the constructed time periods and their logical connections; with the spatial configuration of the segmented scenes depicting the manner in which 'time as form in film'[33] takes shape. Works like Huyghe's *L'Ellipse* label the filmic space as a 'radical elsewhere', as a much more disconcerting presence which cannot even be certified as existing, but rather as 'insisting' or 'enduring', as Hubert Damisch maintains in view of self-reflexive filmic scenes in which the off-screen space and the fictional space dramatically converge,[34] just as the homogenous space-and-time construction of the film invades the extra-fictional off-screen in Huyghe's installation. In that process, the dislocations of the performance context of film icons illuminate the fictional displacement of the real spaces and locations in the filmic fiction. The artistic determination of the relationship of filmic spaces of the imagination to real topographies continues this analysis, sometimes at original locations or at the sites (or shooting locations) of films that have entered the annals of film history.[35] In the confrontation with the ontological status of the existing place, the found-footage installations undertake an attempt to reclaim the ontological conditions of filmic fiction; an attempt in equal measure deconstructive and romantic in regard to the site-specificity of its components. Such conceptual framings of the place- and time-specificity of filmic fictions favour emancipatory spaces of reflection in which the ruptures and production contexts of the filmic aesthetic of illusion are incorporated into the perception,[36] and audio-visual relationships are enabled that present an alternative to the fluctuating, context-negating image formats of contemporary cine-ubiquity, and express a desire to extend the vision of an intensified state to the living environment. Huyghe addresses this desire in granting visibility to the screen as the site where two diverse discourses (on representation and illusion) converge. In his theory of the human gaze, Jacques Lacan has identified these as the 'reversal of consciousness' that can only be confronted in the mode of misconception.[37] The externally directed gaze, which cannot observe itself, follows the function of the desire and leaves the subject in a constitutive nescience about that which exists beyond the beheld world of illusion – in this case that of the film: 'At the same time, its image can by way of the gaze *per se* only be thought of as an anamorphosis.'[38] Huyghe's decentred view on the film screening reveals the image character in a literary epiphanic moment. Comparable to the anamorphosis' effect of conspicuity, the instance of the image/screen renders visible the ability of the gaze and what it refuses at the same time by its constitutive nescience.[39]

These findings move forward from my opening hypothesis, according to which the construction of the time-space relationship is scrutinized and reanimated in artistic installations as a way to highlight the conditions of the screening-out of the ideological and sociocultural dispositions of the film aesthetic. Many found-footage compilations explicitly refer to the cultural role of film as a metaphorical and quasi-mythological space of identification. Framed within installation concepts, adaptations of entire movies or legendary scenes provoke (critical) rereadings of Hollywood classics and their dramaturgical genre stereotypes. On the basis of filmic scenes appropriated in this way, a repetitive momentum is generated by temporal and spatial gradations of the installation screen's choreography. The surplus of meaning thus produced is comparable with a *mise en abyme* that inserts a motif of the narration into the same through imaging processes. The application of this concept to the cinematographic installation possesses great potential as functional differentiation and iconic interpretation of the structural components as pursued in Mieke Bal's essay 'Mise en abyme et Iconicité' (1978).[40] Her argument distinguishes, among others, three forms of this phenomenon that contribute to the development of an iconic *mise en abyme*-theory – that is still lacking in the field of art history and visual studies.[41] The auto-analytic, self-referential, fiction-rupturing and fiction-fracturing operations of the *mise en abyme* can fruitfully be adopted to coherently link the analysis of multiple projection screens placed inside spatial settings to create a complex, and often incommensurable, narrative structure in cinematographic installations. In analogy with Berthold Brecht's *Verfremdungseffekt* ('alienation effect'), in which a character in a play steps outside of the action and addresses the audience in order to explain the author's 'intention', the *mise en abyme* is based on the principle of narrative gradiation that links the staging to the level of discourse. The repetitive structure, which functions as a disruption of illusion, not least through the loop so typical of the cinematographic installation, allows the construction elements of the filmic medium to become visible. A typically Romantic device in that it applies a form of self-reflexive poetry – and accordingly stylizes its own artificiality – the *mise en abyme* is, as Mieke Bal stresses, the 'anachronique par definition'.[42] Often in parallel, the placed picture planes of the cinematographic installation adhere to a logic similar to that of the *mise en abyme*, which looking sideways and backward enforces a mobility of thought in a historically comparing perspective. In contrast to the narrative montage of film sequences that stipulate a linear interpretative direction, artist/film-makers like Harun Farocki deploy editing as a parallel streaming of the picture planes (Figure 2) that hints at the loss of a central axis of meaning

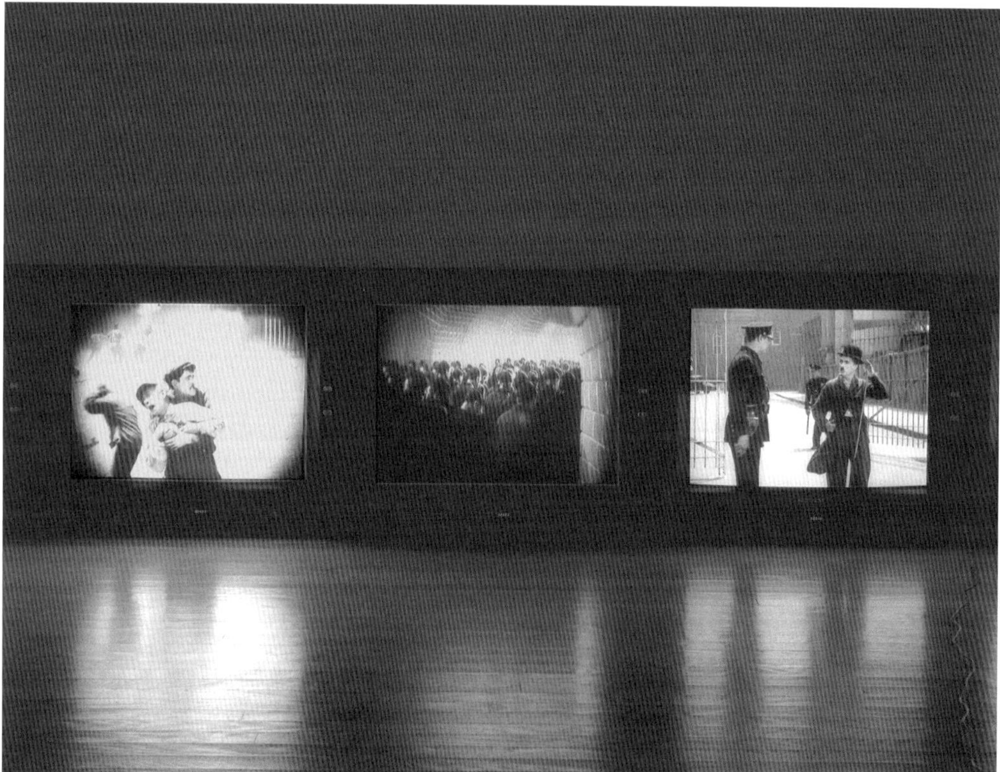

Figure 2: Harun Farocki, *Workers Leaving the Factory in Eleven Decades*, 2006. Courtesy Leonard & Bina Ellen Art Gallery, Concordia University Montréal. Photograph: R-M. Tremblay.

and habitual orders of thought or knowledge.[43] When a number of moving-image planes run parallel, choice-less image consumption is replaced by comparative vision as a critical mode of operation. For each of these updatings of such 'parallel images', the question arises anew as to which intellectual process is being initiated, suggested or expressed in the visual syntax of simultaneous image constellations. Their synchronous movement produces a constantly changing discursive relationship in which the icon-like status of the single scene proves to be a loss of context and a blind spot, both of the aesthetic and also the political difference from the real events. This relationship of interaction on the pictorial level lends weight to the thesis that the 'concrete constitution of the image [...] in every single frame' is to be viewed as a 'political-performative act'.[44] The vanishing of the centre, the 'foregoing of authority', and a linear reading of the events become the starting point of a critical analysis that Mieke Bal identifies in the *mise en abyme* as a tendency toward 'auto-analysis', whereby that which develops dialogically between the picture planes reveals itself to the viewer as the substance.

Revenants

Facilitated by new technical possibilities of reproducing and playing back material, the deployment of found footage from popular movies and auteur films is thematized in its conceptually narrow reference to the filmic space as the paradigmatic place of mimetic reproduction throughout modernity: as a product of reproduction, film itself comes to realization over its recurrent screening. This logic is derived also from the film genre of the 'remake,[45] which in turn amounts to a separate creative category not just in commercial cinema, but also in the installation art concepts. In the cinematographic installation, the (re-)production techniques of the cinema itself are duplicated, assimilated, and reenacted as meta-presentations of a now historical film aesthetic. Reiterations of auratic film scenes or works of film art (richly variegated concepts are evident in the work of artists such as Douglas Gordon, Pierre Huyghe, Steve McQueen, Candice Breitz or Ming Wong) often relate to the context of a film's making as the vanishing point of the artistic analysis. The cultural ubiquity of these films is historically localized and monumentalized in the course of such artistic repetitions. Giorgio Agamben examined this aspect of the film montages of Debord and Godard, remarking that their works were no longer based on the production of images as a prerequisite for constructing a film, but instead demanded merely the repetition and stoppage of film footage.[46] The appropriation of film footage in contemporary installations carries forward the same method.[47] It transposes the cinema to the gallery (or to sites in public space), placing it on display not as an institution, but as a spatial art form with its own historical anchorage, in this way creating references back to the performance contexts of early cinema.[48]

The fragmentation of the visual perspectives in the cinematographic installations, which is thus constitutively linked to the equation of the black box and white cube, on the one hand marks the cultural intersection between transparent, fluid spatial concepts and the cinematographic projection spaces of modernity; on the other hand, it carries forward this historical perspective by relating the dissolution of the space-time continuum in the dislocated mediatized visual constellations of postmodern society to the incoherences of the film-immanent montage aesthetic. With this, a thematic complex is addressed whereby the experience of the cinema (in particular) as the paradigmatic illusionary space of modernity is shifted into the vicinity of the conception of the modern exhibition space – the white cube. These aesthetic spatial models of modernity enter into an 'osmotic relationship' in the contemporary praxis of cinematographic installation spaces – as Gregor Stemmrich has paradigmatically shown by scrutinizing the conceptual concentration of architectural transparency and hermetic space of illusion in Dan Graham's early cinema concept, and suggesting that Graham's complex visual direction, defined by the changing light conditions, might amount to a 'proto-cinematographic installation architecture.'[49] In the manner anticipated by Graham's cinema model (see colour plates, p. 8), the visitor of contemporary installation spaces moves into the visual field of observation and experiences herself as a subject who is constantly aware of being seen. The exhibition space transforms into a stage to whose perceptual conditions the viewing subject reacts habitually in awareness of her visual presence. At the same time, this 'stage' experience orchestrates a mechanism of vision that not only frames the subject aesthetically, but also makes it clear to the subject that she is being co-produced by the ubiquitous image conditions, and contingent visual relationships, of the post-cinematic era.

A sociological dimension that recurrently incorporates the viewer position in installations as a perspective shifting the point of view and, in consequence, the perception and positioning of the artwork, likewise comes to bear in this evident historicity of the media conditions of film and of art. The global experience of cinema has moulded patterns of artistic perception no less than the universalist programmatic of modernity shaped the way space is experienced: meanwhile, the cinematographic experience is no longer restricted to the space of film – that is, the cinema. The motifs, iconographies and impact intensities of cinema are widely scattered and diffuse with the cultural spaces of the present day. While the praxis of film is to be found in different places and on various 'carrier media', the cinematographic installation restages in the museum the role formerly played by film. This apparent 'anachronism' elevates the film, beyond all conventional positionings in either the cinema or in its post-cinematic ubiquity, to the status of art, just as Jacques Derrida's spectres and phantoms adhere neither to the teleology of historical materialism, nor to linear chronology. Similar to the return of Derrida's spectres, the cinematographic installations belong to the time of the unconscious, which is structured and layered differently than the currents of the zeitgeist. Derrida discerned in this 'anachrony' the potential to resist a presence consisting solely in the present, the spectres being always 'future-to-come' and 'coming-back'.[50] In repetitious re-presentations they arrive at the 'survivance' that Derrida comprehends as a living efficiency that cannot be traced back to a rigid antithesis of past and present.

Thus, the aesthetic of the cinematographic installation denotes less a rupture of the notion of the museum and the cinema than a carrying forward throughout the further enabling possibilities of the ideal mobility and autonomy of the viewers. It does so by providing a space of reflection and discursive analysis on the basis of the conventions of the viewing of art, involving 'the staging of "publicness" in contemporary art museums'.[51] By transforming the dissection of the (media) space into a fluctuating ensemble of temporalized factors of viewing and perception, the cinematographic installation aesthetic in the broadest sense reflects Arjun Appadurai's theory of globalization as a multiplication of perspectives and projects. Under the conditions of globalization, the spatial arrangement of modernity is being replaced by a manifoldness of highly differentiated 'mediascapes', 'ethnoscapes', 'financescapes', and 'technoscapes' that make any kind of universal representation of space become obsolete.[52] 'The "individual actor" is the last locus of this perspectival set of landscapes,'[53] as Tom Holert remarks, but must at the same time take issue with the sedimented social realities that run through the globalized realm. This aspect of the factual fragmentation and perspectivization of the architectural, visual, and social-societal relics of modernity comes to light on a meta-plane in installation-based spaces of projection. Their hybrid structures, which deviate from the classical categorizations of the cinema and the white cube as the privileged spaces of perception of modernity, conceptualize an impact-aesthetic that reflects upon the role of the viewer as the actual subject of the placed-in-scene spatial experiences of the present. The viewer, who has up until now found a defined frame of reference and static visual orientation in the museum, is deprived of her secure stance vis-à-vis the object of perception, just as the principle of viewer identification with the camera position, as postulated by the film theorist Christian Metz, loses all validity in view of the multiple projection screens of the installation spaces. This threshold situation, whereby the conceptual fraying-out of the image and the space of perception thematically address the ubiquitary image as well as the visual relationships of the post-cinematic era, allows the visitors to experience the instability of their position as a viewer. Further investigation will be required to establish the extent to which the cinematographic installations in paradoxical combinations of a surplus of visual information with a reduction of sensory stimuli aim to produce a borderline experience of cognitive perceptual structures. Thus, the assertion that we arrive at a state of concentration only through distraction would merit further consideration in connection with Walter Benjamin's reception model.[54] As a productive instrument of exercise (*Übungsinstrument*)[55] of a viewer type new in this sense, however, the cinematographic installation forms confirm neither the visual centring on the artwork along the lines of the traditional white cube aesthetic as affirmation of artistic autonomy, nor can their modes of operation be equated with the distractions of entertainment culture and the arbitrary nature of a contingent stream of images; or even be seen as part of the leveling vortex of cine-visual commodification. Rather, their meta-fictions enable an aesthetic experience in which the spectral visual relationships allow the viewer to enter into the responsibility of an image-critical act of synthesis.

Notes

1 From a philosophical point of view, Juliane Rebentisch develops a sophisticated theory of installation aesthetics, and dedicates a chapter to a lucid analysis of what she termed the 'cinematographic installation', in: Juliane Rebentisch, *Ästhetik der Installation*, Frankfurt am Main: Suhrkamp, 2003, pp. 179–231.

2 Walter Benjamin, 'Das Kunstwerk im Zeitalter seiner technischen Reproduzierbarkeit', in *Gesammelte Schriften*, Vol. 1, Frankfurt am Main: Suhrkamp, 1980, pp. 471–508; Julia Bernhard, 'Malerei als das "Filmisch-Unbewußte"', in Thomas Hensel et al. (eds), *Das Bewegte Bild*, Munich: Wilhelm Fink, 2006, pp. 309–33.

3 Jean-Christoph Royaux, 'Remaking Cinema', in Marente Bloemheuvel (ed.), *Cinéma Cinéma: Contemporary Art and the Cinematic Experience*, Eindhoven: Stedelijk Van Abbemuseum, 1999, p. 21.

4 Bernhard refers to Yve-Alain Bois' essay 'Painting the Task of Mourning' (1990) in which he states that painting, after the 'death' of painting, is evoked by film, after the 'death' of film.

5 Cf. Hubert Damisch, *Fixe Dynamik*, Berlin: Diaphanes, 2004.

6 Peter Weibel describes this chronological transformation as beginning in the 1960s with the extension of cinematographic code with analogue means, continuing in the 1970s with the video revolution based on electromagnetic technology, permitting the modulation and manipulation of image quality, followed in the 1980s and 1990s with the digital apparatus that resulted in 'an explosion of the algorithmic image with completely new features like observer dependency, interactivity, virtuality, programmed behavior, and so forth', in Peter Weibel, 'Preface', in Jeffrey Shaw and Peter Weibel (eds), *Future Cinema: The Cinematic Imaginary after Film*, 2003, p. 18.

7 According to Bense's idea, technology should be regarded not as an addition to human existence, but as a 'mode of its being' (*Seinsweise*), implying that a transition has taken place from using or mastering technology (*Technikhaben*) to technology as a state of being (*Techniksein*): Max Bense, *Technische Existenz: Essays*, Stuttgart: Deutsche Verlags-Anstalt, 1949.

8 The present essay is based on a collaborative research project dedicated to 'Reflections of Cinematographic Aesthetics in Contemporary Art' conducted by the Art History Department of the University of Cologne and funded by the German Science Foundation in the period 2007–12. See also http://kinoaesthetik.uni-koeln.de/index.php?lang=e, accessed 31 July 2013.

9 This also includes the format of the DVD which permits the 'reshuffling' of the order of a film's scenes, as Matthew Clayfield points out, 'demonstrating that the picture's structure as a whole [...] was ultimately reliant on the parts that made it up, thus inverting the traditional hierarchy.' See Clayfield, 'A Cinema Exploded: Notes on the Development of Some Post-Cinematic Forms', 1 May 2010 in http://umintermediai501.blogspot.de/2010/05/cinema-exploded-notes-on-development-of.html, accessed 31 July 2013.

10 Cf. Mark Godfrey, 'Pierre Huyghe's Double Spectacle', in *Grey Room*, No. 32, Summer 2008, pp. 38–61.

11 This argument is also upheld by Rebentisch, 2003, p. 183.

12 Cf. Mieke Bal, 'Mise en abyme et iconcité', in *Littérature*, Vol. 29, 1978, pp. 118–20.

13 Ian White, 'Das Projizierte Objekt', in *kurz und klein. 50 Jahre Internationale Kurzfilmtage Oberhausen*, Ostfildern-Ruit: Cantz, 2004, pp. 191–96.

14 Rebentisch, 2003, p. 183.

15 Hubert Damisch also writes about the 'museum effect of cinema' in Damisch, 2004, p. 234.

16 Cf. Rebentisch, 2003.

17 Cf. Antonia Wunderlich, *Der Philosoph im Museum. Die Ausstellung 'Les Immatériaux' von Jean François Lyotard*, Bielefeld: transcript, 2008.

18 The aforementioned Jean Luc Godard exhibition at the Centre Pompidou in Paris 2006.

19 Guy Debord, *La Société du spectacle*, Paris: Éditions Buchet-Chastel, 1967.

20 Gilles Deleuze, *Cinema 2: The Time-Image* (trans. Hugh Tomlinson and Robert Galeta), London: Athlone Press, 1989.

21 Cf. Boris Groys, *Die Logik der Sammlung*, Munich: Hanser, 1997; Boris Groys, 'In der Autonomie des Betrachters. Zur Ästhetik der Filminstallation', in *Schnitt – Das Filmmagazin*, Vol. 22, 2001, pp. 10–14; Rebentisch, 2003.

22 Rebentisch, 2003. See also Erika Balsom, *Exhibiting Cinema in Contemporary Art*, Amsterdam: Amsterdam University Press, 2013.

23 Deleuze, 1989.

24 Cf. Ursula Frohne, 'Anamorphosen des Kinos: Douglas Gordons *24 Hour Psycho*', in *Kunsthistorische Arbeitsblätter*, Issue 11, 2004, pp. 15–24; 'Double Feature: Filmadaptionen in zeitgenössischer Kunst', in Anne-Kathrin Reulecke (ed.), *Fälschungen. Zu Autorschaft und Beweis in Wissenschaften und Künsten*, Frankfurt am Main: Suhrkamp, 2006, pp. 364–89; 'Dissolution of the Frame: Immersion and Participation in Video Installations', in Leighton, 2008, pp. 355–70; 'Kristallisationen filmischer Temporalität in kinematografischen Installationen', in Ilka Becker et al. (eds), *Just Not in Time. Inframedialität und non-lineare Zeitlichkeiten in Kunst, Film, Literatur und Philosophie*, Munich: Wilhelm Fink, 2011, pp. 267–87; 'Cinema on Display: Film in installativen Konzepten', in Henry Keazor, Fabienne Liptay and Susanne Marschall (eds), *FilmKunst, Studien an den Grenzen der Künste und Medien*, Marburg: Schüren Verlag, 2010, pp. 57–86; 'Moving Image Space. Konvergenzen innerer und äußerer Prozesse in kinematographischen Szenarien', in Ursula Frohne and Lilian Haberer (eds), *Kinematographische Räume. Installationsästhetik in Film und Kunst*, Munich: Wilhelm Fink, 2012, pp. 447–96.

25 Frohne, 2011.

26 Cf. Gertrud Koch and Christiane Voss (eds), *...kraft der Illusion*, Munich: Wilhelm Fink, 2006.

27 This video installation shifts the temporal constitution of the fictional space and the fictional timeline of the filmic narrative into a dialogical relationship with the real locations and the different courses of time. Wenders's film of course used *Ripleys Game* (1974), a novel by Patricia Highsmith, as a model to build upon.

28 Cf. Deleuze, 1989, p. 69.

29 Pierre Huyghe, *Pierre Huyghe – Some Negotiations*, exhibition catalogue, Munich: Kunstverein München, 1999, p. 144.

30 Cf. Roland Barthes, *Camera Lucida: Reflections on Photography* (trans. Richard Howard), New York: Hill and Wang, 1981.

31 Owens, 1992. On the concept of *mise en abyme*, cf. Bal, 1978; Mieke Bal, '*Mise en scène:* Zur Inszenierung von Subjektivität', in Josef Früchtl and Jörg Zimmermann (eds), *Ästhetik der Inszenierung. Dimensionen eines Künstlerischen, Kulturellen und Gesellschaftlichen Phänomens*, Frankfurt am Main: Suhrkamp, 2001, pp. 198–221.

32 Stephen Heath, 'Bemerkungen zur Suture', in Joachim Paech et al. (eds), *Screen Theory. Zehn Jahre Filmtheorie in England von 1971–1981*, Osnabrück: Universität Osnabrück, [1977/78] 1985, pp. 131–46; Kaja Silverman, *The Threshold of the Visible World*, New York & London: Routledge, 1996.

33 Cf. Lorenz Engell, 'Form und Medium im Film', in Jörg Brauns (ed.), *Form und Medium*, Weimar: VDG, 2002, pp. 153–66 (translated by Ursula Frohne).

34 Damisch, 2004.

35 As examples, one might point to Douglas Gordon's installation of his adaptation of John Ford's film *The Searchers* (1954) in his work *Five Year Drive-By* (1995), at the location of the film in the desert of *Twentynine Palms* (2003), or to Dorit Margreiter's installation-based localizations of filmic fictions.

36 Cf. Tom McDonough, *The Beautiful Language of My Century. Reinventing the Language of Contestation in Postwar France, 1945-1968*, Cambridge, MA: MIT Press, 2007; Christa Blümlinger, *Kino aus zweiter Hand. Zur Ästhetik materieller Aneignung im Film und in der Medienkunst*, Berlin: Vorwerk 8, 2009.

37 Cf. Jacques Lacan, *The Four Fundamental Concepts of Psychoanalysis: The Seminar of Jacques Lacan, Book 11* (ed. Jacques-Alain Miller; trans. Alan Sheridan), New York: W. W. Norton & Company, 1998. On Lacan's psychoanalytical investigation of the visual field, cf. Kaja Silverman, 'The Visible World', in Silverman, 1996, pp. 123–227, especially pp. 242–249.

38 Carlo Brune, *Roland Barthes Literatursemiologie und literarisches Schreiben*, Würzburg: Königshausen & Neumann, 2003, p. 122 (translated by Ursula Frohne).

39 Cf. Lacan, 1998. Hans Holbein the Younger managed to wrest a symbolic dimension from this axial paradigm of Alberti's within the famous anamorphosis of his painting *The Ambassadors* (1533). It is most likely more than pure coincidence that this symbolic dimension, that had an impressive and multifaceted theoretical afterlife in Jacques Lacans *objet petit a*, turned up at the bottom of Holbein's tableau in the form of a dead skull. See Lacan, 1998.

40 Cf. Bal, 1978, pp. 118–20.

41 Bal distinguishes the following three categories: 1. *mise en abyme de l'énoncé ou fictionelle*; 2. *mise en abyme de l'énonciation ou narrative*; and 3. *mise en abyme du code ou transcendentale*, in Bal, 1978, pp. 118–20.

42 ibid., p. 120.

43 On Farocki's visual strategies see Ursula Frohne, 'Media Wars. Strategische Bilder des Krieges', in Annegret Jürgens-Kirchhoff, (ed.), *WARSHOTS, Krieg – Kunst & Medien*, Publikation der Tagung des Sonderforschungsbereichs 437: *Kriegserfahrungen – Krieg und Gesellschaft in der Neuzeit, Schriftenreihe der Guernica-Gesellschaft*, Göttingen: V & R Unipress, 2006, pp. 161–186.

44   Michael F. Zimmermann, 'Das Bild als Ausnahmezustand. Nancy und Agamben', in Horst Bredekamp and Gabriele Werner (eds), *Bildwelten des Wissens, Kunsthistorisches Jahrbuch für Bildkritik*, Band 2:1, Berlin: Akademie Verlag, 2004, p. 17.

45   Katrin Oltmann, *Remake/Premake: Hollywoods romantische Komödien und ihre Gender-Diskurse, 1930–1960*, Bielefeld: transcript, 2008; Blümlinger, 2009.

46   Giorgio Agamben, '"Repetition and Stoppage" – Guy Debords Technique of Montage', in Catherine David (ed.), *Documenta X. Documents 2*, Ostfildern-Ruit: Cantz, 1996, pp. 68–75.

47   Nicolas Bourriaud (2005) coined the term 'post-production' for artistic appropriation methods of restaging, sampling, DJ-ing, etc. His analysis of such 're-editing' is based on artistic concepts that directly quote cinematic works and use post-production techniques (sample, toasting, talk over, cutting, playlists, etc.) to reassemble this material as new film-spatial *dispositifs*. Appropriation and re-enactment gives rise to a dialectic of iconophilist and iconoclastic attributes of artistic references to cinema as a technical *dispositif* on the one hand, and a 'mythological' projection space of a mediatized contemporary culture on the other. The latter becomes a focal point of further analysis of the (re-)staging modes of filmic and cinematographic spatial concepts in art.

48   Thomas Elsaesser and Adam Barker (eds), *Early Cinema: Space, Frame, Narrative*, London: British Film Institute, 1990; Thomas Elsaesser, 'Wie der frühe Film zum Erzählkino wurde. Vom kollektiven Publikum zum individuellen Zuschauer', in Irmbert Schenk (ed.), *Erlebnisort Kino*, Marburg: Schüren, 2000, pp. 34–54; Martin Loiperdinger (ed.), *Travelling Cinema in Europe*, Frankfurt am Main: Stroemfeld, 2008.

49   Gregor Stemmrich, *Kunst/Kino. Jahresring 48. Jahrbuch für moderne Kunst*, Köln: Octagon, 2001, illustration 4.

50   Jacques Derrida, *Spectres de Marx*, Paris: Éditions Galilée, 1993.

51   Maeve Connolly, *The Place of Artists' Cinema: Space, Site and Screen*, Bristol & Chicago: Intellect, 2009, p. 63.

52   Arjun Appadurai, *Modernity at Large: Cultural Dimensions of Globalization*, Minneapolis: University of Minnesota Press, 1996.

53   Tom Holert ,'Cinemascape. Distanz und Aufmerksamkeit an einer Straßenecke', in Mark Lewis et al. (eds), *Mark Lewis: Anlässlich der Ausstellung Mark Lewis, 16. April – 3. Juli 2005, Kunstverein Hamburg*, Ostfildern-Ruit: Hatje Cantz, 2005, pp. 25–36; 44.

54   Cf. Anne Ring Peterson, 'Attention and Distraction: On the Aesthetic Experience of Video Installation Art', in *RIHA Journal 0009*, 7 October 2010, http://www.riha-journal.org/articles/2010/ring-petersen-attention-and-distraction, accessed 31 July 2013.

55   Cf. Walter Benjamin, 'Das Kunstwerk im Zeitalter seiner technischen Reproduzierbarkeit', in *Gesammelte Schriften*, Vol. 1, Frankfurt am Main: Suhrkamp, 1980, pp. 471–508.

Chapter 9

Still Life in the Crosshairs, or For an Iconic Turn in Game Studies

Thomas Hensel

Video Games as the Tenth Art

The video game is one of the most complex artefacts to be the subject of art history or media studies. In order to do justice to its manifold aspects – be it narrativity, audio-visuality, inter(re)activity and immersion, ergodicity or ludicity – and its power to integrate all these aspects, game studies test multidisciplinary and polyperspectival approaches, which unite positions from literary studies and information theory, as well as pedagogic and economic perspectives. A glance at current, as well as arguably canonical research literature, nevertheless reveals a distinctive blindness, perhaps maybe even ignorance with regard to another aspect of video games: their visuality and their pictoriality, that is to say their iconicity. The underlying reasons come to light, if one takes a look at a prominent historical paradigm of media studies, with the so-called matrix of interactivity (Figure 1). Here, images, for instance paintings and sculpture, appear as veritable antipodes to video games, and thus as something that has been arrested on a lower step of development in terms of 'interactivity' and 'vividness'.[1]

In fact, one has to concede that a sizeable part of the fine arts has slipped away from media studies as, for a long time, the field of media studies regarded pre-modern visual media – whether they were pictures and frescoes, pamphlets, graphic works, sculptures or buildings – merely as preliminary stages to electronic means of mass communication. The majority of this field de facto cut itself off from its own foundations. With its 'stable' and 'everlasting' material foundation in canvas and oil, wood, marble or metals, art history came into conflict with new concepts of the 'digital', 'virtual' or 'immaterial' media. In contrast to, for example, Marshall McLuhan, for whom an understanding of the fine arts as precursors was practically a prerequisite for the analysis of the latter, a large part of media research remained rather unreceptive to the formal specifics of the image and its historical past layers.[2]

Lebendigkeit (vertical axis, + top to − bottom) / _Interaktivität_ (horizontal axis, − left to + right)

		Gibsons „Simstim"					Gibsons „Cyberspace"	?
3-D Film in odorama	Planetarium	Heiligs „Sensorama"						
	3-D Film							
	Film	HDTV						„Goggles, Gloves, & Headphones"
		TV	Teleshop & TED	Pay-TV	Video	interaktives TV	Videokonferenz	„Goggles & Gloves"
	CD					Karaoke		Video-Spiele
Dias	Viewmaster			Voicemail				
Plastiken	Fotographie			Anruf-beantworter		Telephon	Telephon-Konferenz	CB Funk
Gemälde				FAX				
Bücher	Zeitung	Briefe	dpa Ticker	Email	BBS	UNIX „Talk"	elektr. Konferenzen in Echtzeit	MUD
				Telegraphie		Turings Imitationsspiel		

Figure 1: Matrix of Interactivity.

When, in the following, images are discussed within the context of video games – with the term 'image' denoting all iconic artefacts from paintings to the interactive image of simulation – this happens less with a focus on their perspectivism and spatiality as two of their central characteristics,[3] but more with regard to a third feature that is attributed to artistic images in particular: according to Arthur C. Danto, these are distinguished by the fact that 'they [relate] to "something," but [...] at the same time [address] the means used in the act of relation.'[4] At least since Victor I. Stoichita's major study _The Self-Aware Image_ (1997), the double-coding of images has become generally accepted in art history, and it has become the point of departure for new explorations in game studies as well.[5] The following remarks have to be understood against this background, pertaining to the self-referentiality of media: if one succeeded in describing a video game not only as an image medium – above its purpose as a means of staging digital information – and, going beyond an appreciation of space and perspective, would treat it as an artistic image medium, which displays and reflects its own iconicity, then the analytical tools of game studies would have to be expanded by a further instrument, namely an iconology. However, this would not have to be the kind of iconology as conceived by Aby Warburg or Erwin Panofsky, but rather an iconology understood as a tool used for the examination of the forms, contents and performances of pictorial phenomena irrespective of their media. In the course of this process, video games – apostrophized as the 'tenth art'[6] by media studies – are in no way to be incorporated or colonized and subsumed under their precursors – rather, this is an attempt to mediate between the poles of narratology and ludology[7] and to make some assertions concerning the characteristics of video games in general.

The following deliberations do not aim at a theory of images pertaining to video games; it is a much more modest attempt at comprehending a video game via its images, or, to put it another way, to reflect on a medium – video games – via another medium; here, artistic pictures, specifically the panel painting (although this might appear provocative considering the matrix quoted above). This reflection is based among others on Jay David Bolter's and Richard Grusin's concept of 'remediation'.[8] Remediation contains two components which are dialectically interlaced: immediacy, i.e. the self-neutralization of a medium; and hypermediacy, i.e. the representation of a medium via another medium, which, in contrast to turning it invisible, stages the deliberate exhibition, the reflection on its own 'mediatedness', ultimately, its own performance with regard to mediation. In the following sections, the focus will be on this second component.[9] One point, this much may be said in advance, will show that the medium of the picture does not only outline and contextualize the challenge of the game, thus *framing* it,[10] but that the picture itself *poses* the challenge.[11]

Resident Evil 4 and the Bottle Puzzle

A well-known object is at the centre of the following considerations. It is one of the most popular and critically acclaimed games ever: *Resident Evil 4*, by Capcom in 2005. Its plot line can be summarized in a few words: six years after the 'Umbrella Corporation', the company acting as the *genius malignus* in the *Resident Evil* series, was broken up, Leon Scott Kennedy, known from the second instalment, is working for the US government. He is assigned the task of rescuing the US president's daughter from the grasp of an occult sect called 'Los Illuminados', which tries to achieve world domination by means of an artificial virus. This virus makes monstrous parasites grow within its human hosts, which bestow colossal strength and power.

Resident Evil 4, which can be characterized as a survival horror–third-person shooter–action adventure, and thus appears as a hybrid of many genres, is full of paintings, especially works that belong to so-called 'high art'. These works originate from the most important centres of art of early modern times, which, on the diegetic level, can be explained by the aristocratic taste of the family of the 'Castellan', one of the hero's antagonists. The game design pays its respects to paintings of the Roman and Florentine Early and High Renaissance, for instance Raphael's *The School of Athens* (1510–11) (Figure 2). The range of materials used in the art on display is conspicuous; the suites of the castle are – one might say overabundantly – decked out with oil paintings, as are its halls with frescoes; there are also gobelins, tapestries and sculptures in every imaginable kind of material, up to enamelled terracotta reliefs, which point to works of the family Della Robbia, a dynasty of sculptors.[12]

It would be quite wrong to regard the décor of the setting simply as insignificant padding or eye candy. In fact, the paintings condense and catalyze the narrative. In the second of the

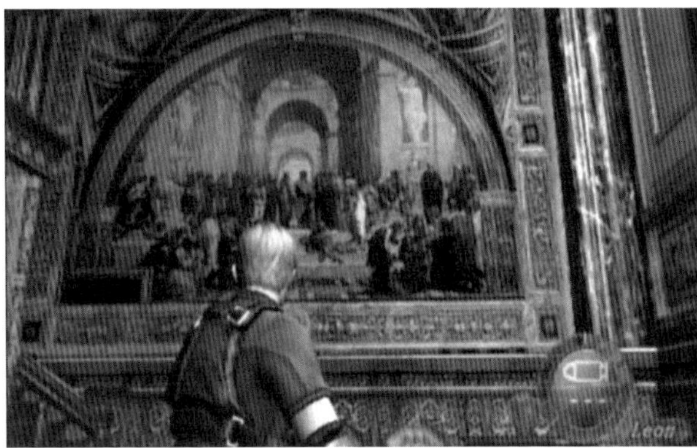

Figure 2: *Resident Evil 4.* Copyright and courtesy: Capcom.

game's three parts, for instance, one encounters a colossal relief showing Bellerophon's battle against the Chimera. Significantly, this relief adorns a gate and, like a puzzle, it has to be completed with three pieces, which the player has to find in order to open the gate and allow the game to progress. While the relief can be regarded on the figurative level as a template for the conflict staged in the game – with Leon Scott Kennedy as Bellerophon and the composite beings of human and parasite as chimeras, themselves mythological hybrids consisting of lion, goat and snake – it also reveals something about the narrative structure of the game itself (similar to the tripartite body of the chimera), put together from discrete parts, which refers to the three topological chapters making up the structure of the game – village, castle, island – each with a boss fight at its end; and the gauntlet which Kennedy has to run in order to find the three pieces of the puzzle appears as a *mise en abyme*, as it recalls the structure of the whole game in miniature. Thus, the relief turns into an image-key, on the one hand in the literal sense – because it clears a gateway as soon as it is completed with the three missing pieces – on the other hand, it also has this function in a metaphorical sense, as a concentration of the narrative, as its explication or anticipation, with a view on just this tripartite structure.

The second example deals with Botticelli's *Primavera* (1480–82), which belongs to the most enigmatic and most widely discussed paintings of western art history – and which, incidentally, also provided a central historic impetus for the development of iconology.[13] Here, too, transformation, the leitmotif of *Resident Evil 4*, is displayed in at least two ways: firstly, in the painting itself – the nymph Chloris turns into the flower goddess Flora after being abducted by Zephyr – but also in front of the painting. Here, during a cutscene which serves as narrative hinge, the protagonist meets an old acquaintance from former days: Ada Wong, herself a shifting figure, as she is involved with 'Los Illuminados', but also shares a bond with Leon Scott Kennedy. Hence, a harmony of contradictions, a dialectical suspension of opposites manifests itself, which will have to be discussed at a later point. But there are also other significant image motifs: for instance the motif of Pygmalion, invoked by various suits of armour and a gigantic stone statue that become alive, or the grotesque,

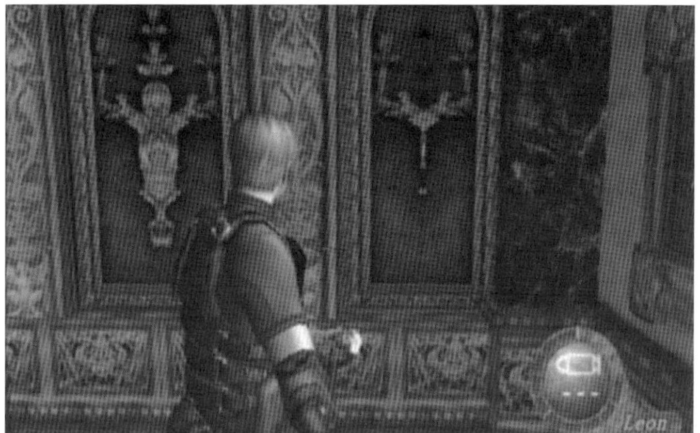

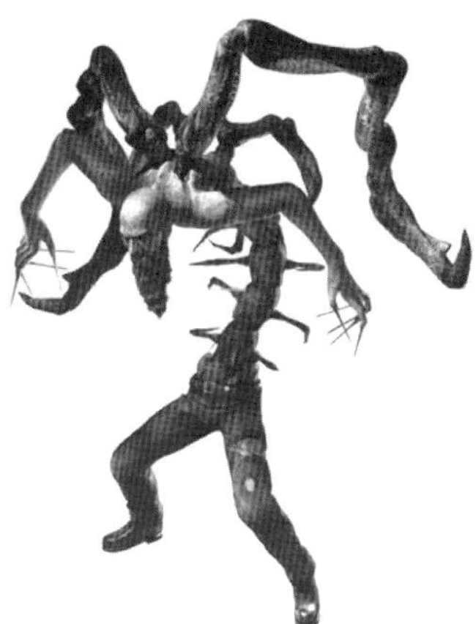

Figure 3a: *Resident Evil 4.* Copyright and Courtesy: Capcom.

Figure 3b: *Resident Evil 4.* Bitores Mendez, Artwork.

which dominates the textures of the rooms as a leitmotif, and also structures the anatomical design of the opponents (Figures 3a and 3b).[14]

Eventually, one encounters picture puzzles and one of the examples which is by far the most spectacular will be analyzed in the following. The so-called bottle puzzle confronts the player with a scenery that evokes a shooting range with its narrow, corridor-like space that has been closed off with a barrier (Figure 4a). As soon as the player follows the incitement to ring a bell, the white wall at the end of the range turns on its axis and presents a magnificent still life on its other side, which obviously functions as a target (Figures 4b and 4c). If the player hits the painting at the wrong spot, it rotates again and turns away from the player's view and his bullets; but if he hits the painted wine bottle or the glass filled with wine, both break into pieces, the fluid runs down the canvas (Figure 4d), and a grille opens close to the avatar, making it possible to move on to the next challenge in the game.

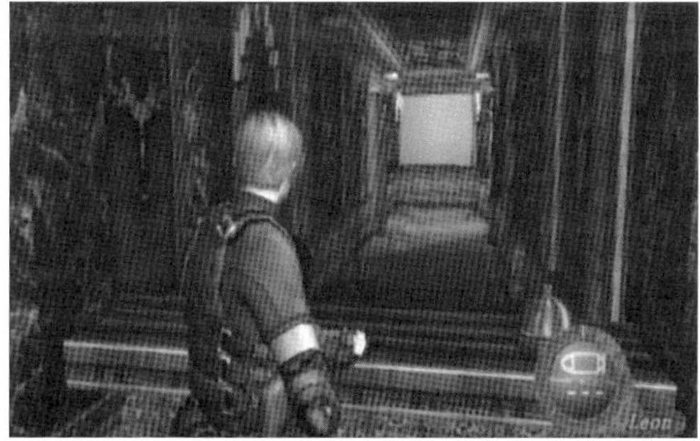

Figure 4a: *Resident Evil 4.* Copyright and courtesy: Capcom.

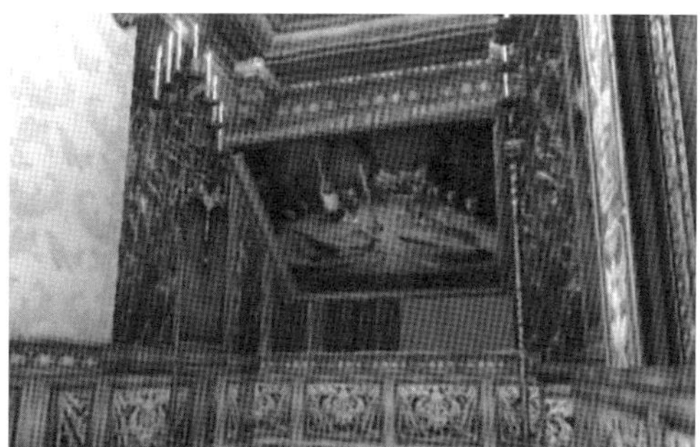

Figure 4b: *Resident Evil 4.* Copyright and courtesy: Capcom.

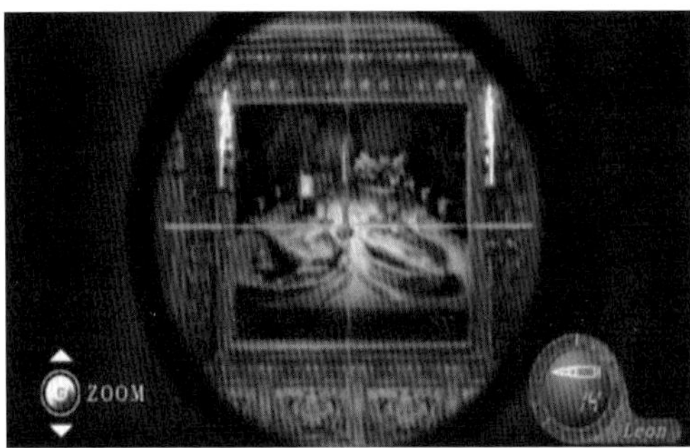

Figure 4c: *Resident Evil 4.* Copyright and courtesy: Capcom.

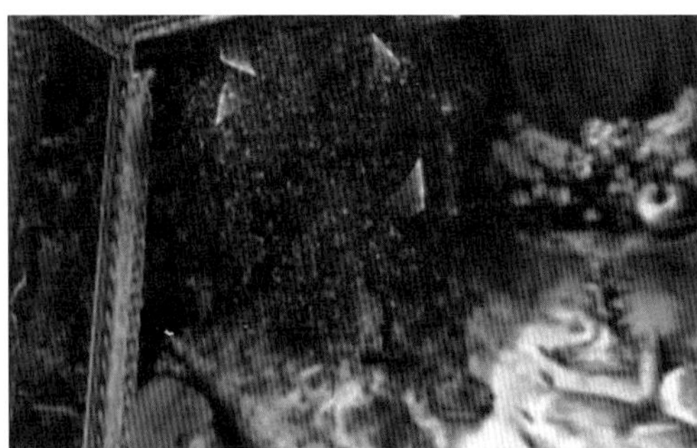

Figure 4d: *Resident Evil 4.* Copyright and courtesy: Capcom.

If one tries to go a bit against the grain of the hectic, nearly seizure-like mood described in relevant depictions of the gameplay,[15] and thus shifts the focus as a player and tries, instead of running and gunning, to stroll through the castle like a contemplative visitor in a museum, then, shortly before reaching that still life, text and picture panels attract one's attention. First of all, four text panels catch the eye due to their explicitness and their plain-spoken text: 'Bread begins the meal of life./ Meat to savor the time at hand./ A dessert to cherish our remaining years./ Our last drink, and the bottle breaks, returning us to the dust from whence we came.' Obviously the panels provide us with a key, enabling us to solve the puzzle – 'Our last drink, and the bottle breaks' (Figure 5) – and endow the still life with a narrative by associating single elements of the painting – bread, meat or a swig of wine – with periods, or more exactly, with life stages.

Analogously, this applies to the picture panels, as they contain a narrative surplus and are presented similarly to the text panels in ostentatious frames, and ordered paratactically in relation to them. The paintings, like the Fates, spin a thread of life: starting with the yet unborn child (prenatal), as implied by the detail of the angel of annunciation (Figure 6a),[16] moving

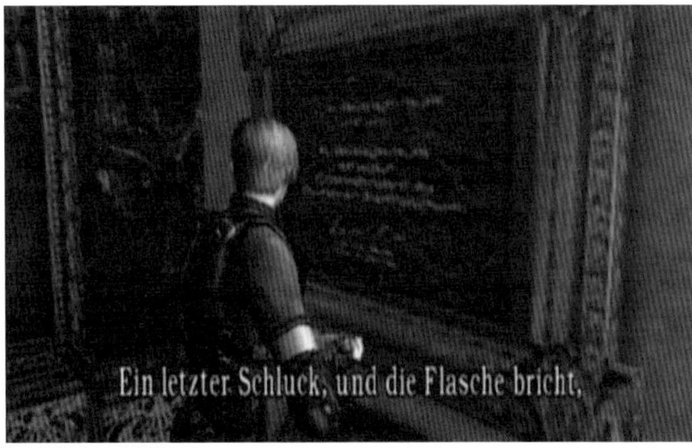

Figure 5: *Resident Evil 4.* Copyright and courtesy: Capcom.

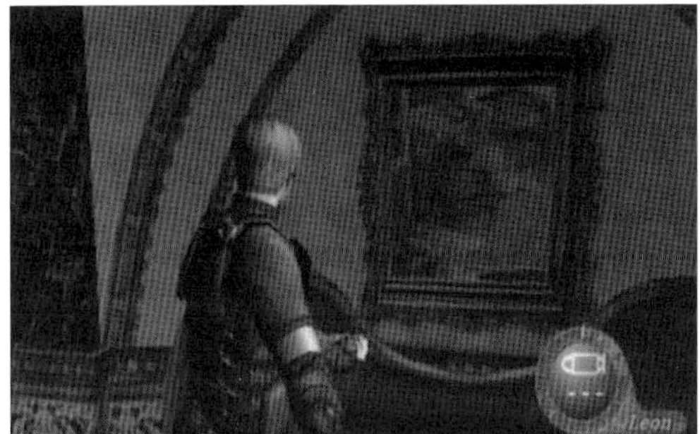

Figure 6a: *Resident Evil 4.* Copyright and courtesy: Capcom.

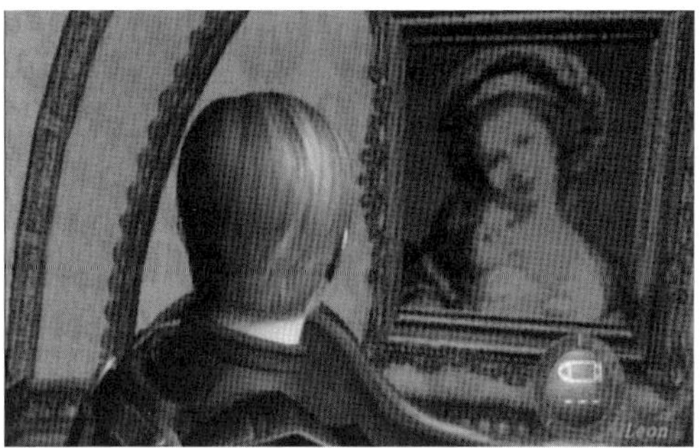

Figure 6b: *Resident Evil 4.* Copyright and courtesy: Capcom.

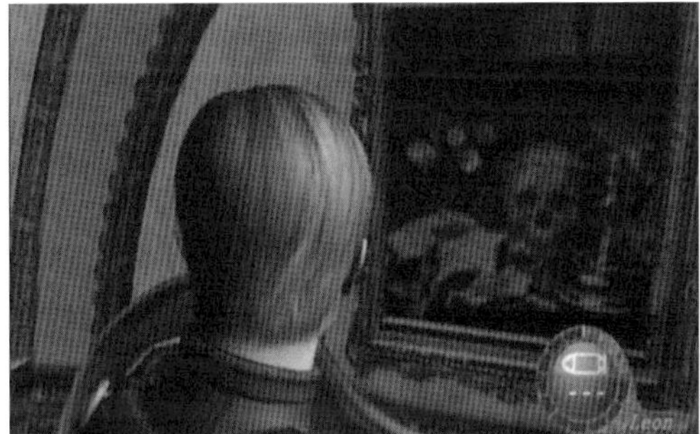

Figure 6c: *Resident Evil 4.* Copyright and courtesy: Capcom.

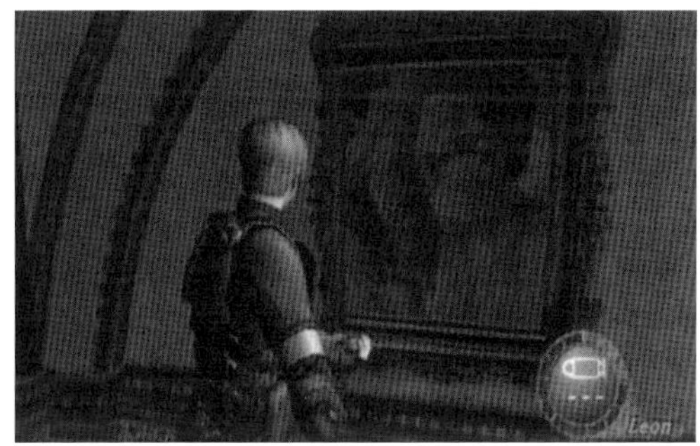

Figure 6d: *Resident Evil 4.* Copyright and courtesy: Capcom.

on to childhood and adolescence, as revealed by a mother-child group (Figure 6b),[17] up to death (post-mortem) (Figure 6c);[18] this last painting adheres to the formula of a vanitas still life or memento mori, and thus also points out the inevitability of one's doom, in this case the doom of the owners of these paintings, 'Los Illuminados'. While, from a narratological perspective, it is therefore possible to speak of a veritable chronotope of passage,[19] it is also the function of the pictures to give a heuristic hint towards a solution of the puzzle: for Botticelli's *Primavera* is the only painting to be cited twice in the whole game – the second time in the form of a detail, significantly the portrait of Chloris, that figure of metamorphosis, showing her head with flowers shooting from her mouth (Figure 6d). Being sensitized to the significance of the images, the message therefore is as follows: focus on the details![20]

While maintaining this perspective, we can allow for a media-archaeological digression and a look at two other historical shot pictures to throw the structural and ontic peculiarity of our still life into relief. The first deals with a video game explicitly created in the context of art and, as it was well known, the designers of *Resident Evil 4* were probably quite familiar with it: *Museum Meltdown* (1996–98) by Palle Torsson and Tobias Bernstrup, a series of site-specific installations of video games. These games were placed in European art museums, employing

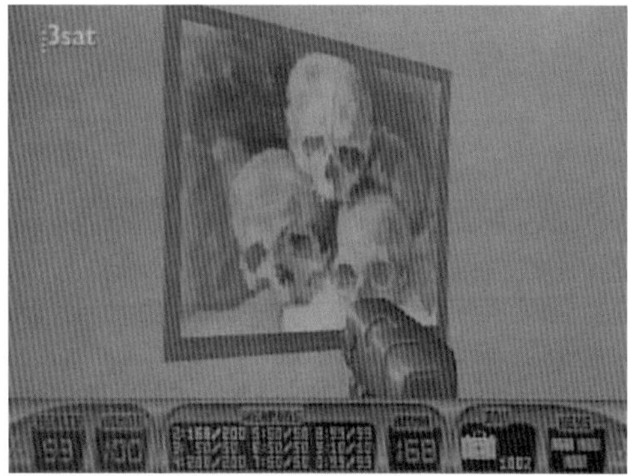

Figure 7: Palle Torsson und Tobias Bernstrup, *Museum Meltdown,* 1996–1998.

the game engines of existing first-person shooters to enable a visitor to walk through a virtual version of the respective museum, where he could shoot at monsters as well as, for instance, Marcel Duchamp's *The Large Glass* (1912–23) or a vanitas still life by Paul Cezanne (Figure 7). In this case, a strong correspondence can be attested on the level of motifs – shooting at a vanitas still life – but only the second example, created by Niki de Saint-Phalle in 1961, sensitizes the observer for our problem of a transgression (Figure 8): titled 'Old Master (Small Shooting

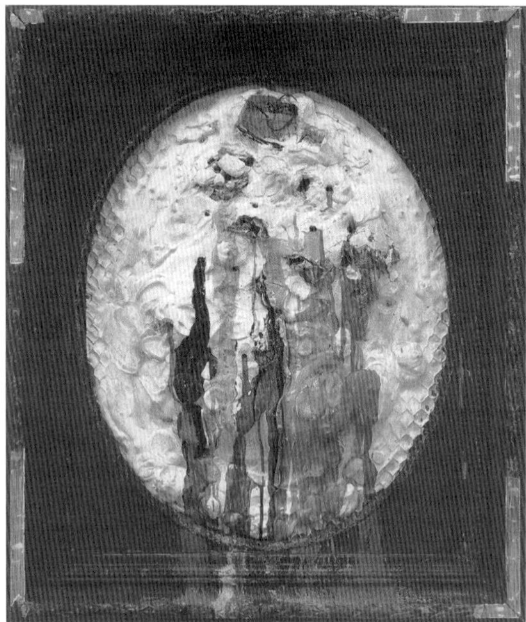

Figure 8: Niki de Saint Phalle, 'Old Master (Small Shooting Painting)', 1961.

Painting)', white plaster bulges from a historic frame, which was cut as an oval, probably for a portrait; a painting which recalls a *tabula rasa*, itself representing the potentiality of all future paintings in the framework of emblematic theory.[21] Niki de Saint-Phalle's iconoclastic gesture, which pits 'low' against 'high', shows some structural similarities with the disposition in *Resident Evil 4*: here, too, a white panel playing with the transgression of its own frame exists, and, similarly, a shot at the panel results in an explosion of colour. However, the transgressive momentum regarding the bottle puzzle presents itself in different categories.

Nature Morte or the Paradox of Paradox

To understand the peculiar paradoxical character of the image displayed in *Resident Evil 4*, it is necessary to take a closer look at the art form of still life, which has a constitutive function for the iconic arrangement of our puzzle. The term 'still life' or *nature morte* is an oxymoron, which ultimately consists of a *contradictio in adjecto*: the adjective 'still' or 'morte/dead' contradicts the essential content of the noun – movement or life.[22] Significantly, the genre of the still life has always dealt with the dialectics of life/death, or put differently, as related to the theory of representation: essence/appearance, truth/illusion, reality/image – since Pliny the Elder at the latest, these are the figurations of artists' competitions in ancient times.[23] A first glance at two prominent exponents of the genre, which were selected more or less arbitrarily, reveals a playful treatment of the picture frame, the 'border guard of the picture'.[24] Here, certain elements – the fruit basket in Caravaggio's case (Figure 9) and the cutting board with knife and spoon in

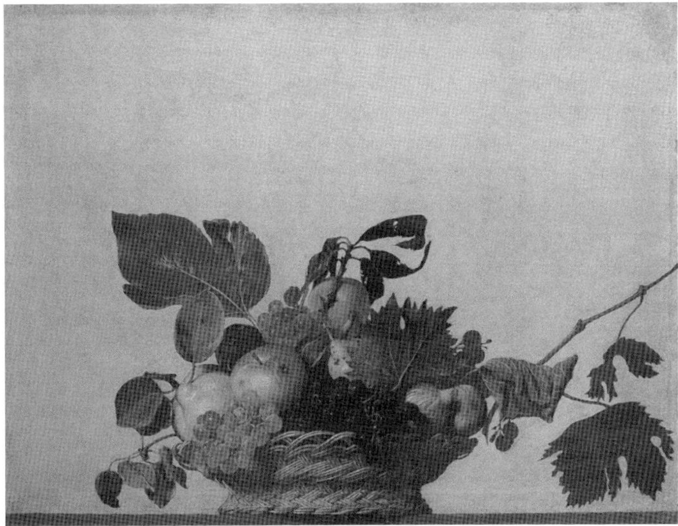

Figure 9: Caravaggio, 'Basket of Fruit', ca. 1596.

Georg Flegel's 17th century still life – transgress the aesthetic border in an illusionistic manner to jump towards the observer.[25]

Like Flegel's painting, the most capricious and exquisite, as well as the greatest examples for the still life and its yearning for transgression, date back to the seventeenth century, 'a period obsessed with the "aesthetic border"',[26] and were created by Cornelis Gijsbrechts.[27] Four examples for his playing with reality and illusion will be subjected to a cursory look. In the first example (Figure 10a), *trompe l'œil* and vanitas are coexistent in a painting that plays on two levels – that of content and that of form, with the ideas of illusion and appearance. While the painting raises the issue of the picture as a cut-out from reality, there is, however, no explicit reflection about representation itself. If one compares this with a second still life by Gijsbrechts, one immediately notices the innovation (Figure 10b): this work features the 'representation of a painting'. A corner of the canvas has become unstuck from the stretcher frame and uncovers it; what we are seeing is the *trompe l'œil* display of a *trompe l'œil* painting, and thus a *trompe l'œil* of the second order. Gijsbrechts not only deals with a doubling of the illusionistic artifice, but also with a doubling of the meditation about vanitas, about the vanity of things. This idea no longer refers just to the objects in the painted image, but has afflicted the painting as such. The dropping canvas reveals its back and exposes the stretcher frame; the only thing we are laying our eyes on is the canvas – the fabric of the material is beginning to fray, its upper right corner is already in tatters. In this case, we are able to study a development from the representation *of* vanitas to the representation *as* vanitas.[28]

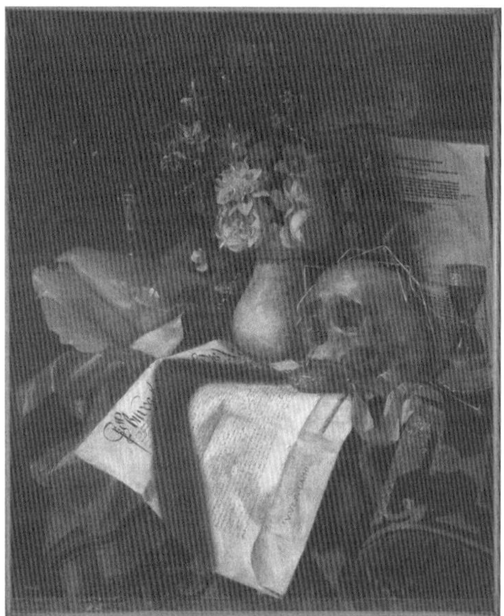

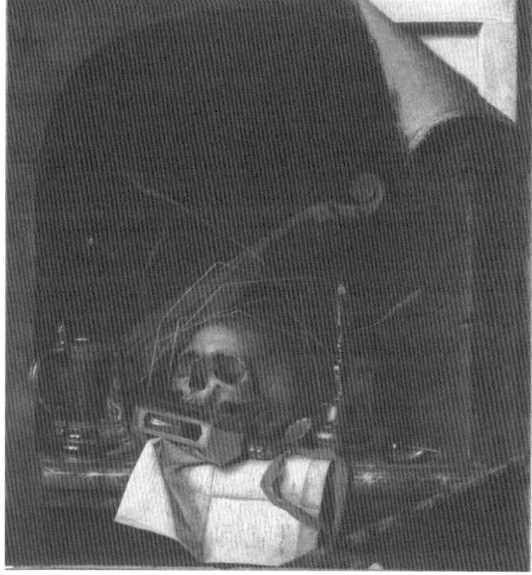

Figure 10a: Cornelis Norbertus Gijsbrechts, 'Vanitas Still Life with Skull and Bunch of Flowers', 1661.

Figure 10b: Cornelis Norbertus Gijsbrechts, 'Vanitas Still Life', 2nd half of the 17th century.

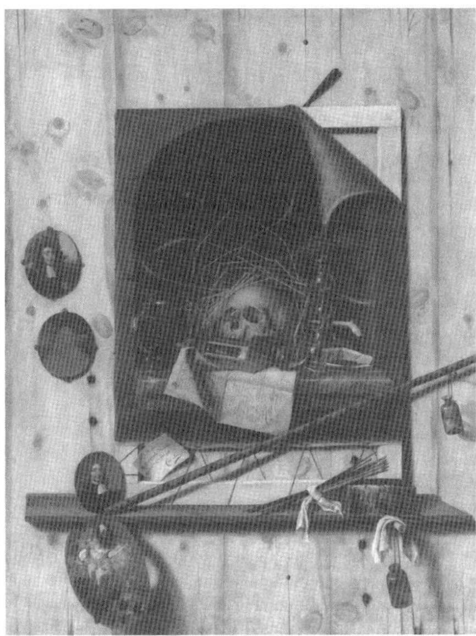

Figure 10c: Cornelis Norbertus Gijsbrechts, 'Trompe-l'œil with Studio Wall and Vanitas Still Life', 1668.

This message becomes more explicit by introducing another of Gijsbrechts' works to this analysis, a work where the sophistication of representation reaches a peak, where the meta-iconic tension nearly arrives at its extremum (Figure 10c). A canvas is in view, which is hung up on a wooden surface. The stretcher frame and the strings tightening the canvas to the frame are visible, as are the tools of the painter jutting into the foreground: palette, hand rest, brush, as well as a self portrait of the artist. In this still life, a paradox reflects the technique of paradox itself – de facto, one is dealing with a painting in the manner of *trompe l'œil*, which presents itself as a simulation of reality; at the same time, however, the painting reveals itself as mere matter (canvas, stretcher frame, paint etc.); but in fact this revelation is a sham exactly because this revelation is presented to us by a painting.[29] Paradoxically, the art of illusion is reinforced by its uncovering, as the disillusionment is accomplished using techniques of illusion.

Thus, the still lifes discussed above, as well as *Resident Evil 4*, display a first, still vague structural analogy, as both employ a 'meta-artistic mechanism that acts as a dialogue between the existential cut and the imaginary cut'.[30] Just as the still life includes a part of the observer's space, i.e. that which according to the norm is on this side of the image, outside of the work, *Resident Evil 4* includes parts of the texture in the gameplay itself, elements which would normally be apart from each other. But Gijsbrechts' panel paintings are also helpful in comprehending another peculiar facet of the bottle puzzle,

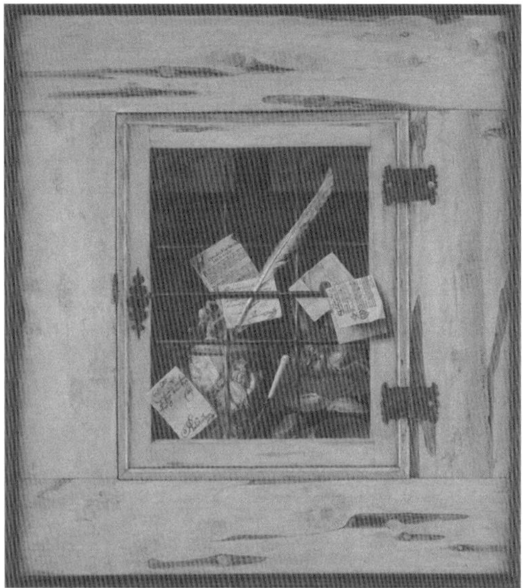

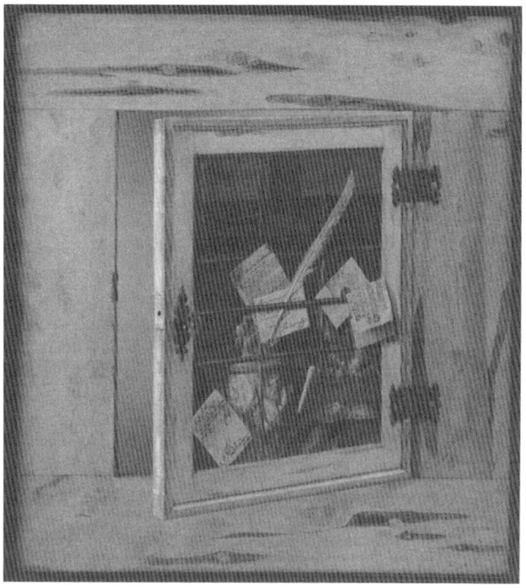

Figure 11a: Cornelis Norbertus Gijsbrechts, 'Trompe-l'œil. A Cabinet of Curiosities with an Ivory Tankard', with closed door, 1670.

Figure 11b: Cornelis Norbertus Gijsbrechts, 'Trompe-l'œil. A Cabinet of Curiosities with an Ivory Tankard', with open door, 1670.

which even eclipses this transgressive performance, and they are useful in highlighting the limitations of the matrix of interactivity invoked at the beginning, which denies interactivity and vividness to images just like those by Gijsbrechts. It is in another *trompe l'œil* depiction, where Gijsbrechts demonstrates how the image-space can merge into a space-image[31] and vice versa, because the illusionistic image-space literally opens up into real space with a cabinet door set into it, which can actually be pivoted. Thus, it subverts the ontological cut, which the frame of a picture performs as the location of a symbolical operation (Figures 11a and 11b). It is exactly this subversion of the ontological cut that manifests itself in the case of our bottle puzzle, here in an actually impossible paradox: where or what is the location of the bottle? In fact, the bottle is a-local or a-situated, it is neither in nor outside the picture, or, posed in the affirmative, it is a part of as well as outside the picture. Apart from the effective conditioning mentioned above, the only purpose of pivoting the picture panel lies in demonstrating that the picture is level and flat, and that there are no objects applied or fastened to it, particularly no bottle or glass (which would spill its content during the pivoting). One could argue that the 'paradox of a "plane depth"',[32] which Gottfried Boehm introduces when he characterizes the image following Leon Battista Alberti's notion of a *finestra aperta* or *velum*, transforms into the paradox of a deep surface – and the other way round, depending on which face of the picture panel one is observing.[33]

Para/ergon, Avatar and Ontological Metalepsis

However, it is not only this shifting between two- and three-dimensionality, between image and reality, which make the still life so valuable for understanding the video game. The entire historical background of the still life is defined by the relation of the *para* to its *ergon*.[34] While it originated as a marginal work, a backside, an accessory, as a framing picture, in a word as a *parergon*, the still life develops into an *ergon* during the seventeenth century.[35] *Para/ergon* is the object which is added to a work and at the same time opposes it:

> A parergon comes against, beside, and in addition to the ergon, the work done [fait], the fact [le fait], the work, but it does not fall to one side, it touches and cooperates within the operation, from a certain outside. Neither simply outside nor simply inside. Like an accessory that one is obliged to welcome on the border, on board [au bard, a bard].[36]

Thus, the prefix 'para' contains a glut of nuances, which are difficult to translate:

> A thing in 'para' […] is not only simultaneously on both sides of the boundary line itself, the screen which is a permeable membrane connecting inside and outside. It confuses them with one another, allowing the outside in, making the inside out, dividing them and joining them.[37]

It is exactly this depiction of an ambiguity or, to establish the tie to the video game, an ontological oscillation, which appears to be a fitting characterization of an avatar as well as a player: however one might define an avatar in particular – as a tool, a sprite, a puppet or a figure –,[38] in the end it is characterized by a paradoxically dual function: it exists as the protagonist of a narrative on the one hand, and functions as the player's tool on the other.[39] This also applies to the player: he/she, too, has factual and fictional facets and is affected by the paradox of a 'double addressing […] as someone who is acting within and outside of diegesis'.[40]

While it is closely related to this double addressing, metalepsis can also be identified as another important structural feature shared by the panel paintings presented above and the images in the video game. Metalepsis is a narrative strategy that blurs the difference between the level of narrating and the level of the narrated acts and events – the narrated world transgresses into the world of narrating and vice versa. Thus, it is a matter of transcending the borders of diegesis on the part of a game figure or the author, which, on the one hand, may stand for the author entering the world he created, or, by the same token, for a figure leaving the narrated world it belongs to and entering the world of its author.[41] Therefore, metalepsis can be understood as a playing with the emphasis on the sensation of reality which, if nothing else, can be considered to be a constitutive factor of the reflexive video game. Just as with the image of a cabinet door by Cornelis Gijsbrechts' brush, the still life in *Resident Evil 4* presents nothing less than a metalepsis *in extremis*; according to Marie-Laure Ryan this is an ontological metalepsis (Figure 12), opening a gateway between

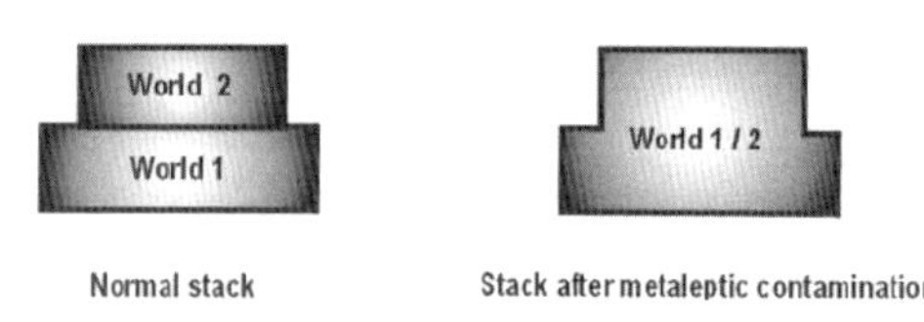

Figure 12: Ontological metalepsis.

the levels, which results in their interpenetration and mutual contamination.[42] The picture of the bottle puzzle in *Resident Evil 4* thus proves to be an iconic *dispositif* that highlights distinctive characteristics of the video game; in turn, those find themselves rooted in the tradition of the panel painting, which is deliberately showcased by *Resident Evil 4*. This tradition thus appears as a perspective on the analysis of video games, which up to now has been completely neglected, but shows itself to be irreducible and cannot be rated highly enough in its potency.

The Video Game as an Inter(re)active Image Act

In concluding, it is worth trying to bridge the gap between the logic of the still life in *Resident Evil 4* and a principal characteristic of the video game: or more exactly, to make an attempt at formulating a point according to representational theory, or, rather, against representational theory.[43] As is generally known, a specific characteristic of the computer's imagery is that it has to be understood less in a representational, but rather in a pragmatic and performative way: 'In hypertexts all kinds of signs become programmable as icons, i.e. as signifiers, which at the pragmatic level produce, with a mouse-click, a connection to what they designate that is no longer merely symbolic, but real.'[44] Thus, the computer image is a visible manifestation of a digital, operative code that subverts the separation between execution (action) and display (representation). One *performs* something in the use of these images, which prove to be image acts in line with John Langshaw Austin and, with regard to Austin's theoretical relevance for the image, German art historian Horst Bredekamp.[45] As is well known, Austin distinguished between 'constative' and 'performative' utterances, which he called 'speech acts'. A constative utterance is a descriptive statement used to make an assessment or observation; a performative utterance, on the other hand, does not state anything, but is the factual execution of the objects and acts it denotes – it constitutes the things it is stating.[46] In a performative utterance, the familiar separation between the means and the objects of representation, between word – or image – and thing is suspended. It is this specific feature that characterizes the still life in *Resident Evil 4*: by stating the existence of the bottle, the image constitutes the bottle itself, just like Cornelis Gijsbrechts' painting of the cabinet door, where the means of representation and its object, image and thing, coincide. But this feature also characterizes the computed image: the image appearing on the computer screen, as a calculated image, turns out to trigger calculations and pragmatic correlations. Thus, the two still lifes presented above, as well as the video game itself, are image acts; they are, in a manner of speaking, images fabricated in and for the moment, which only exist in the instant of their execution.[47] Revealingly, *Resident Evil 4* is a paradigmatic example of exactly this phenomenon, as the fourth part of the *Resident Evil* series was the first to compute all events in real time, meaning that, ultimately, the imagery was produced inter(re)actively[48] by playing the game, while its precursors still had the figures move through pre-rendered environments.

Thus it becomes possible to address *Resident Evil 4* as a game between representation and the self-awareness of representation, where the problematization of representation is elevated to a productive momentum of the depiction itself; and thus it is addressable as a theoretical object that deals with the topics of the image and its performances of transgression and, respectively, remediation. If this is true, then video games are not only defined by their narrativity, inter(re)activity or performativity, but also and especially by their iconicity, which, case by case, is able to incorporate these other potentialities. Thus, it is necessary to perceive the image not only as a function of the ludic, but also, conversely, the ludic as a function of the image. It is a *desideratum* of game studies to perform such an iconic turn; while that of art history lies in recognizing that a new, a tenth art has begun to move into its sphere of authority.

Translated by Jochen Mevius

Notes

1 See Wulf R. Halbach, *Interfaces. Medien- und kommunikationstheoretische Elemente einer Interface-Theorie*, München: Fink, 1994, p. 173. Cf., with regard to this cliché and its rebuttal, Peter Matussek, 'Bewegte und Bewegende Bilder. Animationstechniken im historischen Vergleich', in Christina Lechtermann, Carsten Morsch and Horst Wenzel (eds), *Kunst der Bewegung. Kinästhetische Wahrnehmung und Probehandeln in virtuellen Welten* (Publikationen zur Zeitschrift für Germanistik, Neue Folge, Vol. 8), Bern: Peter Lang, 2004, pp. 1–13.

2 See Horst Bredekamp, 'Bildmedien', in Hans Belting, Heinrich Dilly, Wolfgang Kemp, Willibald Sauerländer and Martin Warnke (eds), *Kunstgeschichte. Eine Einführung*, Berlin: Reimer, 2003, pp. 355–78; Beat Wyss, *Die Welt als T-Shirt. Zur Ästhetik und Geschichte der Medien*, Köln: DuMont, 1997, pp. 23–24.

3 Fruitful analytic approaches concerning these features have been proposed by, for example, Clara Fernández-Vara, José Pablo Zagal and Michael Mateas, 'Evolution of Spatial Configurations in Videogames', in *Proceedings of DiGRA 2005 Conference: Changing Views – Worlds in Play*, http://www.digra.org/dl/db/06278.04249.pdf, accessed 1 October 2011; Stephan Günzel, 'The Spatial Turn in Computer Game Studies', in Konstantin Mitgutsch, Christoph Klimmt and Herbert Rosenstingl (eds), *Exploring the Edges of Gaming. Proceedings of the Vienna Games Conference 2008–2009: Future and Reality of Gaming*, Wien: Braumüller,

2010, pp. 147–56; Michael Nitsche, *Video Game Spaces. Image, Play, and Structure in 3D Worlds*, Cambridge, MA & London: MIT, 2008; Stephan Schwingeler, *Die Raummaschine. Raum und Perspektive im Computerspiel*, Boizenburg: Hülsbusch, 2008; Axel Stockburger, *The Rendered Arena: Modalities of Space in Video and Computer Games*, Doctoral Thesis, University of the Arts, London, 2006, http://www.stockburger.at/files/2010/04/Stockburger_Phd.pdf, accessed 1 October 2011; Steffen P. Walz, *Toward a Ludic Architecture: The Space of Play and Games*, Pittsburgh: ECT Press, 2010; Mark J. P. Wolf, 'Space in the Video Game', in *The Medium of the Video Game*, Austin: University of Texas Press, 2001, pp. 51–75.

4　Arthur C. Danto, 'Das Ende der Kunstgeschichte ist nicht das Ende der Kunst. Karlheinz Lüdeking sprach mit Arthur C. Danto', in *Kunstforum International*, Vol. 123, 1993, pp. 200–08, especially p. 204 (translated by Jochen Mevius). Gottfried Boehm speaks about an 'iconic difference' in this context. See Gottfried Boehm, 'Die Wiederkehr der Bilder', in *Was ist ein Bild?* (Bild und Text), Munich: Fink, 1994, pp. 11–38, especially p. 29.

5　See Britta Neitzel, 'Selbstreferenz im Computerspiel', in Winfried Nöth, Nina Bishara and Britta Neitzel, *Mediale Selbstreferenz. Grundlagen und Fallstudien zu Werbung, Computerspiel und Comics*, Cologne: Halem, 2008, pp. 119–96; Bernhard Rapp, *Selbstreflexivität im Computerspiel. Theoretische, analytische und funktionale Zugänge zum Phänomen autothematischer Strategien in Games*, Boizenburg: Hülsbusch, 2008.

6　Alain and Frédéric Le Diberder, qtd in Dieter Mersch, 'Logik und Medialität des Computerspiels. Eine medientheoretische Analyse', in Jan Distelmeyer, Christine Hanke and Dieter Mersch (eds), *Game over!? Perspektiven des Computerspiels*, Bielefeld: transcript, 2008, pp. 19–41, especially p. 19. For a discussion of video games as an art form, see Andy Clarke and Grethe Mitchell (eds), *Videogames and Art*, Bristol & Chicago: Intellect Press, 2007.

7　Originally, the field of game studies was positioned between these poles: while narratologists regarded video games as narratives and interpreted them like texts, the ludologists rejected any narrow focusing on the contents and emphasized the challenges residing in the game mechanics, for instance the linking between stimulus and response as an element of gameplay. These positions, which were never antagonistic in a strict sense, have started to permeate each other increasingly for some time now.

8　See Jay David Bolter and Richard Grusin, *Remediation: Understanding New Media*, Cambridge, MA: MIT Press, 1999.

9　Intermediality is another concept which is used as a basis for this paper, but which can only be outlined here. This is especially true regarding the concept of intermedial references as developed by Jens Schröter or Irina O. Rajewsky. Cf. Jens Schröter, 'Intermedialität. Facetten und Probleme eines aktuellen medienwissenschaftlichen Begriffs', in *montage/av*, Vol. 7, No. 2, 1998, pp. 129–54; Irina O. Rajewsky, 'Intermediality, Intertextuality, and Remediation: A Literary Perspective on Intermediality', in *Intermédialités/Intermedialities, Vol. 6, 2005*, pp. 43–64.

10　Cf. Mersch, 2008, p. 39.

11　The present paper originates from my postdoctoral thesis entitled 'Das Spielen des Bildes. Zur Ikonizität des Computerspiels', which is positioned at the intersection of art history and media studies, and aims at highlighting various potentialities of iconicity as a constitutive factor of video games, using *Resident Evil 4* and other commercial games as examples.

12 Apart from citations of famous works one also finds new creations by game designers.

13 Cf. Aby Warburg, 'Sandro Botticelli's "Birth of Venus" and "Spring": An Examination of Concepts of Antiquity in the Italian Early Renaissance (1893)', in *The Renewal of Pagan Antiquity: Contributions to the Cultural History of the European Renaissance* (trans. David Britt), Los Angeles: Getty Publications, 1999, pp. 88–156.

14 The motif of Pygmalion and the grotesque are extraordinarily significant with relation to image theory, but cannot be further pursued within the scope of this paper. For the motif of Pygmalion, see Victor I. Stoichita, *The Pygmalion Effect: From Ovid to Hitchcock*, Chicago & London 2008; for the grotesque, see Wolfgang Kayser, *Das Groteske. Seine Gestaltung in Malerei und Dichtung*. With a preface on 'Zur Intermedialität des Grotesken' (trans. 'On the intermediality of the grotesque'), Stauffenburg Bibliothek, Vol. 1, Tübingen, 2004.

15 A pertinent website depicts the gameplay like this: 'The gameplay focuses on fast-paced gunplay, quick controls, and shootouts involving massive crowds of enemies in large open areas', http://capcom.wikia.com/wiki/Resident_Evil_4, accessed 1 February 2011.

16 Sandro Botticelli, *Annunciation* (detail) (1481).

17 Marie Louise Élisabeth Vigée-Lebrun, *Self Portrait with Child* (detail) (1786).

18 Hendrik Andrieszen, *Vanitas Still Life* (1635). I would like to thank Jens Meinrenken and Sabina Mlodzianowski, Berlin, for their help in identifying the paintings.

19 For the concept of 'chronotope', see Michael M. Bachtin, *Chronotopos* (1973), Frankfurt am Main: Suhrkamp, 2008.

20 If we focus on the precarious detail on the still life, the trained eye realizes that bottle and glass are not fitting the perspective, and ultimately look like they have been glued to the surface – which can be regarded as a hint at the solution of the bottle puzzle (Figure 4c). Other hints are the (already described) architecture of the scene which recalls a shooting range, the incitement to ring the bell as well as the causal nexus towards which the player is conditioned: if he shoots and hits the painting, the panel turns or the glass breaks.

21 For the *tabula rasa* motif, see Monika Wagner, 'Die *tabula rasa* als Denk-Bild. Zur Vorgeschichte bildloser Bilder', in Barbara Naumann and Edgar Pankow (eds), *Bilder-Denken. Bildlichkeit und Argumentation*, Munich: Fink, 2004, pp. 67–86.

22 Cf. Victor I. Stoichita, *The Self-Aware Image: An Insight into Early Modern Meta-Painting*, Cambridge: Cambridge University Press, 1997, p. 17.

23 Cf. ibid., p. 29. The famous ancient contest between Zeuxis and Parrhasios is a fitting example in this context. Cf. Hans Körner, Constanze Peres and Reinhard Steiner (eds), *Die Trauben des Zeuxis. Formen künstlerischer Wirklichkeitsaneignung* (Münchner Beiträge zur Geschichte und Theorie der Künste, Vol. 2), Hildesheim, Zürich & New York: Georg Olms, 1990.

24 Georg Simmel, 'Der Bildrahmen. Ein ästhetischer Versuch (1902)', in Rüdiger Kramme, Angela Rammstedt and Otthein Rammstedt (eds), *Aufsätze und Abhandlungen 1901–1908*, Vol. 1 (Complete Edition, Vol. 7), Frankfurt am Main: Suhrkamp, 2000, pp. 101–08, especially p. 106.

25 Cf. Stoichita, 1997, p. 26.

26 ibid., p. 46.

27 Cf. Olaf Koester (ed.), *Illusions. Gijsbrechts – Royal Master of Deception*, Copenhagen: Statens Museum for Kunst, 1999.

28 Cf. Stoichita, 1997, p. 278.

29 ibid., pp. 269–72.

30 ibid., p. 53.

31 For the term and concept of the space-image ('Raumbild'), see Gundolf Winter, Jens Schröter and Joanna Barck (eds), *Das Raumbild. Bilder jenseits ihrer Flächen*, München: Fink, 2009.

32 Boehm, 1994, p. 33.

33 The playing with a two- and three-dimensionality that merge into each other has gained currency, with *Resident Evil 4* being the precedent. Here, I want to briefly point out the puzzle-game *Braid* from 2008, a 2D-side-scroller-jump'n'run, which pays its respects to the bottle puzzle on the intramedial level, although it is far less complex than that puzzle. In each level, the player has to assemble puzzle pieces into a picture – amongst others that of a pair of lovers in deep embrace – which then enables the avatar to proceed. Specifically, the surface of the table standing next to the couple is actually a three-dimensional course element in the picture's perceived two-dimensional surface (which can be imagined to actually jut out of the picture), which the avatar can step on to continue on its way. It can be seen as a tongue-in-cheek reference to the bottle puzzle in *Resident Evil 4* – that it is a bottle, of all things, which is dropping from the table during the tempest of amorous affect.

34 Cf. Stoichita, 1997, pp. 17–29.

35 The term *parergon* (*para* means 'against', *ergon* means 'work, task') is known to be historically grounded: as the ornamental padding added to a speech in the classical rhetoric of, for instance, Quintilian, as, according to Pliny, the decoration of a painting and explicitly as a term for the still life in Franciscus Junius' writings 'De pictura veterum' from 1637.

36 Jacques Derrida, *The Truth in Painting*, Chicago: University of Chicago Press, 1987, p. 54.

37 J. Hillis Miller, 'The Critic as Host', in Jacques Derrida, Harold Bloom, Geoffrey Hartman, Paul de Man and J. Hillis Miller, *Deconstruction and Criticism*, London & New York: Continuum, 1979, pp. 217–53, especially p. 219.

38 For a fundamental introduction, see Rune Klevjer, *What is the Avatar? Fiction and Embodiment in Avatar-Based Singleplayer Computer Games*, http://folk.uib.no/smkrk/docs/RuneKlevjer_What%20is%20the%20Avatar_finalprint.pdf, accessed 1 February 2011.

39 Within the scope of the present paper, the avatar is considered to be an element that is central to the determination of the video game's *differentia specifica*, although games which dispense with an avatar in the narrow sense do exist.

40 Neitzel, 2008, p. 152 (translated by Jochen Mevius).

41 Cf. Jörg Türschmann, 'Die Metalepse', in *montage/av*, Vol. 16, No. 2, 2007, pp. 105–12.

42 See Marie-Laure Ryan, 'Metaleptic machines', in *Semiotica: Journal of the International Association for Semiotic Studies*, Vol. 150, 2004, pp. 439–69, especially p. 442. Painting ('World 1') as well as bottle and glass ('World 2') become 'World 1/2' in the diction of this scheme.

43 In connection with this bridging of the gap, further perspectives would be possible; for instance, one grounded in the sociology of art and design, pointing out that the still life as well as game design bear witness to a pride of the artist, which revels in the luxuriousness of textures and makes the opulence and variance of the simulated artworks mentioned above plausible. Cf. Svetlana Alpers, *The Art of Describing: Dutch Art in the Seventeenth Century,*

Chicago & London: University of Chicago Press, 1983; Norman Bryson, *Looking at the Overlooked: Four Essays on Still Life Painting*, Cambridge, MA: Harvard University Press, 1990.

44 Mike Sandbothe, *Pragmatic Media Philosophy: Foundations of a New Discipline in the Internet Age*, sandbothe.net, 2005, p. 162, http://www.sandbothe.net/pmp.pdf, accessed 1 February 2011. See also Constanze Bausch and Benjamin Jörissen, 'Das Spiel mit dem Bild. Zur Ikonologie von Action-Computerspielen', in Christoph Wulf and Jorg Zirfas (eds), *Ikonologie des Performativen*, München: Fink, 2005, pp. 345–64.

45 See John Langshaw Austin, *How to do things with words: The William James lectures delivered at Harvard University in 1955*, Cambridge, MA: Harvard University Press, 1962; Horst Bredekamp, *Theorie des Bildakts. Frankfurter Adorno-Vorlesungen*, Berlin: Suhrkamp, 2010.

46 According to Austin, weddings, christenings, testaments and bets are examples of performative utterances. See also Sybille Krämer and Marco Stahlhut, 'Das "Performative" als Thema der Sprach- und Kulturphilosophie', in Erika Fischer-Lichte and Christoph Wulf (eds), *Paragrana. Internationale Zeitschrift für Historische Anthropologie*, Vol. 10, No. 1, 2001, pp. 35–64; Thomas Hensel, '"In actu": Performativity and the so-called Media Arts', in *Streams of Encounter – Electronic Media based Artworks. Encounter: Interference, Interaction, Communication. Temporal and Spatial Structures in 'Media Art'*, Taipei: Taipei Fine Arts Museum, 2003, pp. 6–12.

47 For a detailed account, see Thomas Hensel *Nature Morte im Fadenkreuz. Zur Bildlichkeit des Computerspiels*, Trier: Intermedia Design Books 02, 2011.

48 See Dominic Arsenault and Bernard Perron, 'In the Frame of the Magic Cycle. The Circle(s) of Gameplay', in Bernard Perron and Mark J. P. Wolf (eds), *The Video Game Theory Reader 2*, New York: Routledge, 2009, pp. 109–31, especially pp. 119–20.

Chapter 10

Out of Image

Yvonne Spielmann

There are no Images

To introduce the idea of discussing artists' practices that exceed the notion of 'image', I would like to discuss a range of aesthetic-artistic strategies, and also broader creative practices, which I believe can serve as interesting and effective examples of critical interventions into contemporary media landscapes. Let me start by pointing to a few aspects of the present situation, and follow this with a brief discussion of aesthetic strategies in radical arts. First of all, I consider artists' practices as aesthetic interventions where the target is to unveil or reveal, and to make us think about processes in the visual or audio-visual presentation that we usually take for granted, and only question when there is failure and malfunction. In contrast to these failures, aesthetic interventions can be effective instruments in a critical discourse about dominant media cultures, where the arts dissolve and disrupt and rearrange meaningful contexts of mainstream media presentations. The aesthetic means can be subtle, ironic or violent and also compulsive, and they can forcefully dismantle and make visible and audible the raw materials of our highly mediated environments. Secondly, among present creative practices, I feel two important criteria stand out: one is the crossover of different cultural and media elements in dialogical contexts; the other is the interaction of different views, attitudes and realities in open-ended processes – mostly interactive and virtual media applications – wherein we experience variety and diversity beyond and across the dominant modes of image and media productions in commercial and corporate commercial industries. I will return to these criteria below.

In framing this essay, I wish to distance myself from the much debated critical 'turns' in art, media and culture, where the much-vaunted iconic or pictorial turn seems to have fostered a subsequently increasing velocity of shifts. W. J. T. Mitchell's celebrated proposition of a 'pictorial turn'[1] has indeed given rise to a variety of identifiable 'turns'; the most prominent being the 'performative' and the 'postcolonial' turns, each of which represent ruptures in the prevailing theory and discourse deemed urgently required to cope with emerging topics in the humanities and cultural sciences. I do not aim to indicate another new turn to add to the plethora of media and cultural turns we have faced over the past two decades. My interest in visual/audio-visual processing develops in the realm of contemporary interactive and virtual applications and has a different tone. I have coined the title, 'Out of Image', to stress the crossing and expansion of the present that differ from the twentieth-century occupation with the visual that has mainly concentrated on theories of the image. Certainly, the underlying idea is neither to get away from, nor to get away with images. When I suggest that we reflect on strategies to get 'out of the image', I wish to demonstrate strategies that lead to the dissolution of the image in technical terms – not merely as metaphors.

The technical possibilites for an image to be 'out of synch' are primarily rooted in the visual media of film and video, and carry multiple meanings. One needs to synchronize the flow of images in the film projector so that the projection of moving images appears in constant succession of projected light values that are fixed on the material basis of the film strip. In fact, this consists of a series of frames connected and separated by intervals. To generate a consistency in the apparent movement of the series of film frames, the vertical movement of the film strip in front of the projector lamp needs to be adjusted; it must be correctly synchronized with a certain frame rate, which is important in cinema to generate the visual impression of continuously moving images. The frame rate needs to be stabilized at a certain velocity to avoid the unpleasant perception of flicker and maintain the illusion of motion through the effects of the persistence of vision. These mechanisms are well known in cinema studies, and the technical setting has been established since the early days of 'living pictures'.

Perhaps less well known is the fact that, unlike film, video as an electronic medium does not operate with images at all, but uses signal processing for the generation of the visual and audio-visual appearance of electronic imagery and sounds.[2] Video is the first truly audio-visual medium which, in contrast to film, does not generate images as a unit, and does not display the physical delineation of a film strip which makes use of one track for image and one for sound. Thus differentiated, the electronic signal processing realizes – in recording, transmitting, and projecting – unstable states of pictorality, which are variable in terms of their scale, form, directionality and dimensionality. In addition, the audio-visual idiosyncracy of video consists of sound signals that are transformed into image signals and vice versa. The information contained in the video signals can be broadcasted visually and audibly at the same time. The way electronic signals are processed and transformed alternately into video and audio denotes the media-technical conditions for 'realizing' a medium whose open-ended forms derive directly from such electronic signal processes. Furthermore, video signals can, but must not, present electronic 'images'. An image only appears when the horizontal flow of the signal is stopped, and the signal gets adjusted at the end of the line (horizontal synchronization jump), and then the bottom line gets synchronized with the top line (what we call a vertical synchronization jump). Here, we say this is a televisual image; but it is at the same time a violent interruption in the electronic flow that produces an 'image', whereas the flow of signals naturally connotes a horizontal drifting 'out of image'. The forms of image are also not standardized, but come with regional differences: NTSC in the United States; PAL in Europe; SECAM in France and Japan. As a result, various cultural zones have different image forms with their own distinctive chracteristics.

This kind of commerical-corporate endeavour to broadcast internationally and globally is also responsible for the following division of different DVD and mobile/wireless zones, which do not reflect technical necessity, but rather deliberately introduced limitations driven by market needs and interest. In this respect it has to be emphasized that in actuality the so-called digital 'image' does not exist at all. The digital kind of image has no predefined requirements or location of its visual appearance; there is no agreed, standard form or format or specific device of display. Simply, there are no images behind algorithmic processes in the computer that are able to generate the appearance of images just from programming of encoded information. Generating images is only one of the multiple options to use digital computers which – let us recall – were initally designed for processing and calculation of increased masses of data that emerged from the technological drive after World War II. The digital computer was developed as a result of dealing with computer systems as problem-solving machines when military and politics were interested in systems that would process, store, retrieve and link relevant data in the Cold War era.[3]

Digital computers operate by numbers, symbols and codes (analogue computers by signals) – not by text, image and sound. Because this process does not reside physically in recording and reproducing, the digital appearance of images is basically simulation calculated by computers. This opens the field of representation for other dimensions, and the spectrum of relations for innumerable possibilites. By dint of the characteristics of its structure, the digital type of image is essentially synthetic. Whereas electronic transformation includes a process between 'signal states' – notably an in-between – the nature of the process in the digital is such that the electronic transformation switches over to the simulation of this event. Rather, the schema, which every process of transformation needs (in the audio-visual of the electronic process), is itself endlessly manipulated as code, that is simulated in every possible direction and dimension, every possible icon, picture and image. By using computers, the image does not exist any longer, but gives way to the success of simulation of the image in digital and interactive environments of the virtual realities. With the advent of digital computation, the notion of the image has moved out of the constraints of 'an image' as entity – it has become fluid, flexible, instable and endlessly programmable.

In his discussion of contemporary visual media, Mark Poster (2001)[4] has convincingly pointed out that we are not facing an increase of visuality compared to the history of visual media, but rather experiencing a different visual regime distinct from the scopic regimes identified by Martin Jay as characterizing modernity.[5] Nowadays, a visual world would in the first instance need to be determined by the technological setting that enables us to employ calculating machines to generate images by binary coding and algorithms. In face of the technological critieria, the visual is no longer attached to any materiality of the image as a film frame or as a physical form. As Poster argues, the discussion and understanding of visual phenomena can only conribute one strand of expertise to the broader development of information machines. The visual connotes one among multiple aspects when we wish to scrutinize how the integration of different media machines functions in the interrelationship and fusion of sound, image, text and so forth that essentially interact in the digital. It may also be noteworthy to recall here W. J. T Mitchell's research in the early Nineties, in which he analyzed the virtuality of an image that necessarily requires a discussion of the 'pictorial' presence 'as a complex interplay between visuality, apparatus, institutions, discourse, bodies, and figurality.'[6]

It shall be evident by now that, from a technical perspective, electronic media have no images like the analogue recording technologies of photography and film that operate with individual frames. While in the digital domain there are no images that bear the potential of all images in simulation – just codes – encoded information can be displayed visually in endless variety. Nevertheless, these grounding appropriations, which belong to technological constitutents of each medium, and serve to specify the identity of film, video and computer media and so forth in relation and distinction to one another, are not relevant as such. What I find more important to consider here are such technological properties, which are specific to each medium in relation to another level of imagery that is generated 'out of synch'. What I am referring to is related to a deliberate, maybe violent but certainly creative variation in comparison to media standards. These approaches manifest themselves in contrast to forms and formats that we have learnt to accept as conditions of the appearance of certain kinds of media images. Of course, these are shaped by institutions, like television, and corporations, such as mobile phone manufacturers and networks and the computer games industry, and more recently by the standards of Internet providers. The latter produce certain standards wherein the user is allowed to manoeuvre. Standing against these prefigured and determined media environments, e.g. YouTube, Second Life, and so on, media artists have adopted critical positions which oppose, subvert or otherwise evade the ruling standardizations of media. Aesthetic opposition in this respect manifests itself through creative intervention into market-driven and commercially enforced tools, applications and mechanisms that, for the most part, result in the likelihood of almost homogeneous display, output and overflow of media information as it enters private and public zones across the globe.

Alternatively, the goal of aesthetic intervention in the media arts is to demonstrate another focus in treating the visual and audio-visual capacities in virtual and real environments, which are subject to fusion in the digitally-based converging media. What becomes evident in this wide field of crossings and mergers can be characterized as a drifting away from the almost universal aesthetics of industrial image production standards established to serve market interests, and which seem to have taken over. This tendency is displayed in a fast growing variety of applications which, when viewed together, prove rather homegenized aesthetics. The situation, however, is not black and white, but more complex because we do not want to overlook the fact that many artists, scientists, programmers and engineers do depend on having access to the industrial standard of equipment, to cutting-edge tools; and some artists are also fostering close collaborations with the industry for concept development and technical realization. What matters, I suggest, is the direction and level of reflexivity that drive such inventive and creative processes towards intervention, and do not result in adjustment with the given. The creative intervention may be realized on a deliberately low-tech level, and may also involve artist-engineer collaboration with institutions and industries. What is decisive are the levels of effort and desire to foreground and foster the experimental use of technologies and their media manifestations to move in-between forms and standards.

To start with, I would like to draw attention to applications of media technologies, which take advantage of the inconsistent, unstable, non-fixed imagery in electronic culture that sweeps away the concept of a frame where you could cut off a film strip and take out as an individual unit. What interests me here are the various ways in which artists have explored technologies for the use of visualization that according to their technical nature are not meant to be used in image production (e.g. sensors, GPS). In the embryonic and early stages of these 'novel' technologies, it is particularly interesting to scrutinize how artists combine such technologies with other and older tools in favour of creating new visual effects, and sometimes generate images that challenge not only the concept of 'an image', but also the conventional understanding of 'moving images' as we understand cinema. Such deviation and inventive use of computers as multipurpose programmable tools become a means to modify and interfere with standardized, pre-formatted media products emanating from inside the media itself. Sometimes these practices liaise with industries to achieve the deviant aesthetic expression from within the industrial and corporate standard of representation.

Creative Intervention

What I want to discuss as the concept of 'out of image' refers to techniques of mobility and motion, where the artist's intervention and his or her co-creativity with machines and tools (such as computers, LED, GPS, motion and heat sensors and so forth) demonstrates difference to commercial-corporate production of audio-visual information input through cinema, television, Internet and mobile phone displays, and public screens. My starting point is to identify appropriate examples in the contemporary media landscape that can be identified as aesthetic-cultural interventions into electronic culture. These would be creative interventions that address in a reflexive and revealing attitude the products of media cultures that surround us on a global scale. Cultural critic Homi K. Bhabha (1994)[7] has recommended the importance of pursuing creative intervention in 'our cultural contemporaneity', where he sees the partisan role of the artist in a space of intervention. His point of view corresponds to a critique of the global imbalance with regard to 'media realities', and to a critique of commonly shared views of non-western developments as the 'Other' and the outside. Such views were strongly held in the western world until recently. Stuart Hall (1992),[8] for one, has asserted the role of cultural power plays with and through the mass media, and in the formation of cultural analysis as a leading discourse.

Looking generally at the present situation, it is widely agreed that we have reached a level of mediation that has entered many – perhaps too many – areas of our daily lives and activities, so much so that it might sound odd or outdated to seek for a critical position in the arts. Innovation and experiment in the western context is traditionally placed within the history of European avant-garde movements, which predicted a technological future. However, technology is now available to almost everyone. We have reached a level of technological utilization that is available to teenagers in their bedrooms, where production, distribution and consumption intermingle. Furthermore, we have developed technical tools for the remediation of media art, which we can globally distribute and display. As media critic Marshall McLuhan predicted decades ago, media technologies now seem to have become the natural prosthesis of humans and they prolong our bodily and sensorial perception – from the real to the virtual.

Today, most of us are happy to employ these novel technologies, devices and gadgets without much reflection. We do not (usually) refuse to carry all kinds of mini computers around all day long; we do not protest (much) about the talking machines and all the noisy sounds and images that we encounter in almost every public space and place. They come to us without choice or request: we cannot control or stop them in the same way that we can switch off a television. At the same time, we take advantage of all sorts of new applications that demand our ability to constantly adapt to ever-increasingly complex and interconnected operations, while the amount of time and space available to us proportionally decreases. Mobility, flexibility, immediate and permanent accessibility and contactability around the clock are the main characteristics of a situation that extends across the globe, and is greeted by some of us with relief, while others suffer from exhaustion.

This state of affairs is also characterized by contradictions: on the one hand, complex technology has become a smart part of everyday life; while on the other, large sections of our society struggle to cope with the demands of science and technology, which force us to adjust constantly to the growing capacity of networked communication. Computers were introduced to enhance humankind's intellectual capacity; now it's the other way round as we ourselves need to catch up with the digital machines. Beyond this, we cannot ignore the growing imbalance between the kernel of controlling agents – who have hands-on access to, and eventual control of, these new technologies – and the many who remain outside of control, those who are excluded and represent 'the Other'. Dataspace, respectively cyberspace for example, is not an open or free territory somewhere that we can all enter, but another place in extension to the real, with culturally, commercially and politically regulated borders that can be opened or sealed. Moreover, this imbalance is reinforced in critical discourses when debates about media landscapes merely reproduce polarized positions, in particular when they develop viewpoints about the 'before and after', the 'here and there', prolonging the asumptions of the cultural industries without an examination of the underlying attitudes they produce.

As it stands, even critical debate by now seems to have changed its focus as it centres around how to catch up with the latest technological novelties in ways that differ sharply from distanced analysis. The present moment requires a very specific expert knowledge. We are currently facing an abundance of expert debates, which in different tongues and with a growing labyrinth of technical terms and abbreviations delineates the order of the new world. For the most part, these voices manifest hierarchies and differences by discussing, for example, almost exclusively western media as the standard that represents 'us' – thereby deliberately attributing non-western media to 'them', or the 'Other' without much explanation of the justification of this discourse. There seems to be an unspoken unwillingness to engage in a real dialogue that would challenge and reassess such critical presumptions. On the contrary, we face an almost jubilant welcoming of the latest hi-tech consumerism and the innovative products of today's culture industry, which is creating the rules of networked data communication and information, as well as regulation and restriction on a global scale. It has become difficult to determine any critical discourse and argue for aesthetic interventions into complex and diverse media realities. Perhaps the whole project of doing so has become obsolete?

Yet there are other voices that call for radical investigations into these issues, and for an increased awareness of the contexts of media and cultural specificities. Another goal is to dismantle the supposed neutrality of technological developments. These voices are mostly heard from the past and the earlier days of cultural critique, when the digital age and economic globalization were still young and embryonic 'concerns'. Stuart Hall (1992), for example, has sharply detected the simplifying and standardizing mechanisms at work in cultural globalization and the world-system. He observed that while we live with difference and by the same token enjoy pluralism, we also absorb highly concentrated, corporate, and indeed over-corporate, over-concentrated forms of economic power; a living power that manifests itself culturally through the same evocation of difference, and finds pleasure in the incorporation of Otherness as the demonstration of its strength.[9]

Unsurprisingly, it almost goes without saying that the Other and the outside were largely determined as the non-western, exotic entities that nevertheless remain largely unimportant and inferior. One voice in particular can be singled out in providing the answer to the question about where to locate culture between the polarities of self and Other, East and West, inside and outside, in the contemporary situation of crossing, mixing, blending, blurring and other hybridizing combinations: cultural critic Homi K. Bhabha has pointed out that critical engagement beyond such polarities keeps cultural dialogue alive, and inhabits in the in-between zones with dynamic interaction and open-ended processes. In this respect, radical artists' practices will manifest themselves as creative interventions. The artists' intervention is seen as the instrument of interrupting the performances of present media cultures, and the means of fostering multiperspectival views in a variety of combinations and intercultural voices which express lively dialogue, and not dead-end polarities.

By way of further explanation, I would like to discuss some examples of aesthetic-artistic practices in an eastern context, specifically in the Asian-Pacific region, and more precisely in Japan, which may serve as effective approaches to readdress biased discourses that look from here to there, inside to outside, West to East. In contrast to these limited perspectives, I wish to suggest cross-directions and regard it as a matter of course to discuss practices, which are relevant to the topic of intervention and emerge in different cultural contexts. It is necessary to consider both media and cultural specificities where the parameters of these worlds are relevant to understanding the impact of the practices and their targets. The aesthetic practices under discussion here are those which contribute to the overall level of technological media and highlight strategies of artistic intervention. I do not intend to talk about cultural or media specificities and differences as such.

I propose to look in particular at aesthetic practices in Japan, where I find convergent practices regarding the innovative and radical use and application of electronic, computational, interactive and representational modes of presentation that challenge our understanding of 'visual culture' as conceived in the western tradition, based on the notion of an 'image' as a determinable entity. The task is to widen the horizon of discussion and to argue for overcoming some of the still existing barriers between media and cultural discourses, and also between arts and media. This is not about identifying peculiar Japanese media arts; nor is it a discussion of the notion of art. The more interesting question is: what are the overriding, effective and suitable strategies for processes of intervention, dialogue and violation that can cope with standard media tools and technologies that spread out everywhere? On the whole, I think media debates need to be more culturally informed, and cultural debates need to develop their expertise on the processes of mediation. In addition, it may be fruitful for cultural studies to open up discourses beyond the duality of non-western/postcolonial and the western context, and to give stronger consideration to non-western/non-postcolonial fields such as Japan, which play a leading role in shaping contemporary media cultures from a non-western, but nonetheless First World, Asian perspective. Both fields of debate – the media and the cultural studies debates – need to be able to cope with complex contexts: both need to become sensitive to the articulation of difference without pushing its operations to the fore.

With regard to the relation between technologies and visuality, I wish to add a few more preliminary notes to draw the larger picture and then focus on some examples from Japan. Over the past two decades, we can observe an increase of visual technologies that serve to build parallel worlds of viewing, and were strategically placed by military and political power, as well as by commercial industries, in ways that aim to replace older viewing systems, which we have learnt to perceive as representations of an external, physical reality. Here I mean digital simulation techniques, which in the hands of those industries enter the spheres of public images, and tend to create new ways of seeing and perceiving by using the established semiotic systems of reading visual meaning in the media.

Obviously, these new technologies have produced a wealth of imagery that will destabilize representational viewing systems, which were mainly established by cinema and television. The older channels of audio-visual display are challenged by the massive diversity of parallel streams of uninterrupted information on the Internet. But underneath this pseudo-democratic openness of all possible information at the same time at every corner in the world, we find that political and commercial strategies restabilize previously held belief systems of mediated information that have guaranteed the visual order of representation. This structure is now attributed to a different type of visuality, and deployed with the intention to suit a new visual matrix of simulation and computer graphics. Visualization then means an invisible structure that smoothly incorporates binary coded images in conventional presentational forms of viewing, with the result that the viewer can hardly tell the difference. As long as this new type of visuality is presented by and through the older viewing and information systems, the viewers naturally tend to perceive as usual, and attribute visual truth and representational value to these image products of simulation. To understand this problematic positioning of media images, we not only need a critique of the 'image' or the 'visual', but a more precise knowledge of the specificity of the technology underpinning a particular medium and its capacity for visual expression, and also to have multimodal and intermedial capacities. The media that we discuss in view of images such as film, electronic and digital are all determined by technological settings that are specific to the appearance of each medium.

Interestingly, the overall presence of all kinds of technologies that mediate audio-visual, textual and other forms of communication goes hand in hand with a change of size, scale and dimensionality of technological tools, devices and gadgets. Many technologies of daily life have become wearable devices. They fit into the pocket and have multiple functions, most of which are multimodal; the phone is not only ringing by tone, but comes with icons and text, and so forth. Visual tools have been downsized to miniatures and toy formats. The new media machines are predominantly visual; they are pretty, smooth and smart. It has to be noted that the imagery these machines generate are not silent. Not only are sounds attached to support the visual, but sounds and noises accompany machine operations everywhere; input commands come with sounds; machines talk to us in public to attract our attention. In Asia in particular, the public spheres are highly saturated with all kinds of noisy images and sounds that together produce a highly amplified audio-visual sound output to be heard everywhere. The technological apparatus is overwhelming. As Marshall McLuhan noticed in the Sixties when describing the comparatively harmless shift from electric to electronic media, what happens when a new medium arrives is a radical shift of scale, tempo and schema.

Contemporary technologies differ from previous ones with regard to smaller size, faster operation and flexible application. The fixed order of display is abandoned, as is a specific order of the apparatus and a fixed disposition relating the machine to the viewer. We are faced with flexible instead of fixed settings, not a dissolution or decay of visual machines, but rather the opposite. We need to acknowledge that the display of images in a structure with a fixed disposition like in film frames was only one, admittedly very successful and conformist, form of the appearance of visual media. It shall also be clear by now that media are visual, audio-visual or multimodal, and their perception accordingly needs multisensorial awareness.

When I ponder on the research topic of the intersection of technology and desire, I find it important to stress that images that are created by and through technical operations (regardless of how visible they become in the 'end product') are media images. This means that they do have some basic characteristics of their appearance and reappearance. Of interest are the ways in which artists have made use of these mechanisms to express their own ideas, and eventually create another kind of imagery that they desire outside commercial intersts of worldwide corporate media industries.

Japanese Media Arts

I want to take a closer look at artists who employ and combine tools and instruments in their own way, and open up the possibilities of image/-ination through a conceptual departure from standard instrument applications, tools and gadgets that usually serve to construct the conflated private-public media environment we live in. I provide examples of Japanese media artists who create their own desire of using technology, and intervene in dialogical ways with us as audience/consumer and the existing technological landscpapes. The encounter with the digital computer and its multipurpose capacities results in a shared interest to understand the nature of digital computers, as they operate entirely different from any other machine. The key concept for many Japanese media artists, then, is not so much to focus on the use of machines as new media tools, or to simulate older media extensively. The leading idea seems to develop and invent new media. In this view, Masaki Fujihata points out the understanding of media as the 'basic constituents of art'. He also explains how to avoid the trap of the concept:

> Computer technology certainly has a meta level. That's quite special for a technology. It can simulate almost every other previous technology. It can also deal with subjects which seem unrelated to the physical body, theories and concepts. That naturally leads us to come up with ideas such as to simulate human thinking, but simply because of the limits of our own thinking. I guess people get stuck, and end up repeating the same old research, where the results are already known before the experiment is even begun.[10]

In the virtual reality installation *Morel's Panorama* (2003) (Figure 1), Fujihata employs the western image form of the panorma to the projection of a cylindrical screen in a gallery space, where it serves as interface to connect real-time and virtual views of this particular space, that were taken with a panoramic camera. The point is that the camera at the centre captures actual imagery of viewers when they approach the installation, but the real-time projection of their cylindrically distorted moving images gets overlaid with pre-recorded footage showing the artist – who is reading the novel *The Invention of Morel*, which is about the generation of living 3D images. This science fiction novel about the invention of a 3D image system by Adolfo Bioy Casares was published at first in 1940, and became influential

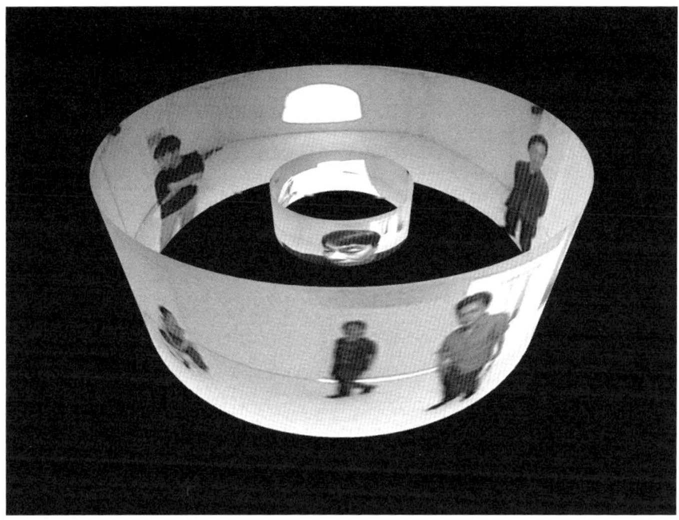

Figure 1: Masaki Fujihata, *Morel's Panorama*, 2003.

in the Eighties in the context of realizing virtual reality.[11] Fujihata's installation immerses viewers into non-localizable experiences through positioning them as if they were inside and outside the projected screen at the same time. There was no real screen in the gallery room of *Morel's Panorama*, but a panoramic camera installed at the centre of two overlaid panoramatic projections that interlace randomly in real time. None of this is possible in any real space based on the physical law of gravity. Clearly, it is useless to speak of images here, although Fujihata conflates image forms that through use of the panorama refer to the western tradition of visual arts. This kind of appropriation can already be seen in Hokusai's woodblock prints and paintings that demonstrate interest in western-style genre and landscape painting. The reference is, however, only a point of departure to rather open-ended forms of imagery, which transgress formal constraints and float freely in the virtual-real spaces that can hardly be experienced in distinction, but elide into an immersive audio-visual environment.

In similar ways, Seiko Mikami's interactive installation, *Desire of Codes* (2007–10) (Figure 2), employs technical tools as models to revitalize the dialogue between the media and human perception. The artist has chosen to combine very small LEDs in 60 moving structures with cameras and lights that move in the direction of the audience, as though the technical and the human are different species and a dialogue between them is possible. The detected movements (by light sensors), distances (ultrasonic sensors) and temperatures (infrared sensors) of the living beings are combined and calculated in the computer in real time and translated into LED intensity that illuminates the space accordingly. The LEDs sit on mobile arms that move like robots or searchlights. With noises reminscent of insects, they seek out their human visitors, who are at the same time causing the emission

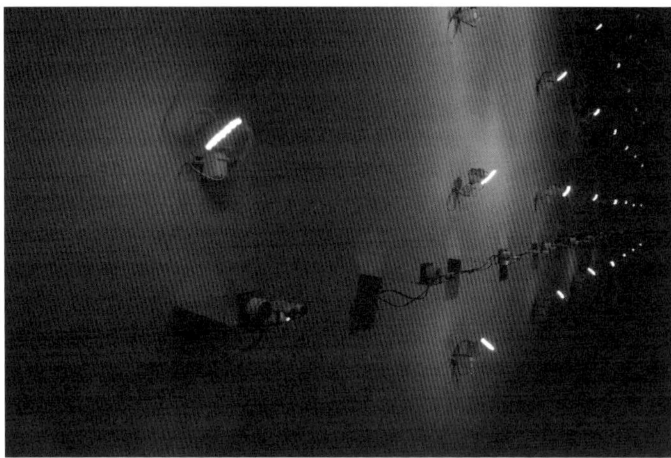

Figure 2: Seiko Mikami, *Desire of Codes*, 2007.

of light and the movement of the structure. In this interactive perceptual circuit, the visitor experiences the mechanism of media surveillance, where human action causes attention and at the same is the subject of its endless, unbroken scrutiny.

One interesting cultural aspect is the reference here to miniaturized computers and gadgets, which have spread like insects through the private and public sectors in Japan. Mikami further highlights a close, intimate and personal relationship between human perception and the individual senses on the one hand, and the humanoid behaviour of machines with sensory instruments on the other. The interface is the space in-between, an intermedium that makes the audience aware of their own experiences of perception. The real-time feedback of the structure provides a model for a dialogical encounter with a machinic environment that stresses the possibilities of the interchange of perception with and within the technologies of our time.

In her solo work, *Desire of Codes*, Seiko Mikami's industrial 'invention', aims to sharpen the viewer's perception and involve him and her physically. In the preceding collaboration with architect Sota Ichikawa, the aesthetic experiment to building one's own perceptual environment reveals as a guiding principle the intervention into the relationship between us and the computers in ways that do not consider computers as Other or outside, but provoke close encounters with the technology and with one another by using technical tools. In their interactive installation *Gravicells* (2004) (Figure 3), Mikami and Ichikawa develop and construct technical tools as models to revitalize the dialogue between the media and human perception. When entering the floor space of the interactive installation, we are invited to experience our position/location data through collected and projected GPS data. Gravity here becomes the interface to combine scientific data with the experience of the human body in a perceptual environment. The walkable installation floor of *Gravicells* resembles the physical experience of one's own gravity: 'On the floor are placed 225 units of

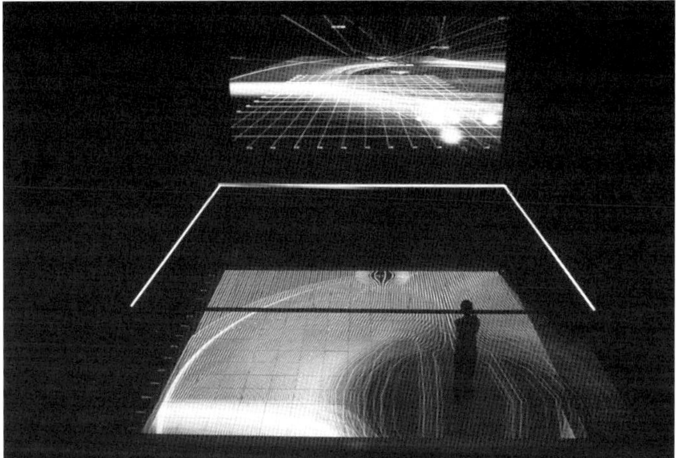

Figure 3: Seiko Mikami and Sota Ichikawa, *Gravicells*, 2004.

40 x 40 cm cell-like grids, in which specially developed sensors (not on/off switches) are fixed to detect instantly and continuously the changing position, weight and speed.'[12]

These data are calculated in the computer and graphically displayed onto the floor in relation to the GPS satellite's position in the sky above, but also in relation to other visitors who walk into the installation. This three-dimensional artwork sits in-between art and architecture, and works with the measured distance of three satellites (that are necessary for the GPS) as an intermedium to connect an observation point from beyond the Earth to our point of subjectivity. The architecture of the installation itself provides a model wherein the rectangular space of the cartographic grid gets reinforced by scientific data that refer to outer space. It gets overruled at the same time by the artists' creativity to modulate the measurement freely in the dataspace of the computer. All the measured data from GPS are represented in the projection of geometrical lines. As the projection of the geometrical scanning image interrelates scientific data of geodesic lines with the participants' activity, the resultant pattern of deformed lines expresses a new aesthetic model of scientific research.

Gravicells also presents a social space in the virtual wherein we experience our relation to Earth gravity and to other people sharing the same space. The work visualizes and materializes non-visual senses and creates an open, flexible and transforming kind of imagery that reflects a wider perceptual experience. The movements and changes made by the participant are then transformed and displayed as movements of sound, light and geometrical images through the sensors. As a result, the complete space is transformed in this interactive installation. Because the position of the actual exhibition space is determined by GPS through antennae on the rooftoop and measured data are included in the projection, the participant can experience his/her locality in relation to the gravity of Earth while walking on the floor that has wired tubes filled with liquid, and is equipped with sensors that detect position, weight and speed. Based on the proximity and distances

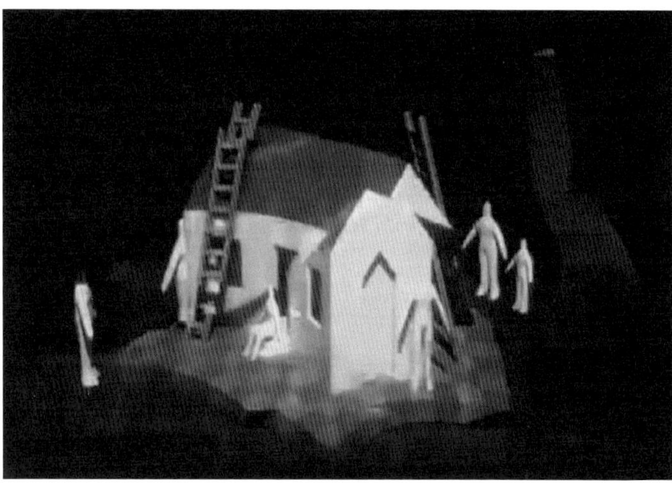

Figure 4: Toshio Iwai, *Morphovision*, 2005.

between the moving participants, their GPS data and the GPS data of the installation site, another space by light, sound and images is generated. The visualization is based on the individual dynamics of the participants and displayed onto the floor, and also projected in 3D on the walls in real time. The installation space is mediating between personal, physical behaviour and the outside environment.

In a similar vein, Toshio Iwai remodels scientific and technical inventions in a media display of deformed and distorted imagery that makes us aware and think of the constructedness of the media world, providing us with data about the real through virtuality. Iwai collaborates closely with Japanese corporations such as Nintendo and Yamaha to develop audio-visual applications and tools that enable the user/viewer to co-creatively generate sound and vision on specifically-designed tools and instruments. Working with Japanese television channel NHK, Iwai has also constructed the 3D image display system *Morphovision* (2005) (Figure 4). Here, the model of a house sits on a turntable, which rotates at high speed while illuminated with special light effects that blend the pulses of the electronic signals from a television with computer-programmed forms of waves (that can be changed by pressing control buttons attached to the installation). This generates the optical illusion of 3D objects transforming and disintegrating. The miniature rotating house can be variously transformed by selecting different patterns of illumination. The light pattern will deform the object like in an animation. The effects result from synchronization of the light that scans the object with the speed of rotation and changing the form of the light (its waveforms) in real time.

Iwai's large-screen public installation, *Bloomberg ICE* (2002) (Figure 5), expresses modification of light display in real time, and also exceeds borders and limitations of image forms. Here, however, the installation is connected to actual and real data

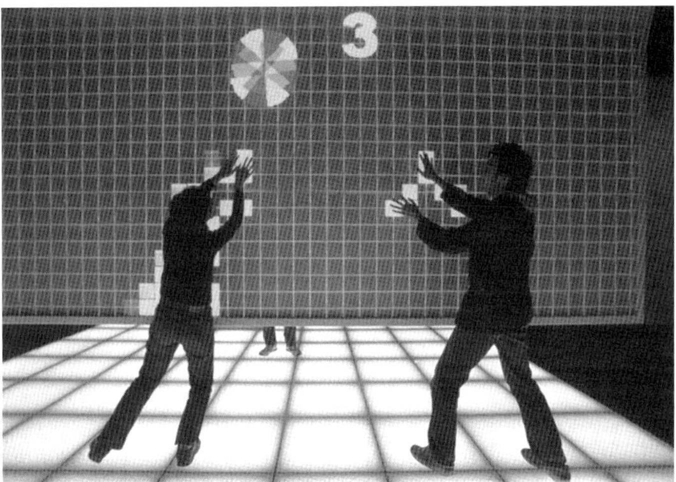

Figure 5: Toshio Iwai, *ICE*, Japan, 2002.

of the stock market that the company Bloomberg displays in the lobby of its Tokyo headquarters. Iwai's installation sits at an interesting intersection of art and commerce, with this permanent interactive artwork accessible in a semi-public space. Stock market figures are audio-visually transformed on a large scale touch screen, which displays actual data streamed in real time from Bloomberg's financial information services. The screen of this installation was designed together with Klein Dytham Architecture for the Bloomberg company building in Marunouchi, Tokyo, and equipped with 800 infrared sensors.[13] Iwai's interface design divides the screen into different segments and lines that display the ticker figures scaling up or down depending on the market values. But the moment the viewer approaches the screen, the sensored body heat changes this virtual visualization of 'real' information to a complex structure of an artist's game that uses the 'real' data as a matrix of animated behaviour. Here, live interaction with real-time information transfigures the abstract data to colourful and moving sound objects. Bubbles, waves and balls move across the screen, and the more players interact, the more the sound and moving pattern of digital waves drives out any recognizable information value of the stock tickers.

I want to close with another approach blending the real and the virtual in an interactive installation by Masaki Fujihata. The field work *Simultaneous Echoes* (2009) (Figure 6) is situated in Londonderry in Northern Ireland. When visiting the region, the Japanese artist felt the need to get acquainted with the field by investigating Irish audio cultures, and thus balance visual and sound information of the field in the installation. As a result, the project was developed in partnership with Irish composer Frank Lyons, who collaborates on media cultural research and the interplay of acoustic and visual scores. Shared concepts were developed through interpersonal dialogue and exchange between the different areas of

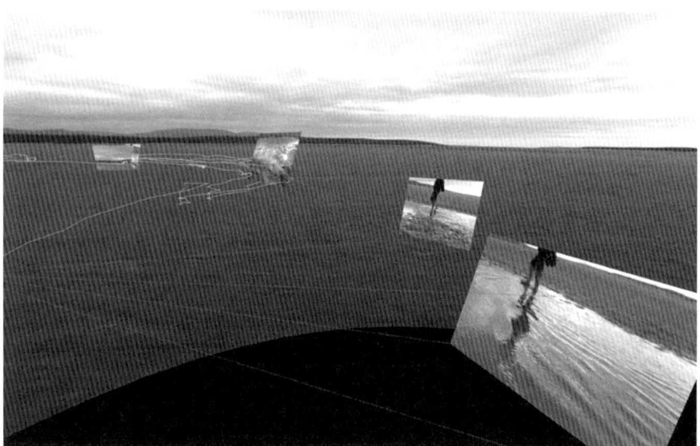

Figure 6: Masaki Fujihata, *Simultaneous Echoes*, 2009.

expertise, resulting in combined aesthetic approaches to record, rework, defamiliarize and recreate/recompose the 'raw materials'.

In the work process of *Simultaneous Echoes*, the interplay of three different types of sound – instrumental sounds of recorded Irish drum and piper players, natural sounds of wind, water and sheep and compositional scores – produce novel 'soundscapes' that have the spatialization of sounds as the main characteristics. In this respect, the mixing, assembling and sampling of different sounds is a way to show a technique of fragmentation and compression as it corresponds to similar compositional activity regarding the design of the visual sequences. Here, different types of video images – one to two minute-long mini-movies of instrument players, natural landscapes, and concise historical landmarks in the vicinity of Londonderry/Derry and the counties of Northern Ireland – are overlaid, converged and presented in a virtual three-dimensional assemblage of panoramas that are interconnected by lines drawn from the GPS data of the recording position.

The computer graphic design demonstrates the distances, connections and crossings of the research journey, but most importantly in the virtual display of the data space there are no borders. This new way of remapping geographical locations constructs an open virtual landscape that enables the artists to control interactively the movement and timing of locations, which were recorded with the images and are now used to compose the audio scores. Corresponding with the raw materials of visual and locational data, the musical composition evolves as a field process and not a coherent, conventional composition. Many elements are overlaid and interact as freely as one manoeuvres in the 3D space.

The general approach of Masaki Fujihata's field projects is to collect exact data of the traces of subjective experiences in a real environment. This information – position data, sounds and images – is presented in the virtual space of the computer as combined artistic-scientific results of actual human behaviour, mobility and communication in the field. This stands in stark contrast to the supposedly objective measuring principles, which are common for standard cartographic representation of the world in maps. Fujihata's unconventionally conceived field data are used as the basis for an aesthetic remapping and remodelling of our perception of location and orientation because he uses recording and display tools to represent the real spaces according to actual subjective parameters and not to cartographic rules. The most subjective views are gained from the public participation of people who inhabit, visit or travel in and through a specific region at different times, and meet with Fujihata's recording team at different locations. All of these activities are registered and the enterprise develops in many directions. It includes diverse forms of communication, interview and intercultural situations with and between locals and foreigners. It also extends to multiple media dimensions, has many visual and auditory layers of recording and display, and through the presentational mode of an interactive installation, reverses subject-object distinction between the artist and his work. Fujihata's field of activity deliberately positions itself in-between, inside and outside the 'objects' of scrutiny; and this encompasses processes of interaction between the observer and the observed.

In this respect, the unique creative collaboration between visual artist Masaki Fujihata and composer Frank Lyons is manifested in an open form of interactive installation work. Therein, processes of deterritorialization lead to novel mappings of locational sounds and images in a specific, unconventional design of virtuality that includes the physical activity of research with regard to the cultural specificity of the presentation and its location. Clearly, we are beyond inside-outside relations here, and any notion of the image or the visual is taken to extremes.

Notes

1   W. J. T. Mitchell, *Picture Theory*, Chicago: The University of Chicago, 1994.
2   Yvonne Spielmann, *Video: The Reflexive Medium*, Cambridge, MA: MIT, 2008.
3   Vannevar Bush, 'As We May Think', in Randall Packer and Ken Jordan (eds), *Multimedia: From Wagner to Virtual Reality*, New York: Norton, [1945] 2001, pp. 135–53; Douglas Engelbart, 'Augmenting Human Intellect: A Conceptual Framework', in Randall Packer and Ken Jordan (eds), *Multimedia: From Wagner to Virtual Reality*, New York: Norton, 2001, pp. 64–90.
4   Mark Poster, *What's the Matter with the Internet*, Minneapolis: University of Minnesota Press, 2001.
5   Cf. Martin Jay, 'Scopic Regimes of Modernity', in Hal Foster (ed.), *Vision and Visuality*, Seattle: Bay Press, 1988.
6   Mitchell, 1994, p. 16.
7   Homi Bhabha, *The Location of Culture*, London: Routledge, 1994.
8   Stuart Hall, 'The West and the Rest', in Stuart Hall and Bram Gieben (eds), *Formations of Modernity*, Cambridge: Polity Press, 1992, pp. 275–320.

9   ibid.

10 Masaki Fujihata, *The Conquest of Imperfection: New Realities created with Images and Media*, Fukushima: Center for Contemporary Graphic Art and Tyler Graphics Archive Collection, 2006, p. 196.

11 Adolfo Bioy Casares, *The Invention of Morel*, New York: New York Review Books, [1964] 2003.

12 Seiko Mikami and Sota Ichikawa, *Gravicells - Gravity and Resistance*, Yamaguchi: Yamaguchi Center for Arts and Media, May to June, 2004.

13 Cf. http://www.klein-dytham.com/project/more/bloomberg/1, accessed 4 October 2012.

PART III

Post-Cinematic Desires: Genealogies of Anthropomorphic Transgressions

Chapter 11

Choreographing the Moving Image: Post-Cinematic Desire
and the Politics of Aesthetics[1]

Isaac Julien

Moving Images beyond the Cinematic Realm

In an increasingly troubled time of emergencies, war and disinformation, moving images in a gallery context could represent an alternative view – one in which images can play a critical role in shaping our understanding of the world, rather than merely being used as a tool for propaganda, or for the art market. If we look at exhibitions such as Mark Nash's recent show at MUSAC – 'One Sixth of The Earth: Ecologies of Image' – the gallery, rather than the cinema, has become an important space for making interventions to review the differing cultural, political and aesthetic perspectives that make up 'moving image' cultures from around the world. After a period of exchange through the 1960s and 1970s, reflected in Chrissie Iles' exhibition 'Into the Light: The Projected Image in American Art 1964–1977' (2001),[2] one can observe both a continuity and an apparent gap between projected installations and experimental film today. Modes of presenting moving images almost seem to separate these two practices; instead of forming a field of interaction, it is as if there are two worlds of the moving image.

This shift brings with it a growing set of questions, including: how do we consider the phenomena of contemporary artists working with film and video today? How did a version of post-cinema become an increasingly common presence within the art gallery context? I would argue that distinctive experimental approaches to visual imagery, once the aesthetic hallmarks of the New Queer Cinema, have transcended this context, moving into the space of the contemporary gallery. See for example the work of Ming Wong, Francesco Vezzoli and Sadie Benning. This growing trend is marked in my own trajectory as an artist and film-maker who, after Derek Jarman's death in 1994, witnessed the end of an independent (queer) film culture in the UK. Regrettably, what film theorist Ruby Rich once rightly crowned New Queer Cinema has long vanished. It can be argued, however, that elements from the genre have reappeared in advertising, mainstream television, and in art galleries today. Through experimentations with film and video, the distinctions between narrative avant-garde and documentary practice have become blurred. At the same time, viewers' experiences have shifted as their viewing habits and subjectivities are influenced by new digital technologies, which blur cognition across several frames. Experimentation is no longer just on the side of the avant-garde.

It is now left to artists to make utopic interventions into spaces that seem to be more open and receptive to thematic and visual experimentation. Contemporary museums and galleries are certainly the main creative spaces where a legacy of cinematic innovation continues, and aesthetic interventions are not only possible, but also recognized. This is my main point: the emerging displacement of cinema, in an art context, can also be viewed as a continuation of some of the concerns of an earlier experimental, independent cinema. Along with installation works from the 1970s, it could be seen as a reconfiguration of sorts: this mutation from one technology to another, from celluloid to digital, makes new interventions possible. Along with this are changes in the nature of spectatorship and subjectivity, due to the ubiquity of digital technologies. Deterritorialization of the gallery means that spectators who come to these spaces may have a different set of expectations, beyond those of a general cinema audience.

Spatial Architecture and the Screens of Projections

In works like *Fantôme Créole* (2005), *Western Union: small boats* (2007) and *Ten Thousand Waves* (2010), I want to address the issues I have just mentioned through the use of multi-screen projections. This is not simply a question of the number of screens – four screens, five screens, now nine screens in *Ten Thousand Waves* – but about breaking away from the normative habits we have in exhibiting and also in looking at moving images. *Western Union: small boats* (Figure 1) is not about 'story-telling' as such, but the migration and movement of people from south to north, and about creating an environment through which an accumulation of sensations – through images and sound – will create a complex, thought-provoking and intriguing piece. The installation is realized in such a way that on the one hand, the viewer will form new, empathetic identifications, while on the other hand, experiencing these images and experiences from an unexpected point of view – from an 'Other' position. It is hoped that spectators will gain a better understanding of the contexts surrounding them. This will be achieved not only through the images and surrounding sound (in 5.1 surround sound), but also through experiencing the design of the installation itself, both in terms of the way one enters the space through five screens, and how the arrangement of images and sounds re-maps a site for witnessing journeys, which may be well known, but are newly being used as the basis for cinematic, video experience in an art gallery context (for example 'Border crossing' at Kunsthallen Brandts in 2012, and 'Unfinished Journeys' at the National Museum of Norway, 2012). The installation of screens and how

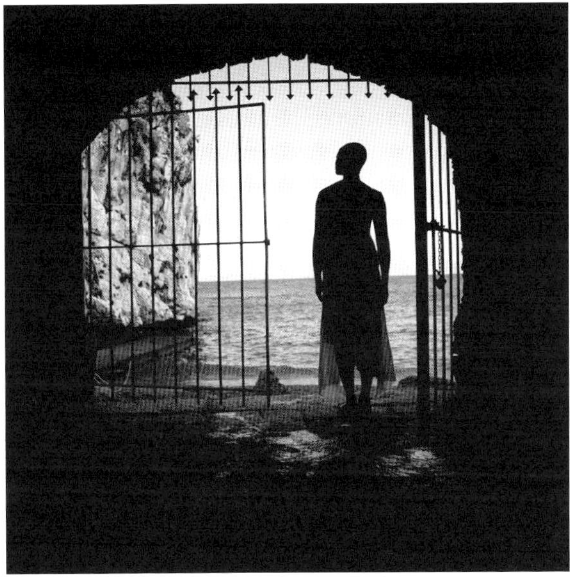

Figure 1: Isaac Julien, *Cast No Shadow (Western Union Series no. 1)*
I, 2007, Duratrans image in lightbox, 120x120 cm. Courtesy of the
artist and Victoria Miro Gallery, London

they interrelate; a work's sound; the relationship of installation and space: all this expands the idea of a screen-projected moving image.

The work of someone like Pipilotti Rist is exemplary in exploring this. She works with an architectural frame where she is interrogating the image, the screen and the sculptural, transforming these elements into a kind of soft architecture. In her presentation at the Hayward Gallery in 2011,[3] there were tiny projections on model buildings (*Suburb Brain*, 1999), or on a spectator's lap (*Lap Lamp*, 2006). There we have this movement away from the idea of projection on a screen as such. In her video works, Pipilotti Rist wants to escape from the confines of the two-dimensional screen, to focus, she says, 'not just in one direction but to open myself up to multiple possibilities.'[4]

Creolité, Cognitive Dissonance and Desire

The question of a creolizing vision, or *creolité*, connected to debates around the francophone usage of the word, and which I have used in my artistic and theoretical research ever since *Documenta 11* (2002),[5] concerning the idea of cognitive dissonance which occurs with certain works such as *Vagabondia* (2000). We can see this in the conversation between Sir John Soane and the architectural aesthetics that he was involved in, and also in the editing, use of sound and use of mirroring as a device.

The question of desire is complicated in my work. The idea that I have been working with is that all films are of a genre, and that there is this orthodox school of thought that films about questions of Otherness and politics should have a realist-documentary form as the default aesthetically-correct mode of presentation. The reason why I challenge this in my practice is precisely because it omits the question of 'desire in images' rather than focusing on aesthetic realism. That more informational realist aesthetic is an approach that could be construed as a 'race relation' discourse, and which at times gets positioned in contemporary art as a defining genre. This ethnographically realist approach is deemed more appropriate and less problematic for identification or non-identification. I am more interested in making a work that is from the perspective of not just the conceptualization of relating experiences in a mode that would be deemed appropriate but inappropriate. I'm talking about the question of the 'inappropriate other',[6] one of Trinh T. Minh-ha's early terms. That inappropriateness has to do with the question: 'What is it that people who are from a background that is not from the dominant group, actually desire to see?' It already starts from that viewpoint. My concerns are connected to 'reparational aesthetics', where I am in dialogue with subjects such as identity and the questioning of what images want, and what artists want from images.

By creating a visual cognitive dissonance I have tried to challenge the idea of what is an 'appropriate' subject or representation of, say, Otherness. It is this kind of visual disturbance that I am interested in effecting via an uncanny moment or the queering of the image through my use of desire.

All of these visual registers ask questions about desire and are part of the act of both constructing images, and then posing certain questions through the construction of those images. They have a poetic relation, or have a relationship to an aesthetic which is not separated from the question of content and aesthetics, bringing those deliberately together as a way of trying to relocate what I see as politically relevant. This might be related to experience, which is also often expressed in another medium; in music and the blues for instance. Being interested in the plasticity, in the over-constructed nature of the image, is a way for me towards a Foucauldian 'regime of truth'. Mark Nash makes this argument about the correlation between realism and materialism in my work that is achieved through an anti-realist strategy. Some critics view the work and claim it is too stylized and lavish and criticize it for that, and one does wonder then what kind of images are we meant to be looking at, or what images do they want to see? So my question of desire plays on the relationship between the spectator's desire, and what is it that they wish to see, and to contradict those ways of seeing. There is a cognitive difference because there is a sophisticated textuality to the image in relation to certain political questions.

The Politics of Representation vs. the Politics of Aesthetics in the Postcolonial Sphere

I have never actually believed in the idea of a black aesthetics separated from aesthetics in general, or from a 'western' aesthetics. Of course there are certain philosophical aesthetic practices (in China for example) where there are long traditions, much longer than European culture, such as the debate about literati aesthetics, which has taken a completely different trajectory to European aesthetics. However, because of the question of slavery and modernity I think it is very difficult to pretend that there is an aesthetics taking place separate from the formation of myself, or from the formation of cultures post-slavery. The violence of slavery demands a reconsideration of how we discuss modernity or aesthetics as terms that are uncontaminated. Of course these problems are seldom addressed.

The politics of aesthetics calls into question what people seem to be obsessed about, which is the issue of representation. The politics of representation has consistently been a spearhead for the way we think about visual art and/or images. Once there is a question about racial formation in the aesthetic construction of images, then people think about a politics of representation, and they forget about the representation and the politics of aesthetics. Lurking behind this is often a method that is still practiced as a certain neoliberal realism, and which has crept into our discussions around representation. The politics of aesthetics, however, is a way to view beyond the politics of representation, which can always only mark the beginning of explorations, not the end of it. The question of realism is always there too, and it is posed to me quite often: how can you make something so sublime out of something that is truly repulsive and traumatic? I think that the question of realism is always there to comment on difference, poetry, imagination, mediation and interpretation. Unfortunately, all of these things, however, often become secondary to the inquiry into representation.

The race relation paradigm guarantees this difference in the aesthetic mode, which is a mode that is set in a documentary framework of how to view the 'Other', and is consumed in a particular manner lending itself to sociological readings.

The idea of the politics of aesthetics makes me think about 'the aesthetics of the sensible' that is posed by French theorist Jacques Rancière.[7] Things do stem from aesthetics, between the alleged binarism of politics and aesthetics and the in-betweenness of things.

The Choreography of the Moving Image

The demand of new technologies means that we cannot separate image and knowledge the way we used to. To my mind, it would seem that the questions of cognition and of who is looking have been altered by new technologies. In this way, the digital revolution has, to a certain extent, democratized the gaze. Take the Arab Spring as an example: this democratization of the gaze implies that we are able to be involved in a number of ways of viewing things simultaneously. Certainly not all parts of the world have access to digital technologies, but a process of rewriting, reframing and reviewing images has taken place in those that have.

We also navigate our own computer screens: a number of frames and screens are open, simultaneously, and that intervisual and intertextual vision develops and seeps into an artist's way of working and making images. All of this has manifested itself in my recent installation in the use of multi-screens, the multiple-temporalities and the simultaneity that can be achieved through the kind of technologies that in return call into question forms of what I call 'neoliberal realism'. In neoliberal realism there is this idea of a new demand for a certain political expediency that viewers connect to race and representation as a means to perform and do a certain form of 'social (or political) work' (take for example the recent riots in England in 2011).

The formation of the choreographic in works like *Ten Thousand Waves* (see colour plates, p. 10) is developed from making and editing multi-screen works, and thinking about the way in which the choreographic becomes part of the architectonic, and also paying attention to the actual images in terms of spatial correlation. Editing the multi-screen work, one is always thinking of how the montage works across the whole space in a lateral sense. This is a way of questioning the ways in which we ordinarily look at moving images, which previously were usually on a single screen. As I said before, now that we consume images through our computer screens, we never look at one window or screen only, but we have several windows open at once. This cognitive rupture, in the way that the screens are interpolating one another, is all part of the idea of the parallel montage. Earlier exhibitions, such as Chrissie Iles' 'Into the Light' (2000), tried to historicize the contemporary by saying that many installation and video artists – such as Bruce Nauman and Joan Jonas – had already been thinking about moving image in a more sculptural sense. The idea of the choreographic is trying to think about the way in which these issues will now be further developed with new digital technologies.

In *Ten Thousand Waves* and earlier works, the idea of montage gets perfected by the spectator. You cannot look at all the images at one and the same time, but you can stand in different vantage points to view the work: a decision has to be made, which inevitably breaks up the panoramic. The spectator is being both part of the work – if you move to view then you add a different unique perspective to each viewing – and s/he is involved in the durational aspect of viewing as well, since it is 50 minutes long.

In *Ten Thousand Waves* there is a 9.2 surround soundtrack that sonically creates routes and maps for how one might view the work. I don't think I want to extrapolate that question of choreography to a 'global choreography', as if to say that the movements that take place in an art exhibition are the same as people moving in a global context. I wouldn't want to trivialize or even mean this as an allegory. With *Ten Thousand Waves* I am basically trying to break down the cognitive relationship that we have to the image, and at the same time to expand upon it. It is also about the idea of trying to immerse the spectator into this haptic relationship to the image: one where s/he is able to develop a kind of new way of 'looking' and to create a new cognitive experience. With some of these experiences I try to hark back to early experiments in cinema, to a particular moment where film-makers were experimenting with the image. Of course spectatorial paradigms in cinema have taken a long period of time to emerge. When the Lumière brothers first screened *L'Arrivée d'un Train au Gare de La Ciotat/The Arrival of a Train at La Ciotat Station* (1895), the audience jumped out of the way.

There is a similar effect with 3D as it tries to resituate the spectator in this early moment of cinema. If we go to see a 3D film, these different elements come very close to our gaze, plunging us into the hyperreal, and exposing the spectator in an almost Brechtian manner. In this way one creates an environment in which we can question the image. At the same time, there is this kind of attraction and seduction to the image, so both things arc happening, which is disorienting, and this disorientation is one of the things I am really interested in producing. All of this is an attempt to grapple with the question of how to view, and of what kind of cognition or vision is being created by these new technologies. The synchronicity that could be achieved is only being made available now; the fact is that it is on high definition and that we were using up to four terabytes of information to drive the whole kind of machinery and filing system. All these different technological innovations are a central preoccupation when making work and trying to push certain questions into that field. These questions around migration and the planetary aspect have been separated from the issue of technological innovation, but I am interested in bringing them together.

Performing the Moving Image

My current interest in choreography stems from an interest I had in dance at an early age, and from thinking about how that might translate into a choreographic use of the camera. And it was by looking at Maya Deren's early work, which had a very lyrical approach to the image, and thinking about that in relationship to movement that I became interested in the body. I saw the body and its representation through film as a way of embellishing the kind of cinema I was interested in. It was like a form of silent cinema, but for video art. And it was through my collaboration with people like Javier de Frutos on *The Long Road to Mazatlán* (1999) and *Vagabondia* that this kind of representation of the body emerged: it is not dance film as such, but utilizes dance as an expression for something else entirely. In *Vagabondia* it could be trauma for example, and in *Western Union: small boats* it's a re-articulation of these questions of migration and journeying. So it's usually about journeying and how to use a different form to represent it, which might seem even incongruous in this context, to use dance to represent migratory journeying and to create this kind of tension. The question of choreography has very much developed into the ideas around making *Ten Thousand Waves*, which was made in conversation with Stephanie Rosenthal, the curator for the exhibition titled 'Move: Choreographing You' (2011), which was shown at Haus der Kunst in Munich in 2011 and then moved to K20 in Düsseldorf. The idea behind that exhibition, which looked at art and dance and movement, was to explore the choreographic movement of the spectator, and how the moving image work can be edited accordingly. So it is how those aspects translate across mediums. Dance is one version but then it gets translated into the choreographic movement of screens, architecture, the kind of notational, rhythmic aspects of a work, and all of these aspects become part of its vocabulary.

Expanded Cinema Revisited

The notion of Expanded Cinema[8] is quite specific. There is a kind of fixation around Expanded Cinema because it has been seen as the exclusive domain for structural film-making of the 1970s, which is terribly Eurocentric and Greenbergian, and it is also seen as something that is only truly achievable on film. There is a kind of essentialism of Expanded Cinema in a particular historic moment, when it came about and within that.

The relationship to the legacy of Expanded Cinema and its retranslation via video projection has served to connect practices generationally through experimental cinema and to reposition it within the new global sphere. Yet the concerns of Expanded Cinema were more abstract compared to those of video projection, which works with the image in a way that is connected to a sculptural presence. In the last couple of years in the UK, we have seen a return to a neoformalism of the single screen in an art world context (not in digital art), and where it is shown. But little has surprisingly been written in the 2000s on Expanded Cinema since it became the lingua franca of contemporary video art. Thinking around the notion of the choreographic and the multi-screen, it is quite complicated to achieve that way of thinking visually. This is a genre that has developed into video art generally and, more recently, a genre that has literally expanded.

The question of the lyrical and the poetic vocabulary enters into the frame. If we think about that in relation to the image, there can be a questioning of the fixity that one might associate with questions of difference and Otherness in moving images. There are a number of film-maker artists, such as Stan Douglas, Fiona Tan and Yang Fudong, who have been working towards the use of both new technology and the use of multi-screens, as well as a certain choreographic approach to questioning the cognitive relationship to images; and that in a way has produced a certain self-reflexive sensibility in artistic works. It has something to do with the fact that these are artists who are trying to question the way that difference is being perceived. In that sense, they are at the same time interested in conceptual frameworks while not seeing the separation between difference and aesthetics. As in the first generation of Expanded Cinema, this is a position that is counteracting a more 'fixed' realist notion of what difference in representational practices moving images might make.

Is there a 'Global Art'?

I don't think global art really exists. What tends to be the case is that there are many different representations of contemporary art, which are competing with the centres, the old Euro-American axis. A totalizing art world in Chelsea, New York, has exploded since the 2000s. This is where you get the most complaints from the October school about the Biennialisation of the art world.

There is a question of the global condition and global technologies. Moving image works do tend to position idea of movement as being very important and a central theme. At the same time, I think we are still in a moment of tension between the medium and globalized networks. I have always seen my work as moving against these tides of globalization. The work is trying to be both two steps in front, and to question the ways in which post-globality is becoming part of networks of dominant hegemonic powers and their various manufacturers – such as image machines – that are being reproduced to circulate certain types of image banks.

I am interested in this tension between the global and the local: the 'glocal'. Translocality is part of the space that I want to inhabit in the sense that I think the idea of movement is not new in my life at all, and necessarily, it has always informed my practice due to the politics of diaspora. We also have this unfinished business of modernism, the competing modernisms, so I think we do have this idea of competing globalisms, which different works are representing.

Poetic Imaginations

Take for example *Paradise Omeros* (2002). I collaborated with Derek Walcott, who wrote the Omeros long poem for which he won the Nobel Prize for Literature. He is a St. Lucianer, which is one of the main reasons why I collaborated with him. I was very attracted to Derek Walcott's poem because obviously it is very much about the sea. His poem, 'The Sea is History', is another work which also influenced the making of *Paradise Omeros*, and that was shot in St. Lucia, the island of my parents' birth. All those kinds of trajectories were presented at *Documenta 11*, a platform to ask questions of 'creolization' and *creolité*. So it was a political as well as an aesthetic and artistic project. With *Ten Thousand Waves* you can see the themes of the seas as histories develop. I commissioned the Chinese poet and writer Wang Ping to write the poem 'Small Boats', and then the 'Mazu' poem. It was very important to think about that work not just as a mere illustration of images but as a springboard. And that is something I have been doing in my work since 1989, with my film *Looking for Langston* (1989), which uses the poems of Langston Hughes. My entrance into Chinese culture was really through the poetry of Wang Ping. When we were filming with Maggie Cheung in the Guangdong Province, Wang Ping started her last poem for the film, which is on Mazu, the Goddess of the Sea. So you have this dialectic approach where one is interpolating the work and vice versa.

Robert Bresson's Theory of Acting

In my early works like *Looking for Langston*, I was very interested in the Bressonian notion of non-actors. For example, there were no professional actors as such in the film. So this idea of models in a non-acting sense was important. And I applied it to *Fantôme Créole* with Vanessa Myrie and Stephen Galloway, a dancer. With Bresson, the history of acting traditions in the English context was something that wasn't useful for thinking about a more lyrical cinema, although Jarman has at times used an overtly theatrical method of performance in his directing of actors for his work. It's certainly a kind of non-naturalist or anti-naturalist approach, working with actors like Tilda Swinton, whose Brechtian approach to performance resonated in a particular way. I'm interested in that notion of breaking down the performance in films like *Peau noire, masques blancs/Frantz Fanon: Black Skin, White Mask* (1996) where there was a Bressonian use of Colin Salmon as a more open-ended sign: he is almost playing Fanon 'in quotation'.

The Mobile Spectator

The idea of the mobile spectator questions the normative habits that spectators may bring to the exhibition space. They are encouraged to unlearn the habits of spectating single-screen cinema – particularly when it comes to moving-image installations. Exploring this concept of the mobile spectator and trying to unfix spectatorial habits developed from single-screen cinema is an important part of my recent work.

It's a double-edged sword because when I make a work, I do so as an artist who is very knowledgeable about film. I'm not so concerned with making work where audiences are screen-tested, so to speak, as in commercial cinema. What I was searching for in a work like *Ten Thousand Waves*, but also in earlier works like *Fantôme Créole*, is how can one really explore the idea of the mobile spectator? In *Fantôme Créole*, a work I made for the Centre Pompidou, the spectators were asked to make sense of the montage which I presented over four screens, surrounding them 360-degrees – four screens in this kind of circular surrounding structure. Mark Nash's description discusses the two actor-protagonists of the work:

> Vanessa Myrie, who also appeared in *Baltimore* (2003), and Stephen Galloway are not characters with dialogue with an implied interiority. Rather they seem to link together scenes between the African city and desert scapes, between the Arctic North and arid South. And the lack of narrative connection signals an intellectual proposition concerning issues connecting these spaces as well as Julien's interest in 'creolized' vision. To create new ideas from new points of connection between spaces. The disjunctive juxtapositions inform parallel montage: they put the spectator in the position of constructing meaning and through a position of the screens which forces the viewer to change the position to grasp the totality of the presentation, fast challenging the fixed position the single-screen work entails.[9]

So, in other words, the spectators would be forced to make their own montage by becoming immobile spectators. But they actually contradicted my intention, instead grabbing the cushions and seats which we had put into the middle of the space and moving right to the back to where they could have a full view of the work. This was very instructional for me.

In *Fantôme Créole* I was interested in the multiple screen projection as a key element for a syntactic articulation of symmetrical and asymmetrical narratives. So utilizing the four screens for me was foregrounding a presentation of a state of 'double consciousness'. I'm borrowing this from W. E. B. Du Bois' term for understanding psychosocial division. The instances of hybridization of space, the ecologies of movement from north to south, would be broken down beyond the simple geographical binaries. In *Fantôme Créole*, the use of four screens was to comment on the context of globalization and the impossibility of drawing rigid visual boundaries between territories. These ideas are translated into the montage strategy of *Fantôme Créole* by a syncopated soundtrack that creates continuities and discontinuities between the separate images that are projected onto the four screens. As art critic Cristina Albu writes:

> The four-screen structure to act as an instrument to form four separated screens with a view to contrasting them, infusing diverse images or representations that also provide a visual poetics of exploring contradictory images which refuse easy readings and direct meanings.[10]

And I would argue that multiple projection has only been made possible in the gallery through the movement to digital. We can only accomplish that attention to detail through this technological precision. This idea of a 'montage of attraction' is being replaced by an 'editing of attractions', taking the Eisensteinian utopian concept of the 'montage of attraction' and juggling different juxtapositions, which have been made across this parallel montage effect. So that's what I'm really excited by: the level of synchronicity and a synchronicity of screens, which can be achieved through computerized editing. I think a work like *Ten Thousand Waves* would be impossible to make without it. But at some point you do need the spectator to become part of the experiment, because you can only see what is really being achieved through your montage if the spectator moves through the space, as s/he does in a work like *Ten Thousand Waves*. Hence, you need to determine both how you structure the screens architecturally within the space and in relation to the 9.2 surround sound. The sound travels across the nine screens or nine speakers and that in a way edges the spectator around this piece as well, but of course spectators are generally still conditioned, when they see moving image works, to participate passively.

From Experimental Cinema to the Gallery Space

Experimental film has occupied quite a marginal position in the UK, yet contesting that very marginality can and will produce something interesting and challenging. In the early 1980s it became important to me to make an intervention into other spaces. By the mid

1990s I felt that the problem experimental film had was around the question of value, and I speak about that in many instances.[11] The question of innovation and its effects were not achieved through experimental film per se, thus I anticipated this move to a gallery context in the early 1990s, and felt that if there was going to be a continuation of my early concerns, it wouldn't take place in the cinema, because it has become this domain where the narrative stronghold – in terms of audience's taste and the question of innovation – had depleted itself. At the same time, digital technology was on the rise and this impacted on the way one was able to make works in a gallery museum context. That is where my interest grew and coincided with creating a new audience for my work. Celluloid to digital has made new interventions possible because of the way you were able to master, as it were, the space of the white cube by turning it into a black box, or even by the idea of introducing projected images in a way that was reminiscent of cinema.

This combination of the way that new technologies redefined how one was able to think about making work in a different location, and the way in which the nature of spectatorship and such activity was also changing, deterritorialized the gallery. It also meant that there could be a different set of spectators that could come to these places with a different expectation beyond the demands of the cinema audience. The question of the genre of moving image works that have been developed in these contexts is radically different to a certain extent, to a positive as much as negative effect. Film theory has been slow to acknowledge this. It is an experience that has to be lived, in the same way as people who have experienced and learned the viewing habits of the cinema.

Spectators have to unlearn habits, particularly when it comes to the moving image installation in contrast to the classical cinema context. With this moment of disruption, it is almost as if the mobile spectator is a distracted subject because of the role of technology such as mobile phones. People no longer have that sort of focused attention. In a sense, my work tries to bring that attention back to the artwork, but certainly the concept of the mobile spectator challenges the more normative habits that we bring to the cinema and the exhibition space. *Ten Thousand Waves* engages with these themes. It is not so much about the number of screens, but it certainly is about trying to break away from normative habits of how we view single-screen works, and trying to create an environment where, through the accumulation of sensations and sound, a complex relationship with the image is created.

This is not achieved through the image itself, but through the design of the installation and the architecture of the space: the construction of the screens and the way this affects the montage of the images, and the sound that traverses across several screens. Hopefully this is re-mapping and creating a place for a re-evaluation of the image. And it is precisely then the question of global migration that I want to re-evaluate, i.e. the news reportage for example, to subvert this genre through a poetic mediation in a gallery context. Connected to that is the use of sound, which makes for a haptic experience. I revive this correlation and hark back to earlier moments in the twentieth century where artists were experimenting with film.

Notes

1. Large portions of this text are based on interviews, which Rania Gaafar conducted with the artist in London.
2. At the Whitney Museum of American Art, New York.
3. 'Eyeball Massage' at the Hayward Gallery in London, curated by Stephanie Rosenthat in 2011.
4. As qtd from Stephanie Rosenthal (ed.), *Pipilotti Rist: Eyeball Massage*, London: Hayward Gallery, 2011.
5. Cf. Isaac Julien, 'Creolizing Vision', in Okwui Enwezor et al. (eds), *Créolité and Creolization: Documenta11_ Platform 3*, Ostfildern: Hatje Cantz, 2003.
6. Trinh T. Minh-ha, 'She, The Inappropriate/d Other', in *Discourse*, No. 8, Winter 1986–87.
7. Jacques Rancière, *The Politics of Aesthetics: The Distribution of the Sensible*, London: Continuum, 2004.
8. Cf. Gene Youngblood, *Expanded Cinema*, New York: Dutton, 1970; A. L. Rees et al. (eds), *Expanded Cinema: Art, Performance, Film*, London: Tate, 2011.
9. As qtd from: www.isaacjulien.com, accessed 29 August 2012.
10. Cristina Albu, 'The Indexicality of the Triptych Video Constructions in Isaac Julien's Installations', in Veit Görner and Eveline Bernasconi (eds), *Isaac Julien: True North – Fantôme Afrique*, Ostfildern: Hatje Cantz, 2006, pp. 73–80.
11. Cf. Maeve Connolly, *The Place of Artists' Cinema: Space, Site and Screen*, Bristol & Chicago: Intellect, 2009.

Chapter 12

Desire, Time and Transition in Anthropological Film-making

Ute Holl

Strategies of colonizing imply the homogenization and standardization of time and space with the help of cultural techniques, scientific instruments and, in the nineteenth century, increasingly technical media such as chrono-photography, cinematography and the gramophone. Technology and media, then, seem to form the arsenal with which an alien culture is measured, described, defined and subjected. The transformation of scientific measuring devices into media of imagination and entertainment, that took place around the turn of the twentieth century, as the history of photography, films or the gramophone record show, also reflects the history of development of a colonial imaginary. Scientific anthropological films of foreign peoples and cultures were screened in cinemas, scientific recordings of languages and voices were played in salons and over the radio not only to educate, but also to entertain the public.[1] As opposed to a distinction made between written scientific reports on the one hand and popular writing on ethnographic issues on the other, films and sound recordings were exposed to scientific societies and a general audience as the same documents of an alien real.

Critical studies of anthropology have stated how the implicit use of normative and western concepts of space and especially of time in anthropology have served to construe and adapt the alien Other through discourse and practices of normative temporality. A transformation of indigenous time forms into a single, standardized western time, which takes place through the process and in the camouflage of objective observation.[2] Thus, the discussion was raised in how far the individual anthropologist themselves were aware of the cultural power they exercised. Technical devices and media appear to be means to maintain the standards of science in anthropology while implicitly exercising political power. The anthropologist could be seen as no more than an agent of larger technological or media configurations. It is here that the question of desire intervenes to hopefully raise the question not merely as moral, but also as a political one.

To introduce the observation of desire and its dynamics in this process is to understand how the topographic and chronological surveyors of colonial grounds and bodies are themselves entangled in this process. Desire, in the sense of structural psychoanalysis, triggered by the fundamental lack of being, links the subject to the Other as reason and resonance of his existence in the world. It thus establishes a temporal form of unconscious dynamics that relates the subject to the expectations and hopes he will have assumed the Other to maintain when facing him. Desire corresponds to the time-form of anticipation and assumption, an orientation into the future and its assumed fulfilment, in the time of the second future, submitting to the desire of the Other. This then is not reducible to the colonial situation, but a relationship that is at the basis of all society.

As opposed to what Johannes Fabian has aimed at in his admirable and seminal study and critique of colonial practices, his demand of a 'radical contemporaneity of mankind'[3] seems too simple a formula to meet the politics of media-time. Considering the entanglement of desire and technology, colonial relations, just as any other power relation, need to be examined more closely in the spatial and temporal constitutions. Rather than reducing these relations to a radical equality in contemporaneity, even a revolutionary use of technological devices and media will challenge linearity and entropic time-forms in favour of relations that are structured by feed-back loops, embroiling the dominant as well as the suppressed into power structures. Technologies of visualization and of acoustic observations in colonial strategies have not just served the 'Domestication of the Savage Mind', as Jack Goody put it, but have also fundamentally changed senses, perception and minds of westerners.[4] In the aesthetics of anthropological film-making, this transformation is negotiated, sometimes as a confusion, sometimes as its negation. To explain this, the phenomenon of trance is traced into its medial prehistory.

Techniques of Travellers

The first contact of travellers with foreign peoples, landscapes and cultures has usually been accounted of as an experience of vertigo, of mirages and distorted perception. To quote from one of the most famous travelogues of the nineteenth century, Francis Galton's *Narrative of an Explorer in Tropical South Africa* (1853), the journal of his travels to Damaraland – today a part of Namibia:

> We passed over a broad flat, flooded in spring-tides, following many waggon-tracks that here seemed so permanent as not to be effaced by years. We were surrounded by a mirage of the most remarkable intensity. Objects two hundred yards off were utterly without definition; a crow, or a bit of black wood, would look as lofty as the trunk of a tree. Pelicans were exaggerated to the size of ships with the studding sails set; and the whole ground was wavy and seething, as though seen through the draught of a furnace.[5]

It was not only the effect of simple heat which irritated Galton, the geographer-gentleman-traveller, but also the constant bouts of fever he suffered from. According to his journal, most of the six months he spent in southern Africa must have been spent in a sheer delirium or fever-trance. Remedies to this sort of vertigo were Sir Galton's constant efforts to measure and map the landscape with the help of compass, sextant, geometry and logarithms. In doing so, he hoped to define the seemingly boundless African planes and to determine distances. This did not only serve his own means and well-being. The data he collected in subordinating African plains to European geometrical space were to be delivered to the British Royal Geographical Society in return for its funding of Galton's trip. In some cases, Galton did more than fulfil the Society's request. Aside from mapping the African countryside, he also proceeded to map the African people. Later on in his travelogue he notes:

> The sub-interpreter was married to a charming person, not only a Hottentot in figure, but in that respect a Venus among Hottentots. I was perfectly aghast at her development and made inquiries upon that delicate point as far as I dared among my missionary friends. The result is, that I believe Mrs. Petrus to be the lady who ranks second among all the Hottentots for the beautiful outline that her back affords [...]. I profess to be a scientific man, and was exceedingly anxious to obtain accurate measurements of her shape; but there was a difficulty in doing this. I did not know a word of Hottentot, and could never therefore have explained to the lady what the object of my foot-rule could be; and I really dared not ask my worthy missionary host to interpret for me. [...] The object of my admiration stood under a tree, and was turning herself about to all points of the compass, as ladies who wish to be admired usually do. Of a sudden, my eye fell upon my sextant; the bright thought struck me, and I took a series of observations upon her figure in every direction, up and down, crossways, diagonally, and so forth, and I registered them carefully upon an outline drawing for fear of any mistake; this being done, I boldly pulled out my measuring-tape and measured the distance from where I was to the place she stood, and having obtained both base and angles, I worked out the results by trigonometry and logarithms.[6]

The mode of observing, the techniques of the observer, are quite simple: while measuring up the natives, the indigenous, the 'Other', the traveller assumed to remain unseen and to have his desires concealed. To himself, any desire remained implemented into an automatism of technical imaging. Of the indigenous men and women we have no testimonies of the anthropologists sight and behaviour. Later in his career, Francis Galton would proceed to be a very proliferous inventor of social disciplinary techniques through more mathematical procedures – statistics – that were to replace scientific forms of subjective judgement in the sciences and social sciences in the course of the nineteenth century.[7] As a founder of social Darwinist thought, eugenics and biometry, Galton later invented the technique of fingerprinting and of composite portraiture, a form of photographic superimposition used to identify physiognomic types in forensic prevention. Galton's techniques to administer and control his sundry physical desires, and to transform them into scientific material for Britain's efforts in colonizing Africa, may have remained obscure to himself as a 'scientific *man*'. They stand out bluntly to the readers of his journal. But while measurements in a universal space are obviously a means to control territories and, as Galton's example illustrates, the people inhabiting it, the approach to standardization and universalization or time is much less obvious and its effects have been haunting anthropological theory, as Johannes Fabian has agued.[8] Distinguishing physical time as a form a prehistorical reconstruction used in 'objective' or "neutral" time scales used to measure demographic or ecological changes' from mundane or typological time-forms, in that it is assumed to be 'not subject to cultural variation'.[9] In a first step Fabian discovers the same procedures in time which Galton had described for spatial measurements in the field: 'In […] Western clock Time, anthropologists have used Physical Time as a distancing device. In most ethnographic studies of other time conceptions the difference between standardized clock time and other methods of measuring provides the puzzle to be solved.'[10] While in written anthropology the traces of what Fabian called 'schizogenic use of Time'[11] has been widely studied, the implementation of temporality as a form of regulating relationships to the Other in anthropological film-making and cinema is more complex.

Techniques of Non-Travellers

Ethnographic film-making in its beginnings simply seems to continue the strategies of nineteenth-century fieldwork: measuring and mapping unknown territories and people, submitting them to symbolic orders in order to master them. If movement such as human or animal locomotion is recorded, transformed, stored and possibly reproduced, the element of time intervenes. Félix-Louis Regnault, a French physician specializing in pathologies of anatomy, is credited for being one of its greatest pioneers. Together with Étienne-Jules Marey and his colleague Charles Comte, Regnault shot chrono-photographic series and short films of African people, from Madagascar and Sudan, as well as of men and women from the Maghreb. He shot chrono-photographic series of their gaits, using a white cloth as a backdrop in order to heighten the photometric contrast in silhouettes, and to be able record the differences in his systematic tabulations and anatomic grids. Although he was a strong promoter of environment or *milieu* in his theoretical approach on peoples and races, he introduced quite a different aesthetics in his photographic set-ups: contrast was the medial clue to legibility and knowledge. And, of course, Regnault never took the trouble to travel to Africa. He did not expose himself to fevers, heat and mirages, since he took his photos at the 'Exposition Ethnographique de L'Afrique Occidentale' at home in Paris, in 1895.[12] Regnault was the perfect observer, one might think, and an early theoretician of the camera gaze as a time machine: 'Cinema expands our vision in time as the microscope gas expanded it in space.'[13] But his images reveal the stage and staging of his gaze. The backdrops, like curtains, clearly reveal the apparatus and its intervention into temporality, but the curtain is also a marker for desire: to see what is behind the curtain introduces the structure of anticipation into the gaze.

Jean Rouch, pioneer of ethnographic film-making himself and for many years the director of the ethnographic film department at the Musée de l'Homme in Paris, described Regnault's work as exhibits designed for a museum, things to be admired in scientific esteem.[14] Regnault expected people to examine his images under strictly scientific conditions, and as far as Étienne-Jules Marey was concerned, photography was a variation of his graphic method; a self-inscription of light to analyze and document movement as a series of still photographies. However, Marey sternly objected to his chrono-photographic images being animated.[15] If they were projected as moving images today, as in some educational collections of early cinema, the audience would be moved by the magic of those early images, by perceiving the unique phenomenon of distance however close the people on the screen might seem. In such examples of early ethnographic filming, analysis and aura, technology and desire are closely interwoven.

Many pioneers of cinema followed that track and technically recorded physical movements of indigenous tribes instead of describing their mores and rituals in words. Thomas Edison, for example, had invited Sioux dancers from Buffalo Bill's Wild West Show into the darkness of his Black Maria. Their chrono-photographed movements could then be animated to be screened as motion pictures in Edison's kinetoscope, and it was reported that in this procedure, the dance was more obvious and visible than the actual dancers. The spirits of the Sioux joined the unknown spirits of the first kinetoscopes, reminding us of Yeats's famous lyrical observation of school children: 'O body swayed to music, o brightening glance, How can we know the dancer from the dance?'[16] Cinematic perception is not only about measuring the Other, strange and alien, but about transforming one's own sense perception an even the structure and coordination of the senses themselves.

Alfred Cort Haddon, a former zoologist – to mention another of the pioneers of ethnographic film-making – employed still cameras, a gramophone with wax cylinders and a Lumière camera during his trip to the Torres Straits on occasion of the Cambridge Anthropological Expedition in 1898. His aim was to 'save vanishing data' of Melanese cultures, not realizing that he was much rather producing data from vanishing cultures. Most of Haddon's material was destroyed due to climate and chemical destruction. Another pioneer among filming ethnographers was the German physician Augustin Krämer who later founded the famous Tübingen Insitute of Ethnology. From 1908 to 1010 he travelled through Melanesia and Micronesia, partly German protectorates at the time. Besides indigenous forms of dancing, the most popular *sujet* of ethnographic film-making, Krämer would shoot people performing various cultural techniques: fire-making, grinding, weaving and producing pottery. Most of the mentioned films were stored in a German archival institution founded in the Fifties: the 'Encyclopedia Cinematographica' at the Institut für den wissenschaftlichen Films in Göttingen (Germany), a post-war institution which paid little attention to concealing its racist epistemes. The idea to store images as documents of other cultures and anthropological facts without discussing the element of time in the gaze seems to lie at the beginning of eliminating, or rather hiding, the aspect of desire from science and knowledge.

Cinematic Motion and Emotion: Gregory Bateson and Margaret Mead

Cinematography fundamentally changed the epistemic frame of anthropology, then a still emerging discipline. As opposed to the strictly symbolic and increasingly calculable means of the old cartographers and their trigonometry and logarithms, longitudes and latitudes, cinema introduced the force of the imaginary into the techniques of the colonizing observer. This fundamentally changed the notion of 'data' from anthropological fieldwork. Certainly not all of the filming ethnographers were aware of the epistemological change they brought about with new practices in new media. In *Tristes Tropiques* (1955), for instance, Claude Lévi-Strauss has been aware of the fact that many typical traits of culture they described were related to the instruments of description they applied. And even less did anthropologists comment on the fact that in using new media in the field they were actually transforming their own cultures from a written universe to an increasingly audio-visually-based 'culture of knowledge', or to use McLuhan's terms, that they were transforming their Gutenberg Galaxy into a Marconi- or Lumière Universe. This is not to claim a determinism of technology or technical media in ethnological thought, but to conceive of a transformation in the notion of behaviour in a larger frame – such as that of technology and desire.

It took years until this epistemological change was clearly addressed, for example by Gregory Bateson, after returning from one of his field trips to Bali, where he had conducted research regarding social behaviour between 1936 and 1939. Bateson and Mead had intentionally used still and 16mm cameras to transform ethnological notation from a written to an audio-visual archive. In Bali, they no longer tried to stage Balinese behaviour, but instead recorded what happened in the moment of intercultural contact:

> We tried to use the still and moving-picture cameras to get a record of Balinese behavior, and this is a very different matter from the preparation of 'documentary' film or photographs. We tried to shoot what happened normally and spontaneously, rather than to decide upon the norms and then get the Balinese to go through these behaviors in suitable lighting. We treated the cameras in the field as *recording* instruments, not as devices for *illustrating* our theses.[17]

Mead and Bateson brought back about 25,000 still photographs and around 22,000 feet (more than 12 hours) of 16mm film. Back in New York, they evaluated this material for their studies on dance and trance rituals.[18] Only after this examination did they realize that filming was just the first step in a revolution of anthropological methods. The problem of editing, of 'making sense' or 'giving meaning' to the evidence on film, remained unsolved, since they did not find an epistemic principle according to which the moving images could be organized. Instead, they published an extraordinarily beautiful photo-book, *The Balinese Character* (1942), as a special edition of the New York Academy of Science's publications, which proves to be an extensive photographic cartography of behaviour. From Bateson's commentaries in this book, we know that in shooting photos and films he tried to abandon

European, or at least western, intentional thinking in favour of a perception 'at random' – a perception which was conceived of as a submission of European intentions and identities to the dynamics of Balinese culture:

> We recorded as fully as possible what happened while we were in the houseyard, and it is so hard to predict behavior, that it was scarcely possible to select particular postures or gestures for photographic recording. In general, we found that any attempt to select for special details was fatal, and that the best results were obtained when the photography was most rapid and almost random.[19]

The order of the photos in the book – images of postures and gestures they found characteristic of Balinese behaviour – illustrates Mead's and Bateson's main argument, which was an enormous political challenge in the 1930s and '40s: Balinese behaviour, they claimed, is organized by principles of non-competitive and anti-rivalizing patterns in all social interactions. Balinese cultural patterns and techniques are designed to avoid acceleration, single goals, competitive growth and climax. This of course had a strong political impact as a criticism of both capitalist and communist societies.

While Bateson's still photography in the publication had been submitted to a readable order, the question of the cinematographic organization of Balinese rituals remained unsolved. Mead and Bateson did not find a higher logic or principle according to which the sequences of movements and dances in their specific duration could be edited. And another specifically cinematic problem arose: Bateson had manipulated the speed of the cameras in order to economize on film stock. He had used slow motion as a temporal microscope – in Regnault's sense – to film more active and interesting moments, while going through less interesting phases in time lapse, not aware of the fact that in filmic perception the emotional expression of the two procedures is completely different, as early film theorists, Arnheim and Panofsky, have observed.[20] The Balinese movements had not only been recorded but at the same time been distorted, displaced and transformed by Bateson's camerawork. Failing to deal with the footage in terms of editing, Mead and Bateson left it to a young New York film-maker, Maya Deren, to see what she could make of it.

Only a few years after their research tour, in 1946, Mead and Bateson participated in the Macy-conferences where new post-war paradigms of social behaviour and social engineering were discussed that took new media, cybernetics and feedback-logics into account. The basic idea was to develop a concept of social change based on characteristic features of cultural organizations. Feedback systems were to be implemented into forms of cultural behaviour instead of simply submitting foreign cultures to American standards. Not only indigenous societies were to be transformed by these techniques, but also fascist and authoritarian cultures of Europe and Japan. The idea of restructuring social practices through cybernetics corresponded to the demands of a post-war administration that was to engage computers in order to predict and organize civil life. While it has been argued that the logics of the enemy ruled cybernetic logics at the core,[21] Mead and Bateson's contributions to the Macy Discussions were based on a non-interventionist model. They firmly believed that in Balinese behaviour they had found patterns for non-aggressive and non-competitive social dynamics and processes, and they also believed that those peaceful Balinese patterns could be applied to other societies, cultures, character formations and behaviours. Also in 1946, Bateson received a Guggenheim Grant to study the 'formulation of a nucleus of theory relating to concepts of culture, personality and character formation and the extension of this nucleus to cover the phenomenon of cultural change'.[22] Teaching at the New School for Social Research in New York, Bateson applied systems theory and cybernetics to social and cultural patterns, and he also used the Bali film material to discuss his considerations. In his lectures and articles Bateson discovered that in the process of childrearing the Balinese behaviour systematically frustrated all 'cumulative interaction', i.e. rivalry, through practices of negative feedback: frustration, deflection and distraction of attention. In these forms of training – techniques of desire themselves – Bateson observed a transformation of competitive behaviour to a continuing plateau of intensity, a concept that Deleuze and Guattari would adopt in the title of their study on schizophrenia and capitalism, *Mille Plateaux*. It is in this period that Bateson started discussing cybernetics and cinematography in anthropology with his younger colleague at the New School, Maya Deren.

Feedback Loops between Technology and Desire: Maya Deren

Maya Deren was rather sceptical about Bateson's plateau-model being a specifically Balinese achievement. In her notebook she considers the idea in respect to cinema, time and duration, drawing further parallels to yet another interesting form of cultural technique. Summarizing Bateson in her own lecture, she observes that the plateau-model is not neutralizing energy, but rather intensifying it:

> [T]he energy which would be required for the ascendent acceleration of a climatic curve is channelized, instead, into a plateau of duration. The duration in time, therefore, is enormously extended and can even withstand interruption, as an accelerating curve cannot. Certainly, this principle applied to sexual activity even in occidental culture is not considered a negation but, on the contrary, valued as a considerable achievement. One might say, in terms of sociological structure, that the purpose of the frustration of climaxes is the channelization of energy which would, in climactic activity, be *spent* and really dissipated in conclusive exhaustion – that it is converted into a tension plateau which serves the continuity both of personal and communal relations.[23]

In fact, Deren will use this model to develop her own film work at the editing table. It is important to note that, for Deren, filmic techniques and technologies are not simple mechanizations of perception, but that they are transformations which translate the rituals filmed (in Bateson's Bali case) into new and unseen cinematic rituals. Slow motion is not, as

Bateson thought of it, a kind of temporal microscope, but it fundamentally transforms the expectations of the audience, transforms its perceptive state: 'It is the phenomenon of duration as tension which explains why slow motion – which may have in it very little activity – often makes for greater tension than normal or rapid motion for the tension consists in our desire to have our anticipation satisfied.'[24]

The technical intervention of editing can produce the exact opposite of what has been intended as effect. Duration in cinema is produced through cutting into movements and motions; continuity is produced on the basis of discontinuity. Here, Deren is actually anticipating Edgar Morin, who discusses the ethnographic analysis of his own culture, the post-war French colonial system, as a product of cinematic devices in his book on cinematic culture, *L'Homme Imaginaire* (1956). He sees the link between cinema and anthropology in the principle of the feed-back: 'J'ai fait en même temps de l'anthropologie du cinéma et de la cinématographologie de l'anthropos, selon le mouvement en boucle: l'esprit humain – éclaire le cinéma – qui éclaire – l'esprit humain etc.'[25] Morin implemented his flow chart between the functions of anthropology and cinema in a film which he shot in 1960 together with Jean Rouch, *Chronique d'un été/Chronicle of a Summer* (1960), and which had been commissioned precisely by the Musée de l'Homme. In this film, Marceline Lorridain, as a very young and beautiful woman, asks men and women of Paris to step before the camera and answer one question – 'Are you happy?' ('Êtes vous heureuses?') – while the film team observes the historical loops that are established in order to answer the question. Young Africans discuss the strange tattoo of numbers on Lorridains wrist: Nazi-administration is taken to the uncanny historical field of interference between technology and desire. Rouch, as always, spares no one.

Maya Deren took Bateson's model to Haiti, where she shot her famous Voudoun material between 1948 and 1951. She never edited it, writing a scientific book on the Voudoun instead, and thus qualifying, in Galton's terms, as a scientific woman. But before going to Haiti, in the times of those 'extended conversations with Mr. Bateson',[26] after Mead and Bateson had given her their Bali footage to see what she could make of it, Deren went through a Galtonian feverish experience before travelling. She experienced the fever at home, in front of her hand-operated 16mm viewing table, turning the cinematic apparatus into a transformation-device. At home, using or rather abusing the Bali-material, Maya Deren would produce an experience of indeterminacy, of mirage and depersonalization, which she would later consider as an initiation into the state of being an artist. Here, a different connection between technology and desire is established, one that does not map or determine the unknown Other, but aims at transforming and changing self-perception. On 16 February 1947, Deren writes in her notebook:

The minute I began to put the Balinese film through the viewer, the fever began. It is a feeling one cannot remember from before, but can only have in an immediate sense. I mean like pain, one remembers having had pain, and even the reaction to the pain – but the exact pain itself, proper, cannot be recreated by memory except rarely – Psychosomatism is the re-creation in immediate terms of unrecollected memory. [...] The immediate physical contact with the film, the nearness of the image, the automatic muscular control of its speed – the fact that as I wound – my impulses and reactions towards the film translated themselves into muscular impulses and so to the film directly with no machine – buttons, switches, etc. – between me and the film – All this seemed for me very important, especially in relation to a film which was not mine. This physical contact creates a sense of intimacy. It is not an image independent of me, projected on a wall, of which I am a spectator. It is immediately, directly, uniquely for my eyes. It comes to life out of the energy of my muscles. Later of course, I shall use the projector to get proper speed, etc. But first this intimate copulation between me and the film must take place and out of it will be born the independent child which will be projected at the Provincetown Playhouse while I sit in a bar across the street.

Truly by 'Maya out of Film' – it is the film machine which is the impregnated woman – .[27]

Turning and watching the Bali footage, attaching her visual and tactile senses to the technical device, Deren makes the experience of being distorted and displaced by Bateson's gaze or at least his camera eye's – just as the Balinese she is watching had been transformed by the camera. The state in which this takes place is the perception of a self which cannot be remembered – like pain, which in a way replaces precisely the self that it affects. It is this notion of transformed perception that links Deren's concept of the cinema to Walter Benjamin's concept of the 'optical unconscious'. In her attachment to the apparatus she remembers something which has never been in her memory, but which obviously stems from an unintentionally and unconsciously formed collective archive – from cinema's memory. To describe this strange link between mental and physical memory she uses the term 'psychosomatism': 'psychosomatism' is the recreation in immediate terms of unrecollected memory. Memory wanders – or rather leaps and skips – into physical realms, somatizes. Memory engrosses, binds and fascinates the body. It is important here that Deren refers to the physical effects of cinema, something Margaret Mead will radically want to exclude from her film work. Deren's term 'psychosomatism' brilliantly describes the film experience as such: the messages transmitted in cinema are necessarily messages that are structured, if not constituted, by the gaps and discontinuities between images, and they necessarily have to take the way of the physical, material matter. In conceiving of this discontinuity in terms of time intervals, not in terms of space, Maya Deren's memory-concept appears as situated halfway between Henry Bergson and Gilles Deleuze.[28]

In her book on the Haitian pantheon, *Divine Horsemen* (1953), Deren describes her own possession by the goddess Erzulie. Erzulie, the patroness of dreams, love and beauty is a complicated personality, outrageous, scandalous, a little embarrassing, and in a truly media-archaeological sense, she might be called a hysteric.[29] Deren's possession occurs as a cinematic disruption, temporal fissure and displacement. In her protocol of possession, Deren describes the first indications for her unusual state of 'psychosomatosis' as an optical deception of narcissistic identification, as an elation and a disaster of the 'mirror-stage'.

The pleasure of seeing her*self* dancing in an illusionary mirror later turns into horror and fear as soon as she realizes that her state is not socially affirmed in the ritual. At this point she needs to accept that the relationship between the dancer and the dance, the 'I' and the mirrored 'self', is volatile. In her protocol Maya Deren writes:

> As sometimes in dreams, so here I can observe myself, can note with pleasure how the white skirt plays with the rhythms, can watch, as if in a mirror, how the smile begins with a softening of the lips, spreads imperceptibly into a radiance which, surely, is lovelier than any I have ever seen. It is when I turn, as if to a neighbor, to say 'Look! See how lovely that is!' and see that the others are removed to a distance, withdrawn to a circle which is already watching, that I realize, like a shaft of terror struck through me, that it is no longer myself whom I watch. Yet it is myself, for as that terror strikes, we two are made one again, joined by and upon the point of the left leg which is as if rooted to the earth.[30]

During the Voudou ritual, the rhythm of the drums supports and holds the decaying 'self'. In the beginning, dancer and dance are welded together, indistinguishably, by the acoustical 'order' of the music that structures time, and the dancing body submits to the rhythm. In the realm of the visual, however, a cleavage occurs that reminds the dancer of its fearful dependency on a mirror-double. This cleavage at the base of all identification is dissolved in the state of possession. Suddenly, the gaze of the dancer turns into a camera eye. The seeing of the cinema's eye proves to be stroboscopic, slowly devolving into slow motion, as if an imaginary mental projection speed was reduced. The film starts to flicker, black holes appear between the images, and the dancing cinematographer is lost in undefined spatio-temporal realms between frames, gaps that must not be perceived in cinema if cinematic perception of movement is to be evoked. Deren continues in her protocol of possession:

> I wrench the leg loose – I must keep moving! I must keep moving! – and pick up the dancing rhythm of the drums as something to grasp at, something to keep my feet from resting upon the dangerous earth. No sooner do I settle into the succor of this support than my sense of self doubles again, as in a mirror, separates to both sides of an invisible threshold, except that now the vision of the one who watches flickers, the lids flutter, the gaps between moments of sight growing greater, wider. I see the dancing one here, and yet in a different place, facing another direction, and whatever lay between these moments is lost, utterly lost. I feel the gaps will spread and widen and that I will, myself, be altogether lost in that dead space and that dead time.[31]

Deren describes her possession as a blackout in terms of a cinematic experience, as well as in technological terms: as the tearing up of the filmstrip inside the projection machine. In cinematic perceptions of the 'Other,' as she conceives of it, technologies are incorporated in a ritualistic process. Creating an immediate reciprocal system between technology and desire, Deren's process of film-making is the exact opposite of the cartographer's method to control desires through techniques of mapping and recording. Hence, Maya Deren's cinema marks a turning point in anthropological film-making, as her films are not about filming and defining the Other, but about transforming the self; transforming to an 'alien Other' under conditions of technical media. Deren's moving images are about becoming 'cinematomorph'. In this cinematic and anthropomorphic transformation, feverish distortions of reality are part of the technique desired.

Notes

1   Cf. Alison Griffiths, *Wondrous Difference: Cinema, Anthropology, and Turn-of-the-Century Visual Culture*, New York: Columbia University Press, 2002. For a German case study, see Britta Lange, *Echt. Unecht. Lebensecht. Menschenbilder im Umlauf*, Berlin: Kadmos, 2006.

2   '[W]e pronounce upon the knowledge gained from such research a discourse which construes the Other in terms of distance, spatial and temporal. The Other's empirical presence turns into his theoretical absence, a conjuring trick which is worked with the array of devices that have the common intent and function to keep the Other outside the Time of Anthropology': in Johannes Fabian, *Time and The Other: How Anthropology Makes its Object*, New York: Columbia University Press, 1983, p. xi.

3   ibid.

4   Cf. Michael Taussig, *Mimesis and Alterity: A Particular History of the Senses*, New York: Routledge, 1993; David MacDougall, *The Corporeal Image: Film, Ethnography and the Senses*, Princeton & Oxford: Princeton University Press, 2006.

5   Francis Galton, *The Narrative of an Explorer in Tropical South Africa*, New York: Reprint Corporation, [1853] 1971, p. 10.

6   Galton, 1971, pp. 53–54. The term 'Venus among Hottentots' is not altogether an innocent one. In 1810, Sarah or Saartjie Baartman, a 20-year-old Khoi girl, was taken to England by Alexander Dunlop, a physician, to be displayed at fairs and side-shows as 'the Hottentot Venus'. She became a famous attraction, rumours spread of her sexual organs, and it is unlikely that Galton would not have heard of her. Later, in France, 'La Venus Hottentote' was made an object of scientific experiments and research, as well as entertainment and an object of scientific techniques and strange desires. Cf. Stephen Jay Gould, 'The Hottentot Venus', in *Natural History*, 1982.

7   Cf. Peter Galison, 'Judgement against Subjectivity', in Caroline Jones and Peter Galison, *Picturing Science, Producing Art*, New York & London: Routledge, 1998, pp. 327–59. Galison claims that the debate about pictorial objectivity in science was initiated precisely around the scientific atlas.

    In the nineteenth century, or more specifically after ca. 1830, both the persona of the natural philosopher and the status of pictorial representation of nature shifted. Instead of a transcendental genius improving or idealizing nature, the desired character of the natural philosopher inverted to one of self-abnegation. Instead of truth to nature, these scientists aspired to let nature 'speak for itself' through a set of instrumentalities that minimized intervention, hamstrung interpretation and blocked artistic license (cf. Galison, 1998, p. 328).

8   Fabian, 1983, p. 32.

9   ibid., p. 22 (emphasis by Fabian).

10 ibid., p. 29.

11 'If one compares uses of Time in anthropological *writing* with the ones in ethnographic *research* he discovers remarkable divergence. I will refer to this as the schizogenic us of Time. I believe it can be shown that the anthropologist in the field often employs conceptions of Time quite different from those that inform reports on his findings': in ibid., p. 21 (emphasis by Fabian).

12 For details on Félix-Louis Regnault's life and work, see Fatimah Tobing Rony, *The Third Eye, Race, Cinema and Spectacle*, Durham & London: Duke University Press, 1996, pp. 21–73. Only later in his life he would travel to India to look at diseases of pilgrims especially, comparing, as Rony observes, the primitive with the pathological (Rony, 1996, p. 32).

13 Félix Regnault, 'L'histoire du cinéma: son rôle en anthropologie', in *Bulletins et Mémoires de la Scoiété d'anthropologie de Paris 3eme tome 7th ser*, Vol. 6, July 1922, p. 65, qtd in Rony, 1996, p. 231.

14 '[I]n 1895 [...] Doctor Félix Régnault, a young anthropologist, decided to use chronophotography for a comparative study of human behavior, including ,ways of walking, squatting, ad climbing, of a Peul, a Wolof, a Diola, or a Madagascan. In 1900 Régnault and his colleague Azouley (who was the first to similarly use Edison cylinders for recording sound) conceived of the first audiovisual museum of man': in Steven Feld (ed.), *Ciné-Ethnography – Jean Rouch*, Minnesota: University of Minnesota Press, 2003, p. 46.

15 Cf. Marta Braun, *Picturing Time. The Work of Étienne-Jules Marey*, Chicago: University of Chicago Press, 1992.

16 William Butler Yeats, 'Among Schoolchildren', in *The Collected Poems of W.B. Yeats*, London: Wordsworth Editions, 2000, p. 185.

17 Gregory Bateson and Margaret Mead, *Balinese Character: A Photographic Analysis*, New York: The New York Academy of Sciences, Vol. 2, 1942, p. 49.

18 Cf. Karl G. Heider, *Ethnographic Film*, Austin: University of Texas Press, 1976, p. 28ff.

19 Bateson et al., 1942, p. 50.

20 Cf. Rudolf Arnheim, 'Bewegung im Film', in Helmut H. Diederichs (ed.), *Kritiken und Aufsätze zum Film*, Frankfurt am Main: Suhrkamp, 1979, pp. 41–45; Erwin Panofsky, 'Style and Medium in the Motion Pictures', in *Critique*, Vol. 1, No. 3, 1947, pp. 5–28.

21 Peter Galison, 'The Ontology of the Enemy: Norbert Wiener and the Cybernetic Vision', in *Critical Inquiry*, Vol. 21, 1994, pp. 228–66.

22 'Thus I had the privilege to participate in the renowned Macy Conferences on Cybernetics. I am indebted to Warren McCulloch, Norbert Wiener, John von Neumann, Evelyn Hutchinson and all other members of the colloquia for everything I have written after the Second World War. My first attempts to synthesize cybernetic conceptions with anthropological data were supported with a Guggenheim grant': in Gregory Bateson, *Ökologie des Geistes*, Frankfurt am Main: Suhrkamp, p. 11 (translated by Rania Gaafar).

23 Maya Deren, 'Notebook', typoscripted, Mugar Library, Boston Unversity, 24 February 1947.

24 Maya Deren, 'Creative Cutting Part I', in *Movie Maker*, May 1947, p. 191.

25 Edgar Morin, *Le Cinéma ou L'Homme Imaginaire. Essai d' Anthropologie Sociologique*, Paris: Nouvelle Edition, [1956] 1977, p. X.

26 'Before I went to Haiti and before this book was even contemplated, I had the good fortune to have many extended conversations with him concerning the cultural organization particularly in reference to Balinese, British and American culture': in Maya Deren, *Divine Horsemen: The Living Gods of Haiti*, Kingston & New York: McPherson & Company, 1953.

27 Maya Deren, 'Notebook', typoscripted, Mugar Library, Boston University, 16 February 1947.

28 Cf. Henning Schmidgen, 'Mind the Gap: The Discovery of Physiological Time', in Annemone Ligensa and Klaus Kreimeier (eds), *Film 1900: Technology, Perception, Culture*, New Barnett: John Libbey Publishers, 2009.

29 Cf. Alfred Métraux, *Le Vaudou Haîtien*, Paris, 1958, pp. 121–22; Deren, 1953, p. 144.

30 Deren, 1953, pp. 258–59.

31 ibid., p. 259.

Chapter 13

Longing in Film: Emotions in Images

Hinderk M. Emrich

How do humans deal with images and how do emotions enter into images? In order to find out about the ways emotions enter images, we initially have to ask: what are images in the first place? Are images constructs? Are they representations of cognitive functions performed by the central nervous system? Are they principally 'geometrical', and therefore representations of 'shapes' that, according to Immanuel Kant, relate to an *a priori* 'spatial' perceptive framework? Are they thus cognitive creations based on categorical performances *ante rem*? Or are images, first and foremost, simply reproductions of the exterior extent of reality as it pertains to the 'actual', i.e. the empirical world that was called the 'resistant' by the transcendental philosopher Johann Gottlieb Fichte? Images are neither confined to being shaped by constructivity, nor by empirical aposteriority alone. They are surely affected by both; and the ways of how they are being influenced is important to the question of how a transgression, how feeling, desire, the sense of longing enter images and, from these, couple into one's own subjectivity. Emphatically speaking, inner images are not 'mimetic' reflections of something, but autonomous 'entities', distinctive archetypal creatures within us, possessing the quality of symbols. Keeping this in mind, images are not primarily reproductions of something, but formations (C. G. Jung, for one, speaks about 'enforming images'); thus it is easier for them to become objects of desire as well as to elicit emotions and longing. Hence, if images possess a partially 'ontological status', then it will be possible to view an image not only as expressing desire, but as something which (as an entity) is also affected by its own 'desire'.

Images cannot be reduced to being reproductions of exterior occurrences, they are in fact semantically charged with psychic contents, which they incorporate themselves as signifiers of emotions. Images are 'mental' phenomena, they are psychically charged, they emit something that is not constituted by them per se, but which they can only evince in so far as they express the mental surplus; and finally because they are supposed to become the latter. This is put across Johann Wolfgang von Goethe's sentence 'In the colourful reflection we have what is life' (German: 'Im farbigen Abglanz haben wir das Leben'). And Johann Gottlieb Fichte writes about 'images which drift by without there being anything by which they drift; images which hang together with images' (German: 'Bildern, die vorüberschweben, ohne daß etwas sei, dem sie vor überschweben; Bilder, die durch Bilder von den Bildern zusammenhängen').[1] Thus, we are dealing with a dialectic, an interplay between archetypal charges, created by us as recipients via a kind of projection – we convert an icon into an icon – but then there is the genuine archetypal character of the images in its primal pictoriality: in other words, on the one hand between the emission going out from something entity-like, apart from us, a 'You' (dealing, so to speak, with an interpersonal relation between the charged object and our subjective sphere); and, on the other hand, the prototypical image within us (Brentano speaks of an 'intentional inexistence' of the object). One of my mentors in philosophy, the philosopher Reinhard Lauth from Munich, delineated this correlation in a lecture about Schelling – regarding the 'interpersonal philosophy'– by speaking of an 'intentional being', which, in the case of 'figurative forms' (and incidentally 'musical forms' as well), would stand between the artist who creates the form and the recipient, constituting a dialectical mediation.

Constitutive Moments of Mediation Between Emotionally-Charged Images and the Subjectivity of the Recipient

If it is true that according to Lauth images are – at least under certain circumstances – existentially 'intentional beings' to the point where one has to admit that they harbour intentions and are out for something, want something for themselves, then the question appears with regard to the actual psychic dimension of images, of what kind of psychic 'dimensions' within this dialectic. What is the nature of this 'transgressive art of moving images'? My focus here draws on mediality and mediation within a psychological/mental context, i.e. psychic vitality, psychic truth. What does 'mediation' mean here? Or put in another way: what is, in the true sense, the 'nature of the mediality of images'?

Here is one example: a young man, nearly a child, catches sight of a blossoming young woman. She is a dancer. She moves, she glances, she is beautiful: is this a being for its own sake, a being for others? Does she invite him to marvel at her, to desire her? Is she, as that what she is, as an image, present for herself? Or is it present as a being for others? Is there a challenge in all of this? Does she want to be acknowledged and approved – in her being? Does she herself desire? And *what* does she desire? And who, ultimately, has this desire?

Longing and Desire in Film

If the assumption is true that the shaped image of the cinema goes far beyond its mimetic quality and virtually represents an 'intentional being' – or is at least supported by it – then one is confronted with the question how this mediation between the collective psyche of the film and the individual psyche of the recipient is accomplished. What is the make-up (the origin) of longing, desire, feeling, the volition (of wanting) in the film? Longing is based upon intentionality appearing as a wish in view of fulfilment. It is about realization. It is about the becoming real, the becoming actual, of sensory experiences; ultimately, happiness in the sense of 'making it happen', of succeeding. It is about the manifestation of a worthwhile, successful life. How is this 'epiphany,[2] as Emmanuel Levinas names it, possible – by 'moving images'? One theoretical approach to this question has been introduced by the anthropologist René Girard as part of his theory of mimesis. As Girard demonstrates, mimetically-mediated wishes become 'stale' when no genuine fulfilment is experienced. According to Girard, the nature of mediality – and this is certainly true for film as well – is actualized/enacted by a mimetic 'linking of wishes'; i.e. the 'mediator' conveys the purpose, the sense, the motive of being-after-something to the subject; the focus is on the 'valorization' of a world, of ambitions, longings, wishes and hopes. But as long as these thematizations do not finally lead to an inner satisfaction, they become moribund, flat, stale, unfulfilling after a short time – and fade away; i.e. a film can only effect such true inner satisfaction if it deals not only with 'sensuality' as such, but brings into being a form of meaning, a creation, a spiritualization in the sense of some form of transcendence towards a meaningful higher reality.

Which examples could one cite in this context? Wong Kar-wai's film *Fa yeung nin wa/In the Mood for Love* (2000) deals with the doubling of a dyadic interconnection. The couple consists of the abandoned partners at their joint meal: the imaginative pictures representing the taste and scent of the food which belongs to the respective partner, the female or male facing the other across the table, create an image of longing concerning intact love and psychic fulfilment. But this image is internally fractured by the reality of infidelity and the implied possibility – in each case, to choose a new mate.

Longing and Touch: Wong Kar-wai's Film *In the Mood for Love* (2000)

In Wong Kar-wai's film *In the Mood for Love* (2000), people are packed together in confined quarters in Hong Kong, after having escaped from Shanghai and the victorious troops of the communists: expulsion and sticky closeness. This situation results in an extreme strain on emotional and social intelligence. As Norbert Bischof describes it in his work *Das RätselÖdipus/The Oedipus Riddle* (1989), human individuation, the maturing towards one's own self as a competent autonomous human subject is, throughout all crises of maturation (especially during the oedipal crisis of puberty), dependent on a specific solution to the problem of proximity and distance, the separation from the parents, the conquest of an interior and exterior terrain belonging to the subject, the uncovering and discovering of an individual space, which can be 'tamed' by the subject. The latter becomes part of the complex 'safety-autonomy-conflict'[3] of the subject, as Bischof puts it. Humans need the feeling of security (proximity to their parents), and at the same time they need autonomy (by 'conquering' the unfamiliar, the Other, the unsafe, and being far away from home).

This opposition between safety and autonomy permeates all crises of maturation and identity, and forms the foundation of the psychic dimension of longing. Longing is an unsatisfied, perhaps partly insatiable, desire for the Other, the absent, the lost, the detached, even to some extent for the completely different/Other, the unreachable and inconceivable, ineffable, inexpressible. Thus, there arguably exist an actual longing and an absolute longing which is detached from the actual: the 'metaphysical desire', as it is represented at the end of the film *Nostalghia* (1983) – longing for home – by Andrei Tarkovsky. Goethe writes these verses in *Wilhelm Meisters Lehrjahre/Wilhelm Meister's Apprenticeship* (1795–96):

You never long'd and lov'd
You know not grief like mine:
Alone and far remov'd
From joys or hopes, I pine:
A foreign sky above,
And a foreign earth below me,
To the south I look all day;
For the hearts that love and know me
Are far, are far away.
I burn, I faint, I languish,
My heart is waste, and sick, and sore;
Who has not long'd in baffled anguish
Cannot know what I deplore [...].

(Nur wer die Sehnsucht kennt,
weiß was ich leide!
Allein und abgetrennt
von aller Freude,
seh ich ans Firmament nach jener Seite.
Ach! Der mich liebt und kennt,
ist in der Weite.
Es schwindelt mir, es brennt
mein Eingeweide.
Nur wer die Sehnsucht kennt
weiß was ichleide!)[4]

These verses disclose a depiction of the sufferings of the lonely – and the longing subject. They ponder a situation of being alone/loneliness, of being forsaken, being disseminated/dispersed in far distance, away from home, a deeply felt joylessness touching upon physical pain. Furthermore, Goethe completes these allegories of pain in another passage of the *Wilhelm Meister* novel with the following poem:

Who longs in solitude to live,
Ah! soon his wish will gain;
Men hope and love, men get and give,
And leave him to his pain.

Yes, leave me to my moan!
When from my bed
You all are fled,
I still am not alone.

The lover glides with footstep light:
His love, is she not waiting there?

So glides to meet me, day and night,
In solitude my care,

In solitude my woe:
True solitude I then shall know
When lying in my grave,
And grief has let me go.

(Wer sich der Einsamkeit ergibt,
Ach! der ist bald allein;
Ein jeder lebt, ein jeder liebt
Und läßt ihn seiner Pein.

Ja! laßt mich meiner Qual!
Und kann ich nur einmal
Recht einsam sein,
Dann bin ich nicht allein.

Es schleicht ein Liebender lauschend sacht,
Ob seine Freundin allein?
So überschleicht bei Tag und Nacht
Mich Einsamen die Pein,

Mich Einsamen die Qual.
Ach, werd ich erst einmal
Einsam im Grabe sein,
Da läßt sie mich allein!)[5]

An eschatology distinctive to the subject is put into the foreground. The longing subject will be solitary in the grave, and even pain will desert him there. In Wong Kar-wai's film about longing and loneliness, the ending comprises a representation of estrangement from the world, a relation to the world characterized by complete self-encapsulation. One of the characters says that reality is experienced as through a window pane. The subject has broken away from all instances of closeness and has entered into a tomb-like virtual space that no longer allows for any kind of closeness, or any kind of contact. The biology of physical contact, the biology of the skin, the development of emotional security via the sensing of closeness is an almost unopened chapter of a physical anthropology which deals with our personal individuation. It is marked by grisly experiments, experiments separating primate babies from their mothers, and experiments featuring surrogate mothers made from plastics, fabric and metal. Emotional security and closeness are not easy to have, cannot easily be replaced, and perhaps they cannot be made the subject of any research. For as soon as one does so, and experiments, one has – like in Heisenberg's quantum mechanics – already destroyed, dissected and dissolved the aforementioned emotional components. Emotional security and closeness are primal archetypal phenomena of our lives and artists try to depict these phenomena, as they wrestle with depictions and reflections like, for instance, Ingmar Bergman's film *Viskningar och rop/Cries and Whispers* (1972).

As I have mentioned before: longing appears in two different manifestations which complete each other. There is, on the one hand, the actual longing for the lost, for unity, closeness and security which once existed, a kind of archetypal state, like the prenatal sense of safety experienced in the womb, the security of resting at one's mother's breast as an infant; and on the other hand, the longing for the undefined, the yearning for one's object of longing, which rests in the uncertain and completely Other, like the longing for the divine in religion, as in the final shot of Tarkovsky's *Nostalghia* (1983), where the dying poet, subjected to the loneliness of being in distant parts, experiences a sense of security in the metaphysical religious sphere after he crosses the water with a burning candle and reaches the far shore.

In this respect, the concept of longing, the phenomenon of longing, is fractured in itself. To always regain what one already had beforehand would not satisfy the longing; the fulfilment of longing would soon become stale, proximity would turn into something unbearable, and closeness and contact would then take on the characteristics of menace. This may be the reason why the maturing child detaches itself from the primal family during the Oedipal crisis of puberty: a world, a new world, where new partners are longed for and have to be embraced. The experience of 'becoming actual', which is based upon contact with parents and siblings, has to be transferred to others, to strangers, to possible partners, who have to be appropriated, introjected and introduced into one's sphere of familiarity and intimacy. But in this, one may also fail.

In monotheistic religion this is the failure of God's proximity: the longing for the absolute cannot be satisfied. Accordingly, the only and invisible God appears to the 'man Moses', as Sigmund Freud calls this founder of religion, as a burning thorn bush, which is still both an image of closeness as well as of distance, an image of the ambiguity present in metaphysical longing. Therefore, in Judaism the image of the Messiah is created; of the redeemer who overcomes the barrier between God and man and dispels man's loneliness, establishing a closeness to God and paradise on Earth. But the Messiah must never appear as an actual fact. In Judaism, the appearance of the Messiah is an eschatology, an utopia of the infinite. Therefore, in the context of Judaism, the arrival of Jesus Christ, the incarnation of the divine spirit, appears as a short circuit, premature, inexcusable. It is only in the state of potentiality that God can create closeness to man, but not as something that is part of reality. Wong Kar-wai reflects upon something quite analogous: the closeness of contact between the yearning and loving partners – between the lovers who have been isolated by their respective spouses' adultery – is delayed again and again, has to stay continually unfulfilled; they must not turn to be 'like the others.' They forego fulfilment and break up with one another.

From the Jewish point of view of the Torah, one would have to comment: if we hastily relinquish our distance to the divine, the invisibility of the absolute, if we accept Jesus Christ as a mediator between God and man – or any mediator at all – then we quickly enter the dimension of the actual or achievable, where the violation of the commandment 'Thou shalt not make for yourself an image of the absolute' results in a kind of idol worship, a deification of the immanent, the worldly, which makes the divine lose its metaphysical quality and leads to a 'dance around the golden calf', in the way Moses experienced it, and which we experience today in the glorification of the Calvinist concept of godly monetary capital.

If the lovers stay caught in their longing for fulfilment, they avoid the dangers lurking in the actualization of satisfaction, in banalization. On the other hand, they also avoid a worthwhile and happy life, and, accordingly, the world has to disappear behind a glass pane. In actively lived Christianity, the presence of the absolute in the immanent, the worldly, the visible, manifests itself in the Holy Communion, in the breaking, sharing and eating of the bread, in the Eucharistic Mass; and Tarkosvky demonstrates this in *Nostalghia* (1983) in the middle part of the film, where, after the longing for the homeland, one's wife, one's dog, one's farm and – although later – the longing for the security of being in God, of being close to God have made their appearance, a subtle Mass is celebrated under the leaking roof of a lunatics' asylum. The Mass takes place under the equation of confluence, of extreme closeness: 1+1 = 1. The language of longing and its fulfilment: *unio mystica*, psychic union.

The motif of longing comprises yet another aspect, which is extraordinarily delicate with regard to contemporary psychology and psychoanalysis: it is the question about the fulfilment of drives and wishes, about the satisfaction of longing. Following Freud, the libido is a biomechanical neuronal energy in the sense of a 'pressure'; a driving force within us, which turns us towards objects of desire and compels the devotion, the closeness, to them. But according to the French psychoanalyst Laplanche this is untrue: he is confident that longing and seduction have to be explained not by a pressure, a push, but by a pull, an attraction. The Other draws us towards itself, because it involves our own attracting imagination that is based on a longing. In his essay about the uncompleted Copernican turn in psychoanalysis, Laplanche comments that Freud falls short when he locates desire, seduction and longing for the 'Other' only in the subconscious, i.e. only in the sphere of the 'id' and the unconscious universe of the drives. In fact, it is the difference between the actual Other and us, the real world of the longed for, which would have to be allowed as something other relating to ourselves. Therefore, exceeding Freud's view, one would have to formulate thus: not only 'Where It was, shall I be', but rather 'Where It was, the Other has to be possible as well.'

With regard to these questions, artists, film-makers, poets are often more advanced than theoreticians. I think that Wong Kar-wai's film is permeated by a firm – maybe romantic – belief in true longing, in the priority of the soul vis-à-vis the drive. The tenderness of near-touches in gestures and gazes, the microscopic of the emotional in smiles, in simple actions with soup, stairs, umbrella – this is the language of an approach towards the psyche and a psychic atmosphere, which takes itself seriously in the way it manifests itself, and experiences itself as something that cannot be reduced to something different, to schemata, to conventions, to mechanisms. In the dominant state of being thrown into confines, into bondage, this actualization of near-closeness manifests a space of freedom. And this is painted in cinematic images, which appear as if a genius had cast them into oil paintings, only to be transformed into a film thereafter.

We find another image of longing in Tarkovsky's film *Solaris* (1972), in the 'elevation' of the avatar. The longing for the realization, the appearance, the epiphany of the psychologist's early love creates – mediated by the 'mare solaris' – the imagination of longing as a transcendence toward another reality.

Here is a third example: in Woody Allen's film *Zelig* (1983), the protagonist finds himself in the situation of being so affected by the aura of his opposite (protagonist), that, like a simulacrum, he starts to resemble that person mimetically. It is, in a sense, the actualization of that very longing to be(coming) the Other which relates to one's self; and to merge with this Other in an act of identifying with her or him. The finding of one's own self only becomes possible through the love of a young woman, a therapist, who enables him to become himself again.

Consequently, one could be tempted to say that images not only express longing, but images 'become' longing, they are themselves in a state of longing for their fulfilment, for their merging and dissolution in the Other, like in Oscar Wilde's *The Portrait of Dorian Gray* (1891), or in the way Mozart's musical inner-images step into reality and want to be heard; to dissolve in the Other and to be fulfilled.

Why is this plausible? It is quite plain: the archetypal images, the 'enforming images' manifest in dreams, in daydreams, in free association and in one's phantasy. And, as Sigmund Freud has shown, these shapes, belonging to the dream and its analogues, press for fulfilment (cf. Lacan's concept of unconscious desire). Regarding the concepts of technology and desire, we might conclude that machines are not the ones harbouring intentions, and they are not after something or long for something. Rather the underlying enforming images, with their semantics and their meaning, hold the desire.

Longing in film does not emerge just because longings that are latently present within us are reactivated, and because film serves as a projection surface for these longings; it rather appears that the pictorial shapes in film are based on intrinsic, basic intentionalities, which, for their part, manifest and envision shapes of reality that are suffused by and based on longing; and that we must be able to experience the literal shocks and commotions, which are created thus, in a downright cathartic manner: this is the only way that processes of psychic maturation and inner transcendence can become possible.

If one summarizes the examples from film, one might say that longing in film always deals with the transgression of boundaries; boundaries which have to be crossed in order to mentally grasp, to get close, to align with the object of longing, the one that is 'longed for'. Longing is about accepting its 'vortex'. It is about the acceptance of hope, and about the transcendence of boundaries towards the Other.

Translated by Jochen Mevius and Rania Gaafar

Notes

1   Johann Gottlieb Fichte, *Die Bestimmung des Menschen/The Vocation of Man* (trans. Peter Preuss), Indiana: Hackett, [1800] 1987, p. 63.

2   Emmanuel Levinas, 'The Trace of the Other', in Mark C. Taylor, *Deconstruction in Context – Literature and Philosophy*, Chicago: University of Chicago Press, 1986, pp. 351–52.

3   Cf. Norbert Bischof, *Das Rätsel Ödipus – Die Biologischen Wurzeln des Urkonflikes von Intimität und Autonomie*, Munich: Piper, 1997.

4   Translation quoted from: http://www.bartleby.com/314/411.html, accessed 20 August 2013.

5   Translation quoted from: http://www.bartleby.com/314/213.html, accessed 13 September 2013.

Chapter 14

The Fever Curve of the Gaze and the Body as (Image) Medium:
Jacques Lacan's Media Theory of Unconscious Desire

Annette Bitsch

For Hinderk Emrich

The following text attempts to answer some pivotal questions concerning the age of images and media which we live in via Jacques Lacan's theory of unconscious desire and the gaze. Our present age of images and the media confronts us with worlds, scintillating between enticement and menace, where images – images transgressively unfettered and liberated, subjectivized and desiring like subjects – reign and circulate. Accordingly, the dynamization and the subjectivity of transmedial images, as well as the connection between the body and the media,[1] are the points structuring these deliberations. The relation between body and media, or – more precisely – the subject, as far as it is conceived as a medium by Lacan and thus differentiated from classical concepts of the conscious and the subject,[2] will serve as an entry into the topic.

Corpsification

Two different eras of thinking, or even two different ontologies, are to be extrapolated hereafter from Lacan's own differentiation between the eyes and the gaze, which traces back to Sartre: a classical ontology and one denoted hereafter as an operational ontology. As the countless and hopeless debates concerning the theory of psychoanalysis as well as philosophy have shown – the reception of the showdown between Heidegger and Cassirer is just one example[3] – ontology is just a term like plutonium or smoking compartment.

But it is Lacan, after all, who writes 'that, of course, I have an ontology – why not? – like everyone else, however naïve or elaborated it may be', although he emphatically adds 'that this [is] a rare, or even unique attempt to give a body to psychical reality without substantifying it.'[4] Accordingly, this is not a classic ontology, nor – to keep to the distinction mentioned above – the assumption occurring under the 'eye' as a figure of thought, which infers a discrete, homogenous and presentifiable origin; an untouchable as well as unchangeable and unmovable archetype, a divine foundation of creation, resting in itself forever and ever. Instead – by starting the passage towards the 'gaze' as a figure of thought – it actually concerns the subversion of such roots of creation and such reasoning about origins by the positioning of a genuine repetition, i.e. a temporal cadence which precedes any illusion of homogeneity, a secondary origin in Jacques Derrida's sense of the term. In short, it concerns the conception of an inaccessible real, which irrevocably eludes any possibility of realization (not least because of its temporality). The static concept of being, which is inextricably interlaced with the 'eye' as a figure of thought, with classic ontology, and which is based on simple dichotomies like being versus non-being; or visible versus invisible – where the invisible can always be uncovered, cleared up, made visible, just as non-being is understood as the simple opposite, the flip side of being – can no longer take hold in a media age, where, with Lacan, one needs to keep in mind that the actual issue is the relation between access and closing as such. As soon as the door opens, it closes. When it closes, it opens. A door needs not to be open or closed; it needs to be open and then closed and then open and then closed. Due to the electric circuit and the inductor circuit which is connected back to itself; that is, due to that what is called feedback, the closing of the door is enough to return it, at once, to the state of opening by an electromagnet, and this is, again, its opening and, again, its closing. In this manner, they generate oscillation, as it is called.[5]

Here, Lacan formulates a medial *a priori* of the unconscious and – as he writes in reference to the concept of implementation as it is found in computer theory – the 'corpsified' subject.[6] He presents a concept of an operationalized and discretized being, which no longer has to be correlated to a static-dichotomous relation, but rather to a temporal-dialectical relation: it is not either 'being' or 'non-being', but rather 'being' followed then by 'non-being' followed by 'being' followed by 'non-being', and so on. Proceeding from an origin that does not hold a totality, but a discrete operational 'two', and therefore can be described more exactly as an original shifting, as the operationalization of an irrevocable discordance between the symbolic and the real;[7] these 'oscillations' of being and non-being, these corpsified significant processes run their course, generating all the images of Jessica Parker in Manhattan, Kate Moss in Carnaby Street, Californian beach girls on Venice Beach and *filles fatales* in Paris; memories of the future, 'Bette Davis Eyes' 2010 and a sushi bar made from laser light. And yet, beneath this fleet of images between glory and symphony, this fleet of image with its scent of electricity and its aroma of the World Wide Web, we encounter a procession of pure signifiers, i.e. discrete elements, ceaseless, blind, colourless and soundless changes between on and off, 0 and 1, or even more precisely within the context of the unconscious subject's desire: between being and non-being.

The moment, where this movement, which continually oscillates or – in Lacan's words – pulses between two discrete states, is brought into being, where the subject is operationalized as a corpsified generator of images and meanings, that moment cannot be grasped or reconciled with the versions of an origin that is part of a classic ontology. This moment where being itself is split, which is situated at the original shifting of the operational ontology governing the subject of the unconscious, no longer occurs under the protective canopy of a divine-metaphysical principle, but in the form of a trauma that is impossible to recall and to reconstruct, even to the point of distraction; a traumatic division of being. As a primordial discretization of being, the division of the subject cannot be thought – respectively objectified – in a spatially concrete context, but is, in contrast, constituted discretely and temporally. The division of being is, according to Lacan, the encounter with the *tuché*, the real, although he also points out that this 'appointment [with the real] to which we are always called' categorically fails due to inherently constitutive reasons, and because the real 'eludes us'.[8]

From this perspective, desire – a continual discrete alternation between being and non-being – appears to be propelled by the impossible wish to purify the unsuccessful encounter which, as a traumatic devastation, is at the root of the world's misfortune that appears symptomatic for the Freudian-Lacanian unconscious – just to miss it and fail at it anew and again and again. But this entirely fatal, Manichean game, this syntactically incorporated compulsion to repeat, does not implement itself without that one side effect that is decisive for the course of the media of destiny, and in turn the fate of the media: instead of that single overexposed epiphany that arrives at a single stroke redeeming everything, secular idols and promiscuous images of the hours are generated in an endless sequence and movement: the young Anna Magnani in a dark red velvet robe with its train set high; a party animal in a camisole, coloured in sugary pastels; a Rockefeller, a Mortimer and the young Andy Garcia in dove-grey suits by Armani. Pictorial emotional outbursts, hunters of the horizon, that uncertain something, stop and glow.

But what is – to finally penetrate the topic – the gaze? The gaze, as one could very briefly describe this theoretical module from Lacan's own discourse concerning computer media, is a subroutine of the unconscious subject's desire delineated above – corpsified, processing via significants and transferring itself in meanings and images.[9] As a movement implemented in the body, the gaze precedes the level of the eye, the phenomenal reality. 'What we have to circumscribe,' writes Lacan, "is the pre-existence of a gaze.'[10]

From the moment of the division of the being, and thus from the digitalization and mediatisation of the subject onwards, the whole world is projected based on this unconscious code of the gaze. But here, on this gallery, where pastel-sugary, Microsoft, surreal and Kafkaesque images weave about, only a single point refers to the subject of the unconscious, the small French *je*, the imaginary French *moi*, the ego of the idealistic central perspective, the common consciousness: 'I see only from one point, but in my existence I am looked at from all sides.'[11] The gaze creates reality with all its ingredients and choreographies: pictures, texts, monitors with changing images in subways, launderettes, airports, shopping malls, well-off households.

In the process, the conscious ego (*moi*) represents nothing more than a projection, tele-controlled by the gaze – and of course this is something that it has to misconceive and deny by all means in order to survive confidently in the Cartesian post-season. Therefore, consciousness and world are situated on the same (imaginary) level: on the stands of reality, on the boards of a phantasm staged by unconscious gazes and thus – because, as we have seen, according to Lacan the unconscious subject is a medium as well – ultimately by the media; a phantasm called reality. The images glittering and flickering across the globe in digitized form do not depict a reality that is immobile and solidly resting in itself. According to the algorithm of Lacan's gaze, they continually show modified and reprogrammed versions, collective phantasms or projections instead, which appear at the place where the original archetype of classic ontology has imploded. Instead of an archetypal image and a divine bedrock, as well as one great and eternal truth that is as unalterable as a Matterhorn, a fluctuation starts to gaze and to blink: continual change, quick progress from Sarah Jessica Parker wearing Anna Magnani's *tailleur*, the young Alain Delon in a black suit by Armani, Popeye at the Fashion Awards New York, the matadors of downtown at Swifty's in Lexington Avenue and, in the harbour of List, Darboven coffee kings and Hanseatic notables, dining on syntheses of turbot and prawn from Sylt. Overstimulating-climate, news-tempest, iPhone-YouTube, image-animals: 'zensitive'.

With the mass media activated at the beginning of the twentieth century, a world- and media age commences that culminates in the universal medium of the Internet, and is no longer determined by a single and only fixed reality grounded in an archetypical origin of images, but – and this represents a distinct dynamic, by which and in which the motion of images is increased – by the periodical update and reconfiguration of this reality; it is no longer determined by truth, but by actuality – an actuality that, since the 1960s, can no longer be distinguished from computer-based simulations and virtual realities. At this point it becomes clear how compatible Lacan's theory of the unconscious gaze is with those numerous theories (from McLuhan, Virilio, Flusser and Baudrillard to constructivism and the current media theory of the virtual) that postulate that our reality is not depicted, but rather constructed by media.

Dynamization

Against this close connection that exists between the theory of the gaze and the media age dominated by a mobilization of images in the world, one could argue that Lacan, when asked to talk about the gaze, nearly always returns to static models with regard to an epoch where images were as fixed and static (and close to chastisement), as tamed and fettered as they could possibly be – central perspective. In the matter of the gaze, Lacan begins a journey to early modern times, where the examinations of Vitruv, Vignola, Dürer and Alberti inaugurated geometrical optics, which turned *ego cogito* into an emperor, and the edges of the picture frame into battlements.[12] Lacan quite diligently notes the simultaneity concerning the emergence of the laws of central perspective in the course of early modern geometrical optics and the rise of a very specific concept of the subject: the Cartesian *cogito*, precursor and prototype of the imaginary consciousness:

> It is not for nothing that it was at the very period when the Cartesian meditation inaugurated in all its purity the function of the subject that the dimension of optics that I shall distinguish here by calling 'geometral' or 'flat' (as opposed to perspective) optics was developed.[13]

And it is there that he discovers a decisive module of his theory of the gaze: the 'geometral point', or 'point of perspective', which puts an image possessing a central perspective (and, not least, the mirror image as well) into focus.

Following Lacan on this expedition, we have created a great distance, temporal as well as conceptual, to those images which – under the technological and medial conditions of the twenty-first century – have galloped wildly and widely from their static image-space, have swarmed outwards. But…are we really that far from Gwyneth Paltrow wearing the statement rosa-style and having a sound massage at the Palazzo Arzaga at Lake Garda, creatures with cinematic appeal at a sublimated Riviera, the grandees of society golfing in Switzerland, losses of control, sensual invasion and image-crackers in the City – to the extent of vacillation, vertigo, and finally de-realization and depersonalization? We are close to what concerns Lacan the most: de-realization and depersonalization. He is concerned with the depersonalization and displacement of the Cartesian consciousness, which is, in its mediality, determined *a priori* by central perspective, along with its sovereign eye which determines and assesses image and world from the zenith of the mirror image; and he is, as a necessary result, also concerned with the liberation of a sequence of images, which, in its accelerating movement spreading to buildings, cities, streets and urban canyons, progressively creates vertigo and feelings of de-realization up to anxiety. The simple equation of gaze and central perspective, which is even common in research on Lacan, thus has to be amended by pointing out that Lacan is not declaring the static image of central perspective to be the matrix of the 'gaze' as a partial drive at all; rather he is concerned about destructing the central perspective, respectively the Cartesian cogito, and transcending the immobile image related to it towards those mobile images which correspond to the movement – the pulsing – of the unconscious subject. Thus, Lacan's true motivation for his research trips back to early modern times, the pertinent study of the laws of geometral optics and, especially, the calculation of the geometral point lies in the prospect of employing the laws for misapplying this optics – something he does *con brio* when studying the anamorphoses of his surrealist friends.[14]

In *Seminar I*, Lacan demonstrates by means of a complex experiment – the experiment with the inverted bouquet of flowers, which can only be mentioned, but not deciphered in detail in this context – that the illusion of central perspective, i.e. the illusion of a reality controlled by an omnipotent fixed point ('I see'), only functions if the subject is positioned exactly in the zenith of the (mirror) image. Only in this position, the point of the conscious *moi* ('I see') can cover the unconscious *je* ('it gazes') exactly and completely, and thus pacify and neutralize it: 'For the illusion to appear, for a world to constitute itself in front of the observing eye [...], [the subject] has to be in a certain position, it has to be in the interior of the cone.'[15]

'I see' has to occupy the geometral point in a literal sense, and, at the same time, repress the 'it gazes' and turn it invisible. This is valid until Lacan's arrival and his approach to suspend the consciousness of classic ontology for the benefit of the subject of operational ontology. Thus, Lacan's actual concern is the decentring of the subject, its displacement from the centre of the image; the fall of the geometral point 'I see' of central perspective for the benefit of the liberation of 'it shows'.

Accordingly, his remark – that one would see poorly at the edges of the image – has to be relativized: vision, insofar as it is arranged according to the static image-world with the eye as its classic sphere of thinking and imagining, indeed worsens and becomes obscure at this point. However, it can only improve in reference to that what 'I would prefer to call the seer's "shoot"/la pousse du voyant',[16] that cataract of light and images, which simultaneously results in addiction and vertigo.

And thus auspicious as well as doom-laden premonitions present themselves: what may happen when the headless *je* ('it gazes') is no longer bound and absorbed by the geometral point *moi* ('I see')? Let us imagine *filles fatales* in a poverty *de luxe*-style in front of a pastel-coloured shop window of a confectioner bristling with vanilla cream *éclairs*, raspberry *petits fours* and pistachio-cream tartlets, and Daisy Duck with Polly Maggoo-sunglasses having lobster soup and delicately melting tuna *parfait* in the harbour of List. Déjà vu, something remembers; was it this? Or was it something different? And who was I? Since the archetype, i.e. the original image, has been split, not only in a merely spatial sense, but in the sense of a temporal movement of origin followed by image followed by origin followed by image, the déjà vu has become operational, anamnesis a delete-rewrite process and the image is a continual remix.

Vintage-Phenomena and Wave Troughs: Lacan and Flusser

Up to this point, the dynamized and strangely animated images, which transgress the *hortus conclusus* of their frame and have swamped whole cities and metropolises, which, in turn, are architectonically and medially constituted in at least equal parts, were examined using Lacan's concept of the gaze, and thus appeared as procedures for the projection of realities, medialized in a real body. But now an additional theory concerning these sequences of images that produce themselves in the fringe between subjectivity and objectivity is going to be delineated and connected to Lacan's concepts. This excursion will introduce Flusser's theory of 'wave troughs' and of the urbanistic revolution in the age of universal mediatisation, and provide another key concept on the dissolution of boundaries and subjectivization. According to Flusser, cities define themselves in the current media neither merely via their topography, nor their material or identifiable elements (of an architectonic or urban-infrastructural kind). Instead, as their constitution is characterized by transportation systems and the propensity for ubiquitous mediality and communication (cars, freeways, the veins of the subway, the cool and controlled labyrinth of the fibre-optic cables, the spectralized skies), they are themselves situated in a hazy area between tarmac-grey reality and the pulse of the global village, between materiality and information.[17] The city as a homogenous entity is literally dissociated and even dematerialized in parts; accordingly, the old division between a public, private and theoretical urban space can no longer be sustained. Flusser writes: '[Now] the three urban spaces [interlock] like fuzzy sets.'[18]

While the old image of the city assumed a traditional idea of man, which can be correlated to the homogeneous, self-related individuality of the classical period, the new 'concept of man' which refers to the new city features completely contrary characteristics. Flusser describes them as such: here 'everything can be divided', but 'not only atoms', also 'every mental phenomenon can be divided into particles, for instance actions into "aktome", decisions into "dezideme", perceptions into "stimuli", imaginations into "pixels".[19] The new city radically diverges from the view offered to the Cartesian *cogito* by the image which was predetermined by its mediality to be based on central perspective and picture frame: a static world of objects where all irritations of the gaze have been pacified and which is cleanly split from the perceiving subject, a *res extensa*. In the new city, these two fortresses – subject and object, I and world – have been irreversibly disintegrated instead insofar as these are understood in the classic sense as fixed instances that can be grasped as singular elements. The objects are superimposed by images in a manner which dissipates the object as an original, material thing – just as if the object was dissolved in a lye made of immaterial codes and pixels; an act of digital cauterization.[20] Thus hybrids develop which have been partially de-ontologized; Flusser calls them 'masks' which can no longer be isolated from the subject in the classic way, but are rather referring to the subject in a determining and formatting manner, namely as mirrors. Lacan's mirror theory seems to resonate in the background when Flusser writes:

When one is observing the image of the city, its 'immateriality' is conspicuous – as long as one has mobilized the necessary imagination. There, one can discern neither houses nor places nor temples; only a mesh of wires, a maze of cables. A walk in Cologne may help to make this image appear a bit more material. While Heine was still of the opinion that it mirrored itself with its holy cathedral in the holy river, we must attempt to have it mirror itself in the relational field. The first things to stick out are the commercial displays, where masks for identification are on offer. On identifies with and as a robe, as a pair of shoes, as a cooking pot. One is – whatever one is – only when one begins to dance in this robe, in this cooking pot. These commercial displays define Cologne as a whole. Such masks are offered everywhere. One dances in the mask of a television image (one identifies with it and identifies oneself in it), in the mask of a party member, an academic title, a family relationship, an art movement, a philosophical position. Cologne proves to be a wave trough in the field of interpersonal relations, where these relations are gathered in masks in order to realize the possibilities inherent in them. Cologne's inhabitants are densely spread swarms of points which dance wearing Cologne masks. Cologne's buildings, places and the cathedral have to be seen as surface phenomena, as congealed, 'materialized' masks, as a kind of archaeological kitchen waste.[21]

And as the subject only maintains relational ties to the masks, it correspondingly restricts itself to the formation of differential and grammatical relationships towards other subjects. Flusser remarks that '"I" is that which is called "you"',[22] and Lacan notes '*I* is a verbal term, and its usage is learned in a specific reference to the other, which is a spoken reference. The *I* is born in the reference to *you*.'[23] Psychoanalysis is explicitly counted among the discourses and spheres of thinking – Flusser lists ecology, molecular biology, computer science, nuclear physics and fractal geometry[24] – which are supported by Flusser's subjects respectively, the 'swarms of points'. And the parallels to Lacan's concept of the unconscious subject, the 'it gazes', are indeed striking. Both Flusser's and Lacan's subject are impossible to unify or to grasp as a singular element; rather, the subject exists exclusively in the intersubjective relation instead – in every case, it is already related to something other, to a significant or to another subject (which, in turn, is nothing but an effect of a significant),[25] to a mask or to the whole 'intersubjective field of relations', which Flusser describes as following in the form of a web of strands: 'We have to imagine a web of interhuman relationships, an "intersubjective field of relations."' The strands of this web have to be understood as channels, through which information like imaginings, emotions, intentions or perceptions flows. These strands knot together provisionally, and generate that which we call 'human subjects'.[26] Strands between dark radiation, moonstruck-white cantor dust, CAD-silk, velvet axons and an algorithm-channel playing in the Hurst-wind weave a web around Sarah Jessica Parker with husky-green Manolos on top of the Tokyo Tower, around Arielle at Piccadilly Circus and around a diplomat's daughter in a knee-length woollen cape with a fur collar and a dark brown Birkin bag in front of Moscow's red town hall. Endangered by longing, fuel for bits, transuranic glances, 'peacockissimo'. Once again the affinity towards Lacan's subject makes itself felt, which is caught up in the web of the signifiers, and in the often highly interlaced structure of symptoms, wishes, dreams and conflicts, and which transfers and projects gazes and desires via the multi-branched channels of the unconscious. Flusser conceives the subject as a medium, just as Lacan presents desire – respectively the gaze – as a code processing in a real body, which initially generates the instinctual life of a city-image consisting of urban canyons, radio waves and surreal oceans of colour and light. It is crucial that these mediatised subjects – as 'intersubjective fields of relations' – are connected with further media and subjects and thus form a web of varying density. Flusser calls particularly dense places in the web, where information accumulates, 'wave troughs in the field, which has to be imagined as oscillating', and ultimately identifies them with the new city itself:

At these dense places, the knots move closer to each other and 'update' each other. In these wave troughs the possibilities inherent in interhuman relationships become 'more current'. These wave troughs have an 'attracting' effect on the field surrounding them (pulling them into the gravitational field); more and more interhuman relationships are attracted by this point. Each wave is a focus for the updating of interhuman contingencies. Such wave troughs have to be called 'cities'.[27]

Flusser represents and presses for a notion of the subject as a medium, which uncompromisingly 'processualizes' the new city; this becomes obvious in his explicit application of the term 'circuit' to the subject that stems from information theory. Regarding the wave troughs, it was important, according to Flusser, 'that the cables of interhuman relations are connected reversibly, not in a bundle, as with television, but in actual webs. [...] These are technical questions, and they have to be solved by urbanists and architects.'[28] Two questions remain unanswered with regard to these subject-media: Lacan's gaze and Flusser's wave trough, which, while they are configured individually on the basis of different theories, are still comparable in many points.

Lacan's theory of the mirror stage, incidentally, re-emphasizes the non-unified, relational constitution of the subject. In this theory, Lacan delineates the narcissistic identification in a mirror image or in the small Other, by means of which the I constitutes itself as I (*moi*), meaning as an integrated, unified and anthropomorphic body image.[29] While this identificational erection of a happiness-support for the ego by a relational reference to an Other has its primal scene in the mirror stage, activated initially between 6 and 18 months and accentuated by emotions shifting between 'hymn' and 'death-halloo', its result – the happiness-support of the ego – is not stable, but disintegrates after a certain period, and therefore necessitates a repeated activation of the mirror phase; respectively a repeated narcissistic identification with an Other. In principle, these loops, the shifts between the loss of ego and its reconstitution, represent a lifelong struggle (for identification) of the subject; hence the decisive question where the specific discarded versions of the ego, the matrices of the self – Lacan calls them 'between-I's'[30] – remain. They are definitely not packed into old suitcases and boxes, stored and locked away, in order to fall into a sleep from eternity to eternity in dark basements and cobwebbed attics. To the contrary: they become clothes, which are perpetually worn in a manner that is asynchronous and always arranged anew. The 'I' is a modern vintage fashion phenomenon:

[It is] the sum of the identifications of the subject [...], with everything this might entail with regards to radical contingencies. If I may describe it figuratively, the *I* resembles different coats worn on top of each other, which are borrowed from the rubbish of a supply shop, as I would call it.[31]

As a pool or depot, this supply shop – which contains the 'between-*I*'s' of a life between Paris Hilton, young Andy Garcia, Sarah Jessica Parker and a Carnaby Street-style Spock in a disaggregated, purely significant form – has a function analogue to the gaze: the signifiers are recombined and synthesized anew in order to transfer one of Flusser's wave troughs, a Mortimer, a Rockefeller, a high-end chaser. This supply shop is, of course, simply a metaphor for Lacan's concept of memory.

Lacan applies the linguistic terms of 'synchrony' and 'diachrony' in order to explain the architecture and the functional principle of this unconscious memory: in all its actions, the subject is determined and instructed by the unconscious codes of desire. In Lacan's version, these codes, the codes of desire and the codes of the unconscious gaze, thereby coincide with memory that is thus defined *in operando*. Memory constitutes itself in diachrony, while at the same time defining the subject in the form of a programme that operates synchronically.[32] The history of the subject is decidedly not the past, insofar as it returns in imaginary recollections, but rather 'history is only the past, if it is historicized in the present – historicized in the present, because it has been experienced in the past.'[33] Memory does not contain the true and only images of the past; rather, memory is the archive that contains the irreducibly past and withdrawn experiences or images in the form of decipherable signifiers. At the same time, it is the code of desire that historicizes a past – which is available in a purely signifying form – in the present; in other words, transforms it, recombines it and transfers it, as described above, as a newly invented history or image story. Thus, one after the other, the clothes of the successive identification partners are acquired, just to become a part of the unconscious memory, the junk shop in diachronic form, and to experience a revelation in synchrony some day: sequences of Lolitas with hair compositions from an elfish dance, shimmering in the colours of meringue and pink tartlets, Bollywood-style *filles fatales* carrying snakeskin messenger bags in fluorescent colours, and Bernhard and Bianca in the Imperial in Castle Bühlerhöhe, dining on quail chops and red mullets in Meaux mustard sauce. Social butterflies, discover the world: deactivation is futile.

Regarding this subject-medium and its functions of retention and transfer, Lacan and Flusser are – in addition to all similarities mentioned above – also conceptually connected by another particular point. According to Flusser, 'the notorious self"[34] is no longer humanely warmed by a core of a deep and true nature, as it was in the epochs of classicism and idealism, as well as, up to recent times, in modern psychology. 'It proves to be,' if anything, 'a shell, and not a core. It keeps the scattered particles [signifiers according to Lacan] together, it "contains" them. […] One realizes this, when one unknots them [the knots which, according to Flusser, constitute the self]. Like onions, they are without a core.'[35] Furthermore, Lacan writes:

> [T]hat the ego is made from the sequence of its identifications with the loved objects which allowed it to take on its form. The ego is an object that is constructed like an onion; one could flense it just to find the successive identifications which constituted it.[36]

And at the core of the crowds of onions fluctuating through London, Paris, New York, Las Vegas, Tokyo and the World Wide Web – an emptiness, the relic of a castration, an *objet petit a*,[37] or a gaze which begins to float through the textures and to transfer Kate Moss in a panné velvet skirt and leather jacket, a young wild-style Steve McQueen and the baroness Jeanne von Oppenheim as a smoke-grey Balenciaga silhouette.

But these new cities, where every picture frame ionizes, and where swarms of points, wave troughs and phosphorescent masks – from Mary Poppins and McDonald's to 'Last Exit to Irreality' circulate – this whole world, governed by a ghostly 'it gazes', which is in a peculiar manner at once deadening as well as subjectified and animated to the point of the dithyrambic: does it still have the ontological status of a classic world of objects, tranquil, stable and reliable? As Flusser notes, the new city, where the mask and the masked person indissolubly amalgamate, most certainly has an aroma of 'immateriality'.[38] Most certainly, the entry into Virilio's third age of the image, the age of virtuality, is implemented with Lacan's theory of the gaze and Flusser's wave trough, according to which subjects become media and transport whole realities.[39] And most certainly all these image-worlds where the gaze becomes 'perceptible' – starting with the surrealist anamorphoses to film images which have become integrated elements of our living environments – appear in an uncanny and other-worldly light. Even while they are completely incompossible to media like central perspective or the picture frame, these new image-worlds are still far from developing towards a de-ontologization of reality or of the cityscape. Operational ontology is not a private mode of classic ontology, and Lacan is incorruptibly strict when he isolates the attributes 'imaginary' or 'virtual' from all purely ideational chimeras, hallucinations, mirages. An imaginary or virtual object – and here his borrowings from Mandelbrot's mathematics of complex numbers appear unmistakable – is composed of a real part (in the case of the subject, this would be the body as the carrier of an image) and an imaginary part, which simply corresponds to the projection transported by the body and created by the gaze.[40] A relativization of central perspective and picture frame is equally necessary and pointing in the same direction – that of an emancipation of operational ontology as a reference towards being; it has to be understood that these are not products of an epoch of a 'more actual' ontology, but that they are nothing but media in principle – media or *Ge-stelle* (frameworks) serving the formatting of a classic world, which is constituted by the strict division of a fixed subject of cognition (*res cogitans*) from a world of objects (*res extensa*) which is just as fixed. Central perspective and picture frame are historically delimited media-*a priori*, and as such, 300 years later in the age of the new city, they are suspended by the media-*a priori* of algorithms implemented in the real, which initially generate subjects, as well as objects as parts of an imaginary reality. This question, which is closely interlocked with the masks and the gaze, with dynamized, subjectivized and transgressive image-worlds, therefore does not concern ontology, or the ontological status or the concept of operational ontology. Instead, it concerns something completely different that was already pointed out at the beginning of this text.

Just like the moment of the division of being or the discretization of the subject, and emerging medialized, i.e. constituted temporally-operationally, the 'medial real' falls into an area of absolute inconceivability and unprethinkability. The unconscious, the real body becoming a medium: this is constitutive for Lacan's theory and prerequisite for any kind of gaze-operation. But the manner and process of this mediatisation remains forever unavailable and elusive, and evades any attempt at a reconstruction that proceeds positively and empirically. The unconscious, and everything taking place at the level of the unconscious, at the other showplace, and thus characterized by an irrevocable withdrawing of conception and cognition, can only be approximated by metaphors and models. Or, with even less of a detour and more suited to Lacan's temperament, by just letting 'it' go and gaze on and initiate gowns like feather clouds, the negligees of *merveilleuses*, complex messages in black on bare skin and young J.F. Kennedy at an opening night of the ballet in Milan. Junk shop passions, lost in onions, gazes like tranquilizer darts. And nothing less is the topic of the conclusion of those passages which Flusser employed to expedite his wave troughs into life and into the cities:

> Because the emerging relational world view, and the anthropology following from it, demand utopian thinking. We have no traditional models for it and have to design them anew. All this was spoken in images. We discussed the cityscapes, the world-image, the conception of man, the mask. This is inevitable. We are no longer able to describe the world and ourselves in it. Discursive language and writing are not suitable to this: Everything is thoroughly calculated, and swarms of dot-like bits are indescribable. But these can be calculated, and algorithms can be re-coded into images. Thus, while the world – and we in it – have become indescribable, they have become calculable and therefore imaginable again. In order to imagine it, we have to mobilize a new imagination, which is based on calculation. We have the devices necessary for this. Accordingly, this lecture has to be understood as an attempt to code synthetic images of algorithms in language. Increasingly, the present interhuman relationships are going to encrypt themselves in such images. Increasingly, our perceptions, imaginations, emotions, intentions, insights and decisions will have to take the shape of such images. Accordingly, all creative disciplines – like science and politics – will become forms of art.[41]

Medial Reveries

The dream is an additional, a different mode, where the subject flees from the eudemonia of the static picture frame, where it escapes the stagnant territorial waters of the geometral point *moi* ('I see'); a mode of cognition which, according to psychoanalysis, is privileged because it is not limited to the conscious signification of logocentrism – 'the dream, founder of any idea of cognition.'[42] In contrast to the punctuality of the *cogito* integrating and fixating the world, there exists no repeater station, no point that centres the system, no sign of reality for the dreaming subject. Lacan writes:

> The subject does not see where it is leading, he follows. He may even on occasion detach himself, tell himself that it is a dream, but in no case will he be able to apprehend himself

in the dream in the way in which, in the Cartesian *cogito*, he apprehends himself as thought. He may say to himself, *It's only a dream.* But he does not apprehend himself as someone who says to himself – *After all, I am the consciousness of this dream.*[43]

The dream system is a radically decentred mesh, in a constant state of movement of Derrida's *différances*, without a fixed point of presence, truth or certainty.[44] The images of the surrealists and numerous other modern artists illustrate this fact as well; in this context, M.C. Escher offers a prominent example. And, as we are propelled through the streets, the floodlit corridors and the avenues bordered by digital oleander of the metropolises and megalopolises of our millennium, does it not appear as a dream, an image-dream, a fever-image-dream?! – escalating fleets of *belles du jour* wearing crime-scene grey Jackie O.-classics, covered by a knee-length woollen cape with a fur collar, or, with the cool sex appeal of the black suit, of urban huntresses with their LA style or their gothic aura, of flamboyant electrified harpies and of a young Marlon Brando with T-shirt, blue jeans, cigarette and a gaze which will have transported the dreamer of this metropolitan fever dream to a final 'protect me from what I want', implored between dignity and delirium, and thus to the ends of reason, of the *cogito*, of the 'I see myself seeing myself.' But the decentring of the subject via its erotization by Marlon Brando's gazes here only appears as a hypostasis for the epistemological shift, and the shift concerning the *a priori* qualities and characteristics of the media, from classic to operational ontology, from the figure of thought 'eye' to the figure of thought 'gaze'; with this shift, the 'I see' of the conscious (*moi*) has been dismissed as the administrative power over world and image in favour of the 'it gazes' of the unconscious subject (*je*), sliding about without any foothold or fence. 'It gazes' on the faces of the big shopping malls and arcades and cinemas in the cities of this world, on myriads of walls in galleries and museums and media centres, on displays in small and big, private as well as super-personal formats.

This happens to such a highly mobilized and dynamized extent that the sequences of the Begum Inaara Aga Khan at the charity gala in New York, Carl-Eduard Graf von Bismarck playing tennis in Boston and Minnie Mouse wearing an American Legend-rovalia mink fur coat on board of the *Queen Elizabeth II*, which continually rotate with and superimpose each other, can no longer be centred by an 'I see' or linked back to an original image, let alone be captured in a picture postcard, in a picture frame or the tableau of the classic *episteme*.

And there is no longer an 'I see' which could fixate and completely acquire these images, employing the logic of representation to link them to the objects existing in the world; there is no longer an 'I think', which, based on a classic Newtonian order of time and space, could proceed to solidify them. Since – and thus this text returns to its beginning in order to gradually prepare for the landing – the medial *a priori* for the operational ontology, which is constitutive for Lacan's gaze, is no longer mechanistic physics with its objectivation of space and time and ego and world.[45] Instead, this role is taken over by electromagnetism, according to which the relation between electric and magnetic field – or being and non-being – is no longer a relation between two complete, self-related, objectifiable states which are thus both static, but rather an infinite temporally-discrete shifting into each other or alternating. Shortly after Faraday's discovery of the principle of electromagnetic induction and of the stroboscopic effect, Faraday's induction coil, Saxton's alternator and Heinrich Daniel Ruhmkorff's induction coil implement a Hegelian bad infinity in the elemental electric changes of direction in alternating current: a timeless-eternal recursion, an oscillating delirium which no longer recognizes any exit conditions – which holds true for the present day as well, insofar as the framework has been implemented here, which at the same moment, at least in the genealogical context, determines the whole of the electrical and computerized media of the twentieth and twenty-first centuries.[46]

Paris Hilton in a robe like a feather cloud and Polly Maggoo-sunglasses at a yoga seminar in Bali, Al Pacino in Armani's bohemian chic at a pool party on Capri, the Printen-making Lambertz family,[47] the marmalade-making Zentis family,[48] and the button-makers of the Pryms, golfing in Switzerland, the Ducks in the grand hotel Schloss Bensberg. Accidental navigation system, one night in Bangkok, Moscow shines, 100 volts in electronic eyes – without any exit conditions, without that final unsettling happy encounter of the symbolic and the real, which would mean salvation, without a holding value, from infinity to infinity.

Subjectivation

And yet – the point were the operational ontology, which starts with the implementation of discrete processes, i.e. the figure of thought 'gaze,' gets into a radical conflict with the classic ontology, the static opposition of the eye and the object captured by it, is not simply situated in this dynamization, which transgresses all temporal and spatial limits towards the infinite. Instead, all these sequences of images sent out from the 'it gazes', these fever curves of an unconscious gaze prove to be massively charged with subjectivity, which distinguishes them fundamentally from classic image-world extracts. And Jacques Lacan is among the first to provide an adequate media theory concerning this subjectivation of the images.

The theory of the unconscious gaze turned out to be the theory of the signifying procedure of desire, which is implemented respectively corpsified in a body. As has been demonstrated thoroughly above, the discrete temporality of the on/off, 0/1 sequence which is implemented in the real, encompasses the real as well in Lacan's view, which means that, from the moment of the division of being onwards, the bodies of the subjects ceaselessly fluctuate between the two states of being and non-being. According to the algorithm of the gaze, they transfer the electronic-eyed images via this infinite, significant process. Images emerge from an unconscious, which in turn can form multimedia systems with technical media. But this unconscious does not depict an existing reality, it does not provide objective images of reality, but generates a reality merging with the images themselves in the highly subjective manner of the 'it gazes' instead. Lacan's perspective acknowledges this new *episteme* and epistemology by no longer proceeding from a discerning philosopher-subject, but from an unconscious subject of desire, which is emitted from the image in form of a gaze.

Conversely, one could point out that Lacan's notions of the mediatized unconscious and the theory of the gaze open up a conception of mediality that is superbly fit to enable the access to the analysis of the specific subjectivity of images in the media age of 2010, and a connection to modern approaches in media studies as they have been developed by German media theorists e.g. Wolfgang Hagen, Astrid Deuber-Mankowsky, Marie Luise Angerer, Claus Pias, Ute Holl etc. Like Lacan, the latter choose the *a priori* antecedent of a perception and experience that is always formatted by media as their point of departure, and focus on the changes 'to which not only our perception of the body, but also our desire is subject to due to the interlacing of the new world of the media.'[49] Media make discontinuities and fractures appear in bodies, media write themselves into bodies, form networks with bodies, deform and reconfigure bodies; or, according to Lacan, bodies become media, and gazes are corpsified. And how could these gaze-generated images possibly be or glow or flicker in a manner that is not highly subjective? Here, the glow of the subjective becomes more intensive, to the same extent that the gatekeeper function of the disembodied-punctual Cartesian 'I see myself seeing myself' (*moi*) is disabled, and, correspondingly, the floodgates are opened to the 'it gazes' (*je*).

For the phenomenon of a subjectivization of images in modernity, which initially appeared enigmatic, and one of the central questions concerning this text, Lacan's theory of the gaze provides a possible approach, as it shows that images are not only transported through the silicon-cool netherworld of the digital machines heartless and indifferent, but also through bodies, where pain and longing and mortal death and the *Dionysia* of the blood seethe.

In conclusion, to turn the carousel of images once again, and to stimulate the gaze once more: where a computer only calculates aseptic sequences of 0 and 1, a body is necessary to experience all the wistfulness, all the recklessness and vertigo that come and go like Kate Moss and Pete Doherty at the Betty Ford Centre. *Filles fatales* between sex and sophistication, and high-end chasers with their Visconti decadence over black trumpet ravioli, and flan from sea urchins with arugula mousse in the harbour of St. Tropez. Rainbow souls, G spot of the eyes, my living: emergency room, blue moon and red poppies, praise the image, the God-descended…

Translated by Jochen Mevius

Notes

1   Concerning this see, for example, Marie Luise Angerer, *Body Options: Körper, Spuren, Medien, Bilder*, Vienna: Turia + Kant, 2000; Sherry Turkle, *Life on the Screen. Identity in the Age of the Internet*, New York: Simon & Schuster, 1995.

2   Cf. Jacques Lacan, *Schriften II* (ed. Norbert Haas and Hans-Joachim Metzger), Weinheim & Berlin: Quadriga, 1991a, pp. 192–95 & 228–29.

3   Cf. Dominic Kaegi (ed.), *Cassirer – Heidegger: 70 Jahre Davoser Disputation*, Hamburg: Meiner, 2002.

4 Jacques Lacan, *Das Seminar XI. Die Vier Grundbegriffe der Psychoanalyse (1963–1964)* (ed. Norbert Haas and Hans-Joachim Metzger), Weinheim & Berlin: Quadriga, 1987, pp. 78–79. (*The Four Fundamental Concepts of Psychoanalysis* (trans. Alan Sheridan), New York & London: Norton, 1998, p. 72).

5 Jacques Lacan, *Das Seminar II. Das Ich in der Theorie Freuds und in der Technik der Psychoanalyse (1954–1955)* (ed. Norbert Haas and Hans-Joachim Metzger), Weinheim & Berlin: Quadriga, 1991b, pp. 382–83 (translated by Jochen Mevius).

6 Jacques Lacan, *Das Seminar XX. Encore (1973–1974)* (ed. Norbert Haas and Hans-Joachim Metzger), Weinheim & Berlin: Quadriga, 1986, pp. 10 & 51.

7 Lacan, 1987, pp. 28–31 (1998, pp. 23–28).

8 ibid., p. 53. Concerning the concept of the division of being, cf. Jacques Lacan, *Schriften I* (ed. Norbert Haas and Hans-Joachim Metzger), Weinheim & Berlin: Quadriga, 1991c, p. 153; pp. 219–21.

9 Concerning Lacan's theory of the gaze in detail, cf. Lacan, 1987, pp. 67–119; Claudia Blümle and Anne von der Heiden (eds), *Blickzähmung und Augentäuschung. Zu Jacques LacansBildtheorie*, Zürich & Berlin: diaphanes, 2009; Hans-Dieter Gondek, 'Eine psychoanalytische Anthropologie des Bildes', in *RISS. Zeitschrift für Psychoanalyse. Freud. Lacan*, No. 48, 2000, pp. 9–28; August Ruhs, 'Triebquelle Auge/Triebobjekt Blick', in *texte. psychoanalyse, ästhetik, kulturkritik*, No. 3, 1999, pp. 107–23.

10 Lacan, 1987, p. 72.

11 ibid.

12 Cf. Lacan, 1987, pp. 85–86. Also cf. Jacques Lacan, *Das Seminar I. Freuds Technische Schriften (1953–1954)* (ed. Norbert Haas and Hans-Joachim Metzger), Weinheim & Berlin: Quadriga, 1990, pp. 98–107, 160–66 & 178–82. Concerning Lacan's optical models, see Blümle et al. (eds), 2009, pp. 7–19. Concerning the window-metaphor, see Joseph Vogl, 'Lovebirds', in Blümle et al. (eds), 2009, pp. 51–64. Cf. p. 56ff in Bernhard Siegert, 'Der Blickals Bild-Störung. Zwischen Mimesis und Mimikry', in Blümle et al. (eds), 2009, pp. 105–08 & 125–28.

13 Lacan, 1987, p. 85.

14 In the context of deconstructing the central-perspectival image, Lacan expressly points out the surrealist anamorphoses. Cf. Lacan, 1987, pp. 70–90.

15 Lacan, 1990, p. 106 (translated by Jochen Mevius).

16 Lacan, 1987, p. 72.

17 Vilém Flusser, *Medienkultur*, Frankfurt am Main, 2005, p. 176 (translated by Jochen Mevius).

18 ibid (translated by Jochen Mevius).

19 ibid., p. 177 (translated by Jochen Mevius).

20 Cf. Flusser, 2005, pp. 179 & 181.

21 ibid., pp. 179–80 (translated by Jochen Mevius).

22 ibid., p. 178 (translated by Jochen Mevius).

23 Lacan, 1990, p. 213 (translated by Jochen Mevius).

24 Cf. Flusser, 2005, p. 178.

25 Lacan expresses this notion in his famous formula, according to which a signifier represents a subject to another signifier (and not another subject!). Cf. Lacan, 1991a, p. 213; Lacan, 1986, pp. 154–55; Lacan, 1987, p. 165.

26 Flusser, 2005, p. 178 (translated by Jochen Mevius).

27 ibid., p. 179 (translated by Jochen Mevius).

28 ibid., p. 180 (translated by Jochen Mevius).

29 Concerning the theory of the mirror stage, cf. also Lacan, 1991c, pp. 63–70 and Lacan, 1991b, pp. 85 & 183–84. Cf. also Peter Widmer, *Angst. Erläuterungen zu Lacans Seminar X*, Bielefeld: transcript, 2004, pp. 11–52.

30 'Between-I' denotes precisely the temporary images of self, respectively Others that the I has identified with in the course of its life, insofar that they are divided into their significant basic elements and thus become storable in the unconscious, which can only account for significants, but no signifiers (images). At the same time, they can be recalled and synthesized anew in dreams for the construction of cover memories or composite personalities. Cf. Jacques Lacan, *Das Seminar III. Die Psychosen (1955–1956)*, Weinheim & Berlin: Quadriga, 1997.

31 Lacan, 1991b, p. 200 (translated by Jochen Mevius).

32 Cf. Lacan, 1990, pp. 20–21; Lacan, 1991b, p. 58.

33 Lacan, 1990, p. 20 (translated by Jochen Mevius).

34 Vilém Flusser, 'The City as Wave-Trough in the Image-Flood', in *Critical Inquiry*, Vol. 31, No. 2, 2005, pp. 324–25.

35 Flusser, 2005, pp. 177–78 (translated by Jochen Mevius).

36 Lacan, 1990, pp. 219–20.

37 Lacan delimits the *objet petit a* as a lack of second order or lack of object from the lack of being ('manque de l'être'), as described above. In the course of being afflicted with this lack of being, the subject becomes discrete: a division is introduced into the real prehistoric-mythic being, enabling it to realize two different discrete states – being and non-being – in a temporal-operational manner, enabling it to oscillate like an electric wire or an electromagnetic wave. If this process was limited to this first operation, life and course of the subject would be a continual, impotent sequence of moments of being/non-being; a bad infinity constituting itself from pure signifiers, which would not be interrupted by a single moment transferring desire via words, sounds or images. Hypercodification is necessary for this purpose, and here the *objet petit a* functions as the decisive operator. Developed from the hypercodification or potentialization of the un-prethinkable and unimaginable lack of being, the *objet petit a* offers the possibility to represent or imagine the lack of being as a factual lack of an object, a vacancy or emptiness. Therefore, at the same time, the subject is enabled to transfer the 'that' of his own discrete dividedness by the way of the *objet petit a* as the invisible integrative centre of the image or, simply, as a gaze, and to project it in infinite and numerous sugar-pastel, surreal, Microsoft and Kafkaesque sceneries. Regarding the *objet petit a* cf. Lacan, 1991a, pp. 9–12, 142–56 & 177–203; Lacan, 1987, pp. 53–64, 136–73 & 263–76; Cf. Slavoj Zizek, *Liebe Dein Symptom wie Dich Selbst! Jacques Lacans Psychoanalyse und die Medien*, Berlin: Merve, 1991, p. 43ff & 81–89; Cf. Slavoj Zizek, *Die Tücke des Subjekts*, Frankfurt am Main: Suhrkamp, 2001, pp. 24–30 & 151–52; Andreas Cremonini, *Die Durchquerung des Cogito. Lacan contra Sartre*, Munich: Fink, 2003, pp. 144–60.

38 Flusser, 2005, p. 179. With reference to Flusser's notion of the duality materiality/immateriality, cf. also the chapter 'Der Schein der Materie', especially pp. 216–22.

39   In his book *La Machine de Vision* (1988), Paul Virilio distinguishes between three ages of the image. The first age of the image is the age of the formal logic of the image; it is realized in painting, etching and architecture, and it corresponds to the level of reality. The age of the dialectal logic of the image is introduced by Virilio as the second age of the image: realized in photography and cinematography, it finds its equivalent in the level of actuality. The third age of the image turns out to be the age of the paradox logic of the image. It is defined by videography, holography as well as infography and can be correlated to the level of virtuality. Cf. Paul Virilio, *Die Sehmaschine*, Berlin: Merve, 1989.

40   Cf. Lacan, 1990, pp. 99–106.

41   Flusser, 2005, pp. 181–82 (translated by Jochen Mevius).

42   Lacan, 1986, p. 37 (translated by Jochen Mevius).

43   Lacan, 1987, pp. 75–76.

44   Cf. Jacques Derrida, 'Die Différance', in *Randgänge der Philosophie*, Vienna: Passagen, 1988, 1996, pp. 29–52.

45   Cf. Károly Simonyi, *Kulturgeschichte der Physik*, Leipzig and Berlin: Urania, 1990, pp. 275–320.

46   Regarding the history and principles of electromagnetism, cf. Simonyi, 1990, pp. 320–55; Wolfgang Hagen, *Das Radio. Theorie und Geschichte des Hörfunks Deutschland – USA*, Munich: Fink, 2005, pp. 6–44; Bernhard Siegert, *Passage des Digitalen. Zeichenpraktiken der Neuzeitlichen Wissenschaften 1500–1900*, Berlin: Brinkmann and Bose, 2003, pp. 341–44.

47   Lambertz is a German biscuit manufacturer.

48   Zentis is a German jam manufacturer.

49   Astrid Deuber-Mankowsky, *Lara Croft. Modell, Medium, Cyberheldin*, Frankfurt am Main: Suhrkamp, 2001, p. 14.

PART IV

Material Specters and the Lives of Images

Chapter 15

The Sequence Image Between Motion and Stillness

Jens Schröter

Introduction: The Sequence Image

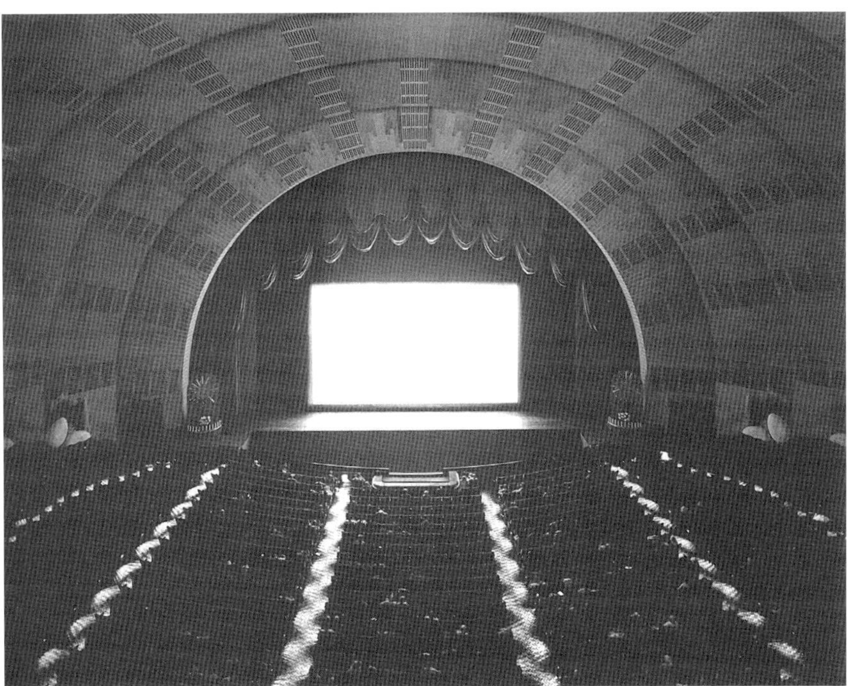

Figure 1: Hiroshi Sugimoto, *Radio Music Hall, NY,* 1978.

We see a room. A curved ceiling, rows of seats, people here and there. A cinema auditorium. However, where we would expect to see the movie playing, there is only a blindingly white rectangle reduplicating the shape of the entire image. This photograph is part of the *Theatres* series by Japanese photographer Hiroshi Sugimoto: *Radio Music Hall, NY* (1978). The series is conceived as a sequence of photographs of cinema auditoriums (as well as open-air cinemas) taken with the shutter opened for the entire length of the film performance. Thus what we see is the motionless image of a movement image and that is: nothing. Or, to be more precise, we see nothing of the film images' movement, only the light from the projected images. In cinematographic films one image follows another. Here, they are layered on top of each other, overexposing the photograph. Their temporal succession is transformed into spatial simultaneousness, and in the process all information is lost. The image shows that an excessive amount of information equals no information at all – white noise: the screen is white, just like a blank canvas. Yet the screen is not simply empty, for it reflects light; only because of this glow is the cinema auditorium visible. The auditorium, as this photograph clearly shows, enfolds the moving or time-based film images like a frame.

Sugimoto's beautiful work demonstrates at least two things.[1] First, there is a fundamental difference between the movement or time image of the cinematographic film and the motionless images of photography. Time and space do not simply translate into each other. Sugimoto demonstrates this by taking the conventional practice of photography to its limits. If he had used a short exposure time – as is standard practice for many applications of photography, and particularly when the inscription of motion blur needs to be minimized – a single image from the projected film would have been visible, a tiny excerpt of the film. The cinema auditorium would have been barely visible or not at all, because far too little reflected light would have been captured. However, Sugimoto prolongs the exposure time, but despite this attempt to capture film adequately, all that remains on the screen is white noise. Second, by making the cinema auditorium, seats, etc. visible, Sugimoto shows that the utterly ephemeral moving images of the film have historically been given a robust architectonic frame in which the conditions of its emergence are manifest: 'As cultural techniques, signifying practices are always connected to individual and specific, institutionally defined *spaces*, special "semiotopes", so to speak'.[2] The architectonic space is not in motion at all – as the long exposure time proves – otherwise the image would be blurred. It embodies the highest degree of immobility, and precisely because of this, it provides space for the movement image. This also applies to the screen itself: if it was moving – if for example it was to change its position constantly – the light from the film would not add up to that brilliant white. In this way, Sugimoto shows that the moving images of film appear in an immobile place.

The emphasis Sugimoto puts on the clear and insurmountable difference between the static and the moving image is, I would argue, not only symptomatic of his 'media archaeology', as one commentator has put it.[3] Nothing seems more obvious than this simple opposition: there are moving and non-moving images. There are no 'slightly moving' images, just as a woman cannot be only 'a bit pregnant', for example.[4] There are, however, overlooked and even suppressed phenomena which confuse the clear delineation of these opposites.

Before I discuss these, I would like to draw attention to the general fact that mainstream media histories tend to neglect a relatively high number of phenomena, and there seem to be at least two reasons for this: an ontological and an empirical reason. Let us take the example of holography: although it does not contribute anything substantial to the problem of the moving image, it needs to be mentioned as an important instance of an excluded image type. To my knowledge, the lens-less image produced by holography is not considered in any history of optical media.[5] In the first place, this is a result of ontological preconceptions: Friedrich Kittler, for example, argues in his book *Optische Medien* (*Optical Media*) that 'all optical media even today' would require 'lens systems'.[6] On this premise, it is hardly surprising that the holographic, lens-less image process, which is wave-optical (and not geometrical-optical) has not become part of the history of optical media. Therefore, it is not included in Kittler's research, either. The second reason, which often overlaps with the first, lies in the conventional centring of media histories on the artistic or the mass media system, or both. All media technologies not established in at least one of these areas simply disappear from media history. Therefore, holography is often classed as too experimental and marginal, a wacky gimmick for tasteless bric-a-brac shops, on the basis of certain aesthetic premises grounded in the art system. It is considered too insignificant, although this is empirically simply not the case. In science (for example, in particle detectors), in the testing of materials, in the scanning devices of supermarket cash registers, on bank notes and credit cards, holography has important and widely used applications, for example for authentification.[7]

To put it briefly, holography is an example of omissions in media history (as a discipline) that permit the construction of essentialist descriptions. The assumption that all optical media are based upon lens systems, and thus on geometrical optics or linear perspective, is such an essentialist description. 'Omissions' and 'suppressions', however, are necessary to create clear and binary oppositions, such as 'analogue' versus 'digital' media.[8] Paraphrasing Bruno Latour, one could say that borderline cases and hybrids are cleared out in order to establish neat distinctions.[9] But what kind of 'omissions' and 'suppressions' in the history of optical media facilitate the construction of an exclusive dichotomy of the moving versus the non-moving image?

In this context, by 'omissions' I do not mean phenomena such as the 'freeze frame'; that is, filmic images that appear to be still images. The moving bits of fluff or scratches on such images make the movement of the image visible, even when the manifest content of the image appears to be static (for example, when photographs are shown in a movie).[10] The phenomena I am referring to hardly ever appear in the history of optical media, and irritate the dichotomy between non-moving and moving image. Three examples spring to mind, but there may be more:

1. The flip book, to which the Kunsthalle Düsseldorf devoted an impressive catalogue in 2005, thus incorporating them into the art system; all of a sudden flip books became a subject of discourse [11]

2. Multiplex holography [12]
3. Certain types of lenticular images.

To begin with, it seems to me that these phenomena, although in many ways entirely different from one another, have the following characteristics in common:

- They show very short sequences of moving images, which, unlike seemingly related examples from very early film,[13] cannot be prolonged for technological reasons.
- More importantly: the emergence of movement depends on the movements of the viewer. Flip books contain a series of still pictures, turning into moving image sequences through small movements of the hands. Certain types of lenticular images are also set in motion only through movements of the hands or through movements of the entire body, and appear static, without movement, to the immobile viewer. This also holds for multiplex holography. Put differently, photographs always appear to be static, no matter how much the viewers move. Films or television images always appear as though in motion, no matter how much the viewers move. In the phenomena that are discussed here, though, the movement of the image depends on the movements of the viewer.

For the time being, I suggest to subsume these phenomena under the rubric 'sequence images'.[14] Two points need mentioning with respect to this rubric: first, the term 'sequence image' may be somewhat irritating because it immediately calls to mind images of comics or cartoons, which I am not referring to here, nor indeed to chrono-photographs. Second, there seems to be a relationship between already mentioned phenomena such as the flip book, and the computer-based images recently – and rather imprecisely – described as 'interactive'. Presumably, there is a kind of fluid transition, although the term 'interactive image' is a very general characterization and ultimately only means tracking the behaviour of a user and computing the image parameters. One option (among many) is to let images move when the viewers move. Furthermore, the movement of these images is not restricted to one short sequence.

In the following section, I shall consider the last of my three examples in more detail: a certain type of lenticular image.

Lenticular Images: History and Applications

The origin of the lenticular image can be traced back to a patent application of 1915. The patent was filed by a man named Walter Hess,[15] and it concerned a process whereby stereoscopic images could be viewed without the necessity of a special pair of glasses. As a result, the patent specification was simply titled 'Stereoscopic Picture'.[16]

First, the author described how the stereoscopic process then in use presented a different image to each eye. This was also the case in Hess' process: 'two ordinary stereoscopic

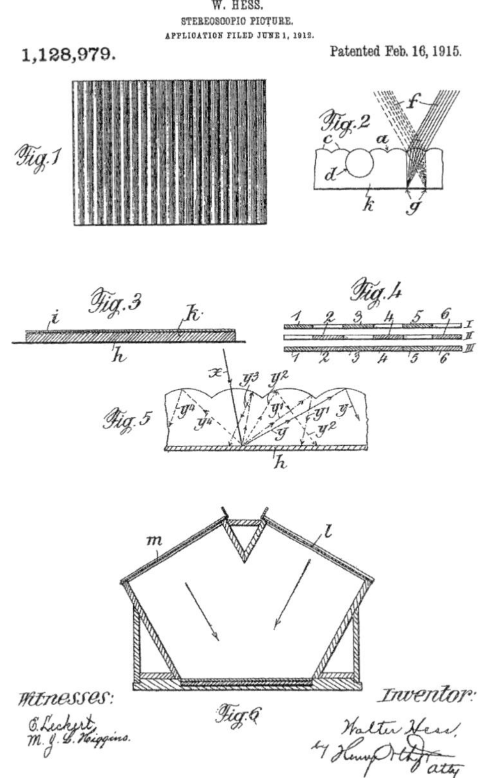

Figure 2: Diagram of a lenticular image.[17]

negatives are used'.[18] The pair of stereoscopic images is used to expose a film, upon which lies an array of cylindrical lenses (Figure 1 in Figure 2 from above; Figure 2 shows the array in cross-section; [d] shows the cylindrical structure). Figure 2 shows how light rays (f) from two different directions are focused on two image points (g) by one of the cylindrical lenses. The two sources of light rays correspond to the two images of a pair of stereoscopic pictures (Figure 6 shows a proposal for a recording device; the two pictures are mounted at the points [m] and [l]). The result is, as Figure 4 shows, that there are pairs of exposed images (I + II) on the light sensitive coating of the film material that form a fine pattern of image strips side by side on the photographic plate (III). When one now looks at the lenticular images, the image strips are directed one at each eye, and a stereoscopic image impression is created without the necessity of special glasses – for this reason lenticular images are also referred to as auto-stereoscopic images.

Obviously, it is not necessary to use a pair of stereoscopic images to create the image strips – one can also use two different images so that when the viewer moves, one image switches to another.[19] Alternatively – and this is the point – one can use two images showing two phases of a motion sequence: when a viewer moves in front of the image, it creates the impression that the image is moving. Within a short time, Hess' process was refined and permitted the recording of more than two images, and thus the storage and playback of short motion sequences became possible. It is impossible, though, to increase the number of images indefinitely – today, the limit is thirty pictures, for, as mentioned above, the sequences in the lenticular process cannot be 'extended' to any length (for example, to a lenticular recording of a two-hour feature film).

With the development of new polymers at the end of World War II, the lenses were further improved and decreased in size. In the USA, the famous magazine *Look* initiated a minor fad for lenticular images when it gave away a postcard-size, stereo-lenticular picture of a bust of Thomas Alva Edison in their issue of 25 February 1964. The process continued to spread with various modifications: lenticular postcards with or without 3D-effects, and with or without animations are still available. Today, one even finds small lenticular pictures on packages of breakfast cereals, for example.[20] Quite recently, these developments wrung a sigh from artist Andrew Hurle, who also works with lenticular pictures: 'Like many innovations in 3D imaging, [the lenticular picture] was hailed as a major leap forward in pictorial representation before failing to develop into anything much more than a novel element in advertising and packaging.'[21]

Precisely these uses – 'advertising' and 'packaging' – are central today, and in what follows, I shall discuss a contemporary example.

Figure 3 shows the Supermotion website of Touchmore Gmbh., a company from Remscheid, a mid-size town in Germany that specializes in innovative advertising products.

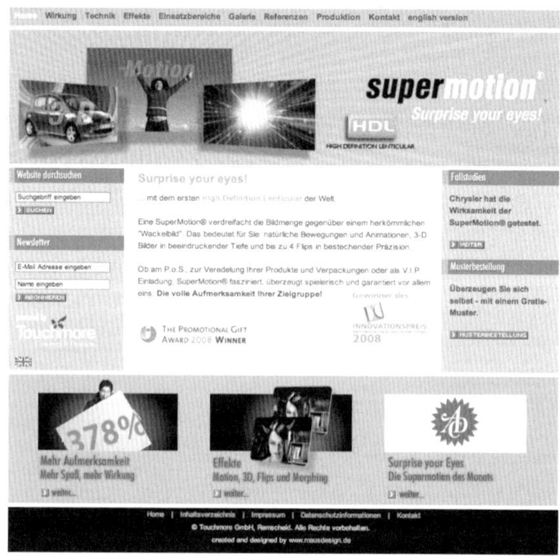

Figure 3: Supermotion website.[22]

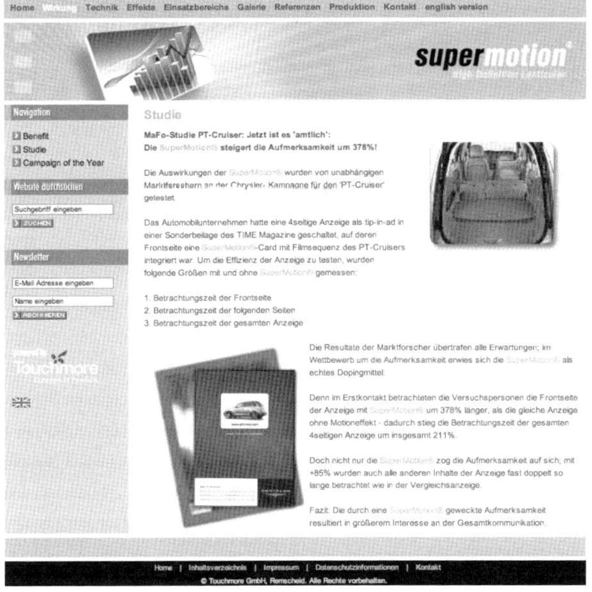

Figure 4: Supermotion website, *Studie* section.[23]

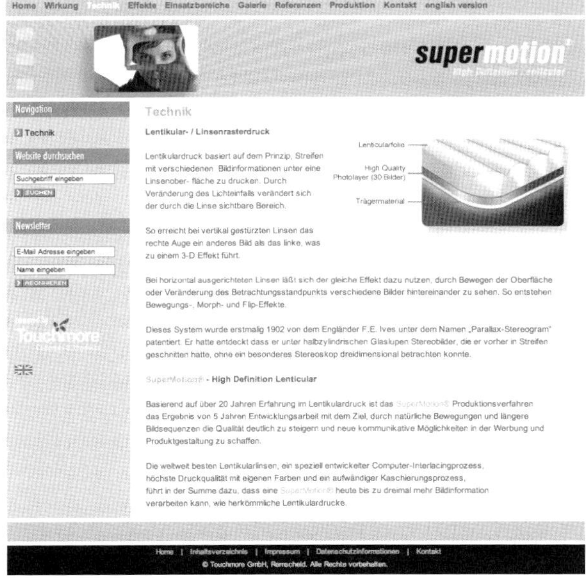

Figure 5: Supermotion website, *Technik* section.[25]

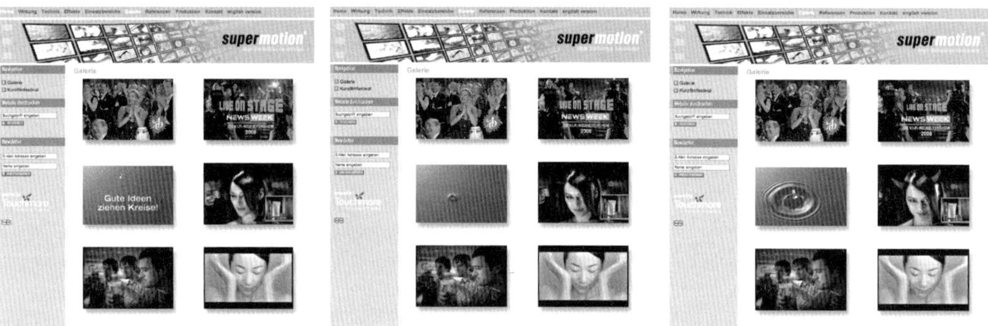

Figures 6a–c: Images from the *Galerie* section.[26]

It is the advertisement for a product called *Supermotion*. The main selling point is the attention that this product – cards the size of telephone or credit cards – attracts. Citing statistical data, Touchmore praises the effectiveness of the 'MotionCard', which – as the technological section of the website makes clear – is a form of the lenticular picture.[24]

On this card, one can see a short motion sequence, whose movement is entirely dependent on the movement of the viewer's hands: a sequence image. That is, movie clips are no longer restricted to an impressive cinema auditorium – its classic 'semiotope' – but can be found in a profane trouser pocket. The gallery of the website presents various examples.

The idea is to put very short advertising spots on these cards and distribute them: the product can be specifically aimed at a presumably male market, like beer, while ads for sexy

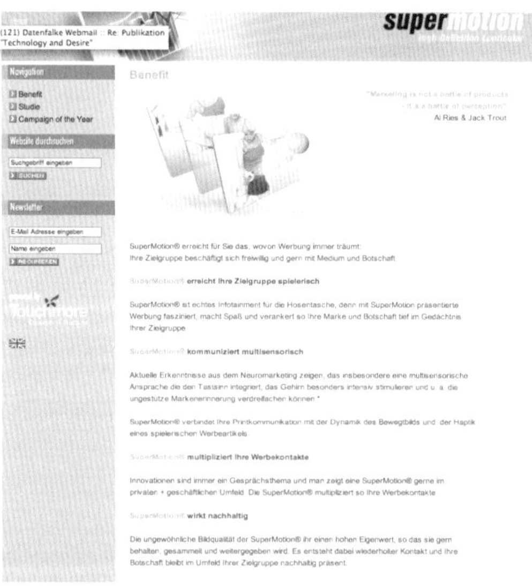

Figure 7: Supermotion website, *Benefit* section.[28]

cosmetics and exorbitantly-priced skin care products promising eternal youth will mostly target women. The advantages of the MotionCard are praised on another web page with reference to McLuhan: 'SuperMotion® achieves for your product what advertising has always dreamed of: your target group devotes itself voluntarily and with pleasure to the medium and the message.'[27] Note that the MotionCard is not intended to focus attention exclusively on the message but also on the medium – the card.

The MotionCard effectively lifts the commercial clip out of the flow of televisual images, where it is usually located, and transforms it into an isolated entity. Only short sequences can be used on the cards so they must be as eye-catching as possible, for in thirty images – slightly longer than one second of film – it is not possible to develop a narrative. Notwithstanding, the isolated status of the clip probably raises viewers' level of attention to the message. And, as the producer correctly says, this effect is enhanced further because the image on this ordinary looking card begins to move when it is moved. Since both media studies and common sense dictate that images are either moving or non-moving, this collapse of categories gives rise to an irritation that, in turn, heightens awareness of the medium itself. Another source of irritation is the sudden appearance of moving images in unlikely places. Unlike Sugimoto's dazzling white screen, these cards are mobile. Normally, one would have to go to a cinema to see moving images, or at least turn on the television or use a smartphone. Here, however, the moving images simply appear out of a trouser pocket, 'without electricity or micro-electronics', and are embedded in an entirely different practice. Lastly, Touchmore proudly names some of their

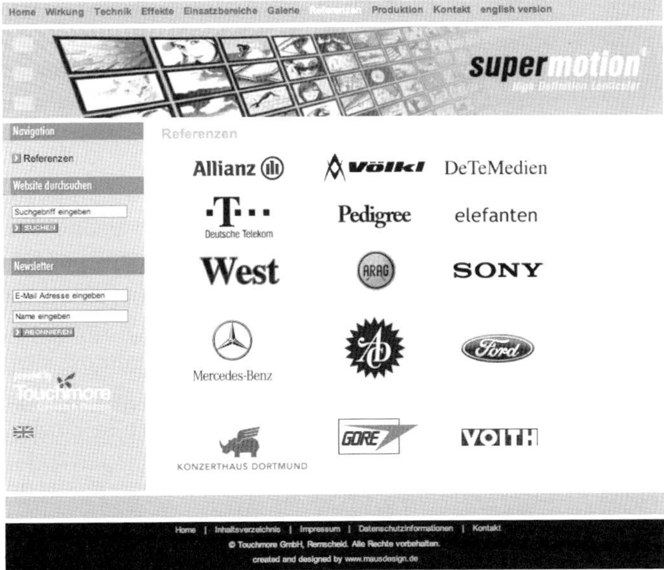

Figure 8: Supermotion website, *Referenzen* section.[29]

customers, among them global players, who already use this product, in order to attract even more interest.

Theoretical Implications and Conclusion

We are concerned here with moving images that have relatively little in common with moving images in cinema, on television, on video, DVD or computer. Unlike the moving images of flip books (and even this does not hold true because of the widely distributed artists' flip books in the twentieth century), these moving images cannot be considered part of the prehistory of 'proper' moving images; that is, the moving images of film, TV, video, DVD and the computer. These images make use of the current state of art technology. What does this mean for theories of the moving image? Any general theory would need to cover all types of moving images and not only specific ones, otherwise a film theory or television theory would suffice. This consideration raises at least two problematic issues: scale and body techniques.

Scale

A theory of the moving image must avoid implicit preliminary decisions concerning the scale of the moving image. Here, I follow Michel Callon and Bruno Latour:

> *There are* of course macro-actors and micro-actors, but the difference between them is brought about by power relations and the constructions of networks that will *elude analysis* if we presume *a priori* that macro-actors are bigger than or superior to micro-actors.[30]

The process of scaling between micro and macro can also be understood temporally: a movement image of one second is as much a moving image as one that moves for two hours. The latter's culturally privileged status is most likely due to the fact that it is able to narrate stories, develop *philosophemes*, evolve characters and modulate formal principles; it connects to literature and literary studies, to art and art history, and to philosophy (cf. for example Gilles Deleuze). The sequence image is, by contrast, almost sheer movement. It conveys scarcely more than rudimentary advertising messages. Its mere unexpected, attention-catching movement is its real message, and therefore in a certain way, it is the prototypical and exemplary 'movement image'. This holds in particular for images in societies organized as market economies, where attention is an end in itself. If it has not yet become the subject of moving image theory, this is due to the preference for semantics or formal structures 'conveyed by' movement, and due to the neglect of movement itself. The 'macro-movement image', therefore, is classified *a priori* as 'bigger than or superior to' the 'micro-movement image' (as the sequence image can also be termed). Instead, one could raise the question how and why the 'superiority' of the 'macro-movement-image' was produced in the first place: by linking bare movement to temporally expanded semantics and/or forms.

Hiroshi Sugimoto's *Theatres* series is a good example to illustrate this. Because the 'macro-movement-image' is inscribed for – let's say – two hours in the static image, it appears as purest white. Sugimoto links the film image with photography in a specific way and so foregrounds the temporal expansion of the movement-image. With this, he renders the difference between the static and the moving image relevant. Artistic strategies of media self-referentiality do not refer to a presupposed ontological difference like, for example, the moving versus the non-moving image – that would be redundant then anyway; rather, they exemplarily produce it.[31] Media theories seeking to define media specificity tend to draw on such examples. In describing the heterogeneous diversity of technological media and their forms there is a desire to reduce this diversity to glaringly simplistic dichotomies – which is why I began this essay with the example of Sugimoto. But strictly speaking, such utterly self-evident argumentative dichotomies ought to be avoided.

Body Techniques

With good reason, Friedrich Kittler once warned about the 'overemphasis on the body, which is fashionable among contemporary scholars'.[32] Still, as I have already pointed out, I believe that a further characteristic of the sequence image is its relationship to the body of the observer. The established and well-discussed types of the 'movement image' move independently of whether the body of the observer moves. Indeed, it is a constitutive feature of watching films that the body is immobilized on seats in a cinema only illuminated by the screen, as shown in Sugimoto's photo: if the spectators' bodies were moving, they would be hardly visible because of the photograph's long exposure time. By contrast, to perceive the sequence image the observer must at least move to a certain extent – I have already mentioned how the representation of the hand tilting the card functions as an 'instruction manual' on the SuperMotion website. The website states: 'Innovations are always a hot topic, and it's fun to show off *SuperMotion*® to business and private acquaintances. And that' show *SuperMotion*® multiplies your advertising contacts.' One shows the card around, draws attention to its curious effect, demonstrates how one has to tilt it, and hands it to someone so they can try it out. Not only is the MotionCard with its movement-images distributed, but also the body techniques that mobilize it. Further, it is also intended to stimulate discourse production about the innovative character of this advertising medium (and *a fortiori* the innovative character of those who employ such an advertising medium): its purpose is to initiate communication – if it succeeds in this, the card will no longer be needed.

It is somewhat problematic, anyway, to analyze the moving image separated from the body techniques in which it is embedded. The lenticular picture on the MotionCard functions like the filmic image, at least with regard to the fact that it results from a sequence of stills. However, even if it was as long as a film, it would still be associated with different body techniques: tilting, showing it around and demonstrating how to tilt it. Naturally, this notion is not an original idea of mine: that the spectators in a cinema are resting in their seats has long been an important theme, for example, in psychoanalytic film theory.[33] Certain spectator activities, though – like eating popcorn – were left out, as Vinzenz Hediger has reminded us in a wonderful essay.[34] Moreover, the difference between the behaviour of television viewers and that of cinemagoers, and the different role of sound has long been an object of study.[35]

In this context, I would like to propose a shift of emphasis: the practices of the movement image are not external to it. The body techniques together with the movement image form a unique, if heterogeneous arrangement. This is shown in an exemplary way by the sequence image: it is not a moving image to which the practice of tilting, showing around, and talking about it is added – it is a movement image if and only if linked with body techniques.

The sequence image offers an opportunity to liberate the discussion of moving images from its implicit centering on cinema and television. And this is the general conclusion to be drawn from my considerations: the apparently marginal and peripheral phenomena of media history – in our case here, sequence images – have the potential to destabilize the theoretical models oriented on the art and mass media system. A general theory of the movement image – to use Deleuze's words – will have to rethink the question of scale and also of body technique in order to arrive at a new concept of the moving image.

Translated by Jochen Mevius and Nicola Glaubitz

Notes

1   Cf. Hans Belting, 'Sugimotos Film', in Thomas Hensel et al. (eds), *Das Bewegte Bild. Film und Kunst*, Munich: Fink, 2000, pp. 283–92.

2   (German translation: 'Zeichenpraktiken sind als Kulturtechniken mit jeweils besonderen institutionell definierten *Räumen* verknüpft, speziellen "Semiotopen", wie man sagen könnte.' Bernhard Siegert, 'Was sind Kulturtechniken? Beschreibung des Lehr- und Fachgebiets', http://www.uni-weimar.de/medien/kulturtechniken/kultek.html, accessed 20 April 2009.

3   Pia Müller-Tamm, 'Double Infinity. Über Anfang und Ende in Sugimotos neuesten Werken', in *Hiroshi Sugimoto*, exhibition catalogue, Ostfildern: Hatje Cantz, 2007, p. 39.

4   Cf. François Albera, 'Vom Standbild zum Bewegungsbild. Über einige neuere Theorien des Films', in *Cinema*, Vol. 30, 1984, pp. 60–69. Albera was already aware that different theorists have very different notions about what the 'essence' of film is (for Deleuze, it is irreducibly movement, whereas for Barthes it is found precisely in the non-moving photogram); however, Albera presupposed these differences as givens.

5   See Ulrike Hick, *Geschichte der optischen Medien*, Munich: Fink, 1999.

6   Friedrich Kittler, *Optical Media: Berlin Lectures*, Cambridge: Polity Press, 2010, p. 71.

7   Cf. Jens Schröter, *3D. Zur Geschichte, Theorie und Medienästhetik des technisch-transplanen Bildes*, Munich: Fink, 2009, Chapter 9.

8   For a critical perspective, see Jens Schröter, 'Analog/Digital – Opposition oder Kontinuum?', in Jens Schröter and Alexander Böhnke (eds), *Analog/Digital – Opposition oder Kontinuum? Zur Theorie und Geschichte einer Unterscheidung*, Bielefeld: transcript, 2004, pp. 7–30.

9   Bruno Latour, *We Have Never Been Modern*, Cambridge, MA: Harvard University Press, 1993.

10 On photography in film, see *Nach dem Film*, No. 8, 'FotoKino', http://www.nachdemfilm.de/no8/no8start.html, accessed 3 January 2008. Cf. Stefanie Diekmann and Winfried Gerling (eds), *Freeze Frames: Zum Verhältnis von Fotografie und Film*, Bielefeld: transcript, 2010.

11 Kunsthalle Düsseldorf (ed.), *Daumenkino. The Flip Book Show*, Düsseldorf: Snoeck, 2005.

12 Cf. Sean Johnston, *Holographic Visions: A History of New Science*, Oxford & New York: Oxford University Press, 2006, pp. 212–16. Cf. Jens Schröter, 'Technologies Beyond the Still and the Moving Image: The Case of the Multiplex Hologram', in *History of Photography*, Vol. 35, No. 1, 2011, pp. 23–32.

13 On the early film as a 'loop' and the revival of this form in digital media aesthetics, see Lev Manovich, *The Language of New Media*, Cambridge, MA: MIT Press, 2001, pp. 314–22.

14 Victor Burgin has also used the notion 'sequence image'; see Victor Burgin, *The Remembered Film*, London: Reaktion Books, 2004, pp. 14–28. But he means something completely different, namely the personal memory of films once seen, often condensed in sequences.

15 I was unable to discover whether his real name was Hess or Hesse – as given in later publications.

16 Cf. Walter Hess, 'Stereoscopic Picture', in Stephen Benton (ed.), *Selected Papers on Three-dimensional Displays*, Vol. MS 162, Bellingham, WA: SPIE Press, 2001, pp. 291–94. In his introduction, Stephen Benton remarks that '[m]any improvements in optical plastics, the design of the single refracting surface available, and fabrication technologies have greatly improved the performance of the simple lenticular sheet, although the basic principle remains as Hess described it': in Benton, 2001, p. xx. There are various theories about the origin of lenticular technology; some writers even date it back to Ives' parallax barrier method of 1902. Although this is a similar approach because two (or more) images are recorded as stripes, however, a battery of lenses is not used. Instead, they are placed behind a series of vertically-aligned opaque and transparent bars; cf. Herbert E. Ives, 'A Novel Stereogram', in *Journal of the Franklin Institute*, Vol. 153, 1902, pp. 51–52; S. H. Kaplan, 'Theory of Parallax Barriers', in *Journal of the SMPTE*, Vol. 59, No. 7, 1952, pp. 11–21.

17 Hess, 2001, p. 294.

18 ibid., p. 291.

19 According to Gerald Oster, the French painter G. A. Bois-Clair had this idea and realized it as early as 1692 – obviously without lenticular lenses. Bois-Clair painted two pictures in strips on two sides of a wooden rod with a triangular cross-section. A passing observer would see one image change into a second picture; see Gerald Oster, 'Optical Art', in *Applied Optics*, Vol. 4, No. 11, 1959, pp. 1359–369.

20 Like the technically very different holograms, such pictures are sometimes affixed to products because they are very difficult or even impossible to copy, and therefore guarantee

that the article is genuine. It is not possible to go into this very interesting aspect of technical non-reproducibility here; see Jens Schröter et al. (eds), *Kulturen des Kopierschutzes*, Vol. 1 & 2, Siegen, 2010.

21 From http://www.andrewhurle.com/28/28.html, accessed 20 April 2009.

22 http://www.supermotion.de/, accessed 20 April 2009.

23 http://www.supermotion.de/wirkung/studie.html, accessed 20 April 2009.

24 This website puts the date of the beginning of lenticular pictures back to Ives' parallax barriers of 1902; cf. footnote 16 above.

25 http://www.supermotion.de/technik/technik.html, accessed 20 April 2009.

26 http://www.supermotion.de/galerie/galerie.html, accessed 20 April 2009.

27 Originally the text on the website is in German. It has been translated here for better readability.

28 http://www.supermotion.de/wirkung/benefit.html, accessed 20 April 2009.

29 http://www.supermotion.de/galerie/referenzen.html, accessed 20 April 2009.

30 Michel Callon and Bruno Latour, 'Unscrewing the Big Leviathan: How actors macrostructure reality and how sociologists help them to do so', in K. Knorr-Cetina and A.V. Cicourel (eds), *Advances in Social Theory and Methodology. Toward an Integration of Micro- and Macro-sociologies*, Boston, MA: Routledge & Kegan Paul, 1981, p. 280 (emphasis by Callon and Latour).

31 See Jens Schröter, 'Das ur-intermediale Netzwerk und die (Neu-)Erfindung des Mediums im (digitalen) Modernismus. Ein Versuch', in Joachim Paech and Jens Schröter (eds), *Intermedialität analog/digital. Theorien, Methoden, Analysen*, Munich: Fink, 2008, pp. 579–601.

32 Kittler, 2010, p. 148.

33 Cf. Christian Metz, *Psychoanalysis and Cinema: The Imaginary Signifier*, London & Basingstoke: Macmillan, 1983, pp. 99–142.

34 Vinzenz Hediger, 'Das Popkornessen als Vervollständigungshandlung der synästhetischen Erfahrung des Kinos. Anmerkungen zu einem Defizit der Filmtheorie', in *montage/av*, Vol. 10, No. 2, 2001, pp. 67–76.

35 Cf. John Ellis, *Visible Fictions. Cinema – Television – Video*, London & New York: Routledge, 1992.

Chapter 16

Gaze and Withdrawal: On the 'Logic' of Iconic Structures

Dieter Mersch

Image and Gaze

It is not always easy to decide whether something is an image or not. Some objects are images without revealing themselves as such, while others are not images at all, and only appear like them. Design objects have a genuine image-like quality, as their iconicity conceals their materiality, while the actual value of the object is assessed according to its form, its exterior appearance. On the other hand – especially in the context of science and technology – we are confronted with iconic textures like maps, blueprints and diagrams which cannot be subsumed under the category of the pictorial, as they are much closer to writings which have to be 'read' than to images which have to be viewed. This does not mean that one cannot talk about 'the image' in general, just because only particular images and objects exist, and their singularity leads beyond the scope of any unified term – although it appears to be problematic to speak of 'the image' in an all-encompassing singular way, in order to gather and collect the characteristics of 'all' images. In contrast, the pictorial is to be understood in the sense of a special 'mediality', the structure of which is to be examined here. On the one hand, this structure participates in a structure of mediality itself; on the other hand, it preserves a characteristic order in this structure. It can be deciphered as an order of 'showing'.[1] It cannot be deduced solely via the structure of representation, or via the symbolic contents of the depiction, or via the techniques of visualization – the methods of making visible and being made visible. An examination of the close interplay of the gaze and the image must be included in the analysis of the pictorial. It is possible to differentiate between at least three levels of the iconic in this context: (1) the actual depiction or representation which, on occasion, may also turn up blank; (2) the methods of visuality with their specific aesthetic and technical strategies; as well as (3) ultimately those conditions which cause the eye to be fettered by a visible object, and allow vision to become aware of a visible in the first place.

This last relationship, however, proves to be extremely tricky and conflicted. Its complexity begins with the fact that the image requires the gaze, while gazes do not inevitably generate images. As Merleau-Ponty points out, the image is primarily connected to invisibility,[2] requiring a particular gaze to initially see something *as* an image – a gaze that one can identify as a 'double vision.' This 'double vision' becomes the subject of the interplay between visibility and invisibility in multiple ways. If one wants to decipher the mediality of the pictorial and its structure, then one needs to proceed from this double gaze and its multiple interlacing between 'withdrawal' and 'excess.'

Pictoriality and Visibility

Initially, to see an image means to perceive something *as* an image as well as to perceive the things shown by the image. The phrasing alone alludes to an instance of duplicity: the 'image as image' as well as the 'image as a thing' that makes 'something' visible or brings it into view, regardless whether it is an object, a figure, a colour or a simple division of a tableau. Thus, a gaping difference exists between pictoriality and the creation of visibility, which nonetheless remains invisible 'in its quality' *as* a difference, because that which becomes visible only does so by virtue of the images themselves creating this visibility. This difference 'marks' the pictorial, as it is constitutive – *as* a difference – for the visibility of the image itself, as far as it represents the prerequisite for the possibility of iconic visuality: that is, an instance of invisibility constitutes a visibility, with a rift running between the visible and the invisible, not right through the image, but rather across it – in another dimension, so to speak. It does not split the image, it does not divide it, but separates it into image and *Ab-Bildung* ('likeness'), or medium and representation – in this context, the terms 'likeness' and 'representation' are to be used in their general meaning, from depiction to indication, from symbolization to that which 'offers' a view to the gaze.[3]

Of course, this difference leads to a number of consequences. First of all, to see an image therefore means to perceive it *as* an image – and not as something else. This finding also allows for an inversion: a thing that can be perceived as an image may alternatively not be seen as such. Accordingly, seeing an image permits a change of attention; the literal 'reflection' of the image as a thing, its construction, its usage, its hanging or its materiality. We are not able to perform this change intentionally, we cannot employ it freely to shift back and forth between perspectives; in fact, complicated medial strategies are necessary at times to carry out this inversion, and art has developed numerous practices to blur and irritate the gaze. While we do not control the gaze and thus the image, it is not unusual for the image to control us, to captivate us and to force its direction upon us, making 'other' means of detachment and distancing necessary to disentangle ourselves from its illusion and its powers of deception.

The other aspect of this difference results in images being less expressive; they are not so much disposed to impart something to the observer, but rather – as has been suggested above – show. Images are certainly quite able to 'tell' something, but where they represent or intimate something, they represent or intimate in a mode of showing. This showing, or indication, differs from observation and also from comprehension because it opens up a view; but the visible generated thus – even if it is the visibility of a thing – is different from merely seeing a thing. René Magritte coined the *apercu* that pictures are viewed differently than objects in space.[4] This suggestion hints at the special medial status of the image, namely the difference between the visible, which is constituted by it and the visual that we encounter. It implies that the visible of the image is different from the visible of the non-image that we face in our visual experience – even if the image itself belongs to the things, which exist in space and can be experienced as such. This also means that the gaze towards the image differs from the gaze in normal perception, even if they both relate to each other. Apparently, some quality must be added so that something can be seen *in* the image, just as, inversely, something normally pertaining to the object is not enough to turn it into an image; in point of fact, the pictorial quality is experienced first and foremost due to a specific 'kind of perception', which turns something into an 'image of something', just as the image has a quality which turns the thing – that one can experience visually – into a 'representation'.

The aforementioned difference is not always easy to spot, particularly since many things which ostensibly do not perform as images can turn into an image if one observes them through the lens of the iconic gaze. This gaze, on the other hand, only exists where images have already been experienced: the view of a landscape, a look through a window, mirrors, photographs, monochrome canvasses, masks, patterns on a wallpaper or geometric figures and simple, coloured rags nailed to a wall. It is their 'framing' which turns these sights into images – although not necessarily, as they can be perceived differently or even not at all. Consequently, the perception of a frame appears as the quality, which has to be added to the gaze, to perception itself, in order to turn it into an iconic experience. At the same time, framing does not automatically refer to that thing which surrounds an image and separates its interior from the exterior, but rather to the *dispositif* – meaning the system of material and non-material conditions which mark a 'border' in numerous possible ways, be it via a real or imagined frame, a certain format or a material medium, like a plate which transforms what is displayed on it invariably into a surface, just to name one of many possible examples. Even images that technically move their edges out of the field of vision, like projections in IMAX cinemas or fulldomes, are characterized by this border, at least by the edge of the screen, the dome, the spatial arrangement and the rows of seats which fix the gaze, and so on; they facilitate the viewing of something *as* the viewing of an image, while they limit the viewing to this function at the same time; their restriction bears comparison with the framing that forces the visual to turn into the iconic and trains or disciplines that which can be tentatively called 'iconic vision'.

All categories of technical illusionism, which can be addressed as the 'immersiveness' of the image, find the source of their dynamic – but also of their futility – in this structure. Its aim amounts to a paradox: the effacement of that which constitutes the viewing of an image – and thus the effacement of pictoriality as a medium. The logic of technological progress exists due to this *telos*: 'a medium that negates its own mediality'.

The Iconic and Discursive 'As'

It is, however, the framing *dispositif* that initially turns the image-like into an image, and produces the duplicity of 'viewing something as an image' and 'observing something in the image'. Every border is marked with a difference, and it constitutes itself along this difference. Here, it can be designated as 'iconic'. Therefore, we encounter a variation that concerns Gottfried Boehm's topic of the 'iconic difference',[5] which originally turned pictorial studies into a philosophical discipline. This also denotes precisely the difference that constitutes the quality of the image as a medium. Consequently, its framing or difference has two results, which coincide directly with the duplicity of the gaze introduced above: first of all, it sets something apart from its surroundings *as* an image and thus emphasizes it; secondly, it makes something visible 'as a representation of something', i.e. it shows something 'as' something. Therefore, along with the pictoriality of the image, it characterizes the representation of something 'as' a specific representation and consequently generates that which can be denoted as an 'iconic as' as distinguished from the 'apophantic' or 'hermeneutic as'. It signifies, even if it generates this significance not in the medium of the sign, but in the medium of the image. Accordingly, 'framing/difference' indicates that which both makes an image possible, and also generates the pictoriality of the image that allows it 'to show', 'represent', 'display something' or make it visible 'as something'. Because this occurs in the visual medium, which is subject to other laws than discursive media like scripts and numbers, it still has to be differentiated from the 'hermeneutic' and thus from the 'semiological' and the 'discursive as'; but initially, such a separation points out nothing more than the necessity of making a distinction between the registers of the 'sayable' and denotable on the one hand, and of the iconic on the other, while its characteristics *as* a distinction still have to be gauged. In turn, this is the distinction that characterizes the medial peculiarity of the image in contrast to text, script and mathematical structures, as well as bestows the image its distinct 'logic', which does not conform to the 'logic' of the symbolic or the discrete and cannot be reduced to them.[6] It reveals that the particular mediality of the image cannot be reduced to a grammatical, semiotic or rhetoric mode; in fact, we are dealing with a systematic incompatibility, which simultaneously raises the question of its describability, which as a discursive description has to remain inadequate with regards to iconic processes.[7]

As an additional consequence, any attempts to reduce 'visual strategies of staging' to rhetoric, and thus to figures which can be traced back to speech, or to simply conceive the image as a metaphor or a method of allegorization appear obsolete.[8] To put it differently: semiotics, hermeneutics or 'iconology' prove to be inadequate approaches for a theory of pictoriality because they disregard precisely the key aspect that would have to be denoted as the mediality of the image in the proper sense. Moreover, the image resists a thorough discursive analysis, as is shown by the failing of *ekphrasis*, which, by interminable utilization of terminology, only shifts and enlarges the gap between discourse and pictoriality instead of closing it. If, alternatively, a discursive analysis is at all possible, if the image can be completely transformed into language, then it would be nothing but a readable text and its observation a continual reading.

In contrast, the approach presented here insists on a fundamental untranslatability, an incommensurability of images and other medial modalities. It suggests taking the gaze as a starting point for deciphering the peculiarity of the pictorial; and thus to place the pictorial in the spectrum of perceptions, which originally don't have a seamless relation with terminology. Consequently, this approach insists on the intuition that the relation between image and gaze defines the specific format of the medium, which requires other means than those borrowed from sign theory, or literary studies and linguistics. The precise examination of this intuition leads to the discovery of a series of divisions that structure the relation between image and gaze; the use of the plural form is meant to underline the fact that this structure consists of a system of differences, of *aporias* and *chiasmi* which evoke varied series of 'perforations'. And the task of a philosophy of the pictorial that bases itself on the gaze has to be committed to reconstructing the mediality of the image and the specific scopophilia it evokes from this inherent system of differences. At the same time, this approach also highlights manifold traces of invisibilities that organize the complex interplay of 'withdrawal' and 'excess' in the image.

Reflexivity and Deframing

The first principle of the gaze's division is constituted by the framing mentioned above. Not only does framing situate a difference via pictorial means, by intersecting or separating, but it is also based upon a material arrangement, which focuses the gaze to the same extent that it indicates and signalizes – be it via the rim of an ocular, the lens of a projector, a screen or spatial boundaries and the like. This has always been utilized or reflected upon by the arts – whether in the form of mirrors that invert or unveil elements not covered by the spatial arrangement, as in the case of Diego Velázquez *Las Meniñas* (1656),[9] or the pastose and expressive quality of colouring that exposes as well as suspends the corporeality of the object in works by Cézanne or Van Gogh. But, at the same time, modernism has pointed out the impossibility of this endeavour. Take, for example, Maurice Denis' plain remark that, before it becomes a 'naked woman' or an 'anecdote', an image is 'essentially a level surface which is covered by paints in a certain arrangement',[10] to which Man Ray adds that:

> [A]s a form of expression, the art of painting – as a simulation of matter or of an arbitrary inspiring subject – [is] characterized by the color and structure of the material, that is by pigments and other materials that can reduced to two dimensions.[11]

If the surface, the materiality of the image – or its *dispositif* – happens to be the prerequisite of presentability – a fact which, when applied to the gaze, becomes the precondition for viewing to literally turn at the borders of pictoriality – then framing, in turn, evolves into the principle of a reflexivity that draws attention to something which is veiled by the image at the same time: the scene of its visualization. The viewing of the image shifts between these two poles. This is the reason why we referred to a 'double' gaze: its viewing, as far as it perceives anything in the image, requires the refraction and inversion of the gaze at the image, in order to make it possible to discern between picture and 'depiction' or medium and representation at any time. The viewing of an image is necessarily reflexive, and this also means that one is able to turn towards the pictoriality of the image itself – and to know at all times that one is viewing an image.

Theoretical possibilities are not real possibilities; in fact other prerequisites are necessary to turn one into the other. For this does not only concern the reflection of the representation's form, but also the exposure of mediality itself; i.e. the appearance of the medium 'as' a medium, which allows an analysis of its structure, just as making it visible includes a paradox. Therefore, the principle of reflexivity is likewise a prerequisite of viewing the image and of the discovery of mediality itself. Only because of this principle does a media theory of the image exists. Art has always capitalized on this – exemplarily in Magritte's reflections on the image in *Les Mots et les Images* (1929) or the indistinguishability of transparency and opacity in Marcel Duchamp's *Grand Verre* (1923),[12] the large window-image which, at the same time enables and obstructs the view through it; the sites of fracture that are present in this work anticipate those interferences that later constituted the actual genre of video art. By deceiving the eyes and other paradoxical strategies it seeks to refract – manifestly as well as latently – the illusionism of pictoriality, as a way to make the elements visible that generate visibility in the first place.

But this can be inverted as well, because the conditions of reflection are simultaneously the conditions of its very negation. The desire for technological perfection in the production of images aims in this direction: in this sphere, iconic reflexivity becomes a tool of illusion. Thus, framing and deframing refer to each other, just like difference and its annulment via 'immersion', which share a similar connection. Both shift like foreground and background in an optical illusion, and terminate the varied history between art and technology. Their correlatives constitute the strategies of visualization concerning the mathematical construction of the image, as well as the device-based manipulation of the field of vision and the systems of optics, which equally direct and blind the gaze. But because reflexivity as the constituent of image-viewing cannot be completely effaced, they also grow to monstrous proportions and turn into a synopsis and totalization of the gaze, as demonstrated most notably by the techniques of illusion prevalent in the nineteenth century: their enhancement and excess exposes an 'iconic claim to power', which Nietzsche and Heidegger have demarcated as a general characteristic of the technological in the shape of a 'will to power'.

It is subject to another shift with relation to the digitalization of the pictorial, its constructability without an index, which photography invariably still left intact. Since this development, effects have written themselves into the visible, without being visible themselves, because no residual traces remain. Image and gaze submit to the regime of those elements that keep themselves unrecognizable as a regime. Accordingly, these 'imagings' use devices and algorithms to install orders of signs that cause the pictorial itself to withdraw, only to generate it anew as an 'iconic grapheme' by means of numerical and statistical methods.[13] But technology does not continue with the classical *illusio*, insofar as this would always relate to a *mimesis* based upon ontology, but as *simulation* that proves to be committed completely to the 'art' of the mathematical, which proceeds syntactically and therefore independent of any discrete content. That which is 'on offer to be viewed' does not conform to immersion or illusion anymore, but turns into fictionality. Here, the term of the 'fictional' does point to literary forms, but refers to the mathematical term existence, which only denotes a possibility subject to the restriction of formal coherence, not a reality. This becomes particularly virulent in the case of digitally generated 'images in science', which do not proceed from mimetic reference, but are based on the computer-aided processing of probabilistic amounts of data, which are used – often with the aid of 'smoothing' and the truncation of extreme values – to make something visible that otherwise would not submit to any kind of visibility. This is not the interplay of generating visibility and invisibility that dominated visualization for centuries, but rather the representation of something non-visual which only follows a 'graphemic' and not a visual 'trace'.[14] As a result, we are dealing with abstract patterns that – as with scanning tunneling microscopy – are generated by scans of distances and their statistical extrapolation, and only function as genuine scriptures. Of course, the explosiveness of an 'iconic ideology' lurks within these depictions, which systematically play with the most prominent characteristic of the image: the power to make something visible and to feign verisimilitude in the process. The image employed as an argument in scientific discourse is in danger of succumbing to this ideology.

Irrepresentability

As the development of the technical generation of images progresses in this manner, from *illusio* to graphemic *simulatio*, it simultaneously follows a 'logic' in which the division of the gaze is annulled; a division that appears as constitutive of the image as a medium. Thus a tendency appears that suggests the erasure of the image as such and its morphing into three-dimensional structures or walkable spaces. But this tendency also exploits the order of framing or difference to the same extent as it is telelogically guided by the images' principle of reflection. Here, the paradox of the endeavour reveals a central feature of the structure of the medial itself. While images are cut by their framing, and their visible elements are raised by *dispositifs* and implemented by technical devices, these remain without outline in the image itself. They do not stand out. The prerequisites of pictoriality thus assert themselves as something that is irrepresentable within the pictorial. Every image is divided by this difference between representation and irrepresentability, which can never be effaced or obliterated by any kind of technical *perfectio*. In other words: the image withdraws its own mediality. It keeps its mediality in the sphere of the invisible. This invisibility corresponds to a 'dialectics of mediality' that consists of the medium's peculiar quality to conceal itself in its appearance.[15] We look by the means of devices, optical appliances or techniques of visualization, but we do not look at them. We recognize or observe something due to the manner of its shape, its colouring, due to a specific direction of the image or choice of detail – but, as modalities of production or enactment, these elements remain merely accompaniments: they show themselves. Even when we encounter only algorithms which calculate images as graphs, we look right through them. While the medium as a medium allows the possibility of refraction and thus a reflection at any time, it forfeits its function concurrent to the degree of its surfacing as a medium: the self-observation turns into a disruption, a dysfunctionality, as has been the topic of e.g. Nam June Paik's early television art which addressed the blindness of the apparatus.

The distinction which thus emerges is preliminary even to the 'iconic difference'; it enters into it as an 'interplay' of appearing and vanishing. It would be possible to speak of a 'difference concerning the difference', although this is not the distinction between picture and 'depiction' – respectively medium and representation – but rather the distinction between medium and mediality, image and pictoriality. It enters into a relation of negativity towards the represented and visible. This explains the reference to invisibility: it points to the contours of a negative aesthetics of the image and the medium. They suggest that only the image as well as its representation appear – but not the mediality: it remains at the back of visibility as something that is always hidden. It constitutes this visibility, but, as a conditional, it does not generate a position in the image, in the field of vision, because it initially opens up and directs the image *as* an image.

This finding is characteristic for every medium qua 'middle' or 'mediation', insofar a genuine dualism is inherent in this 'inbetweenness': to expose itself in the process of representation while not making itself recognizable. While images are able to express or represent something – and in this they appear 'similar to language'[16] to the same extent that they refuse language itself – they cannot represent by what means they represent: this shows itself. The showing conforms to irrepresentability: it is neither able to show at what it is pointing, nor by what means it is showing. Instead, it points in a certain direction, uses allusions, displays or parades itself. Here, the figure of 'showing/concealing' can be borrowed from Wittgenstein's early work. Language, as is formulated in the *Tractatus*, can speak only because of its 'logical form', which, however, cannot be expressed in words. Thus, it is not able to additionally express its own structural or performative format: this 'shows itself'.[17] Images direct the attention in a similar manner, they make something recognizable, they show, but in a way which does not show the modalities of their showing in the process – they elude the visualization of their function where it concerns the creation of visibility.

In the image, showing corresponds to the aesthetic dimension. It points out the duplicity of semblance and appearance and leads – beyond the legible, the *dispositif*, the framing and the 'iconic as' – to the manner of its specific phenomenality. An image, as it represents something, must appear in the same instant, which means that it must show itself in the process of showing and exhibit the means of its representation, its structure as a medium and its materiality, while these suspend and limit the representation at the same moment. The whole complex logic of the 'showable' and the 'unshowable (non-showable)' is linked to this, in a manner which corresponds to the relation between effable and ineffable present in the discursive. Concerning language, Wittgenstein came to the conclusion that 'one [...] [cannot] describe the nature of language employing language';[18] 'Language has to speak for itself.'[19] He adds: 'We are confronted by a kind of theory of relativity pertaining to language.'[20] The philosophy of language fails, because it has to express itself in language about language. Thus, a withdrawal remains, a 'negative mediality of language',[21] which was analogously expressed by Heidegger's tautological aphorism that language is only language: 'Language is language. Language speaks'.[22] This holds also true for the image. '"What the image tells me is itself,"' notes Wittgenstein in his *Philosophical Investigations*, 'That is, its telling me something consists its own structure, *its* own lines and colours.'[23]

The Logic of Showing

Whatever an image shows or incorporates, whatever it says or represents, it does so in the mode of showing. Showing has a different format than telling (itself). Converted and brought close to Nelson Goodman's difference between 'denotation' and 'exemplification',[24] as well as the difference between 'representation' and 'presentation' in the approaches by Susanne Langer, Husserl and Gottfried Boehm,[25] it proves to be fundamental for the analysis of the aesthetic of the pictorial and its structure. At the same time, it indicates another difference, which intersects the image invisibly and irrepresentably, because it precedes every instance of constituting the iconic. Additionally, the specific 'logic' of iconic mediality becomes legible here. Images present – despite all the systems of significance and reconsideration, of symbolization and interpretation which open and domesticate the gaze – and this presentation, this 'making present', also generates their peculiar proximity to evidence. This is the reason for the abundant presence of pictorial strategies; from illustration to allegedly documentary photography and the pictorial character of the news, up to the use of images in the intrinsically image-less natural sciences: they all serve a production of evidence which cannot be generated discursively. The gaze is not only offered something to observe in the image; in fact, it experiences something non-negatable, as in the literal sense of 'evidence' – the true seeing, including that leap into the eyes which cannot be disregarded. Conversely, it is therefore not knowledge or understanding which is characteristic for the pictorial, but the force creating such evidence, which also excludes its negation. This exclusion of negation forms the actual focus of the 'short media theory of the image' as set down by Freud in 'The Means of Representations in Dreams', the pivotal chapter of *The Interpretation of Dreams* (1900).[26] The bizarre forms of dream logic proceed from this. '[I]n any event, a painted, or plastic image, or a film [...] cannot present what is not the case'; thus the corresponding assessment – once more from Wittgenstein's *Philosophical Inquiries* – and the *Big Typescript* adds: 'I am able to draw an image of two men fencing with each other; but not of two men not fencing with each other (meaning an image that represents only this).'[27] This means – as the first characteristic of iconic 'logic' – that the status of negation in the pictorial proves to be precarious, as there is no adequate visual correlative to it: 'One cannot draw the contradictorily negative, but only the contrary (in the sense of representing it positively).'[28]

Above all, showing is not able to withdraw itself; it is unable to negate. This is also due to the fact that the image lacks a grammatical site for the subject. While self-reference exists, it is only possible in a very indirect manner and, again, only while employing the means of visuality; for instance by an image within the image, which refers to the first. This fact implies – as the second characteristic of the logic of the image – an additional format of paradox. While, in the discursive mode, this is based on a connection between a self-reference and a negation, which generates the antinomy in the sentence, the image only allows pareidolia, or metastable interplays between figure and background, as Wittgenstein illustrated with his example of the 'duck rabbit'.[29] Here, both facets of the paradox appear simultaneously, though not in a relationship of affirmation and negation in order to oppose each other; in contrast, they rather demand a continual shifting of attention, which makes their inverse orders exclude each other.[30] While it is possible to paint contrasts and opposites in this way, these are of a different kind than negative 'ipsoflexivities' like 'This is not sentence' or 'This sentence is false'. No image is able to demonstrate that it is not an image; at most it can remove itself like in De Kooning's erased drawing by Robert Rauschenberg (*Erased de Kooning Drawing*, 1953) or resort to cancellations like in Jörg Immendorf's *Hört auf zu Malen* (1965), where the traces of deletion or of the annulled painting are retained and are thus exposed. Even René Magritte's *Ceci n'est pas une Pipe* (1928–29) requires the counteracting sentence; but at the price of an instability developing between image and language, which leaves the observer systematically in the dark about which element has to be given priority.[31] Of course there are 'manipulation', 'retouching' or 'dissemblance', and also 'fogging' and 'blurring', to make something appear indistinct and vague; these techniques stick to the history of images like shadows, but they always retain an affirmative momentum – even when they deliberately intend to deny, denounce or conceal something, they still demonstrate the thing that was denied and denounced in the first place and thus display it as well.

As an additional effect – the third characteristic of an iconic logic – the pictorial lacks any capability of restraint, of distancing consideration: in the process of showing, it has to position itself. Accordingly, an equivalent to the subjunctive in language is missing; therefore the use of images in sciences which debate in the discursive mode appears problematic. The language of the subjunctive is constitutive for the entire rhetoric of the natural sciences, as well as of the empirical social sciences; it embodies not only the discrete ethos of science, but also the latent reservations towards one's own results, the principle of revisability and the parenthetic authority of truth. But because the image is always interlinked with evidence, which becomes manifest or not, scepticism is alien to the pictorial. Certainly, there are occlusion, preliminarity and fragmentariness, but they remain in a mode of presence throughout. The power of pictoriality is based on the magic of such a presence. It imposes itself without reservation and forces the gaze into a scopophilia – an inescapable addiction of the eyes.

The Gaze 'Opened Up'

The lack of negation, metastability, the interplay of pareidolia and an impossible subjunctive are the ciphers of a different 'logic of the image', not indications of its failures that are assigned to position it beneath language, textuality and rational discursiveness. Instead, they delineate the limits of one kind of representability, which provide it with a genuinely affirmative character. "'What the image tells me is itself,'" as Wittgenstein put it, but it also affirms itself. This is the true meaning of evidence: an 'addiction of the eyes' and '*to* the eyes' – the usurpation as well as empowerment of vision. It attracts but also disciplines the gaze. At the same time, it is based on the evocation of a presence that, to the same degree, amounts to the evocation of evidence. Therefore, showing the limits of representability and the production of evidence coincide directly, and consequently define the aesthetic autonomy of the image. Insofar evidence originates from perception, it contains a perception-that (*quod*) before it turns into a perception-of-something (*quid*), as was already pointed out by Kant.[32] It does not concern the witnessing of a thing as such, but rather the 'gift' of becoming visible itself.[33] No kind of seeing may doubt the existence of the 'that' without doubting itself in its role as visual perception, just as – by the way – images are unable to not show something: a specific kind of *ekstasis* is inherent to them. *Ekstasis* stands for 'standing outside one's self' or emerging. The terms 'existence' and 'appearance' mean the same: something appears, something exists. The roots of evidence, especially of evidence as related to pictoriality, can be found in this connection. It is also interlinked with the ability of the image to cause a perception and to captivate the eye.

But this evidence, conceived of in such a way, turns out to be 'fractured evidence'. It shifts between the non-negatability of the iconic showing, which reveals a presence that, on the other hand, is also not present. But it is exactly this gap which forces one to look at the image, to view it. Jacques Lacan has connected this kind of compulsion to desire, which is a desire for visibility as well as a desire *for* the gaze and a desire *of* the gaze. This matches the 'endowment of the gaze' of the image itself, because, as Lacan made it clear, to create an image means to bestow a gaze – and this means, in the same breath, to give oneself, to surrender oneself.[34] In the image itself, such a gaze does not possess a donor, and therefore cannot be answered; it can only be received, i.e. accepted. In a manner of speaking, all painters, creators, directors or video artists surrender their gaze – and it is this surrender that characterizes the hazard of their efforts, just as the image links it to a desire that aims at being looked at to the same extent that it desires to observe seeing itself. It indicates the point that equally 'approaches' and 'addresses' the gaze, just as, on the other hand, looking at an image means paying attention to the gaze's direction while seeing. This is not a definable position or characteristic in the image, this is not something that can be deciphered: the evidence of pictoriality does not possess a decipherable centre.

The difference of *studium* and *punctum*[35] – which goes back to Lacan and was put into focus by Roland Barthes in his philosophy of photography – is connected to this: the *studium*, as an encoded and thus learnable sphere of experiencing an image, allows the reading of the image, while the *punctum* stays uncoded; it denotes the actual irresistible quality, that which, according to Barthes' explicit description, is not identifiable in the image and which approaches and attacks the observer instead.[36] Conforming to the invisibility present in the medium, it both seduces the gaze and forbids it to look away. The captivating quality of the image, this specific intensity, but also power, delineates the characteristic that eludes understanding to the same extent that it 'looks' at the observer and forces him to see. Images and faces share this quality: it is not us who gaze at them, but we are gazed 'at' in return and 'positioned' as well. Being looked at precedes the gaze; this is why Deleuze and Guattari speak of a 'face-like quality' concerning the image,[37] which always contains – however subtle – the 'trace' of the Other. Images are equal to such countenances which do not let go and demand an answer, a 'return of the gaze'.

Therefore, it is possible – apart from the refraction of the gaze at the frame and even beyond the demonstrated duplicity of telling and showing – to detect another principle of the gaze's division: the exchange of gazes between image and observer, which presupposes that gazing at an image always equals answering a gaze. The effects of this exchange point far beyond the *dispositif* of visibility because they do not concern the character of the image as a sign, but rather its 'aura'.[38] This also means that, in media theory, no image can be reduced to its techniques of visualization; instead, it requires the constitution of a theory of the image that proceeds from the gaze, and the examination of the specific exchange of gazes and its effects, because only this displays that momentum concerning the image that, in Walter Benjamin's choice of words, constitutes the gaze's impact.

Chiasm of Gazes

On the other hand this means that a relation to alterity is inherent in every image, insofar as it is marked by the responsive structure of the exchange of gazes. Hence, the actual subject-matter of an aesthetics of pictoriality arises. Psychoanalysis, in particular, tried to fathom the abyssal depth of the pictorial time and again with a string of different approaches. This is particularly true for that Otherness that no gaze can ever perceive, because it constitutes pictoriality in the first place. Images do not only present something to look at; instead, because of the process of showing, an Other gazes out. Thus, two different perspectives cross on the pictorial tableau – making it possible to find a third principle of the gaze's division there, which configures this crossing, a chiasm which first and foremost determinates the mediality of pictoriality in all its intricacy.[39]

John Berger wrote that '[e]very image embodies a specific kind of seeing';[40] thus different kinds of gaze are necessary to decipher them as such, because one must not forget that each different gaze perceives different things, as can be exemplarily demonstrated with a look at Jan Vermeer's *The Art of Painting* (1666). Because the painter is turning his back towards the observer, the painting performs a feat that – according to Lacan – is impossible for a self-portrait: it observes itself 'in the act of observing'. Here, two perspectives make themselves accessible to the observer: that of Vermeer, who is looking at his model and his canvas and that shows the picture in the moment where he has just started to paint; and, on the other hand, one's own, which is observing the painter, while the artist himself is removed from the gaze. No one is able to observe himself from behind; the gaze onto the back remains rather disquieting, and thus the extraordinariness of Johannes Vermeer's *The Art of Painting* is based on the feat of marking the indelibleness of difference by the back view and the double gaze.[41]

Hence, the chiasm of gazes points exactly to this intrusion of an alterity into seeing: the observer's gaze is foiled by a confrontation with an image, just as the gaze of the Other, who is offering himself via his medium, is hit and violated by the observer's vision. In the literal sense, chiasm means a cross-wise intersection. Things that cross each other normally intersect in one point; but if one thinks about the directions of the lines forming the cross spatially – in three dimensions – in the form of 'skewed lines', then there is no point in which the lines intersect. This is pointed out by the way the expression 'chiasm' is normally used. It is a disparity that does not work out anywhere. The 'chiastic' would be that which cannot be aligned, however hard one struggles for identity. Accordingly, a lapse is inherent to it, a fundamental incommensurability.

In this sense, every viewing of an image is a chiastic event, and no construction of the image will ever be able to get hold of it. In other words, the viewing of the image proceeds from there; from something that is at the same time indeterminate and open; from a gap, which, as such, remains unpresentable, and thus inaccessible as well. It points, again, to an instance of invisibility, insofar as the gap bestows a gift that cannot be gazed at. It withdraws itself, while constituting an excess at the same time. The fascination of the image has its source in this excess: for this reason the image always proves to be more than what can be said or construed; and it is also for the same reason that the image approaches me, imposes itself on me, entreats my gaze and lures it, as Lacan expressed it, into its 'trap'[42] – and, once again, it is art that finds its particular domain, its game of mirrors, in this trap and its literal 'reflection'.

Notes

1   Cf. Dieter Mersch, 'Kunst und Medium. Zwei Vorlesungen', in *Gestalt und Diskurs* (Schriftenreihe der Muthesius-Hochschule), Vol. 3, 2003a; Dieter Mersch, 'Wort, Bild, Ton, Zahl. Modalitäten medialen Darstellens', in *Die Medien der Künste: Beiträge zu einer Theorie des Darstellens*, München: Fink, 2003b, pp. 9–49.

2   Maurice Merleau-Ponty, *Das Sichtbare und das Unsichtbare*, Munich: Fink, 1986; Bernhard Waldenfels, 'Spiegel, Spur und Blick', in Gottfried Boehm (ed.), *Homo Pictor*, Munich & Leipzig: Saur, 2001, pp. 14–31.

3   Waldenfels also stresses that this is not only a figure of reflection: 'The enigma of visibility lies in the fact that the becoming as well as the making visible employ the means of the

visible': in Waldenfels, 2003, p. 5. This, on the other hand, gives rise to the question how the constitution of visibility can be become visible in turn.

4 André Blavier (ed.), *René Magritte.Sämtliche Schriften*, Frankfurt am Main et al.: Ullstein, 1985, p. 44.

5 Cf. Gottfried Boehm, 'Die Wiederkehr der Bilder', in *Was ist ein Bild?*, Munich: Fink, 1995, pp. 11–38. Since then the term has had a career in different guises.

6 I have taken a closer look at the hypothesis of the incommensurability between the basic medial formats of writing, images, numbers and sound in my article, 'Wort, Bild, Ton, Zahl. Modalitäten Medialen Darstellens', in Mersch, 2003, pp. 9– 49

7 Cf. regarding this question Gottfried Boehm and Helmut Pfotenhauer (eds), *Beschreibungskunst – Kunstbeschreibung*, Munich: Fink, 1995.

8 Concerning this tightly employed perspective from literary studies, cf. Bettine Menke, 'Bild – Textualität. Benjamins Schriftliche Bilder', in Michael Wetzel and Herta Wolf (eds), *Der Entzug der Bilder*, Munich: Fink, 1994, pp. 47–65.

9 Diego Velázquez' painting *Las Meninas* has brought forth an abundance of interpretations by Michel Foucault, John Searle, Hermann Asemissen and others. Compare with the non-opening imagination of Velazquez in Dieter Mersch, 'Ästhetischer Augenblick und Gedächtnis in der Kunst. Überlegungen zum Verhältnis von Zeit und Bild', in Mersch, 2003b, pp. 151–76.

10 Maurice Denis, qtd in Werner Haftmann, *Malerei des 20. Jahrhunderts*, München: Prestel, 1965, p. 50.

11 Andrea Jahn, Katharina Lepper and HanneloreKersting (eds), *Man Ray*, exhibition catalogue, Stuttgart et al., 1998, p. 35.

12 Cf. Axel Müller, 'Das ist kein Fenster. Überlegungen zu einer zentralen Bildmetapher bei René Magritte und Marcel Duchamp', in Mersch, 2003 b, pp. 127–38.

13 Cf. Dieter Mersch, 'Das Bild als Argument', in Christoph Wulf and Jörg Zirfas (eds), *Ikonologien des Performativen*, Munich: Fink, 2005, pp. 322–44.

14 Cf. Dieter Mersch, 'Visual Arguments: The Role of Images in Sciences and Mathematics', in Bernd Hüppauf and Peter Weingart (eds), *Science Images and Popular Images of the Science*, New York: Routledge, 2008, pp. 181–98.

15 Cf. also Dieter Mersch, 'Medialität und Undarstellbarkeit. Einleitung in eine "negative" Medientheorie', in Sybille Krämer (ed.), *Medialität und Performanz*, Munich: Fink, 2004, pp. 75–96.

16 Theodor W. Adorno insisted on the 'similarity to language' of music in a similar context, but, of course, in a way that this similarity would only manifest itself where music departed from language's function as statement. Cf. Theodor W. Adorno, 'Fragment über Musik und Sprache', in *Musikalische Schriften III*, Vol. 16, Frankfurt am Main: Suhrkamp, 2003, pp. 251–56; Theodor Adorno, 'Musik, Sprache und ihr Verhältnis im gegenwärtigen Komponieren', in ibid., pp. 649–64.

17 Ludwig Wittgenstein, *Tractatus Logico-Philosophicus* (Kritische Edition), in Brian McGuinness and Joachim Schulte (eds), Frankfurt am Main: Suhrkamp, 1989, especially pp. 3.262, 4.022, 4.12–4.1212, 4.126, 5.62, 6.12, 6.36 & 6.522.

18 Ludwig Wittgenstein, *Bemerkungen*, Vol. 3, No. 3, Vienna & New York: Springer, 2000a, p. 30.

19   Ludwig Wittgenstein, *Philosophische Grammatik*, Frankfurt am Main: Suhrkamp, 1973, p. 40.

20   Wittgenstein, 2000a, pp. 33–34.

21   Cf. Dieter Mersch, 'Negative Medialität. Derridas Différance und Heideggers Weg zur Sprache', in *Journal Phänomenologie, Jacques Derrida*, Vol. 23, 2005, pp. 14–22.

22   Martin Heidegger, *Unterwegs zur Sprache*, Pfullingen: Neske, 1975, p. 13.

23   Ludwig Wittgenstein, *Philosophische Untersuchungen/PhilosophicalInvestigations* (trans. G. E. M. Anscombe), Oxford, 1953, pp.143 & 523).

24   Nelson Goodman, *Sprachen der Kunst*, Frankfurt am Main: Suhrkamp, 1995, p. 57ff.

25   Susanne K. Langer, *Philosophie auf neuem Wege. Das Symbol im Denken, im Ritus und in der Kunst*, Frankfurt am Main: Fischer, 1984, pp. 61ff, 172ff & 261ff. On Husserl, cf. Lambert Wiesing, *Artifizielle Präsenz*, Frankfurt am Main: Suhrkamp, 2005. Cf. also Boehm, 'Repräsentation – Präsentation – Präsenz', in Boehm, 2001, pp. 3–13.

26   Sigmund Freud, *Die Traumdeutung*, Frankfurt am Main: Fischer, 1961, p. 259ff.

27   Ludwig Wittgenstein, *The Big Typescript* (ed. Michael Nedo), Vol. 11, No. 4, Vienna & New York: Springer, 2000b, p. 83; Wittgenstein, 2000a, p. 56.

28   Wittgenstein, 2000a, p. 56.

29   Wittgenstein, 1971, p. 228ff.

30   Cf. William J. T. Mitchell, *Picture Theory*, Chicago: University of Chicago Press, 1994, p. 35ff.

31   On René Magritte, see my remarks in Dieter Mersch, *Was sich Zeigt. Materialität, Präsenz, Ereignis*, Munich: Fink, 2002, p. 295ff.

32   Immanuel Kant, *Kritik der Reinen Vernunft*, Hamburg: Meiner, 1956, pp. 225 & 272–73.

33   While the term 'gift' has been made a topic by Derrida – tracing it back to Marcel Mauss – here something completely different is focused upon: the perception of a given as something that is 'given beforehand' and not already constructed by perception. For the usage of the term, cf. Dieter Mersch, *Ereignis und Aura*, Frankfurt am Main: Suhrkamp, 2002, p. 47ff.

34   To show an image thus means to 'provide' a gaze. Cf. Jacques Lacan, 'Linie und Licht', in Boehm 1995, pp. 60–74 .

35   Roland Barthes, *Die Helle Kammer. Bemerkung zur Photographie/Camera Lucida – Reflections on Photography* (trans. Richard Howard), New York: Hill and Wang, 1981.

36   ibid., p. 60ff.

37   Gilles Deleuze and Félix Guattari, *Tausend Plateaus*, Berlin: Merve, 1992, p. 230ff.

38   Cf. Mersch, 2002, p. 75ff.

39   On the crossing of gazes, although understood differently in each case, cf. Maurice Merleau-Ponty, 'Der Zweifel Cézannes', in Boehm, 1995, pp. 39–59; Lacan, 1995, p. 64. However, the crossing of gazes in Lacan is developed from the encounter with alterity.

40   John Berger, *Sehen. Das Bild der Welt in der Bilderwelt*, Hamburg: Reinbek, 1974, p. 10.

41   On Jan Vermeer cf. my remarks in 'Ästhetischer Augenblick und Gedächtnis in der Kunst. Überlegungen zum Verhältnis von Zeit und Bild', in Mersch, 2003b, pp. 151–76.

42   Cf. Lacan, 1995, p. 61.

Chapter 17

The Magical Image in Georges Méliès's Cinema

Lorenz Engell

The following considerations have a double objective. First, I want to delineate the effects of the cinematic image on the things it is showing. I assume that, in the case of the moving images, the effect of the image on the things shown in the image can be spotted by looking at the image itself – that this effect even constitutes the cinematic image to a certain extent, an extent that will have to be determined. In certain cases, film can be understood as the effect on the things it is showing. I want to follow this trace at least with regard to a special case, namely the early cinematic magic, the magic images of Georges Méliès. It may remain speculation whether this allows further conclusions concerning film as a medium in general. On the other hand, however, it is my intention to perhaps bridge, if not close, a gap in theoretical argumentation.

I came across this highly interesting gap in Alfred Gell's work *Art and Agency: An Anthropological Theory*, published in 1998.[1] His theory is instructive for three reasons with regard to the context of 'technology and desire', to which the present volume is dedicated. Firstly, it correlates artworks as concerning the European understanding with magical and cultic objects, resulting in a special type of object, which Gell calls the 'index'. Secondly, it perceives the magical object as a cultural technique and the image as a tool, if not necessarily of desire, or – even less likely – an explicit volition, an intention analogous to consciousness, then at least as a tool for creating and exercising a capacity for action, or 'agency'. Thirdly – and this is its most notable feature – it expressly concedes the possibility to actually attribute an 'agency' to the image itself; an inherent efficacy which cannot be whittled down to originators beyond (or within) the image. It posits that exactly this attribution would take place in the interaction with magical or aesthetical objects.

But Gell does not look closely at this particular attribution, its progression and origination. He simply regards it as a spontaneous 'abduction'. Yet I assume that the practice concerning the abduction of agency, which just cannot happen *ex nihilo*, is particularly interesting with regard to a special case, namely the moving technical image. Therefore, I want to test this theory regarding cinematography and adapt it to the conditions of the moving technical image; in particular with regard to these conditions affecting the point of attribution – and my touchstone is the distinctly magical cinematography of Georges Méliès.

I want to proceed in five steps, dealing with index and causes (in that order); secondly with 'cinemagic' as the position of agency; the third part will take a look at the primacy of vanishing or the negation of agency; while the fourth considers complex scripts; and, finally, the fifth 'cinemagical' operations.

Index and Causes

Thus, images and objects, which are assumed to be the site of intrinsic intention or the instruments of exterior intention, are termed 'index' by Gell. This term originates from Charles Sanders Peirce's semiotics, was taken up by Charles W. Morris, and belongs to the standard repertoire of a theory of signs.[2] Following Gell, an index induces a spectator to assume that it – the index – is caused, in some way, by somebody or something beyond that index.[3] In this case, the actual conditions of causality – and this differs from Peirce's point of view – are initially altogether irrelevant.[4] Only that which the object, the index, refers to in the eyes of the beholder is of importance. According to Gell, this reference to a cause is the prominent function of the index; this, in turn, is important for Peirce as well and, in his view, constitutes a discrete layer of a sign. But this does not apply to all objects, which are actually caused, but ultimately only to the index, by the magical or artistic object. According to Gell, the index is not only perceived as a causal result of, for instance, the laws of nature, but rather as a result of an exercise of power, which, case by case, may remain unknown and unconscious; the index-object might also fail in this or remain mixed up with superimposed other objects. Here, Gell also deviates from Peirce.[5] As conceived by the spectator, the index – the created image or magical object – is neither determinate nor incidental. But this is another direct attribution, which, by the way, might not only affect humans, but other (inanimate) characters, objects, gods and spirits, as well as history and society, too. All these can be held liable as causers (perpetrators) and entities of power.

Furthermore, Gell's index is not only 'caused', but also, for its part, 'causer' ('operator').[6] It is an object which causes the spectator to assume that it will result in consequences, e.g. that it triggers a kind of behaviour, brings about reactions and activities or changes the state of things in some other way. Indiscriminately, the spectator and users, but also other objects, can be the targets of the effect attributed to the index, as understood by Gell. Again, the actual conditions and prerequisites of the causation are completely irrelevant. Gell, using another term by Peirce, states that the 'abduction', meaning the hypothesis or mere assumption of such an effect, suffices.[7] In a kind of linear causal process, the resulting effect is hypothetically ascribed to the index then appears as identical to an exercise of power, or, ultimately, even as an intention, assigned to the putative originator, although this does not have to be true in any way.

Furthermore, Gell states that these two hypothetical relationships – the originator affecting the index and the index affecting the spectator – are both equally invertible as well. As, for example, a patron, the spectator is able to ascribe the origination of a work of art or a magic spell to himself. This is also true for a customer, who is led to assume by a product that it was created according to his wishes and expectations. Furthermore, the index can also be said to possess power over its originator. Like the magic broom, the work can turn against its creator. The inherent logic of a work of art can force the artist to complete it in a way that differs from his original plans. In Gell's words, the agent has then turned into a patient.[8]

In addition to originator, spectator and object (or index), a fourth dimension plays a role in Gells's model. It marks a special case, namely the case of figurative image-works or images in the commonly accepted sense; thus of objects which, just like film images, represent something.

Gell does not spend much effort on the problem of representation. Contrary to Nelson Goodman, he briefly compares Peirce's concept of iconicity with analogy.[9] But he mainly proceeds from the assumption that figurative images lead their spectators to infer the presence of absent objects. The object which is thus present-absent is called 'prototype' by Gell.[10] This is another term that refers to the sphere of Peircean semiotics in an indirect but interesting way. It is important, however, that the 'prototype' itself, the thing represented or otherwise assumed to be present in the image, interferes with the indexical interplay of the causations as well. The 'prototype' would also be able, for instance, to be the origin of the image as well as being produced by the image, or would be able to affect the spectator as well as to allow the spectator, as with a voodoo doll, to affect the 'prototype'. This will suffice, for the moment, as a short introduction to Gell's basic model of magical and artistic objects and their integration into a complex context, a constellation, which, in the following, we want to denote as 'agency'.

Cinemagic: The Position of Agency

What kind of contrasting or validating comment on these propositions is possible from the perspective of cinema and, in particular, Méliès' magic image? In order to briefly test this approach, I want to take a look at a first exemplary film, *L'homme orchestre* (1900). Initially, the film shows an empty stage the spectators would identify as an auditorium (in the cinema). The curtains positioned sideways, as well as the spatial arrangement, are non-ambiguous in this regard. The camera does not change its position, just as a spectator in a theatre would not move from his seat. Additionally, the whole 'scene' remains undisrupted by montage, and proceeds continually, just like in the theatre. A musician holding an instrument steps onto this stage and seats himself on one of the available chairs. As soon as he has taken his seat, a second musician appears. But he does not enter the stage from each side or the background, as it is usually the case in theatre, but arises in front of our eyes out of the first musician as his copy; only with a different instrument in his hands. He detaches from the first musician, who, undaunted, remains seated, and takes place in the next chair. A third musician, identically copied but also carrying a different instrument, detaches from him, and so on and so forth. Step-by-step, seven varyingly identical musicians appear in total. They play an – inaudible – piece with much gestural effort; one of them climbs on his chair to conduct (Figure 1). Afterwards, they all vanish in exactly the same way they appeared: each merges with the figure from which he emerged. In the end, the first one vanishes as well – this time from the middle of the picture.

Initially, this film simplifies things for us because it performs Gell's complete model in the literal sense by putting it on a stage. One can even claim that the model of agency and that of the magical object itself is the 'prototype', the represented object, of this film, just as if it was aware of Gell's model and wanted to show it to us. For this parallel consideration, we initially do not look at the film image itself (more on that later), but rather at that which the filmic image gazes at or, respectively, shows. At first, the film shows a stage and, acting on it, a figure. The figure bows to us or to somebody else, addresses us or somebody else – a series of deictic or, in the sense of sign theory, indexical gestures are employed accordingly – leading us to the inference that – indirectly, invisibly – a recipient, and thus an observer or spectator, is present in the image. Therefore, even though he is invisible, the spectator is literally 'produced' and enters the film as the first hypothetical assumption of Gell's model of agency.

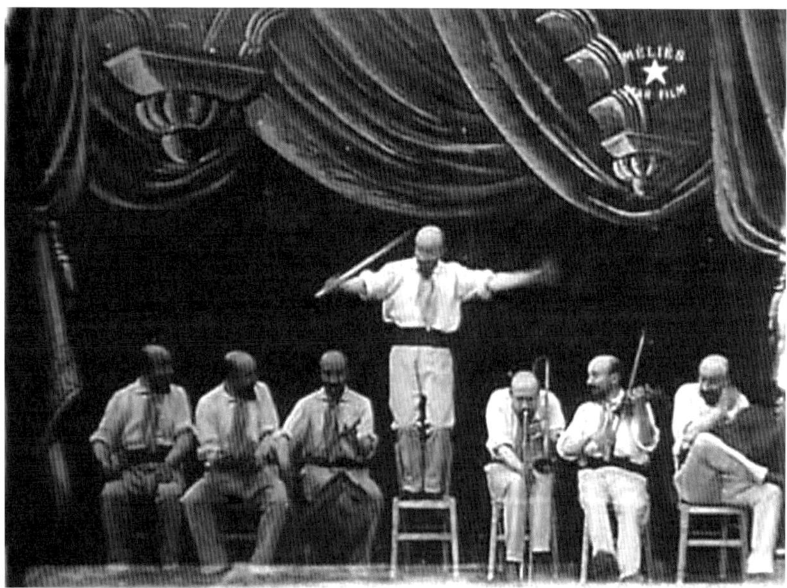

Figure 1: Georges Méliès, *L'homme orchestre*, 1900, 2 min., DVD still.

Next, as the second assumption, Gell's 'prototype' emerges before our eyes: the image-object as a second component of agency, one could say. This takes place in the moment where a second object arises from the first figure, which is very similar to it; the second musician, who nonetheless is the first. The first differs from the second, but is – somehow – present in him and is actually defined by him. Next, a third musician detaches from him – again an identical copy – but with a different musical instrument, and so on. Step by step, seven different versions of the one prototypical musician appear in total. Thirdly, they as a group of seven musicians now function as an orchestra, as an index in Gell's sense of the term. Their orchestra is marked as a creation in the film. Additionally, it is a formation, which prompts us to perceive it precisely as something caused, not as something that has simply emerged – because we assume that the musician, as an agent, duplicates himself as the result of his own efforts, and is not doubled by simple chance or as the patient of an exterior power. Thus, he is the magician, the originator. We conclude this because he presents all actions in the forefront of the image and remains at ease, showing no surprise or resistance with regard to his duplication; but, above all, because the multiplication seems to have an intentional purpose. The seven versions perform an – inaudible – piece with much gestural effort (and, as an ancillary point, while they make us see the cause, they still leave us unable to hear the result).

On the functional level, however, this ancillary point of the absence of the result is very important. Together with the visible purpose, a second hypothesis, a second abduction, is generated by, on the one hand, the silence of the orchestra and, on the other, the ostentatious behaviour of the musicians presenting the piece. It implies the existence of a second effort and a second impact regarding this event, but this time it does not operate among the figures on the screen – it is directed at us, the spectators, and at our astonishment and amusement. Now we shift from the level of the object shown in the image to the level of the film image itself. The figure in the film, the prototype of the film image, but also someone beyond the film, could all be the providers of this effect; and in fact the musician-magician we see is George Méliès himself.

But then the seven versions vanish in exactly the same way in which they appeared: each of them merges with the figure (apparition) he stepped out of. At the end, after he has made the chairs disappear as well, the first musician also fades away. A normal exit is denied to him – we do not know by whom. He tries several doors on the stage and, all of a sudden, finally disappears right from the middle of the image. Only the empty stage remains. This end leads us to suspect that the magician, too, has changed from an agent to a patient during the film. At least we do not have any perceptible reason to believe that it was the intention of the magician to vanish this suddenly; quite to the contrary. It could have been –presumably – an exterior power that has caused this effect. The last thing we see, before the audience applauds, is the empty stage, and thus it is the arrangement of the stage itself, which appears as a possible position of agency, as a magical space with inherent power, full of self-acting traps and barriers.

In 1898, this stage was not only presented as a prototype evoked on a screen by a film image. This screen was actually located on that stage itself, which then became visible in the image on the screen; the stage of the Théâtre Houdin was operated by Méliès and dated back to its founder, the famous magician Houdini.[11] In this theatre, Méliès staged magical revues and fairy-tale pieces, and his film screenings were initially part of that context.

Thus, on the stage of the Théâtre Houdin, the spectators saw a projected image, which showed exactly the same stage on which the image could be seen. Next, this juxtaposition and superimposition of stages is repeated once more in the projected image that we see; it is doubled by the juxtaposition of the musician as 'prototype' and his copies as 'indices', which also appear superimposed and next to each other. By simple spatial proximity, structural analogy and chronological repetition, we are led to assume that the relation of causation which exists between the stage and the stage on the screen is also valid between the musician and his copies. In this manner Méliès's film adopts the motif of the enigmatic, inexplicable origination or agency of a magician facing the magically-produced 'appearances' of the notorious magic stage and the performance of a magician.

With this in mind, it appears interesting that the largest part of Méliès' many films is tied to the framework of stage and staging. While they gradually disengage from the stage, they keep the specifically stage-centred perspective, the framing, and the spatial arrangements of the stage.[12] They, for instance, very often limit the image at the sides by draped curtains, and they do not avoid acting directly in front of the camera (and addressing it in turn). Other films by Méliès, which were created in public spaces, are mainly situated in an urban scenery, and invariably show the settings of public performances and spectacles, the boulevards and squares used for parades, march-pasts, but also fire drills; grand stairways preparing for the reception of guests of state, the promenades of the Bois de Boulogne, where the bourgeoisie showcases their Sunday best. All these spaces are consistently presented in the form of stages, and they evoke the events onstage, or at least contribute to their constitution.

The Primacy of Vanishing: The Negation of Agency

Yet, the end of the orchestra film gives one pause for thought, as the sudden disappearance from the open stage, with neither any further *dispositif* nor any recognizable authorship of the magician, is not part of the established repertoire of the stage, and cannot be attributed to it by any abduction; one that has always been rehearsed and accepted (we might even describe it as an induction). Here, the recognizable logic of the magician causing something – even his own disappearance – meets its limit as well. A still unfamiliar logic becomes effective and is specific to cinematography. Méliès favours it in a particular way; he employs it, especially at the end of his films, again and again, sometimes in an attenuated manner, when the magician turns his wand around to make himself disappear. Not in this case: for a lack of alternatives, we are forced to assume the authorship of neither the magician nor the stage, and especially not of anything visible in the image, but of the image itself – in other words

Gell's index: an artistic, cultic or magical object capable of a response. The disappearance of the magician, as well as our resulting astonishment, can only be an effect of the cinematographic image itself.

And this new hypothesis is confirmed at once. Just as with regard to the juxtaposition of the musicians and the juxtaposition of the stages, the sudden disappearance of the magician-musician from the centre of the image is doubled by the soon following disappearance of the image itself, its own fading after the end of the projection. Here, the cinematographic image leads us to perceive it not only as the cause of the effect it has on us, but also as the cause of the events on the screen themselves, particularly their actual non-appearance. We ascribe agency[13] to the cinematographic image in Méliès's case, and thus possibly up to the present day as well. In a tautological way, this ascription is proven true exactly by the image's ability, its power, to elicit our attribution of agency to it.

This becomes even clearer when we take a look at further cases of creating disappearances in the work of Méliès. The legendary *Escamotage d'une dame/The Conjuring of a Woman at the House of Robert Houdin* and also *Le manoir du diable/The House of the Devil*, both dating from 1896, are very good examples for this particular effect. In *Escamotage d'une dame*, Méliès presents a well-known trick of the stage that has been performed many times. Again, we observe a magic stage; we observe the magician, who directs our attention to his stage and the chair positioned upon it with his gestures. He – gallantly – shows a lady onto the stage, who sits down on the chair. Next, he spreads out a large blanket over her, which covers all of her shape; then, after some short magical gestures, he removes the blanket. The lady is gone. But the lady's disappearance as a result of the magician's manipulation astonishes his audience far less than the exit of the musician-magician right from the centre of the image in the example above (Figures 2–3), because this trick seemed to be quite common and, one suspects, functioned due to the tricks and ruses predisposed by the stage itself. Here, the cinematograph only registers/records. Of course this is also supported by the appearance of a

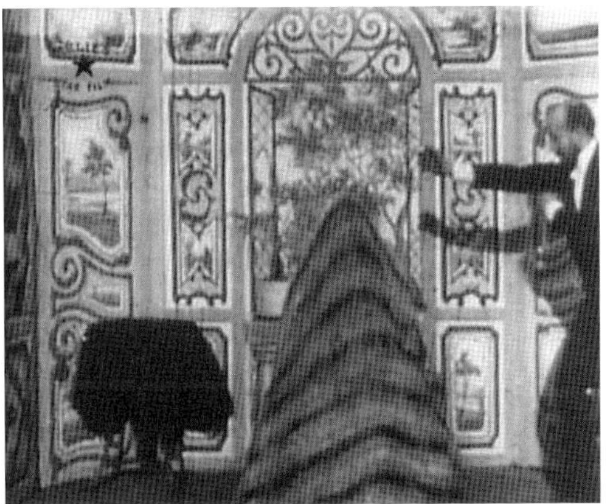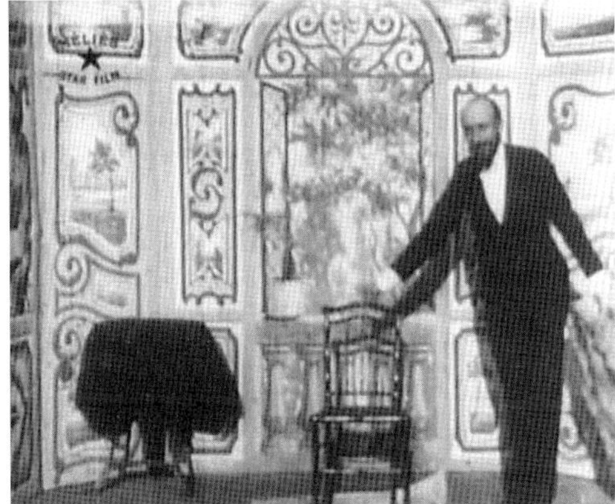

Figures 2–3: Georges Méliès, *Escamotage d'une dame chez Robert Houdin*, 1896, 1 min.

causer, who, as in the other example, acts as the 'prototype' of the magician, and to whom the agency enabling the disappearing act can be ascribed. But there is something peculiar: here, in the film version, the trick itself is just feigned. All the components of the trick, the whole tangible arrangement combining stage, chair, curtain etc., are being put into place, culminating in the little carpet above the trap in the stage, which naturally becomes the method by which the lady disappears during the stage trick. But the stage trick is not performed as such at all; rather, the effect creating the disappearance is caused by the specifically cinematographic means, and is concealed behind the stage trick.

However, it is exactly this method which is prototypical for the magic trick per se: very many tricks employ elaborate material staging and arrangements, which are in no way connected to the detail that actually causes the effect, but cause a distraction from that very detail in return. The special installation visible in the image – again, an index in Gell's sense of the term, a caused cause, a magical constellation – does not have any effect. It is the authorship of those unseen and absent elements of the image which asserts itself in this diversion, this negation of magical agency. It is not the visible in the image which becomes effective, but rather the image itself; this happens in a manner which, initially, is specific to the cinemagical image in particular, but later becomes a characteristic of the cinematographic image in general, namely via the so-called 'stop trick'.

The 'stop trick' and its discovery by Méliès has found its way into the myth-making of film history, and yet it is still reproduced unabatedly in the rigidity of Friedrich Kittler's media-universe as well.[14] Méliès himself describes in his memoirs, how he filmed a plain street scene at the Place de l'Opéra one day.[15] Suddenly, the film got stuck in the camera. Méliès interrupted shooting the film, fixed the camera, and continued recording after a short interruption. When he watched the developed recordings he was deeply baffled: a huge lorry, coming from the margin, went up to the middle of the image – and vanished there without a trace. A closer look revealed that all other figures shown, all passers-by and objects, suddenly vanished at this point of the film as well. But in return, others appeared at other places as if from nowhere. Only the setting of the event, the backdrop of the opera's façade and the scene of the square, remained unchanged. But, as we have seen with regard to the example of the orchestra film above, the film setting-scene might possibly be the causing agent of the appearance of the lorry and the passers-by, but not of their vanishing.

Le manoir du diable (1896)[16] works in exactly the same way: the materially-arranged setting remains stable, just like in the case of the one-man orchestra and its function of the stage; it is out of the question that it functions as the cause for the sudden vanishing and appearance of the characters. In this film, it can only be the work of an initially invisible magician, of an agent, whose interference has to be tolerated by the hero for the moment, putting him into the role of a patient. But using pointing gestures with his rapier, the hero addresses the respective site/position in space, where the vanishing and appearance takes place. Only at the end does the hero regain his agency through the magic of the crucifix.

In *Escamotage d'une dame* (1896), Méliès put the stop trick at the centre of a whole film for the first time. Later, he systematized it extensively and perceived it as the core of his own style of filming, and even of cinematography in general. This is not wholly unjustifiable. The stop trick is still the basis for the classic montage, which is used to this day: a take has to disappear, and everything that has became visible through it, so that there is space for a new one. Effectively, even today every sudden re-cut is a stop trick – and every single framed image (on the film reel) has to vanish in order for a moving image to appear on the screen, twenty-four times a second.

In any case, the vanishing of the cinematographic and the cinemagic can no longer be traced back to the content of the image, the 'prototypes' or the visible settings, like, for example, the painstakingly prepared magic stage. They are not able to make something vanish in the film; it is possible that they disappear themselves, and this, we are forced to assume, is not by their own volition and capability. Thus, an early primacy of vanishing in film establishes itself in this context. It complies with a media-related logic of cinematography. The film image is the only image that is able to deploy its agency by making something vanish, which is also true for its derivatives. In the absence of the magician, it is the image itself which can address single places or points in the image-space, effectively by just making the objects vanish which are positioned at these places. As indices, as caused causations, all possible realizations of images are able to make something that is absent appear as present. This is the 'prototype', and it is at exactly this point that they deploy their agency. But only the film image is, on the one hand, able to bestow presence to this causation, as a temporal object in the image, be it in its continual progress or in the before-after-pattern of the montage.[17] But secondly, and more importantly, it is able to make the object of the image, which is created in this manner, the 'prototype', disappear again. And only this disappearance, which no longer has a cause visible in the image, is able to trigger and to condition the process of abduction, and is sure to make us ascribe its causation to the image itself.

In turn, the cause for this inducement may be that the appearing object, and thus the 'prototype' puts a great demand on our attention during the act of appearance. In the case of vanishing, however, that which disappears is already known; it is only its disappearance, and thus the change, which bothers us. In *Le manoir du diable* (1896), this becomes clear in a changed manner: we do not know the figures that will appear, no more than the protagonists; therefore, we focus on the place of their appearance. The vanishing, on the other hand, concerns the process itself and the power behind it. As soon as a magician, who could have been perceived as responsible, refrains from being present, it is, beyond the visible, only the entity of the cinematographic image itself – the prerequisite with regard to the visibility of the visible – which remains as a possible causer. From this moment on, the cinemagic-cinematographic image operates like a kind of short-circuit: the power of causation or inducement, which we ascribe to it as an index, is verified by it – in terms of a tautological conclusion – exactly by causing us to assume that it has this power at its disposal. It is declared to be the cause, or at least the inducement, for this ascription. In this way, it gains the ability to cause the ascription of causation to itself. The negative version, the negation of agency via making something vanish, emerges as the reflection of the cinemagic image; just as negation generally represents the basic level of reflexivity in logic and other theories, for instance systems theory.[18]

The Script of Agency

Apart from the primacy of vanishing, we are able to gain far more detailed information about the cinematographic image as agency, as a complex instance of causation in its own right, by observing Méliès. This becomes apparent, for example, with regard to Méliès' film *Les cartes vivantes/The Living Playing Cards* (1904). Again, a magician makes his entrance; again, he addresses an audience by looking at the camera and gesturing at the spectators. And, again, he set up a screen on-stage (which appears on the screen), that he, additionally, positions on a pedestal, which itself can be compared to a stage. Next, he pulls out a playing card, which we cannot read due to the great distance. As if he was reacting to calls from the audience, the magician uses a trick to enlarge the card, until we are able to recognize it. Next, he makes the card appear on the screen. In the next trick, he conjures the queen of hearts on the screen in this way – followed later by the king of spades – which he even turns into a real lady of flesh and blood in the end. He guides the lady gallantly from the screen and down the pedestal, and then leads her back up and turns her into a stiff image once more.

How does the image on the screen generate our (self-confirming) belief in its caused authorship (i.e. origination)? This happens in a diachronic sequence and in a synchronic structure. First of all, authorship runs through three phases. Firstly, each is ascribed a different originator during a duplicate process. Authorship is ascribed consecutively; first to the recipient, then to the magician and finally, in a third step, to the image itself. Secondly, the topic of authorship – as the centre of the film – is positioned in the first part, confirmed in the second part by repeating it, and, ultimately, detached from the visible by reversing it in the third part.

It is worthwhile to take a closer look at the dramatic script – which develops in the complex interplay between these two lines of progression in a very short amount of time – in order to gain insights into the anatomy of cinemagic. Due to the addressing gestures of the magician, which we interpret as a reaction to the presence of an audience, the recipients become the invisible prototype of the image, as seen above; they are provided with a site in the real space beyond the image – similarly to Gell, where the offered product appears to us as an answer to our demands.[19]

But in this case, the magician reacts specifically to the prototypical recipient. Thus it is this recipient who causes the magician to enlarge the cards until we can read them. Even though the magician appears as an acting figure, he is, for the time being, still the patient of the scene. And he remains in this role, as he proceeds to remind us in due course, when he enlarges the second and third card specifically for us. Then, in mid-phase, the magician gains agency after all and becomes an agent himself, as he demonstrates to us in a gestural prefiguration what will happen next: the pattern of the card will appear on the screen, the queen will be transformed, the king will replace the queen. In light of the occurring events, we subsequently recognize each preparative gesture of the magician as prefiguration, and due to the repetition, we do not ascribe these prefigurations to a prognostic ability of the magician – something will happen – but perceive them as an expression of an, and of his, intention: 'I will make something happen'. Yet according to Gell, intention and cause are connected directly with each other; the intention even *is* the cause.

This process is supported by gestures of projection; with expressive gestures, the magician literally throws the appearance of the playing card on the screen in one instance, obviously preparing the prototypicality of the image projected on the screen in this manner. Or it is the gesture of contact, when the magician puts the card to the border of the screen, enabling the image to move from here to there, propelled by the force, the pressure of the intention ascribed to the magician. And thirdly the image dissolves into light and smoke, just in order to reappear on the screen across an intermediate space; all these are also obviously variants of the situation of projection characterizing cinema itself.

In the complicated final phase, however, an additional agent enters the scene, as the prototype of the king of spades who unforeseeably materialized from the screen starts to act on his own accord, chases the magician off and takes his place, just like in *L'homme orchestre*. Ultimately, the index itself begins to act: the image shown in the image swallows the magician and releases him again, enabling him to exit the stage in a normal manner. Something that looks like an intentional act of the magician – his leap into the screen – is forced on an altered course by a separate act of the image: the torn image closes behind the body. The magician is unable to perceive this, he has no clue what is happening to him; he is, in fact, vanishing completely from the cinematographic image-space instead of being just physically hidden by the screen present in the image. The magician wants to use the image in order to vanish and reappear, but it is the image which swallows him and releases him again. Additionally, the exit demonstrates that the magician is going to adopt this process as his own intent only after the fact, like a little child who pretends that the unforeseen was his plan all along. Finally, he posits us as the causers of the whole event – he looks at us, his audience, again – and so the circle closes itself.

Thus, ascription of magical or artistic agency cannot be assumed to be a given, but – according to Méliès, and maybe in every other example as well – has to be generated specifically for each single case in its own chronological sequence, following a dramaturgy, a complex script.[20]

This also implies that specifically dramaturgic and time-setting operations, like repetitions, variations, diversions and inversions are indispensable for the process of cinematic magic. Therefore, for films – at least in Méliès' case and possibly for many other instances as well – there exist no inherent magical or artistic objects, indices in Gell's sense, which are always complete and ready, but 'merely' scripts for their fabrication as temporal objects. The technology of desire is cinemagically supported by a dramaturgy of effectuation. For Gell, this simply happens in a cursory manner as 'abduction', more or less without cause; but concerning film, this is the specific operational result of its efforts and its complex scripts. In a strict, Peircean sense, this is no longer an unadulterated abduction; although it is not yet something else, for instance a true induction, it already appears as some kind of induced deduction.

Conclusion: Cinemagic Operations

In light of all this, it seems to be the hallmark of cinema that it does not simply possess energy and effectuation or gets them ascribed like normal indices, but that it acts itself to gain these characteristics and thus contributes to its own agency. This creates an important difference. In order to explain, for example, the presence of the absent, of the prototype, in the image, Gell limits himself, as mentioned above, to the mere existence of an analogy, a relation based on similarity.[21] But regarding cinemagic, it has a preparative, accompanying, framing function at best, like that between the screen placed on the stage and the stage projected on the screen in Méliès' case. It is not the analogy itself or the iconicity which are crucial, but rather the process, the operation of iconization, ultimately, the becoming analogous. This happens via projection in the case of Méliès' magic image, as we have seen. Here, projection functions on three levels at once: in the temporal sense as a catalyst of anticipation; in the physical sense by the casting of the image onto the screen; and, finally, in the technical sense by the effect of lighting. As a result, similarity becomes the effect of an operation, and only as such can it become relevant in the context of agency and decision-making power.

Addressing is, according to Méliès, a second decisive operation for the generation of agency.[22] Here, we have encountered it throughout: from the initial moments of the first example to the final seconds of the last. Addressing can take place via the determination of a point or site in space, as with the disappearance from the image; or via the ascription of a place of performance in the context of complex agency, as in the employment of the spectator as an agent. At least for early films, actions of indication and demonstration, as well as the relations of the gaze and perspectives, are especially important. The removal of such formulas of addressing in late classical film, which identify themselves as the providers of this function, will have the result that classical film – while it is attributed with power effects – does not reveal itself readily as the one agency which leads us to ascribe power to it.

However, there remains to be a third crucial procedure apart from projection and forms of addressing – that of blending, doubling or superimposition. In fact, numerous operations and objects in Méliès's films fulfil functions within the context of projection as well as the context of addressing, starting with the direction of the magic wand and the anticipating gesture up to the leap into the screen. Projection, which is iconic at its core, is interlinked with addressing, which, in turn, is indexical, just the way Peirce described the hallmark of the index: every index also encompasses an icon.[23] In Méliès' case, we are able to shift our focus between these two aspects, just as I have demonstrated above with regard to the questions of 'abduction' and 'induction'. It is ultimately this blurring, a superimposition of the 'second order',[24] which seems to constitute the extraordinary effectiveness of Méliès' magic image, and – to an unknown extent – of cinema in general.

It causes nothing but the things it shows as well; it shows nothing but what it also is, and it is, in fact, nothing but the result of the dramaturgic scripts which characterize it, and of the operations that evoke it; the establishment of agency and the causing of its disappearance and negation, of repetitions and diversions, of variations and inversions, and, finally, of the cinemagic of projection, addressing and superimposition.

Translated by Jochen Mevius

Notes

1   Alfred Gell, *Art and Agency: An Anthropological Theory*, Oxford: Clarendon, 1998.

2   For a history of semiotic terms concerning 'index', see Umberto Eco, *Zeichen. Einführung in einen Begriff und seine Geschichte*, Frankfurt am Main: Suhrkamp, 1977, pp. 60–63; concerning a discussion of the term 'index' as according to Morris and Peirce, see John Dewey, 'Peirce's Theory of Linguistic Signs, Thoughts, and Meaning', in *The Journal of Philosophy XLIII*, No. 4, 1946, pp. 85–95; cf. also Gerhard Schönrich, *Semiotik zur Einführung*, Hamburg: Junius, 1999, p. 105ff.

3   Gell, 1998, pp. 11–16.

4   Charles Sanders Peirce as quoted from a review by Josiah Royce, 'Religious Aspects of Philosophy', in K. O. Apel (ed.), *Schriftenzum Pragmatismus und Pragmatizismus*, Frankfurt am Main: Suhrkamp, 1976, pp. 253–65, especially pp. 256–59.

5   Gell, 1998, pp. 13 & 35ff.

6   ibid.

7   ibid., p.14ff; concerning abduction in detail, see Charles Sanders Peirce, 'Drei Typen des Schlußfolgerns', in Apel, 1976, pp. 395–410; also see Umberto Eco and Thomas A. Sebeok (eds), *The Sign of the Three*, Bloomington: Indiana University Press, 1983; also see Umberto Eco, 'Die Abduktion in Uqbar', in Jorge Luis Borges and Adolfo Bioy Casares, *Gemeinsame Werke*, Vol. 1, München: Hanser, 1983, pp. 271–86.

8   Gell, 1998, p. 21ff.

9   ibid., pp. 25–26.; cf. Nelson Goodman, *Languages of Art*, Indianapolis: Hackett, 1976.

10   Gell, 1998, pp. 25–26.

11   Georges Sadoul, *Georges Méliès*, Paris: Seghers, 1961, p. 20f.; for an overview, also see Fondation Électricité de France, Cinémathèque Française and Cinémathèque Méliès (eds), *Méliès: Magie et Cinema*, Paris: Musées, 2002; Laurent Mannoni and JaquesMalthête (eds), *L'Oeuvre de Georges Méliès*, Éditions de la Martinière & La Cinématheque Française, Paris, 2008.

12   André Gaudréault, *Théâtralité et Narrativité dans L'Oeuvre de Georges Méliès*, Montréal: Presses University 1982; Josef Nagel, 'Frühe Entwicklungstendenzen einer Medienspezifischen Filmsprache', dissertation, Erlangen, 1988; see also Georges Méliès, *Magier der Filmkunst*, KINtop, Vol. 2, Basel & Frankfurt am Main: Stroemfeld/Roter Stern, 1993.

13 The term 'agency' is used in this context as the ability to exercise power, avoiding an overlap with the term 'agency' in the sense of a material and social-institutional organization (of such power).

14 Friedrich Kittler, 'Fiktion und Simulation', in *Ars Electronica* (ed.), *Philosophien der Neuen Technologie*, Berlin: Merve, 1989, pp. 57–79, especially p. 69f; Friedrich Kittler, *Grammophon Film Typewriter*, Berlin: Brinkmann und Bose, 1986, p. 177f.

15 Sadoul, 1961, p. 22; see also Maurice Bardèche and Robert Brasillach, *Histoire du Cinema*, Paris: Denoëlet Steele, 1935, p. 19.

16 In this film, a hero armed with crucifix and rapier vanquishes his attackers, which is not easy at all, because they suddenly disappear from their positions in the room and appear elsewhere in the image.

17 André Bazin, 'Schneiden verboten!', in *Was ist Film?*, Berlin: Alexander-Verlag, 2004, pp. 75–89.

18 Gotthard Günther, *Das Bewußtsein der Maschinen*, Krefeld: Agis, 1957, p. 38ff; cf. Niklas Luhmann, 'Über die Funktion der Negation in Sinnkonstituierenden Systemen', in HaraldWeinrich (ed.), *Positionen der Negativität* (Poetik und Hermeneutik, VI), München: Fink, 1975, pp. 201–08.

19 Gell, 1998, p. 33ff.

20 Regarding the term 'script', see also, among others, Bruno Latour, *Die Hoffnung der Pandora*, Frankfurt am Main: Suhrkamp, 2002, pp. 211–58.

21 Gell, 1998, p. 25.

22 Marc Vernet, 'Le regard à la caméra', in *Figures de l'absence* (*Cahiers du Cinema* essay collection), Paris: Etoile, 1988, pp. 9–28. Incidentally, Vernet provides a very insightful discussion of superimposition as a strategy of absence: ibid., pp. 59–88.

23 Charles Sanders Peirce, 'Vorlesungen über Pragmatismus', in Apel, 1976, p. 362ff.

24 Concerning the term and logic of 'second order', see Heinz von Foerster, *Cybernetics of Cybernetics*, Urbana, IL: University of Illinois Press, 1974; Heinz v. Foerster, *Understanding Understanding: Essays on Cybernetics and Cognition*, New York: Springer, 2003.

Chapter 18

Liminal Spaces: Notes by Film-maker and Artist Malcolm Le Grice

Malcolm LeGrice

In Retrospect: Malcolm Le Grice on...

... key influences of the Expanded Cinema movement in the 1970s on contemporary media art and contemporary video art (film installation art) today?

Expanded Cinema is probably only one part of a general erosion of the strict boundaries between established art media such as painting, sculpture, music, dance, theatre, cinema and literature. Key elements in this were the 'happenings', 'fluxus' and art-technology fusions. This went together with an interest in immersive projection with or without film – Stan Vanderbeek's *Pleasure Dome* (1954) or the *Vortex Concerts* (1957). For my part, film was an extension from, and breaking down of the barriers of, painting. But also, for me, the influence of jazz improvisation on music performance – Cage, Cornelius Cardew and AMM was very important. Art in the 1960s became a melting pot and a realization that there were no boundaries other than cultural habit. So, what was the influence of this on contemporary work? Where in the 1960s we needed to break down the barriers, it is now the normal assumption that there are no constraints to choice of media. This lack of constraint on the forms of art practice is extended through contemporary communications systems: Internet, satellite, mobile phones. Expanded Cinema is no longer a category – all of media and media delivery systems are Expanded Cinema.

... the aspect of the 'presence' of images in Expanded Cinema after film as well as video art have digitalized their production conditions and their filmic moments of projection.

My stress on 'presence' is an attempt to place the immediacy of experience above the conclusiveness (closure) of 'idea'. I react badly to art that becomes quickly closed by the strength and evidence of an intentional 'idea'. Once the idea has been grasped, the experience of the spectator is complete and the work as experience is dead. This, together with a cynical eclecticism, was the biggest problem with postmodernism. So how is presence achieved in work that is digitally produced? My own 'strategy' (actually a psychological desire) has been to continue a tradition of immersiveness, using scale – to engage the spectator in the flow of an event much as music occupies the senses before a concept forms the perception of the spectator. The spectator lives through the experience of a work that may continue to resonate after the work has ended. Indeed, for myself, I resist conclusion and understanding both in the making of a work and in the structures I offer the viewer/listener. Any construction 'belongs' to the viewer and is not merely a reconstruction of my 'intention'.

… the artists that influenced his aesthetic thinking and filming.

My earliest influences from visual art were Monet, Matisse and Picasso, and in the modern period Jasper Johns and Robert Rauschenberg. From music – Louis Armstrong (Hot Five and Hot Seven) then Ornette Coleman and Dizzy Gillespie then in the '60s; of course John Cage and the music group AMM (with whom I have often worked). From literature, by far the greatest influence was from Kafka and from theatre, Beckett. From film the influences are difficult to define. After the 'normal' childhood of Hollywood cinema, as a young artist I became so opposed to narrative cinema that I did not see any film-maker as an influence, particularly opposing Jean Luc Godard (though I saw *Alphaville* [1965] six or seven times and analyzed the script), Alain Resnais etc. So – there were no direct positive influences on my early films coming from other film-makers. After my earliest films – *Castle 1* (1968), *Yes No Maybe Maybenot* (1967) or *Little Dog For Roger* (1967) – I admired and was 'influenced' by Peter Gidal, Birgit and Wilhelm Hein, Stan Brakhage (despite great differences of attitude), and later my colleagues with whom I worked closely, Gill Eatherley, Willam Raban and Annabel Nicolson – the so-called Filmaktion group.

… on the intentionality of the performativity of moving images in Expanded Cinema.

I do not like the idea of 'intention'. Even now, when I make a work it is to explore what I do not know, not to express some existing idea or concept. It remains a complex interaction of desire, serendipity and improvisation. The work is a product of 'working-on' – a very plastic activity. Perhaps the specific clarity of my theoretical writing creates a false impression that my work carries this theoretical 'intention'. This is not true – the art-practice and theory are two different discourses that may run parallel – or not. I do not think about the theory whilst making a work.

… on his film After Lumière (1974). (*After Lumière* is based on *L'Arroseur Arrosé* [Louis Lumière, 1895] – not *L'arrivée d'un train en gare de La Ciotat* [Auguste and Louis Lumière, 1895]).

My main exploration here was related to the 'documental' condition of cinema – the film image as an indexical signifier, but also a 'review' of a minimal narrative where the narrative

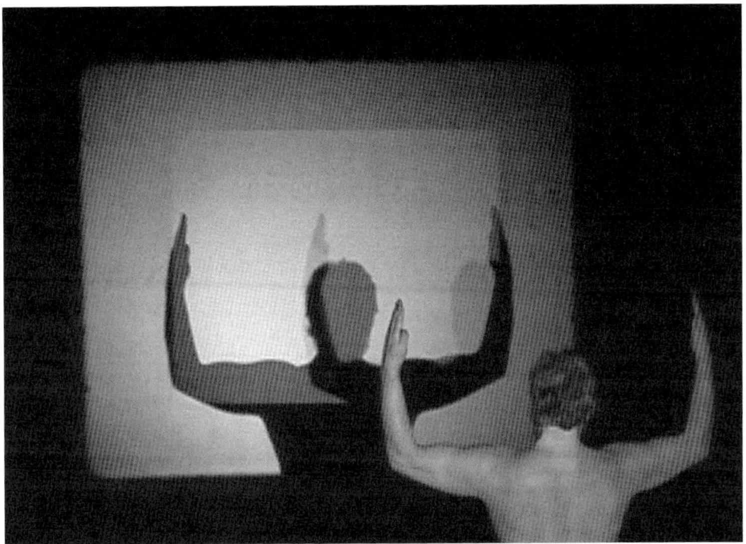

Figure 1: Malcolm Le Grice, still from *Horror Film 1*, 1971. Image courtesy of the artist.

of the film's unfolding for the spectator became more significant (undermines) the internal represented narrative. I see *After Lumière* as a kind of detective story – where the changing repeats, and variations of 'perspective' need to be constantly reviewed and reassessed by the viewer to make sense of the document.

… on his film Threshold (1972). *Colour is a key element in your work. In* Threshold *a liminality of the image is unfolding with interspersed sound elements that reminded me of the kind of visual strategy of 'deferral' that you used in* After Lumière (1895).

The sound is rather denoting an outside of images and a certain kind of displacement or contingency. The sound is no more than a randomized cut up and re-mix of the optical tracks that were on the found footage of the frontier guard sequence. Both the colour sequences and the found footage became raw material for a kind of disco re-mix. This is sort of echoed in the way I now improvise the projector movements of the three-screen version: it is DJ, VJ or F-for-film-J.

Chapter 19

Transgression: The Ethical Turn and the New Politics – Fatih Akin's Cinema and the Multicultural Dilemma

Thomas Elsaesser

For many of my generation, love of cinema has never just been a way of enjoying the twentieth century's favourite form of entertainment. It has always also implied a question: what is the place and potential of 'cinema', in the public sphere that used to be called 'progressive politics?' Since May '68, then November 1989, and especially since September 2001, this question has evolved into engaging through film the seemingly impossible, but necessary demand for 'dialogue': dialogue with the ethnic, the religious or the national Other. Underpinning these encounters with the cultural Other is the hope to keep alive core political issues, such as those of justice and rights, of entitlements and empowerments, of grief and grievances: in a world order that, under the name of liberal democracy and free trade, has tended to cement old inequalities and created new ones.

In Western Europe, the demand for dialogue often expresses itself across the political institutions of the European Union, and its many agencies' efforts to balance (personal, religious) self-determination and (regional, linguistic) autonomy: to 'integrate' those from other backgrounds and beliefs; to promote shared values and equal rights; to harmonize legal frameworks; to maintain health and welfare provisions; to secularize gender-relations, especially with respect to the rights of women; and to set up common institutions that define civility and civic responsibility in an effort to redefine citizenship across the nation state and under conditions of globalization. For some countries outside Europe, it has manifested itself in transitional justice and truth and reconciliation commissions; for yet others, the demand for dialogue articulates itself in the so-called identity wars, and for many more it has remained at the stage of confrontation – either in the form of low-intensity daily attrition, or as high-profile acts of violence and warfare.

Yet the demand for dialogue is also present in the struggles concerning the interpretative authority over, and thus the discursive ownership of the past – the tensions between, for instance, 'history' and 'memory': that is, of how to arbitrate among contested versions of national history as a result of war or political catastrophe (such as in the cases of the legacy of fascism in Italy, Germany or Spain; or of communism in Hungary, the Czech Republic or Poland), of cultural memory of homelands (such as the many examples of expulsion, migration, exile), and of witnessing and testimony (as in the case of crimes against humanity, around genocide or in dealing with the consequences of civil wars and colonialism).

The Ethical Turn

It is in this context that ethics returns as a critical issue, emerging at the juncture where the multiplicity of identities based on markers of difference, and defined as 'cultural' (and thus subsuming nationality, ethnicity, religion, gender), no longer afford a common framework or an agreed basis on which competing claims can be arbitrated or negotiated, other than by bureaucratic forms of redistribution (for instance, 'quotas' or 'affirmative action' in the US; financial grants to foster 'regional autonomy' in the EU; and the administration of a multicultural or diversity agenda at local and community level). Some new standard or category seems to be needed to overcome the deadlock between Enlightenment universalism and regional, ethnic or religious particularism. On the one hand, recognition of the 'Other' is the explicit goal of the politics of multiculturalism, a term that designates the very efforts to mitigate the consequences of Eurocentric essentialism, and to militate for a new tolerance. On the other hand, multiculturalism is not the only philosophy trying to achieve this aim. Ethics, too, has been the name for this encounter with the Other: one thinks of the philosopher Emmanuel Levinas, for whom ethics has little to do with morality, but connotes 'the calling into question of the Same.'[1]

In order to understand what Levinas means by this sentence, and how it relates to the cinema as a vehicle for an ethics after politics, it helps to make a distinction between ethics Mark 1 and ethics Mark 2. 'Ethics' – by common definition, and thus Mark 1 – would be the reasons I give for justifying my actions, the principles that govern the good life; but, etymologically, 'ethics' also refers to the traditions, the customs, habits and values I hold dear. In this sense, ethics is compatible with the aims of multiculturalism, as the harmonious expression of difference. But there is another ethics (hence ethics Mark 2) that does not try to bridge difference, but accentuates it. Such an ethics stands as the recto to the verso of multiculturalism, of which it is both the complement and the missing supplement. Levinas has specified its fundamental principle as follows: 'ethics' encompasses 'the demands that present themselves as necessarily to be fulfilled, but which are neither forced upon me [by morality], nor are they enforceable [by law.]'[2] Such a definition – mapping out a territory separate from but implying law and force, individual and community, necessity and choice – usefully indicates the close interdependence that exists between ethics, politics and multiculturalism. They are communicating vessels in a certain sense, but they are also in mutual competition with each other, and they leave open questions of equality and justice.

For instance, Levinas also insists that an encounter with the Other cannot be reduced to a reciprocal relationship (an exchange, a mutually-agreed contract or bargain, a quid pro quo – as would be suggested when equality is the key aim or demand). Therefore, it is in this second sense that ethics appears as a counter-term to multiculturalism; raising the bar, as it were, by pointing to the latter's failure to specify the precise terms of such an encounter with the Other, prior to (or in the absence of, equality)   ignoring, notably, the risks to selfhood and identity that such an encounter entails, and on which Levinas so forcefully insists.[3]

This ethics Mark 2 is what is usually meant by the 'ethical turn', and besides Levinas, it is associated with the name of Jacques Derrida, for whom ethics signals both an uncoupling from the traditional idea of (party) politics, and a setting up of a critical distance from any form of culturalism, insisting on a distinction between law and justice, but also refusing to pose the question of rights in the terms of identity-politics, i.e. either as a matter of distribution (equality), or of the collective will (democracy). Instead, ethics for both Levinas and Derrida introduces the question of violence, usually excluded from multicultural discourse, as well as re-introducing terms such as 'obligation' or 'demand' generally absent from culturalism; the former terms addressed to the individual in all his/her singularity, while culturalism addresses itself usually to some kind of group or community, i.e. in the plural.[4]

Once More: Double Occupancy and Mutual Interference

This is a summary of how I see the primary logic of the ethical turn: trying to address, if not resolve, the dilemmas of multiculturalism, of (Marxist) left-wing politics, and (new style) NGO-type human rights militancy; each committed to a progressive politics, but on very different philosophical premises. As to its relevance for contemporary cinema, the ethical turn gives me an opportunity to revisit certain positions I put forward in my book on *European Cinema – Face to Face with Hollywood*. There, I also critique concepts such as multiculturalism and diversity politics, for not signalling either the power dynamics in play, or for not specifying the imbrications of inside and out, self and Other that makes inter-ethnic communication and transnational politics often so intractably difficult.[5] Yet if the cinema can do anything well, it is to make an audience experience how much self and Other, inclusion and exclusion are intertwined and dependent on each other, while still allowing for identification with marginal, excessive or transgressive positions and protagonists. Psycho-semiotics, for all its theoretical shortcomings, firmly kept these dynamics in its sights. This is why I made a case for what I called 'double occupancy' and 'mutual interference', intending thereby to displace the discourse of identity as well as the self-Other debate; and instead to argue, even on historical and geopolitical grounds, that the peoples of Europe, however they define themselves – as 'white', 'Christian' or 'Judeo-Christian' (not forgetting that less than a hundred years, it would have been exclusively in terms of nationality) – have always been mixed, and are always already occupied, diasporic, 'diverse' and 'multiple'.

Taken together, my terms 'double occupancy' and 'mutual interference' designate a particular semantic field: one where such 'soft' commands as the need for 'dialogue' and for 'trusting the Other' are understood not so much as 'taking place', either now or in the future, but merely as 'holding open a place', or designating the conditions of possibility, for a much 'harder' mandate, one that does not come for free, but at a cost: namely of 'interfering' and of being 'implicated'; in other words, the active part of 'in-between-ness', of 'entanglement' and of 'hybridity' (to name some of the terms of the postcolonial discourse), and the dangerous part of 'embodiment' and 'situatedness' (to name two terms also much in use in contemporary theory).

Thus, in a second move, I argued that besides the fact that 'mutual interference in the internal affairs of the Other' is a political doctrine by which the European Union wants to arrive at a new definition of sovereignty among its member states, there is a use for the term in the sphere of intersubjectivity, where it becomes relevant for the affective as well as the cognitive dimension of cinematic space. The staple themes of European cinema since the 1990s are narratives that deal with dysfunctional families, with the impossibility of the couple, or they feature the modern metropolis as the site of multi-ethnic desire, violence and power (often symbolized by drugs, music, intense sensations, and out-of-body experiences). In these films – by Scottish, French, German, Italian, Belgian, Swedish or Finnish directors – the idea of mutual interference is challenging in its transgressiveness because it revolves around spaces to be redistributed, and power relations to be renegotiated. Aside from its tragic dimensions, mutual interference also makes room for comedy and, ideally, even holds out hope for taking responsibility for the Other, while not forsaking self-interest (elsewhere I discuss the ethical and political ramifications of so-called non-cooperative games, such as the famous 'Prisoner's Dilemma').

In the chapter dealing with these issues, one of my prime examples, along with Lars von Trier's *Dogville* (2003) was Fatih Akin's *Gegen die Wand/Head-On* (2004). For me, the film seemed symptomatic insofar that, at first glance, it plays with all the clichés of multicultural and hyphenated film-making: Turkish weddings in Hamburg; tanbur-and-reed flute music on the shores of the Bosporus (a recurring tableau-scene acting like a chorus and a framing device); arch-conservative patriarchal fathers (the angry father disowning his daughter); and male double standards when it comes to wives and sex even among the younger generation (strict separation between domestic prudery and public macho lechery). Yet what drives the film's inner dynamic is not at all this ethnic in-betweenness, this cross-cultural fusion of musical styles or intergenerational family feuds. Instead, the story seems propelled by an ethics of transgression which affirms that being true to oneself requires the double occupancy of mutual interference, whatever the consequences. The first half of the film is especially instructive, insofar as the male-female couple seem to compete with each as to who can be more abject, more self-destructive and more non-cooperative. In these moments, cultural differences or the multicultural 'dialogue' between Germans and Turks play hardly any role at all, and instead it is their sense of freedom that comes from having nothing more to lose (to misquote Janice Joplin) that the film forcefully conveys. Both characters meet when they are, in some sense, already dead, having tried to commit suicide and found no reason to live, ejected as the feel themselves to be from their respective social symbolic: a more radical ejection/abjection than either caused or cured by any reassertions of ethnicity. They do not fall in love, but enter into a mutuality contract of non-interference, meant to sustain their respective phantasy-frames – his 'personal independence' and her 'good life' (their 'ethics Mark 1') – thus letting the spectator see what the price of tolerance might be when secured by a bargain. But when one of them encounters the limits of tolerance at the point of interference, a dangerous and violent, but also potentially liberating state opens up, beyond reciprocity and exchange. Ethics Mark 2 clashes with ethics Mark 1, and the couple's trajectory is set on its ultimately tragic, but life-affirming trajectory whose horizon is mutual interference rather than mutual tolerance.

The 'ethical' power of the film, to my mind, comes from the way the film implicitly challenges the politics of identity. *Gegen die Wand* not only does *not* mark any essential difference between 'Turkish' and 'German' culture (the two blend seamlessly) – and thus foregoes all the dramatic (tragic as well as comic) potential that hyphenated identities usually connote in the cinema (*My Big Fat Greek* Wedding, Joel Zwick, 2002; *Monsoon Wedding*, Mira Nair, 2001; *Bride and Prejudice*, Gurinder Chadha, 2004) – but also demonstrates how this non-marking of cultural difference and the non-marking of the phantasy-frame (here the 'contract' that they do not love each other) are mutually interdependent: once they give in to their 'Turkish roots', their ethics of transgression unravels and collapses. The return to Turkey and to cultural identity – even where outwardly 'successful' – leaves them abandoned and isolated, rather than allowing them a 'homecoming' or a 'coming together'. *Gegen die Wand* was therefore almost too perfect a case study of how in contemporary cinema one can find evidence of such antagonistic cooperation around contract as well as how, under conditions of double occupation, mutual interference might be the unattainable horizon of ethical transgression, and even in its failure the preferable alternative to multicultural dialogue or ethnically-based identity politics.

Auf der anderen Seite: Jacques Rancière

However, it is one of Fatih Akin's subsequent films – *Auf der anderen Seite/The Edge of Heaven* (2007) – that is potentially more symptomatic as to the consequences of the ethical turn in cinema. For this, however, I need to call on the 'new politics', the post-Marxist thinking about 'the political' represented by Jacques Rancière and Alain Badiou, two dissenting disciples of Louis Althusser. In particular, I want to introduce Rancière's critique of the 'ethical turn', what he calls the 'tournant ethique dans l'esthetique et le politique'.[6] As a thinker who considers politics and aesthetics as two communicating vessels, Rancière sees the 'politics' of rational management and consensus (such as practiced by the EU) as the very abrogation of politics. The so-called post-ideological politics, such as intervention in the name of 'world opinion', economic sanctions in the name of 'human rights', or humanitarian missions on the back of military actions, seem to him not only a negation of politics; they testify to what he considers a deep (philosophical) nihilism, because they consist of discourses and actions that put victims, fatalities and survivors at the centre of a politics of rights and obligations. They thereby define the purpose of life as living in the presence of death; or rather, they implicitly assume that 'life' has to rescued from all-enveloping death, making 'catastrophe' (historically: the Shoah, the Nakba, the Armenian genocide, the Gulag; environmentally: tsunamis, hurricanes, earthquakes; militarily: 'pre-emptive strikes', 'war on terror') the 'ground' and 'origin' of being from which victimhood emerges as the only form of authentic agency.

This critique of human rights and the culture of commemoration is a tough message, but in keeping with the post-Nietzschean radicalism and 'anti-humanism' in French thinking, from Foucault and Deleuze to Rancière and Badiou. Perhaps even more counter-intuitive and startling, however, is Rancière's claim that the 'ethical turn' associated with Levinas and Derrida is the complement of the same nihilism. Especially in Levinas' formulations, according to Rancière, both action and thought find themselves suspended in the face of pure Otherness. Whether humanist and secular, fixated on health care, welfare and humanitarian aid (as in our western democracies), or religious and messianic, living for the sublime encounter with absolute alterity (as in Levinas), both ethics Mark 1 and Mark 2 are unable to attach positive value to the present, which becomes a site of paralysis and suspension, meaningful only against the foil of death or (natural/man-made) disaster. In other words, the underlying conviction of the 'ethical turn' is that – now in the words of Alain Badiou – 'the only thing that can really happen to someone is death.'[7]

Against this humanist 'state of emergency' (Giorgio Agamben)[8] or Judeo-Christian ethics of alterity (Emmanuel Levinas), Rancière holds on to a radical conception of democratic politics as the thought and action towards equality. Democracy for him is not 'representative', and has nothing to do with substituting or 'standing in for' the people. Predicated on notions such as the distribution of the sensible, dissensus, the articulation of incompatible demands, the dilemmas of impossible choices, and thus on justice and on equality as an active process, Rancière argues that these fundamental aspects of the political can nowadays only be found, if at all, in modern art (Duchamp's ready-mades, conceptual art, installation art), and there in an attenuated, often parodic form: as montage effects, as a love of paradoxes and double-binds. Even relational aesthetics, where the spectator is invited to 'participate' in the creation or completion of the work, which is to say, asked to be present at a miracle or a mystery, is already suspect – as too therapeutic or too metaphysical. Politics must reclaim the territory now occupied by art, and with it, must extend into public space and *occupy* the public sphere, which (museum and gallery) art, and maybe the cinema, precariously inhabit.

In twentieth-century art it is Marcel Duchamp, not surprisingly, who is the champion of this idea of equality, because he has shown how anything can be art if it changes place and category. But for Rancière, it is finally the cinema that is the most appropriate of the arts on the point of becoming 'political', because the cinema is so impure, so mechanical and so lifelike: in short, so 'thwarted'[9] (Rancière's term for the cinema's internally antagonistic forces) that it can bring into being the singularity and visibility (and thus the value) of the ephemeral, the humble, the excluded and the abject. The cinema accomplishes the levelling of differences between art and life, as originally promised by the avant-gardes. At the same time, as the successor to the realist novel, which first made the ordinary, the transitory as well as the abject and the obscene into suitable subjects for art, the cinema has the potential to complete this move in the direction of 'radical equality' in the political sense. Rancière makes clear how much his theory of art is tied to a theory of labour and human agency, which is the reason why he seems to be in covert dialogue with T.W. Adorno and other critical theorists, while objecting to their notions of reification or commodification.

It is this radical but consistent stance on the political as aesthetic and the aesthetic as political – not as antinomic realms (as famously formulated by Walter Benjamin) but as heteronomic relations (of mutual antagonism but also mutual dependence) – which gives Rancière the authority as well as the vantage point of 'the political', from which to deconstruct the ethical, too. In the sphere of politics, conflicts articulate themselves between different part(ie)s of the community in such a way that the antagonism is not only external vis-à-vis an opponent or enemy, but internal and constitutive, touching the individual as a mortal being of body and voice. As Rancière puts it:

> [P]olitics precisely begins when they who have 'no time' to do anything else than their work, take that time that they do not have, in order to make themselves visible as sharing in a common world and prove that their mouths indeed emit common speech instead of merely voicing pleasure or pain.[10]

By contrast, the ethical, as represented by the ethics of human rights, as well as by Levinas' or Derrida's 'ethical turn', seems to be deadlocked or suspended between the idea of a multicultural, but ultimately harmonious community of consensus (what Rancière calls *l'ethique soft*), and the ethics of radical alterity and the state of exception conceived from the perspective of a seemingly forever deferred infinite justice (*l'ethique hard*). But, as Ranciere puts it, somewhat sarcastically, taking a swipe at the 'hard ethics' of Levinas and Agamben: 'a whole trend of thought today dissolves political dissensuality in an archi-politics of exception and terror, from which only a Heideggerian God can save us.'[11]

Auf der anderen Seite: Fatih Akin

With this somewhat summary version of Rancière's thinking on ethics in mind, I want to return to Fatih Akin's *The Edge of Heaven*. As will be clear from what has been said so far, the film's interest for my general argument lies in its triangulation of multicultural encounters, identity politics and ethical dilemmas against a background of several deaths. But what first drew my attention to the film was the presence of Hanna Schygulla, Rainer Werner Fassbinder's muse in so many iconic films from the 1970s, in the role of Susanne, one of the two mothers central to the story. The plot, too, makes more than casual reference to Fassbinder's films: the initial situation is reminiscent of *Angst essen Seele auf/Ali: Fear Eats the Soul* (1974), with a Muslim guest-worker (also called Ali) paying a prostitute not just for sex, but for making him 'proper' food. His accidentally killing her and doing time in prison recalls Franz Biberkopf and Ida in *Berlin Alexanderplatz* (1980), while the lesbian relationship has echoes of *Die Bitteren Tränen der Petra von Kant/The Bitter Tears of Petra von Kant* (1972). Another significant point of contact is that *The Edge of Heaven* was in Germany billed (retroactively) as the second film of a trilogy that was meant to respond, according to the director, to Fassbinder's BRD Trilogy (*Die Ehe der Maria Braun/The Marriage of Maria Braun*, 1979; *Lola*, 1981; *Die Sehnsucht der Veronika Voss/Veronika Voss*, 1979). What the troubled relationship between West Germany and its Nazi past was to Fassbinder, Akin seems to imply, is to him the no less troubled negotiation between 'assimilated' Turks in Germany and their homeland.

As already mentioned, Akin generally avoids the Romeo and Juliet melodramas of multicultural star-crossed lovers and the comedies of mistaken ethnic or national stereotypes, although he co-wrote and co-produced a typical example of both, Arno Saul's *Kebab Connection* (2004), and went on to make *Soul Kitchen* (2009), arguably another riff on the genre. The hyphenation of ethnic or religious identities in such films tends to resolve too comfortably (i.e. in the comic or melancholy modes of resignation), and what remains are messy sets of generational tensions, universal moral dilemmas, emotional ambivalences and split loyalties. Like Fassbinder, Akin is also capable of letting perversely improbable love stories, sadistic scapegoating and suicidal sacrifices prevail. *Auf der anderen Seite* is divided into three parts, each announced by an intertitle, with the first two equally, mercilessly predicting: *Yeter's Death* and *Lotte's Death*. The third part, with the film's title as its intertitle, sees the surviving characters arrive in Turkey, their quests intersecting without actually converging, keeping to parallel tracks and bringing more near misses (with the coffins of Yeter and Lotte crossing at Istanbul airport in opposite directions). This stark and memorable image is a reminder that the film as a whole is conceived in the shape of Moebius strip, or infinite loop, running between the two cities Hamburg and Istanbul, while the six characters criss-cross each others' lives in both directions, or more accurately, on both sides of the Moebius strip: *Auf der anderen Seite* translates literally 'on the other side', leaving open whether this refers to the other side of life/death, of political and national divides, of self/ Other, or – as in my reading/translation – 'on both sides of the same loop'.

The parallels, coincidences, improbabilities and dramatic ironies have irritated several critics, but in all fairness such pointed over-plotting is in keeping with the Douglas Sirk– R.W. Fassbinder genealogy of Hollywood – and maybe even Turkish – melodrama that Akin is inscribing himself into. As the matriarch, Schygulla presides over more than the film's liberal conscience: she is the guardian of a pledge to continue the generational burden of the German-German 'Hollywood' dialogue, extended now into a German-Turkish 'European' dialogue. The ingenuity of the film's dramatic architecture is not in the plotting per se. Consistent with the matrix of melodrama, it manifests itself in a complex moral fabric that is being spun through the story, whose overall design, however – this would be my first argument – might indeed need a third part, to carry the ethical weight that the fable of these six interwoven lives claims for itself. If *Gegen die Wand* (2004) can be said to have been 'political' in Rancière's sense, in that it constantly works towards maintaining the thwarted fable which allows the ordinary to seem extraordinary, *Auf der anderen Seite* is – in reference to my second point – an example of 'l'ethique soft', i.e. of antagonisms, self-division and dissensus working towards acquiescence and resolution, however deferred or suspended at the end.

It should be clear from the plot summary just given that 'transgressions' (of whatever kind: sexual, political, ethnic, religious) are punished in the end. Yet, equally clearly, everyone in *Auf der anderen Seite* demonstrates a will towards sacrifice and self-sacrifice, arising in response to these violations and infractions, even though it does not come from the 'perpetrators' themselves. Instead, attempts at atonement emerge and manifest themselves by way of stand-ins, substitutes and 'representatives'. The son wants to make amends for his father's deed by continuing the payments for which a mother had sacrificed her body and honour, only to die without this sacrifice being known or acknowledged; while another mother wants to become worthy of her daughter's sacrifice, irrespective of whether she believes in the cause that the daughter's lover embraced, a cause that makes the other sacrifices (of 'son' and 'mother') seem very nearly futile. Choices are being made in the name of primary bonds, but the families are incomplete, their missing halves absent, and even the dyad is torn apart: son and father, but no mother; mother and daughter, but no father; mother and daughter, but neither encounter nor recognition.

Evidently, these symmetries, repetition and parallels are carefully established and cleverly worked out. First, the opening scene and the closing one make a temporal bracket and are set during a *bayram*, the national celebration and public holiday that unites secular and religious groups, regardless of their differences. Then, placed near the beginning of the third part, but at the heart of the film and its moral fulcrum, is a scene where Nejat explains to Susanne before an open window – putting it in a frame for contour and emphasis, as it were – the meaning of the procession of young men coming down the steps outside: they are celebrating the memory of Abraham's Sacrifice, a story as meaningful to Muslims as it is to Christians and Jews. In this and other scenes, tolerance and bridge-building, the virtues of Turkey's secular constitution, the shared beliefs of the three 'world religions of the book', the modernizing effects of possible/improbable Turkish entry into the European Union, the shadow of Sharia law on western democracies and several other topical motifs are all closely woven into the destinies of Germans and Turks of the second post-war generations, born like Fatih Akin in the 1970s and now entering public life, often as artists, musicians, intellectuals and academics.

At the same time, Akin seems to hint that there is no easy compromise in sight, and that a price will have to be paid in this generational transfer of first and second generation, of Germans and Turks, of secular liberalism and the long memory of injustice. As Ayten enters a plea bargain with the police to be freed, it means she is betraying her activist comrades, an act that surely cannot remain without consequences. Likewise, the ethics of the various acts of sacrifice are peculiarly New Testament (turning the other cheek, rather than an eye-for-an-eye), based on empathetic identification with the Other and a relay of substitution and place-holding. How does this look from the point of view of the Old Law or of Islam, or indeed, how does this square with the harsher lesson the story of God testing Abraham is meant to teach? Just as dread anticipation of pointless deaths suffuses parts one and two of *The Edge of Heaven*, at the end the viewer is poised for more dread anticipation of the third part of the trilogy announced by Akin, and dealing – after 'Love' and 'Death' – with 'Evil' (in German: *Liebe, Tod und Teufel*). More coincidences, fatal choices, ethical dilemmas and doubtful sacrifices? An incremental increase of suffering and intransigence, of political radicalism and religious hatred? We are not told, and at the end of *Edge of Heaven*, we are left in pending expectation.

In one sense, the film is thus very much in the spirit of Levinas: it places a very high ethical value on sacrifice and substitution. The characters learn and accept their roles as they confront radical Otherness; they become active – leaving their homes, their jobs, their countries – in the service of fulfilling a typically Levinasian demand, namely the necessity to define and find yourself by seeking out an ethical relation of risk and uncertainty. As Levinas maintains in *Otherwise than Being*, in this process, substitution is the very core of subjectivity in the ethical relation. In another sense, *Auf der anderen Seite* – with its implied title 'Death' – also perfectly illustrates the point made by Rancière about such scenarios of substitution and atonement. By seeking to transcend politics (the EU and Turkey), religion and ethnicity (Abraham's sacrifice), such redemptive acts end up with death as the horizon of individual action and decision. The question this raises is whether the film takes such an 'ethical turn' because Akin is committed to this Levinasian ethics, no longer believing either in multiculturalism (which judging by his aversion to hyphenated identities he never did), nor in a negotiated, consensus, EU-style 'political' solution, and therefore settles for the 'harder' version of ethical universalism. Opting for the ethics of victim and sacrifice, of substitution and delegation, the film depicts a specifically Judeo-Christian (if not altogether New Testament-Christian) way of dealing with the issues.

On the other hand, just as plausible is the possibility that Akin is offering a Rancièrean critique of this Levinasian ethics, by making this second film, like the slower counter-movement of a musical piece, after the *furiouso* of the first movement (*Gegen die Wand*), the preparatory antithesis for a third and final part, once more to be played *fortissimo*. Are we being wrong-footed, literally put on the other side, if we accept *Auf der anderen Seite* as a self-enclosed work and 'statement' – endorsing what I called earlier the 'utopian' aspects of mutual interference in the internal affairs of the Other?

Akin certainly uses the dramaturgical resources of melodrama, but avoids the politics of excess typical of Fassbinder (around the abjection and thus the terrible power of victim), and only hints that melodrama, insofar as it is 'failed tragedy', demands justice by performing this 'failure': there is no *anagnorisis* or moment of recognition, no ironic-bitter happy ending (as there is in Sirk), nor the polished but brittle surfaces of Todd Haynes' Sirk remake,

Far From Heaven (2002). All one knows at the end is that a man is waiting for his father at the edge of the Black Sea, on a day that looks calm and serene, but as the fishermen tell him, during a season where you cannot trust the weather.

In fact, remembering how the acts of atonement of Susanne and Nejat are set off against the 'plea-bargaining' of Ayten, how substitution is matched by betrayal, and how Ayten lives in states of exception and abjection (in Germany, initially she has no money, no food, no home), while her political cell is a female 'terrorist' one, it is clear that something ominous is in the offing. It is hard not to recall that Hamburg was the home of Mohamed Atta's conspiratorial cell prior to him setting off to fly a plane into the North Tower of the World Trade Centre in New York. Death is omnipresent; yet while the German and German-Turkish characters live under the sign of actual and symbolic death, the militants in the Istanbul jail (whether belonging to the PKK or some other radical grouping), even though they are potential suicide bombers, are nonetheless full of 'life', of schemes, projected into the future. They have that fierceness of conviction and righteousness, which suggests the possibility of an Antigone-style 'ethical act' (the singular conduct, the terrible choice, the decision taken in the dark night of the soul, putting you outside the law and beyond the pale). On the other hand, Rancière might argue that Ayten's sullen individuality and her comrades' lethal resolve merely instantiate the recto of the verso of the 'ethical turn': the nihilistic need for a permanent state of exception and for the radical but politically voided 'outside.'

The Third Part(y): Alain Badiou and the Nature of 'Evil'

Yet if, as suggested, one considers *The Edge of Heaven* not only as a self-enclosed work, but as part of a trilogy, a further possibility arises. Since it is already known that the first part was under the sign of 'love', the second 'death' and the third will be about 'evil', another reading also becomes possible, this time not following Rancière, but Alain Badiou instead.[12] In such a reading, *Gegen die Wand* becomes an example of one of Badiou's instances of the 'event' (of which there are four instances: love; a scientific breakthrough; a revolution; and a work of art). An event, in Badiou's sense, steals up on you, it strikes you and it changes your life. Love, in *Gegen die Wand* is such an event: when the male hero thinks he is safe because he has a contract that regulates marriage by reducing it to its proper dimensions of sex, money and domestic service, love hits him when he least expects it and when he is least prepared for it. But once it does, he has to be true to the event, no matter what the consequences.

In the case of the second part, *The Edge of Heaven*, a Badiou reading would complement what has been proposed above: with death as both palpable presence and the ethical horizon, Badiou might see the various acts of charity and sacrifice not only as the wrong kinds of love, but as forms of self-betrayal and self-deception, whose major mistake would be to think that good comes after evil, and that such living by proxy can be redemptive, going so far as to imagine that one's exemplary life will make the world a better place. Ayten's betrayal – not so much of her comrades, but of the political event itself; her not being true to her initial commitment of fighting for Kurdish self-determination, universal education, minority rights, or whatever her group is fighting for – would therefore be the crux of the ethical dilemma of the film; or rather, it would have to be the matter to be addressed in the third part, which – by this logic – is rightly advertised as dedicated to the exploration of 'evil'.

But what is 'evil' in the context of the 'ethical turn'? In the war on terror, or in humanitarian missions to Darfur, Somalia, Kosovo or Syria, evil is presumed to pre-exist in the world and has to be fought by the forces of good. This would be the 'soft ethical' position. Rejecting such a turn and reversing its premise, Badiou would argue that for a proper ethical stance, good must be considered as logically and ethically preceding evil. This would be in contrast to Christianity, where the fact of the fallen world means that 'good' is a reactive response to preternatural evil. For Badiou, on the other hand, the good and the true belong together, which means that he associates ethics with the production of universal truths. Evil, instead of being preternatural, would be the consequence of a failure to live up to, or bring into the world, this particular union of the good and the true. As a commentator on Badiou has pointed out, there is a substantial heuristic value, but also risk, to be gained from this stance:

> Positing evil as a derailed truth process is helpful in understanding one of the key questions of the twentieth century – how can ordinary people commit extraordinary acts of evil? – because it demonstrates evil's proximity to progressive and potentially liberating human projects. Evil is thus not easily ghettoized as the [opposite or] 'other' of reason or humanism.[13]

In this light, the 'war on terror', just like the acts of the terrorists, would not only have to be seen as cynical, but as missing its ethical mark, because it shares the deep nihilism which Rancière and Badiou identify around the 'ethical turn', both in its 'soft' and 'hard' variants. With this last thought, I have opened up quite a few ethical dilemmas for myself and have moved from progressive politics to something like transgressive politics. I have also switched from an actual film to one that at the time of writing is still hypothetical, and it is thus a good moment to stop my reflections, before I, too, find myself on the other side: not just beyond hard and soft ethics, but in the realm of pure speculation.

Notes

1   Emmanuel Levinas, *Totality and Infinity: An Essay on Exteriority* (trans. Alphonso Lingis), Pittsburgh: Duquesne University Press, 1969, p. 43.
2   Emmanuel Levinas, *Otherwise than Being: or Beyond Essence*, Pittsburgh: Duquesne University Press, 1998, p. 158.
3   Kwame Anthony Appiah, when arguing for cosmopolitan open-mindedness against parochial universalism, once illustrated the latter by quoting the phrase often attributed

to Fürst Bernhard von Bülow (1903): 'und willst du nicht mein Bruder sein, so schlag ich dir den Schädel ein'/'If you don't want to be my brother, I will bash your head in'.

4 A prominent disciple of Levinas and Derrida, who takes up many of these issues, is Simon Critchley, notably in his book *Infinitely Demanding: Ethics of Commitment, Politics of Resistance*, London: Verso, 2007.

5 Thomas Elsaesser, 'Double Occupancy', in *European Cinema: Face to Face with Hollywood*, Amsterdam: Amsterdam University Press, 2005, pp. 108–30.

6 Jacques Rancière, 'The Ethical Turn of Aesthetics and Politics' (trans. Jean-Philippe Deranty), in *Critical Horizons*, Vol. 7, No. 1, 2006, pp. 1–20.

7 Alain Badiou, *Ethics: An Essay on the Understanding of Evil*, New York: Verso, 2001, p. 35.

8 Giorgio Agamben, *State of Exception* (trans. Kevin Attell), Chicago: University of Chicago Press, 2005.

9 Jacques Rancière, *Film Fables*, New York: Berg, 2006, p. 11.

10 Jacques Rancière, interview on *Aesthetic and Politics*, London: Continuum, 2003, http://www.16beavergroup.org/mtarchive/archives/001877.php, accessed 28 April 2010.

11 Jacques Rancière, *Malaise Dans L'Esthetique*, Paris: Editions Galilée, 2004, p. 148.

12 Alain Badiou, *Ethics: An Understanding of Evil*, London: Verso, 2001, pp. 79–90.

13 Michael Rothberg, 'Review essay of *Ethics: An Essay on the Understanding of Evil*', in Alain Badiou, *Criticism*, Vol. 43, No. 4, Fall 2001, p. 481.

Chapter 20

Radicant Spaces of Enunciation: Visual Art, 'Phenomenotechnique', and 'Criticality' – Towards a Postcolonial Media(l) Theory

Rania Gaafar

Who is Speaking?

The initial idea of this chapter emerged amidst reflections on 'epistemic violence'[1], its interrelation with media, moving images and their scholarly institutionalized reflections in largely Western non-Anglophone cultural studies. There appears to be a need for a 'critical engagement with the specters of the vanished empires, colonies and colonial thinking that still haunt the postcolonial scholarly production' within spaces of knowledge and their very enunciation.[2] The traces and seeming persistency of the invisibility of the Other as a subject of speaking and theorizing in the aftermath of representational theories in art history, film and media studies, and the increasing interest in the visual arts in their postcolonial alteration, signify a paradox to the missing voice of the Other in the academe. The institutionalization of knowledge – despite that of postcolonial studies on the continent – through the very simple yet signifying question (however recognized and all too familiar this may sound at present) 'who is speaking?', and the seeming lack of the agency of the bespoken Other in question in relation to academic knowledge-operation, its constituting authorship and substantially signifying record has emerged as not meeting the reality, eloquence, and experiential veracity of the visual and its transgressively epistemological prospects through the diaphaneity of its emergence. The politically de-colonizing and counter-hegemonic premises – and implementations – of postcolonial theory seem to go astray in its institutional distance to Area Studies mainly and at the same time taking this rift as justifying tool for the lack of Other scholars to participate in the academic institutionalization and knowledge production of post-colonial studies in Western non-English academia in particular.[3] Visual art works and their intricate production of knowledge throughout artistic practices, research and the technological conditions of possibility appear to not only transgress the hegemony of the academe's institutionalized epistemological positionality that maintain forms and functions of the exclusion of Other voices in forming its epistemological canon, but even more so does it provide for the contrapuntal visibility of the Other in all its indeterminacies and theoretical intricacies. The visual pictures the object of knowledge in dynamic alterations as well as agencies and hence transforms the production of theory through what Donna Haraway has come to term 'situated knowledges' (Haraway 1988).

In the following notes the role and potentiality of perceptual, experiential and affective modalities of moving images[4] in their post-cinematographic condition is highlighted, not least as an artistically constituted (research) method to meet the hegemony of (still) (be)speaking the Other (thereby intentionally maintaining her or his invisibility) in academic and textual spheres that are far from signifying forms, functions and effects of embedded methods operating from within institutional practices and knowledge despite the politically imbued cognizance offered by postcolonial theorists from different sides of the spectrum. Yet embeddedness as insinuating structures and forms of transparency nevertheless signify a complicated 'double-bind'[5] method of (neo-colonial) control, and its ideological practices can also serve discourses of maintaining invisibilities of other ethnicities, of race and thus the 'unequal … access to the resources necessary to implement their own voices',[6] their respective knowledge in majoritarian white cultures of scientific and theoretical knowledge.[7] Hence in the following reflections are embedded within what Trinh T. Minh-ha has described as an 'elsewhere within here'[8] – materialized in the signifying practice of the 'hyphenated'[9] identity of not/belonging – that touches upon the experience of Otherness as much as on the epistemology of the spaces of critical enunciation in theory and in artistic practice while upholding a skeptical position to post-racial fantasies in the academe's epistemological spaces of Western European enunciation i.e. scholarship.

Specters of Presence[10]

Axel Honneth elaborates the interrelation between invisibility and the epistemology of recognition[11] in a reference to Ralph Ellison's novel *Invisible Man* (1952) and the opening words of his protagonist in the Prologue[12]. The physical presence, his corporeal existence, is in a fundamental disjunction to the invisible anti-social perception he faces by his environment. Speaking, as it were, the narrator remains nameless and the blindness he detects in his environment is described as a blemished physical feature of the human beings around him: seeing becomes an immanent matter of ideological imaginings rather than mere physical perception. From here, where do we find the conjunction to film and media studies? The apparatus of visibility, of looking, of film and its cinematically ideological discourse, is at the same time psychoanalytically caught in an epistemic relation to race and language, i.e. film-as-text.[13] In cinematic apparatus theory, the ideological illusion of the 'reality effect' in the cinema has formerly positioned the subject-spectator at the centre of an unconscious psychological formation vis-à-vis his place in front of the projection screen. The 'eye-subject' is in need of the film's operator, the camera, to help suture the gaze in film to that of the spectator-subject, yet 'this substitution is only possible on the condition that the instrumentation itself be hidden or repressed'.[14] At the same time, the identification with the film-subjects (i.e. actors) develops a situation of narcissistic fulfilment through the capacity of putting the spectator in a state of regression through the all-absorbing state of illusion that signifies film's ideological 'technique'. It is at this point of intersection where the invisibility of knowledge production and its ideological processing is disclosed in one of the former positions in psychoanalytic film theory. Race as well as gender have not been considered in the beginnings of these theoretically constituting approaches since

> film … lives on the denial of difference: differences are necessary for it to live, but it lives on their negation. This is indeed the paradox that emerges if we look directly at a strip of processed film: adjacent images are almost exactly repeated, their divergence being verifiable only by comparison of images at a sufficient distance from each other… Couldn't we thus say that cinema reconstructs and forms the mechanical model (with the simplifications that this can entail) of a system of writing [*écriture*] constituted by a material base and a counter-system (ideology, idealism) which uses this system while also concealing it?[15]

In the following, I argue toward 'other' experience as an aesthetic position and artistic technique against the background of the missing visibility of knowledge-operation in film to which Baudry referred to as the technical optical instruments referencing the relation of film and its ocular mechanisms and asking in due course: 'Does the technical nature of optical instruments, directly attached to scientific practice, serve to conceal not only their use in ideological products but also the ideological effects which they may themselves provoke? Their scientific base would assure them a sort of neutrality and help to prevent their being questioned.'[16] This invisibility of the ideological formation of film – and vision – speaks to the master territories of knowledge in institutionalized theory, but also to a new way of seeing through the research and production of film and the visual arts and ascribing them new meaning in the light of post-medial performances.[17] The interventions by postcolonial science studies have developed initial approaches to the way other encultured systems of knowledge speak to science and alter its premises and practitioners.[18] This theoretical intervention practises not only the ways the other is no longer spoken, but it inhabits the tacit spaces and affective positions of critical enunciation[19] and hence speaks 'near-by' (Trinh T. Minh Ha) and through the Other. Part of this development and critical awareness seems to be an intentional reassessment of the role and purpose of 'critical distance' and its involvement with epistemic violence, which Iain Chambers indicates: 'To query and undo that so-called critical distance justified in the name of science, knowledge and "truth", and to take the opportunity of the return of the repressed, of the repressed side of modernity in which reason has also and always been accompanied by terror, is to reconfigure the language in which I dwell and which provides me with my home'-.[20]

In his 'semio-pragmatic' approach to film Roger Odin[21] develops the reader actant, whose affects are taken into account by film and its 'socially programmed practices'.[22] It is in light of this acknowledgement to the experience and the origins of the spectator (as well as the author/ artist as producer) that the following ideas develop to revision and revaluate experience and its postcolonial legacy in scholarly research of film and media studies. Through the lens of exilic/diasporic film art and with a view to film and media studies, the following notes offer reflections on experiential and affective possibilities of film (art) whether it can be explored as an experimental concept of a cosmopolitically technological approach to the phenomenology of the Other.

The transformation and subsequent performativity of the cinematic dispositive in moving image installations inside the gallery, as well as the theoretical concepts of the 'mobile spectator', have conceptualized aesthetic forms of cultural alterity as the technological embodiment of experience in film. These changes and transformative knowledge formations have been brought about in an art context mainly. With the latter in mind, this chapter aims to formulate an approach toward a paradigmatic shift in film and media (art) studies by emphasizing and functionalizing the experience of otherness as a form and enunciative method and practice of 'criticality'. Irit Rogoff describes the latter as 'a state of duality in which one is at the same time, both empowered and disempowered, knowing and unknowing':[23]

[Criticality] reflects the search for a practice that goes beyond conjunctives such as those that bring together 'art and politics' or 'theory and practice' or 'analysis and action'. In such a practice we aspire to experience the relations between the two as a form of embodiment which cannot be separated into their independent components. The notion of an 'embodied criticality' has much to do with my understanding of our shift away from critique and towards criticality, a shift that I would argue is essential for the actualisation of contemporary cultural practices.[24]

The radicalization of time and space in moving image art that operates under the ideas, critical reflections and theoretical frameworks of postcolonialism, migration and globalization has been transformed through digital technology (and the influence of imaging technologies in somewhat post-human frames of reference and aestheticism). The development and global improvement of inexorable access to moving image art, social media and often film and video art archives across the globe has produced an enormous outpouring of publications that celebrate the rise and 'multicultural' arrival and embeddedness of artists from both West and East (e.g. Africa, Asia, the Middle East) within 'global' cultural platforms, art spaces, research programs and centres. At the same time the allegedly disappearing boundaries of racialized or genderized spectatorship in the research on contemporary moving image art seem of less interest and relevance today than in the 1990s, when Anglophone cultural theory and film studies brought about paradigmatic turns in gaze theory through the topographies of psychoanalytical desire structures. However, this apparently growing invisibility, the morphing of alterity in the flow of global media and art zones (and capital), as well as the digital distribution of images in the (inevitably) multi-ethnic usage of digital circulation channels and online networks, assume a deceptive transparency, i.e. a self-evident inclusion of 'criticality' in the hypervisibility of images. The need to reflect on the sensitivity and critical knowledge of the image's materiality and its affective economy has been disclosed in what Hito Steyerl has described as the 'poor image' that is the 'contemporary Wretched of the Screen' with its low rendered quality, its ephemeral status in a digitally legal no man's land, as well as its fast circulation in data compressed density.[25] This conceptual embodiment of the image serves as a blueprint to resurrect the slowly effacing relevance of the issues of colonial and postcolonial identities and knowledge hegemony in contemporary moving image art and above all in media theory, as well as in the operating knowledge systems of and through actants of media and film studies. Such reflections have often been absorbed by the ever growing emphasis in curating and the inclusion of non-Western art in biennales in the West (and East), as well as the ensuing inevitably spatial and topographical 'proximity'[26] that contemporary moving image and media art share with art by Western practitioners. This scene of being and 'speaking "nearby"'[27] nevertheless discloses the friction of a confrontation and probing of discourses of the self and Other *in situ*:

> It is a common fact that proximity today is situated at the juncture between two social facts of contact: hostility and hospitality. This concept can also be related to the various ways that different global communities share space. But as distance shrinks, and the border between near and far increasingly dissolves, so does the potential for conflict and contestation become heightened in power relations that define the contact zone of cultures.[28]

The critical pragmatism and 'practical aesthetics' (Jill Bennett 2012) of a concept such as 'proximity' seems to allow for the rendering visible of distance and thus the distance of experiences of otherness/strangeness in artistic (visual) forms of embodiment, which might run the risk of being elided and dismissed in reductionist approaches that merely psychoanalytically universalize the Other as part of the self (or as 'strangers to ourselves' in Julia Kristeva's words).[29] Rather than dwelling on questions of spectatorship and their different perspectives in the visual arts, the notion of 'criticality' extends far beyond the fixed one of 'authorship' (however outdated this term might seem in the present theme), while at the same time it allows thinking the artist as producer and researcher[30] in a space of 'radicant'[31] realism. The term is employed here to lead over to the processual concept of 'phenomenotechnology'[32] (Gaston Bachelard) and its relevance for media theory through the perspective of contemporary art as well as reflecting and conceptualizing the 'radicant' as an intrinsic figure of alterity-in-practice:

> Contemporary art shows how lived experience can be reorganized using mechanisms of representation and production that correspond to the emergence of a new subjectivity that demands its own modes of representation.
> The radicant can without injury, cut itself off from its first roots and reacclimate itself. There is no single origin, but rather successive, simultaneous, or alternating acts of

enrooting. While radical artists sought to return to an original place, radicant artists take to the road, and they do so without having any place to return to. Their universe contains neither origin nor end, except for those they decide to establish themselves.[33]

This idea of 'the radicant' shows the need to reconsider and re-evaluate the epistemologies of a 'conscious subjectivity'[34] (of the artist, scholar, researcher as producer[35]), a political form of life in artistic and theoretical practices (that are not regarded separately here), and its relation to textuality, content and/or form and mediality – as well as in academic research fields of media and cultural studies in the West.[36] Rogoff's reflections on criticality might relate the positions in postcolonial feminism[37] and theory to aesthetic and conceptual practices of artists and film-makers in frameworks that have often been uncritically subsumed so far under the category of 'global art'. It is therefore that postcoloniality and its relation to science studies and technology[38] need to be reconsidered in media and film theory and studies in non-English speaking countries in particular. Back in 1999, María Fernández's critical intervention on the absence of postcolonial discourses in electronic media art, for example, pointed to the interconnectivity of media art and the new market, the progress in technological development and the inevitable rift between First and Third World in this case. Nevertheless, she suggests, of course, the relationship between new media, technology and the identity construction of the colonized subject through apparatuses and their specifically imposing and signifying knowledge system with reference to Edward Said. Fernández assumes that the post-humanist emphasis in new media art at the end of the 1990s perpetually replaced the carnality of the body and thus its experiential flesh. The skin of images, as it were, no longer touches on the body's experience in either colonial life worlds or hegemonic encounters in the West. Fernández focuses on the cyborg as a catalytic hybrid figure (the 'stranger') of (predominantly western) feminist theory, which to a certain extent sought to induce postcolonial feminist theory in gendered discussions in the West (Figure 1).[39]

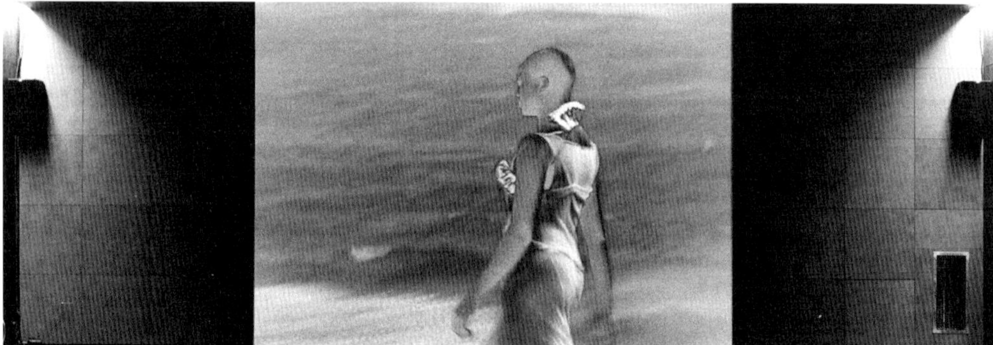

Figure 1: Isaac Julien, *Encore II (Radioactive)*, 2004, colour, Super-8, 3 min. Courtesy the artist and Victoria Miro Gallery, London.

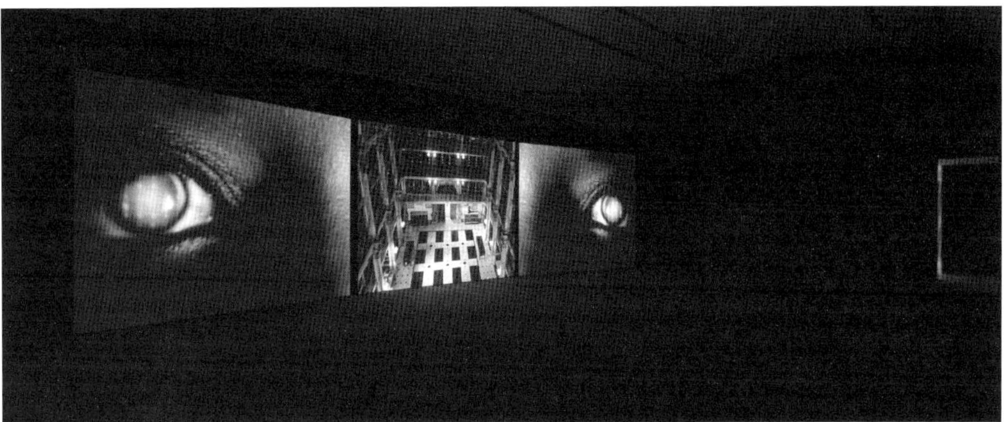

Figure 2: Isaac Julien, *Baltimore,* 2003. Installation view, MCA Sydney, Australia (New Media Collection Centre Pompidou), 2006. Courtesy the artist, Victoria Miro Gallery, London and Metro Pictures, New York.

Even though Fernández focuses on electronic media art theory, the implications of the latter and the parallel formation of the two disciplines – namely that 'postcolonial studies and electronic media theory have developed parallel to one another but with very few points of intersection' – can also be traced in the still dominating interest in 'representations of the Other' in film, media and art contexts (in predominantly non-English speaking countries), however hesitant this approach may seem in sliding up the alleged margins of postcolonial theory.[40] One of the reasons for this separate development seems to be the role of the body and its differing perception and materialization in each of the disciplines mentioned:

> In contrast to this fascination with mechanization and virtualization of the body, postcolonial studies underscores the physiological specificity of the lived body as the realities of subjection are inscribed in the bodies of the colonized peoples: torture, rape, and physical exhaustion, as well as the learning of new bodily grammars and forms of discipline required by colonization and conversion.[41]

The separate progression and maintenance of discourse of these disciplines is a sign of the need to inhabit knowledge for a media theory that embeds the affective subjectivities and perspectives of non-Western culture. It is of interest to historically as well as culturally trace forms of these very lives in affect structures of the economy of cultural and institutional politics in academia, as well as scholarship in film and media theory and philosophy beneath the thresholds of the visible – and the readable. One critical intervention into the field might be an attempt to conceptualize a postcolonial[42] media theory through the lens of contemporary visual art, which seems to be either still marginal or mostly absent in Western (often non-Anglophone) film and media studies. The shift to a reflection and perspective on the moving image's mediality and materiality as a methodological approach toward a postcolonial media theory, and a neo-phenomenological approach to the Other through the spaces of enunciation of other 'interstices' of a new 'historical and theoretical temporality generated by the process of revolutionary transience and transformation.'[43] Both Trinh T. Minh-ha and Homi Bhabha signify the dynamic uncertainty of it, while Bhabha employs it in a Fanonian sense[44] and conceptualizes the space of cultural difference as a performative space of language and knowledge – the 'Third Space of enunciation' that inhabits a 'discursive embeddedness' of (linguistic) difference as well as a 'cultural positionality.'[45] Film and moving image art (which is also at times referred to as media art in a more general sense here) can provide the theoretical involvement for the theory and philosophy of alterity in media and film studies. Film (and moving image art in post-cinematographic forms), as we might conclude then, may even function as a theoretical tool, a theory-as-form in itself, toward the complexities of the 'stranger'[46] and/or 'the inappropriate/d other'[47] who becomes the tilted image of what Nicholas Bourriaud has termed 'the radicant'. Despite the current hype around 'hybridity', 'postcolonialism', 'difference' in the face of globalized media, moving image art and geopolitical and aesthetic translations in conceptual artistic frameworks, the embodiment of (other) experience (also in its technomorphic forms) is a still contested – and less negotiated – area of 'hostility and hospitality'[48] in aesthetic and, above all, film and media philosophical terms.[49]

The mediality of film, its mode of fluid being and thinking as a way to perpetually approach an aesthetic dimension – even methodology – of 'criticality', and its very embodiment through tactility and its sensual consistency looks beyond the very medium of moving images and their subjectively conscious fabric. Thinking in Deleuzian terms of 'enfoldment' (cf. Laura Marks in this volume) and the spatiotemporal memory of the moving image, the fold may also reference 'the topology that rapidly acquires depth when it is bent and deviated by excluded rhythms and dislocating narratives' (Chambers 2008: 18). Laura Marks has termed the conceptualization of Gilles Deleuze's 'plane of immanence' an 'aesthetics of enfolding and unfolding' that materializes on 'three levels – image, information, and the infinite … .' (Marks 2010: 5)-. The digitalization of video art increasingly asks for critical approaches that examine the agency of film (images) and the materiality of experience through the very notion of a 'criticality' that is configured in 'the radicant':

> With its at once dynamic and dialogical signification, the adjective 'radicant' captures this contemporary subject, caught between the need for a connection with its environment and the forces of uprooting, between globalization and singularity, between identity and opening to the other. It defines the subject as an object of negotiation.[50]

Hence the moving image exceeds the confinements of its projection and discloses an insight into questions of critical enunciation and material agency. The performativity of the cinematic dispositive inside the art gallery, as well as the theoretical concepts of artistic research-as-knowledge production and the demands for non-representational theory in postcolonial studies, have disclosed new aesthetic forms of cultural alterity in film and media art. With the latter in mind, these notes aim to instigate a paradigmatic shift in media studies by emphasizing and functionalizing the experience of otherness through the mediality of film and its mode of being as a way to formulate and approach a postcolonial media theory through the assemblage, aesthetics and mediality of film and its paradigms in an art context.

'Phenomenotechnologies' of the Stranger

French philosopher of science Gaston Bachelard outlines a new method and concept for the formation of scientific knowledge, which he terms 'phenomenotechnique' in his work *The New Scientific Spirit* (1934). Thus, laboratory techniques, for instance, and their media produce new knowledge and become theorems in themselves; they form a precondition of knowledge acquisition. It is through technological experiments and their experiential surplus that new phenomena, in e.g. science, are disclosed – not merely by perception or observation. In light of the current interest in artistic research and the material turn in art theory and beyond, in which more than often art and science are interrelated, Bachelard's dynamic concept and methodology discloses new poetic configurations of knowledge. The creation of new knowledge due to the 'epistemic break'[51] that shows in new phenomena is, according to Gaston Bachelard, not merely the result of extensive experimentalizations of 'life' – i.e. in the life sciences and in physics in particular, in the aftermath of Einstein's relativity theory – but it is through experimentation and tension between the imagination, the poetics of art and the rational objectives and aspirations of science that new knowledge is being produced. Thus phenomena – film's specters – are no longer found, but they are being produced – Bachelard's move from the influence of phenomenology to a 'phenomeno*technology*', the conceptual term he implies in his analysis of *The New Scientific Spirit*.[52] This ambivalent, and at the same time dynamically generic, approach toward new phenomena can neither be(come) visible at first sight, nor understood entirely through logic or reason. Rather, it has turned to a trajectory in the juxtaposition of art and science regarding the applied practice of the respective knowledge on both sides. In other words, the tacit ways of knowing and practising the very knowledge acquired through theory, experimentation or artistic research and practice are at the focus of an inquiry that seeks to find the conditions and possibilities of a postcolonial media theory at work through the forms and function of a 'conscious subjectivity'. Given our initial reading of the development of the disciplines of postcolonial studies and media theory, the experimentalization in theorizing becomes as relevant as the artistic aesthetic practice through the material conditions of phenomena: Irit Rogoff, for one, suggests 'approaching Roland Barthes's description of interdisciplinarity not as surrounding a chosen object with numerous modes of scientific inquiry, but rather as the constitution of a new object of knowledge'.[53] Interdisciplinarity then may be thought and enacted within the same parameters of phenomenotechnical methods and practices that constitute new knowledge (as phenomena among others)-. In her artistic practice, Rohini Devasher has developed a generic in situ moment of intertwining art, science and narratives of biological becoming through video feedback and digital prints, combining a nature morte with its movement and transformation through digitization and the vitality of life (see colour plates, p. 1 and 2).

The processual and epistemic rupture in science theory that Gaston Bachelard inducted, and the shift from apparatus-dominated conditions for 'solutions' in science studies to the more complex 'conditions of the construction of objects and phenomena (elementary particles, genes, neuronal networks, protein biosynthesis, immune system etc.)',[54] can be considered in a parallel reading to the 'radicant' premises of moving image art and its aesthetic relation to postcoloniality. Whereas critics (as well as Bachelard himself) have pointed out that 'images' are an obstacle to rational scientific thought,[55] what is of interest for the outline of this chapter is the way the materialization of the imagination is accountable for new knowledge, and how the materialization of imagination is technically evoked by the artist as producer of moving image art. Joan Copjec has highlighted film theory's use of the Foucauldian term *dispositive*, whereas according to Copjec it originally emerged in science epistemology and Gaston Bachelard's writings to counter phenomenology by introducing a 'phenomenotechnology' instead.[56]

Against the background of these generative thoughts and concepts, we can pose the same initial question as Bourriaud in *The Radicant*: '[W]hy is it that globalization has so often been discussed from sociological, political, and economic points of view, but almost never from an aesthetic perspective? How does this phenomenon affect the life of form?'[57] The life of form – or 'how latitudes become form'[58], to quote the title of one of the initial art exhibitions exploring this question a decade ago – can be approached through the kind of radicant method and line of thought that considers the infusion of technology and questions of postcolonial research and alterity in a visual art context (see Figure 2). Tacit as the relation of these concepts may seem, it renders visible the implicit role and perception of the media, and relates it to a perspective on the relation of media and alterity, or even media *as* alterities (cf. Dieter Mersch in this volume).

It is this reflection of the condition of the new as an approach toward an other media epistemology of 'the stranger'[59] and her/his 'other' perspective and, above all, an 'other' spatial (i.e. knowledge harbouring) enunciation that signifies 'how concepts of knowledge, scholarship and science are intrinsically linked to power and racial authority'.[60] Thus an interest and a reflection of what postcolonial media (theory) is or may become needs to take into account and consider the subtle yet signifying embodied spaces of enunciation, of speaking, practicing and showing knowledge – other knowledge – in operation and within the 'interstices' of the conscious medium and its very post-medial dimension and extension, its mediality.

The concept of phenomenotechnology does not only disclose new perspectives onto film's being as (desiring) assemblage[61] that follows a phenomenotechnical method, but subsequently reflects the moving image's desire to become an active agent rather than a passively perceived or produced sign. It also paves the way for a revaluation of the epistemological synthesis between early experiments in technology, the sciences and knowledge. The scientific perspective on film as a prosperous phenomena that emerged out of the physical, machinic and chemical experiments of the nineteenth century traces the history of the invention of 'cinematic desire'[62] through experiments in chrono-photography, movement, perspective, light and finally animation; the first recorded movement experiments through technology to unfold glimpses of cinematic time, space, and later make us aware of the materiality of film. At the same time, phenomenotechnical methods uproot the conclusive results of scientific experiments insofar as they claim to invent the very phenomena in question through experiential experiments, and through technical instruments that are no longer mere utilities to support higher, more meaningful scientific endeavours,[63] This perspective onto the formation of new knowledge, and hence on the possibilities of postcolonial epistemologies in media and film art incorporate the materiality of the very conditions of experiential technology,[64] offer a new impasse and an overdue insight into the aesthetic materiality of alterity in contemporary art and media forms/formats. Thus, the epistemology of form through experience-as-film's-mediality becomes a radicant method to approach a postcolonial media theory. It attempts to do so without succumbing to the pitfalls of a short-sighted reflection on the postcolonial condition as fetishizing and solely ethnically categorizing the Other thereby maintaining the 'substitution of one language for another' in an apparently deadlocked argument – and situation. It is this notorious ex negativo critique that Bourriaud employs to maintain his alternative model of a culture of 'altermodernity'.[65]

Thinking of film as a knowing assemblage through a spatio-temporal paradigm and fluid phenomenotechnically imbued form-as-mediality, its sensual presence creates phenomena on-screen as projections that can be reflected as poetic knowledge. The visual presence of film hence is assembled as a formation of knowledge of sensual experience reflected as a phenomenotechnical method, enhanced through artistic knowledge production/'visual art as knowledge production'[66], the life of material form and the intentionally, technically, functionalized spatio-temporal mediality of film. Bachelard's dynamic experimental methodology and conceptualization of a phenomenotechnology, which he describes as a processual methodology of his 'formation of a new scientific spirit' embodies in an act of self-reflexivity his own approach to a poetics of knowledge, interrelates rationality and poetics, technology and its theoretical as well as practically experimental application in aesthetics and experience. It is in light of the current debate around artistic research as a formation of knowledge in art that Bachelard's concepts can acquire a new perspective and provide new experimental conditions for the constitution of new knowledge, and a technologically and materially-affected epistemological postcolonial culture and its biopolitical significance. Such new formations of knowledge can be disclosed in abstraction and its very form, or in abstract and inductive thought, which creates a 'poetics of relations' (in the words of Édouard Glissant) in which nature and culture are no longer separate entities, but rather signify the relation between science and the arts. These artistic reflections in science and those of science in art can be traced in various structures, but above all in the material structure of perception and experience, in mediality and its formation in the visual arts. This invisibility of the conditions for visualizing matter in immaterially appearing ways has become one of the commons of art in a post-medial context, and it is a feature of the plane of assemblage and its conceptual frameworks that is as materially structural as it is intangible. The visibility of the dispositive in installations has in an act of mediation created new experiments of the real by transforming the apparatus – into a performative mediation of the technical conditions and possibilities of the moving image. These mediations shift the focus to the materialization of images and their projection in spaces of presence. Thus the reflection of the sensitive conventions of media and artistic knowledge production through the relevance of the 'material turn' in an art context have revised the perspective from projections and their curatorial, as well as architecturally inductive, positionalities to the materiality of the visual artworks. These forms of medial transgressions create poetic relations in which the difference between nature and culture merge, as Hans-Jörg Rheinberger emphasizes at the conjunction of art and the history of science: 'the conceptual dynamics of the sciences [and the visual arts] cannot be separated from the emergence of phenomena in which they in turn constitute themselves'.[67]

The various methods to apply and reflect on art and science, span different material forms of media, artworks, graphic or notational manifestations in the sciences, artistic research in the visual arts, or the materialization of light in the chemical substance of the celluloid strip, for example, in analogue 16mm processing. From the visibility of a projected image to the materiality of the digital moving image in its 'post-medial condition' (Rosalind Krauss' term), the structure of different media of artistic production is signified. In moving image installations and projections, film or photography, the materialization of the recording of light is an invisible chemical process that materializes light rays through technical projectors as visible projections. Algorithmic density embodies the digital 'image', being a technically material matrix of visibility-as-invisibility, which becomes the condition for the visual at the same time. Archival practices in research as well as in art (such as digital online archives) further conceptualize knowledge in time and space.

Thus 'representation' of new phenomena in science and the arts no longer rely on their mere visibility, perception or the description of these visible 'objects'. Rather, the technical and aesthetic requirements for 'phenomena' to become visible are under scrutiny here as techniques of knowledge and the relevance and epistemological condition of experimental experience. With all this in mind, 'radicant' methods of the production of the visual arts, and moving images in particular, point to a new (aesthetic) realism of an agential type and a conscious media of film art that is committed to postcolonial knowledge and its epistemological forms.

Notes

1 'Epistemic violence' is reflected here as a structural and habitual maintenance of a hegemony of knowledge through theory and the institutionalisation of agents of speaking knowledge in e.g. the academe and beyond. Nevertheless it also influences the diasporic in Western culture through the looming establishment of 'monocultures of the mind', Gayatri Chakravorty Spivak in Nermeen Sheikh (ed.), *The Present as History: Critical Perspectives on Contemporary Global Power*, New York: Columbia University Press, 2007, pp. 187–188.

Cf. also Gayatri Chakravorty Spivak, 'Subaltern Studies. Deconstructing Historiographies (1985)', in Donna Landry et al. (eds), *The Spivak Reader*, London and New York: Routledge, 1996, pp. 203–237; Gayatri Chakravorty Spivak, 'Three Women's Texts and a Critique of Imperialism', in *Critical Inquiry*, Vol. 12, No. 1, 1985, pp. 243–261.

2   Debjani Bhattacharyya in an unpublished abstract.

3   Cf. instead for an account of academic institutions in which 'diversity practitioners' operate in Australia and the United Kingdom and the experiential credit of a scholar on the discourses of race and gender in these areas: Sara Ahmed, *On Being Included: Racism and Diversity in Institutional Life*, Durham: Duke University Press, 2012.

4   I refer to 'film' when I mean the specifically fluid fabric of moving image art. I reflect film as the conceptualizing form and embodied theory of experiential postcolonial affect.

5   Cf. on 'double-consciousness':' It is a peculiar sensation, this double-consciousness, this sense of always looking at one's self through the eyes of others, of measuring one's soul by the tape of a world that looks on in an amused contempt and pity ff.', W. E. B. Du Bois, *The Souls of Black Folk*, Oxford and New York: Oxford University Press, 2007, p. 8.

6   Grada Kilomba, *Plantation Memories: Episodes of Everyday Racism*, Münster: Unrast, 2010, p. 28 f.

7   Cf. on signifying margins outside the power compendium of knowledge performance: Kalpana Seshadri-Crooks, 'At the Margins of Postcolonial Studies (Part I), in Kalpana Seshadri-Crooks and Fawzia Afzal-Khan, *The Pre-Occupation of Postcolonial Studies*, Durham: Duke University Press, 2000, pp. 3–24; 12–13: 'We can conceive of margin/marginality in two ways. On the one hand, the margin can be conceived as the subject position – the excluded other that must be coaxed into the center through incorporation, inversion, hybridization, revolution. On the other hand, the margin can be conceived as the irreducible remainder – that which is necessarily excluded by every regime of power/knowledge, including that of the discourse of rights. In other words, the margin can be conceived, not so much as that which is external to the power structure, but rather as its constitutive outside, an intimate alterity that marks the limit of power… Such a margin is the province, I argue, of multiculturalism and ethnic studies. The postcolonial margin must be acknowledged as incommensurable and nonrecuperable; on the other hand, given its investment in the critique of the discourses of modernity, this margin produces the very condition for the production of knowledge as such. The margin here functions as the residue of representation, which is discerned when the other is presented as immediately available in its truth and essence. The former notion speaks the positive discourse of rights, the latter the negative discourse of limits.' Also compare for 'neocolonialist knowledge production': Gayatri Chakravorty Spivak: 'Neocolonialism and the Secret Agent of Knowledge', Interview with Robert J. C. Young (1991), www.robertyoung.com, 2007, accessed 1 October 2013, pp. 1–44; 9.

8   Trinh T. Minh-ha, *Elsewhere, Within Here. Immigration, Refugeeism and the Boundary Event*, London and New York: Routledge, 2011, p. 2 and cf. endnote 48.

9   Yan Hairong, 'Position without Identity – An Interview with Gayatri Chakravorty Spivak', in *Positions*, Vol. 15, No., 2007, pp. 429–448.

10 Cf. for a reflection of 'specters' in the Derridean sense: Spivak in Sheikh, 2007, p. 'I take the idea of the spectral from Derrida's very careful distinctions. Spectral is not totally abstract because a ghost has some kind of peculiar body – it is a concept-metaphor – which is not a real body because it is a ghost. Its appearance is periodic but unanticipatable. Inside everything that is data there is the possibility of transformation. Just like money could be realized out of capital in the old days, now in all data there is the possibility of its *real*ization into some actual situation. That is the spectrality because there is some kind of possibility of embodiment (in a trade situation, for instance). On the other hand, that periodicity is not required periodicity (it has to occur every three days or three hours or whatever; doesn't). That concept-metaphor is exactly what spectrality is: embodiment but something other than that...' as well as Jacques Derrida, *Specters of Marx*, London and New York: Routledge, 2006, p. 10; on the 'haunting obsession' of discourse, pp. 45–46; 125 f.

11 Axel Honneth, 'Invisibility: On the Epistemology of Recognition', in Axel Honneth and Avishai Margalit, 'Recognition', in *Proceedings of the Aristotelian Society* (Supplementary Volumes), Vol. 75, 2001, pp. 111–139;

12 'I am an invisible man ... I am a man of substance, of flesh and bone, fiber and liquids – and I might even be said to possess a mind. I am invisible, understand, simply because people refuse to see me. Like the bodiless heads you see sometimes in circus sideshows, it is as though I have been surrounded by mirrors of hard, distorting glass. When they approach me they see only my surroundings, themselves, or figments of their imagination – indeed, everything and anything except me... Nor is my invisibility exactly a matter of a bio-chemical accident to my epidermis. That invisibility to which I refer occurs because of a peculiar disposition of the eyes of those with whom I come in contact. A matter of the construction of their inner eye, those eyes with which they look through their physical eyes upon reality', Ralph Ellison, *Invisible Man*, London: Penguin, 2001, p. 3.

13 'By seizing the apparatus of a regimented look, [Teresa] Brennan argues, one takes possession of the nominal function of language. Language in this schema is engaged in the service of the ego and the foundational fantasy of self-containment,' in Kalpana Seshadri-Crooks, *Desiring Whiteness. A Lacanian Analysis of Race*, London, New York: Routledge, 2000, p. 5.

14 Jean Louis Baudry, 'Ideological Effects of the Basic Cinematographic Apparatus', in Philip Rosen (ed.), *Narrative, Apparatus, Ideology*, New York: Columbia University Press, 1986, p. 295.

15 Jean Louis Baudry, 'Ideological Effects of the Basic Cinematographic Apparatus', in Bill Nichols (ed.), *Movies and Methods*, Vol. 2, Los Angeles: University of California Press, 1985, p. 531; 543; 536.

16 ibid., p. 532.

17 Experimental films of the 'Third Cinema' wave have opposed the hegemony of the gaze between the first and developing world in their aesthetics and production as part of the de-colonizing movements and struggles of the 1960s and 1970s, while more contemporary poetic paradigms of 'visualising theory' through film as an artistic medium have provided a lens to display critical enunciative practices in a moving image art context. One such example is Isaac Julien and Mark Nash's 'poetic documentary' *Frantz Fanon – Black Skin, White Mask* (1996) which combines artistic strategies of transgressing forms of cinematic

identification and visual appropriation through archival footage, photography, performance and their critical reconstruction within the context of Frantz Fanon's life and work in Algeria in an attempt to 'undoing the colonial archive'. Voice-over and its ideology in the cinema, and in colonial cinema in particular, represents a trajectory in *Fanon* for re-inscribing the voice of the Other through different perspectives and critically engaging film in 'the act of visualisation [which] can be seen as a form of theoretical production, one which makes the body in particular a privileged site of imagistic power and mediation', Isaac Julien and Mark Nash, 'Frantz Fanon as Film', in Mark Nash, *Screen Theory Culture*, London: Palgrave Macmillan, 2008, pp.185–196; 189.

18   Cf. Meera Nanda, 'Postcolonial Science Studies – Ending "Epistemic Violence"', in Daphne Patai et al. (eds), *Theory's Empire. An Anthology of Dissent*, New York: Columbia Press, 2005, pp. 575–585.

19   Christian Metz, 'The Impersonal Enunciation, or the Site of Film (In the Margin of Recent Works on Enunciation in Cinema)', in *New Literary History*, Vol. 22, No. 3, Undermining Subjects (Summer, 1991), pp. 747–772.

20   Iain Chambers as qtd from Isaac Julien and Mark Nash, 'Frantz Fanon as Film', in Nash, 2008, pp. 185–196; 194.

21   Cf. Roger Odin, 'A Semio-Pragmatic Approach to the Documentary Film', in Warren Buckland (ed.), *The Film Spectator – From Sign to Mind*, Amsterdam: Amsterdam University Press, 1995.

22   Roger Odin, as qtd from Robert Stam et al. (eds), *A Companion to Film Theory*, Malden, Mass.: Blackwell, 1999, p. 59.

23   Irit Rogoff, '"Smuggling" – An Embodied Criticality', p. 2, http://eipcp.net/transversal/0806/rogoff1/en, accessed 1 February 2013.

24   ibid., p. 1.

25   Hito Steyerl, 'In Defense of the Poor Image', *The Wretched of the Screen*, Berlin: Sternberg Press, 2012, p. 32.

26   Okwui Enwezor, 'Intense Proximity: Concerning the Disappearance of Distance', in Enwezor et al. (eds), *Intense Proximity – An Anthology of the Near and the Far: La Triennale 2012*, Paris: Centre National des Arts Plastiques, 2012, pp. 18–34.

27   Cf. Trinh T. Minh-ha, *Reassemblage: From the Firelight to the Screen*, 1982, voice over by the director.

28   Enwezor, 2012, p. 22.

29   Cf. Sara Ahmed's analysis: 'While identity itself may operate through the designation of others as strangers, rendering strangers internal rather than external to identity, to conclude simply that we are all strangers to ourselves is to avoid dealing with the political process whereby some others are designated as stranger than other others'; *Strange Encounters: Embodied Others in Post-Coloniality*, London & New York: Routledge, 2000.

30   'Where the cultural turn marked a shift from politics and economics to meaning and culture, the "artistic turn" denotes a shift in the processes by which culture comes into being as experience, and through experience as understanding. The cultural turn was not a displacement of the importance of politics and economics, nor of meaning and culture, but rather a means of re-forging interconnections in ways that carried a different emphasis.

The cultural turn allowed for the emergence of difference, of multiple identities. In the same way, the artistic turn is not a displacement of difference or of the possibility of multiple identities. But it does place emphasis differently, seeking to go beneath language and interpretation, accessing the complexity and contradiction of specific experience. Arguably, the artistic turn takes understanding further and deeper towards the singularity of human beings, towards a revaluing oft he individual, artistic and specific experience in a growing "knowledge society". The artistic turn, in this sense, implies a profound questioning of the place of the artist and his or her practice in contemporary society': Kathleen Coessens, Darla Crispin and Anne Douglas, *The Artistic Turn: A Manifesto*, Leuven: Leuven University Press, 2009, pp. 14–15.

31 Nicholas Bourriaud, *The Radicant*, New York: Sternberg Press, 2009.

32 Gaston Bachelard, *The New Scientific Spirit*, Boston: Beacon Press, 1984.

33 Bourriaud, 2009, p. 122; 52.

34 Philomena Essed as quoted from Kilomba, 2010, p. 46.

35 Cf. Okwui Enwezor, 'The Artist as Producer in Times of Crisis', http://www.16beavergroup. org/mtarchive/archives/000839.php, accessed 21 October 2012.

36 Cf. on the role of Other female scholars in Western academe and their experiences: Trinh T. Minh-ha, 'Introduction', *Discourse 8*: *Difference – A Special Third World Woman Issue*, Fall 1986–87, p. 7.

37 On 'difference' as 'division' in feminism, see Trinh T. Minh-ha, *Woman, Native, Other: Writing Postcoloniality and Feminism*, Bloomington & Indianapolis: Indiana University Press, 1989, pp. 82–85.

38 Cf. e.g. Sandra Harding, *The Postcolonial Science and Technology Studies Reader*, Durham & London: Duke University Press, 2011.

39 Mariá Fernández, 'Postcolonial Media Theory', *Art Journal*, Vol. 58, No. 3 (Autumn), 1999, pp. 63–64. Cf. for an exception and attempt to work throughout life science concepts and 'Third World Feminism': Donna Haraway, 'The Promises of Monsters: A Regenerative Politics for Inappropriate/d Others', in *The Haraway Reader*, London: Routledge, 2004, pp. 63–125; and Fernández, 1999, p. 58.

40 Cf. for an inquiry into German colonialism, Shalini Randeria et al. (eds), *Jenseits des Eurozentrismus. Postkoloniale Perspektiven in den Geschichts – und Kulturwissenschaften*, Frankfurt am Main: Campus, 2002.

41 ibid., p. 63.

42 Cf. for a critique of postcolonialism and the consequences of its institutionalization in the academe: 'There are certain dangers attendant upon these perspectives becoming institutionalised, especially within English departments. Ella Shohat points out one negative implication of the very acceptability of the term "postcolonial" in the Western academy: it serves to keep at bay more sharply political terms such as "imperialism", or "geopolitics" (Shohat 1993: 99). Terry Eagelton (1994) makes a related accusation that within "postcolonial thought" one is "allowed to talk about cultural differences, but not – or not much – about economic exploitation". Has "postcolonialism" then begun to function within academia as a term to compromise that allows us to take the easy way out?': Anita Loomba, *Colonialism/ Postcolonialism*, London & New York: Routledge, 1998, pp. xiv–xv.

43 Homi Bhabha, 'Day by Day…with Frantz Fanon', in Alan Read (ed.), *The Fact of Blackness. Frantz Fanon and Visual Representation*, London: ICA, 1996, p. 196.

44 '[Fanon] may yearn for the total transformation of Man and Society, but he speaks most effectively from the uncertain interstices of historical change. From the area of ambivalence between race and sexuality; out of an unresolved contradiction between culture and class; from deep within the struggle of psychic representation and social reality': Homi Bhabha, 'Foreword: Remembering Fanon', in Frantz Fanon, *Black Skin, White Masks*, London: Pluto Press, 1986, p. ix.

45 Homi Bhabha, *The Location of Culture*, London and New York: Routledge, 2005, p. 36: 'The reason a cultural text or system of meaning cannot be sufficient unto itself is that the act of cultural enunciation – the *place of utterance* – is crossed by the *différance* of writing… It is this difference in the process of language that is crucial to the production of meaning and ensures, at the same time, that meaning is never simply mimetic and transparent. The linguistic difference that informs any cultural performance is dramatized in the common semiotic account of the disjuncture between the subject of a proposition (*énoncé*) and the subject of enunciation, which is not represented in the statement but which is the acknowledgement of its discursive embeddedness and address, its cultural positionality, its reference to a present time and a specific age…The production of meaning requires that these two places be mobilized in the passage through a Third Space, which represents both the general conditions of language and the specific implication of the utterance in a performative and institutional strategy of which it cannot 'in itself' be conscious.'

46 'The stranger has a place by being "out of place" at home. The technologies for telling the difference between friends and strangers suggest that this distinction is not only practical but is transformed into an ethics, whereby the proximity of the stranger is seen to risk the very "life" of the family/community and nation […]. Not all those at the borders, such as tourists, migrants, or foreign nationals, are recognized as strangers; some will seem more "at home" than others, someone will pass through with their passports extending physical motility into social mobility. There is no question posed about their origin. The stranger's genealogy is always suspect. The stranger becomes a stranger because of some trace of a dubious origin. Having the "right" passport makes no difference if you have the wrong body or name': Sara Ahmed, *Queer Phenomenology: Orientations, Objects, Others*, Durham, NC: Duke University Press, 2006, p. 141.

47 'We can read the term "inappropriate/d other" in both ways, as someone whom you cannot appropriate, and as someone who is inappropriate. Not quite other, not quite the same […] how can a notion like the "inappropriate/d other" be subject to being effective only at certain times, when its very function is to resist appropriation? It all depends on how the notion is lived and carried on. Since inappropriate(d)ness does not refer to a fixed location, but is constantly according to the specific circumstances of each person, event or struggle, it works differently according to the moment and the forces at work. To relate to this situation in which one is always slightly off, and yet not entirely outside, I've also used the term "elsewhere," to which I've often added "within here" – an elsewhere within here. That is, while you are entirely involved with the now-and-here, you are also elsewhere, exceeding your limits even as you work intimately with them': Trinh T. Minh-ha (with Marina Grzinic),

'Inappropriate/d Artificiality', in Trinh T. Minh-ha, *The Digital Film Event*, London and New York: Routledge, 2005, pp. 125–135; 125.

48   Cf. Richard Kearney and Kascha Semonovitch, *Phenomenologies of the Stranger: Between Hostility and Hospitality*, New York: Fordham University Press, 2011.

49   Further to that, postcolonial critics and scholars have emphasized the ongoing need of critical theory to engage with forms of temporal and contemporary anatomies of the term and discourse of 'postcoloniality': 'Post-colonial concepts (progressive) of radical politics were often domesticated within e.g. German academia to serve certain practices. While radical thinkers have politicised the idea of transculturality, celebrated the third space, hybridity as a site from where to imagine politics as a becoming, when the concept travels to the continent it gets inflected in curious ways whereby it becomes a matter of cultural exchange. Cultural exchange was always a fraught negotiation of power, extremely violent – an epistemological violence rather than a happy barter. The moment we use the unrigorous, broad umbrella term "transcultural flow" we are left bereft of the politics and violence embedded in the process of the entire exchange/flow. What is then the larger premise of the knowledge produced? We propose a critical engagement with the specters of the vanished empires and the colonies and colonial thinking that still haunt the postcolonial scholarly production within the academic spaces of e.g. Germany. We ask the question asked long ago by Black Feminists in the US who showed the problems of talking, thinking, theorizing race without institutional transformation – the same problem Ania Loomba pointed to among North American Academic practices in the 1980s. Why do postcolonial theoretical scholarship produced in English Departments, Art History and Media Studies departments have very little communication with Area Studies departments? What are the methodologies not of decolonizing thought, but making that a practice – an institutional practice? Or are we colonizing the domain of the postcolonial and masquerading it as radical politics to obfuscate those voices and presences amongst our midst for which postcolonial thought sought to make a critical opening?', Debjani Bhattacharyya, unpublished notes to the author, 15 January 2013. This mostly unnoticed seeping development seems to have become a sign of 'post-racial' fantasies and positions that hardly serve postcolonial thought and its original political premises and practices of racial recognition throughout systems of knowledge production such as the academe and science, but rather separate 'experience', its space of enunciation that signifies, and its poetics from the domain of theoretical research – and knowledge. Cf. Kilomba, 2010, pp. 28–29; as well as Trinh T. Minh-ha, 'Difference: A Special Third World Women Issue', in *Feminist Review*, No. 25, 1987, pp. 10–11.

50   Bourriaud, 2009, p. 51.

51   Gaston Bachelard, *Die Bildung des wissenschaftlichen Geistes Beitrag zu einer Psychoanalyse der Objektiven Erkenntnis*, Frankfurt am Main: Suhrkamp, 1984, p. 54.

52   Cristina Chimisso, 'From Phenomenology to Phenomenotechnique: The Role of Early Twentieth-century Physics in Gaston Bachelard's philosophy', in *Studies in History and Philosophy of Science*, Vol. 39, 2008, pp. 384–392.

53   Irit Rogoff, 'Studying Visual Culture', in Nicholas Mirzoeff (ed.), *The Visual Culture Reader*, London: Routledge, 2002, p. 25.

54 Hans Jörg Rheinberger and Michael Hagner (eds), 'Experimentalsysteme', *Die Experimentalisierung des Lebens. Experimentalsysteme in den Biologischen Wissenschaften 1850/1950*, Berlin: Akademie Verlag, 1993, p. 7 (my translation).

55 Cf. Chimisso, 2008, p. 389.

56 Joan Copjec, 'The Orthopsychic Subject: Film Theory and the Reception of Lacan', in *October,* Vol. 49, Summer, 1989, pp. 53–71; 57.

57 Bourriaud, 2009, p. 7.

58 Cf. Vasif Kortun, Hanru Hou (eds), *How Latitudes become Forms – Art in a Global Age*, Minneapolis: Walker Art Center, 2003 (Exhibition Catalogue).

59 I am using the expression in reference to Sara Ahmed's analysis: 'I suggest that we can only avoid stranger fetishism – that is, avoid welcoming or expelling the stranger as a figure which has linguistic and bodily integrity – by examining the social relationships that are concealed by this very fetishism. That is, we need to consider how the stranger is an effect of processes of inclusion and exclusion, or incorporation and expulsion, that constitute the boundaries of bodies and communities, including communities of living (dwelling and travel), as well as epistemic communities': *Strange Encounters: Embodied Others in Post-Coloniality*, London: Routledge, 2000, p. 6.

60 Kilomba, 2010, p. 27. Kilomba's inquiry into the academe as a centre that is 'not a neutral location' is further elaborated by the following questions: 'What knowledge is being acknowledged as such? And what knowledge is not? What knowledge has been made part of academic agendas? And what knowledge has not? Whose knowledge is this? Who is acknowledged to have the knowledge? And who is not? Who can teach knowledge? And who cannot? Who is at the centre? And who remains outside, at the margins?'

61 Cf. Nick Land, 'Machinic Desire', in *Textual Practice*, Vol. 7, No. 3, 1993, p. 473; Félix Guattari, *Chaosophy: Texts and* Interviews *1972–1977*, ed. by Sylvère Lotringer, Los Angeles: Semiotext(e), 2009.

62 Jimena Canales, 'Desired Machines: Cinema and the World in its Own Image', in *Science in Context*, Vol. 24, No. 3, 2011, pp. 329–59.

63 Cf. Gaston Bachelard, *Der Neue Wissenschaftliche Geist*, Frankfurt am Main: Suhrkamp, 1988, p. 18.

64 Cf. Bourriaud, 2009, p. 22.

65 ibid., p. 14; 34; 39.

66 Cf. Sarat Mahraj, 'Know-how and No-How: Stopgap Notes on "Method" in Visual Art as Knowledge Production', in *Art & Research*, Vol. 2, No. 2, 2009, pp. 1–11.

67 Hans Jörg Rheinberger, 'Gaston Bachelard und der Begriff der "Phänomenotechnik"', in id., *Epistemologie des Konkreten*, Frankfurt am Main: Suhrkamp, 2006, pp. 37–55; 40–41; ibid., 'Gaston Bachelard and the Notion of "Phenomenotechnique"', in *Perspectives on Science*, 2005, Vol. 13, No. 3, Massachusetts Institute of Technology.

Biographies of Authors

Annette Bitsch is a media and cultural theorist. She is Associate Professor at the Institute of Cultural Studies at Humboldt University Berlin, and published extensively on media and psychoanalytical theory, cybernetics and on the cultural history of migraine. Her publications include: *Diskrete Gespenster. Die Genealogie des Unbewussten aus der Medientheorie und Philosophie der Zeit*, Bielefeld: transcript, 2009; and *Always Crashing in the Same Car – Jacques Lacans Medientheorie des Unbewussten*, Weimar: VDG, 2001. Her current research is directed towards the field of posthumanism (in the context of media and cultural studies).

Jay David Bolter is the Wesley Chair of New Media at the Georgia Institute of Technology. He is the author of *Turing's Man: Western Culture in the Computer Age* (1984); *Writing Space: The Computer, Hypertext, and the History of Writing* (1991; second edition 2001); *Remediation* (1999), with Richard Grusin; and *Windows and Mirrors* (2003), with Diane Gromala. In addition to writing about new media, Bolter collaborates in the construction of new digital media forms. With Michael Joyce, he created Storyspace, a hypertext authoring system. As a member of the Augmented Environments Lab, Bolter works closely with Prof. Blair MacIntyre, Prof. Maria Engberg, and others on the use of augmented reality to create new media experiences for informal education and entertainment.

Timothy Druckrey is Director of the Graduate Photographic and Electronic Media programme at the Maryland Institute, College of Art. He also works as a curator, writer and editor living in New York City. He lectures internationally about the social impact of photography, electronic media, the transformation of representation, and communication in interactive and networked environments. He co-organized the international symposium *Ideologies of Technology* at the Dia Center of the Arts and co-edited the book *Culture on the Brink: Ideologies of Technology*, New York: New Press, 1998. He also co-curated the exhibition 'Iterations: The New Image' at the International Centre of Photography, and edited the book by the same name published by MIT Press in 1994. He edited *Electronic Culture: Technology and Visual Representation*, Aperture, 1996, and is series editor for *Electronic Culture: History, Theory, Practice* published by MIT Press. He has been a guest professor at the University of

Applied Art, Vienna (2004), and Richard Koopman Distinguished Chair for the Visual Arts at the University of Hartford (2005).

Thomas Elsaesser is Professor Emeritus at the University of Amsterdam and was Visiting Professor at Yale University from 2006 to 2012. Besides over 200 published articles, he has authored, edited and co-edited some twenty volumes, several of which have been translated, notably into German, French, Italian, Hungarian, Hebrew, Korean and Chinese. His most recent publications are: co-edited with Malte Hagener, *Film Theory: An Introduction through the Senses*, London: Routledge, 2010; and *The Persistence of Hollywood*, London: Routledge, 2012.

Hinderk M. Emrich is Professor of Psychiatry and Neurology at Medical School Hannover. He has a doctorate in philosophy and has been teaching on film and TV at the German Academy of Film and TV, at Karlsruhe University of Arts and Design and elsewhere. His publications include: *Welche Farbe hat der Montag? – Synästhesie: Das Leben mit verknüpften Sinnen*, Stuttgart: Hirzel, 2004; *Psyche und Transzendenz*, Würzburg: Königshausen &Neumann, 2002; *Geist, Psyche und Gehirn*, Frankfurt am Main: Peter Lang, 2005; *Identität als Prozeß*, Würzburg: Königshausen & Neumann, 2007; *Scham und Berührung im Film*, Göttingen: Vandenhoeck & Ruprecht, 2008; *Psychiatrische Anthropologie I*, Würzburg: Königshausen &Neumann, 2008.

Lorenz Engell is Professor of Media philosophy and co-director of the Internationales Kolleg für Kulturtechnikforschung und Medienphilosophie (International Centre of Culture Technology and Media Philosophy) at Bauhaus University, Weimar. His publications include (selection): *Fernsehtheorie zur Einführung*, Hamburg: Junius, 2012; *Playtime. Münchener Film-Vorlesungen*, Konstanz: UVK, 2010; *Bilder der Endlichkeit*, Weimar: VDG, 2005; *Bilder des Wandels*, Weimar: VDG, 2003; and is co-editor of *Zeitschrift für Medien- und Kulturforschung*, *Archiv für Mediengeschichte* (2000–10), and *Kursbuch Medienkultur*, Stuttgart: DVA, 1998.

Barbara Flueckiger is Professor of Film Studies at the University of Zurich, Switzerland, since 2007. She has been working internationally as a film professional before she studied film theory and history in Zurich and Berlin. Her research focuses on the interaction between technology and aesthetics, especially in the digital domain. She has published two standard text books on sound design and visual effects, and many articles and book chapters in renowned publications, including peer-reviewed journals. Her most recent research projects AFRESA, 'Film History Re-mastered' and DIASTOR investigate the digitization of archival film. In autumn 2011 and summer 2012 she was a research fellow at Harvard University where she explored material and aesthetic aspects of historical film colours.

Anselm Franke is a curator and critic based in Berlin. He is the Head of the Department of Visual Arts and Film at the Haus der Kulturen der Welt (HKW) Berlin, where he recently curated the exhibitions 'The Whole Earth. California and the Disappearance of the Outside' (with Diedrich Diederichsen), and 'After Year Zero. Geographies of Collaboration after 1945' (both 2013). He was the curator of the Taipei Biennial 2012. Previously he acted as director of Extra City Kunsthal Antwerp, where he curated exhibitions such 'Mimétisme' (2008) and 'Sergei Eisenstein: The Mexican Drawings' (2009). He was co-curator of Manifesta 7 in 2008, and before 2007, curator at KW Berlin. He is a researcher at Goldsmiths College London and writes for Mousse, Parkett, and e-flux journal.

Ursula Anna Frohne is Professor of Art History at the University of Cologne. She has been a curator at the ZKM | Center for Art and Media in Karlsruhe (Germany) from 1995 to 2002, and a lecturer at the University for Art and Design Karlsuhe. She has also been Visiting Professor at Brown University (2001/2002) and Professor for Art History at International University Bremen (Germany) (2002-04). Her selected research grants and fellowships include: the Getty Research Institute (LA), and the Pembroke Center, Brown University, Providence; chair of research project *Reflections of Cinematographic Aesthetics in Contemporary Art* (2007–12) at the University of Cologne, http://kinoaesthetik.uni-koeln. de/. Relevant publications include: *CTRL [SPACE], Rhetorics of Surveillance from Bentham to Big Brother* (co-edited with Thomas Y. Levin and Peter Weibel), Cambridge, MA: The MIT Press, 2002; 'Dissolution of the Frame: Immersion and Participation in Video Installations', in Tanya Leighton (ed.), *Art and the Moving Image: A Critical Reader*, London & New York: Tate Afterall, 2008; *Kinematographische Räume. Installationsästhetik in Film und Kunst* (co-edited with Lilian Haberer), Munich: Wilhelm Fink Verlag, 2012; *Art 'In-Formation': Communication Aesthetics and Network Structures in Art from the 1960s to the Present* (co-edited with Anne Thurmann-Jajes), Hanover: Dartmouth College Press (forthcoming in 2014).

Rania Gaafar is currently a Research Associate in the Media Art department at Karlsruhe University of Arts and Design, and a postgraduate researcher at Goldsmiths College's visual culture department, London. She received a DFG – Ph.D. scholarship from 2006 to 2009 at the Doctoral School *Image, Body, Medium – Towards an Anthropological Perspective* at Karlsruhe University of Arts and Design, and has been a fellow at Akademie Schloss Solitude (April–September 2012) in Stuttgart, Germany. Ph.D. thesis on 'Phenomenotechnologies of Exilic Film Art'. Her current research focus is on postcolonial aesthetic materialities in film and media art. Forthcoming by her is: *Phänomenotechniken in den Visuellen Künsten – Medien, Experiment, Wissen* (Phenomenotechnologies in the Visual Arts – Media, Experiment, Knowledge), Munich: Fink, 2015.

Mark B. N. Hansen is a media and cultural theorist and Professor of Literature and ISIS (Information Science+Information Society) at Duke University. He is author of three books: *Embodying Technesis: Technology Beyond Writing*, University of Michigan Press,

2000; *New Philosophy for New Media*, Cambridge: MIT, 2004; and *Bodies in Code: Interfaces with Digital Culture* New York, London: Routledge, 2006. He is also co-editor of three volumes: *The Cambridge Companion to Merleau-Ponty*, Cambridge: Cambridge University Press, 2005; *Emergence and Embodiment: New Essays in 2nd Order Cybernetics* Durham: Duke University Press, 2009; and *Critical Terms for Media Studies*, Chicago: University of Chicago Press, 2010. His current work focuses on the role of technics and media in the asubjective phenomenology of time.

Janet Harbord is the author of several books on film and philosophies of the moving image, including: *Film Cultures*, Sage, 2002; *The Evolution of Film*, Polity, 2006; and *Chris Marker: La Jetée*, Afterall & MIT Press, 2009. She is recipient of grants from the AHRC, EPSRC and the Leverhulme Trust, and Professor of Film Studies at Queen Mary, University of London.

Thomas Hensel is a Professor of Art and Design Theory at Pforzheim University and a member of the faculty 'Visual Competencies' in the Department for Arts and Image Science, Danube University. Recent books include: *Wie aus der Kunstgeschichte eine Bildwissenschaft wurde. Aby Warburgs Graphien*, Berlin: Akademie Verlag, 2011; *Nature morte im Fadenkreuz. Zur Bildlichkeit des Computerspiels*, Trier: Intermedia Design Books, 2011; (co-edited with Games Coop), *Theorien des Computerspiels zur Einführung*, Hamburg: Junius, 2012; (co-edited with Benjamin Beil), *Game Laboratory Studies*, Siegen: Universi, 2012; (co-edited with Benjamin Beil et al.), *I AM Error. Störungen des Computerspiels*, Siegen: Universi, 2012; (co-edited with Jens Schröter), *Zeitschrift für Ästhetik und Allgemeine Kunstwissenschaft*, Vol. 57, No. 1, 2012.

Ute Holl is a film and media scholar and currently a Professor of Aesthetics of Media at the University of Basel, Switzerland. Her main fields of research are the history of cinema perception, the science history of audio-visual media, media history of acoustics and electro acoustics, as well as the theory and aesthetics of experimental and anthropological cinema. Her work on experimental cinema and its genealogy in nineteenth century psycho-physiological laboratory cultures was published as *Kino, Trance and Cybernetics*, Berlin: Verlag Brinkmann und Bose, 2002. It is currently being translated to English and will be published by Amsterdam University Press.

Isaac Julien is a media installation artist and film-maker. He graduated from St Martins School of Art in 1984, where he studied painting and fine art film. He founded Sankofa Film and Video Collective (1982–92), and was a founding member of Normal Films in 1991. He was nominated for the Turner Prize in 2001 for his films *The Long Road to Mazatlán* (1999), made in collaboration with Javier de Frutos, and *Vagabondia* (2000), choreographed by Javier de Frutos. Earlier works include *Frantz Fanon, Black Skin White Mask* (1996), *Young Soul Rebels* (1991), which was awarded the 'Semaine de la critique prize' at the Cannes Film Festival the same year, and the acclaimed poetic documentary *Looking for Langston* (1989), which also won several international awards. He was Visiting Lecturer at Harvard University's Schools of Afro-American and Visual Environmental Studies, and is a faculty member of the Independent Study Program at the Whitney Museum of American Arts. He was also a research fellow at Goldsmiths College, London, and is currently a Professor of Media Art at Karlsruhe University of Arts and Design in Germany. He was the recipient of the Performa Award (2008), the prestigious mit Eugene McDermott Award in the Arts (2001) and the Frameline Lifetime Achievement Award (2002). He is represented in museum and private collections throughout the world, including the Tate; Museum of Modern Art, New York; Centre Pompidou; the Guggenheim Museum, New York; the Hirshhorn Museum, in Washington; and the Brandhorst Museum, Munich.

Malcolm Le Grice is a media artist and film-maker. He started as a painter, but began to make film and computer works in the mid 1960s. Since then, he has shown regularly in Europe and the USA and his work has been screened in many international film festivals. He has also shown in major art exhibitions like the 'Paris Biennale No.8', 'Arte Inglese Oggi', Milan, 'Une Histoire du Cinema', Paris, 'Documenta 6', 'Kassel' and 'X-Screen' at the Museum of Modern Art, Vienna, and 'Behind the Facts' at the Fondacion Joan Miro, Barcelona. His main work since the mid 1980s is in video and digital media, and includes the multi-projection video installation works *The Cyclops Cycle* and *FINITI*. He has written critical and theoretical work including a history of experimental cinema: *Abstract Film and Beyond*, Cambridge, MA: MIT, 1982; and *Experimental Cinema in the Digital Age*, London: BFI, 2001. Le Grice is a professor emeritus of the University of the Arts London where he was co-founder with David Curtis of the British Artists Film and Video Study Collection.

Laura U. Marks, Ph.D., is an American media theorist and artist. She is Dena Wosk University Professor in Art and Culture studies in the School for the Contemporary Arts at Simon Fraser University, and a Professor at the European Graduate School, where she teaches an intensive summer seminar. She has worked as an editor, curator, professor, critic and scholar. From 1987–91 she was the assistant editor at *Afterimage* magazine. Since 1991 she has been an independent critic, curator and editor. From 1993 to 1995 she was media curator at the Pyramid Arts Centre in Rochester, New York. In 1994, Laura U. Marks was the Rush Rhees Fellow at the University of Rochester. That same year she was a dissertation fellow for the Luce Foundation/American Council of Learned Societies. From 1995–96 she was a Mellon/Pew Fellow in the Division of Critical Studies at the California Institute of the Arts. From 1996–2001 she was an Assistant Professor of Film Studies at Carleton University. She obtained tenure in 2001 at Carleton University. From 2002–03, she was a visiting scholar at the Center for Behavioral Research at the American University in Beirut. Since 2003, she has been a tenured Associate Professor and Dena Wosk University Professor in Art and Culture Studies, School for the Contemporary Arts, at Simon Fraser University.

Dieter Mersch is currently Head of the Theory department at Zurich University of the Arts. He has been Professor for Media Theory at the University of Potsdam from 2004 to 2013. He has studied mathematics and philosophy at the Universities of Cologne and Bochum and received his Ph.D. in philosophy from Technical University Darmstadt (Germany). From 2000–04 he was a guest professor of Philosophy of Arts and Aesthetics at the School of Arts in Kiel; in 2006, he was a guest professor at the University of Chicago; in 2010, a fellow at the IKKM in Weimar; in 2012, a fellow at the ZHdK Zurich. His main areas of interests are media philosophy, aesthetics and art theory, picture theory, semiotics, hermeneutics and post-structuralism. His publications include: *Umberto Eco zur Einführung*, Hamburg: Junius, 1993; *Was sich zeigt*, München: Fink, 2002; *Ereignis und Aura: Untersuchungen zu einer Ästhetik des Performativen*, Frankfurt am Main: Suhrkamp, 2002; *Einführung in die Medientheorie*, Hamburg: Junius, 2006; and *Post-Hermeneutik*, Berlin: Akademie Verlag, 2010.

Jens Schröter is Professor for the Theory and Practice of Multimedial Systems at the University of Siegen. He was director of the graduate school 'Locating Media', http://www.uni-siegen.de/locatingmedia/. He is (together with Prof. Dr. Lorenz Engell, Weimar) director of the research project *TV Series as Reflection and Projection of Change*, http://www.mediatisiertewelten.de/en/projects/tv-series-as-reflection-and-projection-of-change/. His main research topics are: theory and history of digital media, theory and history of photography, theory and history of three-dimensional images, intermediality and copy protection. Recent publications include: *3D. Geschichte, Theorie und Medienästhetik des Technisch-transplanen Bildes*, München: Fink, 2009; editor (with a masters project group) of *Kulturen des Kopierschutzes* I + II, Siegen: Universi, 2010; (co-edited with Marcus Stiglegger), *High Definition Cinema*, Siegen: Universi, 2011; (co-authored with Nicola Glaubitz et al.), *Eine Theorie der Medienumbrüche 1900/2000*, Siegen: Universi, 2011; (co-edited with Thomas Hensel), *Die Akteur-Netzwerk-Theorie als Herausforderung der Kunstwissenschaft?*, Vol. 57, No. 1, 2012, Special Issue of *Zeitschrift für Ästhetik und Allgemeine Kunstwissenschaft*); *Verdrahtet. The Wire und der Kampf um die Medien*, Berlin: Bertz+Fischer, 2012.

Martin Schulz is currently Professor of Art History at the Karlsruhe Institute of Technology. From 2000 to 2009, he was Professor of Art History and Media Theory at Karlsruhe University of Arts and Design, and academic coordinator of the DFG-doctoral School, *Image, Body, Medium – Towards an Anthropological Perspective*. From 2006 to 2012, he was a visiting scholar at the Academy of Fine Arts in Karlsruhe and Düsseldorf; Schiller-University in Jena; University of Heidelberg in the Cluster of Excellence 'Asia and Europe in a Global Context'; the Estonian University in Tallinn; UNAM in Mexico and Tufts University in Boston. He received fellowships from the Internationales Forum Kulturwissenschaften (IFK) in Vienna (Austria) and the Internationales Kolleg für Kulturtechnikforschung und Medienphilosophie (International Center of Culture Technology and Media Philosophy) in Weimar, Germany. He has published widely on contemporary art, photography, media history and picture theory. Selected publications include: (co-edited with Hans Belting), *Quel Corps? Eine Frage der Repräsentation*, Munich: Fink, 2002; (co-edited with Birgit Mersmann), *Kulturen des Bildes*, Munich: Fink, 2006; 'Die Sichtbarkeit des Todes im Medium der Fotografie', in Thomas Macho and Kristin Marek (eds), *Die Neue Sichtbarkeit des Todes*, Munich: Fink, 2007, pp. 289–313; *Ordnungen der Bilder*, Munich: Fink, 2009 (2nd edition); (co-edited with Beat Wyss), *Techniken des Bildes*, Munich: Fink, 2010; 'The Unmasking of Images: The Anachchronism of TV-Faces', in Oliver Grau (ed.), *Imagery in the 21st Century*, Cambridge, MA: MIT, 2011, pp. 32–51.

Yvonne Spielmann, Ph.D., Dr. habil., is the Dean of Faculty of Fine Arts at Lasalle College of the Arts in Singapore. Key foci of her work in media and culture, technology, art, science and communication are: leadership of research, Ph.D. supervision, developing international links within Europe and with the US, instigating networks with partners in South-East Asia, consultancy and curatorship. She holds the 2011 Swedish Prize for Swedish-German scientific co-operation. Milestones of publish research output are four authored monographs and about ninety single authored articles. Her book, *Video, the Reflexive Medium* (published by MIT Press 2008, Japanese edition by Sangen-sha Press 2011, Polish edition in 2012) was rewarded the 2009 Lewis Mumford Award for Outstanding Scholarship in the Ecology of Technics. Her most recent book *Hybrid Culture* was printed in German by Suhrkamp Press in 2010, and in English by MIT Press in 2013. Professor Spielmann's work has been published in German and English and has been translated into French, Polish, Croatian, Swedish, Japanese and Korean.